Making Sense of the Organization

 University of

Making Sense of the Organization

KARL E. WEICK

University of Michigan

Blackwell
Publishing

350 Main Street, Malden, MA 02148-5018, USA
108 Cowley Road, Oxford OX4 1JF, UK
550 Swanston Street, Carlton South, Melbourne, Victoria 3053, Australia
Kurfürstendamm 57, 10707 Berlin, Germany

First published 2001 by Blackwell Publishing Ltd
Reprinted 2001 (twice), 2002, 2003

Library of Congress Cataloging-in-Publication Data

Weick, Karl E.
    Making sense of the organization / Karl E. Weick.
        p. cm.
    Includes bibliographical references and index.
    ISBN 0-631-22317-7 (alk. paper) — ISBN 0-631-22319-3 (pb : alk. paper)
    1. Organizational behavior. 2. Communication in organizations. 3. Psychology,
Industrial.   I. Title.
HD57.7 .W447 2000
158.7—dc21   00-034327

A catalogue record for this title is available from the British Library.

Set in 10 on 12 pt Photina
by Ace Filmsetting Ltd, Frome, Somerset
Printed and bound in the United Kingdom
by T. J. International Ltd, Padstow, Cornwall

For further information on
Blackwell Publishing, visit our website:
http://www.blackwellpublishing.com

Contents

Acknowledgments

The chapters of this manuscript first appeared in other sources. We are grateful to the following publishers for permission to reprint these selections.

Karl Weick (1993). Sensemaking in organizations: Small structures with large consequences. In J. Keith Murnigham (ed.), *Social Psychology in Organizations: Advances
in Theory and Research*, Englewood Cliffs, NJ: Prentice-Hall.

Karl Weick (1985). Sources of order in underorgnized systems. Themes in recent
organizational theory. In Y. Lincoln (ed.), *Organizational Theory and Inquiry: The
Paradigm Revolution*, Beverley Hills, CA: Sage Publications Inc. Reprinted by permission of Sage Publications Inc.

Karl Weick (1993). Organizational redesign as improvisation. In George P. Huber
and William H. Glick (eds.), *Organizational Change and Redesign: Ideas and Insights
for Improving Performance*, Oxford, UK: Oxford University Press. Copyright © 1993
by Oxford University Press Inc. Used by permission of Oxford University Press Inc.

Karl Weick (1993). The collapse of sensemaking in organizations: The Mann Gulch
disaster. *Administrative Science Quarterly*, 38(4).

Karl Weick (1990). The vulnerable system: An analysis of the Tenerife air disaster.
Journal of Management 16(3). Reprinted by permission of Elsevier Science Ltd.

Karl Weick (1990). Technology as equivoque: Sensemaking in new technologies. In
P. S. Goodman and L. Sproull (eds.), *Technology and Organizations*, San Francisco,
CA: Jossey Bass. Reprinted by permission of John Wiley & Sons Inc.

Karl Weick (1977). Enactment processes in organizations. In B. Shaw and G. Salancik
(eds.), *New Directions in Organizational Behavior*, Chicago, IL: St Clair.

Karl Weick (1996). Enactment and the boundaryless career. In Michael B. Arthur
and Denise Rousseau (eds.), *The Boundaryless Career: A New Employment Principle
for a New Organizational Era*, Oxford, UK: Oxford University Press. Copyright ©
1996 by Oxford University Press, Inc. Used by permission of Oxford University
Press Inc.

Karl Weick (1988). Enacted sensemaking in crisis situations. *Journal of Management
Studies*, 25(4). Reprinted by permission of Blackwell Publishers, Oxford, UK.

Richard Daft and Karl Weick (1984). Toward a model of organizations as interpretation systems. *Academy of Management Review*, 9.

Karl Weick and Karlene Roberts (1993). Collective mind in organizations: Heedful interrelating on flight decks. *Administrative Science Quarterly*, 38(3).

Karl Weick (1998). Improvisation as a mindset for organizational analysis. *Organization Science*, 9(5). Reprinted by permission of Institute for Operational Research and the Management Sciences, Linthicum.

Karl Weick and Michel G. Bougon (1986). Organizations as cause maps. In H. P. Sims, Jr. and D. A. Gioia (eds.), *Social Cognition in Organizations*, San Francisco, CA: Jossey Bass. Reprinted by permission of John Wiley & Sons Inc.

Karl Weick (1987). Organizational culture as a source of high reliability. *California Management Review*, 29.

Karl Weick (1987). Substitutes for strategy. In D. J. Teece (ed.), *The Competitive Challenge*, Cambridge, MA: Ballinger.

Karl Weick (1998). The attitude of wisdom: Ambivalence as the optimal compromise. In S. Srivastva and D. L. Cooperrider (eds.), *Organizational Wisdom and Executive Courage*, San Francisco, CA: Lexington.

Karl Weick (1982). Management of organizational change among loosely coupled elements. In P. Goodman (ed.), *Change in Organizations*, San Francisco, CA: Jossey Bass. Reprinted by permission of John Wiley & Sons Inc.

Karl Weick (1977). Organization design: Organizations as self-designing systems. *Organizational Dynamics*, 6(2). Reprinted by permission of the American Management Association.

Karl Weick (1984). Small wins: Redefining the scale of social problems. *American Psychologist*, 39(1). Reprinted by permission of the American Psychological Association.

Karl Weick (1985). Cosmos vs. chaos: Sense and nonsense in electronic contexts. *Organizational Dynamics*, Fall, 14. Reprinted by permission of the American Management Association.

Karl Weick (1999). Sensemaking as an organizational dimension of global change. In J. Dutton and D. Cooperrider (eds.), *The Human Dimensions of Global Change*, Thousand Oaks, CA: Sage Publications Inc. Reprinted by permission of AltaMira Press.

Introduction

It was Bergson's contention that "a true philosopher says only one thing in his lifetime because he enjoys but one contact with the real" (Wagner, 1983). If that's the case then the framing of a set of essays should be pretty straightforward: spot the one contact, describe it, and then tell a tale of variations on a theme, much like a jazz musician playing multiple choruses of a standard melody. My "one contact with the real" may well have been my dissertation research in 1961. The study was an investigation of cognitive dynamics, in which people agreed to do a difficult concept attainment task after they learned that they would get less reward for their participation in the study than they expected (Weick, 1964; see Zanna 1973 for a tighter version of this study). Those who were deprived most severely rated the subsequent task more interesting, but what was most striking was that they were three times more productive at performing it. The interpretation was that people had to resolve a disturbing set of cognitions: I came here to get the rewards they promised me, but I didn't get those rewards, yet I am still participating. How come? Their answer was, because this is such an interesting task. That answer is actually a complex mixture of prospective and retrospective sensemaking. By working hard and solving more problems, they created (enacted) a situation which confirmed the sensibleness of agreeing to participate in the first place. Ontology and epistemology were woven together out of cognitive necessity. We get a glimpse here of the effect of cognition on action, but we also see that action which is public, irreversible, and volitional (Salancik, 1977) is one trigger for justification. Closer attention to the task accompanied by higher effort and careful deployment of aspiration levels literally built the attractive task and the convincing reasons that justified the choice to participate. Having performed the concept attainment task successfully the person infers that he (all participants were male) must have liked the task, which then becomes the reason he agreed to participate in the first place. Cognition lies in the path of the action. There is both the hot cognition of conflict resolution and the cool cognition of inference.

If one is willing to engage in shameless generalization (which may simply be a tactic to deal with having only one contact with the real), then this study may be a microcosm of one way in which people build cosmologies and coherent world views.

Organizations begin to materialize when rationales for commitment become articulated. Notice, that in the very beginning, these rationales may originate in the service of *self*-justification and only later do they become enlarged into collective justifications. Thus, those choices we experience as binding choices may affect retrospective accounts of tasks to which we are attracted, reasons that move us, values we seek to realize, plans we admire, and people we align ourselves with.

I realize that anchoring my intellectual tale in an "ancient" theory – cognitive dissonance theory – and in a quaint methodology – the lab experiment – and in an old experiment at that, is retro and "so 60s" as to risk dismissal. Quaint or not, my choice of that anchor makes some sense of threads that run through this collection of work:

1. The study is about cognitive dynamics and cognition, which has been the theme of subsequent work involving cause maps, sensemaking, self-fulfilling prophecies;
2. The study is about belief-action as the root relationship in the human condition;
3. The study highlights retrospective sensemaking – how can I know what I think of this task until I see how I've done;
4. Reasoning is depicted as motivated behavior driven by concerns of positive self-presentation;
5. Discrepancies, surprise, the unexpected, the dissonant, are implied as the occasion that stirs thought – which is partly why my work seems to contain so little mention of routine/habit/automatic action;
6. Dissonance itself is a term that originated in the world of music, and exploration of jazz improvisation has been a sustained topic of my work as for example in studies of the Minnesota jazz orchestra, the Utrecht jazz orchestra, rehearsals of the Don Ellis and Ladd Macintosh big bands, and more recently, improvisation in smaller groups;
7. The study is about sequence, flow, and process, rather than structure (it does have structuring in it) which has been true of most of my concern with ongoing events (e.g. continuous processes, wildland fires, musical performance);
8. There is the picture of an unsuspecting subject being thrown into something of a mess not of his own making, and making sense of this "thrownness" (Heidegger) in ways that save face and qualify as a small win; and,
9. There is the implied counterpoint that there is more to life than decision making and rational models, and much of this "more than" precedes decision making.

What is *missing* in the original study is much appreciation of the social, interpersonal, multiple actor quality of coordinated activity that characterizes most task performance. That appreciation waxes and wanes in these essays. It waxes in the analysis of the Mann Gulch disaster and in the analysis Karlene Roberts and I published on the "collective mind" of an aircraft carrier. It wanes in the analyses of enactment processes and mental models. And the appreciation is held in tension whenever I discuss requisite variety, the idea that it takes variety to sense and control variety (e.g. reading on culture and high reliability). That idea of requisite variety has been a central assumption throughout my work, but as I work harder to understand what that process is all about, I re-stumble onto the hard dynamic that interpersonal variety begets interpersonal conflict, the reduction of which frequently reduces the variety that one started with. The debacle at Waco is a good example of an incident command team, composed for variety, whose variety quickly disappeared when the incident commander talked to everyone separately in dyadic conversations and was swayed by the last person he talked to, and by the fact that the tactics/operations/swat representatives were the most forceful in their rhetoric. That forcefulness meant that their recommendations dominated those made by people who used more nuanced talk.

The "spirit" that seems to lie behind the work reviewed in the present book is summarized in the preface for the Japanese translation of the second edition of *The Social Psychology of Organizing*. The relevant paragraph reads in part, "Whatever staying power this book has had seems to derive from its persistent emphasis on process, action, recurrent patterns in interaction as the feedstock of organization, social cognition, and on the insistence that organizing is never very tidy or foresightful, despite the necessity of its practitioners to make it appear otherwise. Efforts to maintain the illusion that organizations are rational and orderly in the interest of legitimacy are costly and futile. They consume enormous energy and undermine self-acceptance when managers hold themselves to standards of prescience that are unattainable. To appreciate organizations and their environments as flows interrupted by constraints of one's own making, is to take oneself a little less seriously, to find a little more leverage in human affairs on a slightly smaller scale, and to have a little less hubris and a little more fun. That is the explicit message at the end of the book, rendered in the symbol of a journey to Ithaca. It is also the tacit message throughout the book, a message that has given readers hope rather than despair because it reaffirms what they feel and intuit firsthand as they organize. The flows and ups and downs of social order are tolerable if one feels those are normal fluctuations rather than some kind of testimonial to one's own shortcomings. In the last analysis, organizing is about fallible people who keep going."

As a fallible author, my fear in any collection such as this is that a way of seeing is a way of not seeing. I arranged these articles, all of which touch on sensemaking, into groupings that correspond to stages in the enactment model of organizing. I chose this structure to show the embeddedness of sensemaking and the intertwining of sensemaking and organizing. But no sooner had I created this structure than it became clear that most essays could fit in several places. For example, the analysis of the collapse of sensemaking in Mann Gulch finds its home here in the section on ecological change, the argument being, Mann Gulch firefighters had to make sense of something not of their own making. They faced a dynamic fire environment, had to spot its tendencies, and had to herd the fire and eventually suppress it. But, in coping with the fire, the Mann Gulch firefighters chose which aspects of the fire they noticed to infer its severity (selection), they had prior experience largely with small fires they could suppress in 24 hours (retention), and they treated Mann Gulch as a small fire which was the kind of fire they knew how to handle (use of retained knowledge to guide both action and perception). They treated an equivocal situation as if it were unequivocal. So Mann Gulch is about more than ecological change. The same is true for the other articles in this collection. Although each article has been assigned a specific address, that address does not exhaust its meaning. Sensemaking is not particularly tidy, which means that attempts to portray it may also sprawl. In a way, each of these essays can be read as an effort to find an address for a phenomenon. The persistent struggle in each case is with the question, what is this all about? To take these earlier struggles and now declare arbitrarily that their home has been found, is either an act of hubris or an act of denial . . . or an act of respect for conventions of publishing. Thus, I implore the reader to wade into the essays mindful that they are exercises in reach. In each case I try to make discontinuous worded sense of continuous preverbal flows. These efforts can be read variously. These efforts should be read variously. These multiple readings are themselves the essence of the sensemaking phenomenon that unites this collection.

References

Salancik, Gerald R. (1977). Commitment and the control of organizational behavior and belief. In B. M. Staw and G. R. Salancik (eds.), *New Directions in Organizational Behavior*, pp. 1–54. Chicago: St. Clair.

Wagner, Helmut R. (1983). *Alfred Schultz: An Intellectual Biography*, Chicago: University of Chicago.

Weick, Karl E. (1964). The reduction of cognitive dissonance through task enhancement and effort expenditure. *Journal of Abnormal and Social Psychology*, 68, 533–9.

Zanna, Mark P. (1973). On inferring one's beliefs from one's behavior in a low choice setting. *Journal of Personality and Social Psychology*, 26, 386–94.

I

Organizations as Contexts for Sensemaking

Introduction

The first three chapters describe the organizational context within which sensemaking occurs. For sensemaking purposes, what is significant about organizations is that their work consists of public irrevocable choices that necessitate justification. This work unfolds in loosely coupled systems and often creates ambiguities that need to be reduced. And organizing to reduce ambiguity, itself, involves ongoing efforts to transform general recipes into actions and structures. The embellishment and implementation of general recipes occurs through acts of improvisation that require continuous sensemaking. Obviously there is much more to organizations than justifications, loose coupling, and improvisation. Nevertheless, these are meaningful vantage points from which to examine the resources and challenges for sensemaking that people face in organizations. Whether "in" organizations or not, people still have to come to grips with the fact that "Life is neither meaningful nor meaningless. Meaning and its absence are given to life by language and imagination. We are linguistic beings who inhabit a reality in which it makes sense to make sense" (Batchelor, 1997, p. 39). While it makes sense to make sense in organizations, this is easier said than done. Some settings are more sensible than others. Those variations are the feedstock of these chapters.

Chapter 1, "Sensemaking in Organizations: Small Structures with Large Consequences," was published roughly 30 years after the dissertation research but cognitive dissonance still reverberates in its ideas. The earlier theme of task enhancement reappears in the enlarged idea of commitment. Commitment is placed in the context of interdependent action and is shown to be an important source of organizational character and culture. Value creation, which occurred in the earlier study when people used aspiration levels, problem-solving strategies, and attention, to construct a more engaging task environment, remains a prominent theme. People continue to act in ways that create value and give meaning to their action. Here that process occurs when people engage in important, public, irrevocable, volitional acts that compel a search for justifications. When those justifications are found, they tend to persist and be defended. Hence, people act their way into their values, which paves the way for groups to act their way into their identities, which paves the way for organizations to act their way into their missions. Sensemaking emerges as a retrospective activity that is sensitive to conditions of choice, irrevocability, and visibility. In this chapter we see what an entire organization would look like if it were viewed as a system of commitments.

Chapter 2, "Sources of Order in Underorganized Systems: Themes in Recent Organizational Theory" is one of my all-time favorites. I am fond of this essay because it summarizes a family of related theories into six short themes, it shows how sensemaking is necessitated by the conditions of ambiguity in organized life, it is infused with the imagery of loosely coupled systems which is a depiction of organizations that remains valid, it weaves together ideas such as the presumption of logic and self-fulfilling prophecies and action bias and hindsight that have been mainstays in sensemaking, and it maintains its relevance to current organizational studies through such themes as improvisation (p.34), indeterminacy in adaptive action (p. 38), federations and federalist structures (p. 39), simultaneous loose-tight coupling (p. 43), learning under adverse conditions (p. 44), and self-organizing systems (p. 47). The "sources of order" chapter is focused on a more macro level of analysis and portrays the organizational context in ways that suggest why sensemaking rather than decision making may be the more central organizational issue. Whether there are decisions that need to be made and what those decisions might consist of are products of sensemaking. To be in thrall of decision making is to spend too much time on too narrow a band of issues that crop up too late after most of the important action is already finished. This essay begins to draw attention to earlier pre-decision moments. We see what an entire organization would look like if it were viewed as a loosely coupled system held together by interpretations.

Chapter 3, "Organizational Redesign as Improvisation," again focuses on the entire organization but this time the emphasis is on process, continuous redesign, and what has come to be called the self-organizing organization. What sharpens this exposition is an ongoing contrast between a plausible, empirically based set of assertions consistent with a traditional rational systems view of design and a composite set of assertions that highlight emergent design that focuses more on retrospective sensemaking than on planning and prospective decision making. Since this essay touches on a greater range of organizational activity (e.g. control, change, managerial decision making) it begins to suggest what it means for analysis to take interpretation seriously. Designing is shown to resemble improvisation in the extensive use of retrospect and in the guidance from minimal amounts of precomposed material, suggestions that are amplified in Chapter 12. Repeatedly there is the demonstration that a little structure can go a long way. The power of minimal structures is a pervasive feature of organizing that assumes almost axiomatic status in discussions of sensemaking. It is this pervasive feature, perhaps more than any other, which gives ideas about sensemaking and organizing their quality of fundamentals and broadens their relevance far beyond business organizations. It is this same quality that sustains the belief that individuals can make a difference.

Reference

Batchelor, Stephen (1997). *Buddhism Without Beliefs*, New York: Riverhead.

1

Sensemaking in Organizations: Small Structures with Large Consequences

When scholars evaluate their own work, they often apply unconsciously what I will call the "Schutz Test of Comprehension." In the book *Profound Simplicity*, William Schutz made the following observation about his own writing: "When I look over the books I have written, I know exactly which parts I understood and which parts I did not understand when I wrote them. The poorly understood parts sound scientific. When I barely understood something, I kept it in scientific jargon. When I really comprehend it, I was able to explain it to anyone in language they understood. . . . Understanding evolves through three phases: simplistic, complex, and profoundly simple" (Schutz, 1979, pp. 68–69).

When I applied that same test to the second edition of my book, *The Social Psychology of Organizing* (Weick, 1979), I discovered something that Richard Hackman anticipated on March 27, 1976. Richard and I were exchanging penciled sketches at a meeting of social psychologists to help pass the time more quickly. One of Hackman's drawings shows two gravestones, one for each of us. On his stone is the epitaph, "He saved the world," and on mine is written, "He understood the world," and at the bottom of the diagram is written, "And they both were kidding themselves."

Whether we are kidding ourselves or not, Hackman is still trying to save the world and I am still trying to understand it. What happens in my case is that my own desire to understand the world has led me to attribute the same desire to the world itself. Thus, I view organizations as collections of people trying to make sense of what is happening around them.

The clearest parts of the organizing book (Weick, 1979) were about the process of understanding and included such ideas as (1) understanding involves the tradeoffs among generality, accuracy, and simplicity (pp. 35–42); (2) cause loops create predictability (pp. 74–77); (3) experience is stored in cause maps (pp. 138–143); (4)

order is enacted into the world in ways that resemble self-fulfilling prophecies (pp. 159–164); (5) it takes a complex sensor to understand a complex world (pp. 188–193); and (6) sensemaking is a retrospective process (pp. 194–201).

Behind these ideas were remnants of a mindset that dates back to my dissertation. That mindset originated as an interest in cognitive dynamics (Markus & Zajonc, 1985, pp. 139–141), specifically the effects of cognitive dissonance on performance. Cognitive conflict was the independent variable that was hypothesized to have an effect on performance, because performance would be the means by which the conflict could be resolved.

In the study designed to test this idea (Weick, 1964), people agreed to do a difficult concept attainment task after they learned that they would get less reward for their participation than they expected (see Zanna, 1973 for a tighter version of this study). Those who were deprived most severely rated the subsequent task more interesting and were three times more productive at performing it than were people who felt less deprived. At the time, I felt that the severely deprived people had to resolve a disturbing set of cognitions: I came here to get the rewards they promised me, but I didn't get those rewards, yet I'm still participating. How come? Their answer was, because this is such an interesting task. That answer is actually a complex mixture of prospective and retrospective sensemaking. By working hard and solving more problems, they created a situation that confirmed the sensibleness of agreeing to participate in the first place. Ontology and epistemology were woven together out of cognitive necessity.

What continues to interest me about that study is that not only does it capture the effect of cognition on action, it also captures the effect of action on cognition. It does the latter more by accident than by design. Even though I designed the study to create cognitive dissonance, I also accidentally created the conditions later found to induce strong behavioral commitment. It will be recalled that three conditions are necessary for behavioral commitment: choice, an irreversible action, and public awareness of the action (Salancik, 1977). The dissertation experiment was designed so that people experienced several sources of dissonance. The study was built this way on the assumption that dissonant cognitions are additive and that the more dissonance, the stronger the pressure to do something about it. So negative features were added until the breaking point was reached, when a few people would refuse to participate.

At the time, I was more interested in the number of dissonant elements and did not pay much attention to their content. But now it is clear that the dilemma I created involved *choice* (the person could stay or leave, and four people chose to leave), *irreversibility* (once people agreed to stay, they could not back out halfway through the task), and *public awareness* of the decision (I, the experimenter, knew what the person chose to do, how that person performed, and could tell other people.) So the person made a clear commitment to work on a task, a commitment whose full content was not grasped at the beginning. The person gained a deeper understanding of what that original decision involved when he started to work on that task. Closer attention to the task accompanied by increased effort revealed unsuspected attractions that were given additional substance and credibility by hard work. Hard work literally built the convincing reasons that justified the choice to participate.

Notice the way in which the causal arrow is reversed when this study is reinterpreted as an instance of behavioral commitment. Now, cognition in the form of justification becomes the dependent variable and action is the independent variable from which the person draws inferences about what is happening. Having performed the concept attainment task successfully, the person infers that he must have liked the task, which then becomes the reason the person agreed to participate in the first place – even though he had no idea what the task would be when making the choice. Action affects cognition, which is the opposite direction of causality from that implied by dissonant cognitions affecting action.

The experiment mixes together the hot cognition of conflict resolution with the cold cognition of inference. That interpretation is obviously clearer in hindsight than it was at the time of execution. And both themes are largely buried by a rather heavy-handed set of experimental operations. Nevertheless, a prototype of sensemaking is implied in that study. The purpose of this chapter is to elaborate that prototype in context of organizations and show how it links with other work on sensemaking.

Before we explore the key ideas in depth, let's preview the argument. If we generalize the experiment, it suggests that behavioral commitment is a stimulus to build cosmologies and coherent world views out of whatever resources are at hand. Whenever people act, their actions may become binding if those actions occur in a context of high choice, high irreversibility, and high visibility. If action occurs under these conditions, then subsequent events may be enacted in the service of justification. Thus, justification can become an important source of social structure, culture, and norms. For example, Alan Meyer's (1982) important work on how hospitals adapted to the environmental jolt of a doctors' strike can be read as a series of commitments that were justified by the consolidation and articulation of a consistent culture, strategy, and structure. Each hospital became a more distinct, coherent entity after administrations chose publicly to cope with the strike by weathering the storm, experimenting with contingency plans, or monitoring controls more closely.

Organizations begin to materialize when rationales for commitment become articulated. Since the decisions that stimulate justification originate in small-scale personal acts, organizational rationales often originate in the service of self-justification. Only later does justification become redefined as collective intention. Justifications can easily be transformed into organizational goals because these goals themselves are so general. But collective goals can best be understood as embellishments of earlier direct efforts to validate the soundness of individual commitments on a smaller scale.

From the perspective of commitment, organizations are interesting for a specific reason. To see this, consider Daft's (1986, p. 9) definition of an organization as a social entity that is a goal-directed, deliberately structured activity system with an identifiable boundary. Like most scholars, Daft views an organization as a deliberately structured tool. What is left unspecified is the precise nature of that tool. And that is where commitment becomes important. Organizations are viewed as unique social forms that embody choice, visibility, and irrevocability. Goal direction itself takes on a different meaning: "Goals are discovered through a social process involving argumentation and debate in a setting where justification and legitimacy play important roles" (Anderson, 1983, p. 214).

Thus, organizational action is as much goal interpreted as it is goal directed, and the language of goals is indistinguishable from the language of justification.

Since binding choices can affect the tasks we are attracted to, the reasons that move us, the values we seek to realize, the plans we admire, and the people with whom we align ourselves, commitment helps us to understand organizational life. Organizations are filled with potential committing conditions. In most organizations, people do things that others see (e.g., Tetlock, 1985); people make choices and decisions (e.g., empowerment); choices commit resources to programs and structures that are not reversible; participation is used to raise ownership ("ownership" is simply a synonym for commitment); sunk costs are treated as a variable to be justified rather than a given to be dismissed; and the motivational backdrop for all employment is portrayed as a decision to participate, a decision to produce, and a psychological contract.

Despite the potential sweep of commitment and sensemaking, both concepts refer to events that have relatively small beginnings. Both commitment and sensemaking are promising concepts that can broaden the micro side of macro topics (O'Reilly, 1991, p. 449) and offset the current dominance of macro perspectives in organizational analysis.

To illustrate this promise, the remainder of this chapter addresses the following issues. First, we look more closely at the nature of sensemaking and at equivocality as the basic problem that organizations confront. After an overview of the nature of sensemaking we move, in the second section, to an elaboration of the idea of sensemaking as committed interpretation. After reviewing key ideas about interpretation and commitment, we propose a model by which these two processes interact. In the third section we take a closer look at the commitment process itself and show how interaction is inherently committing. We then look at justification in the fourth section and suggest that it creates social structure in a manner reminiscent of the documentary method of interpretation. In the fifth section, we examine the ways in which justifications are validated, a step that is crucial for organizational analysis even though it is usually ignored. We conclude with a brief discussion of implications.

The Nature of Sensemaking

The central problem of sensemaking is best conveyed by an analogy between sensemaking and the game of Mastermind (Fay, 1990). The object of Mastermind is for a codebreaker to duplicate the exact pattern of colored pegs inserted into holes that has been created by a codemaker but is concealed from the codebreaker by a shield. The codebreaker ventures hypotheses as to what the pattern might be and, on the basis of information supplied by the codemaker, refines the hypothesis until the codebreaker's hypothesis exactly matches the codemaker's original pattern.

Mastermind is precisely what sensemaking is not. People cannot be sure there is a mastercode to be discovered, nor can they be sure what the nature of the code might be, nor even if there is some order in the first place. Even if people do discover the code, they can never be sure they have done so since there is nothing equivalent to the removal of the shield at the end of the game, which reveals the concealed code. Although the basic materials in the Mastermind game are pegs, colors, and holes, the person engaged in sensemaking does not know a priori what the exact building blocks are. "What the world is made of is itself a question which must be answered in terms of the available conceptual resources of science at a particular time" (Fay, 1990, p. 36).

People who try to make sense under these conditions have to differentiate and determine the nature of the materials they are working with, have to look for a unifying order without any assurance that there is a pre-existing order in these materials, have to decide how to represent this order, and have to play indefinitely, never knowing whether they have discovered a unifying order.

The task of sensemaking resembles more closely the activity of cartography. There is some terrain that mapmakers want to represent, and they use various modes of projection to make this representation. What they map, however, depends on where they look, how they look, what they want to represent, and their tools for representation (Monmonier, 1991). The crucial point in cartography is that "there is no 'One Best Map' of a particular terrain. For any terrain there will be an indefinite number of useful maps, a function of the indefinite levels and kinds of description of the terrain itself, as well as the indefinite number of modes of representation and uses to which they can be put" (Fay, 1990, p. 37). The terrain is not itself already mapped such that the job of the sensemaker is to discover this preexisting map. "For mapmakers the idea of a pre-ordered world has no place or meaning" (Fay, 1990, p. 37).

It is the job of the sensemaker to convert a world of experience into an intelligible world. That person's job is not to look for the one true picture that corresponds to a pre-existing, preformed reality. The picture of sensemaking that emerges is not one of the tidy world of Mastermind. Instead, the picture that is suggested is "that there is nobody here but us scratching around trying to make our experience and our world as comprehensible to ourselves in the best way we can, that the various kinds of order we come up with are a product of our imagination and need, not something dictated to us by Reality Itself. There isn't any One True Map of the earth, of human existence, of the universe, or of Ultimate Reality, a Map supposedly embedded inside these things; there are only maps we construct to make sense of the welter of our experience, and only us to judge whether these maps are worthwhile for us or not" (Fay, 1990, p. 38).

The important points implied by the idea of sensemaking as cartography are the indefinite number of plausible maps that can be constructed, the role of imagination and need in the determination of the projections actually used, and the fact that the activity of sensemaking is largely social ("there is nobody here but us scratching around"). The problem of sensemaking is compounded because the terrain keeps changing and the task is to carve out some momentary stability in this continuous flow (Becker, 1986, p. 29). We expand on these points in the next section.

Equivocality in organizational life

Organizations resemble puzzling terrain because they lend themselves to multiple, conflicting interpretations, all of which are plausible (Daft & MacIntosh, 1981). In this equivocal situation of confusion, people are not sure what questions to ask, nor do they expect clear answers even if they do know the right questions (Daft & Lengel,

1986, p. 557). To reduce equivocality, people do not need larger quantities of information. Instead, they need richer qualitative information. "Information richness is defined as the ability of information to change understanding within a time interval. Communication transactions that can overcome different frames of reference or clarify ambiguous issues to change understanding in a timely manner are considered rich. Communications that require a long time to enable understanding or that cannot overcome different perspectives are lower in richness. In a sense, richness pertains to the learning capacity of a communication" (Daft & Lengel, 1986, p. 560). Information richness tends to covary with the extent of face-to-face personal interaction, which is why map making tends to be social.

The dominant form that equivocality takes in organizations is suggested by Gergen's (1982, pp. 62–65) three premises for constructivism, all of which focus on the multiple meanings of action.

1.   The identification of any given action is subject to infinite revision.
       There is no such thing as an ultimate definition, partly because events occur in a continually emerging context that changes the meaning of earlier events, and partly because events occur in an open-ended retrospective context in which all kinds of prior personal and societal history can be invoked to explain what is happening right now. There are no iron-clad rules or logics that guarantee that we will avoid the temptations to infinitely revise.
2.   The anchor point for any given identification relies on a network of interdependent and continuously modifiable interpretations.
       What any action means is seldom self-evident; there is no such thing as a fixed unequivocal observable that allows for "proper identification." Since identification is determined by context, and since context is infinitely expandable into the future and the past, it is not clear which contextual indicators can be trusted among sensemakers. This issue is one that largely has to be negotiated. And whatever agreement people hammer out usually unravels as new events occur and old meanings crumble.
3.   Any given action is subject to multiple identifications, the relative superiority of which is problematic.
       As the number of observers increases, so too does the range of contextual events in which an action can be embedded. And, in the absence of unequivocal observables, there are no grounds other than some kind of consensus or some exercise of power (Smircich & Morgan, 1982) to stabilize what people confront and what it means. To call something "a problem" is no more privileged and no easier to sustain than is the proposal that something is "an opportunity." To make things even more complicated, either proposal can set in motion responses that confirm the label.

Sensemaking in organizational life

If we begin to synthesize these separate images of commitment, retrospect, mastermind, map making, equivocality, rich communication media, and social construction into a coherent perspective on sensemaking, that synthesis would sound a lot like one developed by Morgan, Frost, and Pondy (1983). Sensemaking in the broadest sense is a metaphor that "focuses attention upon the idea that the reality of everyday life must be seen as an ongoing 'accomplishment,' which takes particular shape and form as individuals attempt to create order and make retrospective sense of the situations in which they find themselves. . . . [I]ndividuals are seen as engaged in ongoing processes through which they attempt to make their situations rationally accountable to themselves and others. . . . The sensemaking metaphor encourages an analytical focus upon the processes through which individuals create and use symbols; it focuses attention upon the study of the symbolic processes through which reality is created and sustained. Individuals are not seen as living *in*, and acting out their lives in relations *to*, a wider reality, so much as creating and sustaining images of a wider reality, in part to rationalize what they are doing. They realize their reality, by 'reading into' their situation patterns of significant meaning" (Morgan et al., 1983, p. 24).

In the remainder of this chapter, we pay close attention to several themes in this description:

1. Reality is an ongoing accomplishment: Sensemaking is about flows, a continually changing past, and variations in choice, irrevocability, and visibility that change the intensity of behavioral commitments.
2. People attempt to create order: Through social comparison, expectations, and action, flows become stabilized momentarily.
3. Sensemaking is a retrospective process: Remembering and looking back are a primary source of meaning.
4. People attempt to make situations rationally accountable: Justifications are compelling sources of meaning because they consist of socially acceptable reasons.
5. Symbolic processes are central in sensemaking: Presumptions about patterns that underlie concrete actions constrain interpretation.
6. People create and sustain images of wider reality: Maps are pragmatic images that provide temporary guides for action.
7. Images rationalize what people are doing: Images of reality derive from rationalizations of action, and this mechanism is a central theme in this chapter.

Sensemaking as Committed Interpretation

The description of sensemaking constructed by Morgan, Frost, and Pondy imposed a preliminary order on elements of the sensemaking process. In this section, we impose additional order with the proposal that sensemaking is a process of committed interpretation.

This proposal enlarges on a mechanism first identified by Salancik and Pfeffer (1978), which they described this way: "Commitment binds an individual to his or her behavior. The behavior becomes an undeniable and unchangeable aspect of the person's world, and when he makes sense of the environment, behavior is the point on which constructions or interpretations are based. This process can be described as a rationalizing process, in which behavior is rationalized by referring to features of the environment which support it. Such sense-making also occurs in a social context in which norms and expectations affect the rationalizations developed for behavior, and this can be described as a process of legitimating behavior. People develop acceptable justifications for their behavior as a way of making such behavior meaningful and explainable" (p. 231).

Although this mechanism was discussed (and buried) within a larger discussion of a social information processing approach to job attitudes, I want to highlight and develop it because it provides a compact explanation of sensemaking in organizations. The elaboration developed in this chapter is labeled "committed interpretation," both to highlight the social, symbolic nature of sensemaking and to designate binding action as the object of sensemaking. The concept of committed interpretation combines two mindsets, one involving interpretation and the other involving commitment.

The interpretation mindset

The interpretation mindset is represented by the W. I. Thomas theorem: "If men define situations as real, they are real in their consequences" (Thomas & Thomas, 1928, p. 572). As Shalin (1986, p. 12) suggests, this theorem closely resembles William James's pragmatist dictum that, "We need only in cold blood ACT as if the thing in question were real, and keep acting as if it were real, and it will infallibly end by growing in such a connection with our life that it will become real" (1890, Vol. II, p. 321). In both cases an equivocal situation becomes more stable when definitions are imposed and one among many patterns in the flow of reality is isolated.

What is important to recall is that Thomas, unlike James, did *not* intend the theorem to portray reality construction as a process that varied from individual to individual. Instead, he emphasized that definitions should vary from one *group* to another, that different tribes should define the same situation in different ways, and that things should not have the same meaning for different people in different periods of time and in different parts of the country. The symbolic environment from which definitions arise is always a shared environment and the outlook itself is always a shared outlook that cannot be ignored. The sensemaker's "actions always refer to the world that is already there, the intersubjective universe existing on the intersection of objectively established group perspectives" (Shalin, 1986, p. 13).

The suggestion that the collective condition of human existence is the source of meaning is made explicit in Porac, Thomas, and Baden-Fuller's (1989, p. 398) summary of the four key assumptions in the interpretative approach. These four assumptions comprise the interpretation mindset. Paraphrased, the key ideas include the following:

1. *Activities and structures are determined partly by micro momentary actions of members.* We emphasize the justification of committed actions as our key micro momentary action.

2. *Action is based on interpretations of cues; these interpretations are externalized by concrete activities.* We emphasize that committed action sets the stage for interpretation by narrowing attention to those cues that suggest potential justification, and that justified action then serves to validate and support whatever justification has been chosen to interpret the committed action.

3. *Meaning is constructed when people link received cues with existing cognitive structures.* We emphasize retrospect and the documentary method as the means by which this interpretive process unfolds.

4. *People are reflective and can verbalize the content, and sometimes the process, of their interpretations.* We take seriously people's accounts of how they accomplish interpretation, mindful, however, that retrospective sensemaking involves biased reconstruction of antecedents since outcomes are known at the time reconstruction occurs. This very bias is the strength of retrospect as a method of sensemaking since it edits out false starts and imposes a spurious order on an indeterminate past. But this same editing requires that investigators observe sensemaking as it unfolds if they wish to counteract this bias, which often means that ethnography and use of personal experience are crucial sources of data about interpretation.

The problems in working with an interpretive perspective are not only those of a temptation toward subjectivism and mistaking hindsight bias for efficient information processing, but also, as Keesing (1987) has argued, underestimating the constraints imposed by context, distributed information, differentials in power, and vested interests. Each of these potential blindspots seems to have more effect on the content of justification than on the fact that behavior is the object of interpretation. Context affects the content of acceptable justifications and the choice of features of the environment that support the rationalizing. Context also has an effect on which behaviors are singled out for explanation. However, once the behavior is fixed, the process of sensemaking itself should unfold in essentially the sequence we propose in the next section.

The commitment mindset

Having specified what constitutes an interpretation mindset, we now turn briefly to an explanation of the commitment mindset. The bulk of this chapter elaborates the idea that commitment is a reference point for sensemaking. This idea was implicit in my concept attainment study (Weick, 1964) and in both editions of my organizing book (Weick, 1969, 1979) and was made more explicit by Salancik and Pfeffer (1978).

The basic ideas of commitment are these. Normally, when people act, their reasons for doing things are either self-evident or uninteresting, especially when the actions themselves can be undone, minimized, or disowned. Actions that are neither visible nor permanent are easily explained. As actions become more public and irrevocable, however, they become harder to undo; when actions are also volitional, they become harder to disown. When action is irrevocable, public, and volitional, the search for explanations becomes less casual because more is at stake. Explanations that are developed retrospectively to justify committed actions are often stronger than beliefs developed under other less involving conditions because the search to find these explanations requires more effort and more of the self is on the line. These justifications become tenacious and produce selective attention, confident action, and self-confirmation. Once formed, tenacious justifications then prefigure subsequent perception and action, which means they are often self-confirming.

Commitment focuses the sensemaking process on three things: an elapsed action, socially acceptable justification for that action, and the potential for subsequent activities to validate or threaten the justification. Thus, commitment drives interaction patterns by tying behaviors, explanations, social support, and expectations together in a causal sequence. This sequence can become a causal loop that either stabilizes or amplifies subsequent action patterns. It is these patterns that people come to label as organizational designs. Commitments lead to patterns and, ultimately, to what we see as designs.

To illustrate how the idea of commitment reshapes organizational theory, consider two examples. First, the influential garbage can model of organizations (Cohen, March, & Olsen, 1972) suggests that organizations consist of streams of people, choices, solutions, and problems that intermittently converge, more for reasons of timing than logic. The concept of commitment suggests the possibility of a third basis for order in addition to those of timing and logic. Choice may not be one of four equal determinants of organizational outcomes, as is suggested by the garbage can theory; instead, choice may be the occasion when the other three become organized. Problems, solutions, and people all are potential explanations that justify a binding choice (e.g., "I chose to fire him because he could not meet quality standards;" "We chose this line of technology because it will show the board we are serious about the future;" "We chose to move these people to Texas to bring more imagination to their operations.").

The second example hearkens back to the earlier discussion of equivocality. Staw (1980, p. 71) argues that organizations are often unclear about their goals and theories of causality, and that justification often removes some of this lack of clarity: "Under high levels of ambiguity, justification is necessary to both provide purpose for an organization's membership and rationale for parties external to the organization. In fact, organizations which face a great deal of ambiguity are frequently perceived as more effective when they have developed an elaborate or persuasive set of justifications for their particular goals and technology. ... Thus, in many organizational settings justification can become reality: through justification, perceived sources of ambiguity can be explained away or replaced by shared meaning."

We show next how interpretation and commitment combine to produce sensemaking.

The process of committed interpretation

The model of committed interpretation is straightforward. We preview it here and explore its components in more detail in the remainder of the chapter.

Most action is social, even when the other party is only imagined or implied. This

assumption has two immediate and important consequences. First, when people become bound to acts, those acts tend to be interacts rather than solitary acts (Sandelands
& Weick, 1991). Second, interacts themselves generate their own conditions of commitment since each party's action is public, irrevocable, and volitional relative to the
other party in the exchange. When an interact occurs in a committing context and
also generates its own commitment, the action becomes bound to both parties and a
search for justification intensifies.

Since the committed action is actually a committed interact, the appropriate justifications tend to invoke social entities (e.g., "We did it because our role demanded it,
... because we are colleagues, ... because we are in competition, ... because we
respect each other."). Social justification is the crucial step in the model for organizational theory. Commitments to interacts often are justified by explanations that reify
social structure. Behavioral commitments tend to be justified by constraints and
opportunities, and one of the most convenient and socially acceptable ways to pack-
age constraints and opportunities is (as in terms of) macro entities (e.g., "*They* hoped
we would do it, hinted that it should be done, created the chance to do it.").

Once macro entities are invoked to justify a commitment, people continue to use
them as explanations. And they urge others to use these same explanations. To
support these explanations, people deploy them in a manner that resembles self-
fulfilling prophecies. They expect the social world to be put together the way their
justifications say it is put together, they act as if it is put together this way, and they
selectively perceive what they see as if it were put together the way their justifications say. Through a mixture of reification, enactment, imitation, and proselytizing,
incipient social structure is acted into the world and imposes order on that world.
This process both creates new organization and reaffirms organization already in
place.

Thus, straightforward, small-scale, micro behavioral commitments can have macro
consequences, once we recognize five important properties of these commitments.
First, they begin as commitments to social relationships rather than commitments to
individual behaviors. Second, these social relationships often generate their own conditions of commitment. Third, since social relationships rather than behaviors are
what people become bound to, justifications tend to invoke social entities rather than
individual reasons. Fourth, reifications that justify social commitment tend to set up
expectations that operate like self-fulfilling prophecies. And fifth, efforts to validate
these social justifications tend to spread them to other actors.

Committed interpretation, therefore, is a sensemaking process that introduces stability into an equivocal flow of events by means of justifications that increase social
order. Confused people pay closer attention to those interdependent acts that occur in
conjunction with some combination of choice and/or publicity and/or irrevocability.
(Commitment is an additive process that develops gradually [Salancik, 1977, p. 4].)
As they become more fully bound to these interdependent actions, people are more
likely to invoke some larger social entity to justify the commitment. This act of
justification, which often resembles reification, invokes a presupposed order such as a
role system, institution, organization, group, or imputed interest group that explains
the action.

The residue from an episode of committed interpretation is a slight increase in social order plus a partial articulation of what that order consists of (e.g., role system, professional norms, group pressure, collective preference). When people act on behalf of these committed interpretations and their reified content, their actions become more orderly, more predictable, and more organized. As a result of this tightening, their actions have more impact on others and are more likely to be imitated. Thus, both the form and substance of organization become more distinct and the world momentarily becomes slightly less chaotic. And all because some action first stuck out as more public, more irrevocable, and more attached to a set of actors than were other actions.

In the remainder of this chapter, we expand on three themes mentioned in this overview of committed interpretation: interacts as the object of commitment; reification as the content of justification; and validation as the outcome of justification.

The Commitment to Interacts

Commitment is a reference point for sensemaking, and the object of that commitment is a double interact, not an act. When an action by Person A evokes a specific action in Person B, an interact exists (e.g., author makes an assertion and editor criticizes assertion). If we then add in A's response to B's reaction, a double interact exists (e.g., author modifies assertion in response to criticism). Hollander and Willis (1967) argue that the double interact is the basic unit of analysis for social influence, because it can distinguish among conformity ($A_xB_yA_y$), anticonformity ($A_xB_xA_y$), independence ($A_xB_yA_x$), and uniformity ($A_xB_xA_x$).

The double interact is itself a committing context, because it contains all four variables that bind a person to action. *Volition* is present at two points, both when A takes an initial action and when A decides what to do in response to B's reaction. A's initial action is also *public*, because it is observed by B, and *explicit*, because B is able to see that a reaction is warranted. A's second action is *irrevocable* in that he or she had an opportunity to change the first act and has now responded to new information with the second action.

If we simply take the $A_1B_1A_2$ sequence one step further and add B_2 (a triple interact), we now have a sequence in which there should be more commitment to actions A_2 and B_2, because actions A_1 and B_1 created the conditions for commitment.

The potential for an interact to become a committing context when it extends to a double and triple interact may explain why it is so important to retain a *social psychology* of organizations. The smallest unit within which all four conditions of commitment can occur at the same time is the double interact. Conceivably, any action performed within this setting can dominate the actor's attention and draw justifications. If this is plausible, then whatever happens within double and triple interacts should have a disproportionately large effect on meaning and interpretation.

From interacts to collective structures

While the basic forms of interaction – the interact, double interact, and triple interact – have relevance to commitment because they embody conditions that can bind people to actions, we have said little about the content of the actions to which people become bound. This content is the sense that people feel and share.

Content becomes more salient if we reexamine the concept of collective structure (Weick, 1979, chap. 4). Allport (1962) argues that collective structure forms whenever "there is a pluralistic situation in which in order for an individual (or class of individuals) to perform some act (or have some experience) that he 'desires' to perform (or for which he is 'set') it is necessary that *another* person (or persons) perform certain acts (either similar or different and complementary to his own)" (p. 17).

Collective structures form when self-sufficiency proves problematic. This idea is the same starting point for organizational analysis that Barnard (1938) adopted in his famous analogy of men coordinating their actions to move a stone (pp. 86–89). If we translate Allport's description into the ABAB sequence of the triple interact, then all we need to do is argue that A_1 and B_1 are instrumental acts, A_2 and B_2 are consummatory acts, and that B must do B_1 if A is to enjoy A_2, and A must do A_1 if B is to enjoy B_2. Neither A nor B has direct control over their outcomes, and they must entice someone else to contribute a means activity to get their own desired outcomes. For example, editors need good manuscripts if they are to print issues of a journal on time, and authors need to have their work printed if they want to achieve wider dissemination of their ideas. The instrumental actions of writing manuscripts and providing journal space allow both parties to experience outcomes that they cannot control directly. Writing allows editors to print, and printing allows writers to influence.

When authors write and editors publish, these acts are part of longer strings of action. As writing proceeds, the author becomes bound, not just to the writing itself, but also to the subsequent steps of evaluation and dissemination. As editing proceeds, the editor becomes bound, not just to providing space for print, but to filling that space with interesting text and doing so in a timely manner. Thus, each party gets bound to a larger number of actions and contributions by other people.

These additional actions and people tend to be included in whatever justification is adopted. And this wider inclusion increases the possibility that justifications will invoke roles or other social forms as the explanation for the commitment. Commitment to interdependent behaviors, justified as roles in an emerging collective structure, sets the stage for these justifications to become entities.

In other words, people commit to and coordinate instrumental acts (means) before they worry about shared goals (Weick, 1979, pp. 91–95). But shared goals do emerge as people search for reasons that justify the earlier interdependent means to which they have become bound. And those reasons tend to be variations on the theme, "We did those things *because they were roles in a system*" (Katz & Kahn, 1978, chap. 7). Both the roles and the system that requires them (Wiley, 1988) are created and given substance when people justify a collective structure that was originally built around interdependent means.

From behavioral commitment to social commitment

Committed interpretation, thus, is distinctly social in at least three ways. First, the act that is the object of commitment tends to be a double interact rather than an act. For example, strategic conversations, defined as "verbal interactions within superior–subordinate dyads focusing on strategic generalities" (Westley, 1990, pp. 337–338), are double interacts in which top managers and middle managers co-determine strategic outcomes. Their joint efforts to synthesize feelings and frames into implemented strategy are volitional, public, irrevocable interacts that bind both parties and necessitate an explanation that justifies the relationship.

The second sense in which committed interpretation is social is that the justifications chosen to explain the committed interact are socially acceptable within the setting where the commitment occurred. For example, the interaction order among radiologists and technicians that Barley (1986) documented differed among hospitals and across time, and different rationales for dominance or cooperation were invoked in each setting.

The third sense in which committed interpretation is social is that social structure is often invoked to justify commitments. For example, social movement organizations often coalesce when "aggregates of individuals who share common grievances and attributional orientations" (Snow, Rochford, Worden, & Benford, 1986, p. 464) justify their actions by invoking silent constituents for whom they serve as agents of change. The justification lends form to these "unmobilized sentiment pools" and suggests the existence of an organizational base for expressing their discontent and pursuing their interests. The social movement becomes a social form constituted as justification for commitments to double interacts involving grievance.

In their description of sensemaking, Morgan et al. (1983) argued that images of reality tend to derive from rationalization. What we have suggested is that it is interacts rather than acts that are rationalized. This, in turn, suggests that the resulting images of reality will be social images. Previous work on individual commitment tends to overlook the degree to which commitment is grounded in social relationships and is justified by social entities. Once this possibility is entertained, then commitment becomes a more powerful tool to track sensemaking and the emergence of social structure in organizations.

The Justification of Committed Interacts

When people justify interacts, those justifications routinely acknowledge the existence of interdependence (e.g., Zanna & Sande, 1987). The justifications lend substance to the interdependence and reify it into a social entity. For example, I can justify becoming bound to an interdependent sequence by arguing that it was expected; it was my role; it demonstrated that I trust you and am myself trustworthy; it accomplished something neither of us could have done alone; I am subordinate to you; it is our duty; we were told to do it; or we had the same interest. Each of these justifications affirms that a social act was the object of commitment, and each justification lends substance to that social entity.

The point is that reification of a collectivity justifies commitment. Having become bound to interdependent action, if the person says, "That's the way we do things in this culture, in this firm, in this family, or when women are involved," then cultures, firms, families, and gender are invoked as macro sources of micro constraints.

This line of argument resembles Knorr-Cetina's (1981) explanation of a possible linkage between micro and macro phenomena. The macro is not a distinct existential level that emerges from micro events. Instead, the macro is constructed and pursued *within* micro interaction. Micro interaction is constrained by representations of macro entities alleged to exist as a distinct layer of social reality (e.g., see avoided test in Weick, 1979, pp. 149–152). But aside from their effects as mediated through representations that are treated as if they were real, macro "entities" have no separate existential effects.

Participants "continually employ notions and engage in actions whose mutual intelligibility appears to be based upon their presupposition and knowledge of broader societal units" (Knorr-Cetina, 1981, p. 12). Thus a binding interdependent action is made intelligible and justified by presupposition of societal institutions and collective sentiments. Macro constructions such as organization, family, state, media, or market are created in micro situations, often in the form of justifications for interdependent actions ("We did it to preserve freedom, gain competitive advantage, create jobs, influence the market"), and then treated as if they were real constraints to be honored, resisted, bypassed, rationalized, reversed, or ignored.

As we will see later, reification is an *initial* move in an extended chain of validating actions, many of which lend substance to what originally was a mere presumption of social structure. As both Thomas and James made clear, presumptions taken seriously often become self-validating (see Weick, Gilfillan, & Keith, 1973, for a demonstration of this effect). When people presuppose societal institutions, expectations, constraints, and explanations that transcend the committed interact are activated and inform an institution's development.

Symbols and justification

To understand the role of reification in justification, we need to take a closer look at Morgan et al.'s (1983) suggestion that sensemaking involves "symbolic processes through which reality is created and sustained" (p. 4). To understand this phrase, we need to look both at symbols and at the way in which they become linked with concrete actions.

The content of sensemaking comes from preexisting symbols, norms, and social structures (Isaac, 1990, p. 6) that people reproduce and transform rather than create from scratch (Bhaskar, 1978, p. 13). Sensemaking itself is often described as sculpting done by a clever bricoleur (Harper, 1987, p. 74; Levi–Strauss, 1966) who uses whatever materials and tools are at hand to fashion whatever sense is needed. So, although we persist, as do Morgan et al. (1983) in using the verb *create* to describe sensemaking, we do so mindful that the activity itself is shaped by presuppositions and precedents (Smircich & Stubbart, 1985, pp. 732–733) as well as discoveries.

When Morgan et al. (1983, pp. 4-5) talk about symbols in the context of organizations, they emphasize the quality of bricolage: "The word *symbol* derives from Greek roots which combine the idea of sign, in the sense of a mark, token, insignia, means of identification, with that of a throwing and putting together. A symbol is a sign which denotes something much greater than itself, and which calls for the association of certain conscious and unconscious ideas, in order for it to be endowed with its full meaning and significance. A sign achieves the status of a symbol when it is interpreted, not in terms of strict resemblance with what is signified, but when other patterns of suggestion and meaning are 'thrown upon' or 'put together' with the sign to interpret it as part of some much wider symbolic whole. . . . Any object, action, event, utterance, concept, or image offers itself as raw material for symbol creation, at any place, and at any time."

Although organizational symbols can take many forms, the simple classification proposed by Czarniawska-Joerges and Joerges (1990) is a reasonable starting point. They suggest that people use at least three verbal tools to invest experience with meaning: labels, metaphors, and platitudes. "Labels tell *what* things are, they classify [e.g., decentralization, leadership excellence]; metaphors say *how* things are, they relate, give life [e.g., personal development as gardening, organization as garbage can]; platitudes conventionalize, they standardize and establish *what is normal* [e.g., democracy must be built anew in each generation]" (p. 339). Labels, metaphors, and platitudes link the present with the past, impose past definitions on present puzzles, and provide compelling images *if* those images are shared.

The probability of sharing is increased if socialization processes in organizations focus on language (Jablin, 1987; Louis, 1980). "Perhaps the most important context in which definitions of organizational reality are created and shaped is the socialization of new members" (Eisenberg & Riley, 1988, p. 136). Newcomers are exposed to a whole new vocabulary and grammar of symbols, jargon, ideology, attitudes, stories, private jokes, and restricted words, which shape their inclination to label events and which produce a trained incapacity to see the world differently.

Documentary method and justification

Once this vocabulary of symbols is in place, it becomes the language of justification. These symbols become linked with committed interacts through a process called the "documentary method" (Garfinkel, 1967, p. 78). Morgan et al. (1983) anticipated this process when they observed, "Symbols, when approached upon the basis of this perspective [sensemaking], assume principal significance as constructs through which individuals concretize and give meaningful form to their everyday lives" (pp. 24–25). The documentary method, which Heritage (1984, p. 84) has called the "constituent task of making sense," speaks to the linkage of concrete events with meaningful forms. The symbol simultaneously refers to the here and now and to the larger social scene, and the documentary method is the means by which these two worlds are connected.

Garfinkel (1967) defined the documentary method in the following manner: "The method consists of treating an actual appearance as 'the document of,' as 'pointing to,' as 'standing on behalf of' a presupposed underlying pattern. Not only is the pattern derived from its individual documentary evidences but the individual evidences, in their turn, are interpreted on the basis of 'what is known' about the underlying pattern. Each is used to elaborate the other" (p. 78).

Several parallels between the process of justification and the documentary method are suggested. The committed interact is the equivalent of the actual appearance or the document. The justification is the equivalent of an underlying pattern that presupposes a macro context. Neither the interact nor the underlying pattern are labeled initially. Instead, each fleshes out the other. The interact suggests a derived pattern, and the interact then takes its meaning from this derivation, which itself has become strengthened because there appears to be another tangible outcropping that exemplifies it; each is used to elaborate the other. The connection of a cryptic current interact with a presupposed pattern is the key interpretive procedure that reduces equivocality.

Leiter's (1980, pp. 165–189) extended discussion of the documentary method suggests the following nuances of this interpretive procedure. The method itself is deceptive in its apparent simplicity, since it appears to assert simply that people treat a set of appearances as standing on behalf of an underlying pattern. In the context of committed interpretation, we assert that the appearance that gets attention is a committed interact, that the pattern invoked to justify it is a feature of social structure consistent with the interact, that each elaborates the other through enactment into the world, and that through enactment into the world the pattern gains validity and the interact gains meaning. Precisely *which* pattern is likely to be invoked cannot be specified in advance simply because the content is sensitive to context and depends on which explanations are salient at the moment an accounting is required.

A subtle but crucial feature of the documentary method is that it lends factual character to a transient social world. The presupposed pattern creates a sense of stable social structure that is consistent across time and confers meaning on concrete acts that seem to occur under its aegis. The interacts literally become meaningful because they occur in a stable context, even though this stability is itself a construction. Precisely because the here and now can be "connected to the transcendent social scene" (Leiter, 1980, p. 168), the person is protected from having to deal with a continuing string of idiosyncratic, random appearances. "The members' sense of social structure involves, and depends upon, the stability of the object over and in spite of variations in situational appearances" (p 169).

To use the documentary method is to presume and rely on the facticity of the social world while simultaneously creating that facticity. The world must be assumed to be real for it to be made real. Thus, the ability to assume a factual social world is necessary for facticity to be created. It is the joint effect of being bound to an interact and of being exposed to symbols that portray a presumably factual social world, which, in the case of organizational members, make it relatively easy to use this process of interpretation.

An important implication is that the documentary method is crucial for micro organizational analysis beyond its appropriateness for the concept of committed interpretation. The documentary method suggests a means by which organizational structure itself is created. Earlier, we suggested that justifications often reify social entities. Committed actions can be justified as macro necessities (e.g., "This is a partnership."). Once invoked as justifications, these macro entities then materialize when they are treated as if they are real constraints.

Although the earlier discussion of reification was confined to interacts, the relevance of reification for organizational sensemaking extends beyond these small units. A suggestion of this broader relevance is to be found in Hilbert's (1990) description of how skills used in the documentary method create the macro structures that make sense of micro events: "Microevents are classified into existence even as they are used to document the reality of macroevents of which they are examples. Macrostructures, then, are idealizations or typifications that are documented, filled out, and continually reproduced and modified by their microexamples, these examples being exactly what they are by affiliation with the very macropatterns they are used to document" (p. 803).

To return to the starting point for this chapter, sensemaking is an attempt to produce micro stability amidst continuing change. People produce micro stabilities by social commitment, which means that interacts become meaningful and that both the interacts and the meanings will be repeated. Stated more abstractly, micro stability is produced when people "orient to a presupposed social-structural order, reifying and reproducing it in the course of their activity and imposing its reality on each other as they do" (Hilbert, 1990, p. 796). Thus, reification starts with the documentary method. People presume that something concrete, often their own committed behavior, is a document of some larger pattern that, having been presumed, proceeds to flesh out both the particular and the general.

Illustrations of sensemaking using the documentary method are relatively common in the organizational literature. For example, Westley's (1990) discussion of middle managers and strategy presumes a mechanism similar to that of the documentary method: "Strategy is a meaning generating activity concerned with integrating and interpreting information. As such it is abstracted from specific tactics, policies, or operational procedures while being intimately concerned with relating these into an overall pattern" (p. 342). Strategy is the underlying pattern; tactics, policies, and procedures are the documents; and each relates to and integrates the other in the interest of meaning.

Westley describes a female middle manager who is excluded from the inner circle of people who know the strategic pattern thoroughly, and who, as a result of this exclusion, finds sensemaking difficult. When given a 2-inch pile of memos to digest and comment on, this person finds herself "searching for strategic generalities and the total picture so that she can make sense of the specific particular decisions that are passed along to her" (p. 343). She literally has documents in search of patterns. Having been excluded from strategic activity, she has not even a clue about the larger context of these memos.

Other examples of the documentary method can be cited. Daft and Weick (1984, p. 286) describe organizations as interpretation systems that tie external events (i.e., "documents") to internal categories (i.e., "underlying patterns"). Ranson, Hinings, and Greenwood (1980) state explicitly that "the 'rational' panoply of roles, rules, and procedures which make up organizational design is not pregiven in the organization but is the skilled, practical, and retrospective accomplishment of members. . . . Prescribed roles, rules, and authority relations are drawn upon retrospectively to locate and validate the emergent action within the wider context of meaning" (pp. 2, 5). Roles and rules are the underlying patterns that render the documents of "emergent action" more meaningful. Porac et al. (1989) suggest that specific transactions involving what to produce, what to purchase, and whom to target as customers are all documents that gain their meaning from a mental model of the environment that consists of identity beliefs and causal beliefs (p. 399). This mental model contains the underlying patterns that inform and explain the technical and material transactions.

The central role of justification in sensemaking has often been overlooked because traditionally the process has been labeled "*self*-justification" (e.g. Aronson, 1980, pp. 7–10). This phrase carries a connotation of defensiveness and distortion (e.g., Staw, 1980, p. 59), which deflects attention from the more neutral meaning that "a rational reason for doing something is merely rationalizing done within socially acceptable bounds" (Salancik & Pfeffer, 1978, p. 235, footnote 3). Furthermore, even the qualifier, "self" is misleading, since the self is socially defined and takes many forms (e.g., Simmel, 1971, pp. 10–11). If there are multiple selves, then the phrase *self-justification* specifies little.

The preceding analysis suggests that one way to understand the statement "symbolic processes create and sustain reality" is to argue that organizations begin to materialize when social rationales for social commitments are created. Not all justifications consist of reification, although all committed behaviors are social. This social character of commitment is always available as a cue that can guide the search for an underlying pattern toward social forms and macro entities. Since organizational settings are multiactor social forms, it seems safe to presume both that reification is a common route that justification will take initially, and that action initially explained by reification soon generates the reality that replaces the reification with substance.

The Validation of Justification

Many justifications are not fully formed immediately after commitment occurs. Instead, they are worked out over time as the implications of the action are gradually discovered and new meanings of the action are created. Thus, the tendency for people writing about commitment to dwell on the immediate justification seems too limited because it focuses on too short a time interval. Key effects of commitment can also be observed later in the period, which we label postjustification action. There is evidence that once a justification begins to form, it exerts an effect on subsequent action (e.g., Penner, Fitch, & Weick, 1966; Weick & Prestholdt, 1968).

Justification is not a brief moment in sensemaking. Instead, it shapes and is shaped by action subsequent to the commitment. Thus, if a person justifies a decision to accept an unpleasant assignment with the explanation that it will be a challenge and an opportunity, that person often can create just such attractions and solidify the justification by the way he or she performs the assignment. The person acts so as to turn the assignment into an opportunity; these actions validate the rationale by actually creating opportunities, which further intensifies action; and the result is a justification whose validity is demonstrable and under the control of the actor. This scenario shows most clearly how justifications gain their tenacity and validity.

The way in which postjustification action contributes to validity can be illustrated if we extend a straightforward example of postaction justification. Salancik (1977, p. 27) describes a man who goes to a sales convention in Hawaii and justifies that action in different ways to different audiences. To himself he says he needed a vacation, to his wife he says it was a business obligation, and to his boss he says he wanted to survey the competition. The point we want to add is that, having made these justifications, he now will act more like vacations are important, conventions are a necessity, and surveying the competition is crucial. Justifications can turn into preferences that control subsequent attention and action (Weick, 1966, 1967). Detecting this outcome requires that we pay closer attention to the ways in which repeated use of a justification reaffirms its value and begins to transform it into a stable frame reference. Sensitivity to these outcomes requires, in turn, that we look for the ways in which actions following commitment are used to create and solidify an emergent justification.

Postdecision validation

Our focus on the postdecision period shows the continuing impact on organizational behavior of Leon Festinger and others who worked with cognitive dissonance theory. While dissonance theory per se has been increasingly bounded (e.g., Cooper & Fazio, 1989; Scher & Cooper, 1989), theorists of sensemaking continue to elaborate the basic insight that postdecision behavior differs markedly from predecision behavior (Jones & Gerard, 1967). During the predecision period, people pay equal attention to alternatives in an effort to reduce their ignorance. If there is differential attention to alternatives, they pay more attention to the alternatives they eventually reject. This is the pattern of information processing that Daft and Lengel (1986) associate with uncertainty.

Once the decision is made, the problem shifts from ignorance to confusion. This counterintuitive outcome – How can people be confused *after* a decision? – occurs because people temporarily face multiple, conflicting definitions of what their decision means. Not only does it mean that they will receive the positive features of their chosen alternative and avoid the negative features of their unchosen alternatives; it also means they will receive the negative features of their chosen alternative and forgo the positive features of their rejected alternative. Thus, when the decision means many different conflicting things, the problem is one of too many meanings, not too few, and the problem shifts from one of uncertainty to one of equivocality (Daft & MacIntosh, 1981). The decision has become an equivoque (Weick, 1979, p. 174), an event with two or more possible meanings. This may explain in part the much-discussed "regret" that often follows decision making.

We see that equivocality enters the sensemaking process at two points: before a committing action occurs, and immediately after a committed action becomes someone's responsibility but has not yet been justified.

Validation and action intensity

After the committed action has been chosen, there is little advantage to reflecting on the advantages of the rejected alternative or disadvantages of the chosen alternative. Once a decision is made, action is more effective when probabilistic information is treated as if it were deterministic and beliefs that are only relatively true are treated as if they were absolutely true (Brickman, 1987, p. 36). "Commitment marshals forces that destroy the plausibility of alternatives and remove their ability to inhibit action. These forces are nonrational, though their use is functional. . . . We may choose our actions in the first place on the rational basis of their standing in our informational system, but we drive them, energize them, and justify them on the nonrational basis of our motivational commitment to them" (Brickman, 1987, pp. 40–41).

Intensity facilitates the justification of commitments because it helps people accept activities that are not the best they might obtain and allows them to turn forgone possibilities into enhancement of the chosen alternative. People who pursue a chosen alternative unequivocally and with intensity often uncover unexpected attractions (Brickman, 1987, p. 54), with the result that the committed person is no longer greatly troubled by the thought that there might be more attractive alternatives.

Intense actions justify commitment by synthesizing positive and negative consequences of the chosen alternative. But intense actions also enable people to enact realities in which the justifications become accurate stories about how the world actually works. Consider an example proposed by Henshel (1987, p. 34).

Suppose a judge makes a public, irrevocable choice to dispose of juvenile delinquency cases on the basis of whether the defendant comes from an intact or broken home. The judge justifies this choice on the basis that broken homes produce delinquents who are incorrigible. The justification is a theory and a reification as well as a prediction that can be confirmed or disconfirmed. When the judge sends those from broken homes to prison more often than those from intact homes, this action exposes those in broken homes to prison experience, they find it harder to get jobs once they are released, and they resort more quickly to more serious crimes. As a result, official crime statistics now contain more cases that confirm the theory. Broken homes now do in fact correlate with a higher recidivism rate, which leads people to invoke the justification with more confidence. Judges resort to even more differential sentencing based on data about conditions at home because the "facts" show that home conditions make a difference.

A justification with little intrinsic validity comes to be seen as more valid because powerful people believe in it and act on these beliefs (Snyder, 1984). For these people, the world has become sensible. What they underestimate is their role in producing this sense. What has happened is that a justification has created a serial self-fulfilling prophecy that builds confidence in the prophecy through a deviation-amplifying causal loop (Maruyama, 1963). Under these conditions, both the justification and the action mutually strengthen one another, and the result is intense action that enacts a portion of the environment people confront. Thus, intensity guided by commitment can change the environment to resemble more closely the justification that was first imposed on it.

Similar scenarios are found throughout the organizational literature. Starbuck (1976, p. 1081), for example, argues that organizations play an active role in shaping their environments, partly because they seek environments that are sparsely inhabited by competitors, partly because they define their products and outputs in ways that emphasize distinctions between themselves and their competitors, partly because they rely on their own experience to infer environmental possibilities, and partly because they need to impose simplicity on complex relationships. A key mechanism in all of these scenarios is that perceptions and actions validate one another in ways that resemble self-fulfilling prophecies: "It is primarily in domains where an organization believes it exerts influence, that the organization attributes change to its own influence, and in domains where an organization believes itself impotent, it tends to ignore influence opportunities and never to discover whether its influence is real. ... Moreover, it is the beliefs and perceptions founded on social reality which are especially liable to self-confirmation" (Starbuck, 1976, p. 1081).

Writing about political institutions, March and Olsen (1989) observed that "much of the richness of ecological theories of politics stems from the way in which the actions of each participant are part of the environments of others. The environment of each political actor is, therefore, partly self-determined as each reacts to the other. ... When environments are created, the actions taken in adapting to an environment are partly responses to previous actions by the same actor, reflected through the environment. A common result is that small signals are amplified into large ones, and the general implication is that routine adaptive processes have consequences that cannot be understood without linking them to an environment that is simultaneously, and endogenously, changing" (p. 46).

Thus, political actors, as well as organizational actors in general, choose and create some of their own constraints, particularly when they justify committed interacts and then treat these justifications as prescriptive and factual and important.

Conclusion

A dominant question for scholars of organizing is, How do people produce and acquire a sense of order that allows them to coordinate their actions in ways that have mutual relevance? The answer proposed here is, by concrete communicative interaction in which people invoke macro structures to justify commitments. Thus, social order is created continuously as people make commitments and develop valid, socially acceptable justifications for these commitments. Phrased in this way, individual sensemaking has the potential to be transformed into social structures and to maintain these structures. Commitment is one means by which social structure is realized. This proposal suggests a possible mechanism by which structuration (e.g., Barley, 1986; Giddens, 1984) actually works.

The preceding analysis also implies the following:

1. Sensemaking is focused on those actions around which the strongest commitments form.
2. The content of sensemaking consists of justifications that are plausible to,

advocated by, sanctioned within, and salient for important reference groups with which the actors identify.

3. Actions "mean" whatever justifications become attached to them. Committed actions are equivocal (Daft & MacIntosh, 1981) since they have multiple meanings; the justification process reduces this confusion (Daft & Lengel, 1986).

4. Organizing begins with moments of commitment. These moments determine the meanings that are available to make sense of events that fill the other noncommitting periods. The generation of meaning is a discontinuous process that is activated when important actions coincide with settings in which those actions are performed volitionally, publicly, explicitly, and irrevocably. Among our many actions, few occur under conditions that are binding. Most organizations, most of the time, activate few of these committing conditions. When they do, they activate them only for a handful of people. Since commitment is an additive process, commitments strengthen slowly and incrementally. Furthermore, new justifications and new meanings are slow to emerge as they are grounded in old meanings that persist even though they are outdated. As a result, organizational life may be experienced by many as empty and meaningless. This sense of anomie should decline the more action is encouraged and the more committing the context within which that action unfolds.

5. Presuppositions, expectations, and even faith are important engines in the sense-making process, especially when actors are confident and environments are malleable. In understructured settings such as temporary systems, small firms, and entrepreneurial ventures, motivated presuppositions can exert influence and alter interaction patterns. Alteration is even more likely when the presuppositions and actions form a deviation-amplifying feedback loop. Micro dynamics have the potential to create sensibleness by actually stabilizing the environment, and this is the point of analyzing what happens *after* a justification is formulated. Justification is not just head work. Thoughts are acted into the world (Porac et al., 1989, pp. 398–401).

6. Organizations are ideal sites for committed interpretation because they generate action, champion accountability, make choices, value good reasons, and scrutinize everything. But organizations also exaggerate their intentional nature and thus often miss the fact that their interpretations are focused on their commitments. People *do* know best that to which they are committed, but not because they knew it and then became committed. It is just the opposite. Action leads the sensemaking process; it does not follow it. People need to be less casual about action since whatever they do has the potential to bind them and focus their sensemaking. Inaction, repetitive action, and idiosyncratic action all have direct effects on what people know and how well they know it. Action *is* intelligence, and until it is deployed, meaning and sense will be underdeveloped.

7. Social psychology is crucial for organizational analysis because it is the one discipline that does not fall prey to the error of assuming that large effects imply large causes. Social psychology is about small events that enlarge because they are embedded in amplifying causal loops, are acted into networks where they spread (Porac et al., 1989), become sources that are imitated,

resolve important uncertainties at impressionable moments, make discontinuous changes in performance (Chambliss, 1989), and so on. Organizations are not monoliths. Instead, they are loosely coupled fragments (Orton & Weick, 1990) just as individuals are. This fragmentation means that the relevant unit of analysis is small in size though not in influence, that small events spread intermittently and fortuitously, and that macro perspectives are hollow unless linked with micro dynamics.

It is important to reiterate the way in which commitments serve to guide organizational behavior. Our challenge as researchers is not to predict exactly what will happen in each organizational moment. To attempt that is to attempt to predict the path of a bouncing football (Kuhn & Beam, 1982, pp. xxi–xxii): It is neither necessary nor possible. Instead, what we need to understand are those events that give direction and meaning to the stream of organizational moments.

That is what commitments do. Once a person makes a commitment, then subsequent events often are interpreted in ways that confirm the soundness of that commitment. Thus, commitments constrain the meanings that people impose on streams of experience.

The picture of an organization that emerges from these ideas is that of a stream of problems, solutions, and people tied together by choices. What happens over time is that choices mobilize reasons and justifications, which people then use to make elements in these streams more orderly. Organizing starts with a set of choices and streams. When the streams converge, people pay attention and construct explanations for the convergence. Their explanations vary depending on their needs, their associates, and their prior choices. The stream of consciousness in organizations takes the tangible form of streams of people, solutions, and problems that become organized to justify choices. When we say that people construct reality, what we mean is that they use commitments to guide their efforts at sensemaking. Commitments are what they start with. And commitments are what shape their continuing search for sensible work in a sensible setting.

References

Allport, F. H. (1962). A structuronomic conception of behavior: Individual and collective. *Journal of Abnormal and Social Psychology, 64*, 3–30.

Anderson, P. A. (1983). Decision making by objection and the Cuban missile crisis. *Administrative Science Quarterly, 28*, 201–222.

Aronson, E. (1980). Persuasion via self-justification: Large commitments for small rewards. In L. Festinger (Ed.), *Retrospectives on social psychology* (pp. 3–21). New York: Oxford.

Barley, S. (1986). Technology as an occasion for structuring: Evidence for observations of CAT scanners and the social order of radiology departments. *Administrative Science Quarterly, 31*, 78–108.

Barnard, C. I. (1938). *The functions of the executive.* Cambridge, MA: Harvard University Press.

Becker, H. (1986). Dialogue with Howard S. Becker. In H. S. Becker (Ed.), *Doing things together* (pp. 25–46). Evanston, IL: Northwestern University Press.

Bhaskar, R. (1978). On the possibility of social scientific knowledge and the limits of natural-
ism. *Journal for the Theory of Social Behavior, 8*, 1–28.

Brickman, P. (1987). *Commitment, conflict, and caring.* Englewood Cliffs, NJ: Prentice Hall.

Chambliss, D. F. (1989). The mundanity of excellence: An ethnographic report on stratifica-
tion and olympic swimmers. *Sociological Theory, 7*(1), 70–86.

Cohen, M. D., March, J. G., & Olsen, J. P. (1972). A garbage can model of organizational
choice. *Administrative Science Quarterly, 17*, 1–25.

Cooper, J., & Fazio, R. H. (1989). Research traditions, analysis, and synthesis: Building a faulty
case around misinterpreted theory. *Personality and Social Psychology Bulletin, 15*(4), 519–
529.

Czarniawska-Joerges, B., & Joerges, B. (1990). Linguistic artifacts at service of organizational
control. In P. Gagliardi (Ed.), *Symbols and artifacts: Views of the corporate landscape* (pp. 339–
364). Berlin: de Gruyter.

Daft, R. L. (1986). *Organization theory and design* (2nd ed.). St. Paul, MN: West.

Daft, R. L., & Lengel, R. H. (1986). Organizational information requirements, media richness
and structural design. *Management Science, 32*(5), 554–571.

Daft, R. L., & MacIntosh, N. B. (1981). A tentative exploration into the amount and equivocality of information processing in organizational work units. *Administrative Science Quarterly,
26*, 207–224.

Daft, R. L., & Weick, K. E. (1984). Toward a model of organizations as interpretation systems.
Academy of Management Review, 9, 284–295.

Eisenberg, E. M., & Riley, P. (1988). Organizational symbols and sensemaking. In G. M. Goldhaber
& G. A. Barnett (Eds.), *Handbook of organizational communication* (pp. 131–150). Norwood,
NJ: Ablex.

Fay, B. (1990). Critical realism? *Journal for the Theory of Social Behaviour, 20*, 33–41.

Garfinkel, H. (1967). *Studies in ethnomethodology.* Englewood Cliffs, NJ: Prentice Hall.

Gergen, K. J. (1982). *Toward transformation in social knowledge.* NY: Springer-Verlag.

Giddens, A. (1984). *The constitution of society: Outline of the theory of structuration.* Cambridge,
England: Polity Press.

Harper; D. (1987). *Working knowledge.* Chicago: University of Chicago.

Henshel, R. L. (1987, September). *Credibility and confidence feedback loops in social prediction.*
Paper presented at the Plenary Session of the VII International Congress of Cybernetics and
Systems, University of London.

Heritage, J. (1984). *Garfinkel and ethnomethodology.* Cambridge, England: Polity Press.

Hilbert, R. A. (1990). Ethnomethodology and the micro–macro order. *American Sociological
Review, 55*, 794–808.

Hollander, E. P., & Willis, R. H. (1967). Some current issues in the psychology of conformity
and nonconformity. *Psychological Bulletin, 68*, 67–76.

Isaac, J. C. (1990). Realism and reality: Some realistic considerations. *Journal for the Theory of
Social Behaviour, 20*, 1–32.

Jablin, F. M. (1987). Organizational entry, assimilation, and exit. In F. M. Jablin, L. J. Putnam,
K. H. Roberts, & L. W. Porter (Eds.), *Handbook of organizational communication* (pp. 679–740).
Newbury Park, CA: Sage.

James, W. (1890). *The principles of psychology. Vol. II.* New York: Holt.

Jones, E. E., & Gerard, H. B. (1967). *Foundations of social psychology.* New York: Wiley.

Katz, D., & Kahn, R. L. (1978). *The social psychology of organizations.* New York: Wiley.

Keesing, R. M. (1987). Anthropology as interpretive quest. *Current Anthropology, 28*, 161–
176.

Knorr-Cetina, K. D. (1981). The micro-sociological challenge of macro-sociology: Towards a reconstruction of social theory and methodology. In K. Knorr-Cetina & A. V. Cicourel (Eds.), *Advances in social theory and methodology* (pp. 1–47). Boston: Routledge & Kegan Paul.

Kuhn, A., & Beam, R. D. (1982). *The logic of organization.* San Francisco: Jossey-Bass.

Leiter, K. (1980). *A primer on ethnomethodology.* New York: Oxford.

Levi-Strauss, C. (1966): *The savage mind.* Chicago: University of Chicago.

Louis, M. R. (1980). Surprise and sensemaking: What newcomers experience in entering unfamiliar organizational settings. *Administrative Science Quarterly, 25,* 226–251.

March, J. G., & Olsen, J. P. (1989). *Rediscovering institutions: The organizational basis of politics.* New York: Free Press.

Markus, H., & Zajonc, R. B. (1985). The cognitive perspective in social psychology. In G. Lindzey & E. Aronson (Eds.), *Handbook of social psychology* (Vol. 1, 3rd ed., pp. 137–230). New York: Random House.

Maruyama, M. (1963). The second cybernetics: Deviation-amplifying mutual causal processes. *American Scientist, 51,* 164–179.

Meyer, D. A. (1982). Adapting to environmental jolts. *Administrative Science Quarterly, 27,* 515–537.

Monmonier, M. (1991). *How to lie with maps.* Chicago: University of Chicago.

Morgan, G., Frost, P. J., & Pondy, L. R. (1983). Organizational symbolism. In L. R. Pondy, P. J. Frost, G. Morgan, & T. C. Dandridge (Eds.), *Organizational symbolism* (pp 3–35). Greenwich, CT: JAI Press.

O'Reilly, C. A., III. (1991). Organizational behavior: Where we've been, where we're going. *Annual Review of Psychology, 42,* 427–458.

Orton, J. D., & Weick, K. E. (1990). Loosely coupled systems: A reconceptualization. *Academy of Management Review, 15,* 203–223.

Penner, D. D., Fitch, G., & Weick, K. E. (1966). Dissonance and the revision of choice criteria. *Journal of Personality and Social Psychology, 3,* 701–705.

Porac, J. F., Thomas, H., & Baden-Fuller, C. (1989). Competitive groups as cognitive communities: The case of scottish knitwear manufacturers. *Journal of Management Studies, 26,* 397–416.

Ranson, S., Hinings, B., & Greenwood, R. (1980). The structuring of organizational structures. *Administrative Science Quarterly, 25,* 1–17.

Salancik, G. R. (1977). Commitment and the control of organizational behavior and belief. In B. M. Staw & G. R. Salancik (Eds.), *New directions in organizational behavior* (pp. 1–54). Chicago: St. Clair.

Salancik, G. R., & Pfeffer, J. (1978). A social information processing approach to job attitudes and task design. *Administrative Science Quarterly, 23,* 224–253.

Sandelands, L. E., & Weick, K. E. (1991). *Social commitment and organizing.* Unpublished manuscript, University of Michigan.

Scher, S. J., & Cooper, J. (1989). Motivational basis of dissonance: The singular role of behavioral consequences. *Journal of Personality and Social Psychology, 56,* 899–906.

Schutz, W. (1979). *Profound simplicity.* New York: Bantam.

Shalin, D. N. (1986). Pragmatism and social interactionism. *American Sociological Review, 51,* 9–29.

Simmel, G. (1971). How is society possible? In D. H. Levine (Ed.), *George Simmel on individuality and social forms* (pp. 6–22). Chicago: University of Chicago.

Smircich, L., & Morgan, G. (1982). Leadership: The management of meaning. *Journal of Applied Behavioral Science, 18,* 257–273.

Smircich, L., & Stubbart, C. (1985). Strategic management in an enacted world. *Academy of Management Review, 10*, 724–736.

Snow, D. A., Rochford, E. B., Jr., Worden, S. K., & Benford, R. D. (1986). Frame alignment processes, micromobilization, and movement participation. *American Sociological Review, 51*, 464–481.

Snyder, M. (1984). When belief creates reality. In L. Berkowitz (Ed.), *Advances in experimental social psychology* (Vol. 18, pp. 247–305). New York: Academic Press.

Starbuck, W. H. (1976). Organizations and their environments. In M. D. Dunnette (Ed.), *Handbook of industrial and organizational psychology* (pp. 1069–1123). Chicago: Rand McNally.

Staw, B. M. (1980). Rationality and justification in organizational life. In B. M. Staw & L. L. Cummings (Eds.), *Research in organizational behavior* (Vol. 2, pp. 45–80). Greenwich, CT: JAI Press.

Tetlock, P. E. (1985). Accountability: The neglected social context of judgment and choice. In L. L. Cummings & B. M. Staw (Eds.), *Research in organizational behavior: Vol. 7* (pp. 297–332). Greenwich, CT: JAI Press.

Thomas, W. I., & Thomas, D. S. (1928). *The child in America: Behavior problems and programs.* New York: Knopf.

Weick, K. E. (1964). The reduction of cognitive dissonance through task enhancement and effort expenditure. *Journal of Abnormal and Social Psychology, 68*, 533–539.

Weick, K. E. (1966). Task acceptance dilemmas: A site for research on cognition. In S. Feldman (Ed.), *Cognitive consistency* (pp. 225–255). New York: Academic Press.

Weick, K. E. (1967). Dissonance and task enhancement: A problem for compensation theory? *Organizational Behavior and Human Performance, 2*, 189–208.

Weick, K. E. (1979). *The social psychology of organizing* (2nd ed.). Reading, MA: Addison-Wesley.

Weick, K. E., Gilfillan, D. P., & Keith, T. (1973). The effect of composer credibility in orchestra performance. *Sociometry, 36*, 435–462.

Weick, K. E., & Prestholdt, P. (1968). Realignment of discrepant reinforcement value. *Journal of Personality and Social Psychology, 8*, 180–187.

Westley, F. R. (1990). Middle managers and strategy: Microdynamics of inclusion. *Strategic Management Journal, 11*, 337–351.

Wiley, N. (1988). The micro–macro problem in social theory. *Sociological Theory, 6*, 254–261.

Zanna, M. P. (1973). On inferring one's belief from one's behavior in a low-choice setting. *Journal of Personality and Social Psychology, 26*, 386–394.

Zanna, M. P., & Sande, G. N. (1987). The effects of collective actions on the attitudes of individual group members: A dissonance analysis. In M. P. Zanna, J. M. Olson, & C. P. Herman (Eds.), *Social influence* (Vol. 5, pp. 151–164). Hillsdale, NJ: Erlbaum.

2

Sources of Order in Underorganized Systems: Themes in Recent Organizational Theory

Because new ideas are often hard to grasp, authors sometimes use metaphors to introduce them. One recurring metaphor that has been used to suggest an alternative view of organizations portrays an unconventional soccer game played on an unconventional soccer field. There are at least two versions of this metaphor in the published literature. Although both versions suggest a new way of thinking, they differ in significant ways.

Version 1 of the soccer metaphor appears on page 1 of my 1976 article in *Administrative Science Quarterly* entitled "Educational Organizations as Loosely Coupled Systems." Version 1 reads as follows:

> Imagine that you're either the referee, coach, player or spectator at an unconventional soccer match: the field for the game is round; there are several goals scattered haphazardly around the circular field, people can enter and leave the game whenever they want; they can say "that's my goal" whenever they want to, as many times as they want to, and for as many goals as they want to; the entire game takes place on a sloped field, and the game is played as if it makes sense.

Version 2 of the soccer metaphor appears on page 276 of the March and Olsen book titled *Ambiguity and Choice in Organizations* (1976) in a chapter that March coauthored with Pierre Romelaer. The second version reads as follows:

> Consider a round, sloped, multi-goal soccer field on which individuals play soccer. Many different people (but not everyone) can join the game (or leave it) at different times. Some people can throw balls into the game or remove them. Individuals while they are in the game try to kick whatever ball comes near them in the direction of the goals they like and away from the goals that they wish to avoid. The slope of the field produces a

bias in how the balls fall and what goals are reached, but the course of a specific decision and the actual outcomes are not equally anticipated. After the fact, they may look rather obvious; and usually normatively reassuring.

The difference between the two versions can be understood by focusing on the second version. In it

(1) many people can join the game, but not everyone;
(2) people can either leave the game or join it;
(3) some people can throw balls into the game, but others can't;
(4) some people can remove balls from the game, but others can't;
(5) players do not kick the ball in just any old direction; they kick it in the direction of goals they like and away from goals they wish to avoid;
(6) there is just one slope to the field, not many slopes, and this slope produces a consistent bias in which goals are reached easily; but some goals are usually reached.

Goal setting is more haphazard in version 1, in which people lay claim to whatever goals they wish, whenever they wish. In version 2 goal setting is more stable and is defined in terms of things people like and things they wish to avoid.

Version 2 states that the course of decisions and the nature of actual outcomes are not easily anticipated, whereas version 1 makes no mention at all of decisions, outcomes, or anticipations.

Both versions state that people try to make sense of this confusing world. Version 1 states that people play the game "as if it makes sense." Version 2 states that decisions and outcomes may look "obvious" and "reassuring," but only after the fact (retrospectively). In both versions any sense that people make of these events is contained in their heads rather than in events and is superimposed on the events. The subtle difference is that in version 1 active efforts to make sense of the confusion occur while the game is being played (the presumption of logic), whereas in version 2 sense is superimposed after the game concludes and the outcome is known.

Version 2 states explicitly that people understand that they are playing soccer (see sentence 1). This constraint is not explicitly stated in version 1, which says only that people play some game as if it makes sense, although it's not clear that all participants have soccer in mind as the game they are playing.

Goals are "multiple" in version 2, but are scattered haphazardly in version 1. In version 2 there might or might not be some order in the way the goals are arranged.

The slope of the field in version 1 essentially adds one more complication for the confused player, whereas in version 2 the slope of the field seems to influence which balls reach which goals, a consistent influence that introduces some order.

In each of these comparisons version 1 contains less order than version 2. It's as if the author of version 1 thought that the key point about organizations is that they contain no order at all. Others have made the same mistake. Starbuck (1982, p. 16), for example, observed that "although the garbage-can model (which is the theoretical context within which March originated his version of the soccer metaphor), captures some aspects of real life, it puts too much emphasis on randomness."

The soccer game portrayed in version 2 is far from random. Small, subtle pockets of order occur in several places. Order resides in timing, participation, ideology, language, shared images, overlapping individual goals, stable a priori preferences, and a consistent environment for the game itself (imparted by the slope of the field). Less prominent as sources of order in the soccer games are the usual trappings of administration such as rules, regulations, standard operating procedures, constant surveillance, lines of authority, clear narrow job descriptions, detailed specifications of desired outcomes, official goals, and organizational charts. Not only is order present in unexpected places, but the small amount of order that does exist seems to be sufficient.

There is room in the soccer game for improvisation, change, redefinition, new goals, experimentation, even as there is also an elementary structure within which people get their bearings. Any temptation to "tighten up" the soccer game would not be an obvious improvement and could, in fact, undo the structure that is there.

The point in dissecting the two versions of the soccer game is that the newer models of organization suggest that order occurs in unexpected places and spans fewer people for shorter periods than we thought. These newer proposals, however, do not claim that order is completely absent. Organizations may be anarchies, but they are *organized* anarchies. Organizations may be loosely coupled, but they are loosely coupled *systems*. Organizations may resort to garbage can decision making, but garbage cans have borders that impose some structure.

Themes

Although there is enormous variation among newer proposals of what organizations are like, there are at least six themes that are found in most of them. I will describe these themes in an effort to give an overview of one alternative to the rational bureaucratic model of organizations that has been the prevailing paradigm up to now. The themes I will discuss include the following:

(1)   There is less to rationality than meets the eye.
(2)   Organizations are segmented rather than monolithic.
(3)   Stable segments in organizations are quite small.
(4)   Connections among segments have variable strength.
(5)   Connections of variable strength produce ambiguity.
(6)   Connections of constant strength reduce ambiguity.

There is less to rationality than meets the eye

There are growing doubts about the importance of formal rationality in organizations (see Anderson, 1983; Manning, 1983). The complaint is not that rationality is ill-conceived but, rather, that the conditions under which it works best are relatively rare in organizations. Starbuck (1982, p. 16) is representative when he notes that "very rarely, if ever, does an organization begin action by perceiving a problem, then define this problem carefully, next generate possible actions solely because they might solve the stated problem, and finally, select a single course of action solely on the ground that it ought to be the best way to solve the problem."

Adherence to the prescriptions of a rational model can improve decision making if the environment changes slowly (Starbuck, 1982, p. 5), if there are few social groups, and if the situation is reasonably well controlled by agents with centralized authority (Kling, 1980, pp. 90, 100). Rational procedures work where stable means can be identified that are instrumental to stable ends in an environment in which these stable means–ends linkages will not be disrupted by unexpected events.

Rationality in newer formulations is still discussed, but in the context of a narrower set of issues. Rationality is viewed (1) as a set of prescriptions that change as the issue changes, (2) as a facade created to attract resources and legitimacy, and (3) as a postaction process used retrospectively to invent reasons for the action.

The suggestion that rationality is issue-specific is made concrete in Westerlund and Sjöstrand's (1979, p. 91) observation that rationality is an honorific label "given to the individual or group acting in the manner the evaluator wishes." Rational decisions typically mean "managerially rational," which means rational in the eyes of the people on top, the owners, the current dominant coalition. When these stakeholders change, the definition of rational conduct also changes.

As a rule, many theorists now try to preface all generic references to rationality with a qualifier (see March, 1978, pp. 591–593 for an example). It is no longer acceptable to state that an action is rational or nonrational. Instead, an adjective is used to qualify the sense in which the action is judged rational. Thus, actions are described as class-rational, gender-rational, resource-rational, value-rational, labor-rational, decision-rational, and action-rational. There are forms of rationality such as contextual-rationality, process-rationality, or calculational rationality (Dyckman, 1981).

To describe some action as rational within a specific context is to suggest that it may be seen as less rational in a different context. To specify rationality in this narrower sense is to strip it of some of its inflated value as the major criterion of effective performance and to suggest that it is sometimes a rhetorical claim buttressed by little more than brashness on the part of the claimant and inattentiveness on the part of the target.

Organizations use rationality as a facade when they talk about goals, planning, intentions, and analysis, not because these practices necessarily work, but because people who supply resources believe that such practices work and indicate sound management (Pfeffer, 1981, pp. 194–196). The appearance of rational action legitimates the organization in the environment it faces, deflects criticism, and ensures a steady flow of resources into the organization.

> An educational organization, for example, must go through the rituals approved in the environment for assuring legitimacy: hiring a ritually approved staff, offering a conventionally established curriculum, and granting the usual range of credentials, that is, degrees. None of these performances assure that a meaningful or substantively integrated educational experience will ensue. In fact, the organization takes pains to insulate its core teaching–learning activity from external evaluation or accountability. (Benson, 1983, p. 47)

Organizations are often heavily invested in the dramatization of their efficiency even though such displays often restrict actual efficiency. Elaborate public efforts to make rational decisions can often undermine the vigor and speed of subsequent action. However, if less deliberation occurs, the firm runs the risk that it will be judged impulsive, erratic, or, worst of all, unpredictable.

To meet the contradictory demands of deliberated decision and decisive actions, organizations often decouple the outside from the inside (Meyer & Rowan, 1977). The appearance of deliberation is fostered for public consumption while a different set of procedures is used to get work done. Thus, every organization has a visible president, hierarchy, and strategic plan; but internal functioning often ignores these trappings.

The final sense in which rationality is used by newer theorists is as a post hoc rationalizing device (Staw, 1980). "Societal ideologies insist that actions ought to be responses – actions taken unreflectively without specific reasons are irrational and irrationality is bad. . . . So organizations justify their actions with problems, threats, success or opportunities" (Starbuck, 1983, p. 94). The sequence in this quotation is the key point. First action occurs, and then the "reasons" why the action occurred are invented and inserted retrospectively into the organization's history. The action is reframed as a response to a threat, a solution to a problem that becomes clear only after the action was finished, a response to something that no one realized was a stimulus until the outcome became evident.

Starbuck suggests that retrospective justification is done for external consumption, but retrospective processes also serve important internal needs for understanding and prediction. It is not just outsiders who live by the theory that every action ought to be a response to some earlier stimulus. Organizational members impose the same logic on themselves. Insiders need reasonable reasons just as much as do outsiders. Insiders use the existence of action and an outcome as the occasion to initiate their own search for reasons. As the search backward for explanations of the action occurs in a very different context than when the action was first initiated (e.g., the outcome is known), the reasons singled out retrospectively are likely to be of less help for the next prospective action because they underestimate the vast amount of uncertainty that was present during the early stages of acting.

Organizations are segmented rather than monolithic

Not only do theorists qualify any reference they make to rationality, they also avoid the definite article "a" or "the" when referring to an organization. No organization is monolithic, yet continued references in the literature to "the organization" often suggest otherwise. People persist in referring to *the* organization due to a combination of failure to discount for hindsight bias, casual sorting of organizations into undifferentiated categories, routine aggregation of individual survey responses to create nominal organizations, and preoccupation with central tendencies (the mean) rather than dispersion (variation).

These tendencies have introduced inaccuracy into most analyses of organizations. Organizations are seen as more unified actors than they are, operating in more homogeneous environments than exist, and capable of longer lines of uninterrupted action than in fact they can mobilize.

The impression that organizations are orderly is fostered in part by hindsight bias. Experiments show that people consistently overestimate the predictability of past events, once they know how they turned out (Fischoff, 1975; Fischoff & Beyth, 1975; Slovic & Fischoff, 1977). Once a person knows the outcome, the reasons for that outcome seem obvious and the person cannot imagine any other outcome (hindsight bias).

Second guessing of warnings about the imminence of Pearl Harbor represents one example in which such biases are especially evident (Fischoff & Beyeth-Marom, 1976; Chan, 1979). When people look back at prior events once they know the outcomes of those events, they "see" an orderliness and inevitability that suggests that the events unfolded in a rational manner and could be managed by a simple application of rationality. Observers come away from their analysis with a strong impression that there is sufficient order to sustain rational analysis and rational management.

But hindsight is not the only bias that tempts us to view organizations as monolithic. March and Olsen (1976, p. 19) identify an even more generic bias that leads people to exaggerate the orderliness in organizations. The bias involves assumptions about reality, intention, and necessity.

(1)   The reality assumption is that what appeared to happen did happen.
(2)   The intention assumption is that what happened was intended to happen.
(3)   The necessity assumption is that what happened had to happen.

The assumption that what appeared to happen did happen neglects the importance of interpretation in organizational perception. What appears to happen happens as a function of the different a priori beliefs that members impose on basically ambiguous data (believing is seeing). Given that interpretations tend to emphasize order rather than disorder, the reality assumption favors the impression that organizations are unified, predictable actors.

We have already seen an example of the second assumption (what happened was intended to happen) in the earlier discussion that people feel pressure to invent retrospectively, the stimuli to which their actions are a "response." It is usually assumed that action occurs when people translate the stimulus of an intention into actions. Different intentions produce different outcomes, better intentions produce better outcomes.

March and Olsen argue that there are at least three reasons why intentions alone seldom control action. First, action often produces decisions that are intended by no one and desired by no one. Second, action often occurs in response to duty and obligation rather than in response to intention. Third, intention is often overwhelmed by exogenous factors such as when firms become bankrupt even though top management had no intention of folding the firm.

The third assumption (what happened had to happen) essentially states that the observed outcome is inevitable and substantially different from other outcomes that might have occurred. The flaw in this assumption is that substantial "differences in final outcomes are sometimes produced by small (and essentially unpredictable) differences in intermediate events leading to the outcomes" (March & Olsen, 1976, p. 20). Thus, alternative outcomes were highly probable and chance, rather than design, produced the actual outcome that was observed.

When people impose each of the preceding three assumptions, they fail to grasp the indeterminacy that inheres in adaptive action. Blind to the effects of these assumptions, observers conclude that rational models work and that organizations are tightly coupled systems. When asked to explain why organizations are effective, people identify rational designs, failing to realize that such designs are retrospective intentions that were not present while the action unfolded. The steps actually responsible for effectiveness seldom can be discovered after the event has occurred (an exception is the instant replay).

The perceptual distortions we have described have an effect on practice as well as research. Practitioners often conclude that effectiveness is the result of rational, orderly action. That conclusion is often an artifact of hindsight – we know what happened before we look back to discover why it happened. What we fail to see when we use hindsight are the experiments, false starts, and corrections that enabled people to learn and improve. It is the opportunity to learn from mistakes that we need to build in when we start our next novel action. But the necessity for those opportunities is the very thing we don't see when we reconstruct a smooth, defensible line of action after the fact. When we design our next action, we don't build in enough chances to learn, experiment, improvise, and be surprised. Furthermore, we start with unrealistically high expectations about how smoothly the activity will unfold. We are not prepared for all the disruption that occurs and often do a poor job rebounding from it.

When practitioners and researchers are better able to identify and compensate for some of the perceptual biases we have mentioned, they are more likely to see segments than unity. To understand more fully why unity is impossible, consider that top management in complex organizations does not design operating structures, it designs decision structures. Top management divides the organization into segmented subunits, which then design the operating structures. The importance of this distinction is that management does not actually manage the organization. Instead, it manages the process that manages the organization (Kuhn & Beam, 1982, pp. 325–326 refer to this as metamanagement).

To design a decision structure, top management selects the people who will be in the decision-making group. Even this is a tricky process. As top management doesn't know enough to make some decisions, which is why they formed the decision structure in the first place, they also probably do not know enough to say who the members of the decision-making group should be or who they might need for advice. If top management acknowledges this reality, they are forced to give up some of their control over the list of people who will be their agents.

Although top management is accustomed to saying, "Do what I tell you and I will reward you in proportion as you do it to my satisfaction," they adopt a different philosophy to manage segmented complexity. They now say essentially

> Do what you collectively think best in light of the objectives I have stated. I will try to reward you collectively as I will have no real way of knowing which persons will have

had what effect in your decisions. In fact, you are probably better judges than I of whether your methods were the most effective available and which of your members is the most effective. All I can do is to tell you whether your accomplishment as a group strikes me as reasonably satisfactory relative to my purposes. (Kuhn & Beam, 1982, p. 327)

This revised job description for the decision-making group essentially says, "see what you can do and do your best." The manager retains some control over the purse strings and over decisions to hire, fire, and promote people. However, as individual contributions are concealed within the group product, even personnel decisions are difficult to make.

The manager still exerts some influence by seeing that wider organizational considerations are kept in mind when decisions are made between units, keeping decision makers informed of relevant constraints, replacing agents, and handling situations that exceed the range for which the group was designed.

An unusual twist implicit in the description of segmented control is that the organizational form looks very much like the control structures found in universities (Bess, 1982). The president of a university is unable to evaluate whether the intellectual products of the faculty are worthwhile. The best research goes the way the researcher wants it to go, not the way the administrator wants it to go. Administrators cannot directly manage the pursuit of hunches, so they say, "keep busy and do research." Segments within the university decide key issues, such as teaching and admissions requirements, and the only control presidents have over these subgroups is money and final approval of personnel decisions.

Questions of authority, legitimacy, and insubordination are greatly attenuated in universities, but the same is true in other organizations in which the ties among subsystems are loose and responsibility is delegated to groups rather than to individuals. Although people often object that much organizational theory has been drafted to explain university organizations and therefore has limited generality, in fact the loosely coupled university structure is a prototype for all complex organizations in which lower-level segments act like top management. The structures that result from strong delegation resemble a federation, a market, a holding company, or a confederacy that tries to keep from getting overly organized.

A school, for example, can be understood as a federation of dissimilar segments. Schools have taken what is basically a two-person interaction between a teacher and a learner, and have added all kinds of tasks, responsibilities, and activities onto this basic core relationship. Each item that is added represents a segment rather than an integrated part. Thus, there is no such thing as *the* school or *a* school. What the additions do is loosen the basic teacher–learner relationship. This basic relationship becomes complicated to the point where segments have only modest dependence on one another. To treat the school as a single organization is to miss most of how it functions.

Stable segments in organizations are quite small

New perspectives emphasize not only that organizations are segmented, but also that the segments are both small and stable. Whenever complex organizations unravel, they fall back into these small stable units.

The logic for predicting this outcome was captured by Simon in a fable about two watchmakers named Hora and Tempus, who were continually being interrupted while they assembled watches. Simon's original fable has been recast by Kuhn and Beam (1982, pp. 249–250) in a more accessible form that makes even more clearly the point that stability resides in small entities.

> Your task is to count out a thousand sheets of paper, while you are subject to periodic interruptions. The interruption causes you to lose track of the count and forces you to start over. If you count the thousand as a single sequence, then an interruption could cause you, at worst, to lose count of as many as 999. If the sheets are put into stacks of 100, however, and each stack remains undisturbed by interruptions, then the worst possible count loss from interruption is 108. That number represents the recounting of the nine stacks of 100 each plus the 99 single sheets. Further, if sheets are first put into stacks of ten, which are then joined into stacks of 100, the worst possible loss from interruption would be 27. That number represents nine stacks of 100 plus nine stacks of ten plus nine single sheets. Not only is far less recounting time lost by putting the paper into "subsystems" of tens and hundreds, but the chances of completing the count are vastly higher.

The list of forces within organizations that can unravel large, complex entities is long. They include things like high mobility of people among positions, faulty memories, attempts to cope with overload by lowering the standards of acceptable performance, public compliance undercut by private deviation, sudden changes in authority or job descriptions, merging of odd product lines, and the like. All of these can interrupt complex interdependencies and cause the complex states to revert to simpler, more stable configurations.

The question then becomes, what are some of these small stable segments in organizations? Mintzberg (1973) and others have suggested that, on the average, managers can work for about nine minutes before they are interrupted. That finding can be interpreted as one instance of small segmented stability in organizations. Life in organizations is lived in nine-minute bursts. Activities lasting less than nine minutes are relatively free from disruption, whereas activities that last longer are more vulnerable to interruption.

It is difficult for people to maintain more than ten strong pairwise relationships. The instability of a three-person group in which two can pair against the third makes the point that stable social relations inhere in small entities, often involving only two or three people. When a large group is under pressure, stable pairwise interactions will become the most common structure.

People have limited thinking capacity. They are described as serial information processors rather than parallel processors. They can do only one thing at a time. This means that on those rare occasions when a person is successful in doing several things simultaneously, this is an unstable condition and any interruption or sudden change will cause the person to drop all but one project.

Given that managers do little reading, people who talk about managerial writing emphasize the necessity for brevity, as in the one-page memo, the one-page executive summary, the one unshakeable fact. In each of these cases the stable segment is a very small number of words. Longer presentations often are ignored, misread, skimmed, or otherwise dismissed. Again, stability lies in small, short segments.

Other examples could be described, but the point is that small segments are not necessarily disorderly. Instead, what seems to be true within organizations is that coherence occurs in smaller sized entities than may be true in other settings. As an analogy, consider sentences and paragraphs. Individual sentences can be well crafted, clear, and self-explanatory. Sets of sentences, however, may be harder to assemble, less sensible when assembled, and confusing when read as if they were coherent paragraphs. If people work with individual sentences, there is no problem. Each sentence makes sense. When, however, people combine sentences to make longer, more complex arguments, the structures become more flimsy and often collapse back into separate assertions.

Organizations built of small stable segments make sense over shorter spans of time, involving fewer people than we thought. Once these temporal and spatial boundaries are exceeded, orderliness, predictability, and sensibleness decline. This outcome is the straightforward consequence of the basic instability of complex structures and the tendency for complex structures to change into simpler, more stable structures. Most of the time most segments of organizations will be found in these simpler states. It is these simpler structures that become linked and supply the basic orderliness found in organizations.

Connections among segments have variable strength

Organizations often are described as systems, and the principal graphic used to portray this description is a set of boxes connected by arrows:

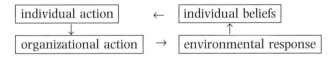

This form of illustration is deceptive, because it suggests that the connections have constant strength and are tight. In most organizations, however, connections among segments are variable rather than constant.

The idea of variable strength can be illustrated in several ways. In a diagram such as the one at the beginning of this section, if we estimate the probability that each variable will trigger the next variable within one day and multiply these values, we find that longer chains are looser than shorter chains.

In the same kind of diagram weak connections exist when the variables share few variables in common and when the variables they do share are themselves weak. If people express doubts about whether one variable has significant effect on another variable, this is an indication of weaker connections. If individual variables can vary over a large range, chains of these variables will be connected more tightly than is true in chains in which the range of a variable is small. Variables with little room to vary soon become frozen and fail to pass variation along to the other variables with which they are connected.

Loose coupling can be observed in many places. Connections among parts are loosened when solutions are inserted into organizations that have no problems requiring that solution. Computer purchases are a good example. Most computer sales are vendor-driven ("look what this will do for you"). The customer seldom asks, "Do I really need that capability?" Instead, in order to keep up with the competition, hardware is purchased and then employees are urged to use the hardware in order to justify the purchase.

Thus, the machine now becomes a required step in every process. Existing controls are disrupted and parts of the system that previously had been self-regulating are disconnected. No one knows what is occurring and everyone knows less about the organization than they did before, because interdependencies have been made more variable.

Variable connections come from managerial self-interest. People at the top of the organization frequently make decisions that maximize income to members in the dominant coalition (Kuhn & Beam, 1982, pp. 332–348), which means that there are tight ties among a handful of people, but looser ties between the managers and stockholders.

Loose coupling is evident in schools. Only a limited amount of inspection and evaluation occurs in schools. A principal who visits a classroom too frequently is accused of "harassment." Professionals are reluctant to give one another unsolicited feedback. As a result, poor performance persists in the name of professional autonomy.

The goals of education also are indeterminate, which makes them difficult to use as hard standards to evaluate individual performance. Administrators and instructors work on variable raw materials with little control over the supply; they have no firm standards by which to judge the impact of their work and no clear theory of causation that specifies the effects of the things they do.

Schools have large spans of control. There are few employees and many students. Teachers find it hard to keep track of the students, let alone of one another. Because the technology of education is not clear, educators try many different things and find it difficult to tell what works. Schools make extensive use of specialists; every time a specialist is inserted between a teacher and a student, the control over the student is loosened.

Some aspects of schools – the bus schedule, for example – are tightly coupled. Students and drivers know where people are supposed to be and whether buses are running late or early; principals know when to expect certain people for certain things. How people get paid is tightly coupled. When the payroll clerk fouls up, the system grinds to a halt. People raise their voices, and something gets done fast. Open classrooms are tightly coupled in the sense that one person's actions cannot easily be ignored by others; visual and aural dependencies exist whether or not people want them.

We have already mentioned some features of organizations that suggest why connections vary in strength (e.g., frequent changes in top management, ill-specified job descriptions, large spans of control), but there are at least four general features of organizations that directly affect the strength of connections:

(1) *Rules*: Rules vary in severity, number, latitude for deviations, and clarity. Connections become tighter and less variable as all four of these properties intensify.
(2) *Agreement on rules*: The more agreement there is on the content of rules, the nature of violations, and how violations will be handled, the tighter the coupling.
(3) *Feedback*: The sooner people learn about the effects of their actions, the tighter the coupling.
(4) *Attention*: As attention becomes more constant, connections become more stable (when attention shifts due to changes in salience or need, connections become more variable).

Obviously, these four characteristics are not the only sources of connections. Even if more items are added to the list, the point remains the same. An organization is neither entirely loose nor entirely tight. Most organizational segments contain a mixture of tightness and looseness (e.g., vague rules, minimal agreement, swift feedback, and highly focused attention). This combination means that although there is some order in the organization, it is less pervasive than rational bureaucratic models would suggest. Organizations are imperfect systems within which there is indeterminacy, but there is some order. In the language of systems theory, organizations are represented as

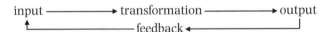

and this constitutes a rudimentary system. It is rudimentary because the connections among those four components may be activated "(1) suddenly (rather than continuously), (2) occasionally (rather than constantly), (3) negligibly (rather than significantly), (4) indirectly (rather than directly), and (5) eventually (rather than immediately)" (Weick, 1982, p. 380). Even though the connections are indeterminate, sooner or later the system completes a cycle and produces something approximating what it was designed to produce. If people watch the system long enough, they will see that the components are connected and that eventually everything gets processed.

The image of a loosely coupled system is important more as a summary description of a way to think about organizations than as a precise technical description of a specific quality of organizational structure. The phrase "loosely coupled system," in other words, is useful for what it connotes as well as for what it denotes. Diverse images that people associate with the phrase all include qualities that are visible when entities are less orderly, less predictable. Whatever people think of when they imagine a loosely coupled system is often what we actually see when we study the indeterminacies within an organization.

One set of connotations evoked by the label "loosely coupled system" is visible in the following description:

A loosely coupled system is a problem in causal inference. For actors and observers alike, the prediction and activation of cause–effect relations is made more difficult because relations are intermittent, lagged, dampened, slow, abrupt, and mediated.

Actors in a loosely coupled system rely on trust and presumptions, are often isolated, find social comparison difficult, have no one to borrow from, seldom imitate, suffer pluralistic ignorance, maintain discretion, improvise, and have less hubris because they know the universe is not sufficiently connected to make widespread change possible.

A loosely coupled system is not a flawed system. It is a social and cognitive solution to constant environmental change, to the impossibility of knowing another mind, and to limited information-processing capabilities. Loose coupling is to social systems as compartmentalization is to individuals, a means to achieve cognitive economy and a little peace (adapted from Weick, 1982, pp. 404–405).

Connections of variable strength produce ambiguity

The presence of variable connections means that ambiguity is likely to be high, superstitious learning is probable as it is more difficult to attach specific outcomes to specific prior causal actions, communications will be delayed and distorted, people may find it difficult to learn because feedback is delayed beyond the point at which someone is able to understand precisely what prior action is relevant to the feedback, and there may be a high incidence of giving up and resignation when systems are not responsive to demands.

Variability makes it difficult to anticipate, plan, implement, coordinate, and control. Even though variability makes it hard to be rational, it has the benefit of enabling people to stumble onto adaptive actions they had not thought of. Nevertheless, stumbling bothers most organizations. They dislike ambiguity even more than they like adaptation. If organizations dislike ambiguity, they will probably also dislike self-determination, delegation, and differentiation, because each one is associated with loose connections, and loose connections are a source of ambiguity.

McCaskey (1982) has identified twelve sources of ambiguity (see Table 2.1) and March and Olsen (1976, p. 12) have identified four sources – intention: organizations have inconsistent and ill-defined objectives; understanding: unreliable connections between actions and their consequences; history: no single version of past events exists; and organization: participation and attention vary.

Ambiguity is found in all aspects of organizational activity. It can be found in changing and complex environments, nonroutine tasks, and networks that have dense interdependencies. Ambiguity is present when people cannot understand raw materials or do not know when a product or service is finished, and when people convert raw material into a finished product on the basis of intuition and chance rather than logic (Gerwin, 1981, p. 6).

Even though ambiguity is common, it is not sufficient to say simply that people try

Table 2.1 Characteristics of ambiguous, changing situations

Characteristic	Description and comments
Nature of problem is itself in question	"What the problem is" is unclear and shifting. Managers have only vague or competing definitions of the problem. Often, any one "problem" is intertwined with other messy problems.
Information (amount and reliability) is problematical	Because the definition of the problem is in doubt, collecting and categorizing information becomes a problem. The information flow threatens either to become overwhelming or to be seriously insufficient. Data may be incomplete and of dubious reliability.
Multiple, conflicting interpretations	For those data that do exist, players develop multiple, and sometimes conflicting, interpretations. The facts and their significance can be read several different ways.
Different value orientations, political/emotional clashes	Without objective criteria, players rely more on personal and/or professional values to make sense of the situation. The clash of different values often politically and emotionally charges the situation.
Goals are unclear, or multiple and conflicting	Managers do not enjoy the guidance of clearly defined, coherent goals. Either the goals are vague, or they are clearly defined and contradictory.
Time, money, or attention are lacking	A difficult situation is made chaotic by severe shortages of one or more of these items.
Contradictions and paradoxes appear	Situation has seemingly inconsistent features, relationships, or demands.
Roles vague, responsibilities unclear	Players do not have a clearly defined set of activities they are expected to perform. On important issues, the locus of decision making and other responsibilities is vague or in dispute.
Success measures are lacking	People are unsure what success in resolving the situation would mean and/or they have no way of assessing the degree to which they have been successful.
Poor understanding of cause–effect relationships	Players do not understand what causes what in the situation. Even if sure of the effects they desire, they are uncertain how to obtain them.
Symbols and metaphors used	In place of precise definitions or logical arguments, players use symbols or metaphors to express their points of view.
Participation in decision-making fluid	Who the key decision makers and influence holders are changes as players enter and leave the decision arena.

to reduce it. Because ambiguity is never fully removed, it is part of the normal context of organizational action. Ambiguity gives form to much of what occurs.

For example, individual actions often affect organizational actions, but organizational actions less often have a determinate effect on the environment. Nevertheless, individuals often believe that what they do brings about direct changes in the environment. This erroneous interpretation is called "superstitious learning." As Hedberg (1981, p. 11) describes it,

> complex interactions between organizations and their environments exceed people's cognitive capacities for mapping so that faulty inferences are drawn. Superstitious learning thus, in effect, separates one subsystem that produces actions from another subsystem that forms beliefs. Organizational learning proceeds but the coupling between actions and knowledge is weak.

Although it is tempting to say that superstitious learning is simply one more instance of organizational pathology, it seems more productive to ask, "How can organizational members continue to act and learn even though their descriptions of reality, causality, and the instrumentality of action have low validity?"

The concept of self-fulfilling prophecies contains a partial answer to the question. Members who mistakenly see a change in the environment as caused by their own action build into their causal theories the belief that they are able to change environments. This apparent efficacy is an error in the sense that it is an incorrect interpretation of what actually happened. What is more interesting, however, are those occasions when environments are sufficiently malleable that, acting on this mistaken belief, people can create a reality that makes the belief true. In changeable environments superstitious learning can set in motion a sequence of activities that transforms the superstitious conclusion into correct perception.

Self-fulfilling prophecies (Jones, 1977) tend not to be appreciated for the profound sense in which they provide insight into how organizations function. An original prophecy is incorrect and may result from a mistaken perception that an environmental outcome was caused by an individual action. Later, when the person acts as if the prophecy were correct, the prophecy can become correct and the environment becomes responsive to the individual action rather than to some other exogenous factor. Thus, the incorrect theory of action becomes self-correcting. It sets into motion a set of events that validate what was originally an invalid belief.

Notice that in the case of superstitious learning, ambiguity is partially dealt with when the person draws an inference about cause and effect and stores that inference in a cause map. That step represents an avoidance of uncertainty because no clarification actually occurs. But when that inference then becomes a constraint on subsequent action, uncertainty is actually reduced. When the person acts as if the stored inference is true, a previously loose relationship between cause and effect becomes tightened, and the uncertainty surrounding that effect becomes reduced.

Organizations can learn in the face of ambiguity because superstitious learning can be self-correcting in ways that are moderately adaptive.

To understand ambiguity, however, is not simply to become fascinated with the self-fulfilling properties of superstitious learning. Ambiguity also increases the extent to which action is guided by values and ideology. When ambiguity is present, people who can resolve it gain power. The values of these powerful people often affect what the organization becomes. When ambiguity increases, the person best able to resolve it gains power, as does that person's vision of the world and the organization. Ambiguity thus becomes the occasion when ideology may be shuffled. An organization may "reset" itself whenever there is an important, enduring ambiguity that is resolved by someone whose actions have surplus meaning. Those actions may implant a more pervasive set of values.

When new values are introduced into an organization, a new set of relevancies and competencies are created that can provide a badly needed source of innovation. An organization can learn new things about itself and about its environment when ambiguity is present. If an organization continues to act even though it does not know for certain what it is doing, there is a chance that the organization will emerge from its confrontation with ambiguity in slightly different shape than when it started to cope. In this way ambiguity can produce innovation and greater utilization of resources.

Continuous ambiguity also exerts continuous pressure on organizations to modify their structure so that coping is more successful. If Burns and Stalker's organic system is treated prescriptively as an arrangement capable of dealing with uncertainty, we would expect to see organizations pressured by ambiguity to demonstrate more use of specialized professional skills (high complexity), continual redefinition of individual tasks (low formalization), development of more ad hoc centers of authority located closer to the source of a problem (low centralization), and movement toward a network structure (this list is adapted from Gerwin, 1981, p. 6).

Although it is not new to argue that ambiguity determines structure, what is new is the suggestion that when organizations face chronic ambiguity, their ongoing activities can be interpreted as continuing efforts to move from a less appropriate mechanistic structure to a more appropriate organic structure. Thus, organizations may be responding not just to the substance of a particular ambiguity (e.g., a possible hint of a takeover), but to the more generic reality of ambiguity itself. Organizational action may be a partial attempt to deal with an immediate problem, but it may be better understood as a strong ongoing effort to redesign the organization so that it can handle whatever ambiguities occur in the future.

Thus, when members become more and more conscious of networks, this can be read as a specific attempt to reduce dependence on a single supplier of a scarce resource. But this same action can be interpreted more broadly as an effort to deal with the larger issue of interdependence as a continuing source of ambiguity. Efforts to enlarge a network reduce the power of specific interdependencies.

Again, what is happening can be understood as something more than simple effort to reduce uncertainty. The actions can be understood as attempts to accept ambiguity, live with it, and take advantage of some of the unique opportunities for change that occur when ambiguity increases.

All of these efforts are modestly patterned and can account for some regularities in organizational activity. To say that variable connections create ambiguity is to describe a prominent background characteristic to which organizations accommodate. As they accommodate, organizations assume predictable forms.

Ambiguity is prominent in organizations, but before organizations reduce it, ambiguity has already had some immediate impact on the processes and structures found in them. To understand ambiguity is to understand these immediate effects as well as the more active attempts to reduce ambiguity that are described in the next section.

Connections of constant strength reduce ambiguity

Given the existence of ambiguity produced by connections of variable strength, managers need to reduce ambiguity to tolerable levels. As Athos states, "good managers make meanings for people, as well as money" (Peters & Waterman, 1982, p. 29).

Whether one refers to organizations as garbage cans (Cohen, March, & Olsen, 1972), anarchies (Cohen & March, 1974), loosely coupled systems (Glassman, 1973), negotiated realities (Hall, 1973), or arenas (Berg, 1979), the point remains that managers work amid a great deal of disorder.

One way managers cope with disorder is by presuming that there is a logic by which events cohere. These presumptions of logic are evident in the inferences about cause and effect that are assembled into cause maps (e.g., Ashton, 1976, Bougon, Weick, & Binkhorst, 1977; Goodman, 1968; Axelrod, 1977; Roos & Hall, 1980; Porac, 1981).

When managers then act as if loosely coupled events are tied together just as they are in a cause map, events often become more tightly coupled, more orderly, and less variable.

For example, the head of an extended care unit in a hospital (Roos & Hall, 1980) may believe that if he has more contact with influential outsiders, there will be less pressure on him from the chief administrator in the hospital to cut his budget. Having presumed that the world contains this causal connection, the head of extended care spends more time away from the hospital, which makes him more visible to outsiders. The outsiders pay more consistent attention to the hospital, which means that their actions become more predictable and focused.

Through the simple act of becoming visible, the head makes the "environment" with which the entire hospital must deal more homogeneous and more predictable.

The hospital becomes constrained by an environment that did not exist until the head of extended care changed the salience of events for significant others, who then intensified their demands on the hospital. Events became more orderly under the influence of interaction that itself was launched on the basis of presumptions that just such orderliness existed.

At the time the action was started, there was no guarantee that orderliness would be "there" to validate the initial presumption. Confident action addressed to a presumptively logical world gave it a tangible form that resembled the presumptions stored in the administrator's cause maps.

It is crucial to see that the issue here is *not* one of accuracy. Cause maps could be wrong and still be an important part of managerial action. The important feature of a cause map is that it leads people to anticipate some order "out there." It matters less what particular order is portrayed than that an order of *some* kind is portrayed. The crucial dynamic is that the prospect of order lures the manager into ill-formed situations that then accommodate to forceful actions and come to resemble the orderly relations contained in the cause map. The map animates managers, and the fact of animation, not the map itself, is what imposes order on the situation.

Thus, trappings of rationality such as strategic plans are important largely as binding mechanisms. They hold events together long enough and tight enough in people's heads so that they do something in the belief that their action will be influential. The importance of presumptions, expectations, justifications, and commitments is that they span the breaks in a loosely coupled system and encourage confident interactions that tighten settings. *The conditions of order and rightness in organizations exist as much in the mind as they do in the field of action.*

To review, there are several ways to regain constancy when it is lost through variable connections. Three that are of special interest are language, action, and interaction.

Organizations have been described as a "set of procedures for argumentation and interpretation" (March & Olsen, 1976, p. 25). A significant portion of the environment consists of nothing more than talk, symbols, promises, lies, interest, attention, threats, agreements, expectations, memories, rumors, indicators, supporters, detractors, faith, suspicion, trust, appearances, loyalties, and commitments, all of which are more intangible and more influenceable than material goods (Peters, 1980; Gronn, 1983; Weick, 1980).

Words induce stable connections, establish stable entities to which people can orient (e.g., "gender gap"), bind people's time to projects ("Al, I'd like you to spend some time on this one"), and signify important information. Agreement on a label that sticks is as constant a connection as is likely to be found in organizations.

Labels carry their own implications for action, and that is why they are so successful in the management of ambiguity. Consider these labels: that is a cost (minimize it), that is spoilage (reduce it), that is overhead (allocate it), that is a transfer price (set it), that is a variance (investigate it), that is a surplus (distribute it), that is a need (fill it), that is a problem (solve it), that is a decision (make it), that is a bluff (challenge it), that is feather-bedding (remove it), that is stupidity (exploit it), and so forth. In each of these instances a label consolidates bits and pieces of data, gives them meaning, suggests appropriate action, implies a diagnosis, and removes ambiguity.

Much ambiguity occurs because there are events floating around that seem to bear no relation to one another. Because it is not clear what is going on, it is even less clear what ought to be done about it. Labels (sometimes any old label) serve to focus attention and shrink the number of possibilities as to what might be occurring. A mere hint as to what the connection might be may be all that is needed to connect diverse events, give them a theme, and allow them to be managed.

Given that so much of what happens in organizations can be understood as a self-fulfilling prophecy, labels often are sufficient to mobilize a response that fulfills the prophecy made by the label (e.g., they will be hostile). The reason prophecies fulfill themselves so often in organizations is that events are sufficiently disconnected and ambiguous that they can absorb quite different labels. People who find a vivid label and then push it persistently often are able to redirect organizational action, because they have gained control over how the organization defines itself and what it says it is up to.

Connections of variable strength can be stabilized by action as well as by language. Action can simplify environments, can make environments more orderly, can create linkages where none existed, and can construct feedback loops.

Action can stabilize a situation of high variability, if it is forceful, persistent, and confident. However, to develop a strong basis for action, people often need to sacrifice decision rationality. They need to analyze few alternatives, consider only the positive characteristics of the chosen actions, and choose as their objectives consequences that are likely to occur (Brunsson, 1982).

If people consider many alternatives, or both positive and negative alternatives, or argue over objectives, these all raise uncertainty that can lower motivation, commitment, and impact.

Action rationality contains a dilemma for everyone who administers an organization. If the decision process is made more rational and alternatives are considered more carefully, people may discover a better alternative, but in doing so they dissipate some of the energy that could help implement the better alternative. Thus, a good idea gets carried out less forcefully than it might have, and fails to solve the problem as adequately as it seemed it would when it was discussed. The disappointing outcome occurs, not because of a defect in deliberation, but because of a defect in implementation. In trying to discover the good alternative, people lost some of the commitment that they needed to put it into action.

The potential contradiction between choosing the right thing and getting it done can be examined as a problem in requisite variety. The principle of requisite variety states that no sensing device can control input that is more complicated than the sensing device. Thus, in a landscape scene with numerous gradations in texture and color, fine-grain film has more variety than does coarse-grain fast film, and the more varied film will register more of the variety in the complicated scene.

The relationship between requisite variety and action rationality is that organizations can use two quite different strategies to reduce ambiguity in complicated environments. First, they can try to register the fine grain of the environment and then choose an action that is sensitive to subtle but potentially important regularities in that complicated environment. This path is the path of decision rationality.

But there is another way to deal with complicated environments. This alternative strategy is to wade in, take vigorous action, and simplify the environment so that relatively crude analyses are sufficient to keep track of the main things that are happening. In an environment made simple by action, decision rationality is unnecessary. You don't have to worry about registering subtle nuances if your action simplifies that environment and removes the nuances.

The choice between action and deliberation often is irreversible. If you choose in favor of accurate sensing, you reduce your capability to take strong action. Therefore, the analysis must be accurate and identify some small action that can remedy the problem that is sensed (small actions can be executed with less commitment). It is often the case that the more fully a problem is understood, the smaller will be the change necessary to solve it. All solutions do not require massive action (Weick, 1984). However, if only a relatively small action is available to correct a problem, detail and accuracy are crucial.

If you decide to take strong action in order to simplify the situation, you forgo any chance of learning more about the situation as it originally existed and about small changes that could produce big effects.

It is relatively hard to gain the best of both worlds. Administrators run the risk of knowing their world well but being unable to do anything about it, or they run the opposite risk of making some decisive change in the world only to discover that they changed the wrong thing and the problem got worse. Both outcomes represent a decrease in ambiguity.

The third classic response to ambiguity is to turn to another person and, in common, build some idea of what is occurring (see Schachter, 1959). Larger entities act in an analogous manner. Divisions come to look like one another because they imitate one another and build consensual definitions (DiMaggio & Powell, 1983).

It may seem unusual that two groups, both equally in the dark, could get clarity by watching one another. Apparently, the observer assumes that the person being watched understands the situation more fully. Having made this assumption, the observer then imposes meaning on what is observed and attributes the meaning to the observed person rather than the observer.

A great deal of interactive ambiguity reduction takes place inside individual heads rather than between heads. Puzzles become resolved into sensible constructions when people elaborate a grain of truth into a full-blown explanation. And people often discover these grains of truth when they compare their views with those of other people who see things in a slightly different way.

Social interaction seems to reduce ambiguity in the following way:

Two things are interesting about this solution. First, ambiguity created by loose connections is managed by increased interdependence between people. As depicted, once the variability has been reduced, people will revert back to more solitary action, in which there is less discussion. That prediction may not be accurate, especially if ambiguity reduction is reinforcing and people become closer to those who satisfy important needs. Thus, persistent mutual ambiguity reduction could tighten a previously loose social system.

A second implication of the diagram is that people may perceive that whereas they don't know what is going on, everyone else does. Having made this assumption, confused people tell no one about their confusion. These assumptions would be represented by a negative relationship between ambiguity and discussion: The more ambiguity an individual perceives, the less that person talks to others in the belief that others would view him or her as inept, unperceptive, stupid. If a second negative relationship is introduced, the cycle becomes unstable and a vicious circle results.

To illustrate, variability increases, which increases ambiguity, which decreases the amount of discussion that occurs, which causes variability and ambiguity to intensify, until the reluctant talker will have generated a situation that he or she simply cannot tolerate any longer.

On rare occasions instability can move in the opposite direction. Suppose variability declines. In the microcosm that has been drawn ambiguity also would decline, the person responds to a reduction of ambiguity with an increase in discussion, which further reduces variability, until, theoretically, no variability or ambiguity would remain. Although that might seem desirable, the likelihood of that occurring in an organization with variability is quite low.

Implications for Administration

Several implications for practice flow from the preceding analysis, and they are summarized below. The flavor of these suggestions is anticipated by Padgett (1980, p. 602), who warned, "don't expect orthodoxy where ambiguity is salient."

(1) Look for small pockets of order and protect them, grow them, or diffuse them. A little order can go a long way, so don't overdo it.
(2) Assess when decision rationality works in your setting and when it doesn't. Build your own ad hoc contingency theory of decision rationality.
(3) Don't treat rationality as a universal prescription. If you live by rationality alone, you lose options (use of intuition, quick response, trial and error) and you lose nondeliberated sources of variety (hunches).
(4) Retrospective explanations are poor guides to prospective action. We know relatively little about how we actually get things done. We don't know what works, because we misremember the process of accomplishment. We will always underestimate the number of false starts that went into the outcome. Furthermore, even though there were dead ends, we probably did learn from them – we learned more about the environment and about our capabilities. Keep good records during a process, because hindsight will gloss over most of the difficulties you had while striving for the outcome. Failure to see difficulties may result in unrealistic expectations about how fast and how easily the next goal can be achieved.
(5) Intention is neither a necessary nor a sufficient condition for action.
(6) Practice enlightened delegation through control of the staffing process.
(7) Don't dismiss universities as mere ivory towers, at least until you understand more about how they actually function. They resemble your organization more closely than does a military organization. Think of your organization as a federation, market, or holding company.
(8) Design around the stable subsystem. Assign critical tasks to small stable units. For any task ask, "Can this task be done in nine minutes by two people who attend to one thing at a time?" If the answer is yes, you have assigned critical tasks to a stable unit. If you can't embed critical assignments in small, stable entities, then shield people against interruptions, simplify their tasks so stress has less disruptive effects on performance, or help people increase their tolerance for stress.
(9) Don't expect long chains of events to make sense. Sense occurs only in small bursts in organizations.
(10) Be patient: Systems are sluggish and slightly disorderly, but they do eventu-

ally act in a systemlike manner. If you persist, you may create connections that are more continuous, constant, significant, direct, and immediate. If you persist, this "both increases the likelihood that a proposal will be current at an opportune time and creates a diffuse climate of availability and legitimacy for it" (March & Olsen, 1982, pp. 25–26). A persistent recommendation will fit some situation sooner or later ("every rain dancer brings rain if he dances long enough"), the recommendation remains salient ("well, we could always do x"), the recommendation may accrue legitimacy ("we always hear about x, so at least it must have a place in this organization in someone's view"), and persistence signifies that some people value whatever is affirmed repeatedly.

(11)   View loose coupling descriptively before you view it evaluatively, in order to see the functions it plays (generates variation, preserves autonomy, localizes trouble, is understandable to fallible minds).

(12)   Accuracy is less important than animation. Any old map or plan will do, if it gets you moving so that you learn more about what is actually in the environment. A map is not the territory; a plan is not the organization.

(13)   Anticipations matter; don't adopt them casually. They tend to fulfill themselves.

(14)   Labels are a powerful means to reduce ambiguity. Impose them with caution and deliberation because they can direct action.

(15)   To manage meaning is to view your organization as a set of procedures for arguing and interpreting. In any organizational assessment, ask questions such as these: How do we declare winners of the argument? When do we interpret? What interpretations do we tend to favor (blind spots?)? Whose interpretations seem to stick?

(16)   To get things done, it is more important to capture a person's attention than a person's intention. People act in response to salient concerns (e.g., deadlines). So to control action, you need to control salience.

(17)   To learn about your goals, preferences, and capabilities, act and treat your actions as conjectures about what these goals, preferences, and capabilities are.

(18)   Be willing to leap before you look. If you look before you leap, you may not see anything. Action generates outcomes that ultimately provide the raw material for seeing something. Before action takes place, the meaning of any situation is essentially limitless. The situation could become anything whatsoever and therefore it is everything and nothing. The situation takes on distinct form and meaning only when action is inserted into it. When people examine the action they took, they see more clearly what the situation was and what it meant. By acting, often without the safety of knowing what the action will look like or amount to or come to mean, people learn something meaningful, even though what they learn may not be what they expected.

(19)   You can optimize either deliberation or action, but not both.

As this chapter began with a metaphor, it seems appropriate to end with one. In the final analysis managing may be more like surfing on waves of events and decisions (Westerlund & Sjöstrand, 1979, p. 121) than like either of the two versions of soccer mentioned at the beginning. People who surf do not command the waves to appear, or to have a particular spacing, or to be of a special height. Instead, surfers do their best with what they get. They can control inputs to the process, but they can't control outcomes. To ride a wave as if one were in control is to act and have faith. The message of newer perspectives often boils down to that.

Note

This chapter was written while I held the Thomas F. Gleed Chair of Business and Finance at Seattle University, and this support is gratefully acknowledged. Portions of this chapter were presented at a career development seminar entitled, "Linking New Concept of Organizations to New Paradigms for Inquiry," Overland Park, Kansas, November 4–5, 1983.

References

Anderson, P. A. (1983). Decision making by objection and the Cuban missile crisis. *Administrative Science Quarterly, 28*, 201–222.

Ashton, R. (1976). Deviation-amplifying feedback and unintended consequences of management accounting systems. *Accounting, Organizations, and Society, 1*, 289–300.

Axelrod, R. (1977). Argumentation in foreign policy settings. *Journal of Conflict Resolution, 21*, 727–756.

Benson, J. K. (1983). Paradigm and praxis in organizational analysis. In L. L. Cummings & B. M. Staw (Eds.), *Research in organizational behavior* (Vol. 5). Greenwich, CT: JAI.

Berg, P. O. (1979). *Emotional structure in organizations.* Farnborough: Teakfield.

Bess, J. L. (1982). *University organization.* New York: Human Science Press.

Bougon, M., Weick, K. E., & Binkhorst, D. (1977). Cognition in organizations: An analysis of the Utrecht Jazz Orchestra. *Administrative Science Quarterly, 22*, 606–639.

Brunsson, N. (1982). The irrationality of action and action rationality: Decisions, ideologies, and organizational actions. *Journal of Management Studies, 19*, 29–44.

Chan, S. (1979). The intelligence of stupidity: Understanding failures in strategic warning. *American Political Science Review, 73*, 171–180.

Cohen, M. D., & March, J. G. (1974). *Leadership and ambiguity.* New York: McGraw-Hill.

Cohen, M. D., March, J. G., & Olsen, J. P. (1972). A garbage can model of organizational choice. *Administration Science Quarterly, 17*, 1–25.

DiMaggio, P. J., & Powell, W. W. (1983). The iron cage revisited: Institutional isomorphism and collective rationality in organizational fields. *American Sociological Review, 48*, 147–160.

Dyckman, T. R. (1981). The intelligence of ambiguity. *Accounting, Organizations, and Society, 6*, 291–300.

Fischoff, B. (1975). Hindsight and foresight: The effect of outcome knowledge on judgement under uncertainty. *Journal of Experimental Psychology: Human Perception and Performance, 1*, 288–299.

Fischoff, B., & Beyth, R. (1975). "I knew it would happen": Remembered probabilities on once-future things. *Organizational Behavior and Human Performance, 13*, 1–16.

Fischoff, B., & Beyeth-Marom, R. (1976). Failure has many fathers. *Policy Sciences, 7*, 388–393.

Gerwin, D. (1981). Relationships between structure and technology. In P. C. Nystrom & W. H. Starbuck (Eds.), *Handbook of organizational design* (Vol. 2). New York: Oxford University Press.

Glassman, R. B. (1973). Persistence and loose coupling in living systems. *Behavioral Sciences, 18*, 83–98.

Goodman, P. S. (1968). The measurement of an individual's organization map. *Administrative Science Quarterly, 13*, 246–265.

Gronn, P. C. (1983). Talk as the work: The accomplishment of school administration. *Administrative Science Quarterly, 28*, 1–21.

Hall, P. M. (1973). A symbolic interactionist analysis of politics. *Sociological Inquiry, 42*, (3–4), 35–75.

Hedberg, B. (1981). How organizations learn and unlearn. In P. C. Nystrom & W. H. Starbuck (Eds.), *Handbook of organizational design* (Vol. 1). New York: Oxford University Press.

Jones, R. A. (1977). *Self-fulfiling prophecies*. Hillsdale, NJ: Erlbaum.

Kling, R. (1980). Social analyses of computing: Theoretical perspectives in recent empirical research. *Computing Surveys, 12*, 61–110.

Kuhn, A., & Beam, R. D. (1982). *The logic of organization*. San Francisco: Jossey-Bass.

Manning, P. K. (1983). *Queries concerning the decision-making approach to police research*. Paper presented to the British Psychological Society.

March, J. G. (1978). Bounded rationality, ambiguity, and the engineering of choice. *Bell Journal of Economics, 9*, 587–608.

March, J. G., & Olsen, J. P. (1976). Organizational choice under ambiguity. In J. G. March & J. P. Olsen (Eds.), *Ambiguity and choice in organizations* (pp. 10–23). Bergen: Universitetsforlaget.

March, J. G., & Romelaer, P. J. (1976). Position and presence in the drift of decisions. In J. G. March & J. P. Olsen (Eds.), *Ambiguity and choice in organizations* (pp. 251–276). Bergen: Universitetsforlaget.

McCaskey, M. B. (1982). *The executive challenge: Managing change and ambiguity*. Marshfield, MA: Pitman.

Meyer, J. W., & Rowan, B. (1977). Institutionalized organizations: Formal structure as myth and ceremony. *American Journal of Sociology, 83*, 340–363.

Mintzberg, H. (1973). *The nature of managerial work*. New York: Harper & Row.

Padgett, J. F. (1980). Managing garbage can hierarchies. *Administrative Science Quarterly, 25*, 583–604.

Peters, T. J. (1980). Management systems: The language of organizational character and competence. *Organizational Dynamics, 9* (1), 3–26.

Peters, T. J., & Waterman, R. H. (1982). *In search of excellence*. New York: Harper & Row.

Pfeffer, J. (1981). *Power in organizations*. Marshfield, MA: Pitman.

Porac, J. F. (1981). Causal loops and other intercausal perceptions in attributions for exam performance. *Journal of Educational Psychology, 73*, 587–601.

Roos, L. I., & Hall, R. I. (1980). Influence diagrams and organizational power. *Administrative Science Quarterly, 25*, 57–71.

Schachter, S. (1959). *The psychology of affiliation*. Stanford, CA: Stanford University Press.

Slovic, P., & Fischoff, B. (1977). On the psychology of experimental surprises. *Journal of Experimental Psychology: Human Perception and Performance, 3*, 544–551.

Starbuck, W. H. (1982). Congealing oil: Inventing ideologies to justify acting ideologies out. *Journal of Management Studies, 19*, 3–27.

Starbuck, W. H. (1983). Organizations as action generators. *American Sociological Review, 48*, 91–102.

Staw, B. M. (1980). Rationality and justification in organizational life. In B. M. Staw & L. L.

Cummings (Eds.), *Research in organizational behavior* (Vol. 2). Greenwich, CT: JAI.

Weick, K. E. (1976). Educational organizations as loosely coupled systems. *Administrative Science Quarterly, 21,* 1–19.

Weick, K. E. (1980). The management of eloquence. *Executive, 6* (3), 18–21.

Weick, K. E. (1982). Management of organizational change among loosely coupled elements. In P. Goodman (Ed.), *Change in organizations* (pp. 375–408). San Francisco: Jossey-Bass.

Weick, K. E. (1984). Small wins: Redefining the scale of social problems. *American Psychologist, 39,* 40–49.

Westerlund, G., & Sjöstrand, S. E. (1979). *Organizational myths.* New York: Harper & Row.

3

Organizational Redesign as Improvisation

A way of seeing is a way of not seeing.
G. *Poggi*, The British Journal of Sociology, *December, 1965*

Today is not yesterday – We ourselves change – How then can our works and thoughts, if they are always to be the fittest, continue always the same.
Thomas Carlyle

One mistake the arts would never make is to presume that a part or role can be exactly specified independent of the performer, yet this is the idea that has dominated work organizations for most of the twentieth century.
Peter B. Vail, Managing as a Performing Art, *1989: 124*

I suspect that much organizational illness can be attributed to the contrived (though time honored) ways in which humans are differentiated, constrained, controlled and directed, rewarded and punished, and limited to tasks that others have decided are appropriate to a given job. The illusion is that there is no alternative.
(McEachern, 1984: 81)

The activity of architectural design often serves as the metaphor for organizational design, as in Khandwalla's (1977: 260) statement that "the formed world is the only habitable one." In its earliest stages, the overarching study, called the CODE study, was itself described using imagery consistent with this metaphor.[1] Organizational design modeled along the lines of architectural design is viewed as a bounded activity that occurs at a fixed point in time. The activity is largely decision making, concentrated in a small group, which translates intentions into plans. The plans are based on assumptions of ideal conditions and envision structures rather than processes. The structures are assumed to be stable solutions to a set of current problems that will change only incrementally.

While the metaphor of architecture is a compelling model for organizational change, it is not the only one. I hope to demonstrate that an alternative metaphor, design as improvisational theater, corrects many of the blind spots induced by the metaphor of architecture. The idea of design as improvisation would suggest that Khandwalla's statement should be rewritten to read, "the forming world is the only habitable one." The revised assumptions that lie behind this rewrite include such ideas as redesign is a continuous activity, responsibility for the initiation of redesign is dispersed, interpretation is the essence of design, resourcefulness is more crucial than resources, the meaning of an action is usually known after the fact, and a little structure goes a long way.

In a group of improvisational players, there are always more possible meanings for their actions than the group can ever use, so their problem is to agree on a sufficient number of meanings to make coordinated action possible. But agreements are held to a minimum so that people retain the capability to make individual adjustments to local irregularities. In improvisational theater, coordination occurs not so much because people have identical views of "the" design, but because they have equivalent views of what is happening and what it means. Equivalence allows both coordination and individual expression to occur simultaneously. As a result, people are able to accomplish collectively what they could not do individually, but also to cope individually with unexpected problems by virtue of their diverse capabilities. The design that produces this complex mixture tends to be emergent and visible only after the fact. Thus, the design is a piece of history, not a piece of architecture.

The remainder of this chapter explicates the idea of organizational design as improvisation, by contrasting it with the idea of organizational design as architecture. The vehicle for this contrast is a statement, written in the early stages of the CODE study, which addressed the question, "Why study organizational design?" This statement implies several assumptions that are consistent with the idea that design resembles architecture. Several of these implied assumptions are identified, and then they are rewritten to illustrate the idea that design resembles improvisation. The meaning of each rewritten assumption is then discussed in the adjacent text.

The complete text of the 16-line CODE statement is shown in Table 3.1. The specific portions of this text from which the implied assumptions are drawn, are identified throughout by the line number(s) where these portions are stated.

Images of Improvised Design

CODE PHRASE: "The design of an organization determines" (line 1).

Implied assumptions
1. A design is a blueprint.
2. A design is constructed at a single point in time.
3. Designs produce order through intention.
4. Design creates planned change.

Alternative assumptions
1.1 A design is a recipe.

Table 3.1 Why study organizational design?

- 1 To a great extent, the design of an organization determines the distribution of resources, authority, and information.
  2 As a consequence, it directly impacts the ability of individual managers to make and to implement
  3 timely, technically and economically sound, and organizationally acceptable decisions.
  4 The ability to make and implement such decisions, in turn, affects the effectiveness of the organization.

- 5 Related to the reason above, the design of an organization directly affects a manager's ability to
  6 coordinate and control the activities of subordinates in order to enhance organizational performance.
  7 Proper organizational design can therefore make the difference between having an effective, well-run organization
  8 and having one with recurrent crises and organizational inefficiencies.

- 9 Organizational environments are changing more rapidly than ever before. Because the effectiveness of
  10 an organizational design erodes over time as the environment changes, the organization must be designed
  11 to fit current and future environments, not the environment of the past.

- 12 Innovative technologies are continuously being introduced in modern organizations. The effectiveness of
  13 different organizational designs depends on the technology and how the work is done.

- 14 Modern communication and computing technologies facilitate the process of coordination and control
  15 and make new organizational designs feasible. New communication and computing technologies can also
  16 increase organizational effectiveness in current or previously abandoned organizational designs.

  2.1   Designing is continuously reconstructed.
  3.1   Designs produce order through attention.
  4.1   Design codifies unplanned change after the fact.

The phrase *organizational design* contains a trap. The trap is that the word design can be used as a noun as well as a verb. When people in organizations talk about the design of an organization, they tend to equate it with things like organization charts, written procedures, and job specifications. Features of organizations that are less thing-like and more continuous, fleeting, and emergent, are easily overlooked. As a result, organizational designs tend to focus on structures rather than processes and to contain few provisions for self-correction.

Improvisation is about process and about designs that are continuously reconstructed. Starbuck and Nystrom (1981: 14) captured this idea perfectly when they said, "a well-designed organization is not a stable solution to achieve, but a developmental process to keep active." Kilmann, Pondy, and Slevin (1976: 7) made essentially the same point when they argued that one-time design strategies make sense if the environment is basically placid, but continuous redesign is necessary when the environment becomes turbulent. If the architecture metaphor tempts people to introduce the design process at only a few fixed points in time, then this should lead to lower performance as the rate of environmental change accelerates.

Designs as recipes

One way to shift attention from the static to the dynamic in organizational design is to move from the assumption that a design is a blueprint to the assumption that a design is a recipe. Simon (1962) used the contrast between blueprints and recipes to illustrate two different ways to describe complex systems. Complex systems can be described using descriptions that resemble blueprints (e.g., a circle is the locus of all points equidistant from a given point) or by descriptions that resemble recipes (e.g., to construct a circle, rotate a compass with one end fixed until the other arm has returned to its starting point). Blueprints, organizational charts, musical scores, pictures, diagrams, and chemical formulae all capture the way we sense the work. These devices help us identify and label what we see. For example, an organizational chart helps us see who is at the center and who are at the periphery of information flows.

But what blueprints can't do is capture how that sensed world came into being. It takes a recipe to do that. Recipes, organizational values, expressive notations in music, self-actuated museum demonstrations, strip maps, and differential equations all describe actions that generate the objects specified in blueprints.

To many designers, a blueprint is the goal and the recipe is the means to get there. As Simon puts it, the basic problem in design is, given a blueprint, what is the corresponding recipe that will achieve it? That way of formulating the question is too narrow. It illustrates the limits of the architectural metaphor. Blueprints are assumed to exert control over more of the design process than is consistent with what we know about either organizations or people. Architects may treat blueprints as givens, but people who improvise treat them as emergents. The givens for people who improvise are the recipes and routines by which they generate actions that could become any one of several different blueprints.

A typical recipe for design sounds like this: Take a hierarchy and flatten it; take an executive committee and enlarge it; find an elite and join it; turn these five notes into a composition. In each case a starting point is specified – hierarchy, committee, elites, musical notes. And an action is also specified – flatten, enlarge, join, compose. But what is not specified in advance are the structures that will emerge as these actions and starting points are mixed together. Even when detailed blueprints supposedly drive the design process, this same open-ended quality is present. Events are set in motion, but the orderliness they will create remains to be discovered.

Design, viewed from the perspective of improvisation, is more emergent, more continuous, more filled with surprise, more difficult to control, more tied to the content of action, and more affected by what people pay attention to than are the designs implied by architecture. Even though improvisation may involve more uncertainty, it does not thereby become any less effective. Emergent, continuous designing is sensitive to small changes in local conditions, which means the design is continuously updated as people and conditions change.

If we view designing as improvisation and designs as recipes, then there are at least three additional implications that run counter to traditional views of organizational design.

Designs as attention

The notion of improvisation implies that attention rather than intention drives the process of designing. As we saw earlier, blueprints portray the world we sense and recipes portray the way that world is enacted. Since the only things we can sense are enacted events that have already taken place, attention rather than intention becomes central to the design process. The importance of attention is often missed since in organizations as in architecture, design is focused on the future (see lines 10 and 11 of the CODE statement) and blueprints are treated as tools of intention. In actuality, design is focused on the past and blueprints are tools of attention. Design is focused on extrapolations of the past since the past contains the only data we have to work with. And blueprints influence attention rather than intention because they contain categories and relationships that are imposed on elapsed actions to make them more sensible.

This complex mixture of attention, designs formed in retrospect, and sensemaking that always occurs "too late" is visible in Mintzberg and McHugh's (1985: 160) analysis of the Canadian Film Board between 1939 and 1975. They found that the periods that unfolded as if they were the result of intended designs actually consisted of patterns that emerged gradually, sometimes fortuitously, out of elapsed actions made sensible after the fact. The patterning of film board actions, and the designs in which those actions were imbedded, were the product of attention rather than intention. The key point is that designing often consists of a shifting pattern of attention and meaning imposed on an ongoing stream of social activity, rather than a stable pattern of intention imposed a priori on events initiated to achieve an outcome.

As a variation on this point, it is important to note that design often codifies previous unplanned change rather than creates future planned change. The assumption that design creates planned change is implicit in a question asked in much of the research reported: "When was it definitely decided to make this change?" Respondents could have been asked, "When was it definitely decided that this change had been made?", a question that more closely taps the emergent, retrospective origin of many designs. The idea that design is a process of codification starts with the notion that events often simply unfold. When viewed retrospectively, with a specific framework in hand, elapsed events seem to cohere as if they had been designed. The coherence is partly an artifact of selective attention and partly the artifact of actions which themselves fall into habits, patterns, and routines. It is not that the coherence is undesigned. Rather, the source of the coherence in the design lies elsewhere than in intention. There was not a transition from imagination, through intention, into execution. Instead, there was an imaginative interpretation of execution that imputed sufficient coherence to the execution that it could easily be mistaken for an intention.

Designs as bricolage

Design is clearly a process of sensemaking that makes do with whatever materials are at hand. This is perhaps our sharpest point of departure from the architectural view, so it needs to be spelled out explicitly. From the perspective of improvisation, designing is synonymous with bricolage, and the designer acts like a bricoleur. The terms bricolage and bricoleur come from Levi-Strauss's (1966) research on the savage mind.

The French word *bricolage* (which has no precise equivalent in English) means to use whatever resources and repertoire one has to perform whatever task one faces. Invariably the resources are less well suited to the exact project than one would prefer but they are all there is. The person who engages in bricolage is called a *bricoleur*, which means roughly a jack-of-all-trades or someone who is a professional do-it-yourself person (Levi-Strauss, 1966: 17). A bricoleur should not be confused with an odd job man, because considerably more knowledge about materials is assumed in the case of the bricoleur.

The defining characteristic of a bricoleur is that this person makes do with whatever tools and materials are at hand. These resources are always heterogeneous because, unlike the materials available to the engineer, the bricoleur's materials have no relation to any particular project. Elements are collected and retained on the principle that they may come in handy (p. 18). Engineers take on only those projects for which they have the necessary raw materials and resources, whereas bricoleurs do not similarly restrict themselves. The bricoleur's materials are not project-specific, but, instead, they represent the contingent result of all of the previous uses to which those items have been put. The materials, in other words, mean whatever they have been used for in the past. The more diverse these uses, and the more fully the materials themselves are understood, the more innovative will the bricoleur be in improvising new designs from this stock of materials.

When the bricoleur begins to work on a project, "his first practical step is retrospective" (p. 18). He interrogates the existing set of materials to see what it contains. What it contains is defined in large part by the uses to which it has been put up to that point. It is these prior uses (what the object signifies) that are manipulated and recombined in an effort to advance the project. Through the use of generalization, analogies, and comparisons, the bricoleur assembles new arrangements of elements. Prior history can preconstrain the ways in which the materials are interpreted, but this limitation is not unique to bricoleurs.

Two recent discussions of the bricoleur each have added some nuances to our understanding of this improvisational mode of design. Harper (1987) found the embodiment of the bricoleur in a small backwoods garage in upstate New York, a man named Willie who improvised Saab automobile repairs, wood burning stoves, tractor parts, and solutions to whatever problems people brought him, using odds and ends that he had accumulated over the years. Willie's genius is apparent in his "tractor" – a vehicle made from a 1929 International truck rear axle and seat, a 15-horsepower motor from a hay baler, front wheels from a Chevrolet car, a steering box from a 1942 one and one-half ton truck, and a gas tank from an outboard motor. The tractor could pull enormous loads in superlow, yet travel up to 40 miles per hour. What Harper's analysis shows is that the bricoleur is a thinker who makes creative use of whatever builds up during the process of work.

Thayer's (1988) recent discussion of bricolage in the context of leadership provides a second extension of the basic concept. He argues that the main function of any leader is to draw organization out of the raw materials of life (p. 239) by using ingeniously whatever is at hand. Each instance that the leader faces is a unique combination of resources and beliefs. And other than the recipe to "make do," there is no fixed procedure that the leader can follow to convert that assortment of resources into a more meaningful organization. As Thayer puts it: "The leader's function is . . . fixing things on the spot through a creative vision of what is available and what might be done with it" (p. 239). The act of drawing organization out of whatever is at hand is not a random exercise. What makes for skilled bricolage is intimate knowledge of resources, careful observation, trust in one's intuitions, listening, and confidence that any enacted structure can be self-correcting if one's ego is not invested too heavily in it.

If there is a key to success as a bricoleur it is buried in Levi-Strauss's statement that objects "are not known as a result of their usefulness; they are deemed to be useful or interesting because they are first of all known" (p. 9). Willie does not know about hay baler motors because they are useful ways to power a tractor. It's the other way around. Because he knows these motors so well, he is able to see that the one he has in hand can help him solve the problem of finding power for his tractor. Exhaustive observation and systematic cataloging of relations and connections (Levi-Strauss, 1966: 10) are necessary for successful bricolage.

With this background in place, we can now return to the issue of organizational design. If we think of designers as people who improvise, then the materials they have available to work with are the residue of their past experience and the past experience of people in their design group, the meanings attached to this past experience, observational skills, and their own willingness to rely on imaginative recombination of these materials. These elements are focused more on the past than on the future. And they are affected more by the ways in which people have codified the past than on how they envision the future. From the perspective of the bricoleur, efforts to improve organizational design fail for at least five reasons: (1) people are too detached and do not see their present situation in sufficient detail; (2) past experience is either limited or unsystemized; (3) people are unwilling or unable to work with the resources they have at hand; (4) a preoccupation with decision rationality makes it impossible for people to accept the rationality of making do; and (5) designers strive for perfection and are unable to appreciate the aesthetics of imperfection (Gioia, 1988).

Willie's tractor had post hoc orderliness, which suggested that it must be the product of intentional design. Some intention clearly was involved since he did not assemble the pile of junk in his back lot into a piece of sculpture, a buzz saw, or a boat anchor. But the important point is that he did not collect his junk pile and then add to it to fit some preconceived plan of how to make a tractor. Instead, he essentially looked at the pile of junk, said to himself, "somewhere in that pile of junk is a tractor," and then proceeded to discover the tractor in the set of materials which, up to that point, had not been organized under this concept. By saying in essence, what I have here is enough for my purposes, Willie transformed himself from an engineer into a bricoleur. And, in doing this, Willie developed his tractor into properties which an engineer working with blueprints and imagined constraints, might well have said were impossible to attain in a vehicle of this size and weight. This is not to argue that bricolage is superior to engineering. Only that it is not demonstrably worse. The connotations of the word design have tempted many people to overlook that possibility.

There are more routes to orderliness than the one through intention, planning, and implementation. Orderliness can also result from improvisation based on intimate knowledge of resources. Intimate knowledge often suggests artful recombinations of seemingly miscellaneous materials, which can make a large difference. It is that theme to which we turn next.

Myths Surrounding the Design Process

CODE PHRASE: "The design of an organization determines the distribution of resources, authority, and information" (line 1).

Implied assumptions
5. An organization has only a single design.
6. The design determines the distribution of resources.
7. Designs are large structures that are stabilized.

Alternative assumptions
5.1 An organization has multiple designs.

6.1   The distribution of resources determines the design.
7.1   Designs are small structures that are amplified.

If we take the position that design is often emergent, improvised, locally rational, and built from whatever resources are at hand, then design loses some of its force as a driving condition for organizational change. If design becomes fully formed, visible, and influential relatively late in the history of a group, then it should strongly reflect the effects of events that occurred earlier in its history. Very few of those events will be directed explicitly to issues of design. Instead, most of them will be related simply to doing the work.

If design is essentially an outcome of work, rather than an input to it, then several designs should exist in any one organization since several different kinds of work occur simultaneously. Furthermore, the distribution of resources to do the work will determine the designs, and small, early events will have a disproportionately large effect on the content of the eventual design. Each of these three mechanisms reflects a different assumption than is visible in the CODE statement. And each of these alternative assumptions is consistent with the idea that organizational design is an exercise in improvisation.

The myth of singular design

An organizational design is not a monolithic entity. Any reference to "the" organizational design is misleading because it makes the "assumption of homogeneity" (Dornbusch and Scott, 1975: 77). This is the assumption that the technology of an organization is essentially the same across tasks and occupational groups and the social structure is the same across work units. Typically, however, multiple structures and designs are found within a single organization, which means it is more accurate to describe organizations as a group of groups, a set of shifting coalitions, or as a federation of subcultures. This means that designs usually characterize smaller groups of people doing more specific tasks than is usually implied when people describe an organizational design as if it fits the organization as a whole.

Any attempt to construct "the" design is doomed because there is no such thing. Instead, designers need to answer the question, "Design in whose view?" To answer that question, they need to know what stream of activities, produced by what people, in the service of what goals, over what time period, has had some design attributed to it retrospectively, and now needs to have that design respecified.

The myth of resource dependence

The second assumption about monolithic design that we need to reexamine is the idea that designs determine the distribution of resources. Within organizational theory, one of the more influential theories concerning resources is the view that organizations can be understood if we know the pattern of their resource dependence. Pfeffer and Salancik (1978) argue that social actors become powerful when they control resources that are critical to the organization's survival, especially when these resources cannot be obtained elsewhere. Since organizational designs tend to form around coalitions that control scarce resources, there is reason to question the idea that design determines resource distribution.

Hall (1984), in his study of the demise of the *Saturday Evening Post*, found that between 1940 and 1947 the magazine faced critical problems of supplies and printing capacity due to wartime conditions. The production operations coalition rose to power during this period since they were able to reduce some of the uncertainty concerning the critical resources of paper, ink, and printing. Their ascendance was reflected in the emergent design. After the war, when supplies were no longer a problem, the critical uncertainty became declining circulation. The coalition concerned with circulation and promotion gained ascendance, operations people lost influence, and the design shifted once more. Thus, the idea of resource dependence suggests that the distribution of resources determines design, rather than the other way around.

But we can go one step further. The concept of bricolage implies that resources are not as scarce, nor are they distributed as unevenly, as Pfeffer and Salancik suggest. The discussion of bricolage sensitized us to the possibility that there are many more potential resources, in many more places in organizations, than we usually assume. The reason we miss this possibility is that we maintain narrow definitions of what constitutes a resource. And we assume that a resource has a fixed meaning and there is limited substitutability of one resource for another one.

If we adopt a view of resources that is more consistent with the idea of bricolage – resources are pragmatic and are defined by the conditions of their use – then the distribution of the skills of bricolage, rather than the distribution of resources, should affect how the organization functions. It is the ability to combine old resources in new ways to reduce new uncertainties that determines organizational effectiveness. Thus, designs don't determine resource distribution; it's the other way around. Further, it is not the resources per se that determine design, but the capability to create resources from the residue of past experience.

Whether we adopt the idea of resource dependence or the idea of resource improvisation, resources become influential in the determination of design. To redesign an organization means that people need to redefine the crucial uncertainty facing the organization, to specify the critical resources needed to address that newly identified uncertainty, and then to encourage people either to find or to improvise the resources required. Resort to bricolage as a means to resolve critical new uncertainties should be more apparent in organizations that favor generalists than in organizations that favor specialists.

The myth of large causes

The third assumption about monolithic design that we need to reexamine concerns the size and stability of designs. A design modeled after architecture typically covers many units, is worked out in some detail, and represents a relatively stable large structure that is put in place intact. The picture of design that is implied by the combination of improvisation, retrospect, and emergent orderliness is somewhat different. The primary image in this alternative view is summarized in this recipe: a little structure goes a long way (Weick, 1989).

To grasp the sense in which small structures can generate large designs, consider a self-fulfilling prophecy. Self-fulfilling prophecies are just another way of saying that expectations make a difference. A self-fulfilling prophecy was defined by Robert Merton as "an unconditional prediction or expectation about a future situation such that, first, had it not been made, the future situation envisaged would not have occurred, but because it is made, alterations in behavior are produced which bring about that envisioned situation, or bring that envisioned situation to pass" (cited in Henshel, 1987: 2).

The key event in a self-fulfilling prophecy involves an expectation that causes an envisioned situation to materialize. Prophecies, therefore, become tools of design. They set forces in motion which produce determinant structures that weren't there before. New structures are created because the prophecy alters behaviors, and the altered behaviors are the means by which the prophecy is fulfilled.

To see how this works, consider a bandwagon effect in an election (Henshel and Johnston, 1987). A bandwagon effect occurs when the predicted winner in an election poll gains additional votes as a result of the publication of the poll. The poll is a prophecy, and it becomes a self-fulfilling prophecy when it leads people to alter their behavior in ways that lend validity to the prophecy. Henshel and Johnston (1987) found that poll forecasts do alter behavior, but not in the ways we thought. Poll forecasts that reach some level of credibility and accuracy lead key individuals to increase their financial contributions, volunteerism, and endorsements, and these three inputs modify campaigns. It is these altered campaigns that affect voters and lead them to alter their behaviors so the prophecies of the polls are fulfilled. Notice that there is nothing mysterious or nonrational about the way this mechanism works. Choices to increase support for a candidate based on polls are rational choices made by people who stand to benefit if the candidate is elected.

The bandwagon effect is an even better example of emergent designs with small beginnings than may be apparent. So far, we have suggested that expectations make a difference. But they make even more of a difference when they recycle. Once an election poll gains credibility, it becomes more likely that the forecast will alter behavior even more quickly and even more strongly, which makes it even more accurate, which raises its credibility even more, and so on. If one expectation is a source of a design, then a self-confirming expectation that recycles and amplifies should produce a more stable design that organizes an increasingly large set of resources. Something that started small in the form of an expectation grows into a complex structure of interdependent people because a self-fulfilling prophecy became a *serial* self-fulfilling prophecy. Small initial increments in funds, people, and endorsements were amplified into more powerful variables that determined outcomes. The self-fulfilling prophecy and the events it triggered became the design, although no one intended this outcome. Furthermore, it would be hard to predict the size of the structure that eventually emerged, given the inconspicuous events with which it started.

The scenario we have described is not confined to election campaigns. It is the essence of emergent design. The things designers *expect* will happen may predict the designs they achieve better than will their statements about what they plan to have happen. Creating a bandwagon through serial self-fulfilling prophecies that amplify is not that much different from creating a social movement or becoming an idea champion. In both cases, the incipient design starts small but enlarges rapidly. The beginning creates the conditions for its own perpetuation and enlargement. While it is possible to design an expectation that amplifies, it is more likely that elements combine with less deliberation around smaller starting points that are more capricious. Again, the resulting design is no less orderly nor is it necessarily any less effective. What it is, however, is less bound by the limits of the designer's imagination, more subject to the vagaries of improvisation, and more likely to assume unexpected shapes.

Managers and Improvised Design

CODE PHRASE: Design "impacts the ability of individual managers" (line 2).

Implied assumptions
   8.   Design affects managerial ability.
   9.   Managerial action is individual.

Alternative assumptions
   8.1 Managerial ability affects design.
   9.1 Managerial action is social.

Organizational designs can have an impact on managerial ability, as the CODE statement suggests, in the sense that formalized relationships make it easier or harder to get things done, in the sense that designs provide more or less discretion to do what one is best able to do, and in the sense that designs carry provisions for more or less corrective feedback. But the idea of design as improvisation highlights the opposite direction of impact – namely, ability has an impact on design. It is important to understand this opposite relationship because it suggests determinants of design that people often overlook.

Managerial ability and design

The idea that ability affects design was implicit in the previous discussion of bricolage. People who have skills at bricolage often are able to transform a large number of miscellaneous resources into a small number of critical resources through imaginative recombination. These recombinations may remove critical uncertainties. If they do, this means that the people who built the critical resources acquire more power and a bigger say over what form the organization will take. The skilled bricoleur affects design because people defer to, seek out, comply with, and attribute power to those who are able to reduce critical uncertainties. These acts of deference can become stabilized into repetitive sequences that then become a new emergent structure.

The idea that ability affects design is also implicit in the choice to deal with technical complexity through greater complexity of the performer rather than greater complexity of the structure. Scott (1987: 236) has called this choice a watershed in organizational design. Rather than divide the work and parcel it out to differentiated groups, designers keep the work intact and assign it to complex, flexible performers called professionals. When the work is handled by professionals, organic structures tend to replace mechanistic structures (Weick and McDaniel, 1989), the locus of authority is task-specific, and interdependence is intermittent rather than constant. Regardless of what designs professionals enact, the point is that complex skills embodied in a single actor have an impact on organizational design.

But ability affects design in a still more basic sense. Ability affects perception: people see those things they can do something about (Jervis, 1976: 374–375). And ability affects goal setting: people feel they should do what they can do (Dornbusch and Scott, 1975: 86). People see the world as filled with projects that fit their capabilities, and they see these projects as the ones that need doing. If the content of design is affected by what people notice, and if people notice those things about which they can do something, then generalists – people such as a bricoleur who are able to do many different things – should notice more options and enact a greater variety of designs than specialists see and do. Improvements in design expertise should come not so much from direct schooling in blueprints for design as from development of a larger response repertoire.

Managerial self-efficacy and design

While actual skill development is an important determinant of design, one's *perception* of that level of skill development may be equally influential in the determination of design, as is suggested by the work of Bandura and his associates (1986). The sense of self-efficacy experienced by designers should affect the designs they produce. The key ideas about efficacy include the following.

When people transform their knowledge and abilities into action, this transformation is mediated by thoughts about themselves and their capabilities. These thoughts concern such things as perceived capability to mobilize motivation, to control perturbing thoughts, to persevere, to bounce back from failure, and to exert some control over the environment. These beliefs affect how much of one's skills will actually be mustered to cope with the demands of a task. Thus, given the same level of skill, a person will perform poorly, adequately, or extraordinarily, depending on self-efficacy (Bandura and Wood, 1989). High self-efficacy is associated with a rapid recovery from failure and reverses (Bandura, 1990: 317), persistence in the face of obstacles, the effective control of intrusive thoughts that focus attention on the self rather than on the task, a perception of the environment as controllable, the likelihood of setting higher goals and remaining committed to them for longer periods, and the increased ability to visualize the future in terms of scenarios of success rather than scenarios of failure.

The relevance of efficacy to organizational design is the following. To construct designs in dynamic environments requires that information from diverse sources be integrated, that design options be identified, and that exploratory learning occur, concurrently with management of the ongoing organization. There is a need for the creative and persistent use of complex sets of capabilities in order to exercise some control over the environment and the organization. Success in forming and enacting these complex capabilities is mediated by self-referential thought:

> Operative self-efficacy is a generative capability in which multiple subskills must be continuously *improvised* [italics added] to manage ever-changing circumstances. . . . (I)ndividuals who believe themselves to be inefficacious are likely to effect limited changes even in environments that provide many opportunities. Conversely, those who have a firm belief in their efficacy, through ingenuity and perseverance, figure out ways of exercising some measure of control in environments containing limited opportunities and many constraints. (Bandura and Wood, 1989: 805–806).

Beliefs about self-efficacy and the controllability of the environment trigger something akin to a self-fulfilling prophecy for design. People who believe the environment can be enacted and that they have the capabilities to do so, are motivated to make strong, persistent efforts to control it, which increases their chance for success. If they succeed, this validates their sense of efficacy and their perception of controllability. If they fail, the effects of the failure are transient and become the occasion for learning rather than self-doubt (Elliott and Dweck, 1988). People who doubt their efficacy and view environments as uncontrollable exert less effort for shorter periods, which thwarts successful control. Unfortunately, this confirms their prophecy that things are uncontrollable and that they don't have sufficient skills to change this reality (Bandura and Wood, 1989: 811).

If we assume that better design comes from focusing on the task than from focusing on the self, then high self-efficacy is an important antecedent of design because it encourages people to pay attention to the task. People with lower self-efficacy doubt their problem-solving capabilities, the controllability of the environment, and their likelihood of success, and these doubts become self-confirming through their debilitating effects on action. The doubts suggest that redesign is fruitless, and these doubts become intrusive thoughts, which make it that much harder to visualize and enact any design that is an improvement. The design process becomes impoverished, not because people lack the skills for design, but because they lack the beliefs that convert those skills into action.

Managerial groups and design

One outcome of the CODE assumption that design impacts the ability of individual managers is a blind spot regarding the ways in which ability rather than the environment shapes design. But another, more subtle, blind spot lurks in the phrase "individual manager" because it presumes that there is such a thing. In many ways, the idea of an individual manager is a fiction. Managing is a composite of partial contributions made by many individuals whose identity is defined by their social relations. Management work is profoundly social, which means that the dispersion and meaning of a design is not easily controlled. Designs don't create social systems; they are created by social systems. And design effectiveness is determined by the existing social relationships that are engaged by the design.

Organizational design is social rather than individual in the obvious sense that it is built of social entities such as the top management team (Hurst, Rush, and White, 1989), the interact (Weick, 1979), the vertical dyad linkage between superior and subordinate (Graen and Scandura, 1987), or the interaction order (Barley, 1986: 101). In all of these cases, the important point is that "decisions are made either in the presence of others or with the knowledge that they will have to be implemented, or understood, or approved by others" (Burns and Stalker, 1961: 118).

But organizational design is also social in the less obvious but more fundamental sense that the individual is not separable from the human whole: "'Society' and 'individuals' do not denote separable phenomena, but are simply collective and distributive aspects of the same thing, the relation between them being like that between other expressions, one of which denotes a group as a whole and the other the members of the group, such as army and the soldiers, the class and the students" (Cooley, 1964: 37). If a person goes off alone into the wilderness, that person goes with a mind formed in society, and communication continues through memory, imagination, and books (p. 49). The imagined presence of others is no less real than their actual presence. Individuals who retrospectively label some pattern as a design speak on behalf of their associates (Chatman, Bell, and Staw, 1986), speak through the language they were socialized into, speak from a place in a social structure complete with reputation and status and expectations, and speak to prove their entitlement to continue to be regarded as a member in good standing.

When Allport (1954: 5) crafted his influential definition of social psychology as "an attempt to understand and explain how the thought, feeling, and behavior of individuals are influenced by the actual, imagined, and implied presence of other human beings," he provided a framework that is useful also for the scholar of organizational design. The thought, feeling, and behavior that go into the construction of a design, and that are reciprocally shaped by that design, are never individual and solitary. Designs are shaped in the service of others who matter, just as those others who matter are themselves shaped by the designs they construct. Designs reflect social interests, and they also structure social interests. Any act by an "individual manager" is actually an act by a representative, whose stature and membership are on the line. Whether high stakes are involved depends on the availability of alternative social resources. The smaller the number of alternatives, the higher the need to enact designs that are acceptable in the eyes of those who matter. Even if this drama is played out in imagination, it is no less real. What is unreal is to regard it as the activity of just one person.

Interpretation and Improvised Design

CODE PHRASE: Designs affect "the ability to make and implement" "timely, . . . sound, and . . . acceptable decisions" (lines 2–3).

Implied assumptions
    10. Decisions determine effectiveness.
    11. The purpose of design is to facilitate decision making.
    12. People decide and then they act.

Alternative assumptions
    10.1 Interpretations determine effectiveness.
    11.1 The purpose of design is to facilitate interpretation.
    12.1 People act and then they interpret.

Improvisation is largely an act of interpretation rather than an act of decision making. People who improvise have to make sense of unexpected events that emerge, which means they are more concerned with interpreting what has happened than with deciding what will happen. They may decide to start some activity, such as implementing a design, and they may also try to control how the activity will unfold. Nevertheless, this control is never complete, and unintended consequences are commonplace. These unintended consequences force people to revise their sense of what is happening and what can be accomplished. And it is these revised interpretations, rather than the initial decisions, that guide action and constitute the actual design in use. That design in use is shaped more by action than by plans, and more by interpretations than by decisions. In this section, we look briefly at the role of interpretation in design.

Interpretation and decision making

To interpret means to encode external events into internal categories that are part of the group's culture and language system (Daft and Weick, 1984). The act of interpretation involves creating maps or representations that simplify some territory in order to facilitate action. A common simplification is the interpretation that events require some kind of decision to be made. It is this sense in which design becomes an issue of interpretation before it becomes an issue of decision making. As Brown (1978: 376) has shown, power in organizations is exercised by those who design the frameworks, which then determine what it means to "make decisions." Frameworks affect what we see and what we ignore, which then affect the scope and content of decision making.

    The way in which interpretation takes precedence over decision making can be illustrated using the idea of decision strategies put forward by Thompson and Tuden (1959). They argued that decision makers need to use different strategies to make decisions, depending on whether their associates agree or disagree on their preferences for outcomes and whether these associates agree or disagree about the causal structure of the problem (i.e., which means leads to which outcomes). If people agree on both preferences and means-ends relations, then the appropriate design for decision making is one that allows for a programmed, routine response. If people agree on preferences but not on causal structure, a case that is common among professionals, then the appropriate design is one in which collegial interaction among equals results in a judgment. Disagreement on preferences with agreement on causal structure favors a design in which people can work out a compromise among the various representatives who favor different preferences. Complete disagreement requires a design that increases the probability that some inspiring vision will emerge on which people can agree.

Each of these four decision strategies – computation, judgment, compromise, and inspiration – favors a different design, but the prescribed design presumes that preferences and causal structure are fixed. To design for interpretation means that we back up one step. The designer now asks the question, "What design will enable people to achieve more agreement on preferences and causal structure so that they can make greater use of computation and routine to make decisions?" The design prescription implied here is that people and responsibilities should be distributed so that people find it easier to agree on preferences and/or causation.

If the environment is loosely coupled and indeterminant, then there may be no conceivable design that will improve agreements about causal structure. In that case, the designer who is sensitive to interpretation should encourage patterns of interaction that make it more likely that people will come to some agreement in their preferences for outcomes. The current push to change corporate culture (e.g., O'Reilly, 1989) can be understood as an effort to increase agreement on preferences in the face of an inability to get much agreement about what leads to what in a turbulent world. The push for more agreement on preferences is a push for conditions that favor collegial, professional interaction and a more thorough use of informed judgment to make tough decisions.

Notice that most organizations have preferred decision strategies already in place from earlier design exercises. For example, they may have a representative structure, such as in union–management negotiations, where they hammer out a compromise, given their dissimilar preferences and similar views of causal structure. But, as the pace of environmental change intensifies and as novel competitive pressures arise, old views of causal structure no longer work and dominant new views are hard to come by. As a result, the old pattern of agreements on causal structure that made compromise a plausible decision strategy now breaks down, even though the strategy of compromise is retained. The situation has changed into one in which inspiration is appropriate, yet the people involved continue to act as if compromise still makes sense.

What is needed in the face of this impasse is a design that does one of two things. Either it enables people to learn more about their environment and rebuild some agreements about causal structure – in which case they can continue to use compromise – or it enables them to generate truly novel solutions that are so compelling and so elegant that they inspire commitment from everyone. These two designs have points of overlap. In both cases, an openness to information and experimentation is beneficial. But the inspirational design requires more attention to persuasion, passion, and conversion, and thus it is more like a social movement than is the more incremental, more deliberate, more dispassionate, more cumulative design involved in rebuilding solid agreements about the nature of causation in a complex world.

In all of these scenarios, interpretation is a key to effectiveness, and the purpose of design is to facilitate interpretation. Once an interpretation is stabilized, then people can design for decision making. In the face of causal indeterminacy, many designs for interpretation help people adopt "the mantle of professionalism" and become more sensitive to issues of value (Ranson, Hinings, and Greenwood, 1980: 6). The design issue is not how to apply judgment to decision making. The design issue is how to construct a capability for judgment in the first place. That issue is an act of interpretation, because it necessitates an effort to get agreement on preferences. In order to construct such a framework, people have to encode events into a common set of values and implications. Once that commonality is achieved, then they can begin to act like professionals.

Organic organizational structures often turn out to be excellent generic designs, not so much because they are better suited to deal with high environmental uncertainty, but because they encourage the dense interactions that enable people to come to agreements about preferences and sometimes even causal structures (Weick and McDaniel, 1989). It is these agreements which then make it possible for people to use decision strategies that are better suited to deal with uncertainty. When interpretation is the issue, people need to design for agreement rather than for effectiveness. Effectiveness focuses too much attention on decision making and rationality and too little attention on what assumptions, frameworks, and resources people impose that give shape to that decision making.

Interpretation and sensemaking

If organizational design is to generate unequivocal interpretations, as well as effective decisions, then it must provide a way to focus the interpretation process. Otherwise, people are flooded with plausible interpretations for what their elapsed actions mean. One way to focus interpretation is through the use of behavioral commitment. The idea is that if a design creates structural conditions in which a behavior is difficult to change, then interpretation will focus on those socially acceptable reasons that justify the irrevocable action. Organizational design incorporates a sensitivity to the interpretation process when it creates those conditions in which specific behaviors become the anchor around which expectations, beliefs, and attitudes form.

The background for this proposal lies in Salancik's (1977) discussion of behavioral commitment. The basic ideas are these. Normally, when people act, their reasons for doing things are either self-evident or uninteresting, especially when the actions themselves can be undone, minimized, or disowned. Actions that are neither visible nor permanent can be explained with casual, transient explanations. As those actions become more public and irrevocable, however, they become harder to undo; and, when those same actions are also volitional, they become harder to disown. When action is irrevocable, public, and volitional, the search for explanations becomes less casual because more is at stake. Explanations that are developed retrospectively to justify committed actions are often stronger than beliefs developed under other, less involving, conditions. A tenacious justification can produce selective attention, confident action, and self-confirmation. Tenacious justifications prefigure both perception and action, which means they are often self-confirming.

Commitment focuses sensemaking on three things: an action, a socially acceptable justification for that action, and the potential of subsequent activities to validate the justification. Thus commitment is an outcome of improvised design that facilitates interpretation. Commitment ties together behaviors, explanations, social support, and expectations into a plausible causal sequence. This sequence can become a causal loop that either stabilizes or amplifies the pattern. It is these patterns which people come to label as sensible episodes. Different commitments lead to different patterns and a different sense of what is happening.

The importance of design in sensemaking can be illustrated using Smircich and Morgan's (1982: 258) description of the management of meaning; they propose that "leadership lies in large part in generating a point of reference, against which a feeling of organization and direction can emerge." An improvised design creates a point of reference around which meaning forms. To redesign is to respecify this generative point. Our proposal is that behavioral commitment is one way to create this point of reference. Thus, commitment is important because it sets sensemaking in motion and imposes some constraints on the form it will take.

Commitments can persevere, diffuse, and enlarge. And it is this capability which makes them important for design. Staw (1982: 116) has described this possibility in a way that unites several themes we have been developing: "When technology is ambiguous and products are value laden, commitment to goals and procedures, whatever they are, may be sufficient for proper adjustment to the environment. At the extreme, a 'school of thought' may be created (as in university life) where successful organizational leaders are those who can convince others that their own commitments are the standard to be achieved."

Several points are worth noting in Staw's description. First, commitment enables people to cope with turbulent environments. Second, commitment is a way to cope with unclear cause-effect relationships ("technology is ambiguous") and disagreement about preferences ("products are value laden"). Third, any old commitment can trigger the process of interpretation – all we need is something that animates people so they begin to generate actions, which can then become patterned. Fourth, although Staw says that commitment encourages "adjustment to" the environment, the phrase "creation of" could be substituted just as easily to allow for the possibility of enactment. Fifth, commitments to goals and procedures may stimulate justifications which turn into a "school of thought," a paradigm, or a system of interpretation. Sixth, leaders who try to persuade others to adopt the leader's commitment as a standard are managing interpretation. Seventh, commitment to goals and procedures represents a basic act of organizing, since consciously constructed procedures to reach goals are the defining property of organizations for many analysts.

Interpretation and action

Commitment becomes a more plausible tool of design when we assume that people act their way into meaning. When people improvise and then look back over their actions to see what they might have meant, they often discover decisions that they apparently made, although they didn't realize it at the time (Garfinkel, 1967). Thus, action is decision-*interpreted*, not decision-driven. Actions are crucial because they constrain meaning and structure and organizational form. It is these constraints that people seem to lose sight of when they assume that decisions affect action.

Think back to the earlier example of bandwagon effects. Serial self-fulfilling prophecies create a trail of public, irrevocable, voluntary actions by pollsters, contributors, and candidates, which become justified into an "organized campaign." The organized campaign is an emergent design that forms out of irrevocable forecasting, contributing, and campaigning that become linked into causal sequences that amplify. As the linkages among these actions become tighter, expectations become stronger, action is shaped more fully by expectations, and actions become less variable – all of which represent an increase in social order.

Actions can be an important source of meaning and structure that hold a system together, but only when these actions become salient anchors for justification. When attention is focused on a handful of actions, the process of interpretation also becomes focused. Designs in the service of interpretation differ materially from designs in the service of decision making. Designs for interpretation presume that people are confused rather than ignorant, and that confusion is reduced by interaction, opportunities for consensual validation, self-organizing, collective memory, conversation, and narratives (Orr, 1990) – in short, by rich communication media. A growing number of organizational observers identify phenomena such as paradox (e.g. Quinn and Cameron, 1988) dilemmas (Aram, 1976), and dualities (Munch, 1982) as everyday accompaniments of decision making. The problem with environments is no longer solely one of uncertainty, with a corresponding need for increased quantities of information. Advanced information technologies (e.g., Huber, 1990) have lessened this problem. The problem now is more one of multiple meanings.

Designs that help people remove equivocality are needed to cope with multiple meanings. Those designs tend to be more social, more tolerant of improvisation, and more affected by action than is true for designs grounded in decision making.

Forms of Control in Improvised Design

CODE PHRASE: "Manager's ability to coordinate and control the activities of subordinates" (lines 5–6).

Implied assumptions
 13. Control is differentially distributed.
 14. People impose controls.
 15. Activities are the object of control.

Alternative assumptions
 13.1 Control is equally distributed.
 14.1 Ideas impose controls.
 15.1 Ideas are the object of control.

The model of control usually assumed by designers is that it is unilateral, top down, tied to positions, hierarchical, and formal. Some individuals exert control over other ones, and either the process or the outcome of activities is the object of control. When Perrow (1986: 129) discussed first-order controls, such as giving orders, direct surveillance, and imposition of rules, and second-order bureaucratic controls, such as specialization and standardization, he described the two forms of control that are usually associated with design.

If we adopt the idea of design as improvisation, then direct control becomes more difficult, partly because people do not have exact standards against which improvised performance can be measured. Instead, when people improvise they often discover the standards for performance simultaneous with the discovery of what the actions produce in the first place. Direct control of improvisation is also difficult because it is self-defeating to standardize performance. The advantage of improvisation is that it is responsive to ongoing change in the organization and the environment, and stand-ardization removes this advantage. Since the essence of improvisation is that people use many different means to accomplish outcomes, behavior control (Ouchi, 1979) is meaningless. And since realized outcomes often differ from intended outcomes, out-come control may also be difficult.

Control by premises

Given the many ways in which an improvised performance is ambiguous, any at-tempt to impose control over this performance using traditional forms of control is apt to fail. Surveillance of improvisation is difficult, and it is unclear what one is looking for even if surveillance is possible.

But improvisation is not without control. It is controlled by frames of reference (Shrivastava and Mitroff, 1984) that participants take for granted. Perrow (1986) calls these third-order controls. They are embodied in such things as the vocabulary of the organization, procedural and substantive routines, preferred communication channels, selection criteria, meeting agendas, and socialization practices. Control through premises is just as influential in shaping behavior as is control through rules or bureaucratic standardization. But premise control is also less obtrusive, more cognitive, more tied to language, and more volitional, since "the subordinate *voluntarily* restricts the range of stimuli that will be attended to ('Those sorts of things are irrelevant,' or 'What has that got to do with the matter?') and the range of alternatives that would be considered ('It would never occur to me to do that')" (Perrow, 1986: 129).

The ways in which third-order controls affect behavior are subtle and easily over-looked by the designer who finds it easier to see the material controls represented by tangible orders, rules, surveillance, standardization, specialization, and hierarchy. Third-order controls are more subtle but no less forceful because:

> They limit information content and flow, thus controlling the premises available for decisions; they set up expectations so as to highlight some aspects of the situation and play down others; they limit the search for alternatives when problems are confronted, thus ensuring more predictable and consistent solutions; they indicate the threshold levels as to when a danger signal is being emitted . . .; they achieve coordination of effort by selecting certain kinds of work techniques and schedules." (Perrow, 1986: 128).

We have already been introduced to third-order controls in the previous discussion of behavioral commitment. We saw that people act their way into meanings when they try to explain elapsed actions. If some of those important elapsed actions were done publicly and irrevocably and volitionally, they will be especially salient since they are clearly the responsibility of the people who did them. The reasons people invoke to justify these visible behaviors become potential third-order controls for other actions. Not only do these justifications explain the committed action, they also are often communicated to other personas as premises they can use to express themselves and to interpret the actions of other people. The justifications become a crucial part of the cognitive infrastructure that articulates and gives substance to the organization. The organization actually becomes defined in part by the recurrent justifications that people adopt to express and interpret organizational action. Justifications that deviate from these conventions can call into question the person's tacit claim that he or she is a member in good standing.

The importance of justification as a tool for design is suggested by Lucas's (1987: 147) statement that "organizations define and think themselves out through repertoires of patterned actions, a capacity to develop, implement, and maintain justifications for structures of existing repertoires, and through negotiating rules for changing these repertoires." Justifications are one of many forms by which organizations define and think themselves into existence. Justifications are socially acceptable reasons people give themselves for choosing to do something in public that is irrevocable. As these reasons accumulate into patterns of affirmation, restriction, and permission, they guide people and enable them to judge others and justify themselves to those others. Sets of justifications should form coherent and workable systems of interpretation that create a corporate culture. To describe the organization in this way is to suggest that control is widely rather than narrowly dispersed, that ideas rather than people impose controls, and that ideas rather than activities are the object of control.

If we argue that organizations *are* cultures, rather than *have* cultures, as does Meek (1988: 459), then everyone in the organization, including those at the top, is equally subject to third-order control: "Most anthropologists would find the idea that leaders create culture preposterous: leaders do not create culture. It emerges from the collective social interactions of groups and communities. . . . The chief is as much a part of a local culture as are his tribal or clan compatriots." The notion that control is differentially distributed tends to be associated with the view that organizations have cultures that can be changed from the top. Cultures are not that easy to change, nor are they the exclusive property of people at the top. As ideas diffuse through the organization, control also becomes diffused since people now adopt similar premises for their decisions.

While it is obvious that resources such as expertise and capital are differentially distributed, there are general capabilities such as bricolage and improvisation that enable people to reduce some of this differential. Because ideas can originate anywhere within the organization and diffuse to any other part, third-order controls are potentially available to a much larger number of participants than are the controls of rules and standardization. This means that redesign can be initiated in a wider variety of places, and that anyone with a compelling framework is a potential designer.

As organizations come more and more to resemble networks (e.g., Miles and Snow, 1986), the notion of dispersed design becomes more plausible.

Control by paradigms

If ideas rather than people impose control, then we must learn more about what form these compelling ideas take. A recurrent suggestion is that systems of ideas in organizations resemble paradigms in science (Shrivastava and Mitroff, 1984: 19; Brown, 1978; Bresser and Bishop, 1983: 598–592; Pfeffer, 1982). If we assume that paradigms contain organizational designs and guide action, then we have a vehicle by which ideas, interpretations, and justifications exert control.

Pfeffer (1982: 227–228) describes a paradigm as a "technology, including beliefs about cause-effect relations and standards of practice and behavior, as well as specific examples of these, that constitute how an organization goes about doing things." Since justifications often take the form of beliefs about cause-effect, standards, and examples, they are important elements in paradigms. Paradigms tend to be closed systems, closed in the sense that they are not just a view of the world, but also contain procedures for inquiring about the world and categories to collect the observations that are stimulated by these inquiries. Paradigms are powerful tools of interpretation.

Paradigms can create strong preconceptions that prefigure observation. This possibility suggests that paradigms could produce behavioral confirmation in ways similar to those reviewed earlier in the context of serial self-fulfilling prophecies. Justifications might do more than simply provide rationales for designs that are internally compelling. They might also shape actions in ways that validate the rationales.

The way in which specific justifications may generate an organizational design, preserved in a paradigm, is suggested by Ross and Staw's (1986) careful study of Expo 86. The explanations adopted to justify the investment of more resources into Expo 86 included such justifications as the following: we will inject 15,000 man-years of jobs into the economy; this will show that Vancouver is the equal of Toronto and Montreal; British Columbia will be seen as the province that completes its projects; this shows what the Social Credit government can do; and Expo 86 will increase our chances to get a major league baseball team. These justifications gave meaning to the sponsor's decision to proceed with funding of Expo 86, but they also provided evocative images that defined the event for people who were unclear about what it was and what it meant.

These justifications for Expo 86 can be viewed evaluatively as biased statements that reflect an escalation of unrealistic expectations. But they can also be viewed descriptively as reasons held for a reason, which diffused and organized people who were originally both detached from and puzzled by the initial commitment. The justifications replaced disorganization with organization, and microcommitments with macroconsequences. Justifications of a few imposed an order, focus, and meaning on many. The justifications that accumulated around Expo 86 gradually became a set of third-order controls that shaped how people thought about the event and how they acted to validate these thoughts.

Control by enacted stability

When justifications become combined into paradigms, they often have effects similar to those of formal structure: "Since robust ideologies incorporating harmonious values elicit self-control and voluntary cooperation they can substitute for formal structures designed to achieve the same ends" (Meyer, 1982: 55).

Contingency theories (e.g., Lawrence and Lorsch, 1967) begin with some variation of the theme that mechanistic structures are best suited to stable environments, while organic structures are more appropriate for changing environments. Typically, environmental change is viewed as something largely outside the influence of organizations. The position we are developing suggests a different conclusion. Justifications, assembled into paradigms, can be enacted into a changing environment, thereby imposing some stability on it. Perception guided by a coherent paradigm can prefigure an environment. And confident action based on that prefiguring can actually move the environment in the direction of those paradigmatic preconceptions. That possibility is the important design point that is implicit in serial self-fulfilling prophecies.

But the key point is not that environments can be enacted so they become more consistent with preconceptions. The key point is more basic than this. Any environment that becomes more consistent with preconceptions also becomes more stable and more predictable. And as the environment becomes more stable and predictable, it becomes better suited to mechanistic organizational forms. The effect of paradigms on the environment may depend less on the content of the paradigm than on the fact that the paradigm represents a plausible map of the environment and helps stabilize the environment. If the paradigm stabilizes the environment and makes it more predictable, then mechanistic organizational forms become more appropriate.

In a way any old paradigm will do. As long as the paradigm improves prediction, allows a higher level of agreement on cause-effect relations and/or preferences, and encourages people to act as if their prophecies are valid, then the result will be more environmental stability, a more favorable setting for mechanistic structures, and a setting in which application of a rational model will be more appropriate. Recall that in the bandwagon example, decisions to increase financial contributions, work, and endorsements were rational responses to increases in polling accuracy produced by self-fulfilling prophecies.

Thus, we wind up in the same place as do many designers, with their highly specified designs and mechanistic structures animated by rational procedures. But we get there through a very different route. Essentially, we argue that people enact stability and rationality into the environment when they justify behavioral commitments engage in subsequent activities that reaffirm earlier justifications, pool justifications into paradigms, and deploy these paradigms like serial self-fulfilling prophecies. Stability comes from tight coupling between action and cognition that is created by the necessity to explain behavioral commitments to oneself and to important peers. This tightened coupling represents a focused actor, engaged in focused action, that can change existing environments and enact new ones. Persistent action that is backed by a supportive paradigm can stabilize environments and make reasoning and formalization more successful.

Strong paradigms built from justifications impose perceptual as well as material stability on the changing environment, at least for short periods of time. These temporary stabilities allow the activation of short-term routines to deal with inputs. And these temporary stabilities tend to be the dominant forms of control in improvised designs.

Sources of Change in Improvised Designs

CODE PHRASE: "Proper organizational design can therefore make the difference between having an effective, well-run organization and one having recurrent crises and organizational inefficiencies" (lines 7–8).

Implied assumptions
   16. An effective organization has few crises and inefficiencies.
   17. Recurrent crises and inefficiencies reduce current effectiveness.
   18. Proper organizational design reduces current inefficiency.

Alternative assumptions
   16.1 An effective organization has many crises and inefficiencies.
   17.1 Recurrent crises and inefficiencies increase future effectiveness.
   18.1 Proper organizational design exploits crises and inefficiencies.

One of the ironies of a successful organizational design is that its very effectiveness makes redesign and learning more difficult. If crises and inefficiencies are held to a minimum in the interest of order and high performance, then this creates the wrong context for learning and redesign. Redesign is stimulated by trial and error, experiments, failures, rough edges, and novel juxtapositions, if people aren't overwhelmed by anxiety when old designs fail and new ones are not yet obvious (Weick, 1985). Continued effectiveness in a changing environment requires continuous redesign. And continuous redesign requires both crises that suggest new ways of operating and resilient people who are able to spot these new ways of operating. A system in which crisis and efficiency are muted in the name of effective operation has lost some of its capability for adaptation, creativity, and learning (Weick, 1977). Crisis and inefficiency benefit redesign, but this possibility is often lost on designers who measure the quality of their design by how well things seem to be running right now.

Inefficiency as a source of change

To rethink the role of crisis and inefficiency in organizational design, we first need to reexamine the concept of effectiveness. Discussions of design tend to treat effectiveness criteria as fixed criteria of performance that reflect adaptation. An alternative way to view effectiveness criteria is as variable sources of sensemaking that preserve adaptability. Adaptive organizations often change scorecards so that they measure what their current design makes possible. Thus, when confronted with ineffective performance, people are just as likely to change their criteria of effectiveness as they are to change their designs. They act, and then treat the consequences of their actions as their intentions. As a result, their existing organizational design is reaffirmed as an appropriate design.

Effectiveness, viewed in the context of improvisation, is simply one kind of explanation that is used to make sense of elapsed action. Effectiveness has little meaning a priori (Cummings, 1983: 193) because there is nothing for it to explain until action takes place. Once action occurs, then effectiveness is one of many categories that suggest what the action may have meant. But notice an interesting twist. All action is effective with respect to some criterion. The problem is simply to locate that criterion, to use it to interpret one meaning of the action, and then to convince other people that this is a plausible meaning for what occurred. The problem of interpretation involved in judgments of effectiveness is no different from the problem of interpretation involved with behavioral commitment. In both cases, the goal is to explain the elapsed action.

This line of argument has several implications for design. First, it suggests that there is nothing magical about "effectiveness," especially considering that Campbell (1977: 36–39) found 30 different indices of effectiveness that have been used by researchers and practitioners. With that much diversity in indicators, judgments of effectiveness are nothing but an exercise in interpretation. Second, crises and inefficiencies stimulate learning and reinterpretation. Actions that prove hard to justify often stimulate a wider, more vigorous search for explanations that may uncover novel rationales for design (Grandoori, 1987). Third, there can be value in inefficient actions. Starbuck and Nystrom (1983: 152–153), who have written extensively on this theme, reflect the flavor of these discussions when they note:

> Benefits can arise from accepting goal disagreements, shifting attention from one goal to another, using sophisticated forecasting techniques while distrusting their forecasts, questioning strategies and procedures that have clearly succeeded, altering constraints that define acceptable behavior, and lowering goals after failures or unsuccessful searches. Such actions sharpen perceptions, encourage experimentation, and foster improvements. Judgments about organizational effectiveness generally undervalue information, discovery, and learning. Effectiveness that falls below the best performance attainable is nevertheless desirable if it includes information about better criteria or better methods. Conversely, superficially optimal effectiveness is actually undesirable if it forecloses learning.

Consider the example of information overload. Among the responses to information overload are omission, greater tolerance for error, queueing, filtering, abstracting, use of multiple channels, escape, and chunking (Miller, 1978: 131-152). While each of these responses is an inefficient use of information input, each also may reveal that some of that input is actually dispensable, as well as that new ideas in the form of new priorities, new methods of coping, and different categories, make more sense in the context of current problems.

Collateral organization as a source of change

In general, the willingness to cultivate inefficiency and crisis to improve design is motivated by doubts that any one design can anticipate change and stimulate ongoing innovation. Crises and inefficiencies expand repertoires and update understanding of the environment. But they also make ongoing functioning more difficult, which is why Huber (1984: 941) proposed the importance of the collateral organization. Two organizations, with the same members, operate side by side, one being the experimenting organization and the other being a set of more mechanistic roles and procedures to exploit the discoveries of the experimenting organization. The concept of simultaneous participation in more than one organization structure is a valuable means to preserve the divergence necessary for change and the convergence necessary for stability.

Collateral organizations, however, make sizeable demands on people, require clear switching rules, and can create nightmares of accountability (e.g., which system did you think you were in when you made that blunder?). At a minimum, design efforts should target inefficiencies as both a threat and an opportunity, and then inquire thoroughly which of those two possibilities best preserves the adaptability of the organization. Inefficiencies often preserve a diverse response that might prove beneficial in a different environment. If the environment is changing rapidly and might soon assume some quite different form, and if the inefficiencies can be isolated from the rest of the system, then they might well be protected from designers and accountants alike since they may comprise the core of the next generation of design.

Dynamics of Change in Improvised Design

CODE PHRASE: "Organizational environments are changing ... rapidly ... [which] erodes [the effectiveness of an organizational design] over time" (lines 9–10).

Implied assumptions
 19. Environments change more rapidly than do organizations.
 20. Designs construct organizations to fit environments.
 21. Designs are relatively permanent.

Alternative assumptions
 19.1 Organizations change more rapidly than do environments.
 20.1 Designs construct environments to fit organizations.
 21.1 Designs are relatively transient.

Rapid environmental change is often the impetus for organizational redesign. Use of the word "erodes" in the CODE statement to describe the effect of this environmental change on the organization implies a gradual, almost imperceptible, loss of fit over a long period of time. The imagery of erosion also implies that periods of redesign are infrequent. There should be intermittent small changes in design intended to prop up those features that seem to be losing their value. The overall picture is one of permanency with minor variations in the same form rather than a change from one form to a very different form (Greenwood and Hinings, 1988). The implication is that it is hard to change an organization. And once it is changed, it's hard to change it again. Thus, the rapidly changing environment usually outruns the less rapidly changing organization.

But that difference in the speed of change makes sense only when designers draw a sharp boundary between organizations and environments. What they miss is the arbitrariness of the line separating organization from environment. They miss this because they neglect the ways in which people construct the environments that supposedly outrun them.

Change in enacted environments

Starbuck (1976: 1069) made the case that organizations construct their own environments: "Organizations' environments are largely invented by organizations themselves. Organizations select their environments from ranges of alternatives, then they subjectively perceive the environments they inhabit. The processes of both selection and perception are unreflective, disorderly, incremental, and strongly influenced by social norms and customs."

But the issue of the environment is not simply one of perception. It also involves action. As Starbuck shows later (p. 1081), organizations play an active role in shaping their environments – partly because they seek environments that are sparsely inhabited by competitors; partly because they define their products and outputs in ways that emphasize distinctions between themselves and their competitors; partly because they rely on their own experience to infer environmental possibilities; and partly because they need to impose simplicity on complex relationships. The key mechanism in all of this, a mechanism specified earlier, is that these perceptions and actions validate one another in ways that resemble self-fulfilling prophecies: "It is primarily in domains where an organization believes it exerts influence that the organization attributes change to its own influence, and in domains where an organization believes itself impotent, it tends to ignore influence opportunities and never to discover whether its influence is real. . . . Moreover, it is the beliefs and perceptions founded on social reality which are especially liable to self-confirmation" (p. 1081).

March and Olsen (1989: 46), writing about political institutions, observed that the actions of each participant often are part of the environment of others. This means that the environments of each person are partly self-determined as each reacts to the other. When environments are created, actions taken in "adapting to" an environment are partly responses to one's own previous actions reflected through the environment. A common result is that small signals are amplified into large ones.

If people enact their environments, then a loss of fit between the organization and the environment takes on a new meaning. A loss of fit means that the organization has developed capabilities, resources, and limitations that have not yet been acted into the environment. The environment continues to demand from the organization capabilities that it no longer possesses. But the origin of this mismatch lies inside the organization, not outside. The problem is not a turbulent environment. The problem is a turbulent organization. Since the organization is changing faster than the demands it faces, the remedy is a more forceful, more intense application of the organizational design now in place to modify that environment.

When an organization has developed more rapidly than has an environment, it may take some redesign to ensure that the organization has a more forceful impact on the environment and shapes it toward newly acquired competencies. The advanced organization confronting an outdated environment needs essentially to strengthen what it already has in place. It needs to strengthen its culture, become more proactive, act like a true believer, intensify action rationality, and reaffirm its commitments, all in an effort to change the beliefs and actions of those people who comprise the environment (Eccles and Crane, 1988).

Change in the enactor of environments

If we assume that the purpose of design is to construct environments to fit organizations, then the key question is not so much "What is out there?" as "What is in here?" What the organization has available affects what it sees out there, as we saw in assumption 8.1, "Managerial ability affects design." And what the organization has available is something that can only be known by action, not by thinking (Mintzberg, 1990). Designs that facilitate the construction of environments encourage bricolage, deutero-learning (Bateson, 1979), rich assessment of situations (Daft and Lengel, 1986), rotation among assignments to discover and create strengths, careful attention to the interpersonal linkages that comprise the environment (Eccles and Crane, 1988), efforts to raise confidence and self-efficacy (Weick, 1983), development of a culture that promotes enacting rather than reacting, and the accomplishment of small wins (Weick, 1984). Designs that fit environments to organizations encourage gerrymandering. The boundaries of environments are drawn in such a way as to benefit the organization's interests and current strengths. Once interests are acted into the environment, the organization becomes constrained by requirements that are tailored more closely to its strengths.

If redesign is driven more by changes that originate inside the organization than by changes that originate outside, then any one design should have a short life, since there are so many prods to internal change. With frequent internal changes, there is more demand for these frequent changes to be expressed. Any one design is relatively transient because competence, experience, insight, resilience, and aspirations change often. While routines may freeze an organization and erode only under constant pressure from the environment, there are many routines designed explicitly to keep an organization unfrozen (Weick, 1977). By definition, designs based on improvisation will reflect a continually changing set of competencies as resources are recombined in increasingly novel ways. As people are encouraged to grow and develop, the basis for new designs will also expand.

If designs originate in ideas, interaction, shifting competencies, and retrospect, then organizations should be characterized by a succession of short-lived designs that evaporate rather than erode. Designs disappear abruptly rather than fade because they are competence-specific. As competence changes, so too does design.

The possibility that designs are transient seems to lie just below the surface even in formulations dedicated to the discovery of optimal long-term designs. For example, Huber, Ullman, and Leifer (1979: 568) note that, "it may be that the closest we can come to an optimum design in a real organization is a *situation* where an organization designer's goals are maximized because *momentarily* and as far as anyone can determine, his constraints are satisfied" [italics added].

Transient designs are visible in the class of organizations that Lanzara (1983) labels as "ephemeral." He observed organizations that emerged immediately after a violent earthquake in southern Italy in 1980 and concluded that the most basic feature shared among them was that "they do not assume their own survival or permanence as a requirement for identity and effectiveness of performance. In other words, ephemeral organizations are there to disappear, after displaying a great deal of activity. They have no past and no future, they live in the present. They do not tell stories about themselves and do not project their own image into the future, but take the chance of the present" (p. 88). Contrasts between formal and ephemeral organizations are listed in Table 3.2.

Ephemeral organizations have only local intelligence that is short-sighted. Their level of intervention is the street level (p. 92). This implies action rationality, abrupt rather than gradual changes in effectiveness, sensitivity to local conditions, and insufficient duration for anything like erosion to occur. While any one ephemeral organization has minimal adaptability since it is tailored to meet local needs and the needs of the creator for self-expression (pp. 79–80), the form itself has considerable adaptability. Following the earthquake disaster, official institutions and government relief agencies were slow to mobilize and inept once they did mobilize (p. 74). The unresponsiveness and vulnerability of large systems, structured strictly by formalized procedures, became visible immediately in extreme situations. Unless procedures are loosened, commitments to action are strengthened, and role identities are broadened, nothing gets done.

As Lanzara concludes: "In a world which has suddenly become turbulent, unreliable, unpredictable, and where the value of the 'precedent', once indisputable, is becoming of little help for present and future action, it would not be surprising if human societies and their members relied less and less on formal, longstanding institutions and procedures, and more and more on informal, ephemeral arrangements" (p. 92).

Improvised designs such as those made visible by ephemeral organizations start small, enlarge quickly, disappear abruptly, and reappear often. The fate of these designs is more dramatic and fitful than is suggested by the term "erosion." Furthermore, people rather than environments may be the impetus to that erosion. If designs are capacity-driven, then changes in experience, perception, and ability, rather than changes in the environment, should be the focus of attempts to diagnose declining effectiveness.

Table 3.2   Contrast between formal and ephemeral organizations

Traits	Formal organizations	Ephemeral organizations
Boundaries	Clear	Fuzzy
Leadership	Central locus, relatively constant	Shifting, lacking
Membership and recruitment	Contractual	Permeable, fluid, noncontractural
Commitment	External; extrinsic reward	Internal; self-reinforcing intrinsic reward
Size	Large organisms	Small units
Organizational structure	Formal, unusually hierarchical, (tree-like)	Informal, heterarchical (network-like)
Division of work	Highly differentiated, bureaucratic	Rudimentary
Tasks	Specialized, high expertise required	Nonspecific, low expertise required
Roles	Prescribed by authority	Self-prescribed
Rules and procedures	Explicitly mapped out; only partially internalized	Implicit, not mapped, and varying; fully internalized
Activities	Institutionalized, routine, domain-induced	Ad hoc, informal, need-induced
Performance	Measured by "accounting" (economic efficiency)	Measured by "organizing" (practical effectiveness)
Memory	Long-ranged	Short-spanned
Intelligence	Global; central locus	Local; distributed; short-sighted
Information flows	Vertical	Horizontal

Source: Adapted from Lanzara, 1983: p. 88.

Conclusion

Vaill (1976: 77) expressed many of the same reservations about the metaphor of architecture that I expressed when he observed:

> Design behavior is, in fact, much more creative and unpredictable than our culture would have us believe. The term "engineering" derives from the same root as "ingenuity." What is it that the designer is really doing? Terms like "groping," "intuiting," "experimenting," come readily to mind. Perhaps the design of physical and/or mechanical entities is a quasi-deductive process, but the designs of organizations in which human beings are going to live and work certainly is not. How is it, then, that we are unable to look at organization designs for what they are – highly imperfect and tentative representations of what the world should be like, with debatable values buried down inside them (sometimes deliberately disguised), representations whose principal defensi-

ble function is that they trigger off debate among real men about real problems? This is about the most that can be said of organization designs. Why do we experience such a strong compulsion to let these designs exert more influence than this? [italics removed from original].

I have tried to show that good designs are those designs that incorporate the intuiting, experimenting, and arguing that are prominent in improvisation. Designing occurs more often but is less conspicuous than the metaphor of architecture implies. To design is to notice sequences of action that are improvements, call attention to them, label them, repeat them, disseminate them, and legitimize them.

People who construct one-time intentional, deliberated designs, construct entities that are imposed on social settings that they neither control nor fully understand. In doing this, they overlook the improvisational character of organizational design. They overlook the emergent designs that bubble up when capability changes. They overlook the ways in which interdependent actors become self-organizing in the face of underspecified designs. They overlook the power of retrospect. And they overlook the way in which action generates its own meaning.

In turbulent periods, orderliness is limited to short-lived transactions, intelligence is reduced to local expertise, and determinacy covers only those events close together in time and space. While no one questions that it would be desirable to have grand and stable designs in times of turbulence, the organization is not sufficiently homogeneous to support concerted action, nor is the environment sufficiently determinant to encourage accurate, long-term prediction. Instead, the way out of turbulence may lie in continuous improvisation in response to continuous change in local details. Designing replaces design.

Note

1. This study is hereafter referred to as the CODE study and is described in Glick, Huber, Miller, Doty, and Sutcliffe (1990).

References

Allport, G. W. 1954. The historical background of modern social psychology. In Lindzey, G. (Ed.), *Handbook of social psychology*, Vol. 1 (pp. 3–56). Reading, MA: Addison-Wesley.

Aram, J. D. 1976. *Dilemmas of administrative behavior*. Englewood Cliffs, NJ: Prentice-Hall.

Bandura, A. 1986. *Social foundations of thought and action: a social cognitive theory*. Englewood Cliffs, NJ: Prentice-Hall.

Bandura, A. 1990. Conclusion: reflection on nonability determinants of competence. In Sternberg, R. J., and Kolligian Jr., J. (Eds.), *Competence considered* (pp. 315–362). New Haven: Yale University.

Bandura, A., and Wood, R. E. 1989. Effect of perceived controllability and performance standards on self-regulation of complex decision-making. *Journal of Personality and Social Psychology*, 56: 805–814.

Barley, S. 1986. Technology as an occasion for structuring: evidence from observations of CAT scanners and the social order of radiology departments. *Administrative Science Quarterly*, 31: 78–108.

Bateson, G. 1979. *Mind and nature*. New York: Dutton.

Bresser, R. K., and Bishop, R. C. 1983. Dysfunctional effects of formal planning: two theoretical explorations. *Academy of Management Review*, 8: 588–599.

Brown, R. H. 1978. Bureaucracy as praxis: toward a political phenomenology of formal organizations. *Administrative Science Quarterly*, 23: 365–382.

Burns, T., and Stalker, G. M. 1961. *The management of innovation*. London: Tavistock.

Campbell, J. P. 1977. On the nature of organizational effectiveness. In Goodman, P. S., and Pennings, J. M. (Eds.), *New perspectives on organizational effectiveness* (pp. 13–55). San Francisco: Jossey-Bass.

Chatman, J. A., Bell, N. E., and Staw, B. M. 1986. The managed thought: the role of self-justification and impression management in organizational settings. In Sims Jr., H. P., and Gioia, D. A. (Eds.), *The thinking organization* (pp. 191–214). San Francisco: Jossey-Bass

Cooley, C. H. 1964. *Human nature and the social order*. New York: Schocken.

Cummings, L. L. 1983. Organizational effectiveness and organizational behavior: a critical perspective. In Cameron, K. S., and Whetten, D. A. (Eds.), *Organizational effectiveness* (pp. 187–203). New York: Academic Press.

Daft, R. L., and Lengel, R. H. 1986. Organizational information requirements, media richness and structural design. *Management Science*, 32: 554–571.

Daft, R. L., and Weick, K. E. 1984. Toward a model of organizations as interpretation systems. *Academy of Management Review*, 9(2): 284–295.

Dornbusch, S. M., and Scott, W. R. 1975. *Evaluation and the exercise of authority*. San Francisco: Jossey-Bass.

Eccles, R. G., and Crane, D. B. 1988. *Doing deals*. Cambridge, MA: Harvard Business School.

Elliott, E. S., and Dweck, C. S. 1988. Goals: an approach to motivation and achievement. *Journal of Personality and Social Psychology*, 54: 5–12.

Garfinkel, H. 1967. *Studies in ethnomethodology*. Englewood Cliffs, NJ: Prentice-Hall.

Gioia, T. 1988. *The imperfect art*. New York: Oxford University Press.

Glick, W. H., Huber, G. P., Miller, C. C., Doty, D. H., and Sutcliffe, K. M. 1990. Studying changes in organization design and effectiveness: Retrospective event histories and periodic assessments. *Organization Science*, 1(3): 293–312.

Graen, G. B., and Scandura, T. A. 1987. Toward a psychology of dyadic organizing. In Cummings, L. L., and Staw, B. M. (Eds.), *Research in organizational behavior*, Vol. 9 (pp. 175–208). Greenwich, CT: JAI Press.

Grandoori, A. 1987. *Perspectives on organization theory*. Cambridge, MA: Ballinger.

Greenwood, R., and Hinings, C. R. 1988. Organizational design types, tracks, and the dynamics of strategic changes. *Organization Studies*, 9: 293–316.

Hall, R. I. 1984. The natural logic of management policy making: its implications for the survival of an organization. *Management Science*, 30: 905–927.

Harper, D. 1987. *Working knowledge*. Chicago: University of Chicago Press.

Henshel, R. L. 1987. Credibility and confidence feedback in social prediction. Paper presented at the Plenary Session of the Vll International Congress of Cybernetics and Systems, University of London.

Henshel, R. L., and Johnston, W. 1987. The emergence of bandwagon effects: a theory. *Sociological Quarterly*, 28: 493–511.

Huber, G. P. 1984. The nature and design of post-industrial organizations. *Management Science*, 30(8): 928–951.

Huber, G. P. 1990. A theory of the effects of advanced information technologies on organizational design, intelligence, and decision making. *Academy of Management Review*, 15: 47–71.

Huber, G. P., Ullman, J., and Leifer, R. 1979. Optimum organization design: an analytic-adaptive approach. *Academy of Management Review*, 4: 567–578.

Hurst, D. K., Rush, J. C., and White, R. E. 1989. Top management teams and organizational renewal. *Strategic Management Journal*, 10: 87–105.

Jervis, R. 1976. *Perception and misperception in international politics*. Princeton, NJ: Princeton University Press.

Khandwalla, P. N. 1977. *The design of organizations*. New York: Harcourt, Brace, Jovanovich.

Kilmann, A. H., Pondy, L. R., and Slevin, D. P. 1976. Patterns and emerging themes in organization design. In Kilmann, R. H., Pondy, L. R., and Slevin, D. P. (Eds.), *The management of organization design*, Vol. 1, (pp. 1–15). New York: North-Holland.

Lanzara, G. F. 1983. Ephemeral organizations in extreme environments: Emergence, strategy, extinction. *Journal of Management Studies*, 20: 71–95.

Lawrence, P., and Lorsch, J. W. 1967. *Organization and environment*. Boston: Harvard University Business School.

Levi-Strauss, C. 1966. *The savage mind*. Chicago: University of Chicago Press.

Lucas, R. 1987. Political-cultural analysis of organizations. *Academy of Management Review*, 12: 144–156.

March, J. G., and Olsen, J. P. 1989. *Rediscovering institutions: the organizational basis of politics*. New York: Free Press.

McEachern, A. W. 1984. *Organizational illusions*. Redondo Beach, CA: Shale.

Meek, V. C. 1988. Organizational culture: origins and weaknesses. *Organization Studies*, 9, 453–473.

Meyer, A. D. 1982. How ideologies supplant formal structures and shape responses to environments. *Journal of Management Studies*, 29: 45–61.

Miles, R. E., and Snow, C. C. 1986. Organizations: new concepts for new forms. *California Management Review*, 28(3): 62–73.

Miller, J. G. 1978. *Living systems*. New York: McGraw-Hill.

Mintzberg, H. 1990. The design school: reconsidering the basic premises of strategic management. *Strategic Management Journal*, 11: 171–195.

Mintzberg, H., and McHugh, A. H. 1985. Strategy formation in an adhocracy. *Administrative Science Quarterly*, 30: 160–197.

Munch, R. 1982. Talcott Parsons and the theory of action: II. The continuity of the development. *American Journal of Sociology*, 87: 771–826.

O'Reilly, C. 1989. Corporations, culture, and commitment. *California Management Review*, 31(4): 9–25.

Orr, J. E. 1990. Sharing knowledge, celebrating identity: community memory in a service culture. In Middleton, D., and Edwards, D. (Eds.), *Collective remembering* (pp. 169–189). London: Sage.

Ouchi, W. G. 1979. A conceptual framework for the design of organizational control mechanisms. *Management Science*, 25: 833–848.

Perrow, C. 1986. *Complex organizations: a critical essay*, 3rd ed. New York: Random House.

Pfeffer, J. 1982. *Organizations and organization theory*. Boston: Pitman.

Pfeffer, J., and Salancik, G. R. 1978. *The external control of organizations*. New York: Harper and Row.

Quinn, R. E., and Cameron, K. S. 1988. *Paradox and transformation*. Cambridge, MA: Ballinger.

Ranson, S., Hinings, B., and Greenwood, R. 1980. The structuring of organizational structures. *Administrative Science Quarterly*, 25: 1–17.

Ross, J., and Staw, B. M. 1986. Expo 86: an escalation prototype. *Administrative Science Quarterly*, 31: 274–297.

Salancik, G. R. 1977. Commitment and the control of organizational behavior and belief. In Staw, B. M., and Salancik, G. R. (Eds.), *New directions in organizational behavior* (pp. 1–54). Chicago: St. Clair.

Scott, W. R. 1987. *Organizations: rational, natural, and open systems*, 2nd ed. Englewood Cliffs, NJ: Prentice-Hall.

Shrivastava, P., and Mitroff, I. I. 1984. Enhancing organizational research utilization: the role of decision makers' assumptions. *Academy of Management Review*, 9: 18–26.

Simon, H. A. 1962. The architecture of complexity. *Proceedings of the American Philosophical Society*, 106(6): 467–482.

Smircich, L., and Morgan, G. 1982. Leadership: the management of meaning. *Journal of Applied Behavioral Science*, 18: 257–273.

Starbuck, W. H. 1976. Organizations and their environments. In Dunnette, M. D. (Ed.), *Handbook of industrial and organizational psychology* (pp. 1069–1123). Chicago: Rand McNally.

Starbuck, W. H., and Nystrom, P. C. 1981. Why the world needs organizational design. *Journal of General Management*, 6: 3–17.

Starbuck, W. H., and Nystrom, P. C. 1983. Pursuing organizational effectiveness that is ambiguously specified. In Cameron, K. S., and Whetten, D. A. (Eds.), Organizational effectiveness (pp. 135–161). New York: Academic Press.

Staw, B. M. 1982. Counterforces to change. In Goodman, P. S. and Assoc. (Eds.), *Change in organizations* (pp. 87–121). San Francisco: Jossey-Bass.

Thayer, L. 1988. Leadership/communication: a critical review and modest proposal. In Goldhaber, G. M., and Barnett, G. A., (Eds.), *Handbook of organizational communication* (pp. 231–264). Norwood, NJ: Ablex.

Thompson, J. D., and Tuden, A. 1959. Strategies, structures, and processes of organizational decision. In Thompson, J. D., Hammond, P. B., Hawkes, R. W., Junker, B. H., and Tuden, A. (Eds.), *Comparative studies in administration* (pp. 195–216). Pittsburgh: University of Pittsburgh.

Vaill, P. B. 1976. The expository model of science in organization design. In Kilmann, R. H. Pondy, L. R., and Slevin, D. P. (Eds.), *The management of organization design*, Vol. 1 (pp. 73–88). New York: Holland.

Weick, K. E. 1977. Re-punctuating the problem. In Goodman, P. S., and Pennings, J. M. (Eds.), New perspectives on organizational effectiveness (pp. 193–225). San Francisco: Jossey Bass.

Weick, K. E. 1979. *The social psychology of organizing*, 2nd ed. Reading, MA: Addison-Wesley.

Weick, K. E. 1983. Managerial thought in the context of action. In Srivastava, S. (Ed.), *The executive mind* (pp. 221–242). San Francisco: Jossey-Bass.

Weick, K. E. 1984. Small wins: redefining the scale of social problems. *American Psychologist*, 39: 40–49

Weick, K. E. 1985. A stress analysis of future battlefields. In Hunt, J. G. (Ed.), *Leadership and future battlefields* (pp. 32–46). Washington: Pergamon-Brassey's.

Weick, K. E. 1989. Organized improvisation: 20 years of organizing. *Communication Studies*, 40: 241–248.

Weick, K. E., and McDaniel, R. R. Jr. 1989. How professional organizations work: implications for school organization and management. In Sergiovanni, T. J. and Moore, J. H. (Eds.), *Schooling for tomorrow* (pp. 330–355). Boston: Allyn and Bacon.

Components of Sensemaking

Introduction

"How can I know what I think until I see what I say." That phrase has haunted me most of my professional life. This entire book could be read as a gloss on where that phrase has taken me. And the insertion of plural pronouns into that phrase shows the close ties between organizing and sensemaking: how can we know what we think (or want or feel) until we see what we say (or do). The phrase can be read as a recipe for organizing or as a recipe for sensemaking. Read as a recipe for organizing, we could say that when something unexpected occurs and there is an *ecological change*, people often *enact* something, *select* portions of the enactment to take seriously, and *retain* some meaning of what they enacted. Subsequently, they may then apply or alter what they retain in their next enactments and selections. Read as a recipe for sensemaking, we could say that when people in an *ongoing social* setting experience an interruption, they often *enact* something, *retrospectively* notice meaningful *cues* in what they previously enacted, interpret and retain meaningful versions of what the cues mean for their individual and collective *identity*, and apply or alter these *plausible* meanings in subsequent enactment and retrospective noticing.

When executed in a forward direction, the sequence enactment–selection–retention is consistent with the idea that doing is knowing. When executed in a backward direction, with retention having an effect on enactment and selection, the sequence is consistent with the idea that knowing is doing. And if these opposite directions of execution are combined into an ongoing cycle, then doing is knowing is doing is . . . (etc.). Organizing "and" sensemaking turn out to have a closer affinity than is signified by the word "and." It seems more useful to talk about organizing "as" sensemaking, organizing "through" sensemaking, or organizing "for" sensemaking. To make sense of something is to begin to provide a plausible platform for sharing mental models, coordinating activities, and interacting to produce relationships. To organize around something is to converge on an event whose articulation and preservation feels beneficial and of joint relevance. Sense makes organizing possible. And organizing makes sense possible.

Even in the face of all of this explication, sensemaking remains a subtle, elusive phenomenon. To force-fit it into arbitrary definitions at this stage of conceptual development seems counter-productive. It is sufficient to cite Prus's (1996) description of sensemaking to draw a crude boundary around the phenomenon of interest. Sensemaking is the "meaningful linkaging of symbols and activity, that enables people to come to terms with the ongoing struggle for existence" (p. 232). While that statement is quite general, it does touch the basics. The statement reiterates that continuous action is central to sensemaking (linkaging, activity, ongoing struggle); it identifies symbols as a crucial sensemaking tool; it reaffirms that sensemaking is about creating meaningful linkages; and it portrays the goals of sensemaking as acceptance and coming to terms rather than control and manipulation, suggesting once again that sensemaking is about existence that precedes essence. Sensemaking generates understanding that is provisional, plausible, subject to revision, swift, directed toward continuation of interrupted activity, ready-to-hand (see discussion of Heidegger in Weick, 1999), tentative, infused with ignorance, and sufficient for current purposes. Most of the time sensemaking is all we have, especially considering that the world is both unknowable and unpredictable (McDaniel, 1997). Sensemaking starts out as a momentary, expedient understanding. But the sense thus created often lingers and gets stored as if it were the product of a far more deliberate, intentional analysis. Sensemaking is about small pockets of sense, often pragmatically helpful, that lie behind our "larger" understandings. When people act their way into their values, these moments are seldom epiphanies. Instead, they are usually small, everyday committing moments. These moments are the feedstock of sensemaking. That is why students of sensemaking get so worked up over the small acts that may have large consequences.

If we hearken back to the recipe, "how can I know what I think until I see what I say," then organizing and the residues of order it throws off, have importance for sensemaking. Organizations shape what people say and do, shape what people notice in their deeds and discourse, and shape the thoughts, presumptions, and labels that people treat as their beliefs. It is these beliefs that have a continuing effect on subsequent saying and seeing. This cycle is not a closed cycle because the retained knowledge that affects subsequent sensemaking is reconstructed, recalled imperfectly, and colored by hindsight.

Given the close relationship between organizing and sensemaking, I have arranged the next 15 chapters into five categories that correspond to different emphases in organizing: ecological change, enactment, selection, retention, doubt. I refer to these categories as "emphases" rather than "stages" or "steps," because they do not always occur in a lockstep sequence and because more than one emphasis tends to operate at any one moment.

References

McDaniel, Reuben R., Jr. (Winter 1997). Strategic leadership: A view from Quantum and chaos theories. *Health Care Management Review*, 21–37.

Prus, Robert (1996). *Symbolic Interaction and Ethnographic Research*, Albany: SUNY.

Weick, Karl E. (1999). That's moving: Theories that matter. *Journal of Management Inquiry*, 8(2): 134–142.

Ecological Change

Top management in business organizations is notorious for its aversion to surprise. Yet surprise, interruption, and discrepancy are mainstays of organizational experience. A cornerstone of organizational studies is Mintzberg's (1973) finding that on average managers work for a mere 9 minutes before they are interrupted. What we see at work here is a basic feature that creates occasions for sensemaking. Our perceptual system is tuned to the detection of differences, which means we continually experience "the ubiquity of discrepancy" (Mandler, 1997, p. 74). We have strong reactions either when there is the unexpected appearance of irrelevant objects or the unexpected absence of important objects (p. 70). These are the noticeable changes that we try to normalize (e.g. Vaughan, 1996) through sensemaking. The following three chapters provide a flavor of the raw materials involved in ecological changes that trigger sensemaking. The raw materials that are prominent in these chapters include a dynamic active environment of wildland fire that is being altered by complex interactions among terrain and heat and wind; a dynamic active environment of oversize aircraft moving around without radar contact or centerline lights in deteriorating weather; and a dynamic active environment of continuous process technology that generates equivocal patterns of dial readings that reflect complex interactions that are tough to model. In each case, ongoing projects are interrupted, actions shape the interruption toward normalcy so that the project can be resumed, and these efforts at sensemaking prove inadequate in the case of the wildland fire and takeoffs at an alternate airport, and generally more adequate in the context of monitoring technology.

Chapter 4, "The Collapse of Sensemaking in Organizations: The Mann Gulch Disaster," shows the importance for collective sensemaking of experience, interpersonal familiarity, and leadership. This chapter imposes a sensemaking frame on Norman Maclean's powerful story of 13 young men who lost their lives when they were unable to outrun an exploding wildland fire. The crew leader, Wagner Dodge, invented a way to save the crew at the last possible moment – an escape fire that cleared an area so the fire would burn around the crew – but he was unable to persuade the crew to use it. When the crew parachuted into the location of this fire, they expected that they would suppress it by 10:00 the next morning. This expectation colored their interpretation of a fire that was actually beginning to escape and turn ugly. Their preference for a safer explanation of what they faced, their efforts to explain away discrepancies, and their reluctance to update their belief that the fire was small, led to the sudden appearance of more than they could handle. This is a powerful allegory of what can happen unexpectedly in organizational life. The chapter describes several ways to make sensemaking structures more resilient and better able to update their situational awareness. As with most chapters in this book, the reader encounters themes that crop up repeatedly, albeit in different settings. One such theme is the importance of a well-developed capability for improvisation and another is the central role of doubt in sensemaking (see "The Attitude of Wisdom" p. 112; ch. 16, p. 361). In the most vivid terms possible, Mann Gulch shows the folly of arguing that sensemaking is a relativistic perspective which implies that any old interpretation is just as good as any other. What Mann Gulch shows is that labels matter. Firefighters linger too long near an exploding fire they can't control, in the belief that it is a "10:00 fire" they can control. The words, as well as the fire, determined their fate.

The second exhibit of ecological change, Chapter 5, "The Vulnerable System: An Analysis of the Tenerife Air Disaster," is a vivid illustration of the ways in which excess arousal, built from discrepancies that accumulate, can shape what is noticed in one's surroundings. That which is noticed is that which is made sensible. Most sensemaking, because of its proximity to interruption, occurs when people are in heightened states of arousal. The Tenerife disaster shows just how important that dynamic can be. As pressure mounts at Tenerife, we see people try to normalize threatening events toward less threatening interpretations. We see this in air traffic controllers acting as if large planes can make sharp turns in small spaces. We see this in a KLM first officer desperately trying to make sense of a captain who begins a takeoff roll without clearance from air traffic control. And we see this in the KLM captain himself, quietly – but perhaps no less desperately – trying to proceed with a takeoff despite growing hints that the takeoff runway is occupied and further delays are imminent. In the Mann Gulch analysis we focused on resilience. In the Tenerife analysis we focus on the flip side, vulnerability. Either way it becomes clear that speaking up in the face of overlooked discrepancies is vital for collective sensemaking. It is easy to get swept up in the rhetoric of "trust" and conclude that once it is established, effective system functioning is assured. Trust without trustworthiness and self-respect is not sufficient. The plight of the first officer at Tenerife makes that point forcefully. And tragically.

Chapter 6, "Technology as Equivoque: Sensemaking in New Technologies," is another favorite because it takes a "golden oldie" in organizational analysis, technology, and recasts it using imagery compatible with a sensemaking perspective. Technology does not lose its materiality in the process of this translation. It still can bruise toes when it is kicked. But what "it" refers to becomes more problematic, especially when people try to model "its" functioning. Making sense of complex invisible interactions has become an increasingly common experience as information technology becomes more dominant. And it is the models as well as the machinery that concerns us, just as it was 10:00 label as well as the flames that concerned us in

Mann Gulch. The general theme is that as newer technologies have become more stochastic, continuous, and abstract, more of their operation has become a problem of sensemaking. This shift has meant that analysts now have to pay closer attention to such concepts as structuration, affect, interactive complexity, and premise control, if they want to comprehend how technology works. The discussion of Perrow's (1984) important concept of interactive complexity mates that phenomenon with arousal and expands the treatment in the Tenerife analysis.

Taken together, these three chapters provide a picture of the kind of ecological change that intensifies the activity of sensemaking. People are thrown into events that are both constraining and constrained by enactment. It is misleading to call these events "external" because they are a mixture of imposed models, fixed properties, and malleable properties modified by intrusive actions. It is also misleading to call them "stimuli" because prior actions frequently shape the appearance of ecological changes which means that they are just as much responses as they are stimuli. To treat these changes instead as interruptions, surprises, or discrepancies is to encourage closer attention to ongoing activities, projects, and surprises.

References

Mandler, George (1997). *Human Nature Explored*, New York: Oxford University Press.

Mintzberg, Henry (1973). *The Nature of Managerial Work*, New York: Harper & Row.

Perrow, Charles (1984). *Normal Accidents*, New York: Basic Books.

Vaughan, Diane (1996). *The Challenger Launch Decision*, Chicago: University of Chicago Press.

4

The Collapse of Sensemaking in Organizations: The Mann Gulch Disaster

The purpose of this chapter is to reanalyze the Mann Gulch fire disaster in Montana described in Norman Maclean's (1992) award-winning book *Young Men and Fire* to illustrate a gap in our current understanding of organizations. I want to focus on two questions: Why do organizations unravel? And how can organizations be made more resilient? Before doing so, however, I want to strip Maclean's elegant prose away from the events in Mann Gulch and simply review them to provide a context for the analysis.

The Incident

As Maclean puts it, at its heart, the Mann Gulch disaster is a story of a race (p. 224). The smokejumpers in the race (excluding foreman "Wag" Wagner Dodge and ranger Jim Harrison) were ages 17–28, unmarried, seven of them were forestry students (p. 27), and 12 of them had seen military service (p. 220). They were a highly select group (p. 27) and often described themselves as professional adventurers (p. 26).

A lightning storm passed over the Mann Gulch area at 4PM on August 4, 1949, and is believed to have set a small fire in a dead tree. The next day, August 5, 1949, the temperature was 97 degrees and the fire danger rating was 74 out of a possible 100 (p. 42), which means "explosive potential" (p. 79). When the fire was spotted by a forest ranger, the smokejumpers were dispatched to fight it. Sixteen of them flew out of Missoula, Montana at 2:30PM in a C-47 transport. Wind conditions that day were turbulent, and one smokejumper got sick on the airplane, didn't jump, returned to the base with the plane, and resigned from the smokejumpers as soon as he landed ("his repressions had caught up with him," p. 51). The smokejumpers and their cargo were dropped on the south side of Mann Gulch at 4:10PM from 2,000 feet rather than the normal 1,200 feet, due to the turbulence (p. 48). The parachute that was connected to their radio failed to open, and the radio was pulverized when it hit the ground. The crew met ranger Jim Harrison who had been fighting the fire alone for four hours (p. 62), collected their supplies, and ate supper. About 5:10 (p. 57) they started to move along the south side of the gulch to surround the fire (p. 62). Dodge and Harrison, however, having scouted ahead, were worried that the thick forest near which they had landed might be a "death trap" (p. 64). They told the second in command, William Hellman, to take the crew across to the north side of the gulch and march them toward the river along the side of the hill. While Hellman did this, Dodge and Harrison ate a quick meal. Dodge rejoined the crew at 5:40PM and took his position at the head of the line moving toward the river. He could see flames flapping back and forth on the south slope as he looked to his left (p. 69).

At this point the reader hits the most chilling sentence in the entire book: "Then Dodge saw it!" (p. 70). What he saw was that the fire had crossed the gulch just 200 yards ahead and was moving toward them (p. 70). Dodge turned the crew around and had them angle up the 76-percent hill toward the ridge at the top (p. 175). They were soon moving through bunch grass that was two and a half feet tall and were quickly losing ground to the 30-foot-high flames that were soon moving toward them at 610 feet per minute (p. 274). Dodge yelled at the crew to drop their tools, and then, to everyone's astonishment, he lit a fire in front of them and ordered them to lie down in the area it had burned. No one did, and they all ran for the ridge. Two people, Sallee and Rumsey, made it through a crevice in the ridge unburned, Hellman made it over the ridge burned horribly and died at noon the next day, Dodge lived by lying down in the ashes of his escape fire, and one other person, Joseph Sylvia, lived for a short while and then died. The hands on Harrison's watch melted at 5:56 (p. 90), which has been treated officially as the time the 13 people died.

After the fire passed, Dodge found Sallee and Rumsey, and Rumsey stayed to care for Hellman while Sallee and Dodge hiked out for help. They walked into the Meriwether ranger station at 8:50PM (p. 113), and rescue parties immediately set out to recover the dead and dying. All the dead were found in an area of 100 yards by 300 yards (p. 111). It took 450 men five more days to get the 4,500-acre Mann Gulch fire under control (pp. 24, 33). At the time the crew jumped on the fire, it was classified as a Class C fire, meaning its scope was between 10 and 99 acres.

The Forest Service inquiry held after the fire, judged by many to be inadequate, concluded that "there is no evidence of disregard by those responsible for the jumper crew of the elements of risk which they are expected to take into account in placing jumper crews on fires." The board also felt that the men would have been saved had they "heeded Dodge's efforts to get them to go into the escape fire area with him" (quoted in Maclean, p. 151). Several parents brought suit against the Forest Service, claiming that people should not have been jumped in the first place (p. 149), but these claims were dismissed by the Ninth Circuit U.S. Court of Appeals, where Warren E. Burger argued the Forest Service's case (p. 151).

Since Mann Gulch, there have been no deaths by burning among Forest Service firefighters, and people are now equipped with backup radios (p. 219), better physical conditioning, the tactic of building an escape fire, knowledge that fires in timber west of the Continental Divide burn differently than do fires in grass east of the Divide, and the insistence that crew safety take precedence over fire suppression.

The Methodology

Among the sources of evidence Maclean used to construct this case study were interviews, trace records, archival records, direct observation, personal experience, and mathematical models.

Since Maclean did not begin to gather documents on Mann Gulch until 1976 (p. 156) and did not start to work in earnest on this project until his seventy-fourth birthday in 1977, the lapse of almost 28 years since the disaster made interviewing difficult, especially since Dodge had died of Hodgkin's disease five years after the fire (p. 106). Maclean located and interviewed both living witnesses of the blaze, Sallee and Rumsey, and persuaded both to accompany him and Laird Robinson, a guide at the Smokejumper base, on a visit back to the site on July 1, 1978. Maclean also knew Dodge's wife and had talked to her informally (p. 40). He attempted to interview relatives of some who lost their lives but found them too distraught 27 years later to be of much help (p. 154). He also attempted to interview (p. 239) a member of the Forest Service inquiry team, A. J. Cramer who, in 1951, had persuaded Sallee, Rumsey, and ranger Robert Jansson to alter their testimony about the timing of key incidents. Cramer was the custodian of seven or eight watches that had been removed from victims (p. 233), only one of which (Harrison's) was released and used as the official time of the disaster (5:56PM). To this day it remains unclear why the Forest Service made such a strong effort to locate the disaster closer to 6:00PM than to 5:30, which was suggested by testimony from Jansson, who was near the river when the fire blew up, and from a recovered watch that read 5:42. Maclean had continuing access to two Forest Service insiders, Bud Moore and Laird Robinson (p. 162). He also interviewed experts on precedents for the escape fire (p. 104) and on the nature of death by fire (p. 213).

The use of trace records, or physical evidence of past behaviors, is illustrated by the location during a 1979 trip to the gulch, of the wooden cross that had been placed in 1949 to mark the spot where Dodge lit his escape fire (p. 206). The year before, 1978, during the trip into the gulch with Sallee and Rumsey, Maclean located the rusty can of potatoes that had been discarded after Hellman drank its salty water through two knife slits Rumsey had made in the can (p. 173). He also located the flat rocks on which Hellman and Sylvia had rested while awaiting rescue, the juniper tree that was just beyond the crevice Sallee and Rumsey squeezed through on the ridge (p. 207), and Henry Thol, Jr.'s flashlight (p. 183). Considering the lapse of time, the destructive forces of nature over 28 years, and the power of a blowup fire to melt and displace everything in its path, discovery of these traces is surprising as well as helpful in reconstructing events.

Archival records are crucial to the development of the case, although the Forest Service made a considerable effort after its inquiry to scatter the documents (p. 153) and to classify most of them "Confidential" (p. 158), perhaps fearing it would be charged with negligence. Records used by Maclean included statistical reports of fire suppression by smokejumpers in Forest Service Region 1 (e.g., p. 24); the report of the Forest Service Board of Review issued shortly after the incident (dated September 29, 1949, which many felt was too soon for the board to do an adequate job); statements made to the board by people such as the C-47 pilot, parents of the dead crew (p. 150), and the spotter on the aircraft (p. 42); court reports of litigation brought by parents of smokejumpers against the Forest Service; photographs, virtually all of which were retrieved for him by women in the Forest Service who were eager to help him tell the story (p. 160); early records of the smokejumpers organization, which was nine years old at the time of the disaster; reports of the 1957 task force on crew safety (p. 221); and contemporary reports of the disaster in the media, such as the report in the August 22, 1949 issue of Life magazine.

Direct observation occurred during Maclean's three visits to Mann Gulch in 1976, 1977, and 1978 (p. 189), trips made much more difficult because of the inaccessibility of the area (pp. 191–192). The most important of these three visits is the trip to the gulch with Sallee and Rumsey, during which the latter pair reenacted what they did and what they saw intermittently through the dense smoke. When their accounts were matched against subsequent hard data (e.g., their estimation of where Dodge lit his escape fire compared against discovery of the actual cross planted in 1949 to mark the spot), it was found that their reconstruction of events prior to the time they made it to safety through the crevice is less accurate than their memory for events and locations after they made it to safety. This suggests to Maclean that "we don't remember as exactly the desperate moments when our lives are in the balance as we remember the moments after, when the balance has tipped in our favor" (p. 212). Direct observation also occurred when Maclean and Robinson themselves hiked the steep slopes of Mann Gulch under summer conditions of heat and slippery, tall grass that resembled the conditions present in the disaster of 1949. The two men repeatedly compared photos and maps from 1949 with physical outcroppings in front of them to see more clearly what they were looking at (e.g., photos misrepresent the steepness of the slope, p. 175). There were also informal experiments, as when Rod Norum, an athlete and specialist on fire behavior, retraced Dodge's route from the point at which he rejoined the crew, moved as fast as possible over the route Dodge covered, and was unable to reach the grave markers as fast as the crew did (p. 67). During these trips, Maclean took special note of prevailing winds by observing their effect on the direction in which rotted timber fell. These observations were used to build a theory of how wind currents in the gulch could have produced the blowup (p. 133).

Personal experience was part of the case because, in 1949, Maclean had visited the Mann Gulch fire while it was still burning (p. 1). Maclean also was a Forest Service firefighter (not a smokejumper) at age 15 and nearly lost his life in the Fish Creek fire, a fire much like the one in Mann Gulch (p. 4). Maclean also reports using his practical experience as a woodsman to suggest initial hypotheses regarding what happened at Mann Gulch (e.g., he infers wind patterns in the gulch from observations of unusual wave action in the adjacent Missouri River, p. 131).

Having collected data using the above sources, but still feeling gaps in his understanding of precisely how the race between fire and men unfolded, Maclean taught himself mathematics and turned to mathematical modeling. He worked with two mathematicians, Frank Albini and Richard Rothermel, who had built mathematical models of how fires spread. The group ran the predictive models in reverse to see what the fire in Mann Gulch must have been like to generate the reports on its progress that were found in interviews, reports, and actual measurements. It is the combination of output from the model and subjective reports that provide the revealing time line of the final 16 minutes (pp. 267–277).

If these several sources of evidence are combined and assessed for the adequacy with which they address "sources of invalidity," it will be found that they combat 12 of the 15 sources listed by Runkel and McGrath (1972: 191) and are only "moderately vulnerable" to the other three. Of course, an experienced woodsman and storyteller who has "always tried to be accurate with facts" (p. 259) would expect that. The rest of us in organizational studies may be pardoned, however, if we find those numbers a good reason to take these data seriously.

Cosmology Episodes in Mann Gulch

Early in the book (p. 65), Maclean asks the question on which I want to focus: "what the structure of a small outfit should be when its business is to meet sudden danger and prevent disaster." This question is timely because the work of organizations is increasingly done in small temporary outfits in which the stakes are high and where foul-ups can have serious consequences (Heydebrand, 1989; Ancona and Caldwell, 1992). Thus, if we understand what happened at Mann Gulch, we may be able to learn some valuable lessons in how to conceptualize and cope with contemporary organizations.

Let me first be clear about why I think the crew of smokejumpers at Mann Gulch was an organization. First, they have a series of interlocking routines, which is crucial in Westley's (1990: 339) definition of an organization as "a series of interlocking routines, habituated action patterns that bring the same people together around the same activities in the same time and places." The crew at Mann Gulch have routine, habituated action patterns, they come together from a common pool of people, and while this set of individual smokejumpers had not come together at the same places or times, they did come together around the same episodes of fire. Westley's definition suggests it doesn't take much to qualify as an organization. The other side is, it also may not take much to stop being one.

Second, the Mann Gulch crew fits the five criteria for a simple organizational structure proposed by Mintzberg (1983: 158). These five include coordination by direct supervision, strategy planned at the top, little formalized behavior, organic structure, and the person in charge tending to formulate plans intuitively, meaning that the plans are generally a direct "extension of his own personality." Structures like this are found most often in entrepreneurial firms.

And third, the Mann Gulch crew has "generic subjectivity" (Wiley, 1988), meaning that roles and rules exist that enable individuals to be interchanged with little disruption to the ongoing pattern of interaction. In the crew at Mann Gulch there were at least three roles: leader, second in command, and crewmember. The person in the lead sizes up the situation, makes decisions, yells orders, picks trails, sets the pace, and identifies escape routes (pp. 65–66). The second in command brings up the rear of the crew as it hikes, repeats orders, sees that the orders are understood, helps the individuals coordinate their actions, and tends to be closer to the crew and more of a buddy with them than does the leader. And finally, the crew clears a fire line around the fire, cleans up after the fire, and maintains trails. Thus, the crew at Mann Gulch is an organization by virtue of a role structure of interlocking routines.

I want to argue that the tragedy at Mann Gulch alerts us to an unsuspected source of vulnerability in organizations. Minimal organizations, such as we find in the crew at Mann Gulch, are susceptible to sudden losses of meaning, which have been variously described as fundamental surprises (Reason, 1990) or events that are inconceivable (Lanir, 1989), hidden (Westrum, 1982), or incomprehensible (Perrow, 1984). Each of these labels points to the low probability that the event could occur, which is why it is meaningless. But these explanations say less about the astonishment of the perceiver, and even less about the perceiver's inability to rebuild some sense of what is happening.

To shift the analytic focus in implausible events from probabilities to feelings and social construction, I have borrowed the term "cosmology" from philosophy and stretched it. Cosmology refers to a branch of philosophy often subsumed under metaphysics that combines rational speculation and scientific evidence to understand the universe as a totality of phenomena. Cosmology is the ultimate macro perspective, directed at issues of time, space, change, and contingency as they relate to the origin and structure of the universe. integrations of these issues, however, are not just the handiwork of philosophers. Others also make their peace with these issues, as reflected in what they take for granted. People, including those who are smokejumpers, act as if events cohere in time and space and that change unfolds in an orderly manner. These everyday cosmologies are subject to disruption. And when they are severely disrupted, I call this a cosmology episode (Weick, 1985: 51–52). A cosmology episode occurs when people suddenly and deeply feel that the universe is no longer a rational, orderly system. What makes such an episode so shattering is that both the sense of what is occurring and the means to rebuild that sense collapse together.

Stated more informally, a cosmology episode feels like vu jàdé – the opposite of déjà vu: I've never been here before, I have no idea where I am, and I have no idea who can help me. This is what the smokejumpers may have felt increasingly as the afternoon wore on and they lost what little organization structure they had to start with. As they lost structure they became more anxious and found it harder to make sense of what was happening, until they finally were unable to make any sense whatsoever of the one thing that would have saved their lives, an escape fire. The disaster at Mann Gulch was produced by the interrelated collapse of sensemaking and structure. If we can understand this collapse, we may be able to forestall similar disasters in other organizations.

Sensemaking in Mann Gulch

Although most organizational analyses begin and end with decision making, there is growing dissatisfaction with this orthodoxy. Reed (1991) showed how far the concept of decision making has been stretched, singling out the patching that James G. March has done in recent discussions of decision making. March (1989: 14) wrote that "decision making is a highly contextual, sacred activity, surrounded by myth and ritual, and as much concerned with the interpretive order as with the specifics of particular choices." Reed (1991: 561) summarized March this way: "decision making preferences are often inconsistent, unstable, and externally driven, the linkages between decisions and actions are loosely-coupled and interactive rather than linear; the past is notoriously unreliable as a guide to the present or the future; and . . . political and symbolic considerations play a central, perhaps overriding, role in decision making." Reed wondered aloud whether, if March is right in these descriptions, decision making should continue to set the agenda for organizational studies. At some point a retreat from classic principles becomes a rout.

There have been at least three distinct responses to these problems. First, there has been a shift, reminiscent of Neisser and Winograd's (1988) work on memory, toward examining naturalistic decision making (Orasanu and Connolly, 1993), with more attention to situational assessment and sensemaking (Klein, 1993). Second, people have replaced an interest in decision making with an interest in power, noting, for example, that "power is most strategically deployed in the design and implementation of paradigmatic frameworks within which the very meaning of such actions as 'making decisions' is defined" (Brown, 1978: 376). And third, people are replacing the less appropriate normative models of rationality (e.g., Hirsch, Michaels, and Friedman, 1987) based on asocial "economic man" (Beach and Lipshitz, 1993) with more appropriate models of rationality that are more sophisticated about social relations, such as the model of contextual rationality (White 1988).

Reed (1991) described contextual rationality as action motivated to create and maintain institutions and traditions that express some conception of right behavior and a good life with others. Contextual rationality is sensitive to the fact that social actors need to create and maintain intersubjectively binding normative structures that sustain and enrich their relationships. Thus, organizations become important because they can provide meaning and order in the face of environments that impose ill-defined, contradictory demands.

One way to shift the focus from decision making to meaning is to look more closely at sensemaking in organizations. The basic idea of sensemaking is that reality is an ongoing accomplishment that emerges from efforts to create order and make retrospective sense of what occurs. Recognition primed decision making, a model based in part on command decisions made by firefighters, has features of sensemaking in its reliance on past experience, although it remains grounded in decision making (Klein, 1993). Sensemaking emphasizes that people try to make things rationally accountable to themselves and others. Thus, in the words of Morgan, Frost, and Pondy (1983: 24), "individuals are not seen as living in, and acting out their lives in relation to, a wider reality, so much as creating and sustaining images of a wider reality, in part to rationalize what they are doing. They realize their reality, by reading into their situation patterns of significant meaning."

When the smokejumpers landed at Mann Gulch, they expected to find what they had come to call a 10:00 fire. A 10:00 fire is one that can be surrounded completely and isolated by 10:00 the next morning. The spotters on the aircraft that carried the smokejumpers "figured the crew would have it under control by 10:00 the next morning" (Maclean, p. 43). People rationalized this image until it was too late. And because they did, less and less of what they saw made sense:

1. The crew expects a 10:00 fire but grows uneasy when this fire does not act like one.
2. Crewmembers wonder how this fire can be all that serious if Dodge and Harrison eat supper while they hike toward the river.
3. People are often unclear who is in charge of the crew (p. 65).
4. The flames on the south side of the gulch look intense, yet one of the smokejumpers, David Navon is taking pictures, so people conclude the fire can't be that serious, even though their senses tell them otherwise.
5. Crewmembers know they are moving toward the river where they will be safe from the fire, only to see Dodge inexplicably turn them around, away from the river, and start angling upslope, but not running straight for the top. Why? (Dodge is the only one who sees the fire jump the gulch ahead of them.)
6. As the fire gains on them, Dodge says, "Drop your tools," but if the people in the crew do that, then who are they? Firefighters? With no tools?
7. The foreman lights a fire that seems to be right in the middle of the only escape route people can see.
8. The foreman points to the fire he has started and yells, "Join me," whatever that means. But his second in command sounds like he's saying, "To hell with that, I'm getting out of here" (p. 95).
9. Each individual faces the dilemma, I must be my own boss yet follow orders unhesitatingly, but I can't comprehend what the orders mean, and I'm losing my race with the advancing fire (pp. 219–220).

As Mann Gulch loses its resemblance to a 10:00 fire, it does so in ways that make it increasingly hard to socially construct reality. When the noise created by wind, flames, and exploding trees is deafening; when people are strung out in a line and relative strangers to begin with; when they are people who, in Maclean's words, "love the universe but are not intimidated by it" (p. 28); and when the temperature is approaching a lethal 140 degrees (p. 220), people can neither validate their impressions with a trusted neighbor nor pay close attention to a boss who is also unknown and whose commands make no sense whatsoever. As if these were not obstacles enough, it is hard to make common sense when each person sees something different or nothing at all because of the smoke.

The crew's stubborn belief that it faced a 10:00 fire is a powerful reminder that positive illusions (Taylor, 1989) can kill people. But the more general point is that organizations can be good at decision making and still falter. They falter because of deficient sensemaking. The world of decision making is about strategic rationality. It is built from clear questions and clear answers that attempt to remove ignorance (Daft and Macintosh, 1981). The world of sensemaking is different. Sensemaking is about contextual rationality. It is built out of vague questions, muddy answers, and negotiated agreements that attempt to reduce confusion. People in Mann Gulch did not face questions like where should we go, when do we take a stand, or what should our strategy be? Instead, they faced the more basic, the more frightening feeling that their old labels were no longer working. They were outstripping their past experience and were not sure either what was up or who they were. Until they develop some sense of issues like this, there is nothing to decide.

Role structure in Mann Gulch

Sensemaking was not the only problem in Mann Gulch. There were also problems of structure. It seems plausible to argue that a major contributor to this disaster was the loss of the only structure that kept these people organized, their role system. There were two key events that destroyed the organization that tied these people together. First, when Dodge told Hellman to take the crew to the north side of the gulch and have it follow a contour down toward the river, the crew got confused, the spaces between members widened appreciably, and Navon – the person taking pictures (p. 71) – made a bid to take over the leadership of the group (p. 65). Notice what this does to the role system. There is now no one at the end of the line repeating orders as a check on the accuracy with which they are understood. Furthermore, the person who is leading them, Hellman, is more familiar with implementing orders than with constructing them or plotting possible escape routes. So the crew is left for a crucial period of time with ill-structured, unacknowledged orders shouted by someone who is unaccustomed to being firm or noticing escape routes. Both routines and interlocking are beginning to come apart.

The second, and in some way more unsettling threat to the role system occurred when Dodge told the retreating crew "throw away your tools!" (p. 226). A fire crew that retreats from a fire should find its identity and morale strained. If the retreating people are then also told to discard the very things that are their reason for being there in the first place, then the moment quickly turns existential. If I am no longer a firefighter, then who am I? With the fire bearing down, the only possible answer becomes, an endangered person in a world where it is every man for himself. Thus, people who, in Maclean's words, had perpetually been almost their own boss (p. 218) suddenly became completely their own boss at the worst possible moment. As the entity of a crew dissolved, it is not surprising that the final command from the "crew" leader to jump into an escape fire was heard not as a legitimate order but as the ravings of someone who had "gone nuts" (p. 75). Dodge's command lost its basis of legitimacy when the smokejumpers threw away their organization along with their tools.

Panic in Mann Gulch

With these observations as background, we can now look more closely at the process of a cosmology episode, an interlude in which the orderliness of the universe is called into question because both understanding and procedures for sensemaking collapse together. People stop thinking and panic. What is interesting about this collapse is that it was discussed by Freud (1959: 28) in the context of panic in military groups: "A panic arises if a group of that kind [military group] becomes disintegrated. Its characteristics are that none of the orders given by superiors are any longer listened to, and that each individual is only solicitous on his own account, and without any consideration for the rest. The mutual ties have ceased to exist, and a gigantic and senseless fear is set free." Unlike earlier formulations, such as McDougall's (1920), which had argued that panic leads to group disintegration, Freud, reversing this causality, argued that group disintegration precipitates panic. By group disintegration, Freud meant "the cessation of all the feelings of consideration which the members of the group otherwise show one another" (p. 29). He described the mechanism involved this way: "If an individual in panic fear begins to be solicitous only on his own account, he bears witness in so doing to the fact that the emotional ties, which have hitherto made the danger seem small to him, have ceased to exist. Now that he is by himself in facing the danger, he may surely think it greater."

It is certainly true in Mann Gulch that there is a real, palpable danger that can be seen, felt, heard, and smelled by the smokejumpers. But this is not the first time they have confronted danger. It may, however, be the first time they have confronted danger as a member of a disintegrating organization. As the crew moved toward the river and became more spread out, individuals were isolated and left without explanations or emotional support for their reactions. As the ties weakened, the sense of danger increased, and the means to cope became more primitive. The world rapidly shifted from a cosmos to chaos as it became emptied of order and rationality.

It is intriguing that the three people who survived the disaster did so in ways that seem to forestall group disintegration. Sallee and Rumsey stuck together, their small group of two people did not disintegrate, which helped them keep their fear under control. As a result, they escaped through a crack in the ridge that the others either didn't see or thought was too small to squeeze through. Wag Dodge, as the formal leader of a group he presumed still existed, ordered his followers to join him in the escape fire. Dodge continued to see a group and to think about its well-being, which helped keep his own fear under control. The rest of the people, however, took less notice of one another. Consequently, the group, as they knew it, disintegrated. As their group disintegrated, the smokejumpers became more frightened, stopped thinking sooner, pulled apart even more, and in doing so, lost a leader-follower relationship as well as access to the novel ideas of other people who are a lot like them. As these relationships disappeared, individuals reverted to primitive tendencies of flight. Unfortunately, this response was too simple to match the complexity of the Mann Gulch fire.

What holds organization in place may be more tenuous than we realize. The recipe for disorganization in Mann Gulch is not all that rare in everyday life. The recipe reads: Thrust people into unfamiliar roles, leave some key roles unfilled, make the task more ambiguous, discredit the role system, and make all of these changes in a context in which small events can combine into something monstrous. Faced with similar conditions, organizations that seem much sturdier may also come crashing down (Miller, 1990; Miles and Snow, 1992), much like Icarus who overreached his competence as he flew toward the sun and also perished because of fire.

From Vulnerability to Resilience

The steady erosion of sense and structure reached its climax in the refusal of the crew to escape one fire by walking into another one that was intentionally set. A closer look at that escape fire allows us to move from a discussion of what went wrong at Mann Gulch, to a discussion of what makes organizations more resilient. I want to discuss four sources of resilience: (1) improvisation and bricolage, (2) virtual role systems, (3) the attitude of wisdom, and (4) respectful interaction.

Improvisation and bricolage

The escape fire is a good place to start in the search for sources of resilience simply because it is clear evidence that, minimal though the organization of the crew might have been, there still was a solution to the crisis inside the group. The problem was, no one but Dodge recognized this. The question then becomes, How could more people either see this escape fire as a solution or develop their own solution? This is not an easy question to answer because, from everything we know, Dodge's invention of burning a hole in a fire should not have happened. It should not have happened because there is good evidence that when people are put under pressure, they regress to their most habituated ways of responding (e.g., Barthol and Ku, 1959). This is what we see in the 15 people who reject Dodge's order to join him and who resort instead to flight, a more overlearned tendency. What we do not expect under life-threatening pressure is creativity.

The tactic of lighting a fire to create an area where people can escape a major prairie fire is mentioned in James Fenimore Cooper's 1827 novel *The Prairie*, but there is no evidence Dodge knew this source (Maclean, p. 104). Furthermore, most of Dodge's experience had been in timbered country where such a tactic wouldn't work. In timber, an escape fire is too slow and consumes too much oxygen (p. 105). And the fire that Dodge built did not burn long enough to clear an area in which people could move around and dodge the fire as they did in the prairie fire. There was just room enough to lie down in the ashes where the heat was less intense (p. 104).

While no one can say how or why the escape fire was created, there is a line of argument that is consistent with what we know. Bruner (1983: 183) described creativity as "figuring out how to use what you already know in order to go beyond what you currently think." With this as background, it now becomes relevant that Dodge was an experienced woodsman, with lots of hands-on experience. He was what we now would call a bricoleur, someone able to create order out of whatever materials were at hand (e.g., Levi-Strauss, 1966; Harper, 1987). Dodge would have known at least two things about fires. He would have known the famous fire triangle – you must have oxygen, flammable material, and temperature above the point of ignition to create a fire (Maclean, p. 35). A shortage of any one of these would prevent a fire. In his case, the escape fire removed flammable material. And since Dodge had been with the Forest Service longer than anyone else on the crew, he would also have known more fully their four guidelines at that time for dealing with fire emergencies (p. 100). These included (1) start a backfire if you can, (2) get to the top of a ridge where the fuel is thinner, (3) turn into the fire and try to work through it, and (4) don't allow the fire to pick the spot where it hits you. Dodge's invention, if we stretch a bit, fits all four. It is a backfire, though not in the conventional sense of a fire built to stop a fire. The escape fire is lit near the top of a ridge, Dodge turns into the main fire and works through it by burning a hole in it, and he chooses where the fire hits him. The 15 who tried to outrun the fire moved toward the ridge but by not facing the fire, they allowed it to pick the spot where it hit them.

The collapse of role systems need not result in disaster if people develop skills in improvisation and bricolage (see Janowitz, 1959: 481). Bricoleurs remain creative under pressure, precisely because they routinely act in chaotic conditions and pull order out of them. Thus, when situations unravel, this is simply normal natural trouble for bricoleurs, and they proceed with whatever materials are at hand. Knowing these materials intimately, they then are able, usually in the company of other similarly skilled people, to form the materials or insights into novel combinations.

While improvised fire fighting may sound improbable, in fact, Park Service fire-fighters like those stationed at the Grand Canyon approximate just such a style. Stephen Pyne (1989), a Park Service firefighter, observed that people like him typi-cally have discretion to dispatch themselves, which is unfathomable to the Forest Service crews that rely on dispatchers, specialization, regimentation, rules, and a conscious preference for the strength of the whole rather than the versatility and resourcefulness of the parts. Forest Service people marvel at the freedom of move-ment among the Park people. Park Service people marvel at how much power the Forest Service is able to mobilize on a fire. Pyne (1989: 122) described the Park Service fire operations as a nonstandard "eclectic assembly of compromises" built of discretion and mobility. In contrast to the Forest Service, where people do everything by the book, "The Park Service has no books; it puts a premium on the individual. Its collective behavior is tribal, and it protects its permanent ranks." If improvisation were given more attention in the job description of a crew person, that person's receptiveness to and generation of role improvisations might be enhanced. As a result, when one organizational order collapses, a substitute might be invented im-mediately. Swift replacement of a traditional order with an improvised order would forestall the paralysis that can follow a command to "drop your tools."

Virtual role systems

Social construction of reality is next to impossible amidst the chaos of a fire, unless social construction takes place inside one person's head, where the role system is reconstituted and run. Even though the role system at Mann Gulch collapsed, this kind of collapse need not result in disaster if the system remains intact in the individual's mind. If each individual in the crew mentally takes all roles and therefore can then register escape routes and acknowledge commands and facilitate coordination, then each person literally becomes a group (Schutz, 1961). And, in the manner of a holograph, each person can reconstitute the group and assume whatever role is vacated, pick up the activities, and run a credible version of the role. Furthermore, people can run the group in their head and use it for continued guidance of their own individual action. It makes just as much sense to talk about a virtual role system as it does to talk about a virtual anything else (e.g., Bruner, 1986: 36–37). An organization can continue to function in the imagination long after it has ceased to function in tangible distributed activities. For the Mann Gulch fire, this issue has bearing on the question of escape routes. In our research on accidents in flight operations off nuclear carriers (Weick and Roberts, 1993), Karlene Roberts and I found that people who avoid accidents live by the credo, "never get into anything without making sure you have a way out." At the very last moment in the Mann Gulch tragedy, Dodge discovered a way out. The point is that if other people had been able to simulate Dodge and/or his role in their imagination, they too might have been less puzzled by his solution or better able to invent a different sensible solution for themselves.

The attitude of wisdom

To understand the role of wisdom (Bigelow, 1992) as a source of resilience, we need to return to the crew's belief that all fires are 10:00 fires. This belief was consistent with members' experience. As Maclean put it, if the major purpose of your group is to "put out fires so fast they don't have time to become big ones" (p. 31), then you won't learn much about fighting big fires. Nor will you learn what Maclean calls the first principle of reality: "little things suddenly and literally can become big as hell, the ordinary can suddenly become monstrous, and the upgulch breezes can suddenly turn to murder" (p. 217). To state the point more generally, what most organizations miss, and what explains why most organizations fail to learn (Scott, 1987: 282), is that "Reality backs up while it is approached by the subject who tries to understand it. Ignorance and knowledge grow together" (Meacham, 1983: 130). To put it a different way, "Each new domain of knowledge appears simple from the distance of ignorance. The more we learn about a particular domain, the greater the number of uncertainties, doubts, questions, and complexities. Each bit of knowledge serves as the thesis from which additional questions or antithesis arise" (Meacham, 1983: 120).

The role system best able to accept the reality that ignorance and knowledge grow together may be one in which the organizational culture values wisdom. Meacham (1983: 187) argued that wisdom is an attitude rather than a skill or a body of information:

> To be wise is not to know particular facts but to know without excessive confidence or excessive cautiousness. Wisdom is thus not a belief, a value, a set of facts, a corpus of

knowledge or information in some specialized area, or a set of special abilities or skills. Wisdom is an attitude taken by persons toward the beliefs, values, knowledge, information, abilities, and skills that are held, a tendency to doubt that these are necessarily true or valid and to doubt that they are an exhaustive set of those things that could be known.

In a fluid world, wise people know that they don't fully understand what is happening right now, because they have never seen precisely this event before. Extreme confidence and extreme caution both can destroy what organizations most need in changing times, namely, curiosity, openness, and complex sensing. The overconfident shun curiosity because they feel they know most of what there is to know. The overcautious shun curiosity for fear it will only deepen their uncertainties. Both the cautious and the confident are closed-minded, which means neither makes good judgments. It is this sense in which wisdom, which avoids extremes, improves adaptability.

A good example of wisdom in groups is the Naskapi Indians' use of caribou shoulder bones to locate game (Weick, 1979). They hold bones over a fire until they crack and then hunt in the directions to which the cracks point. This ritual is effective because the decision is not influenced by the outcomes of past hunts, which means the stock of animals is not depleted. More important, the final decision is not influenced by the inevitable patterning in human choice, which enables hunted animals to become sensitized to humans and take evasive action. The wisdom inherent in this practice derives from its ambivalence toward the past. Any attempt to hunt for caribou is both a new experience and an old experience. It is new in the sense that time has elapsed, the composition of the hunter band has changed, the caribou have learned new things, and so forth. But the hunt is also old in the sense that if you've seen one hunt, you've seen them all: There are always hunters, weapons, stealth, decoys, tracks, odors, and winds. The practice of divination incorporates the attitude of wisdom because past experience is discounted when a new set of cracks forms a crude map for the hunt. But past experience is also given some weight, because a seasoned hunter "reads" the cracks and injects some of his own past experience into an interpretation of what the cracks mean. The reader is crucial. If the reader's hunches dominate, randomization is lost. If the cracks dominate, then the experience base is discarded. The cracks are a lot like the four guidelines for fire emergencies that Dodge may have relied on when he invented the escape fire. They embody experience, but they invite doubt, reassembly, and shaping to fit novelties in the present.

Respectful interaction

The final suggestion about how to counteract vulnerability makes explicit the preceding focus on the individual and social interaction. Respectful interaction depends on intersubjectivity (Wiley, 1988: 258), which has two defining characteristics: (1) Intersubjectivity emerges from the interchange and synthesis of meanings among two or more communicating selves, and (2) the self or subject gets transformed during interaction such that a joint or merged subjectivity develops. It is possible that many role systems do not change fast enough to keep up with a rapidly changing environment. The only form that can keep up is one based on face-to-face interaction. And it is here, rather than in routines, that we are best able to see the core of organizing. This may be why interaction in airline cockpit crews, such as discussed by Foushee (1984), strikes us so often as a plausible microcosm of what happens in much larger systems. In a cockpit under crisis, the only unit that makes sense (pun intended) is face-to-face synthesis of meaning.

Intersubjectivity was lost on everyone at Mann Gulch, everyone, that is, but Sallee and Rumsey. They stuck together and lived. Dodge went his own individual way with a burst of improvisation, and he too lived. Perhaps it's more important that you have a partner than an organization when you fight fires. A partner makes social construction easier. A partner is a second source of ideas. A partner strengthens independent judgment in the face of a majority. And a partner enlarges the pool of data that are considered. Partnerships that endure are likely to be those that adhere to Campbell's three imperatives for social life, based on a reanalysis of Asch's (1952) conformity experiment: (1) Respect the reports of others and be willing to base beliefs and actions on them (trust); (2) Report honestly so that others may use your observations in coming to valid beliefs (honesty); and, (3) Respect your own perceptions and beliefs and seek to integrate them with the reports of others without deprecating them or yourself (self-respect) (adapted from Campbell, 1990: 45–46).

Earlier I noted a growing interest in contextual rationality, understood as actions that create and maintain institutions and traditions that express some conception of right behavior and a good life with others (Reed, 1991). Campbell's maxims operationalize this good life with others as trust, honesty, and self-respect in moment-to-moment interaction. This triangle of trust, honesty, and self-respect is conspicuously missing (e.g., King, 1989: 46–48) in several well-documented disasters in which faulty interaction processes led to increased fear, diminished communication, and death. For example, in the Tenerife air disaster (Weick, 1990), the copilot of the KLM aircraft had a strong hunch that another 747 airplane was on the takeoff runway directly in front of them when his own captain began takeoff without clearance. But the copilot said nothing about either the suspicions or the illegal departure. Transient cockpit crews, tied together by narrow definitions of formal responsibilities, and headed by captains who mistakenly assume that their decision-making ability is unaffected by increases in stress (Helmreich et al., 1985), have few protections against a sudden loss of meaning such as the preposterous possibility that a captain is taking off without clearance, directly into the path of another 747.

Even when people try to act with honesty, trust, and self-respect, if they do so with little social support, their efforts are compromised. For example, linguists who analyzed the conversations at Tenerife and in the crash of Air Florida flight 90 in Washington concluded that the copilots in both cases used "devices of mitigation" to soften the effects of their requests and suggestions:

> A mitigated instruction might be phrased as a question or hedged with qualifications such as "would" or "could." . . . (I)t was found that the speech of subordinate crew members was much more likely to be mitigated than the speech of captains. It was also found that topics introduced in mitigated speech were less likely to be followed-up by

other crew members and less likely to be ratified by the captain. Both of these effects relate directly to the situation in which a subordinate crew member makes a correct solution that is ignored. . . . The value of training in unmitigated speech is strongly suggested by these results. (O'Hare and Roscoe, 1990: 219)

If a role system collapses among people for whom trust honesty, and self-respect are underdeveloped, then they are on their own. And fear often swamps their re-sourcefulness. If, however, a role system collapses among people where trust, hon-esty, and self-respect are more fully developed, then new options, such as mutual adaptation, blind imitation of creative solutions, and trusting compliance, are cre-ated. When a formal structure collapses, there is no leader, no roles, no routines, no sense. That is what we may be seeing in Mann Gulch. Dodge can't lead because the role system in which he is a leader disappears. But what is worse, Dodge can't rely on his crewmembers to trust him, question him, or pay attention to him, because they don't know him and there is no time to change this. The key question is, When formal structure collapses, what, if anything, is left? The answer to that question may well be one of life or death.

Structures for Resilience

While the answer to that question is not a matter of life or death for organizational theorists, they do have an interest in how it comes out. A theorist who hears Maclean's question, "what the structure of a small outfit should be when its business is to meet sudden danger and prevent disaster," might come back with a series of follow-up questions based on thinking in organizational studies. I look briefly at four such questions to link Mann Gulch with other concepts and to suggest how these linkages might guide further research.

First, there is the follow-up question, Is "small" necessarily a key dimension, since this group is also young and transient? Maclean calls the 16–person smokejumper crew "small;" except that it is conventional in the group literature to treat any group of more than 10 people as large (Bass, 1990: 604). Because there is so little commu-nication within the crew and because it operates largely through obtrusive controls like rules and supervision (Perrow, 1986), it acts more like a large formal group with mediated communication than a small informal group with direct communication.

It is striking how little communication occurred during the three and a half hours of this episode. There was little discussion during the noisy, bumpy plane ride, and even less as individuals retrieved equipment scattered on the north slope. After a quick meal together, people began hiking toward the river but quickly got separated from one another. Then they were suddenly turned around, told to run for the ridge, and quickly ran out of breath as they scaled the steep south slope. The minimal communication is potentially important because of the growing evidence (e.g., Eisenhardt, 1993: 132) that nonstop talk, both vocal and nonverbal, is a crucial source of coordination in complex systems that are susceptible to catastrophic disasters.

The lack of communication, coupled with the fact that this is a temporary group in the early stages of its history, should heighten the group's vulnerability to disruption.

As Bass (1990: 637) put it, "Groups that are unable to interact easily or that do not have the formal or informal structure that enables quick reactions are likely to experience stress (Bass, 1960). Panic ensues, when members of a group lack superordinate goals – goals that transcend the self-interests of each participant." While the smokejumpers have the obvious superordinate goal of containing fires, their group ties may not be sufficiently developed for this to be a group goal that overrides self-interest. Or Bass's proposition itself may be incomplete, failing to acknowledge that unless superordinate goals are overlearned, they will be discarded in situations of danger.

Second, there is the follow-up question, Is "structure" what we need to understand in Mann Gulch, or might structuring also be important? By structure, I mean "a complex medium of control which is continually produced and recreated in interaction and yet shapes that interaction: structures are constituted and constitutive . . . of interpersonal cognitive processes, power dependencies, and contextual constraints" (Ranson, Hinings, and Greenwood, 1980: 1, 3). Structuring, then, consists of two patterns and the relationships between them. The first pattern, which Ranson et al. variously described as informal structure, agency, or social construction, consists of interaction patterns that stabilize meaning by creating shared interpretive schemes. I refer to this pattern as shared provinces of meaning, or meaning. The second pattern, variously described as configuration, contextual constraints, or a vehicle that embodies dominant meanings, refers to a framework of roles, rules, procedures, configured activities, and authority relations that reflect and facilitate meanings. I refer to this second pattern as structural frameworks of constraint, or frameworks.

Meanings affect frameworks, which affect meaning. This is the basic point of the growing body of work on structuration (e.g., Riley, 1983; Poole, Seibold, and McPhee, 1985), understood as the mutual constitution of frameworks and meanings (Ranson, Hinings, and Greenwood, 1980) or relations and typifications (DiMaggio, 1991) or structures and structuring (Barley, 1986). Missing in this work is attention to reversals of structuration (Giddens, 1984). The use of descriptive words in structuration theory such as "continually produced," "recreated in interaction," "constituted," and "constitutive" directs attention away from losses of frameworks and losses of meaning. For example, Ranson, Hinings, and Greenwood (1980: 5) asserted that the "deep structure of schema which are taken for granted by members enables them to recognize, interpret, and negotiate even strange and unanticipated situations, and thus continuously to create and reenact the sense and meaning of structural forms during the course of interaction." The Mann Gulch disaster is a case in which people were unable to negotiate strangeness. Frameworks and meanings destroyed rather than constructed one another.

This fugitive quality of meaning and frameworks in Mann Gulch suggests that the process of structuring itself may be more unstable than we realized. Structuring, understood as constitutive relations between meaning and frameworks, may be a deviation-amplifying cause loop (Maruyama, 1963; Weick, 1979) capable of intensifying either an increase or decrease in either of the two connected elements. Typically, we see instances of increase in which more shared meanings lead to more elaborate frameworks of roles, which lead to further developments of shared meaning, etc. What we fail to realize is that, when elements are tied together in this direct manner, once one of them declines, this decline can also spread and become amplified as it does so. Fewer shared meanings lead to less elaborate frameworks, less meaning, less elaborate frameworks, and so on. Processes that mutually constitute also have the capability to mutually destroy one another.

If structuration is treated as a deviation-amplifying process then this suggests the kind of structure that could have prevented the Mann Gulch disaster. What people needed was a structure in which there was both an inverse and a direct relationship between role systems and meaning. This is the only pattern that can maintain resilience in the face of crisis. The resilience can take one of two forms. Assume that we start with an amplifying system like the one in Mann Gulch. The role system lost its structure, which led to a loss of meaning, which led to a further loss of structure, and so on. This is the pattern associated with a deviation-amplifying feedback loop in which an initial change unfolds unchecked in the same direction. One way to prevent this amplification is to retain the direct relation between structure and meaning (less role structure leads to less meaning, more structure leads to more meaning) but create an inverse relation between meaning and structure (less meaning, more structure, and vice versa). This inverse relationship can be understood as follows: When meaning becomes problematic and decreases, this is a signal for people to pay more attention to their formal and informal social ties and to reaffirm and/or reconstruct them. These actions produce more structure, which then increases meaning, which then decreases the attention directed at structure. Puzzlement intensifies attentiveness to the social, which reduces puzzlement.

The other form of control arises when a change in structure, rather than a change in meaning, is responsible for counteracting the fluctuations in sensibleness. In this variation, less structure leads to more meaning, and more meaning then produces more structure. The inverse relationship between structure and meaning can be understood this way: When social ties deteriorate, people try harder to make their own individual sense of what is happening, both socially and in the world. These operations increase meaning, and they increase the tendency to reshape structure consistent with heightened meaning. Alienation intensifies attentiveness to meaning, which reduces alienation.

What is common to both of these controlled forms is an alternation between attention to frameworks and attention to meanings. More attention to one leads to more ignorance of the other, followed by efforts to correct this imbalance, which then creates a new imbalance. In the first scenario, when meaning declines, people pay more attention to frameworks, they ignore meaning temporarily, and as social relations become clearer, their attention shifts back to meanings. In the second scenario, when social relations decline, people pay more attention to meaning, they ignore frameworks temporarily, and as meanings become clearer, attention shifts back to frameworks. Both scenarios illustrate operations of wisdom: In Meacham's words, ignorance and knowledge grow together. Either of these two controlled patterns should reduce the likelihood of disaster in Mann Gulch. As the smokejumpers begin to lose structure they either also lose meaning, which alerts them to be more attentive to the structure they are losing, or they gain individual meaning, which leads them to realign structure. The second alternative may be visible in the actions taken by Dodge and Rumsey and Sallee.

This may seem like a great deal of fretting about one single word in Maclean's question, "structure." What I have tried to show is that when we transform this word from a static image into a process, we spot what looks like a potential for collapse in any process of social sensemaking that is tied together by constitutive relations. And we find that social sensemaking may be most stable when it is simultaneously constitutive and destructive, when it is capable of increasing both ignorance and knowledge at the same time. That seems like a fair return for reflecting on a single word.

Third, there is the follow-up question, Is "outfit" the best way to describe the smokejumpers? An outfit is normally defined as "a group associated in an undertaking requiring close cooperation, as a military unit" (Random House, 1987: 1374). The smokejumpers are tied together largely by pooled interdependence, since the job of each one is to clear adjacent portions of a perimeter area around a blaze so that the fire stops for lack of fuel. Individual efforts to clear away debris are pooled and form a fire line. What is significant about pooled interdependence is that it can function without much cohesion (Bass, 1990: 622). And this is what may have trapped the crew. Given the constantly changing composition of the smokejumping crews, the task largely structured their relations. Simply acting in concert was enough, and there was no need to know each other well in addition. This social form resembles what Eisenberg (1990: 160) called nondisclosive intimacy, by which he meant relationships rooted in collective action that stress "coordination of action over the alignment of cognitions, mutual respect over agreement, trust over empathy, diversity over homogeneity, loose over tight coupling, and strategic communication over unrestricted candor." Nondisclosive intimacy is a sufficient ground for relating as long as the task stays constant and the environment remains stable.

What the Mann Gulch disaster suggests is that nondisclosive intimacy may limit the development of emotional ties that keep panic under control in the face of obstacles. Closer ties permit clearer thinking, which enables people to find paths around obstacles. For example, when Rumsey squeezed through a crevice in the ridge just ahead of the fire, he collapsed "half hysterically" into a juniper bush, where he would have soon burned to death. His partner Sallee stopped next to him, looked at him coldly, never said a word, and just stood there until Rumsey roused himself, and the two then ran together over the ridge and down to a rock slide where they were better able to move around and duck the worst flames (Maclean, p. 107). Sallee's surprisingly nuanced prodding of his partner suggests the power of close ties to moderate panic.

One might expect that the less threatening the environment, the less important are relational issues in transient groups, but as Perrow (1984) emphasized in his normal accident theory, there are few safe environments. If events are increasingly interdependent, then small unrelated flaws can interact to produce something monstrous. Maclean saw this clearly at Mann Gulch: The colossal fire blowup in Mann Gulch was "shaped by little screwups that fitted together tighter and tighter until all became one and the same thing – the fateful blowup. Such is much of tragedy in modern times and probably always has been except that past tragedy refrained from speaking of its association with screwups and blowups" (Maclean, 1992: 92).

Nondisclosive intimacy is not the only alternative to "outfit" as a way to describe the smokejumpers. Smith (1983) argued that individual behaviors, perceptions of reality, identities, and acts of leadership are influenced by intergroup processes. Of special relevance to Mann Gulch is Smith's reanalysis of the many groups that formed among the 16 members of the Uruguayan soccer team who survived for 10 weeks in an inaccessible region of the Chilean Andes mountains after their aircraft, carrying 43 people, crashed (see Read, 1974 for the original account of this event). Aside from the eerie coincidence that both disasters involved 16 young males, Smith's analysis makes the important point that 16 people are not just *an* outfit, they are a social system within which multiple groups emerge and relate to one another. It is these intergroup relationships that determine what will be seen as acts of leadership and which people may be capable of supplying those acts. In the Andes crash, demands shifted from caring for the wounded, in which two medical students took the lead, to acquiring food and water, where the team captain became leader, to articulating that the group would not be rescued and could sustain life only if people consumed the flesh of the dead, to executing and resymbolizing this survival tactic, to selecting and equipping an expeditionary group to hike out and look for help, and finally to finding someone able to explain and rationalize their decisions to the world once they had been rescued.

What Smith shows is that this group of 16 forms and reforms in many different directions during its history, each time with a different coherent structure of people at the top, middle, and bottom, each with different roles. What also becomes clear is that any attempt to pinpoint *the* leader or to explain survival by looking at a single set of actions is doomed to failure because it does not reflect how needs change as a crisis unfolds, nor does it reflect how different coherent groupings form to meet the new needs.

The team in the Andes had 10 weeks and changing threats of bleeding, hygiene, starvation, avalanche, expedition, rescue, and accounting, whereas the team in Mann Gulch had more like 10 minutes and the increasingly singular threat of being engulfed in fire. Part of the problem in Mann Gulch is the very inability for intergroup structures to form. The inability to form subgroups within the system may be due to such things as time pressure, the relative unfamiliarity of the smokejumpers with one another compared with the interdependent members of a visible sports team, the inability to communicate, the articulation of a common threat very late in the smokejumpers' exposure to Mann Gulch, and ambiguity about means that would clearly remove the threat, compared with the relative clarity of the means needed by the soccer players to deal with each of their threats.

The point is, whatever chance the smokejumpers might have had to survive Mann Gulch is not seen as clearly if we view them as a single group rather than as a social system capable of differentiating into many different sets of subgroups. The earlier discussion of virtual role systems suggested that an intergroup perspective could be simulated in the head and that this should heighten resilience. Smith makes it clear that, virtual or not, intergroup dynamics affect survival, even if we overlook them in our efforts to understand the group or the "outfit."

As a fourth and final follow-up question, If there is a structure that enables people to meet sudden danger, who builds and maintains it? A partial answer is Ken Smith's intergroup analysis, suggesting that the needed structure consists of many struc-

, maintained by a shifting configuration of the same people. As I said,
e makes sense when time is extended, demands change, and there is no
at the beginning of the episode. But there is a leader in Mann Gulch,
.. There is also a second in command and the remaining crew, which
e is a top (foreman), middle (second in command), and bottom (remaining
/e take this a priori structure seriously, then the Mann Gulch disaster can
stood as a dramatic failure of leadership, reminiscent of those lapses in
leaders..ip increasingly well documented by people who study cockpit/crew resource
management in aircraft accidents (e.g., Wiener, Kanki, and Helmreich, 1993).

The captain of an aircrew, who is analogous to a player coach on a basketball
team (Hackman, 1993: 55), can often have his or her greatest impact on team
functioning before people get into a tight, time-critical situation. Ginnett (1993) has
shown that aircraft captains identified by check airmen as excellent team leaders
spent more time team building when the team first formed than did leaders judged as
less expert. Leaders of highly effective teams briefed their crewmembers on four issues: the task, crew boundaries, standards and expected behaviors (norms), and
authority dynamics. Captains spent most time on those of the four that were not
predefined by the organizational context within which the crew worked. Typically,
this meant that excellent captains did *not* spend much time on routinized tasks, but
less-excellent captains did. Crew boundaries were enlarged and made more permeable by excellent captains when, for example, they regarded the flight attendants,
gate personnel, and air traffic controllers as members of the total flight crew. This
contrasts with less-excellent captains, who drew a boundary around the people in the
cockpit and separated them from everyone else.

Excellent captains modeled norms that made it clear that safety, effective communication, and cooperation were expected from everyone. Of special interest, because
so little communication occurred at Mann Gulch, is how the norm, "communication
is important," was expressed. Excellent crews expect one another to enact any of
these four exchanges: "(1) I need to talk to you; (2) I listen to you; (3) I need you to
talk to me; or even (4) I expect you to talk to me" (Ginnett, 1993: 88). These four
complement and operationalize the spirit of Campbell's social imperatives of trust,
honesty, and self-respect. But they also show the importance of inquiry, advocacy,
and assertion when people do not understand the reasons why other people are
doing something or ignoring something (Helmreich and Foushee, 1993: 21).

Issues of authority are handled differently by excellent captains. They shift their
behaviors between complete democracy and complete autocracy during the briefing
and thereafter, which makes it clear that they are capable of a range of styles. They
establish competence and their capability to assume legitimate authority by doing the
briefing in a rational manner, comfortably, with appropriate technical language, all
of which suggests that they have given some thought to the upcoming flight and
have constructed a framework within which the crew will work.

Less autocratic than this enactment of their legitimate authority is their willingness to *disavow perfection*. A good example of a statement that tells crewmembers they
too must take responsibility for one another is this: "I just want you guys to understand that they assign the seats in this airplane based on seniority, not on the basis
of competence. So anything you can see or do that will help out, I'd sure appreciate

hearing about it" (Ginnett, 1993: 90). Notice that the captain is not saying, I am not competent to be the captain. Instead, the captain is saying, we're all fallible. We all make mistakes. Let's keep an eye on one another and speak up when we think a mistake is being made.

Most democratic and participative is the captain's behavior to *engage the crew*. Briefings held by excellent captains last no longer than do those of the less-excellent captains, but excellent captains talk less, listen more, and resort less to "canned presentations."

Taken together, all of these team-building activities increase the probability that constructive, informed interactions can still occur among relative strangers even when they get in a jam. If we compare the leadership of aircraft captains to leadership in Mann Gulch, it is clear that Wag Dodge did not build his team of smokejumpers in advance. Furthermore, members of the smokejumper crew did not keep each other informed of what they were doing or the reasons for their actions or the situational model they were using to generate these reasons. These multiple failures of leadership may be the result of inadequate training, inadequate understanding of leadership processes in the late 1940s or may be attributable to a culture emphasizing individual work rather than group work. Or these failures of leadership may reflect the fact that even the best leaders and the most team-conscious members can still suffer when structures begin to pull apart, leaving in their wake senselessness, panic, and cosmological questions. If people are lucky, and interpersonally adept, their exposure to questions of cosmology *is* confined to an episode. If they are not, that exposure stretches much further. Which is just about where Maclean would want us to end.

Note

This is a revised version of the Katz-Newcomb lecture presented at the University of Michigan, April 23–24, 1993. The 1993 lecture celebrated the life of Rensis Likert, the founding director of the Institute for Social Relations. All three people honored at the lecture – Dan Katz, Ted Newcomb, and Ren Likert – were born in 1903, which meant this lecture also celebrated their 90th birthdays. I am grateful to Lance Sandelands, Debra Meyerson, Robert Sutton, Doug Cowherd, and Karen Weick for their help in revising early drafts of this material. I also want to thank John Van Maanen, J. Richard Hackman, Linda Pike, and the anonymous *ASQ* reviewers for their help with later drafts.

References

Ancona, Deborah G., and David F. Caldwell (1992). "Bridging the boundary: External activity and performance in organizational teams." *Administrative Science Quarterly*, 37: 634–665.
Asch, Solomon (1952). *Social Psychology*. Englewood Cliffs, NJ: Prentice-Hall.
Barley, Stephen R. (1986). "Technology as an occasion for structuring: Evidence from observations of CT scanners and the social order of radiology departments." *Administrative Science Quarterly*, 31: 78–108.

Barthol, R. P., and N. D. Ku (1959). "Regression under stress to first learned behavior." *Journal of Abnormal and Social Psychology*, 59: 134–136.

Bass, Bernard M. (1960). *Leadership, Psychology, and Organizational Behavior*. New York: Harper.

Bass, Bernard M. (1990). *Bass and Stogdill's Handbook of Leadership*. New York: Free Press.

Beach, Lee R., and Raanan Lipshitz (1993). "Why classical decision theory is an inappropriate standard for evaluation and aiding most human decision making." In Gary A. Klein, Judith Orasanu, Roberta Calderwood, and Caroline E. Zsambok (eds.), *Decision Making in Action: Models and Methods*: 21–35. Norwood, NJ: Ablex.

Bigelow, John (1992). "Developing managerial wisdom." *Journal of Management Inquiry*, 1: 143–153.

Brown, Richard Harvey (1978). "Bureaucracy as praxis: Toward a political phenomenology of formal organizations." *Administrative Science Quarterly*, 23: 365–382.

Bruner, Jerome (1983). *In Search of Mind*. New York: Harper.

Bruner, Jerome (1986). *Actual Minds, Possible Worlds*. Cambridge, MA: Harvard University Press.

Campbell, Donald T. (1990). "Asch's moral epistemology for socially shared knowledge." In Irwin Rock (ed.), *The Legacy of Solomon Asch: Essays in Cognition and Social Psychology*: 39–52. Hillsdale, NJ: Erlbaum.

Daft, Richard L., and Norman B. MacIntosh (1981). "A tentative exploration into the amount and equivocality of information processing in organizational work units." *Administrative Science Quarterly*, 26: 207–224.

DiMaggio, Paul (1991). "The micro-macro dilemma in organizational research: Implications of role-system theory." In Joan Huber (ed.), *Micro-macro Changes in Sociology*: 76–98. Newbury Park, CA: Sage.

Eisenberg, Eric M. (1990). "Jamming: Transcendence through organizing." *Communication Research*, 17: 139–164.

Eisenhardt, Kathleen M. (1993). "High reliability organizations meet high velocity environments: Common dilemmas in nuclear power plants, aircraft carriers, and microcomputer firms." In Karlene H. Roberts (ed.), *New Challenges to Understanding Organizations*: 117–135. New York: Macmillan.

Foushee, H. Clayton (1984). "Dyads and triads at 35,000 feet." *American Psychologist*, 39: 885–893.

Freud, Sigmund (1959). *Group Psychology and the Analysis of the Ego*. (First published in 1922.) New York: Norton.

Giddens, Anthony (1984). *The Constitution of Society*. Berkeley: University of California Press.

Ginnett, Robert C. (1993). "Crews as groups: Their formation and their leadership." In Earl L. Wiener, Barbara G. Kanki, and Robert L. Helmreich (eds.), *Cockpit Resource Management*: 71–98. San Diego: Academic Press.

Hackman, J. Richard (1993). "Teams, leaders, and organizations: New directions for crew-oriented flight training." In Earl L. Wiener, Barbara G. Kanki, and Robert L. Helmreich (eds.), *Cockpit Resource Management*: 47–69. San Diego: Academic Press.

Harper, Douglas (1987). *Working Knowledge: Skill and Community in a Small Shop*. Chicago: University of Chicago Press.

Helmreich, Robert L., and Clayton Foushee (1993). "Why crew resource management? Empirical and theoretical bases of human factors training in aviation." In Earl L. Wiener, Barbara G. Kanki, and Robert L. Helmreich (eds.), *Cockpit Resource Management*: 3–45. San Diego: Academic Press.

Helmreich, Robert L., Clayton H. Foushee, R. Benson, and W. Russini (1985). "Cockpit re-source management: Exploring the attitude-performance linkage." Paper presented at Third Aviation Psychology Symposium, Ohio State University.

Heydebrand, Wolf V. (1989). New organizational forms." *Work and Occupations*, 16: 323–357.

Hirsch, Paul, Stuart Michaels, and Ray Friedman (1987). "'Dirty hands' vs. 'clean models': Is sociology in danger of being seduced by economics?" *Theory and Society*, 16: 317–336.

Janowitz, Morris (1959). "Changing patterns of organizational authority: The military estab-lishment." *Administrative Science Quarterly*, 3: 473–493.

King, Jonathan B. (1989). "Confronting chaos." *Journal of Business Ethics*, 8: 39–50.

Klein, Gary A. (1993). "A recognition-primed decision (RPD) model of rapid decision making." In Gary A. Klein, Judith Orasanu, Roberta Calderwood, and Caroline E. Zsambok (eds.), *Decision Making in Action: Models and Methods*: 138–147. Norwood, NJ: Ablex.

Lanir Zvi (1989). "The reasonable choice of disaster: The shooting down of the Libyan airliner on 21 February 1973." *Journal of Strategic Studies*, 12: 479–493.

Levi-Strauss, Claude (1966). *The Savage Mind*. Chicago: University of Chicago Press.

Maclean, Norman (1992). *Young Men and Fire*. Chicago: University of Chicago Press.

March, James G. (1989). *Decisions and Organizations*. Oxford: Blackwell.

Maruyama, Magorah (1963). "The second cybernetics: Deviation-amplifying mutual causal process." *American Scientist*, 51: 164–179.

McDougall, William (1920). *The Group Mind*. New York: Putnam.

Meacham, John A. (1983). "Wisdom and the context of knowledge." In D. Kuhn and J. A. Meacham (eds.), *Contributions in Human Development*, 8: 111–134. Basel: Karger.

Miles, Ray E., and Charles C. Snow (1992). "Causes of failure in network organizations." *California Management Review*, 34(4): 53–72.

Miller, Danny (1990). *The Icarus Paradox*. New York: Harper.

Mintzberg, Henry (1983). *Structure in Fives: Designing Effective Organizations*. Englewood Cliffs, NJ: Prentice-Hall.

Morgan, Gareth, Peter J. Frost, and Louis R. Pondy (1983). "Organizational symbolism." In L. R. Pondy, P. J. Frost, G. Morgan, and T. C. Dandridge (eds.), *Organizational Symbolism*: 3–35. Greenwich, CT: JAI Press.

Neisser, Ulric, and Eugene Winograd (1988). *Remembering Reconsidered: Ecological and Tradi-tional Approaches to the Study of Memory*. New York: Cambridge University Press.

O'Hare, David, and Stanley Roscoe (1990). *Flightdeck Performance: The Human Factor*. Ames, IA: Iowa State University Press.

Orasanu, Judith, and Terry Connolly (1993). "The reinvention of decision making." In Gary A. Klein, Judith Orasanu, Roberta Calderwood, and Caroline E. Zsambok (eds.), *Decision Making in Action: Models and Methods*: 3–20. Norwood NJ: Ablex.

Perrow, Charles (1984). *Normal Accidents*. New York: Basic Books

Perrow, Charles (1986). *Complex Organizations*, 3rd ed. New York: Random House.

Poole, M. Scott, David R. Seibold, and Robert D. McPhee (1985). "Group decision-making as a structurational process." *Quarterly Journal of Speech*, 71: 74–102.

Pyne, Stephen (1989). *Fire on the Rim*. New York: Weidenfeld & Nicolson.

Random House (1987). *Dictionary of the English Language*, 2d ed.: Unabridged. New York: Random House.

Ranson, Stewart. Bob Hinings and Royston T. Greenwood (1980). "The structuring of organi-zational structures." *Administrative Science Quarterly*, 25: 1–17.

Read, P. P. (1974). *Alive*. London: Pan Books

Reason, James (1990). *Human Error*. New York: Cambridge University Press.

Reed M. (1991). Organizations and rationality: The odd couple." *Journal of Management Studies*, 28: 559–567.

Riley, Patricia (1983). "A structurationalist account of political culture." *Administrative Science Quarterly*, 28: 414–437.

Runkel, Phillip J., and Joseph E. McGrath (1972). *Research on Human Behavior*. New York: Holt, Rinehart, and Winston.

Schutz, William C. (1961). "The ego, FIRO theory and the leader as completer." In Louis Petrullo and Bernard M. Bass (eds.), *Leadership and Interpersonal Behavior*: 48–65. New York: Holt, Rinehart, and Winston.

Scott, W. Richard (1987). *Organizations: Rational, Natural, and Open Systems*. Englewood Cliffs, NJ: Prentice-Hall.

Smith, Ken K. (1983). "An intergroup perspective on individual behavior." In J. Richard Hackman, Edward E. Lawler, and Lyman M. Porter (eds.), *Perspectives on Behavior in Organizations*: 397–408. New York: McGraw-Hill.

Taylor, Shelby E. (1989). *Positive Illusions*. New York: Basic Books.

Weick, Karl E. (1979). *The Social Psychology of Organizing*, 2d ed. Reading, MA: Addison-Wesley.

Weick, Karl E. (1985). "Cosmos vs. chaos: Sense and nonsense in electronic contexts." *Organizational Dynamics*, 14(Autumn): 50–64.

Weick, Karl E. (1990). "The vulnerable system: Analysis of the Tenerife air disaster." *Journal of Management*, 16: 571–593.

Weick, Karl E., and Karlene H. Roberts (1993). "Collective mind in organizations: Heedful interrelating on flight decks." *Administrative Science Quarterly*, 38: 357–381.

Westley, Frances R. (1990). Middle managers and strategy: Microdynamics of inclusion." *Strategic Management Journal*. 11: 337–351.

Westrum, Ron (1982). "Social intelligence about hidden events." *Knowledge*, 3: 381–400.

White, S. K. (1988). *The Recent Work of Jürgen Habermas: Reason, Justice, and Modernity*. Cambridge: Cambridge University Press.

Wiener, Earl L., Barbara G. Kanki, and Robert L. Helmreich (1993). *Cockpit Resource Management*. San Diego: Academic Press.

Wiley, Norbert (1988). "The micro-macro problem in social theory." *Sociological Theory*, 6: 254–261.

5

The Vulnerable System: An Analysis of the Tenerife Air Disaster

There is a growing appreciation that large-scale disasters such as Bhopal (Shrivastava, 1987) and Three Mile Island (Perrow, 1981) are the result of separate small events that become linked and amplified in ways that are incomprehensible and unpredictable. This scenario of linkage and amplification is especially likely when systems become more tightly coupled and less linear (Perrow, 1984).

What is missing from these analyses, however, is any discussion of the processes by which crises are set in motion. Specifically, we lack an understanding of ways in which separate small failures become linked. We know that single cause incidents are rare, but we don't know how small events can become chained together so that they result in a disastrous outcome. In the absence of this understanding, people must wait until some crisis actually occurs before they can diagnose a problem, rather than be in a position to detect a potential problem before it emerges. To anticipate and forestall disasters is to understand regularities in the ways small events can combine to have disproportionately large effects.

The purpose of the following analysis is to suggest several processes that amplify the effects of multiple small events into potentially disastrous outcomes. These processes were induced from an analysis of the Tenerife air disaster in which 583 people were killed. The processes include, the interruption of important routines, regression to more habituated ways of responding, the breakdown of coordinated action, and misunderstandings in speech-exchange systems. When these four processes occur in the context of a system that is becoming more tightly coupled and less linear, they produce more errors, reduce the means to detect those errors, create dependencies among the errors, and amplify the effects of these errors.

These processes are sufficiently basic and widespread that they suggest an inherent vulnerability in human systems that, up until now, has been overlooked. The processes suggest both a research agenda for the next decade as well as a managerial agenda.

Description of Tenerife Disaster

On March 27, 1977, KLM flight 4805, a 747 bound from Amsterdam to the Canary Islands, and Pan Am flight 1736, another 747 bound from Los Angeles and New York to the Canary Islands, were both diverted to Los Rodeos airport at Tenerife because the Las Palmas airport, their original destination, was closed because of a bomb explosion. KLM landed first at 1:38 PM, followed by Pan Am which landed at 2:15 PM. Because Tenerife is not a major airport, its taxi space was limited. This meant that the Pan Am plane had to park behind the KLM flight in such a way that it could not depart until the KLM plane left. When the Las Palmas airport reopened at 2:30, the Pan Am flight was ready to depart because its passengers had remained on board. KLM's passengers, however, had left the plane so there was a delay while they reboarded and while the plane was refueled to shorten its turnaround time at Las Palmas. KLM began its taxi for takeoff at 4:56 PM and was initially directed to proceed down a runway parallel to the takeoff runway. This directive was amended shortly thereafter and KLM was requested to taxi down the takeoff runway and at the end, to make a 180-degree turn and await further instruction (see Figure 5.1).

Pan Am was requested to follow KLM down the takeoff runway and to leave the takeoff runway at taxiway C3, use the parallel runway for the remainder of the taxi, and then pull in behind the KLM flight. Pan Am's request to hold short of the takeoff runway and stay off it until KLM had departed, was denied. After the KLM plane made the 180-degree turn at the end of the takeoff runway, rather than hold as instructed, it started moving and reported, "we are now at takeoff." Neither the air traffic controllers nor the Pan Am crew were certain what this ambiguous phrase meant, but Pan Am restated to controllers that it would report when it was clear of the takeoff runway, a communique heard inside the KLM cockpit. When the pilot of the KLM flight was asked by the engineer, "Is he not clear then, that Pan Am?" the pilot replied "yes" and there was no further conversation. The collision occurred 13 seconds later at 5:06 PM. None of the 234 passengers and 14 crew on the KLM flight survived. Of the 380 passengers and 16 crew on the Pan Am plane, 70 survived, although 9 died later, making a total loss of 583 lives.

A brief excerpt from the Spanish Ministry of Transport and Communication's investigation of the crash, describes interactions among the KLM crew members immediately before the crash. These interactions, reconstructed from the KLM cockpit voice recorder (CVR), are the focus of the remainder of our analysis.

As the time for the takeoff approached, the KLM captain "seemed a little absent from all that was heard in the cockpit. He inquired several times, and after the copilot confirmed the order to backtrack, he asked the tower if he should leave the runway by C1, and subsequently asked his copilot if he should do so by C4. On arriving at the end of the runway, and making a 180-degree turn in order to place himself in takeoff position, he was advised by the copilot that he should wait because they still did not have an ATC clearance. The captain asked him to request it, and he did, but while the copilot was still repeating the clearance, the captain opened the throttle and started to takeoff. Then the copilot, instead of requesting takeoff clearance or advising that they did not yet have it, added to his read-back, "We are now at takeoff."

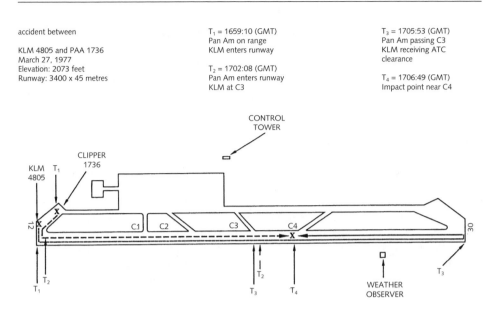

accident between

KLM 4805 and PAA 1736
March 27, 1977
Elevation: 2073 feet
Runway: 3400 x 45 metres

T_1 = 1659:10 (GMT)
Pan Am on range
KLM enters runway

T_2 = 1702:08 (GMT)
Pan Am enters runway
KLM at C3

T_3 = 1705:53 (GMT)
Pan Am passing C3
KLM receiving ATC
clearance

T_4 = 1706:49 (GMT)
Impact point near C4

Figure 5.1   Tenerife airport diagram

The tower, which was not expecting the aircraft to take off because it had not been given clearance, interpreted the sentence as, "We are now at takeoff position." (When the Spanish, American, and Dutch investigating teams heard the tower recording together and for the first time, no one, or hardly anyone, understood that this transmission meant that they were taking off.) The controller replied: "O.K., . . . stand by for takeoff . . . I will call you." Nor did the Pan Am, on hearing the "We are now at takeoff," interpret it as an unequivocal indication of takeoff. However, in order to make their own position clear, they said, "We are still taxiing down the runway." This transmission coincided with the "Stand by for takeoff . . . I will call you," causing a whistling sound in the tower transmission and making its reception in the KLM cockpit not as clear as it should have been, even though it did not thereby become unintelligible.

The communication from the tower to the PAA requested the latter to report when it left the runway clear. In the cockpit of the KLM, nobody at first confirmed receiving these communications until the Pan Am responded to the tower's request that it should report leaving the runway with an "O.K., we'll report when we're clear." On hearing this, the KLM flight engineer asked, "Is he not clear then?" The captain did not understand him and he repeated, "Is he not clear that Pan American?" The Captain replied with an emphatic "Yes." Perhaps influenced by his great prestige, making it difficult to imagine an error of this magnitude on the part of such an expert pilot, both the copilot and flight engineer made no further objections. The impact took place about 13 seconds later (*Aviation Week*, 1978b: 71).

Tenerife as a Stressful Environment

Stress is often defined as a relation between the person and the environment, as in Holyroyd's and Lazarus's (1982) statement that "psychological stress requires a judgment that environmental and/or internal demands tax or exceed the individual's resources for managing them" (22). Their use of the word *judgment* emphasizes that stress results from an appraisal that imposes meaning on environmental demands. Typically, stress results from the appraisal that something important is at stake and in jeopardy (McGrath, 1976).

There were several events impinging on people at Tenerife that are likely to have taxed their resources and been labeled as threatening. These events, once appraised as threatening, had a cumulative, negative effect on performance (George, 1986). After we review some of the more prominent of these events, we look more closely at which concepts used in the stress literature help us most to make sense of the Tenerife disaster. It is these concepts that deserve closer attention in subsequent research on how crises are mobilized. The concepts to be discussed include size of discrepancy between demands and abilities, regression to first learned responses, and interruption as the occasion for stress. First, however, we review the demands at Tenerife.

Environmental demands at Tenerife

The KLM crew felt growing pressure from at least three sources: Dutch law, difficult maneuvers, and unpredictable weather. Because the accident took place near the end of March, members of the KLM crew were very near the limits of time they were allowed to fly in one month. This was more serious than a mere inconvenience because in 1976 the Dutch enacted a tough law on "Work and Rest Regulations for Flight Crews" (Roitsch, Babcock, & Edmunds, 1979: 14) that put strict limits on flight and duty time. The computation of these limits was complex and could no longer be done by the captain nor did the captain have any discretion to extend duty time. Therefore, the KLM crew faced the possibility of fines, imprisonment, and loss of pilot license if further delays materialized. The crew was informed that if they could leave Las Palmas by 7 PM their headquarters thought they could make it back to Amsterdam legally, but headquarters would let them know in Las Palmas.

Further pressure was added because the maneuver of turning a 747 around (backtracking) at the end of a runway is difficult, especially when that runway is narrow. It takes a minimum width of 142 feet to make a 180-degree turn in a 747 (Roitsch et al., 1979: 19) and the Tenerife runway was 150 feet wide.

Finally, the weather was unpredictable, and at Tenerife that creates some unique problems. Tenerife is 2073 feet above sea level and the sea coast is just a few miles away. This means that clouds rather than fog float into the airport. When KLM's crew backtracked, they saw a cloud 3000 feet down the runway moving toward them at 12 knots (Roitsch et al., 1979: 12), concealing the Pan Am plane on the other side. Pan Am was taxiing inside this cloud and passed its assigned runway exit because it could not see it. KLM entered that same cloud 1300 feet into its takeoff roll and that is where the collision occurred. The tower did not see the collision or the resulting fire because of the cloud, nor could the firefighters find the fire at first when they were summoned. The density of the cloud is further shown by the fact that when the firefighters started to put out the fire on one plane, the KLM plane, they didn't realize that a second plane was on fire nearby because they couldn't see it (*Aviation Week*, 1978a: 117–119).

The KLM crew was not the only group that was under pressure. Las Palmas airport had reopened for traffic at 2:30, barely 15 minutes after Pan Am had landed at Tenerife. Pan Am was ready to leave Tenerife immediately except that they were blocked by KLM 4805 and continued to be blocked for another 2.5 hours. Reactions of the Pan Am crew to the lengthening delays undoubtedly were intensified by the fact that they had originally asked to circle over Las Palmas because they had sufficient fuel to do so, a request that was denied by Spanish controllers. The Pan Am crew also saw the weather deteriorating as they waited for KLM to leave. They had been on duty 11 hours, although they were not close to the limits of their duty time.

Controllers at Tenerife were also under pressure because they were shorthanded, they did not often handle 747s, they had no ground radar, the centerline lights on the runway were not operating, they were working in English (a less familiar second language), and their normal routines for routing planes on a takeoff and landing were disrupted because they had planes parked in areas they would normally use to execute these routines.

Research leads to be pursued

The events at Tenerife provide a pretext to think more carefully about discrepancy size, regression, and interruption as components of stressful environments. These three concepts figure prominently in the events we have just reviewed, and by implication, they may also be a source of system vulnerability in other environments.

McGrath (1976) has shown that the traditional formulation of stress as a discrepancy between demands and ability operates differently from what most people thought. The highest arousal occurs when abilities are only slightly less than what is demanded and there is a chance that the person can cope. Small discrepancies create the most intense stress.

Despite all of the pressures operating at Tenerife, and despite all of the ways in which demands were mounting, the people involved were nearly able to cope successfully. Abilities almost matched demands. When the KLM captain saw the Pan Am plane in front of him on the runway, he pulled back fully on the control column in an attempt to fly over it. The tail of his plane scraped the runway and left a 66 foot long streak of metal embedded in the runway. It was only the KLM's wheels that hit the right wing and rear cabin of the Pan Am plane (which the Pan Am pilot had almost been able to steer off the takeoff runway) (Roitsch et al., 1979: 13), and when the KLM settled back on the runway after the collision, it was intact. Ignition of the extra fuel taken on to speed up departure from Las Palmas caused the KLM fatalities.

Tenerife is important, not just because it illustrates that small discrepancies can have large effects, but even more important because it seems to be an unusually clear example of the much discussed, but seldom pursued idea that stress can produce regression to first learned responses (Allnutt, 1982: 11; Barthol & Ku, 1959). If there is a key to understanding the Tenerife disaster, it may lie in this principle.

The pilot of KLM 4805 was Head of the Flight Training Department of KLM. He was a training captain: the flights he was most familiar with were those which followed a script, had fewer problems, and were shorter in duration. Furthermore, he had not flown on regular routes for 12 weeks. The importance of this background becomes evident in the context of a footnote in the Spanish Ministry's report:

> Although the captain [KLM captain] had flown for many years on European and inter-continental routes, he had been an instructor for more than 10 years, which relatively diminished his familiarity with route flying. Moreover, on simulated flights, which are so customary in flying instruction, the training pilot normally assumes the role of controller: that is, he issues takeoff clearances. In many cases no communications whatsoever are used in simulated flights, and for this reason takeoff takes place without clearance (*Aviation Week*, 1978a: 121).

Pressure leads people to fall back on what they learned first and most fully. In the case of the KLM pilot, this was giving himself clearance to takeoff. Giving clearance is what he had done most often for the last 10 years when sitting at the head of a runway and it is the response he may have reverted to as pressures mounted at Tenerife.

Both the Pan Am crew and the air traffic controllers seem also to show evidence of regression. The Pan Am captain wanted to hold short of the active runway, but he was asked to proceed down the active runway by a ground controller who spoke with a heavy accent and who did not seem to comprehend fully what Pan Am was requesting. Rather than attempt a potentially more complex negotiation to get permission to hold short, the Pan Am captain chose the more overlearned option of compliance with the controller's directive. Controller communiques also became more cryptic and harder to understand as controllers tried to cope with too many aircraft that were too big. These pressures may have made their use of English, a language which they used less frequently, more tenuous and increased the likelihood that more familiar Spanish language constructions would be substituted.

The more general implication of the disruptive effects of regression is that more recently learned complex rationales and complex collective responses are all more vulnerable to disruption than are older, simpler, more overlearned, cultural and individual responses. Requisite variety (Zeleny, 1986) is much harder to achieve than it looks. When people acquire more complex responses so that they can sense and manage more complex environments, they do not become more complex all at once. Instead, they develop their complexity serially. Under pressure, those responses acquired more recently and practiced less often, should unravel sooner than those acquired earlier, which have become more habitual. Thus, requisite variety may disappear right when it is most needed. Hypothetically, the KLM pilot had high requisite variety because he was both a training pilot and a line pilot. In reality, however, his more recent habits of line flying disappeared under pressure and were replaced by his older habits of flying under training conditions.

Among the many theories of stress that could be applied to the incidents at Tenerife, one of the most fitting is Mandler's (1982) because it encompasses so many properties of Tenerife, including interruption, limited information processing, cognitive narrowing, interpretation, plans, and autonomic arousal.

The centerpiece of Mandler's theory is the idea that interruptions trigger activity in the autonomic nervous system. This autonomic activity absorbs information processing capacity, which then decreases the efficiency of complex thought processes. By way of background, the autonomic nervous system (ANS) is the branch of the peripheral nervous system that regulates the body's internal environment and maintains homeostasis. The sympathetic branch of the ANS, through the secretion of adrenaline and noradrenaline, mobilizes the common symptoms of stress such as accelerated heart rate, increased blood pressure, and increased glucose secretion (Frankenhauser, 1986).

In Mandler's theory, autonomic activity is triggered by interruption, which he defines as "Any event, external or internal to the individual, that prevents completion of some action, thought sequences, plan, or processing structure" (92). Both action structures and intrapsychic cognitive structures can be interrupted, either when an expected event fails to occur or an unexpected event occurs.

The degree of autonomic activity that occurs following an interruption depends on two factors: first, the degree of organization of the action or thought process that is interrupted (invariant, habituated actions with high degree of expectancy among parts create a sharp increase in autonomic activity when interrupted); and second, the severity of interruption (high external demand to complete an action, coupled with repeated attempts to restart the action and repeated interruptions combine to facilitate arousal).

The autonomic activity triggered by an interruption focuses attention on two things, both of which consume considerable information processing capacity. Attention is focused on the interrupting event, and if it is not altered, on the internal autonomic activation itself. When autonomic arousal consumes scarce information processing capacity, this reduces the number of cues that can be processed from the activity that was underway at the time of the interruption.

In Mandler's model, stress is an interruption that signals an emergency and draws attention to events in the environment. In the short run, this signalling is adaptive and improves coping. Autonomic activity alerts people to the existence of threatening events, but if the threat is not dealt with and the arousal continues, then it registers in consciousness and interferes with ongoing cognitive activity. Thus, consciousness becomes the arena for troubleshooting, but unless the diagnosis and coping is swift, and the response being interrupted is weak in its organization, the troubleshooting consumes information processing capacity and this leads to the omission of important cues for task performance and an increase in cognitive inefficiency.

If we apply Mandler's concepts to the situation of the KLM pilot, we pay closer attention to such aspects as the following. The diversion to Los Rodeos was an interruption of the plan to get back to Amsterdam legally. And the cloud moving down the runway toward the KLM plane represents a potential interruption of a lower order plan to leave Las Palmas. Because neither interruption can be removed directly, autonomic arousal increases, displaces more information processing capacity, and decreases attention to peripheral cues such as radio transmissions. The severity of the interruption should be substantial because a well organized takeoff routine is interrupted, but most of all because there is a continuing, intense demand to complete the interrupted action (there is no realistic substitute activity that will get the passengers to Las Palmas unless they leave Los Rodeos on KLM 4805).

The pilot's potential focus on the interruption created by the diversion to Los Rodeos and on the consequent lengthening of duty time, coupled with potential awareness of his own internal agitation (which would be hard to label as "pleasure" but easy to label as "frustration" or "fear"), all use up information processing capacity. This leaves little remaining capacity for the immediate task of taxiing the plane to a difficult takeoff position and then flying it safely off the runway. Furthermore, there would appear to be little remaining capacity available to process cryptic, nonstandard, sometimes noisy transmissions from the tower and other aircraft.

Thus, to use Mandler's phrase, consciousness became "the arena for troubleshooting," but the troubleshooting was devoted to the question of a legal return to Amsterdam, a higher order plan, rather than to the immediate plan of leaving Los Rodeos. Attention devoted to interruption of the higher order plan used up the major share of attention that could have been allotted to the lower order, more immediate plan.

The point I want to demonstrate is that crises in general typically involve the interruption of plans or cognitive structures or actions that are underway. Because interruption is a generic accompaniment of crisis, a theory of stress and emotion that uses interruption as the point of departure is ideally suited for further investigation and application to settings involving crisis. Furthermore, susceptibility to interruption is an important predictor of system vulnerability.

The Breakdown of Coordination Under Stress

The phrase "operator error" is misleading in many ways, but among the most subtle problems is the fact that the term is singular (Hayashi, 1985). An operator error is usually a collective error (e.g., Gardenier, 1981), but it is only recently that efforts have been made to understand the ways in which team interaction generates emergent potentialities for and remedies of local failures (e.g, Hirokawa, Gouran, & Martz, 1988). The crew in the KLM cockpit provides a unique glimpse of some ways in which crises become mobilized when crew interaction breaks down.

Individualism in the cockpit

The setting in the KLM cockpit was unusual, not only because the captain was the head of flight training and a member of the top management team, but also because this captain had given the co-pilot (first officer) his qualification check in a 747 just two months earlier. This recently certified first officer made only two comments to try to influence the captain's decision during the crucial events at the head of the runway. The ALPA report of the crash describes those comments this way:

The KLM first officer was relatively young and new in his position and appeared to be mainly concerned with completing his tasks so as not to delay the captain's timing of the takeoff. He only made two comments in order to try to influence the captain's takeoff decision. When the captain first began pushing up the thrust levers, he said, "Wait a minute, we do not have an ATC clearance." The captain, rather than admitting to an oversight, closed the thrust levers and responded by saying, "No, I know that, go ahead ask." The second occurrence was at the end of the ATC clearance readback. The KLM first officer observed that the captain had commenced the takeoff and finished the ATC clearance readback by stating, "We are, uh, taking off" or "We are at takeoff" over the radio. After many hours of replaying the tapes, it is difficult to be sure what statement the first officer made. For this reason, we assume that neither the approach controller nor the Pan Am crew were positive about what was said. The Study Group believes that this ambiguous statement by the first officer was an indication that he was surprised by the KLM captain's actions in commencing the takeoff. We believe the first officer thought something was wrong with the takeoff decision by the captain, and tried to alert everyone on frequency that they were commencing takeoff. The KLM captain did not comment on his first officer's radio transmission but rather became immediately involved in setting takeoff power and tracking the runway centerline. (Roitsch et al., 1979: 18)

The first officer is not the only person acting in a manner that is more individual than collective (Wagner & Moch, 1986). The same was true for the engineer. The flight engineer was the first and current President of the European Flight Engineers Organization. There is an odd statement about him in the ALPA documents. It says that he was not in favor of integrating the functions of the engineering position with those of the pilot crewmembers, such as communication, navigation, and general monitoring of the operation of the flight. "He is said to have felt that flight engineering should consist of specialized emphasis on power plant and systems analysis and maintenance consideration" (Roitsch et al., 1979:5). Recall that the engineer was the last point where this accident could have been prevented when he asked, "Is he not clear then, that Pan Am?" Recordings suggest that he made this statement in a "tentative manner" (Roisch et al., 1979: 22) just as the plane entered the thick cloud and the pilots had their hands full keeping the plane on the runway.

Research leads to be pursued

These several observations suggest that the KLM crew acted less like a team (Hackman, 1987) than like three individuals acting in parallel. That difference becomes important in the context of an important generalization suggested by Hage (1980): "Microsociological hypotheses usually require limits. The human scale is much smaller than the organizational one – at least as far as hypotheses are concerned. Beyond this the 'world' of the individual appears to be dominated by normal curves where too much of a good thing is as bad as too little. In contrast, linearity appears to be a good first approximation in the organizational 'world'" (202).

We should expect that most microhypotheses are curvilinear and most macrohypotheses are linear. McGuire's (1968) model of individual persuasion, for example, is curvilinear and predicts that people with moderately high intelligence are more persuasible than are those who are higher or lower in intelligence. Dailey (1971) argues that individual perceptual accuracy is curvilinear and reflects a tradeoff between increasing confidence in one's own judgment and decreasing openness to new information.

When we move from individual to group, we move from micro in the direction of macro and should expect to find fewer curvilinear relationships and more linear relationships. For example, the recurrent finding that the relationship between stress and performance is curvilinear, holds for individuals, but when it is examined as a group phenomenon, the relationship is found to be more linear (Lowe & McGrath, 1971). Thus, as we move from individual to group, increases in stress should lead to increases in performance, not decreases. However, this shift is dependent on whether individuals coalesce into a team that is a distinctive entity exhibiting distinctive functional relationships or whether they merely act in the presence of another and respond and fall apart, more like individuals than like groups.

A KLM crew that is not a team is subject to curvilinear relationships, whereas a crew that is a team is more subject to linear relations. It is conceivable that more stress improves team performance but degrades individual performance, because teamwork lowers task complexity. A well-functioning team may face a simpler task than does a poorly functioning team. And research on the Yerkes-Dodson (e.g., Bregman & McAllister, 1982) law shows that performance of simple tasks is less susceptible to the disruptive effects of arousal than is performance of complex tasks.

What Hage describes resembles what Hackman (1987) seems to have in mind when he describes group synergy: synergy "refers to group-level phenomena that (1) emerge from the interaction of group members, and (2) affect how well a group is able to deal with the demands and opportunities in its performance situation" (324). Group synergy creates outcomes that "may be quite different from those that would be obtained by simply adding up the contributions of individual members" (321–322). Synergy can be either positive or, as appears to be the case with the KLM crew, negative: negative synergy is described as "a failure of coordination within the group so severe that *nobody* knows what he or she is supposed to be doing" (322). Although it is true that the plane was accelerating in a mechanically correct manner and the crew had in hand a clearance routing them to Las Palmas, lingering uneasiness about pilot judgments was neither voiced nor resolved until it was too late. What is unclear is whether the KLM crew represents a case of negative synergy with a defective group interaction process, or a case of three individuals who never became a group in the first place, or a case where a group became transformed into a collection of separate individuals when stress led the three people to fall back on dissimilar idiosyncratic ways of responding (Lazarus & Folkman, 1984: 104).

Hackman's model seems to suggest that the KLM crew in the Tenerife disaster is an example of a group where there was a slight deficiency of knowledge and skill (pilot unfamiliar with route flying, first officer recently certified on 747) but mainly a deficiency in the performance strategies (328–331) they adopted to review their design and their process and to alter it to fit the abnormal demands created by the diversion.

Helmreich's continuing research on flightcrew behavior has direct relevance to our understanding of the Tenerife disaster. As part of this program, Helmreich has assessed the managerial aspect of flight operations using a 25-item "Cockpit management attitudes survey" (Helmreich, 1984). The instrument, administered to more than 5000 pilots, has been validated on pilots classified as high and low in resource management (Helmreich, Foushee, Benson, & Russini, 1985) and covers such topics as personal reactions to stress (e.g., "pilots should feel obligated to mention their own psychological stress or physical problems to other flight-crew personnel before or during a flight"), interpersonal communication (e.g., "the pilot flying the aircraft should verbalize his plans for maneuvers and should be sure that the information is understood and acknowledged by the other pilot"), and crew roles (e.g., "There are no circumstances [except total incapacitation] where the first officer should assume command of the ship").

The items in the survey are of special interest in the context of Tenerife. It was found (Helmreich, 1984: 586) that captains and first officers differed significantly in their answers to item 5, which read, "First officers should not question the decision or actions of the captain except when they threaten the safety of the flight." The first officers agreed with the contention significantly more often than did the captains. However, on item 6, which read "Captains should encourage their first officers to question procedures during normal flight operations and in emergencies," captains were significantly less enthusiastic about encouraging input than were first officers. Thus, the idea of coordinated activity and coordinated decision making in the cockpit is a source of ambivalence and a potential source of errors that could enlarge.

These two items remained diagnostic in the validation study, because they were 2 of the 6 items that discriminated most sharply between 114 pilots rated below average or outstanding by evaluators, who actually rode with these pilots and evaluated their flight crew performance. Pilots evaluated as outstanding felt more strongly that first officers should be encouraged to question their decisions and that the first officers should question decisions other than those that threaten the safety of the flight. Pilots with below average performance held the opposite attitudes. Parenthetically, it should be noted that the item that discriminated most sharply between the outstanding and the below average was the item that read, "My decision-making ability is as good in emergencies as in routine flying situations." Below average pilots agree with this item; outstanding pilots disagree with it. Thus, not only do the outstanding pilots realize that their ability to make decisions can change under stress, but in realizing this, they may become more receptive to inputs from others that will help the crew cope.

Speech-Exchange Systems as Organizational Building Blocks

KLM as an airline is in large part constituted by its speech exchanges. When people employed by KLM talk among themselves and with outsiders, not only do they communicate within an organization, they also construct the organization itself through the process and substance of what they say. As their talk varies, the solidity and predictability of the organization itself varies. Conversations with headquarters about duty time, conversations with the KLM agent at Las Palmas about ways to hasten the departure, conversations (or the lack of them) among crew members that construct the hypothesis that the runway is empty, all are the building blocks of the order and disorder that is the hallmark of organized activity.

The unfolding of the Tenerife disaster reminds us that macroprocesses such as centralization are made up of repetitive microevents that occur frequently and in diverse locations. Organizations are built, maintained, and activated through the medium of communication. If that communication is misunderstood, the existence of the organization itself becomes more tenuous.

The Tenerife disaster was built out of a series of small, semi-standardized, misunderstandings, among which were the following:

1.   KLM requested two clearances in one transmission (we are now ready for takeoff and are waiting for ATC clearance). Any reply could be seen as a comment on both requests.
2.   The controller, in giving a clearance, used the words "after takeoff" ("maintain flight level niner zero right after takeoff proceed with heading zero four zero until intercepting the three two five radial from Las Palmas"), which could have been heard by the KLM crew as permission to leave. The ATC Manual (7110.650, October 25, 1984) clearly states, under the heading "Departure Terminology" that controllers should, "Avoid using the term 'takeoff' except to actually clear an aircraft for takeoff or to cancel a takeoff clearance. Use such terms as 'depart,' 'departure,' or 'fly' in clearances when necessary" (heading 4–20: 4–5). Thus, the Tenerife controller could have said "right turn after departure" or "right turn fly heading zero four."
3.   As we have seen, the phrase "We are now taking off" is nonstandard and produced confusion as to what it meant.
4.   When the controller said to KLM, "Okay . . . stand by for takeoff . . . I will call you," a squeal for the last portion of this message changed the timbre of the controller's voice. This may have led the KLM crew to assume that a different station was transmitting and that the message was not intended for them.
5.   The controller did not wait to receive an acknowledgement (e.g., "Roger") from KLM after he had ordered them to "standby for takeoff." Had he done so, he might have discovered a misunderstanding (Hurst, 1982: 176).
6.   Shortly before the collision, for the first and only time that day, the controller changed from calling the Pan Am plane "Clipper 1736" to the designation "Pappa Alpha 1736." This could sound like the controller is referring to a different plane (Roitsch et al., 1979: 22).

The point to be emphasized is that speech exhange and social interaction is an important means by which organization is built or dismantled. This is not to say that social interaction is a local, self-contained production that is unaffected by anything else in the setting. There clearly are "noninterpretational foundations of interpretation in social interaction" (Munch & Smelser, 1987: 367). The interpretation process itself is shaped by shared language, authority relationships that assign rights of interpretation, norms of communication, and communication. The meanings that actors co-construct are not self-created. So microanalysis cannot go it alone without macroinput. As Mead put it, people carry a slice of society around in their heads

(Alexander & Giesen, 1987: 9). But to acknowledge that slice, is also to acknowledge the carrier and the fact that the slice is realized, made visible, and given shape, in discourse.

Research leads to be pursued

We have already discussed several issues regarding communication and here will merely supplement those by suggesting that (a) communication is necessary to detect false hypotheses and (b) crises tend to create vertical communication structures when, in fact, lateral structures are often more appropriate for detection and diagnosis of the crisis.

In any crisis situation, there is a high probability that false hypotheses will develop and persist. It is largely through open exchange of messages, independent verification, and redundancy, that the existence of false hypotheses can be detected. There are at least four kinds of situations in which false hypotheses are likely to occur and in which, therefore, there is a premium on accuracy in interpersonal communication (O'Reilly, 1978). These four, identified by Davis (1958), are the following:

1. Expectancy is very high. If a pilot hears a distorted message and knows the tower would not say something meaningless, then the pilot tries to fill in the gaps, and hears the message he or she "should" have heard. This tendency increases the likelihood that a dubious hypothesis will be preserved. Applied to Tenerife, because the crew was expecting takeoff clearance and because they wanted to hear takeoff clearance, it is probable that when the tower said, "Okay, stand by for takeoff, I will call you," and when a squeal accompanied the middle portion of that message, they could have heard "OK, takeoff," which is what they expected to hear.

2. The hypothesis serves as a defense. People interpret communiques in ways that minimize anxiety. In nuclear power plant control rooms, for example, "it is easy for each operator to assume the other knows best, and, in being a good fellow, to reinforce the other's misperceptions. Thus error probabilities for people working together may be better or worse than error probabilities for individuals working independently and not communicating" (Sheridan, 1981: 23). Occasionally, a pilot's seniority and status "may be an even greater bar to admitting his mistakes – and he will only publicly reject his false hypothesis when it is too late" (Allnutt, 1982: 9). Applied to Tenerife, the hypothesis that there is no one on the runway, given the limited amount of current information present in the radio traffic that had been processed, could easily be bolstered if the pilot and the first officer both assumed that, if there were someone on the runway, surely the head of flight training would know it.

3. Attention is elsewhere. We have already encountered this explanation in the context of Mandler's theory. Allnutt (1982: 9) supplements the earlier discussion when he notes that, "if a pilot has a number of immediate tasks, and if one of those requires special attention, he is likely to be less critical in accepting hypotheses about other components of the work load." Thus a person may

ignore information that conflicts with the prevailing hypothesis when it comes from instruments that are on the periphery of attention. Applied to Tenerife, the pilot was undoubtedly more focussed on the takeoff including the approaching cloud, the difficult backtrack maneuver, and tracking the centerline on the runway without the help of lights than he was on the radio communiques that were being handled by the first officer.

4. It is after a period of high concentration. There is often a let-up near the end of a journey, when the most difficult part of the procedure has been completed. False hypotheses can persist in the face of this decreased attentiveness. Applied to Tenerife, the Spanish Ministry report of the accident actually raised this possibility: "Relaxation – after having executed the difficult 180-degree turn, which must have coincided with a momentary improvement in the visibility (as proved by the CVR, because shortly before arriving at the runway approach they turned off the widescreen wipers), the crew must have felt a sudden feeling of relief which increased their desire to finally overcome the ground problems: the desire to be airborne" (*Aviation Week*, 1978a: 121). The false hypothesis that the runway was clear was something the crew expected to be true, something they wanted to be true, something they dimly felt might not be true, but in the context of hierarchical communications was something they jointly treated as if it were true.

The likelihood that crises impose hierarchical constraints (Stohl & Redding, 1987) on speech-exchange systems is a straightforward extrapolation from the finding that stress leads to centralization (see Staw, Sandelands, & Dutton, 1981). This finding traditionally has been interpreted in a way that masks a potentially key cognitive step that allows us to understand Tenerife more fully. Before stress creates centralization, it must first increase the salience of hierarchies and formal authority, if it is to lead to centralization. It is the increased salience of formal structure that transforms open communication among equals into stylized communications between unequals. Communication dominated by hierarchy activates a different mindset regarding what is and is not communicated and different dynamics regarding who initiates on whom. In the cockpit, where there is a clear hierarchy, especially when the captain who outranks you is also the instructor who trained you, it is likely that attempts to create interaction among equals is more complex, less well learned, and dropped more quickly in favor of hierarchical communication, when stress increases.

What is especially striking in studies of communication distortion within hierarchical relationships (Fulk & Mani, 1985), is that the "types of subordinate message distortion [to please the receiver] are quite similar to the strategies used to address message overload. They include gatekeeping, summarization, changing emphasis within a message, withholding, and changing the nature of the information" (Stohl & Redding, 1987: 481). The similar effects of hierarchy and overload on communication suggests that one set of distortions can solve two different problems. A mere change in emphasis in a communication upward can both reduce message overload and please the recipient. These mutually reinforcing solutions to two distinct problems of crises – overload and centralization should exert continuing pressure on communication in the direction of distortion and away from accuracy.

Interactive Complexity as Indigenous to Human Systems

As the day unfolded at Tenerife after 1:30 in the afternoon, there was a gradual movement from loosely coupled events to tightly coupled events, and from a linear transformation process to a complex transformation process with unintended and unnoticed contingencies. Human systems are not necessarily protected from disasters by loose coupling and linear transformation systems, because these qualities can change when people are subjected to stress, ignore data, regress, centralize, and become more self-centered.

Thus it would be a mistake to conclude from Perrow's (1984) work that organizations are either chronically vulnerable to normal accidents or chronically immune from them. Perrow's (1984: 63) structural bias kept him from seeing clearly that, when you take people and their limitations into account, susceptibility to normal accidents can change within a relatively short time.

Several events at Tenerife show the system growing tighter and more complex:

1. Controllers develop ad hoc routing of two jumbo jets on an active runway because they have no other place to put them (Roisch et al., 1979: 8).
2. Controllers have to work with more planes than they have before, without the aid of ground radar, without a tower operator, and with no centerline lights to help in guiding planes.
3. Controllers keep instructing pilots to use taxiway "Third Left" to exit the active runway, but this taxiway is impossible for a 747 to negotiate. It requires a 148-degree left turn followed by an immediate 148-degree right turn onto a taxiway that is 74 feet wide (Roisch et al., 1979: 19). Thus, neither the KLM pilot nor the Pan Am pilot are able to do what the controller tells them to do, so both pilots assume that the controller really means for them to use some other taxiway. Nevertheless, the KLM pilot may have assumed that the Pan Am pilot had exited by taxiway third left (Roisch et al., 1979: 24).
4. The longer the delay at Tenerife, the higher the probability that all hotel rooms in Las Palmas would be filled, the higher the probability that the air corridor back to Amsterdam would be filled with evening flights, occasioning other air traffic delays, and the greater the chance for backups at Las Palmas itself, all of which increased the chances that duty time would expire while the KLM crew was in transit.
5. Throughout the afternoon there was the continuing possibility that the terrorist activities that had closed Las Palmas could spread to Tenerife. In fact, when the tower personnel heard the KLM explosion, they first thought that fuel tanks next to the tower had been blown up by terrorists (Roisch et al., 1979: 8).

Research leads to be pursued

Stress paves the way for its own intensification and diffusion because it can tighten couplings and raise complexity. Each of the several effects of stress that we have reviewed up to this point either increases dependencies among elements within the system or increases the number of events that are unnoticed, uncontrolled, and unpredictable. For example, the same stress that produces an error due to regression paves the way for that error to have a much larger effect by increasing the complexity of the context in which the error first occurred. As stress increases, perception narrows, more contextual information is lost, and parameters deteriorate to more extreme levels before they are noticed, all of which leads to more puzzlement, less meaning, and more perceived complexity. Not only does stress increase the complexity, it also tightens couplings. Threat leads to centralization, which tightens couplings between formal authority and solutions that will be influential, even though the better solutions may be in the hands of those with less authority. Notice how the same process that produces the error in the first place, also shapes the context so that the error will fan out with unpredictable consequences.

Normally, individual failures stay separate and unlinked if they occur in a linear transformation system where they affect only an adjacent step and if they occur in a loosely coupled system where that effect may be indeterminate (Perrow, 1984: 97, characterizes "airways" as linear, modestly coupled systems). If the couplings become tighter (e.g., slack such as excess duty time is depleted) and if the linear transformation process becomes more complex through the development of a greater number of parallel events having unknown but multiple logic entailments (Douglas, 1985: 173), then more failures can occur and they can affect a greater number of additional events.

Cost cutting at the Bhopal plant prior to the disastrous gas leak illustrates the subtle way in which minor changes can tighten couplings and increase complexity:

> When cost cutting is focused on less important units [in Union Carbide], it is not just decreased maintenance which raises susceptibility to crisis. Instead, it is all of the indirect effects on workers of the perception that their unit doesn't matter. This perception results in increased inattention, indifference, turnover, low cost improvisation, and working-to-rule, all of which remove slack, lower the threshold at which a crisis will escalate, and increase the number of separate places at which a crisis could start. As slack decreases, the technology becomes more interactively complex, which means there are more places where a minor lapse can escalate just when there are more minor lapses occurring. (Weick, 1988: 313)

The point of these details is that "normal accidents" may not be confined to obvious sites of technical complexity such as nuclear power plants. Instead, they may occur in any system that is capable of changing from loose to tight and from linear to complex. As we have suggested, any system, no matter how loose and linear it may seem, can become tighter and more complex when it is subjected to overload, misperception, regression, and individualized response.

Implications and Conclusions

Although we have examined closely only a single incident, we have done so in the belief that Tenerife is a prototype of system vulnerability in general. Among the generic properties of Tenerife that are likely to be found in other systems, we would include the interruption of important routines among and within interdependent systems, interdependencies that become tighter, a loss of cognitive efficiency due to autonomic arousal, and a loss of communication accuracy due to increased hierarchical distortion. This configuration of events seems to encourage the occurrence and rapid diffusion of multiple errors by creating a feedback loop which magnifies these minor errors into major problems.

Implications for both research and practice of the processes observed in this prototype have been scattered throughout the preceding account and I conclude by reviewing some of those which seem especially important. The concepts that I found most helpful were concepts that have been around for some time. The good news is that much of the old news about crises and behavior remains viable news. What I have basically done is gather these bits and pieces of understanding in one place, sort through them for their relevance to a single dramatic event, and then propose that the resulting assemblage represents a plausible configuration that explains the genesis of a large crisis from small beginnings. The account I have assembled is as much a reminder of tools already in hand as it is a set of speculations about new variables.

Nevertheless, in assembling, editing, and reformulating existing ideas, several themes for future research were identified and I review seven of them below.

First, the concept of temporary systems (e.g., Bryman, Bresnen, Beardsworth, Ford, & Keil, 1987; Goodman & Goodman, 1976; Miles, 1964) has been around for some time, but seems worth resuscitating because air crews, task forces, and project teams are both plentiful and doing increasingly consequential work. It is not just air crews with their constantly changing personnel that form an odd mix of the mechanistic and the organic. Any group with a transient population is subjected to some of the same dynamics (e.g., see Gaba, Maxwell, & DeAnda, 1987 on mishaps during anesthesia administration). Thus, it would be instructive to learn to what extent parallels of Tenerife occur in the larger category of organizational forms called temporary systems.

Second, it goes without saying that we must continue to refine and make more precise the concept of stress. The concept plays an important role. It blends together emotion, anxiety, strain, pressure, and arousal. This blending can be troublesome because of the resulting ambiguity, but the global concept of stress nevertheless serves the important function of reminding investigators that affect is a vital part of experience and the human condition (Kemper, 1987). That reminder is worth whatever terminological distress it may occasion.

Third, there appears to be an important but little understood tradeoff between cohesion and accuracy in groups (e.g., Weick, 1983). Janis's (1982) important research on groupthink demonstrates the many insidious ways that sensing and criticism can be sacrificed in the service of group maintenance. Tenerife reminds us again of how delicate this balance can be and of the necessity to see the conditions under which the dilemma can be accommodated.

Fourth, in a related vein, we may need to restudy the possibility that pluralistic ignorance (Miller & McFarland, 1987) is a potential contributor to early stages of crisis. Pluralistic ignorance applied to an incipient crisis means I am puzzled by what is going on, but I assume that no one else is, especially because they have more experience, more seniority, higher rank. That was the error with the Enterprise at Bishop Rock (Roberts, in press) (i.e., "surely the captain knows that is a rock just ahead") as well as with the KLM takeoff (i.e., "surely the captain knows that the runway may not be clear").

The first officer, who is reluctant to take off for Las Palmas but assumes no one else is, may not be all that different from the person who is reluctant to ride to Abilene (Harvey, 1974) on a sticky Sunday afternoon, but assumes no one else is. The conditions under which that paradox gets resolved before damage is done remain important to articulate.

Fifth, if the elements that form the pre-crisis context become tightly coupled and more complex, then failures occur more often because of complexity and spread farther and more quickly because of tighter couplings. That is important, but fairly obvious. What is less obvious, and what the analysis of Tenerife suggests, is that persistent failures (those that remain unresolved and lead to a buildup of autonomic arousal) can also tighten couplings and increase complexity. Failures use up information processing capacity. With less information processing capacity, people ignore more central cues, invoke simpler mental models that leave out key indicators, and become more tolerant of unexplained and unpredicted entailments. Failures make authority structures, divisions of labor, and assigned responsibilities more salient. This can tighten the coupling between assigned roles and role behavior in the crisis, even though such in-role behavior may be dysfunctional. Notice that this tightening between assigned pre-crisis roles and action during crisis is especially likely if those pre-crisis roles are overlearned. Even though improvisation might reduce the impact of a crisis, it is difficult when arousal is high and when, as Helmreich (1984) demonstrated, captains are wary of the idea that there are times when first officers should override their judgment. This wariness surely does not get lost on ambitious first officers.

Special attention should be directed at systems that are either loose/linear, loose/complex, or tight/linear, because they all are potentially vulnerable to small failures that are difficult to contain. The fact that so many systems are included within these three categories is the basic point being emphasized.

If tightening and complication of systems can be blocked, slowed, or dampened, or if people can be trained and rewarded to redesign the performance strategies when both their context and their structure become tighter and more complex, then failures should stay small and local.

Sixth, we need to see whether, as group interaction improves, task complexity (Wood, 1986) decreases? If so, we then need to see if this is a plausible means by which cohesive groups are less susceptible to disruption from stress than are uncohesive groups? This may be one means by which cohesive groups continue to function productively even though they are subjected to very high levels of stress.

And seventh, we need to see whether an increment in stress increases the salience of formal structure and authority relations. If so, this may be a considerable deterrent to expertise rather than position controlling the content of an early diagnosis. Given the tendency for communication among equals to turn hierarchical under stress, it would appear necessary that those at the top of the hierarchy explicitly legitimate and model equal participation, if they are to override that salience of hierarchy.

Implications for practice

Again, the implications for practice that emerge from an analysis of Tenerife are not unusual, but they bear repeating because we are likely to see many more situations in the future that assume the outlines of Tenerife.

First, part of any job requirement must be the necessity for talk. Strong, silent types housed in systems with norms favoring taciturnity can stimulate unreliable performance because misunderstandings are not detected. Of the four implications for managerial practice derived by Sutton and Kahn (1987) in their influential stress review, three concern talk: be generous with information, acknowledge the information functions of the informal organizations, do not hold back bad news too long. LaPorte, Rochlin, and Roberts (e.g., LaPorte & Consolini, 1989) find that reliable performance and amount of talk exchanged co-vary.

What our analysis of Tenerife has uncovered is the possibility that with communication a complex system becomes more understandable (you learn some missing pieces that make sense of your experience) and more linear, predictable, and controllable.

The recommendation that people should keep talking is not as simple as it appears, because one of the problems at Three Mile Island (TMI) was too many people in the control room talking at one time with different hunches as to what was going on. The din created by tense voices plus multiple alarms, however, would make it all but impossible to single out talk as uniquely responsible for confusion, misdiagnosis, and delayed responding. The crucial talk at TMI should have occurred in hours before the control room got cluttered, not after.

If things do not make sense, speak up. This is the norm that needs to be created. Only by doing so can you break pluralistic ignorance (i.e., "you too, I thought I was the only one who didn't know what was going on").

Second, cultivate interpersonal skills, select people on the basis of their interpersonal skills, and devote training time to the development of interpersonal skills (Helmreich, 1983). As technologies become more complex than any one person can comprehend, groups of people will be needed to register and form collective mental models of these technologies. Requisite variety is no longer an individual construct; it must be viewed as a collective accomplishment (Orton, 1988). But to create collective requisite variety, leaders must create a climate in which trust, doubt, openness, candor, and pride can co-exist and be rewarded.

Third, remember that stress is additive, and that off the job stressors cumulate with those that arise on the job. Encourage norms that people under stress should alert others who are dependent on them that their performance may be sub-par. That norm is hard to implant in a macho culture where coping is perceived as grounds for promotion and an admission of problems is seen as grounds for being plateaued.

Fourth, treat chaos as a resource and reframe crises into opportunities to demonstrate and reaffirm competence as well as to enlarge response repertoires. One of the most important contributions of chaos theory (e.g., Gleick, 1987) as well as the counsel to "thrive on chaos" (Peters, 1987) is that they suggest that disorder contains some order; therefore, prediction, if not control, is possible. If chaos theory is not convincing on those instrumental grounds, then at least it suggests that chaos is indigenous, patterned, normal, and to be expected. Appreciation of those aspects of chaos may cushion the arousal that occurs when it becomes the source of interruption. Any response is seen as susceptible to interruption: one never becomes wedded to a single strategy but instead, repeatedly cultivates options and alternative routes by which projects can be completed.

Fifth, controllability makes a difference (Karasek, 1979; Sutton & Kahn 1987), which means discretion must be generously distributed throughout the system. The removal of the KLM pilot's discretion to extend duty hours increased the severity of the interruption occasioned by the diversion to Tenerife and may have produced more cognitive narrowing than would have occurred had the effects of that interruption been bypassed by an extension of duty time.

Sixth, if a strong case can be made that new complex skills should be learned to replace old skills that are no longer appropriate, then the new skills should be overlearned, but with a clear understanding of the tradeoffs involved. It is important to overlearn new skills to offset the tendency for that skill to unravel in favor of earlier learning under pressure of stress. But, overlearning is a mixed blessing. It reduces the likelihood of regression, but in doing so it heightens the disruptive effects of an interruption because overlearning makes the sequence of the response more invariant. The remedy would seem to be to give people more substitute routes by which an interrupted response can be carried to completion and inoculate people against the disruptive qualities of interruption. Help them expect interruption and give them a mindset and actions to cope with interruption.

And seventh, forewarn people about the four conditions under which they are especially vulnerable to false hypotheses. Remind people to be mindful when they are most tempted to act in a mindless fashion (i.e., when they expect something, when they want something, when they are preoccupied with something, and when they finish something).

In conclusion, small details can enlarge and, in the context of other enlargements, create a problem that exceeds the grasp of individuals or groups. Interactive complexity is likely to become more common, not less so in the next few decades. It is not a fixed commodity, nor is it a peculiar pathology confined to nuclear reactors and chemical plants. It may be the most volatile linkage point between micro and macro processes we are likely to find in the next few years.

Note

Early abbreviated versions of this article were presented at the dedication of the Stanford Center for Organizational Research, at the School of Library and Information Management at Emporia State University, and at the Strategic Management Research Center at the University of Minnesota. Animated discussions with people at all three locations contributed immeasurably to the final product, and I deeply appreciate the interest and help of those people.

References

Alexander, J.C. & Giesen, B. 1987 From reduction to linkage: the long view of the micro-macro debate. In J.C. Alexander, B. Giesen, R. Munch, & N.J. Smelser (Eds.), *The macro-micro link*: 1–42. Berkeley: University of California.

Allnutt, M. 1982. Human factors: basic principles. In R. Hurst & L.R. Hurst (Eds.), *Pilot error* (2nd ed.): 1–22. New York: Jason Aronson.

Aviation Week and Space Technology. 1978a. Spaniards analyze Tenerife accident. November 20: 113–121.

Aviation Week and Space Technology. 1978b. Clearances cited in Tenerife collision. November 27: 69–74.

Barthol, R.P, & Ku, N.D. 1959. Regression under stress to first learned behavior. *Journal of Abnormal and Social Psychology*, 59: 134–136.

Bregman, N.J. & McAllister, H.A. 1982. Motivation and skin temperature biofeedback: Yerkes-Dodson revisited. *Psychophysiology*, 19: 282–285.

Bryman, A., Bresnen, M., Beardsworth, A.D., & Ford, J. & Keil, E.T. 1987 The concept of the temporary system: the case of the construction project. *Research in the Sociology of Organizations*, 5: 253–283.

Dailey, C.A. 1971. *Assessment of lives*. San Francisco: Jossey-Bass.

Davis, R.D. 1958. Human engineering in transportation accidents. *Ergonomics*, 2: 24–33.

Douglas, M. 1985. Loose ends and complex arguments. *Contemporary Sociology*, 14 (2): 171–173.

Frankenhauser, M. (1986). A psychological framework for research on human stress and coping. In M.H. Appley & R. Trumbull (Eds.), *Dynamics of stress*: 101–116. New York: Plenum.

Fulk, J., & Mani, S. 1985. Distortion of communication in hierarchical relationships. In M. McLaughlin (Ed.), *Communication yearbook 9*: 483–510. Newbury Park, CA: Sage.

Gaba, D.M., Maxwell, M. & DeAnda, A. 1987 Anesthetic mishaps: breaking the chain of accident evolution. *Anesthesiology*, 66: 670–676.

Gardenier, J.S. 1981. Ship navigational failure detection and diagnosis. In J. Rasmussen & W.B. Rouse (Eds.), *Human detection and diagnosis of system failures*: 49–74. New York: Plenum.

George, A.L. 1986. The impact of crisis-induced stress on decision making. In F. Solomon & R.Q. Marston (Eds.), *The medical implications of nuclear war*: 529–552. Washington, DC: National Academy of Science Press.

Gleick, J. 1987 *Chaos: Making a new science*. New York: Viking.

Goodman, R.A., & Goodman, L.P. 1976. Some management issues in temporary systems: a study of professional development and manpower – the theater case. *Administrative Science Quarterly*, 21: 494–501.

Hackman, J.R. 1987 The design of work teams. In J.W. Lorsch (Ed.), *Handbook of organizational behavior*: 315–342. Englewood Cliffs, NJ: Prentice-Hall.

Hage, J. 1980. *Theories of organizations*. New York: Wiley.

Harvey, J.B. 1974. The Abilene paradox. *Organizational Dynamics*, 3 (1): 63–80.

Hayashi, K. 1985. Hazard analysis in chemical complexes in Japan – especially those caused by human errors. *Ergonomics*, 28: 835–841.

Helmreich, R.L. 1983. *What changes and what endures: the capabilities and limitations of training and selection*. Paper presented at the Irish Air Line Pilots/Aer Lingus Flight Operations Seminar, Dublin.

Helmreich, R.L. 1984. Cockpit management attitudes. *Human Factors*, 26: 583–589.

Helmreich, R.L., Foushee, H.C., Benson, R., & Russini, W. 1985. *Cockpit resource management: exploring the attitude – performance linkage*. Paper presented at Third Aviation Psychology Symposium, Ohio State University, Columbus.

Hirokawa, R.Y., Gouran, D.S., & Martz, A.E. 1988. Understanding the sources of faulty group decision making: a lesson from the Challenger disaster. *Small Group Behavior* 19: 411–433.

Holroyd, K.A. & Lazarus, R.S. 1982. Stress, coping, and somatic adaptation. In L. Goldberger & S. Breznitz (Eds.), *Handbook of stress*: 21–35. New York: Free Press.

Hurst, R. 1982. Portents and challenges. In R. Hurst & L.R. Hurst (Eds.), *Pilot error* (2nd ed.): 164–177 New York: Jason Aronson.

Janis, I.R. (1982). *Victims of groupthink* (2nd ed.). Boston: Houghton-Mifflin.

Karasek, R.A. 1979. Job demands, job decision latitude and mental strain: implications for job redesign. *Administrative Science Quarterly*, 24: 285–308.

Kemper, T.D. 1987 How many emotions are there? Wedding the social and the autonomic components. *American Journal of Sociology*, 93: 263–289.

LaPorte T., & Consolini, P.M. 1989. *Working in practice but not in theory: theoretical challenges of high reliability organizations*. Unpublished manuscript, Department of Political Science, University of California at Berkeley.

Lazarus, R.S., & Folkman, S. 1984. *Stress, appraisal, and coping*. New York: Springer.

Lowe, R., & McGrath, J.E. 1971. *Stress, arousal, and performance: some findings calling for a new theory*. Project report, AF1161–67, AFOSR, University of Illinois.

Mandler, G. 1982. Stress and thought processes. In L. Goldberger & S. Breznitz (Eds.), *Handbook of stress*: 88–104. New York: Free Press.

McGrath, J.E. 1976. Stress and behavior in organizations. In M.D. Dunnette (Ed.), *Handbook of industrial and organizational psychology*: 1351–1395. Chicago: Rand-McNally.

McGuire, W.J. 1968. Personality and susceptibility to social influence. In E.F Borgatta & W.W. Lambert (Eds.), *Handbook of personality theory and research*: 1130–1187 Chicago: Rand-McNally.

Miles, M.B. 1964. On temporary systems. In M.B. Miles (Ed.), *Innovation in education*: 437–490. New York: Teachers College Bureau of Publications.

Miller, D.T. & McFarland, C. 1987 Pluralistic ignorance: when similarity is interpreted as dissimilarity. *Journal of Personality and Social Psychology*, 53: 298–305.

Munch, R., & Smelser, N.J. 1987 Relating the micro and macro. In J.C. Alexander, B. Giesen, R. Munch, & N.J. Smelser (Eds.), *The macro-micro link*: 356–387 Berkeley: University of California.

O'Reilly, C.A. 1978. The intentional distortion of information in organizational communication: a laboratory and field approach. *Human Relations*, 31: 173–193.

Orton, J.D. 1988. *Group design implications of requisite variety*. Unpublished manuscript, School of Business Administration, University of Michigan.

Perrow, C. 1981. Normal accident at Three Mile Island. *Society*, 18 (5); 17–26.

Perrow, C. 1984. *Normal accidents*. New York: Basic.

Peters, T.J. 1987 *Thriving on chaos*. New York: Knopf.

Roberts, K.H. in press. Bishop Rock dead ahead: the grounding of U.S.S. Enterprise, *Naval Institute Proceedings*.

Roitsch, P.A., Babcock, G.L. & Edmunds, W.W. 1979. *Human factors report on the Tenerife accident*. Washington, D.C.: Airline Pilots Association.

Sheridan, T.B. 1981. Understanding human error and aiding human diagnostic behavior in nuclear power plants. In J. Rasmussen & W.B. Rouse (Eds.), *Human detection and diagnosis of system failures*: 19–35. New York: Plenum.

Shrivastava, P. 1987 *Bhopal: Anatomy of a crisis.* Cambridge, MA: Ballinger.

Staw, B.M., Sandelands, L.E., & Dunon, J.E. 1981. Threat-rigidity effects in organizational behavior: a multilevel analysis. *Adminstrative Science Quarterly,* 26: 501–524.

Stohl, C. & Redding, W.C. 1987 Messages and message exchange processes. In F.M. Jablin, L.L. Putnam, K.H. Roberts, & L.W. Porter (Eds.), *Handbook of organizational communication:* 451–502. Newbury Park, CA: Sage.

Sutton, R.I. & Kahn, R.L. 1987 Prediction, understanding, and control as antidotes to organizational stress. In J. W. Lorsch (Ed.), Handbook of organizational behavior: 272–285. Englewood Cliffs, NJ: Prentice-Hall.

Wagner, J.A. & Moch, M.K. 1986. Individualism collectivism: concept and measure. *Group and Organization Studies,* 11:280–304.

Weick, K.E. 1983. Contradictions in a community of scholars: the cohesion-accuracy tradeoff. *The Review of Higher Education,* 6(4): 253–267.

Weick, K.E. 1988. Enacted sensemaking in crisis situations. *Journal of Management Studies.* 25: 305–317.

Wood, R.E. 1986. Task complexity: definition of the construct. *Organizational Behavior and Human Performance,* 37: 60–82.

Zeleny, M. 1986. The law of requisite variety: is it applicable to human systems? *Human Systems Management,* 6: 269–271.

6

Technology as Equivoque: Sensemaking in New Technologies

New technologies, such as complex production systems that use computers (Ettlie, 1988; Majchrzak, 1988; Susman and Chase, 1986; Zuboff, 1988), create unusual problems in sensemaking for managers and operators. For example, people now face the novel problem of how to recover from incomprehensible failures in production systems and computer systems. To solve this problem, people must assume the role of failure managers who are heavily dependent on their mental models of what might have happened, although they can never be sure because so much is concealed. Not only does failure take on new forms, but there is also continuous intervention improvement, and redesign, which means that the implementation state of development never stops (Berniker and Wacker, 1988, p. 2).

Problems like these affect organizational structure in ways not previously discussed by organizational scholars. To understand new technologies and their impacts, we need to supplement existing concepts. Thus, the purpose of this chapter is to describe features of new technologies that necessitate a revision in the concepts we use to understand their place in organized life and then to suggest what some of those revised concepts might be.

The central idea is captured by the phrase *technology as equivoque*. An *equivoque* is something that admits of several possible or plausible interpretations and therefore can be esoteric, subject to misunderstandings, uncertain, complex, and recondite. New technologies mean many things because they are simultaneously the source of stochastic events, continuous events, and abstract events. Complex systems composed of these three classes of events make both limited sense and many different kinds of sense. They make limited sense because so little is visible and so much is transient, and they make many different kinds of sense because the dense interactions that occur within them can be modeled in so many different ways. Because new technologies are equivocal, they require ongoing structuring and sensemaking if they are to be managed.

The effects of these equivocal properties on organizations can be grasped more readily if analysts talk about structuration rather than structure, affect rather than analysis, dynamic interactive complexity rather than static interactive complexity, and premise control rather than behavioral control.

To flesh out this analysis, we will briefly examine prevailing thought about technology, after which we will discuss properties of new technologies and then four conceptual shifts that help us understand the organizational implications of these properties. We will conclude by reframing the main argument.

Definitions of Technology

Three definitions of technology provide a context that illustrates strengths and weaknesses of prevailing thought about technology:

1. "We define technology as the physical combined with the intellectual or knowledge processes by which materials in some form are transformed into outputs used by another organization or subsystem within the same organization" (Hulin and Roznowski, 1985, p. 47).
2. Technology is "a family of methods for associating and channeling other entities and forces, both human and nonhuman. It is a method, one method, for the conduct of heterogeneous engineering, for the construction of a relatively stable system of related bits and pieces with emergent properties in a hostile or indifferent environment" (Law, 1987, p. 115).
3. "Technology refers to a body of knowledge about the means by which we work on the world, our arts and our methods. Essentially, it is knowledge about the cause and effect relations of our actions. . . . Technology is knowledge that can be studied, codified, and taught to others" (Berniker, 1987, p. 10).

Definition 1 is representative in the sense that it includes the components of skills, equipment, and knowledge mentioned by most scholars of technology. In contrast to many other definitions, however, explicit mention is made of raw materials and a transformation process, items that are often implicit in other definitions. Also novel to this definition is the mention that output might be used within the same organization. Inclusion of this contingency makes it possible to talk about multiple, diverse technologies within the same organization. Finally, this definition is noteworthy because of its emphasis on processes rather than on static knowledge, skills, and equipment. By equating technology with process, the authors alert us to the importance of changes over time and sequence.

Definition 2 is rather unusual. The definition highlights the contentious, adversarial environment of multiple constituencies that have a stake in the design and operation of technology (for example, see Perrow's [1984] discussion of production pressures for one source of contention). The definition captures better than most the fact that, both in its design and in its operation, technology is a partially fortuitous emergent outcome of a relatively stable network of relations among quite diverse elements. The definition counterbalances those definitions of technology that depict the process as deliberate, rationalized, homogeneous, planned, systematized, and controlled by prospective rationality. The design and operation of technology do share some of those qualities, but they do not exhaust the character of the process when it unfolds in politicized organizations, and Law's (1987) definition allows us to describe technology in a way more compatible with this quality of organizations.

Definition 3 becomes most sensible when it is supplemented by the author's definition of a technical system as "a specific combination of machines, equipment, and methods used to produce some valued outcome . . . Every technical system embodies a technology. It derives from a large body of knowledge which provides the basis for design decisions" (Berniker, 1987, p. 10).

By differentiating between the opportunities provided by knowledge ("technology") and the choice of one combination from this larger set as "the" technical system, Berniker makes the design of technology a more explicit, more public process that need not be left to engineers. Definitions such as definition 1 fold together knowledge, design, and a specific manifestation of technology, with the result that technology becomes a given, rather than a variable. As we will see shortly, the very complexity and incomprehensibility of new technologies may warrant a reexamination of our knowledge of cause-effect relations in human actions and the choice of a different combination of machines, equipment, and methods to produce the outcomes for which new technologies are instrumental.

Berniker's portrait, however, is not without problems, since technology often follows rather than precedes a technical system. Especially with new technologies, a specific technical system is often the vehicle to discover cause-effect linkages in human action that we had not seen before, but which can now be used in subsequent designs. Thus, technology is both an a posteriori product of lessons learned while implementing a specific technical system and an a priori source of options that can be realized in a specific technical system.

While we will try in our subsequent discussion to distinguish between technology as knowledge and a technical system as a specific subset of that knowledge, this will often be difficult, precisely because new technologies have considerable overlap between their technology and their technical systems. Given their short history and novel engines, the size of the understanding is not much larger than the size of any one technical system. This in no way cuts down the number of combinations that are possible in technical systems involving new technology, but it does mean that these combinations are informed by hunches rather than by well-developed knowledge, that considerable improvisation is involved, and that design and operation have a strong core of experimentation and unjustified trial and error. The very fact that new technologies have technologies and technical systems that are roughly similar in size recommends their description as equivoques.

Definitions of technology similar to those just reviewed have been translated into survey items intended to capture variations in skills, equipment, and technique. Scott (1987) and Hancock, Macy, and Peterson (1983) provide helpful summaries of the measurement that has been attempted.

One of the more influential frameworks to capture variations in technology is Perrow's (1967) attempt to differentiate technologies on the basis of the number of exceptions that performers encounter and the extent to which the exceptions they do encounter are analyzable. Lynch (1974) and Withey, Daft, and Cooper (1983) have developed instruments that assess these two dimensions. Perrow (1986, p. 143) has suggested that the essence of his notion can be tapped informally with this interview question: "Ask people about the frequency with which they come across problems for which there is no ready solution at hand, and about which no one else is likely to know much." While this line of questioning may elicit reactions to such accompaniments of technology as uncertainty, unpredictability, and variability, it obscures important details of this variability. For example, the item assumes that people know when they come across problems, and yet many of the newer technologies, such as nuclear power generation, have as one of their distinguishing properties the fact that operators often do not even realize that problems exist for which they need solutions. Thus, to ask people about exceptions and analyzability misses key aspects of newer technologies characterized by interactive complexity (Perrow, 1984). The Perrow items also bury other organizational information that becomes important in the context of newer technologies. When a person reports that there is no ready solution at hand, that may reflect the technology but it also may reflect aspects of the respondent, such as trained incapacity, specialization in some other technology, limited experience, low self-esteem, low cognitive complexity, and so on. The report of no ready solution at hand may also reflect organizational dimensions. For example, one of the many streams found in organized anarchies is a steady stream of solutions in search of problems. If people report that solutions are not at hand, this could mean that existing access structures are funneling solutions away from the respondent or funneling novel problems toward that person.

When respondents report not only that they do not know of solutions but also that no one else is likely to know either, that may say something about the technology but it also may mean that people have no network, or that they have a network but it has no weak ties, or that they are reluctant to ask for help, or that they are not reluctant but instead assume that no one has the answer, a prophecy that becomes fulfilled when they seek out no one and remain without an answer.

As technologies become more automated, abstract, continuous, flexible, and complex, they may become less analyzable and encounter more exceptions. These changes in analyzability and exceptions should be patterned, but the question is whether our concepts and instruments are sufficiently sensitive to capture these patterns and to differentiate degrees of routineness (Perrow, 1986) and degrees of analyzability. The answer seems to be no.

Properties of New Technologies

The purpose of this section is to single out three qualities of newer technologies – stochastic events, continuous events, and abstract events – that, while present in older technologies, seem now to be more prominent and to have distinctive organizational implications. Furthermore, these three properties seem not to be reflected in existing measures of technology, which means they are not yet important independent variables in organizational explanations. All three properties also underscore why it is now more crucial than ever to articulate the micro side of technology and to link it with macro concepts.

Stochastic events

Davis and Taylor (1976) suggest that previous industrial-era technologies were deterministic, with clear cause-effect relationships among what was to be done, how it was to be done, and when it was to be done. Newer automated technologies no longer are dominated by determinism. Instead, "people operate in an environment whose 'important events' are randomly occurring and unpredictable" (Davis and Taylor, 1976, p. 388).

For example, Buchanan and Bessant (1985) describe the difficulties people had replacing batch production of pigments with computerized process controls, because their understanding of the mechanisms of pigment chemistry was weak. Neither the speed of the reactions nor the nature of the side effects was well understood, which meant that manufacturing was closer to alchemy than anything else. A world of alchemy is a world of stochastic events. Berniker (1987) describes technical systems built around poorly understood processes and notes as an example the lingering uncertainty involved in smelting aluminum from bauxite and in bonding metal parts in aircraft. Technical systems that involve dense interaction (such as military command and control systems) are continually vulnerable to unexpected interruptions from staff who request explanations, justifications, revisions, or attention to the fact that they exist (Roberts, forthcoming; Metcalf, 1986).

While technologies have always had stochastic events – for example, steam boilers did blow up (Burke, 1972) – the unique twist in new technologies is that the uncertainties are permanent rather than transient. All technologies surprise operators at first, but as learning develops, surprises recede. That normal development, however, occurs less often with new technologies, because of their poorly understood processes and raw material, continuous revision of the design of the process, and the fact that implementation often is the means by which the technology itself is designed. Furthermore, with increased dependence on computers, there is the dual problem that computers often do not give a complete and accurate picture of the state of the process and, when they do, "operator state identification and control activities gradually become decoupled from actual process state as a function of execution problems or the unexpected" (Woods, O'Brien, and Hanes, 1987, p. 1741).

Existing concepts in organizational theory are generally insensitive to sources and consequences of stochastic events, referring instead simply to variable inputs and outcomes, to unanalyzable exceptions (Perrow, 1967), or to unclear cause-effect relations that require the decision strategy of judgment (Thompson and Tuden, 1959). The problem is not that these concepts are wrong but rather that they lump together diverse, crucial properties of new technologies that have diverse consequences. For example, Berniker (private communication) has suggested that stochastic events can occur in one of four forms. They can either be understood or not be understood, and they can occur either once or recurrently. Stochastic events that occur once and are understood are the most common and are not especially arousing. Single events that are not understood are outside the organization's experience and are much more stressful. If puzzling events occur repeatedly, then there is some chance for learning, but only if the organization operates in an experimental mode, which can be dangerous with some technologies (Weick, 1988a). While all four forms have unclear cause-effect relations, the implications for adaptation, learning, and structuring are quite different among them.

If new technologies have a larger stochastic component, this suggests several things. Concepts need to be tuned more finely, to differentiate among forms that stochastic events can take. Campbell's (1988) elaboration of forms of task complexity is a move in this direction. Dornbusch and Scott's (1975) concept of the active task incorporates distinctions that are relevant to understanding stochastic events. They argue that tasks vary in predictability of resistance ("Can I predict the problems to be encountered?"), efficacy ("Can I handle the problems I predict?"), and clarity ("Are the goals to be realized by my performance clear?"). (See Dornbusch and Scott, 1975, p. 106, for items to measure these dimensions.) The attractiveness of their dimensions is the separation of diagnosis, action and such organizational constraints as performance pressure. As we will see, new technologies are hard to diagnose because of the substantial mental demands they make on operators and the many ways in which surprises can occur; but new technologies are also hard to control because of interactive complexity, and they are hard to measure because people disagree about what constitutes effective performance.

The skill requirements of a stochastic environment are unique. A large repertoire of skills must be maintained, even though they are used infrequently; people are usually on standby, giving special attention to startup and to anticipating faults that may lead to downtime; the distinction between operations and maintenance is blurred; skills in monitoring and diagnostics are crucial; people must be committed to do what is necessary on their own initiative and have the autonomy to do so; and people have now assumed the role of "variance absorber, dealing with and counteracting the unexpected" (Davis and Taylor, 1976, pp. 388–389).

As we noted earlier, stochastic environments represent a moving target for learning because they can change faster than people can accumulate knowledge about them. When recurrence is scarce, so is learning, which is why stochastic events have become a permanent fixture of new technologies.

The preceding descriptions, with their emphasis on chronic surprise, suggest the possibility that operators and managers alike should be tense during much of the time they interact with these technologies. That suggestion will be amplified throughout this chapter, but here we simply note that a stochastic environment can be an arousing environment. Furthermore, since new technologies typically represent a division of labor in which routine tasks are automated and nonroutine tasks are left for human judgment, humans face a complex task composed of an unbroken string of tough decisions. Evidence shows that performance of complex tasks is more vulnerable to disruption from excessive arousal than is performance of simple tasks. Those disruptions that do occur (for example, perception narrows, and dominant responses dominate) tend to reduce learning and induce error.

Continuous events

An expanded version of Woodward's (1965) continuous process technology provides a prototype that captures additional properties of new technologies. Traditionally, process production has been illustrated by batch production of chemicals, by continuous-flow production of gases, liquids, and solids, and by description of the outputs as dimensional products measured by width, capacity, or volume, rather than as integral products that can be counted (Scott, 1981). Continuous process production tends to be more heavily automated than the mechanized process of mass production (Mintzberg, 1983), which means that some of the issues discussed as stochastic events still apply when we emphasize continuity rather than unpredictability. While continuity and stochastic events covary, we intend to pry them apart as much as possible because they represent distinct issues in new technologies.

Continuous processes impose their own imperative – the reliability imperative – and this sets them apart from stochastic events. This shift from efficiency to reliability may constitute the single most important change associated with new technologies. Reliability is salient in continuous processing because the overriding requirement is to keep the process doing what it is supposed to do. This means there is a premium on maintaining the continuity and integrity of the process. "Responsibility for assuring operations continuity is more important than responsibility for effort" (Adler, 1986, p. 20).

Reliability has recently been highlighted as an issue of safety in the context of dangerous technologies (for example, nuclear power plants), but the issue of reliability is larger than the question of safety. Most of the technologies associated with safety issues are part of a larger group of technologies, all of which involve continuous processes. The problems posed by continuous processing are more visible and consequential in such technologies as nuclear reactors, but the problems are indigenous to all members of this class. Thus, the current concern with issues of reliability is not just a reaction to an increase in the number of dangerous technologies; it is symptomatic of a larger set of unique issues associated with postindustrial technology in general. While efficiency was the hallmark of deterministic industrial-era technology, reliability is the hallmark of stochastic, continuous technology associated with the postindustrial era.

There are numerous examples of an upswing in continuous processing. Bank tellers now deal with a level of automation that is qualitatively higher than that of continuous flow chemical refineries (Adler, 1986). When transaction entries are made, adjustments are made instantaneously to all relevant bank accounts. Since the data base is on line for entry and access, any error means that the bank uses inaccurate data for all subsequent operations and calculations. Air traffic control in heavily loaded sectors requires continuous processing (Finkelman and Kirschner, 1980). Activities that normally look like mass production, such as the production of soap operas (Intintoli, 1984), in fact turn out to resemble continuous production more closely.

Transaction processing in general has become more continuous, as is evident in automatic teller machines, computerized reservation systems, toll-free phone numbers that can be switched from one answering location to another according to the time of day, and point-of-sale debit machines that can support continuous transaction processing in direct sales. Unlike previous continuous process technologies, which were confined to one location (such as a factory or refinery) newer technologies use communication technology and construct organization without location. New technologies knit separate actors, transactions, and locations together into a continuous process.

One of the most interesting examples of continuous processing is flexible, automated manufacturing. The fascinating quality of this technology is that it allows continuous processing of customized products. Less standardized low-volume unique products, usually made in a job shop, can now be made by a quasi-continuous process (Adler, 1988). This capability lends new significance to the similarities that Woodward (1965) observed between unit production systems and process production systems. She found that both systems employed more organic structures than did mass production. As Miles states, "Both appear to be organized into small production groups or teams, with more general role responsibilities and greater informality and autonomy in task-related interactions. Elaborate controls and sanctions are not feasible in the highly routine unit-production system, and they are not needed in the process technologies because they are built into the throughput system itself" (Miles, 1980, p. 59).

A technology that combines craft and continuous processing (a combination that is possible, given some of the similarities observed by Woodward) may provide a core image to understand newer technologies. Denison (personal communication) has suggested that reliability assurance becomes the craft. As the supervisor of continuous processing pays more attention to the process and the product than to people, he or she may often become the most skilled worker, or someone very much like a person involved in unit production (Davis and Taylor, 1976).

People confronted with problems of continuity and reliability need a different set of sensitivities and skills than do people confronted with problems of discreteness and efficiency. It is important, for example, for them to visualize and think in terms of processes rather than products. Burack (cited in Davis and Taylor, 1976) has suggested that such aptitudes as high attention to work processes, rapid response to emergencies, ability to stay calm in tense environments, and early detection of malfunctions are crucial. Adler (1986) argues that newer technologies, which put a premium on continuous processing, require that people assume higher task responsibility, deal comfortably with higher levels of abstraction, and develop a deeper appreciation for the qualitatively higher levels of interdependence involved in their work.

Perrow's (1984) diagnosis that the coincidence of tight coupling and technological complexity has created conditions of interactive complexity and a new family of failures (called "normal accidents") may be an early recognition that continuous processing in general presents unique problems that require unique structures. Classical examples of continuous processing technologies, such as chemical plants, are described by Perrow (1984, p. 97) as "interactively complex," although he describes other process technologies, such as drug and bread production, as "linear, tight." As we will argue shortly, a linear, tight system is vulnerable because if members lose some comprehension of cause and effect, the system becomes more interactively complex and more prone to failure. All agree that continuous processes, by definition, have no buffers, which compounds the problems created by more frequent stochastic events and higher mental workloads.

The coexistence of stochastic events and continuous events creates several problems of analysis. For example, it could be argued that stochastic events – which have been around as long as technology itself – are no more common in new technologies than they were before but simply seem that way because they stand out more vividly against the background of more continuous processing. The argument throughout this chapter is that the combination of increased cognitive demands, increased electronic complexity, and dense interdependence over larger areas increases the incidence of unexpected outcomes that ramify in unexpected ways. These unexpected ramifications need not be synonymous with failure because they may also be occasions for innovation and learning. The point is that we assume there are more stochastic events with new technologies, rather than more salience for relatively the same number of stochastic events as were associated with older technologies; but we could be wrong.

Abstract events

More and more of the work associatedwith new technologies has disappeared into machines, which means that managers and operators experience increased cognitive demands for inference, imagination, integration, problem solving, and mental maps to monitor and understand what is going on out of sight. Buchanan and Bessant (1985, p. 303) argue that people who work with new technologies have to have a complex understanding of at least four components: "1. the process – its layout, sequence of events and interdependencies; 2. the product – its key characteristics, properties, and variability of raw materials; 3. the equipment – their functions, capabilities and limitations; 4. the controls – their functions, capabilities and limitations, and the effects of control actions on perfomance." These four understandings are crucial because the technology is partially self-controlled, and people have to handle the unexpected and provide backup control when automatic control systems fail. People need sufficient understanding of abstract events so that they can intervene at any time and pick up the process or assemble a recovery.

The unique and sizable cognitive demands imposed by new technologies suggest that the concept of operator error is misleading and should be replaced. Part of the argument for replacement is that operators are often blamed for errors that lie with designers and systems (Perrow, 1984). In Berniker's (private communication) colorful language, "Operator error is the fig leaf of scoundrels promoting complex systems." Thus, at the minimum, we should talk about operating error rather than operator error.

Aside from that issue, I want to argue that new technologies foster operator *mistakes* rather than operator errors. The difference is not trivial. An error occurs when a person strays from a guide or a prescribed course of action through inadvertence and is blameworthy, whereas a mistake occurs when there is a misconception, a misidentification, or a misunderstanding. Some problems in new technologies do occur when operators stray from rote procedures and err in executing an intention, but a more frequent and more serious source of problems develops when people form their intentions in the first place.

Mistakes that arise during the formation of intentions have many sources, but one of the most crucial is the control philosophy of "one measurement – one indicator" (Woods, O'Brien, and Hanes, 1987, p. 1728). When implemented, this philosophy means that each dial and meter in a control room registers the output of one sensor out in the plant. Information is provided to the operator at the lowest level of detail which means that integration, pattern recognition, and diagnosis are wholly dependent on human processing and on whatever models and experience the operator brings to the monitoring task. Inadequate sampling of displayed information, inattention to information on the periphery, and distractions during the building of a representation of a problem all can affect the formation of an intention.

The problem of distractions, in particular, deserves closer attention because of its subtlety and its tendency to amplify, and because it is a prototype of the issues that arise because of the tight association between new technologies and computer controls. Integration of single indicators into a recognizable pattern is easier when data are presented simultaneously rather than serially. Operators who are able to sweep visually across an array of dials can create and execute novel search sequences with relatively little effort. They can see immediately the rate at which indicators are changing, as well as relative rates of change among dials, and they can test hypotheses by rapid inspection. They can also stumble onto odd readings that they were not looking for. This pattern of visual search changes sharply when indicators are displayed on separate screens of video display terminals. To access indicators in a novel sequence, operators must consciously execute a novel set of commands, which can be distracting, and they must remember what the earlier screens have registered and hope that the readings have not changed while subsequent screens were being accessed. Serendipitous diagnosis based on accidental discovery of an anomalous reading is less likely, and the skill required to transform a serial data presentation into a parallel presentation is not trivial (the transformation resembles that required for an air traffic controller to mentally transform a two-dimensional display on a flat radar screen into a three-dimensional picture of airplanes converging from different altitudes).

Mistakes in the formation of an intention tend to be surprisingly resistant to change, as was evident at Three Mile Island (Perrow, 1984); at Tenerife, when the pilot of KLM flight 4805 persisted in his hypothesis that the cloud-shrouded runway was clear for takeoff (Weick, 1988b); and in several studies of operator performance (Woods, O'Brien, and Hanes, 1987). These mistakes usually are not corrected until a "fresh viewpoint enters the situation" (Woods, O'Brien, and Hanes, 1987, p. 1745).

While we could cite numerous other examples of the ways in which new technologies have become more abstract, with a corresponding higher mental workload, we need instead to highlight the significance of this change. New technologies are basically dual rather than singular. They involve the self-contained, invisible material process that is actually unfolding, as well as the equally self-contained, equally invisible imagined process that is mentally unfolding in the mind of an individual or a team. There are relatively few points at which the mental representation can be checked against and corrected by the actual process. True, there are hundreds of discrete sensors that track fluctuations, but those readings do not convey a direct picture of relationships, be they cause-effect, goals-means, or physical relationships. Relational information is the most crucial information when the object being monitored is a continuous process.

Thus, unlike any other technologies that have been used previously as predictors by organizational theorists, the new technologies exist as much in the head of the operator as they do on the plant floor. This is not to argue that one technology is more important than another, but it is to argue that cognition and microlevel processes are keys to understanding the organizatiorial impact of new technologies.

An operator's representation of a process technology, and the resulting formation of intentions and choice of control activities, can gradually become decoupled from the actual process state, so that the operator's control intervention literally creates a new technical system that is understood neither by the operator nor by the devices for self-control originally designed into the material technology. The human construction is itself an intact and plausible view. The decoupling is gradual. The immediate consequences of decoupling are invisible except for dial fluctuations that could be errors, separate independent deviations of separate sensors, or a single problem with multiple symptoms. Therefore, it is not surprising that so-called mistakes persist.

New technologies are parallel technologies involving a technology in the head and a technology on the floor. Each is self-contained. Each is coordinated with the other intermittently rather than continuously. Each corrects the other discontinuously. Each can have a sizable effect on the other, and the parallel technologies have a constant amount of mystery that is due to the invisibility of the processes each contains.

Conceptualizing New Technologies

Such concepts as structure, analysis, complexity, and behavior control have been prominent in previous discussions of deterministic, mechanized, physical technologies that impose their imperatives on organizational functioning. As technologies become more stochastic, continuous, and abstract, those same concepts no longer explain as much as they used to. In their place, we now need to talk more about structuration, affect, dynamic interactive complexity, and premise control. The following discussion shows why.

From structure to structuration

Deterministic, stable technology is compatible with deterministic organizational structure, but the shift toward stochastic, automated technology requires that we pay more attention to structuration and structuring. Structuration is defined as "the production and reproduction of a social system through members' use of rules and resources in interaction" (Poole, n.d., p. 6). The important ideas in that statement are that systems are built from interactions and rules; that such resources as action are the tools people use to enact their organizations; and, most important, that structures are both the medium and the outcome of interaction. People create structural constraints, which then constrain them (Turner, 1987). Structuration pays equal attention to both sides of that structuring process (constraining and being constrained), whereas earlier notions emphasized one side and neglected the other.

The idea that structure constrains action (Khandwalla, 1974) dominated earlier discussions of mechanized technology, but this emphasis was flawed because it treated structure as a given and underestimated the degree to which human action can alter it. The opposite emphasis, represented by the idea that structure is an emergent property of ongoing action (Weick, 1969), made the opposite error. It suggested that ongoing action unfolds free of any preconceptions, and it underestimated the degree to which institutional patterns impose prior constraints on the action from which structures emerge.

The concept of structuration is exemplified by Goffman's marvelous observation that "in everyday life actors are simultaneously the marks as well as the shills of social order" (cited in Barley, 1986, p. 79): the same person is both the shill who constructs the game and the mark who is drawn in by the game that has been constructed; victimizer becomes victim through frameworks laid down during prior interaction.

An illustration of how technology affects structuration has been supplied by Barley's (1986) analysis of two radiology departments that adopted CAT scanners. In one department, initial expertise was lodged in the technicians (Suburban Hospital); in the other, expertise was lodged in radiologists (Urban Hospital). The new technology introduced in both settings was identical – a Technicare 2060 whole-body computed topography scanner. This technology is stochastic (for example, bone artifacts sometimes appear unpredictably in pictures of the basal brain area, which makes interpretation difficult) and continuous (for example, the timing of injections of dye to highlight portions of the body affects the conclusions that may be drawn), and the mental workload is substantial because the system uses novel diagnostic signs. The technology is hypothesized to affect structuration in the following manner. At first the technology is exogenous. When translated into a technical system, it either confirms ingrained interaction patterns or disturbs and reformulates them. These patterns are carried by scripts – "standard plots of types of encounters whose repetition constitutes the setting's interaction order" (Barley, 1986, p. 83) – which create reciprocal links between structure and action. Thus, the technology ratifies or alters scripts that have grown up as a result of previous structuring. When the new body-imaging technologies were introduced to both departments, radiologists and technicians alike drew on traditional, institutionalized patterns of signification, legitimation, and domination (see Riley, 1983) to construct roles to deal with this technology and to interpret the strange products that it produced. However, the traditional pattern of technicians' deference to professional radiologists proved inadequate, especially at Suburban, because radiologists had only modest understanding of the technology. The puzzling technology introduced slippage between the idealized patterns of dominance and legitimation built up from past practice and the immediate problem of trying to discover what the novel diagnostic signs meant. Given this slippage, new patterns of action emerged and were incorporated into scripts that made a lasting change in institutional structure.

To understand how structures were both created and altered by interactions between radiologists and technicians, we need to look more closely at the scripts that emerged from actions involving the new technology. Some of these scripts, such as direction giving, countermands, usurping the controls, direction seeking, and expected criticisms, ratified traditional institutional forms. Other scripts, such as preference stating, clandestine teaching, role reversal, and mutual execution, modified these traditional forms. Each script was built from actions evoked by the technology, but the influence of the technology on structure occurred through the ratio of ratification scripts to modification scripts, not through some more static vehicle, such as workflow rigidity. For example, the ratio of preference stating (a modification script) to direction giving (a ratification script) was lower at Suburban (1:1.7) than at Urban (1:4.7), which meant that the same technology produced more structural change at Suburban than at Urban and did so because it led to the construction of a different social order. Direction giving is a straightforward enactment of the prevailing institutionalized dominance of radiologists over technologists; direction giving is a pure expression of existing structure. But as the frequency of this pure enactment is moderated by scripts that place greater emphasis on collegiality, the traditional form is changed. Ongoing affirmations and modifications such as these are the means by which technology both shapes structure and is itself shaped by structure when different techniques are built and used to run it.

The relationships between structuration and technology can be diagrammed into the deviation-amplifying system shown in Figure 6.1. The linkage from C to D

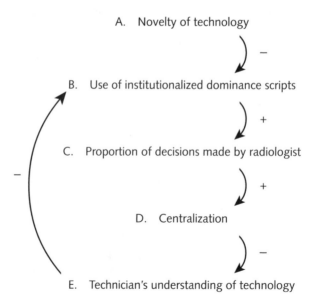

Figure 6.1   Structuration and technology

represents action as a constraint on structure. The linkage from E to B represents institutional constraints on action. Scripts are found at steps B and C, and either ratification or modification can occur at each of those two stages. Notice that when we depict the structural effects of technology in this way, once technology provides the initial "kick" to the process, its effects are then dependent on how it becomes woven into the process of action. This embedding is a mixture of action, scripts, and institutional forms, but the technology itself becomes something different, according to how these three components interact. That is the central point of the structuration hypothesis, and it is an important point to maintain as technologies become more fluid and more difficult to comprehend, with less transparent effects on shifting organizational structures.

There are several ways to enlarge Barley's (1986) analysis and bring in additional dimensions of technology. The point at which technology is introduced is the point at which it is most susceptible to influence (Winner, 1986), and Barley's analysis shows why. When conceptualized in the context of structure, technologies are treated as self-evident artifacts to which people accommodate, rather than as open-ended artifacts that accommodate to interactions. Structuration sensitizes the observer to look for an ongoing redefinition among structure, action, and technology. Beginnings are of special importance for structuration because they constrain what is learned about the technology and how fast it is learned (for example, Urban Hospital technicians learned less and learned more slowly, even though it was assumed that they understood the technology).

Barley's (1986) description could be parsed with concepts other than structuration, partly because uncertainty is such a prominent part of the events and varies between the two settings. Uncertainty seemed to be higher at Suburban Hospital than at Urban Hospital because Suburban added the uncertainty of a new social order, in which technicians had more expertise than medical professionals did, to the uncertainty of a novel technology, which was shared with Urban.

Contingency theories of power (Hickson and others, 1971) are relevant to Barley's analysis because the radiologists at Urban and the technologists at Suburban both were in a position to resolve important uncertainties. This powerful position was consistent with a division of labor traditional at Urban but not at Suburban. While these power differentials are evident, contingency theory does not spell out explicit mechanisms by which these differences will affect interaction, technology definition, and structure, which is why structuration is a useful complementary perspective.

The uncertainty connected with a CAT scanner might also be viewed as a stimulus for the development of new coordinating mechanisms, such as mutual adjustment, lateral communication, and meetings (Van de Ven, Delbecq, and Koenig, 1976), and more of these should be developed at Suburban than at Urban. This prediction is consistent with the data, although the process implied is not sufficiently sensitive to history and institutional mechanisms to predict how coordination was built and what the implications were for performance.

While there are other ways than structuration to understand Barley's data, none of them preserve quite so succinctly the point that technology is both a cause and a consequence of structure. This dual role of technology occurs because structuring is an ongoing process that shapes the meaning of artifacts through scripts, interaction, and tradition and is itself shaped by those meanings. The ability to treat structure in this manner is an important conceptual change that we need for understanding the effects of new technologies.

From analysis to affect

Throughout the preceding discussion, we have implied that new technologies trigger strong feelings. These feelings have a substantial effect on the operation of the technologies. Thus, we need to understand not only how operators solve problems within the bounds of their mental maps but also how they do so under pressure. Problem solving under pressure means coping both with interruptions and with excessive arousal. We review these two issues in that order.

When a continuous process begins to fail, in an environment where excessive deviation in one measurement – one indication is signaled by one alarm, operators are hit with an "avalanche" of alarms (Woods, O'Brien, and Hanes, 1987, p. 1735). In the first few minutes after a sudden change in a parameter, two hundred alarm points may be active. Since the alarms are hardwired and not conditioned by multivariable patterns, the operator gets no help in pattern recognition from the alarms themselves. Furthermore, the search for patterns is carried out amidst considerable distraction.

The theorizing about emotion done by Berscheid (1983) and Mandler (1984) suggests that interruptions, similar to those that alarms create, are a sufficient and possibly necessary condition for arousal and emotional experience. Since interruption is a chronic threat to continuous processing, and since stochastic events are a chronic source of interruptions, we may expect that strong emotions are coexistent with new technologies.

This conjunction of strong emotions and new technologies can be understood if we look more closely at the relationship between arousal and interruption. A necessary condition for emotion is arousal, or discharge in the autonomic nervous system. Arousal has physiological significance because it prepares people for fight-or-flight reactions. Of even more importance is the fact that arousal also has psychological significance. The perception of arousal provides a warning that there is some stimulus to which attention must be paid in order to initiate appropriate action. This signal suggests that one's well-being may be at stake.

An important property of arousal, often neglected by those who do research on stress, is that it develops slowly. Arousal occurs roughly two to three seconds after a stimulus has occurred, and this delay gives time for a more appropriate direct action to occur. Thus, the autonomic nervous system is a secondary, backup, support system, which is activated largely when direct action fails. When heightened arousal is perceived it is appraised, and some link between the present situation and relevant prior situations is established to impose meaning on the present. Arousal leads people to search for an answer to the question "What's up?" Answers differ according to socialization.

The variables of arousal and cognitive appraisal are found in many formulations dealing with emotion, but the unique quality of Mandler's (1984) and Berscheid's

(1983) research is their emphasis on the interruption of action sequences as the occasion for emotion. Organized action sequences in organizations are illustrated by standard operating procedures (SOPs), continuous processing, scripts, and roles. All of these tend to become more tightly organized the more frequently they are executed. The interruption of an ongoing SOP or plan is a sufficient and possibly necessary condition for arousal of the autonomic nervous system.

Interruption is a signal that important changes have occurred in the environment; thus, a key event for emotion is the interruption of an expectation. It makes good evolutionary sense to construct an organism that reacts significantly when the world is no longer the way it was.

Emotion is what happens between the time that an organized sequence is interrupted and the time at which the interrupting stimulus is removed or a substitute response is found that allows the sequence to be completed. Until either event occurs, autonomic arousal increases. When interruption first occurs, there is redoubled effort to complete the original interrupted sequence, which means that both redoubled effort and subjective emotional experience may occur at the same time. The more tightly organized an interrupted action sequence is, the greater the arousal. If there are many different ways in which an interrupted sequence can be completed, then arousal is not likely to build very much. This suggests that people who are able to improvise should show less emotional behavior and less extreme emotions. They can create more substitute behaviors, and so their arousal should not build to the same high levels that are experienced by people who have fewer substitute behaviors. Finally, the interruption of higher-order and more pervasive plans should be more arousing than the disruption of lower-order plans.

If we apply these propositions to new technologies, we start by asking, "What is the distribution of interruption in technology? Where are interruptions most likely to occur, and how organized are the actions and plans that are likely to be interrupted?" If we can describe this, then we can predict where emotional experiences are most likely to occur and how intense they will be. For example, systems with newer, less well-organized response sequences, settings with fewer standard operating procedures, and settings that are more loosely coupled should be settings in which there is less emotion because interruptions are less disruptive. Settings in which there are few developed plans should be less interruptible and therefore should elicit less emotion.

So far, we have talked only about the frequency of emotion, not about the kind of emotion that occurs. Negative emotions are likely to occur when an organized behavioral sequence is interrupted unexpectedly and the interruption is interpreted as harmful or detrimental. If there is no means to remove or circumvent the interruption, the negitive emotion should become more intense the longer the interruption lasts.

To summarize the key points, "emotion is essentially a non-response activity, occurring between the awareness of the interrupting event and an action alternative that will maintain or promote the individual's well-being in the face of an event" (Berscheid, Gangestad, and Kulakowski, 1984, p. 396). When people perform an organized action sequence and are interrupted, they search for an explanation and a remedy. The longer they search, the higher the arousal and the stronger the emotion. If people find that the interruption has slowed the accomplishment of a sequence, they are likely to experience anger. If they find that the interruption has accelerated accomplishment, then they are likely to experience pleasure. If they find that the interruption can be circumvented, then they experience relief. If they find that the interruption has thwarted a higher-level plan, then the anger is likely to turn into rage, and if they find that the interruption has thwarted a minor behavioral sequence, then they are likely to feel disappointment or minor irritation. All of these emotional experiences are accompanied by redoubled effort to complete the original sequence that was interrupted.

Other than redoubled effort, what other behavioral consequences of emotion might we expect in new technologies? To ask this question is to confront the venerable issue of whether emotion disrupts adaptive functioning or energizes it. Given the staying power of this controversy, we must assume that both views are partially correct and that we must specify when emotion disorganizes and when it energizes. To do so, we make the controversial assumption that the relation between emotion and performance follows the inverted U curve associated with the Yerkes-Dodson law (Broadhurst, 1957). While Neiss's (1988) review raises important questions about the notion of global arousal and reminds us that motor performance is overdetermined, we retain the concept of arousal throughout this chapter as shorthand for the idea that uncertainty about something important (McGrath, 1976) affects performance in a manner analogous to the Yerkes-Dodson law. Since uncertainty about something important seems to be an apt description of what people face when they operate stochastic, continuous, abstract new technologies, we find it useful to retain the concept of arousal and the inverted U hypothesis as an orderly starting point to think about these issues.

This starting point consists of the basic idea that an increase in emotional intensity from some zero point produces an increase in the quality of performance up to some point, beyond which performance deteriorates and finally is disorganized. "The optimal point is reached sooner, that is to say, at lower intensities, the less well-learned or more complex is the performance; increase in emotional intensity supposedly affects finer skills, finer discriminations, complex reasoning tasks, and recently acquired skills more readily than routine activities" (Frijda, 1986, p. 113).

Thus, the question of whether emotion energizes or disorganizes depends on whether one is ascending (energizes) or descending (disorganizes) the inverted U. To move beyond the coarse grain of the inverted U toward a more specific understanding of the relationship between emotion and performance, we must ask additional questions.

1. Are the unlearned, better-practiced, dominant responses that become salient in an emotional situation task-relevant (emotion improves performance) or task-irrelevant (emotion degrades performance)?
2. Does emotion reduce attentional capacity (Weltman, Smith, and Egstrom, 1971) only moderately, so that peripheral cues for performance are ignored but central cues continue to be noticed (emotion improves performance), or does it reduce attentional capacity significantly, so that both peripheral and some central cues are ignored (emotion degrades performance)?
3. Does emotion induce a regression toward a more primitive, simpler, overlearned

way of behaving, with corresponding abandonment of newer, more complex, less fully learned responses (Eysenck, 1982)? Darwin called emotions states of functional decortication, by which he meant that lower centers overrule higher ones. Frijda (1986) notes that stubbornly persisting in behavior one is used to can be considered a regressive response mode. It will be recalled that perseveration in simple diagnoses is a persistent problem in control-room diagnoses.

The key point for technology is that the breadth of attention varies in response to fluctuations in emotion (Weltman, Smith, and Egstrom, 1971; Berkun, 1964; Wachtel, 1967). This variation could affect both task conceptions and performance. Assuming that people try to make sense of whatever they notice, as the breadth of their attention varies, so should their descriptions of what they are doing. Thus, task conceptions themselves, not just task performance, should change as arousal changes. Unreliable performance may persist because the operator is performing a different task than observers realize. The point is that this discrepancy in conception may be due to differences in pressure rather than to differences in authority and position.

There is a clear example of this possibility in Barley's (1986) data. Technicians at Urban Hospital were the object of a steady stream of directives, imperative speech, puzzling countermands, sarcasm, and usurped control generated by radiologists. These could easily have raised the level of threat and arousal experienced by technicians, which in turn could have narrowed their attention, made complex learning more difficult, and actually altered their conception of what kind of task CAT-scanner technology posed for them. These effects could have slowed their learning, which should then have intensified the pressure that radiologists imposed, making further learning even more difficult.

This scenario of obstructed learning produced by heightened arousal places less emphasis on differences in position, authority, and structure and more emphasis on the disruptive effects of emotions, such as threat and fear, when they occur under conditions of high arousal and complex technology. Since ongoing learning is so much a part of new technologies, anything that obstructs learning, such as arousal, is of considerable importance.

Since new technologies make greater demands for abstract mental work, we must pay as much attention to the fact that there is an increase in demands as to the fact that those demands are mental. To cope with mental workloads is an arousing, emotional experience, which means that mental processes will be modified by affect. New technologies have properties that seem likely to intensify affect. If that intensification occurs, then affect can shape the technology because it attenuates the attention directed at it. As attention varies, so do conceptions of the technology and the effectiveness and reliability of performance. To change how people cope with this technology requires an understanding of these fluctuations in attention. As we have suggested, these fluctuations are driven by uncertainties that seem to affect people in a manner analogous to those postulated for the concept of global arousal.

From static to dynamic interactive complexity

The fact that stochastic, continuous processing occurs under conditions of high arousal has implications beyond the individual level of analysis. This can be illustrated by an extension of Perrow's (1984) concept of interactive complexity. Figure 6.2 contains the essential ideas. From top to bottom, Perrow (1984) categorizes organizations on the basis of complexity (linear, complex) and coupling (loose, tight); interactive com-

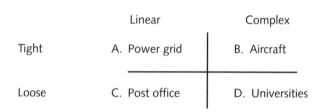

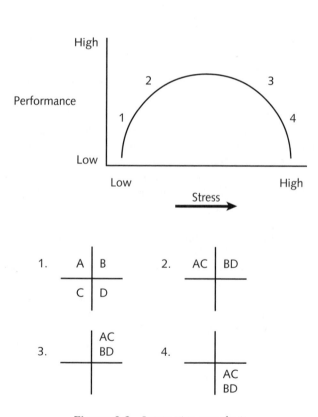

Figure 6.2   Interactive complexity

plexity occurs in cell B, where aircraft, nuclear power reactors, and chemical processing plants are assigned. In the middle of Figure 6.2 is the classical inverted U curve relating performance and arousal. The numbers spaced along this curve represent four different stages of arousal (1 = lowest, 4 = highest), and these numbers retain this same meaning in the set of four diagrams at the bottom of Figure 6.2. The four diagrams at the bottom show what may happen to diverse systems when people in them experience increasing levels of stress. For example, diagram 2 asserts that when stress increases from point 1 on the curve to point 2, loosely coupled systems become more tightly coupled. Diagram 3 asserts that as stress increases even more, linear systems become complex. And diagram 4 asserts that when stress intensifies still more, complex interactive systems fall apart into complex arrangements of loosely coupled parts.

The processes responsible for these organizational and technological changes are those observed to accompany changes in arousal. When arousal increases from step 1 to step 2, there is a tendency for groups to become more centralized (Hermann, 1963), and there is a tendency for individuals to ignore peripheral cues in task performance and to focus on central cues (Easterbrook, 1959). As people become more task-oriented, performance improves and interdependencies become tightened. Loosely coupled relations become tighter, but there is no change in technical complexity because all cues that are crucial for task performance are still being monitored.

When pressure increases still more, as in diagram 3, then people, operators and managers alike, begin to ignore cues that are central to task performance. They lose sight of some information they need to know, which means that everything becomes more complex and less comprehensible than it normally is. When people ignore information that is central to performance, existing interactions between variables are ignored or misperceived, and through their interventions new interventions may be triggered inadvertently. The situation becomes both more complex and more tightly coupled, which means that all organizations, not just those that start with interactive complexity, experience this condition. Perrow's analysis implies that once an organization is assigned to one of his four cells, it remains there. That implication overlooks the important effects that arousal can have on task conceptions. The combination of centralization, perceptual narrowing, and regression produced by increased arousal can alter perceptions of tasks and structures, thereby altering combinations of coupling and complexity.

By making the assignment of an organization to one of Perrow's four categories more fluid, as a result of arousal, we can extend his analysis. Organizations that routinely function as tightly coupled complex systems (cell B) should know more about that condition and be better able to cope with it than organizations that routinely function in the other three cells. Organizations in cell C (loose/linear) know the least about interactive complexity (tight/complex), which means that when they become tighter and more complex, they should be the most unsettled by this experience and cope with it least adequately. Organizations in cells A and D should cope with interactive complexity equally well – better than C, but worse than B.

One index of inability to cope with interactive complexity might be the speed with which organizations disintegrate and move from cell B to cell D. If we assume that those with less experience with interactive complexity deteriorate more quickly, then loose linear organizations should exit from cell B first, followed by loose/complex and tight/linear organizations. Organizations that are accustomed to interactive complexity will fold eventually in the face of continuing extreme arousal, but they should survive longer, making better decisions than any other form of organization.

Whether increases in arousal come from resource scarcity (Lawrence and Dyer, 1983), demands on attention (March and Olsen, 1986), or from "contradictory information, unexpected and mysterious interactions, and the need to follow rigid procedures that are written by the experts and that may be inappropriate in a particular instance" (Perrow, 1984, p. 151), these increases are likely to be more frequent, more intense, and more disruptive when they occur in conjunction with continuous processing, stochastic events, and a higher mental workload.

Interactive complexity is not a fixed commodity tied to specific technologies, such as nuclear reactors. Since arousal tends to increase when control and prediction become problematic, and since newer technologies alter many of the processes of control and prediction that people are accustomed to, arousal is likely to accompany many of the newer technologies much of the time. What makes this so serious is that virtually all of the effects of arousal on the already complex newer technology are in the direction of making it even more complex. Stochastic events become even more so when the few patterns that are still visible in them vanish in the face of perceptual narrowing.

When we argue that interactive complexity is dynamic rather than static, this does not give researchers license to study perception and ignore material artifacts and structure. Material artifacts set sensemaking processes in motion; sensemaking is constrained by actions, which themselves are constrained by artifacts; and sensemaking attempts to diagnose symptoms emitted by the technology. What we are trying to emphasize in recasting the concept of interactive complexity is that the increased mental workload created by new technologies forces people to impose more of their own interpretations to understand what is occurring. These interpretations are necessarily incomplete, which means that a greater number of material events interact longer, with potentially more severe consequences – out of sight but, more seriously, out of mind. When people use fallible models to cope with stochastic, continuous, abstract events under conditions of excessive arousal, interactive complexity is one consequence.

The gradual decoupling of a mental model of a process from the actual steps that occur in that process allows events to unfold that ramify in their consequences and grow increasingly incomprehensible. These outcomes potentially occur whenever excessive arousal contracts attention and allows events to interact unnoticed and unmonitored, so that a new technical system and a new set of interactions are created, without any person intending it. It is in this sense that humans can transform a simple linear system into one that is interactively complex, and it is in this sense that interactive complexity and new technologies are closely associated.

The point of all this is not to lay one more shortcoming at the door of the human operator; quite the opposite. What we are suggesting is that the design of technical systems often fails to moderate arousal levels, make complex judgment tasks simpler, distribute responsibilities among team members, reduce distractions, provide incentives for early reporting of error and problem solving, reduce production pressure, heighten perceptions of control, and add slack capacity to attention.

Considering what they face, it is remarkable that operators do as well as they do. If, after three years, teams of professional analysts still were not completely certain of what had happened at Three Mile Island, then we can hardly fault a handful of operators who had thirteen seconds to decide what had happened. As Frijda (1986, pp. 476–477) observes, "A human being cannot have been made to stand and withstand all contingencies life presents. What can you expect from a system that only takes nine months to produce and merely weighs about 70 kilograms? . . . One may assume that humans have been fitted out with provisions to deal effectively with a number of important contingencies. There is necessarily a cost to this. Several emotion provisions, for instance, are emergency provisions. They produce response fast, and upon a minimum of information processing. If the system can do that, one should not complain that its information processing on these occasions is truncated, or that response is being made when finer meaning analysis might have shown it to be unnecessary."

From behavior and output control to premise control

As new technologies increasingly take on the form of abstract working knowledge, they move deeper inside the operator's head, which means that effective control over these technologies will be exerted by cognitive variables and unobtrusive controls. Obtrusive controls, such as orders, rules, regulations, specialization, or hierarchy (Perrow, 1977), require more observables than are ordinarily present with new technologies. For example, behavior control (Ouchi and McGuire, 1975) is more difficult in new technologies because visible behaviors comprise a smaller portion of the actual inputs. Thus, behavior is a less meaningful object of control: there is less behavior to monitor, the effects of observed behaviors are mystified by interactive complexity, and the same behaviors may be mediated by private diagnoses that vary widely in their accuracy. All of these complications mean that observed behaviors are less diagnostic of how well the process is progressing.

Output control is also difficult, for many of the same reasons. Visible outputs are less meaningful because so many unobservable determinants other than operators' actions can affect them. While an operator can be held accountable for the output, that accountability is empty if neither the operator nor the monitor understand what is occurring or why.

Obtrusive managerial controls, such as direct surveillance and standardization, are relatively ineffective ways to influence the operation of new technologies because less obtrudes to be monitored or standardized. This does not mean that obtrusive controls have disappeared in organizations with new technologies, but it does mean that unobtrusive controls in the form of decision premises (for example, managerial psychosocial assumptions incorporated into work arrangements) should have more impact. Decision premises have become more crucial now that more of the organization is carried in the head and less of it is carried by visible, sensible, transparent artifacts. Cognition is an increasingly important determinant of organizational outcomes because, with fewer visible artifacts, more of the organization has to be imagined, visualized, and filled in from cryptic cues. All of this fleshing out is cognitive and is affected by decision premises.

When premises underlying action are controlled, according to Perrow (1986, p. 129), "the subordinate *voluntarily* restricts the range of stimuli that will be attended to ('Those sorts of things are irrelevant' or 'What has that got to do with the matter?') and the range of alternatives that would be considered ('It would never occur to me to do that')." Premise controls are important when work is nonroutine, which is why we have highlighted them in the context of stochastic technologies.

Premise controls are often created when managerial psychosocial assumptions are incorporated into technological and organizational designs. As Dornbusch and Scott (1975, p. 89) note, work arrangements, which consist of such components as allocation of responsibility, procedures for the evaluation of performance, and rules governing task performance, usually "are messages concerning the nature of the tasks from those who control to those who perform." At the center of these messages is either a delegation premise (that performers can make nontrivial decisions regarding a course of action) or a directive premise (that they cannot). These premises may be unconsidered choices by managers, but that does not make them any less potent.

Much of the potency of managerial assumptions derives from the fact that they act like self-fulfilling prophecies. Davis and Taylor (1976, p. 412) provide the example of "when assumptions are held that a system is comprised [sic] of reliable technical elements and unreliable social elements, then in order to provide total system reliability, the technical design must call for parts of people as replaceable machine elements to be regulated by the technical system or by a superstructure of personal control. On the other hand, if the system designers' assumptions are that the social elements are reliable, learning, self-organizing, and committed elements, then the technical system will require whole, unique people performing the regulatory activities. Experience has shown that in the latter case such a technical system design produces effects markedly different than [in] the former."

It becomes more plausible to link technology with determination by self-fulfilling prophecies when a sizable portion of the technology exists in the form of decision premises. Self-fulfilling prophecies are themselves decision premises, which become realized when they are treated as if they were true.

An interesting puzzle in technology may be the result of a self-fulfilling prophecy incorporated into managerial assumptions. American implementation of flexible manufacturing systems differs dramatically from Japanese implementation of the same systems. Thurow (1987) observes that the average American system makes ten parts while the average Japanese system makes ninety-three different parts. Adler (1988) cites data showing that American systems produce eight parts, on average, whereas those in Japan produce an average of thirty parts and those in Germany as many as eighty-five parts. In other words, flexible manufacturing systems in the United States show a remarkable lack of flexibility. Although flexible manufacturing is more like batch or continuous processing, managers may still assume it is a long-linked assembly line and embed the system in a mechanistic structure, which fulfills the prophecy that it is simply an electronic assembly line. Again, the imposed premises define, flesh out, and actualize a portion of the technology.

It does not matter that the operators are more sensitive to nonroutine qualities of the technology that the manager overlooks. Managerial assumptions typically dominate, and this is especially serious when managers underestimate the skills required for operation of new systems (Adler, 1986). This underestimation is not trivial, since it is backed up with directives rather than with delegation. These directives either squeeze out the flexibility that was designed into the technology or, more seriously, restrict perception and make it harder for people to operate the technology in a reliable manner.

Our point is that managers and designers are able to exert substantial influence over the form of new technologies because key parts of these technologies exist in the form of decision premises, which makes these forms more vulnerable to the premises imposed by managers.

If those premises are imposed by managers who feel threatened by the potential loss of their authority (Davis and Taylor, 1976) or by designers who want to centralize decisions, promulgate rules, and differentiate tasks (Scott, 1981), then technologies will be run with less judgment than is necessary to manage and comprehend their complexity. As a result, these technologies will become more interactively complex because directives will make it harder for operators to monitor, learn about, and respond to the full range of states that a machine can assume. The artificial restriction of perception and action by directives does not stop elements of the technology from interacting, but it does curtail comprehension of these interactions, which means the technology becomes more complex and more puzzling.

Thus, interactive complexity can be a social construction, as well as an indigenous feature of new technologies. This is why, throughout this chapter, it is assumed that interactive complexity is more common, more easily created, and more pervasive as an accompaniment of newer technologies than has previously been recognized. Furthermore, decision premises are an important source of interactive complexity. Designers whose assumptions issue in directives create more interactive complexity than do designers whose assumptions issue in delegations.

Conclusions

The preceding analysis suggests that an important pathway by which new technology affects organizations is variation in the ability of people to reason about the deep structure of new systems. Reasoning of some sort is mandatory because the systems are equivocal. The adequacy of reasoning depends on the extent to which the mental models used by people who work with new technologies are equivalent to the processes they model. These models represent an imagined technology that people assume parallels the actual technology, which they can see only through its punctate sensors.

Reasoning about new technologies can have a consequential effect on the way those technologies function. Our recurrent theme has been that technical systems and organizational constraints can reduce meaning, control, and predictability, which raises arousal, which affects the material interactions that are set in motion, which affects the outcome, which then feeds back and has a further effect on meaning, control, and predictability. The cycle can be broken, reversed, or dampened at any one of these points. Part of what we have tried to articulate is ways in which people can gain some control over the increasingly private, increasingly equivocal new technologies, which often test the limits of human comprehension.

This rephrasing of the main argument is an attempt to articulate the implications for individuals, as well as for organizations, of a set of technological qualities that we have not seen together before in quite this combination. Just as the novel combination of complex structures and tight coupling has produced interactive complexity and normal accidents at the organizational level, so has the novel combination of stochastic events and continuous processes produced cognitive emotional complexity and operator mistakes at the individual level. More important, normal accidents and operator mistakes derive from analogous assumptions and mechanisms, the one set emphasizing macro material determinants and the other emphasizing micro perceptual determinants.

New technologies are fascinating because, in their complex equivocality, they force us to grapple with a key issue in technology – namely, how to apply perceptual perspectives to a material world. In the preceding discussion, I have tried to blend the material and the perceptual, the micro and the macro. In the process, the picture that has emerged is one in which fallible people prove to be more resourceful and more adaptable than any control system yet fabricated. At the same time, these people are also so skilled at sensemaking that it is hard for them to detect when a mental model is becoming decoupled from the process they are trying to model and control. The model that is gradually becoming decoupled remains sufficiently plausible that the prospect of a mismatch between it and the actual process seems remote. Ironically, that very remoteness may be so reassuring to people that they remain only moderately aroused; their attention may range more widely, and they may then notice the incipient decoupling and correct it. Such are the oddities associated with new technologies: they may become least comprehensible when people worry most about comprehending them.

New technologies are paradoxical, as well as equivocal. These descriptions are not intended merely as clever phrases. Instead, they speak to the core issues we need to resolve if we want to understand technologies in which mental representation plays a central role in operation.

New technologies introduce a set of issues in technology that organizational theorists have yet to grapple with. Unless they do, the power of technology as a predictor of organizational functioning will diminish. That has been the message of this chapter.

Note

I acknowledge with gratitude the valuable comments of George Huber, Dan Denison, Chet Miller, and especially Eli Berniker on earlier drafts of this chapter.

References

Adler, P. "New Technologies, New Skills." *California Management Review*, 1986, *29*, 9–28.

Adler, P. S. "Managing Flexible Automation." *California Management Review*, 1988, *30*, 34–56.

Barley, S. R. "Technology as an Occasion for Structuring: Evidence from Observations of C T Scanners and the Social Order of Radiology Departments." *Administrative Science Quarterly*, 1986, *31*, 78–108.

Berkun, N. M. "Performance Decrement Under Psychological Stress." *Human Factors*, 1964, *6*, 21–30.

Berniker, E. "Understanding Technical Systems." Paper presented at Symposium on Management Training Programs: Implications of New Technologies, Geneva, Switzerland, Nov. 1987.

Berniker, E., and Wacker, G. "Advanced Manufacturing Systems." Unpublished manuscript, 1988.

Berscheid, E. "Emotion." In H. H. Kelley and others (eds.), *Close Relationships*. New York: W. H. Freeman, 1983.

Berscheid, E., Gangestad, S. W., and Kulakowski, D. "Emotion in Close Relationship: Implications for Relationship Counseling." In S. D. Brown and R. W. Lent (eds.), *Handbook of Counseling Psychology*. New York: Wiley, 1984, 435–476.

Broadhurst, P. L. "Emotionality and the Yerkes-Dodson Law." *Journal of Experimental Psychology*, 1957, *54*, 345–352.

Buchanan, D. A., and Bessant, J. "Failure, Uncertainty, and Control: The Role of Operators in a Computer-Integrated Production System." *Journal of Management Studies*, 1985, *22*, 292–308.

Burke, J. G. "Bursting Boilers and the Federal Power." In M. Kranzberg and W. H. Davenport (eds.), *Technology and Culture: An Anthology*. New York: Schocken, 1972.

Campbell, D. J. "Task Complexity: A Review and Analysis." *Academy of Management Review*, 1988, *13*, 40–52.

Davis, L. E., and Taylor, J. C. "Technology, Organization, and Job Structure." In R. Dubin (ed.), *Handbook of Work, Organization, and Society*. Skokie, Ill.: Rand-McNally, 1976.

Dornbusch, S. M., and Scott, W. R. *Evaluation and the Exercise of Authority*. San Francisco: Jossey-Bass, 1975.

Easterbrook, J. A. "The Effect of Emotion on Cue Utilization and the Organization of Behavior." *Psychological Review*, 1959, *66*, 183–201.

Ettlie, J. E. *Taking Charge of Manufacturing: How Companies Are Combining Technological and Organizational Innovations to Compete Successfully*. San Francisco: Jossey-Bass, 1988.

Eysenck, M. W. *Attention and Arousal*. New York: Springer-Verlag, 1982.

Finkelman, J. M., and Kirschner, C. "An Information-Processing Interpretation of Air Traffic Control Stress." *Human Factors*, 1980, *22*, 561–567.

Frijda, N. F. *The Emotions*. New York: Cambridge University Press, 1986.

Hancock, W. M., Macy, B. A., and Peterson, S. "Assessment of Technologies and Their Utilization." In S. E. Seashore, E. E. Lawler III, P. H. Mirvis, and C. Cammann (eds.), *Assessing Organizational Change*. New York: Wiley, 1983.

Hermann, C. F. "Some Consequences of Crisis Which Limit the Viability of Organizations." *Administrative Science Quarterly*, 1963, *8*, 61–82.

Hickson, D. J., and others. "A Strategic-Contingencies Theory of Intraorganizational Power." *Administrative Science Quarterly*, 1971, *16*, 216–229.

Hulin, C. L., and Roznowski, M. "Organizational Technologies: Effects on Organizations' Characteristics and Individuals' Responses." In L. L. Cummins and B. M. Staw (eds.), *Research in Organizational Behavior*. Vol. 7. Greenwich, Conn.: JAI Press, 1985.

Intintoli, M. J. *Taking Soaps Seriously: The World of "Guiding Light."* New York: Praeger, 1984.

Khandwalla, P. N. "Mass-Output Orientation of Operations Technology and Organizational Structure." *Administrative Science Quarterly*, 1974, *19*, 74–97.

Law, J. "Technology and Heterogeneous Engineering: The Case of Portuguese Expansion." In W. E. Bijker, T. P. Hughes, and T. J. Pinch (eds.), *The Social Construction of Technological Systems*. Cambridge, Mass.: MIT Press, 1987.

Lawrence, P. R., and Dyer, D. *Renewing American Industry*. New York: Free Press, 1983.

Lynch, B. P. "An Empirical Assessment of Perrow's Technology Construct." *Administrative Science Quarterly*, 1974, *19*, 338–356.

McGrath, J. E. "Stress and Behavior in Organizations." In M. D. Dunnette (ed.), *Handbook of Industrial and Organizational Psychology*. Skokie, Ill.: Rand-McNally, 1976.

Majchrzak, A. *The Human Side of Factory Automation: Managerial and Human Resource Strategies for Making Automation Succeed*. San Francisco: Jossey-Bass, 1988.

Mandler, G. *Mind and Body: Psychology of Emotion and Stress*. New York: Norton, 1984.

March, J. G., and Olsen, J. P. "Garbage Can Models of Decision Making in Organizations." In J. G. March and R. Weissinger-Baylon (eds.), *Ambiguity and Command*. Marshfield, Mass.: Pitman, 1986.

Metcalf, J., III. "Decision Making and the Grenada Rescue Operation." In J. G. March and R. Weissinger-Baylon (eds.), *Ambiguity and Command*. Marshfield, Mass.: Pitman, 1986.

Miles, R. H. *Macro Organizational Behavior*. Santa Monica, Calif.: Goodyear, 1980.

Mintzberg, H. *Structure in Fives*. Englewood Cliffs, N.J.: Prentice-Hall, 1983.

Neiss, R. "Reconceptualizing Arousal: Psychobiological States in Motor Performance." *Psychological Bulletin*, 1988, *103*, 345–366.

Ouchi, W. G., and McGuire, M. A. "Organizational Control: Two Functions." *Administrative Science Quarterly*, 1975, *20*, 559–569.

Perrow, C. "A Framework for the Comparative Analysis of Organizations." *American Sociological Review*, 1967, *32*, 194–208.

Perrow, C. "The Bureaucratic Paradox: The Efficient Organization Centralizes in Order to Decentralize." *Organizational Dynamics*, Spring 1977, pp. 3–14.

Perrow, C. *Normal Accidents: Living with High-Risk Technologies*. New York: Basic Books, 1984.

Perrow, C. *Complex Organizations*. (3rd ed.) New York: Random House, 1986.

Poole, M. S. "Communication and the Structuring of Organizations." Unpublished manuscript, n.d.

Riley, P. "A Structurationist Account of Political Culture." *Administrative Science Quarterly*, 1983, *28*, 414–437.

Roberts, K. H. "Bishop Rock Dead Ahead: The Grounding of U.S.S. *Enterprise*." *Naval Institute Proceedings*, forthcoming.

Scott, W. R. *Organizations: Rational, Natural, and Open Systems*. Englewood Cliffs, N.J.: Prentice-Hall, 1981.

Scott, W. R. *Organizations: Rational, Natural, and Open Systems*. (2nd ed.) Englewood Cliffs, N.J.: Prentice-Hall, 1987.

Susman, G. I., and Chase, R. B. "A Sociotechnical Analysis of the Integrated Factory." *Journal of Applied Behavioral Science*, 1986, *22*, 257–270.

Thompson, J. D., and Tuden, A. "Strategies, Structures, and Processes of Organization Decision." In J. D. Thompson (ed.), *Comparative Studies in Administration*. Pittsburgh, Pa.: University of Pittsburgh Press, 1959.

Thurow, L. C. "A Weakness in Process Technology." *Science*, 1987, *238*, 1659–1663.

Turner, J. H. "Analytical Theorizing." In A. Giddens and J. H. Turner (eds.), *Social Theory Today*. Stanford, Calif.: Stanford University Press, 1987.

Van de Ven, A. H., Delbecq, A. L., and Koenig, R. "Determinants of Coordination Modes Within Organizations." *American Sociological Review*, 1976, *41*, 322–338.

Wachtel, P. L. "Conceptions of Broad and Narrow Attention." *Psychological Bulletin*, 1967, *68*, 417–429.

Weick, K. E. *The Social Psychology of Organizing*. Reading, Mass.: Addison-Wesley, 1969.

Weick, K. E. "Enacting Sensemaking in Crisis Situations." *Journal of Management Studies*, 1988a, *25*, 305–317.

Weick, K. E. "We Are at Takeoff: Lessons from Tenerife." Paper presented at Stanford University, Nov. 1988b.

Weltman, G., Smith, J. E., and Egstrom, G. H. "Perceptual Narrowing During Simulated Pressure-Chamber Exposure." *Human Factors*, 1971, *13*, 99–107.

Winner, L. *The Whale and the Reactor*. Chicago: University of Chicago Press, 1986.

Withey, M., Daft, R. L., and Cooper, W. H. "Measures of Perrow's Work-Unit Technology: An Empirical Assessment and a New Scale." *Academy of Management Journal*, 1983, *26*, 45–63.

Woods, D. P., O'Brien, J. F., and Hanes, L. F. "Human Factors Challenges in Process Control: The Case of Nuclear Power Plants." In G. Salvendy (ed.), *Handbook of Human Factors*. New York: Wiley, 1987.

Woodward, J. *Industrial Organization: Theory and Practice*. London: Oxford University Press, 1965.

Zuboff, S. *In the Age of the Smart Machine: The Future of Work and Power*. New York: Basic Books, 1988.

Enactment

"Ready, fire, aim" is a moment of sensemaking that makes rationalists cringe, interpretavists smile, and lay people shrug. The moment has too little deliberation and deliberation in the wrong place for rationalists. The moment has enough "text" for interpretavists to work with. And the moment is not that different from all the other moments of normal natural trouble that lay people are thrown into. In each case, what is disturbing or soothing is that people act their way into explanations. This is trial and error with a twist. These are trials in search of what it means to make an error. This is doing that produces knowing. It is also doing that may be informed by prior knowing. Enactment brackets something to be made sensible which means that people are inextricably part of the data they puzzle over. My brackets seldom correspond to yours. And it would be hard for me to insure that they do. The placement of enactment near the beginning of sensemaking imparts an "action bias" to the activity, which is one reason it fits neatly into organizations that are themselves "action generators" (Starbuck, 1983).This early placement also accounts for the pragmatic quality of sensemaking since actions tend to be embedded in projects, and sense seems to follow the contours of ongoing projects. As I mentioned earlier, sensemaking is about continuation, journeys rather than destinations, and normalizing. Left to its own devices (i.e. guided largely by retained knowledge and routines) sensemaking is the infrastructure of organizational inertia. The reason it remains a conservative force is that action keeps singling out evidence that confirms prior sense, much in the manner of a self-fulfilling prophecy.

But action is not always surgical. It usually throws off unanticipated consequences. And it is these consequences that provide a pretext to develop new ways of seeing. Once again, we see that sensemaking occurs amidst a continuing stream of unique data that invite updating, although those data are not always noticed. Whether noticed or not, what remains noteworthy from a sensemaking perspective is the extent to which people are both proactive and reactive toward their surroundings. They create their own constraints, whether they do so by normalizing or by enacting self-fulfilling prophecies, or by simply messing up "the scene of the crime" thereby making it impossible to see what really happened. These are all instances of enactment. In each case people put a personal imprint on what is "out there." This perspective on action and enactment is explored in the following three chapters: Chapter 7 which bounds the phenomenon, Chapter 8 which personalizes the phenomenon in terms of career development, and Chapter 9 which portrays the role of enactment in crises such as the Bhopal disaster.

Chapter 7, titled "Enactment Processes in Organizations," is focused on organization–environment relationships and makes the case that environments are constituted by action and stored in the head as cause maps. The density and diversity of examples in this chapter provides an invitation for induction and do-it-yourself theorizing. Where else, for example, are you likely to discover the origin of the word "glitch," a translation of Piaget, and a truckload of canaries, all mustered to make a basic argument that we need to conceptualize organizational environments differently. Enactment is treated as a more influential engine in sensemaking than is "the environment." The reasoning is that externalities, such as music notation on a sheet of paper, are nothing but moments in a stream until they are bracketed by the actions of performance. It is the played notes "surging in extension of the musician's activities," not the written notes, that affect subsequent rehearsing. The use of reasonableness, plausibility, and warranted arbitrariness as criteria of validity in sensemaking is illustrated throughout this chapter. There is also the idea that self-talk, here described as "soliloquies," is an important contribution individuals make to organizational functioning. The note acknowledging Michel Bougon's impact on this essay needs to be underscored. Extensions of some of these themes are evident in his continuing work on congregate maps (e.g. Bougon, 1992).

Chapter 8, "Enactment and the Boundaryless Career: Organizing as We Work," represents a "fast forward" from the era of Polaroid's stock price, Mercury-Atlas 9, and charades in the first chapter to the era of spiral careers, flat hierarchies, and the individual as the corporation. But the basic perspective remains the same. People act their way into clearer identities by learning from retrospective interpretations of the improvisations necessary to handle discontinuous work assignments. The unusual assertion in this chapter is that these improvisations are a crucial mechanism by which organizational level learning takes place. This possibility, one that has also been discussed by James March, Anne Miner, and Barry Staw, is a good example of small structures that have large, diffuse consequences. In this chapter, I argue that improvisation in the face of discontinuity and weak situations leaves an orderly structural residual that is momentarily well adapted to current contingencies. This is structuration driven by improvisation. When it occurs, both the individual and the structure learn and are updated. Thus, in a surprising inversion, hierarchies no longer enact careers. Instead, careers enact hierarchies. As organizational life becomes more defined as a life of projects (e.g. Fast Company), individual initiatives enact more of what those projects mean.

Chapter 9, "Enacted Sensemaking in Crisis Situations," hints at the tension involved when understanding lags behind enactment. We see what we think only *after* we say it and perhaps harm someone in the saying. We know what our rifle shot has hit and what we were "aiming" for only *after* we fire. We know what our career was only *after* it's too late to change. If cognition lies in the path of the action, and becomes clearer as a result of the action, then this could have ominous implications for crisis management. People who stumble onto an escalating set of symptoms face the question, how can I know what I face until I start to treat it and see how it responds? That's the sensemaking dilemma in an unfolding crisis. Treating the crisis in order to diagnose it could make things better or worse. Unfortunately, one seldom has the option to call "time out" and deliberate. Something has to be done. And people have to develop some immediate sense of what they face. An unfolding crisis is almost an ideal setting in which to watch the dynamics of sensemaking under pressure, which may be one of the reasons my work looks so much like "ambulance chasing." In this chapter, the Bhopal disaster is used as the pretext to explore ways in which enactment in the service of sensemaking can reduce, contain, or accelerate a developing crisis. The issue here is not so much decision making or building a safety culture, as it is one of comprehension. People who operate organizations that are capable of catastrophic outcomes make sense using the same processes as everyone else does. Neither their routines nor their procedure manuals anticipate everything that operators face in those organizations. The only things we can count on are that surprises will continue to occur, people will continue to act their way into understanding, and actions and understanding will continue to contract in ways associated with threat-rigidity cycles (Staw, Sandelands, and Dutton, 1981). Given these "constants," an important relationship in sensemaking is the effect of capability on perception. People see those events they feel they can handle. And we don't see what we can't handle. Pediatricians who were unable to deal with parents who battered their own children, didn't "see" child abuse until social workers who did know how to handle abusive parents, joined their treatment teams (Westrum, 1993). A perceived lack of individual capability can often be offset by increased collective capability that heightens collective sensing and sensemaking. This prospect is why organizing processes and collective sensemaking are central issues in organizations that run high-risk technologies and why the discussion of "capacity" in this chapter is a starting point to think through these relationships.

References

Bougon, Michel (1992). Congregate cognitive maps: A unified dynamic theory of organization and strategy. *Journal of Management Studies*, 29, 269–89.

Starbuck, William H. (1983). Organizations as action generators. *American Sociological Review*, 48, 91–102.

Staw, Barry M., Sandelands, Lance E., and Dutton, Jane E. (1981). Threat-rigidity effects in organizational behavior: A multi-level analysis. *Administrative Science Quarterly*, 26, 501–24.

Westrum, Ron. (1993). Thinking by groups, organizations, and networks: A sociologist's view of the social psychology of science and technology. In W. Shadish and S. Fuller (eds.), *Social Psychology of Science*, New York: Guilford, pp. 440–58.

7

Enactment Processes in Organizations[1]

With the introduction of open systems analyses into organization theory, it has become fashionable to talk about the interaction between organizations and their environments. One byproduct of this has been a potential overestimation of the ease with which distinct organizations can be differentiated from their distinct environments. The presence of explicit boundaries separating distinct, internally-constrained entities has been assumed so that investigators could move on to other issues. These assumptions of distinct units, however, have influenced the form that other arguments about organizations take. For example, having assumed that boundaries are not problematic, investigators have examined issues such as how things "cross" boundaries, how organizations react to their environments and occasionally try to influence them, and how organizations go about learning what is really out there that they have to deal with.

The perspective to be developed in this chapter argues that organizations[2] are more active in constructing the environments that impinge on them than is commonly recognized. That is, organizations often impose that which subsequently imposes on them. From this perspective, organizational scholars should pay particular attention to the conditions under which organizations implant that which they later rediscover and call "knowledge" or "understanding" of their "environment." The nature of the processes whereby organizations create the environments that subsequently constrain their actions can be illustrated using banks, physicians, and actors as examples.

Enacted Investment

Large banks are institutional investors in the stock market. they collect money from individual clients and use it to purchase stock, bonds, and other securities for their clients' benefit. These large institutional investors account for a sizeable portion of the trading that occurs on the exchanges (currently, almost 60 percent of the shares traded). Presumably, the interaction between these investors and the market could be examined as one of investors reacting to market fluctuations in such a way as to raise the probabilities that their investments will be profitable.

The sheer size of these investors, however, also means that their activities can he understood as the creation of the environments that then impose on them. The fate of Polaroid Corporation stock during 1972 is a good example. During 1972 Polaroid sold for as much as $149 per share,

> . . . a price that reflected near unanimous agreement among institutional investors that Polaroid was a growth company with hot consumer prospects: After all, it had just developed a new color camera that would ultimately be in every household. Yet sometime that year, the fund managers who thought so highly of Polaroid began wondering how they could ever unload the huge Polaroid blocks they had accumulated, since at that point anyone who was likely to buy Polaroid stock had probably already done so. Suddenly, institutions began to bail out of Polaroid, causing the price to fall. This drop led other institutions to sell ever-larger blocks of Polaroid shares, causing the price to drop even more sharply. At one point in 1972, Polaroid dipped as low as $86; last year it bottomed out at $15. (Rottenberg, 1976, pp. 21–22)

Doubts concerning the attractiveness of Polaroid investments created the environment which then was imposed on investors and made Polaroid stocks less attractive to hold, thereby validating the initial definition that they might be less attractive than originally thought – a self-fulfilling prophecy.

This example of an enacted environment in banking illustrates the more general case that there may be a closed-loop quality to much organizational "sensemaking." There are conditions under which organizations do not act like open systems, conditions under which they create the environment that they make sense of. Campbell (1975) has made a similar observation:

> Adaptive evolution is a negative feedback steering device, and therefore works best when the evolving social organization is a small part of the total environment, so that variations in the social organization do not substantially change the selective system, that is, the overall environment. It is on these grounds that one might well doubt that any adaptive social evolution is going on at the level of nations today. Major nations are so few in number, and so much the dominant part of each other's environment, that each variation initiated by one nation may fundamentally change the overall system, thus altering the selective system and creating something closer to a runaway positive feedback rather than a stabilizing negative feedback. (p. 1106)

Unless an evolving organization is only a small part of the environment, then, its actions will change the selection system. As an organization increases in size it becomes more and more its own selection system and finally quite literally does impose the environment that imposes on it. As should also be apparent, the distinction between organization and environment becomes hopelessly blurred under these ultimate conditions, a blurring that was apparent in the Polaroid sell-off.

Enacted Medicine

Physicians also create some of the environments that impose on them. A particularly clear example of this enactment is "physician-induced disease" (iatrogenics). The concept of iatrogenics has been invoked by Scheff (1965) in his studies of errors in medical diagnosis. He notes that the predominant decision rule in medicine is, "When in doubt continue to suspect illness." If we use the language of "type 1" errors and "type 2" errors, a type 1 error would occur when the physician dismisses a patient who is actually ill and a type 2 error would occur when a physician retains a patient who is not ill.

Scheff presents considerable data demonstrating that physicians overwhelmingly make type 2 errors. The chief medical errors, in other words, consist of the physician diagnosing someone as sick who in fact is really well. This preference for type 2 errors seems to rest on two assumptions: (1) "Disease is usually a determinant, inevitably unfolding process, which if undetected and untreated, will grow to a point where it endangers the life or limb of the individual, and, in the case of contagious diseases, the lives of others" (p. 71); (2) "medical diagnosis of illness, unlike legal judgment, is not an irreversible act which does untold damage to the status and reputation of the patient" (p. 71). These two assumptions which buttress a preference for type 2 errors imply that type 2 errors are relatively harmless. It is this conclusion to which Scheff takes strong objection.

He argues that it is possible for a physician to create illness where none exists by inadvertently giving labels to his patients at a time of high suggestibility. In response to this labeling, patients then proceed to act out a career of chronic illness. Had the labels not been available, had the person's symptoms remained unorganized (see Miller, Hampe, Barrett, and Noble, 1970), and had the person not been as suggestible, then a career of illness would not necessarily have occurred. The effects of a diagnosis of false positive may be much more serious than is now realized in the medical profession.

To carry the analysis one step further, among physicians it is probably the case that they can be sorted into those who favor active intervention to alleviate sickness and those who prefer to "let nature take its course." The proposition suggested by this categorization is that those who favor active intervention will make more type 2 errors than those who view intervention as a means to assist natural processes. The "interventionists" more frequently impose a world that subsequently presents them with medical environments requiring their skills.

Enacted Theater

Actors, especially those who engage in improvisational theater, frequently impose environments which then organize their subsequent activities. A good example of theatrical enacted environments is Keith Johnstone's "Theatre Machine" company in London (Jencks and Silver, 1973, pp. 144–45). In one routine, two performers are given a deck of cards with one sentence of dialogue written on each card. The deck is shuffled, after which the actors take turns reading lines from the cards and trying to make dramatic sense of them. In another sketch two players improvise dialogue while two additional players move the speakers' body parts through "suitable" actions. Obviously the body movements always lag slightly behind the words that are being said thereby creating some striking incongruities. Members of the company also create a situation where two actors mime something in slow motion while a third person comments on it. "A scene like this involves triple discoveries, with each performer supplying information to the others that he then uses in some generally unexpected way; successive transformations take place" (p.145).

In each of these instances, the players build up an environment that informs their subsequent actions. Frequently, the actors do not know what they have done until the action is completed. A person, for example, who tries to make random dialogue meaningful, may not know what he has just said until he hears the tone of voice used by his partner in the next remark. The actors steadily build up a plausible world, but it is a world of their own design put in place by their own actions and then rediscovered as something to which they accommodate their subsequent actions. The actors are literally talking to themselves, but in doing so, they are not becoming more confused. Quite the contrary. Their world is developing a sense of sorts.

Conclusion

In all three cases – investment policies, iatrogenics, and improvisational theater – people had a major role in creating the world toward which they subsequently "responded." The separations between the organization and the environment were decidedly blurred in each case (e.g., the physician sees himself when his diagnosis implants a "disease" which is then presented to him for treatment). Sensemaking in each of these cases often involves individuals examining reflectively their own actions in order to discover what they've done and what the meaning of those actions is. Finally, the process of sensemaking in each case is better understood by examining what is in people's heads and imposed by them on a stream of events than by trying to describe what is "out there."

Conceptualizatlons of Enactment

We will now try to locate the phenomenon we are interested in by means of organizational concepts. Relevant assertions made by Filley, House, and Kerr (1976), Katz and Kahn (1966), and Piaget (1962) will be examined.

Control imagery

In the examples of banks, physicians, and actors, there was an activist imagery. Organizations were proactive toward their environments rather than reactive to them.

The theme that organizations try to control their environments whenever possible has appeared often in the organizational literature:

> Organizations seek to control environments by increasing their power over environmental units, and seek to adapt to environments by monitoring environmental demands and by designing structures and practices to permit effective response to such demands. (Filley, House, and Kerr, 1976, p. 299).

Generally, organizations that face complex, unpredictable environments tend to have complex structures, including high differentiation among units and high decentralization of decision making.

The enactment perspective used in this chapter highlights different features in organization–environment interactions than are emphasized by Filley, House, and Kerr. For example, distinctions between *the* organization and *the* environment are treated as more problematic (see the following discussion of Katz and Kahn), and the activity of controlling is also viewed differently. The importance of control from an enactment perspective lies in the fact that to control something is to take actions with respect to it. These actions become the raw materials from which a sense of the situation is *eventually* built. The controlling actions are what the organization examines retrospectively to see what it is up to. Filley, House, and Kerr also say little about how the organization knows what it faces. The environment portrayed in this proposition is already thick with meaning, and the problem we are interested in is how organizations invest their settings with meaning and modify these understandings over time. In a sense, Filley, House, and Kerr intercept the problem of adaptation later than we do. They assume that the organization "knows" its environment and can then decide which portions can be controlled and which require accommodation. The question we focus on is how does the organization even come to use labels such as "controllable" or "coercive" to punctuate its stream of experience? Why not other labels? Why assume organizations strive to control environments rather than their own perceptions (Powers, 1973)?

Organizations have to build their environments before they can even have the luxury of controlling them. The ways in which they construct them cognitively will have strong effects on their actual actions of control. Furthermore, in the act of controlling their constructed environments, organizations learn quite vividly what those environments consist of. It is the understanding and sensemaking which accompany the Filley, House, and Kerr controlling and adapting activities that are given most attention in the enactment perspective.

Systems imagery

Some of the issues broached in the preceding section concerning boundaries can be illustrated in terms of open systems theory. As mentioned earlier, in their enthusiasm for the imagery of organizations as open systems, some investigators have taken as a given the distinction between an "organization" and its "environment." They have been vague, however, about what that environment is toward which those organizations are open and where it "begins." Thus, much of the talk about environments faced by organizations suffers from misplaced concreteness. As a result, boundaries are drawn between the supposed "environment" and the supposedly corresponding "organization" with more certainty than seems warranted.

To illustrate the issue of misplaced concreteness, consider the following statement:

> The first problem in understanding an organization or a social system, is its location and identification. How do we know that we are dealing with an organization? What are its boundaries? What behavior belongs to the organization, and what behavior lies outside it? (Katz and Kahn, 1966, p. 14)

In their first sentence, Katz and Kahn declare that the identification and location of systems are problematic. In their second sentence the problem is said to be epistemological (i.e., a problem in the acquisition of knowledge). But in their third and fourth sentences Katz and Kahn ignore the caveat imposed by the first two sentences; they assume the *existence* of boundaries, insides, and outsides – an existence which they had just declared problematic. Predictably, in their following section Katz and Kahn also ignore their caveats and talk about inputs and outputs that take place between *an* open system and "*the* external environment" (p. 19, emphasis added). Inclusion of the article "the" before "external environment" implies a unique, objective environment that exists independent of actors and actions and that appears similar to all observers. Furthermore, the qualifier "external" placed before the word "environment" implies that there is another environment, presumably labeled "internal," that is not to be confused with the external one.

While the categories external/internal or outside/inside exist logically, they do not exist empirically. The "outside" or "external" world cannot be known. There is no methodological process by which one can confirm the existence of an object independent of the confirmatory process involving oneself. The outside is a void, there is only the inside. A person's world, the inside or internal view, is all that can be known. The rest can only be the object of speculation. Therefore, when we object to internal/external or inside/outside as arbitrary partitions that tend to confuse issues, what we mean is simply that logical distinctions in this case do not necessarily correspond to empircal distinctions. Actors immersed in experiential streams organize and punctuate those streams by positing organizations and environments (and gods and traits), however, and the last thing we want to do is define away their solutions to sensemaking by imposing for them the logical but empirically empty distinction between internal and external worlds. *If* organizational members discover that inside/outside is a useful punctuation, and impose it, and retain it because it allows them to take reasonable actions, fine. We simply don't want to put words in their mouths or images in their eyes.

The misplaced concreteness of talk about *the* organization and *the* environment diverts the attention of organizational theorists from crucial problems. If one asserts the existence of a mythical entity, then observers are tempted to search for its properties rather than treat its "existence" as problematic. If it were viewed as problematic, the more crucial questions would consist of queries such as under what conditions its "existence" is posited, what that positing accomplishes for the positer, and how people operate when they punctuate their streams of experience with other nouns than "the external environment."

Environments are problematic, but not their substances and properties and parts. It is their existence as an entity that is problematic. How does it come to pass that an organization finds it useful to say of its flow of experience, "we face an environment" or "we face the environment"? To what questions asked by organizational members is the positing of an environment or the environment an answer? Yet organizational theorists don't worry about problems such as this. They act as if it is obvious what the environment is and where it is. Given these a priori certainties, what investigators tend to dismiss is the assertion that the environment is located in the mind of the actor and is imposed by him on experience in order to make that experience more meaningful. It seldom dawns on organizational theorists to look for environments inside of heads rather than outside of them. Neither Filley, House, and Kerr, nor Katz and Kahn, sensitize organization watchers to this issue. One person, however, who has taken seriously the possibility that environments are in the head, waiting to be imposed, is Jean Piaget.

Cognitive imagery

An unusually thorough summary of the sensemaking mechanism we are proposing is found in the following phrase translated from Piaget (1962, pp. 191–3):

> . . . the initial universe [of a person] is not a network of causal sequences, but a simple collection of events surging in extension of *his* own activities. (pp. 191–92, emphasis added)[3]

Virtually all of the elements that we associate with enacted sensemaking are found in that sentence. The closest approximation to the enactment process per se is contained in the phrase, "surging in extension of his own activities." The imagery of surging suggests that things are not well delineated, they change as a consequence of the intensity and nature of an individual's activities, and that what a person does is what he eventually will know.

The process of transforming these enacted raw data into information is suggested by Piaget to be a two-stage affair. First, there is a crude punctuation phase in which the undifferentiated flow is turned into "a simple collection," a phrase that implies that portions are bracketed and separated (the flow of the stream of experience has been frozen and divided into units), that only the crudest relations, if any, have been established among the units, and that a modest transformation from raw data into information has occurred. One might even argue that this crude breaking up of a stream into a simple collection of events lies somewhere between bracketing a portion of the stream of experience for further work and labeling and connecting that which has been bracketed.

The second stage of the transformation from raw data to information, however, is the more influential one for conduct. The person continues to do cognitive work on the collection of events until they become transformed into a "network of causal sequences." The final product of enactment, therefore, will be a causal map (Weick, 1975) depicting how the events in the simple collection are causally related.

It is interesting that Piaget describes the events as surging rather than emerging, implying that these events occur suddenly rather than gradually. The course of sensemaking implied here is jagged and discontinuous rather than smooth and continuous. Surprises should be plentiful and puzzles more dogged than any actor would wish. Again it should be emphasized that the person is active, both cognitively and physically, when the environment is organized. The person is not a data collector, is not accumulating replicas of the environment, and is not copying outside events. Instead, the person is punctuating and enacting the flow of experience, the results of these activities being retained in a network of causal sequences or causal map.

The key ideas in Piaget's description can be illustrated by considering the following stream of experience:[4]

adhadhadhadhadhadhadJameswhileJohnhadhadhadhadhadha
dhadhadhadhadhadmoreinterestfortheteacherhadhadh.

Enactment is partially the process of stumbling onto that string. Enactment also means bracketing some portion of that stream as in the following:

JameswhileJohnhadhadhadhadhadhadhadh
adhadhadhadmoreinterestfortheteacher

These dual enactment activities of generating and bracketing occur at the initial stage of sensemaking, can be constrained by past experience, produce raw data rather than information, and partially constrain sensemaking because they exclude portions of the stream of experience. So far, we have an exhibit of what exists as "extensions of a person's own activities."

Once a person has generated/bracketed part of the stream, then the activities of punctuation and connection (parsing) can occur in an effort to transform the raw data into information. One way to punctuate that stream is to separate it by equal spaces into 19 "words," an arbitrary, reasonable, initial way to organize that stream. The result looks like this:

James while John had had had had had had had
had had had had more interest for the teacher

Now, we have a "simple collection of events," namely words, but we have no idea how they might be connected or organized in terms of meaningful "causal sequences."

Even though the initial puctuation was reasonable, it did not prove to be sensible. We still don't know what is being asserted. Therefore, we try another form of punctuation, this time using unequal spaces between the words.

James while John had had had had had had h
ad had had had had more interest for the teacher

The use of unequal spacing as a punctuation scheme looks promising, because connections among sets of words are suggested. If we insert punctuation marks in place of the unequal spaces to concretize the connections, we arrive at the following display:

James, while John had had "had had," had had "had."
"Had had" had had more interest for the teacher.

Punctuated in that manner, the work produced by John was found more interesting by the teacher than was James' work. John has "caused" an increase in the teacher's interest. A meaningful causal sequence has appeared. Exactly the opposite conclusion can be reached if we punctuate those same raw data like this:

James, while John had had "had," had had "had had."
"Had had" had had more interest for the teacher.

Now James, rather than John, becomes the favored person and James, rather than John, is responsible for heightening the teacher's interest.

Notice some salient properties of this episode of sensemaking. There is a certain arbitrariness to the activity. One set of punctuations and connections is frequently as plausible as another. Those punctuations that are made are also consequential; the identity of the favored person in this example changes depending on which punctuation scheme is used. Furthermore, the enactment of the reader-actor was initimately woven into that final information both by means of the activity of punctuation and by means of the initial bracketing.

Enactment processes generated and bracketed the raw data; punctuation and connection processes (parsing) transformed the raw data into information – and the *result* was an enacted environment. Notice that the enacted environment is something more than a simple collection of events. Depending on how the initial sequence is parsed, either James or John "caused" a change in the teacher's interest. It is not just that each of the two men possesses some "had hads" and the teacher possesses more interest; rather it is the fact that these assorted possessions have become causally linked. They were not intrinsically or inherently causally linked. Instead, the sequences became causally related only as an extension of the actor's own activities of bracketing and parsing.

It is important to note that even though enactment looks like a relatively insignificant portion of the process of doing interpretations, in fact it is of major importance. The only possible raw materials that are available for subsequent parsing and retention, are those materials initially generated and/or bracketed by enactment processes. Enactment drives everything else in an organization. *How enactment is done is what an organization will know.* Even though parsing and enactment are constrained by past experience (e.g., I will often do what I can label), what I am trying to specify are those processes that affect the invention of environments, in order to see more clearly how organizations generate self-validating knowledge of those environments.

Characteristics of Enacted Sensemaking

This chapter represents working notes about a class of phenomena, the observation of which will allow observers to render these observations obsolete. That is, a definitive characterization of enacted sensemaking remains to be written. It is possible, however, to state some preliminary considerations that may be relevant to defining the concept.

Reality is treated metaphorically

Elsewhere I have noted that "reality is a metaphor" (Weick, 1969a). By that I meant that talk about "a reality" is simply one way that people try to make sense out of the stream of experience that flows by them. To say that there is a reality, an environment, and then to search for and discover underlying patterns in those superimposed structures is one way to make sense of that stream. But the tenuousness of this process, as well as the actor's central role in its execution are captured only if we remain attentive to reality *as* metaphor. Failure to view reality in these terms Is usually associated with underestimation of the ways in which individuals contribute to the worlds they think they see.

Literally, to enact an environment can mean to "create the appearance of an environment" or to "simulate an environment for the sake of representation." Those two meanings are compatible with the position taken in this chapter. Members act as if they have environments, create the appearance of environments, or simulate environments for the sake of getting on with their business. These organizing acts are acts of invention rather than acts of discovery, they involve a superimposed order rather than underlying order, and they are based on the assumption that cognition follows the trail of action.

One of the more dramatic examples of the metaphorical quality of reality is found in attempts by technicians, engineers and astronauts at NASA to make sense out of unaccountable electrical phenomena

> ... like the light on an instrument panel suddenly turning on when the machine it serviced was most definitely off. That was sometimes not merely hard to explain, but impossible to explain. So they called it a glitch. God's own luminescence was in the switch! Give a better explanation! "I just threw a glitch into the light when I was turning my warning lights off and on," said Gordon Cooper during the flight of Mercury-Atlas 9 when a gravity signal showed on his switchboard during an orbital freefall. Cooper was renowned for his phlegm, but one butterfly of the night must have beat its wings in his throat when he looked at a dial, which showed the force of gravity was present at a time when he knew he must be without weight. Yet note: Whether it is with vanity, woe, or awe, he still takes credit for throwing the glitch. Who indeed has not felt the force of his own personality before a sensitive machine? (Mailer, 1970, pp. 167–68)

NASA brackets (generates?) a puzzling portion of its stream of experience and invents the label "glitch" as an explanation for the origins of and causal connections among mysterious phenomena. "God's own luminescence was in the switch." The enacted environment of "glitch" is then retained as one more causal map available to be superimposed as an "explanation" for puzzles such as those which confronted Cooper. When the normal presumption of an "earthly" reality proved inadequate as a means for NASA to organize what it thought it saw, the extraordinary presumption of an additional, more ethereal reality was introduced, after which it was again sensemaking, as usual. NASA may not have treated reality as a metaphor prior to "glitch," but it's a safe bet that they now hedge their epistemological and metaphysical bets, given a glitch's "existence."

Soliloquies define cognition

"An explorer can never know what he is exploring until it has been explored" (Bateson, 1972, p. xvi). The organizational equivalent of that assertion is "an organization can never know what it thinks or wants until it sees what it does." In the case of organizations, what they say and what they do provide the displays which can be examined reflectively after their occurrence in order to understand what is occurring. The sequence in that prototypical soliloquy is crucial. Talk or some kind of action occurs first and provides the occasion for an eventual articulation of cognitions and desires.

Consider the following question, one commonly uttered by organization members in the interest of sensemaking: "How can I know what I think until I see what I say?"

If we apportion the several activities in that sentence among the organizing processes of retention, selection, and enactment (Weick, 1969b), the apportionment will be as follows. "Know what I think . . ." is the outcome and conclusion of an effort at sensemaking. Knowledge of what one thinks, therefore, is stored in the retention process in the form of an enacted environment. Thus, an enacted environment is the residue of a sensemaking episode that is stored in the retention process as past wisdom. An enacted environment is the output from an episode of sensemaking, not the input to it.

Environments enacted on previous occasions can constrain contemporary enactment. When it is said that an organization is influenced by what it already knows, we mean that contemporary activities of generating and bracketing are affected as well by the present stream of experience as by environments that have been enacted on previous occasions.

The phrase, "until I see" is the process of selection and involves the activities of punctuation and connection. Punctuation means chopping the stream of experience into sensible, namable, and named units, and the activity of connection involves imposing relationships, typically causal relationships, among the punctuated elements. Another way to describe the selection activity is to say that it involves parsing. To parse something means to analyze and describe it grammatically, which also means to point out parts and their interrelations. Pointing out the parts is the activity of punctuation; interrelating these parts is the activity of connection; and the joint activities of punctuation and connection are the activity of parsing.

Other investigators (e.g., Watzlawick; Beavin, and Jackson, 1967, pp. 54–59) have also talked about the activity of punctuation, but their analyses imply that punctuation involves imposing different relationships among given variables. Never specified in these discussions is how the variables become singled out and named in the first place. Instead, it is argued that people can see different sequences in a long stream of pre-punctuated activities. What I wish to emphasize is the fact that punctuation involves chopping a stream of experience into event-variables that are labeled but that these labels are rather arbitrary. Once the variables have been named, the individual has not yet completed the sensemaking activities because the events must be grouped in some meaningful way. This grouping activity was referred to as "connection" by David Hume (1748; reprinted, 1955) and there is no reason to depart from his term. The activity of *seeing* what one has said implies for us organizing, in meaningful ways, raw data of letters and words.

This means that the phrase, "what I say" contains the enactment process. Raw talk is the data on which subsequent sensemaking operates. The talk – the saying, the soliloquizing – is what is meant by the activity of enactment.

Thus, taken in reverse order, there is the enactment process of saying, which is followed by the selection process of transforming the saying into information, a process that involves parsing (punctuation and connection). Once the enacted stream of talk has been parsed, an enacted environment exists. This enacted environment is something that the organization's members momentarily "know" and "feel they understand." The retained enacted wisdom may, on future occasions, serve as a constraint on actions that generate and bracket the stream of experience and/or as a constraint on the labels, punctuation marks, and relationships that are imposed on new chunks of raw data.

When it is asserted that organizations talk to themselves and engage in soliloquies, that shorthand expression maps across the process of enactment, selection, and retention in the manner specified above. That mapping suggests that the enacted environment is primarily an output rather than an input, that enactment generates raw data rather than information, and that the so-called "serious" work of sensemaking involves parsing which occurs as a selection activity.

Organizing soliloquies can affect such diverse phenomena as motivation, decision making, and communication. Robert Faris, for example, suggests the motivational importance of retrospecting soliloquies:

> The reward for the mountain climber, as well as for the pursuer of many a distant goal, must then be spread over a process of imagination extending over a long period of time in which images of past and future intermingle. In the months before the activity begins, for example, the climber not only imagines the experience of climbing, but relishes the more distant future when he can look back on the adventure. . . . Sometimes, at the moment of consummation of a long-term project, the event goes by so quickly that the person hardly experiences it, and has afterward only a confused memory. Such is often reported for weddings and graduation exercises which presumably culminate long periods of effort and planning. . . . It may be that even when a brief sense of ecstasy is felt, its power and influence yet lie in the longer term of anticipation and retrospection in imagination. It is the suggestion of this argument, in any case, that motivation for long-range goals is mainly, perhaps entirely, in the time-extending anticipatory and retro-

spective imagination, along with anticipation of retrospection and retrospection of anticipation, applied not only to the moment of goal consummation, but to various significant stages of the process of activity before and after. (1968, p. 66)

Thus, what may sustain interest in activities with brief moments of consummation, are the anticipation of retrospection and retrospecting the anticipation. Not only do soliloquies stretch the duration of the activity but they also make a larger portion of it sensible.

The potential importance of soliloquies in decision making has been described by Garfinkel:

In place of the view that decisions are made as the occasions require, an alternative formulation needs to be entertained. It consists of the possibility that the person defines retrospectively the decisions that have been made. *The outcome comes before the decision.* . . . The rules of decision making in daily life . . . may be much more preoccupied with the problem of assigning outcomes their legitimate history than with the question of deciding before the actual occasion of choice the conditions under which one, among a set of alternative possible courses of action, will be elected. (1967, p. 114)

The game of charades is a superb metaphor for enacted sensemaking as it affects communication. In charades, an actor enacts an environment which puzzled observers try to parse. Imagine that you are the person in charades who must act out the title of a movie and imagine that you are given, as your title, the movie *Charade*. As the presenter, you probably would try somehow to get "outside" of the game and point to it so that the observers would see that the answer is the very activity they are now engaged in. Alas, the observers are likely to miss this subtlety and instead to shout words like, "pointing," "finger," "excited," "all of this," and so forth.

There are several interesting features of enactment in charades. The person doing the gesturing knows what he is perceived as enacting only after he hears the observers' guesses. That is, the actor produces a soliloquy, the punctuation of which is done by others. The actor produces an enacted environment as an output but the observers are faced with a display which they can punctuate and connect in numerous ways. The actor imposes meanings on his environment that come back and organize his activities, except that the observers see these implanted meanings as puzzles rather than certainties. If the actor has enacted a puzzling or complicated or subtle environment, that enactment comes back and organizes him in the sense that he has to do enormous work to salvage, patch up, and redirect the observers' efforts to invent plausible constructions for his subtleties.

Notice that in mountain climbing, historicizing an outcome, and charades, the actual actions available for sensemaking are loosely organized. They remain susceptible to numerous interpretations, interpretations that will be imposed after the fact. Organizations talk to themselves in order to clarify their surroundings and learn more about them. These soliloquies frequently are closed systems. Organizations examine retrospectively the very displays that initially they created as pretexts for sensemaking. Organizations talk in order to discover what they are saying, act in order to discover what they are doing.

Enactment brackets raw data

In another work (Weick, 1969b) I described enactment in a rather confusing manner: "The enactment process creates the information that the system adapts to, and in doing so removes a small amount of equivocality" (p. 91). If that sentence had contained the words "raw data" instead of "information," the meaning would have been clearer. While I am retaining the ideas that enactment is an active process and that it creates some of what the organization has to deal with, it is also clear that the creation of information occurs later in the process of organizational sensemaking than I realized. In the earlier analysis, enactment simultaneously put an environment before the organization and partially labeled that environment. For the sake of clarity, I think the activities of enacting the raw data and of labeling it need to be separated so that it is possible to get a clearer idea of what affects each activity. In the earlier example involving James, John, the teacher, and a host of "hads," information appeared quite late in the example when, finally, "words" were identified and separated. Left unexplained was the genesis of the raw data on which meanings were superimposed. That same questionable origin of raw materials available for sensemaking is present in my description of enactment quoted at the beginning of this paragraph.

The temptation is strong to conclude that the analysis is complete once an environment has been described in terms of information. What is left out by this description is an explanation of how the raw data were generated and bracketed in the stream of experience as potential candidates for sensemaking. The concept of enactment, as a sensemaking activity, is now being assigned exclusively to the initial steps when experience is both generated and bracketed under the partial constraint of retained wisdom.

The distinctions among information, raw data, meaning, and communication have been illustrated by Thayer (1967):

> A [manufacturing] plant does not operate on the basis of the existence of certain raw materials, but on the basis of certain *information* about the condition, place, price, utility, and so on, of those raw materials: ". . . any characteristic of an operation that can be observed and recorded constitutes potential information for the communication network" (Miller and Starr, 1960). Materials and parts are thus legitimate units of information. (p. 92)

It could be argued, as I did in 1969, that enactment is the process by which an organization generates its own information. However, that usage obscures the crucial distinction between data and information. As Thayer (1967) said:

> It is not the "things" of the world – material or nonmaterial with which we deal. We deal with "information" about these things . . . the things themselves are physical data that are sensed and transduced by the individual sensorium to provide him with raw sensory data. The function of the psychological system, at this point, is to select out and convert that raw data into information – i.e, into "mental" material for thought or "decision." It is this event or occurrence – that of consciously or unconsciously ascribing meaning or significance to raw sensory data and thus of converting it to information –

that I prefer to call "communication." Thus communication *occurs* when some raw data input has been meaningfully related to some portion of the total psychological system for immediate or later use in thought or action. It follows from this, and other notions of intrapersonal functioning, that the *meaning* of *any* experience is constituted by the very process of its accommodation into the dynamic psychological system. (p. 89)

Given the distinction between raw data and information, I want to argue that enactment involves generating the raw data which is eventually transformed by other processes into information and action. Enactment processes shape an organization's experience at the raw data stage, not at the information stage. Influences from enactment are there from the beginning and it is this sense in which enactment involves the creation of an orginization's environment.

When people talk about organizations operating on information as an environment, they often fail to specify what the raw data are or how they were created. This failure makes it difficult to understand how organizations do interpretation, how they know, or what they know. The concept of an enactment process tries to fill that gap by highlighting the difference between raw data and information and by asserting that actions generate the raw data that eventually may be parsed into sensible experiences.

Thus, when it is asserted that enactment processes generate raw data, this means that actions serve to bracket and single out some portions of the stream of experience for further examination. The bracketing is exceedingly crude in the sense that it involves nothing more than the suggestion that observers should pay more attention to *this* ill-defined portion of the stream than to that one.

Enactment, viewed as the generation and bracketing of raw data, can also be described using imagery associated with an evolutionary epistemology. If we consider the common sequence of trial and error, then enactment is pure trial with no judgments of error being made. Perception of error is a selection activity. Error is a particular way of parsing the ongoing stream of experience under the constraint of retained wisdom. Enactment generates raw data from which one may conclude that an error has been made, but those very same data might just as easily be punctuated as a truth has been spoken, a truism has been blurted, an absurdity has been confirmed, and so forth. If you cannot mentally disentangle truth from error in a sequence of trials, then you've got the image of what is meant by an enactment process and you can begin to sense the modest constraints that shape it.

Implications of the point that enactment is largely unconstrained can be seen if we examine the assertion that organizations engage in lots of random actions. Members of organizations often do things with little warrant and it is often these episodes of bumbling and galumphing that produce rich variations which can be serendipitously parsed into novel definitions of what has occurred (Weick, 1976). Enactment is the organizational equivalent of unjustified variation (Campbell, 1974), and is often only weakly constrained by retention and causal maps. It is that sense in which "galumphing" is an accurate description of what happens in enactment. Miller (1973, p. 92) has described galumphing as the "patterned voluntary [i.e., controlled by retention and causal maps] elaboration or complication of process, where the pattern is not under the dominant control of goals."

Activities that are not under the predominant control of retention and causal maps are activities that can wrap themselves in novel ways around novel "objects" in the environment, thereby providing occasions for novel parsing and adaptation. The veneer of rationality that overlies much talk about organizations tends to minimize the role of random activities. If enactment is described as pure trial, as random activity, as indiscriminate bracketing, as generating raw data, and as loosely coupled actions, as well as activity that may be constrained by previous enactment, then the subtle mixture of chaos and order that seems to characterize this initial process has been captured.

Reasonableness supersedes accuracy

If one assumes that sensemaking involves invention rather than discovery, then validation takes on a different appearance. One cannot say that a superimposed order is right or wrong. Such a judgment would presume an underlying order that is waiting to be discovered. Validation of superimposed patterns involves judgments of reasonableness, and if one superimposed order is reasonable and is no less plausible than some other imposed order, then the imposition is valid.

The notion that reasonableness is the appropriate criterion of validity in superimposed orders is found in our research on model cultures (Weick and Gilfillan, 1971). We composed three-person groups, implanted a specific strategy that the founders were to use in solving the Common Target Game, and then steadily for 11 generations replaced these founders one at a time with naïve subjects. The question was, what would happen to the initial strategies or punctuations that were implanted? Previous research suggested that the implanted strategies would disappear by about the sixth generation due to spontaneous innovations introduced by newcomers. What we found was that this occurred in one condition but not in another. It all depended on the kind of tradition present. One form of punctuation was perpetuated indefinitely. Thus, spontaneous innovation does not inevitably erode a tradition or displace an enacted environment.

When a culture started with a strategy that was just as good as another one they could have used, this strategy persisted. Even when occasional subjects tried to revolt against this "reasonable" strategy and replace it, these efforts were never successful. We labeled this type of strategy, "warranted arbitrary." By this we mean that arbitrarily choosing this particular strategy is warranted or reasonable because no real-world criteria exist that suggest it is any worse than other ones. Other similar strategies are equally functional and it's a toss-up as to which one should be used. Thus, the choice among these equivalent strategies can legitimately be made on grounds such as personal preference, esthetic qualities, whatever.

But if a less functional strategy is adopted (its dysfunctions outweigh its functions), it will rapidly disappear due to counterpressures from reality. We have labeled this kind of item "unwarrantedly arbitrary." A group is in trouble if it ignores rational criteria and adopts a strategy that is *not* obviously as good as other ones it can imagine. The group is in trouble because this strategy is vulnerable to spontaneous innovations and will soon disappear. This is fortunate in the sense that there seems to be a self-correcting mechanism that operates in a group even when its personnel is changing. It is less fortunate because these changes expose the group to uncertainty and low productivity during the intervals when the unwarranted strategy is gradually being replaced.

We were struck by the fact that this apparent cultural wisdom in the choice and perpetuation of strategies clearly is not tied to specific people. By the fourth generation in all cultures, no one knows precisely what strategy that culture started with and all participants know that their task is to hit the target numbers in any way they please. Nevertheless, naïve subjects continue to use the exact strategy their culture started with *if* that strategy is just as good as any other one, and refuse to use the initial strategy the culture started with if there are alternative strategies that are more reasonable. Once the poorer strategies have been replaced by more reasonable ones, the replacements also become resistant to spontaneous innovation.

Thus, to state that an organization makes reasonable punctuations of its experience is not a bland assertion. To make reasonable punctuations is the best that an organization can do when it constructs an enacted environment.

It will be recalled that parsing is an act of invention, not an act of discovery. It is an invention in the sense that decisions about punctuation and connection single out an economical network from the few networks posited which, in turn, are but a handful of all possible causal networks that could have been invented. A crucial property of an invented network or causal map is that its validity cannot be proven in a logical sense. Instead, the only assertion that can be made about conclusions contained in the map are that they are as likely, as possible, and as reasonable as some other conclusion.

Thus, when it is stated that an imposed structure is reasonable, that description carries a great deal of meaning. It means that we are talking about inductions rather than deductions, about likelihoods rather than certainties, about contingencies rather than necessities, about plausible explanations rather than proofs, about exceptions rather than uniformities, about invention rather than discovery, and about the pragmatically sensible rather than the strictly logical. Reasonableness, not accuracy, is the topic of interest in enacted sensemaking.

Ideas are real-ized

One of the best ways to capture the nuances in the view that environments are enacted is to say that people act out and real-ize their ideas. In the processes of acting out and of real-izing their ideas, they create their own realities. The crucial phrase is "real-izing their ideas." By this I mean literally that people make real, or turn into a reality, those ideas that they have in their heads. It is that sense in which the phrase, "believing is seeing" is more than a play on words; it captures part of the mechanism by which organizing processes unfold and create their own environments.

Similar imagery suggesting that ideas control what is seen is found in the following quotation from Popper (1962):

> Without waiting, passively, for repetitions to impress or impose regularities on us, we actively try to impose regularities upon the world. We try to discover similarities in it,

and interpret it in terms of laws invented by us. Without waiting for premises, we jump
to conclusions. These may have to be discarded later, should observation show that they
are wrong. (p. 73)

Thus, people invent organizations and their environments and these inventions
reside in ideas that participants have superimposed on any stream of experience. This
contrasts with the view that organizations and environments consist of underlying
structures that are revealed to inquisitive discoverers. The one quibble I have with
Popper involves the last sentence. The phrase "should observation show that they are
wrong" implies a reality underlying the appearances, an implication that I find dispensable. I don't think observation would suggest that something should be discarded because it is wrong. Instead, I think observation would simply suggest that
there are alternative, arbitrary ways to make sense out of a stream of experience, and
that these alternative-imposed regularities might be more useful or more esthetic or
more pleasant or more novel than the regularities currently being imposed.

Another way to phrase the issue of ideas being real-ized is to say that sensemaking
is an efferent activity. The modifier "efferent" means "centrifugal" or "conducted
outward." The person's idea is extended outward, implanted, and then rediscovered
as knowledge. The discovery, however, originated in a prior invention by the discov-
erer. In a crude, but literal sense, one could talk about efferent sensemaking as
thinking in circles. Action, perception, and sensemaking exist in a circular, tightly-
coupled relationship.

This tight coupling between enactment and selection processes, has been talked
about in the guise of several concepts. Perhaps the most common one is the notion of
the self-fulfilling prophecy (e.g., Archibald, 1974; Bateson, 1951; James, 1956; Kelley
and Stahelski, 1970; Merton, 1948; Henshel and Kennedy, 1973):

> A self-fulfilling prophecy may be regarded as the communicational equivalent of "beg-
> ging the question." It is behavior that brings about in others, the reaction to which the
> behavior would be appropriate reaction. For instance, a person who acts on the premise
> that "nobody likes me" will behave in a distrustful, defensive, or aggressive manner to
> which others are likely to react unsympathetically, thus bearing out his original
> premise. . . . Pragmatically, we can observe that this individual's interpersonal behavior
> shows this kind of redundancy, and that it has a complementary effect on others, forcing
> them into certain specific attitudes. What is typical about the sequence and makes it a
> problem of punctuation, is that the individual concerned conceives of himself only as
> reacting to, but not as provoking, those attitudes. (Watzlawick, Beavin, and Jackson,
> 1967, pp. 98–99)

The essence of efferent sensemaking is summarized in the last sentence of that quotation.

People frequently isolate particular items, presume that they are indicators of
some underlying pattern, and use this tentative pattern identification both to search for
and to label subsequent particulars which, in turn, flesh out the underlying pattern
which, in turn, fleshes out the sensibleness of current particulars, etc. This kind of tight
circularity is what has been called, the "documentary method of meaning."

The [documentary] method consists of treating an actual appearance as "the document of," as "pointing to," as "standing on behalf of" a presupposed underlying pattern. Not only is the underlying pattern derived from its individual documentary evidences, but the individual documentary evidences in their turn, are interpreted on the basis of "what is known" about the underlying pattern. Each is used to elaborate the other. (Garfinkel, 1967, p. 78)

Eloquent exhibits of the documentary method in operation are found in McHugh's (1968) experimental counseling protocols. He had subjects, under the guise of testing a new format for counseling, pose questions to a concealed counselor about their current problems that the counselor could answer with a yes or no. The counselor decided whether to answer yes or no by flipping a coin. The phenomenon of interest is how the troubled subjects make do with the fragments of contradictory and disjointed advice that they get from the counselor such that they transform the "interaction" into a sensible occasion. Clients literally real-ize their own ideas when they overlay them on the counselor's equivocal display.

There's an eerie sense in which McHugh's "random counseling" resembles client-centered counseling (Rogers, 1951). The client-centered counselor basically reflects back to the patient whatever the patient says and little more. Thus, the client is forced to impose new meaning on very little new data. In fact, the client may find the reflected comments to be almost as puzzling as are the bits and pieces of advice purveyed by the coin-flipping counselor. It is conceivable that client-centered counseling is nothing more or less than intensified usage of the documentary method.

That possibility aside, however, the point I wish to make is that how people make sense of randomized counseling may be prototypic of organizational sensemaking. In random counseling, the subject generates a display that is susceptible to multiple punctuations, gets an answer from the counselor which is even more puzzling than his initial enactinent, and then visibly has to repunctuate, readjust, and reemphasize all that has accumulated up to that point. In the McHugh studies (and those done by Garfinkel) the subject thinks out loud while trying to make sense of the counselor's cryptic advice and these protocols are unusually rich displays in which one can examine punctuation, repunctuation, and alternative attempts at connection. Garfinkle presents detailed analysis of what people are doing when they try to make sense of the counselor's remarks (1967, see pp. 89–94), and similar detailed analyses are found in McHugh, the latter study being of interest because McHugh varied the proportion of yeses and noes that occurred during the exchanges.

Concepts such as real-ized ideas, self-fulfilling prophecies, and the documentary method share an imagery of efferent sensemaking. The documentary method perhaps most clearly contains the elements of a tight coupling between retention and punctuation that, working in the manner of a closed loop, generates a self-validating and compelling interpretation of the world. Efferent sensemaking assumes that an idea is projected or imposed and then discovered and punctuated by the imposer.

I think prevailing images of organizations incorporate too much passivity. The organizations are thought of as sitting back and examining a presuinably separate, prestructured environment in order to figure out how to adapt to that environment. If we shift to a more self-conscious efferent imagery and if we blur the boundaries between organizations and environments, and if we selectively use open systems imagery, then we put ourselves in a better position to say that a substantial number of the enacted environments associated with organizations consist of personal ideas that are extended outward, implanted, and rediscovered.

Enacted Sensemaking in Orchestral Organizations

The purpose of the present section is to give an extended example of how one talks about enactment in an organization; that is, to demonstrate what observers notice when they take seriously the possibility that organizations enact many of their environments and how observers label, punctuate, and connect what they notice. Although the illustration describes orchestras, the ideas apply more broadly to other kinds of organizations.

In a field experiment (Weick, Gilfillan, and Keith, 1973), 38 musicians in two functioning jazz orchestras rehearsed three compositions written by composers whose attributed credibility was given as either high or low. Composer credibility is of potential importance in music making because it is thought to influence the amount and kind of effort a musician will put forth to comprehend a new piece of music. Meyer has argued that efforts to comprehend new music are mediated by the "presumption of logic." "Without faith in the purposefulness of, and rationality of art, listeners would abandon their attempts to understand, to reconcile deviants to what has gone before or to look for their *raison d'être* in what is still to come" (1956, p. 75). We predicted that musicians would find it difficult to presume logic when a composer was portrayed as nonserious. Consequently, the musicians would make more errors when they played that composer's music due to initial indifference or doubts, would downgrade the worth of the music, and would forget it sooner. However, when the *very same* piece of new music was given to a comparable orchestra and was attributed to a serious composer, we expected that the musicians would presume the music was purposeful and would expend more effort to comprehend it. This greater effort would be evident in such things as fewer errors and higher evaluation and better memory for the tune relative to its fate when attributed to a nonserious composer.

The predicted difference in errors occurred on the first play-through of the new music but disappeared on the second play-through, due to a combination of additional nonserious rehearsing plus direct observation that the composition itself was purposeful (the three selections were written by two established jazz composers, Alf Clausen and Don Piestrup). The predicted difference in evaluation did not occur, but when assessed by a recognition test the compositions given as written by serious composers were remembered significantly better 24 hours after the rehearsal. These data suggest that the attribution of credibility can be self-confirming. Closer attention to the work of the credible composer resulted in fewer errors and a better-sounding performance relative to the work of the noncredible composer, thereby confirming the credibility prophecy. When the musicians believed that the music was of higher quality, they generated, by their own heightened attentiveness, a better-sounding tune, which then constrained their subsequent playing.

Viewed more broadly, any orchestra rehearsal where musicians process new music is an ideal setting in which to observe the ways in which a strange piece of music is made more sensible. There are numerous sources of equivocality when new music is rehearsed. The music itself is equivocal because it is unknown, it contains some amount of musical complexity, it contains certain amounts of *calculated* or intentional disorder, many of its performance characteristics (such as the tempo where it plays well) have to be established, it is equivocal relative to the style in which the band prefers to play, and the tune shows a greater or lesser departure from convention in music. These and other questions are what an orchestra tries to resolve when it rehearses.

The environment that the orchestra members face is not simply the composition placed in front of them, but rather what they do with that composition when they play it through for the first time. The musicians don't react to an environment, they *enact* the environment. In the credibility study the enacted environment available to the musicians after their first play was an undifferentiated "soup." As observers, we might label this soup with nouns such as "sounds," "tempos," "themes," "shadings," and "errors." The first play-through of the composition could be made sensible by participants in a variety of ways. The crucial point is that the play-through, not the sheets of music, was the environment the musicians tried to make sensible.

Once musicians enact an environment, they then punctuate or break that environment into discrete events that are available for relating (e.g., "those 12 notes are thrilling," "those 6 bars are impossible," "that portion is ugly," "the notes are hard to read," "the tempo at which we start seems to be crucial"). Essentially, the musicians punctuate the stream of enacted music into reasonable nouns and then try to relate or connect the nouns in a reasonable manner. It is important to emphasize that (1) punctuation is arbitrary, (2) punctuation is a precondition for sensemaking, and (3) punctuation imposes a figure-ground relationship on the enacted environment, thereby making it more manageable.

Once a musician parses the stream of experience into a set of variables, he is able to make the inference that some of these punctuated variables co-vary. When one of the punctuated variables changes its value, one or more other variables are seen to move also, and these movements may be in the same or opposite directions. Based on these movements the observer then infers a connection among the variables and may also infer, in the case of temporally separated but co-moving variables, a relationship of "causality." It is crucial to note that this act of connection is based on the experience of recurrent co-movement among the variables of interest and takes place in the mind of an individual participant. In a like manner, the organization is in the mind.

It is at this point in the argument where the thinking of David Hume (1748) is especially pertinent.

> All events seem entirely loose and separate. One event follows another, but we can never observe any tie between them. They seem *conjoined*, but never *connected*. . . . But when one particular species of events has always, in all instances, been conjoined with another, we make no longer any scruple of foretelling one upon the appearance of the other, and . . . we then call the one object "cause," and the other "effect." We *suppose* [emphasis added] that there is some connection between them, some power in the one by which it infallibly produces the other and operates with the greatest certainty and

strongest necessity. . . . The mind is carried by habit, upon the appearance of one event, to expect its usual attendant and to believe that it will exist. This connection, therefore, *which we feel in the mind* [emphasis added], this customary transition of the imagination from one object to its usual attendant, is the sentiment or impression from which we form the idea of power or necessary connection. . . . This is the sole difference between one instance, from which we can never receive the idea of connection, and a number of similar instances by which it is suggested. (Hume, 1955, pp. 85–86)

Returning to the musicians who perform music by high- or low-credibility composers, they might punctuate this experience into seven variables: (1) attributed credibility; (2) playing effort exerted; (3) tolerance for errors; (4) attention to notes; (5) willingness to reconcile deviant notes; (6) willingness to suspend judgment; and (7) quality of tune when judged retrospectively. These seven variables are specified solely to illustrate the argument. It should be apparent that we can maintain consistency in our argument only if these variables are specified by the participant, *not* by an observer.

Given these seven variables, it is possible for the musician to connect them causally. For example, on the basis of repeated experience he might note that as credibility decreases, playing effort and attention to notes decrease and tolerance for error increases; when effort decreases, this decreases both the judged quality of the tune and the attention that the musician pays to the notes; when the tolerance for errors increases, this serves to decrease the attention to the notes, the willingness to reconcile deviant notes, and the willingness to suspend judgment about the tune; and finally the musician may note that all of these relationships may decrease the perceived quality of the tune, which then leads to a further lowering of credibility. If these connections are summarized graphically then we would obtain the set of causal connections shown in Figure 7.1. This is a causal map. It summarizes those punctuations and connections that are inferred by a person after repeated exposures to a stream of experience.

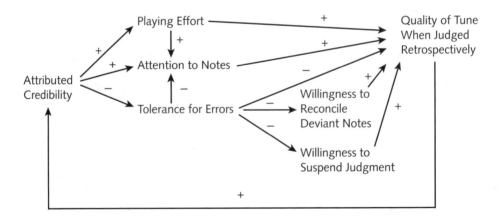

Figure 7.1 Causal map

We assume that musicians, as well as people in general, retain causal maps in their minds. These maps, in the case of musicians, are superimposed on flows of experience that involve music making. What the maps do in part is suggest which variables can be punctuated out of that flow of experience (e.g., "I should single out from the flow of experience the amount of effort I am exerting because this is a significant portion of this experience"). These maps also suggest which punctuated variables are connected with which other punctuated variables. Notice that the map in Figure 7.1 is an overlay or a template that the individual imposes on a stream of enacted experience to separate portions of that display into a figure-ground relationship.

It is an interesting property of superimposed structures that they are often self-validating structures. To see this, reexamine the causal map of Figure 7.1. It contains several loops by which one can start with the variable "attributed credibility" and trace a path that returns to the starting variable. The interesting property of each pathway is that it is a positive feedback loop. For example, if credibility decreases, this causes an increase in the tolerance for errors, which causes a decrease in the judged quality of the tune, which causes a further decrease in credibility, and so forth. A musician who imposes this particular structure on his music making will generate self-fulfilling prophecies that reinforce the map and confirm the initial attribution of credibility. If we treat "presumption of logic" as a variable, this means that a musician may find it easier or harder to presume that the composer is credible and that his composition will be serious or reasonable. If the musician increases the presumption of logic, then he raises the level of attributed credibility and through the imposition of the causal map produces the higher-quality tune – which confirms the initial presumption. If, however, he doubts the presumption of logic, then this lowers the !evel of credibility and *through the very same causal map* produces the lower quality tune which confirms the initial doubts about credibility.

The point is, the causal map in Figure 7.1 may *be* the orchestra. If we then ask where that orchestra is, the answer is, in the minds of the musicians. It exists in the minds of the musicians in the form of the variables they routinely punctuate and the connections they routinely infer among these variables. These maps are then superimposed on any gathering where the announced agenda is music making.

So far, most of the points made deal with processes that take place in the minds of solitary actors. Within the orchestra it is true that the causal maps differ among 38 musicians and it is also true that any one musician has his own doubts about the stability of some of the punctuations and connections he makes. These differences and doubts suggest two things. First, there should be residual equivocality even after individuals impose their own idiosyncratic versions of what has happened. Second, coordination will be problematic until some agreements can be reached among the participants as to what has happened and what should be done about it.

Elsewhere, we have argued (Weick, 1969b) that equivocality removal is essentially an interpersonal process and involves at least two members interlocking some behaviors to accomplish this removal. Using the ideas already presented, we can state more precisely how interlocked behaviors remove equivocality. The crucial collective act in organizations may consist of members trying to negotiate a consensus on which portions of an enacted display are *figure* and which are *ground*. More specifically, members collectively try to reach some workable agreement as to which portions of elapsed streams should be punctuated into variables and which connections among which variables are reasonable.

Thus when we assert that equivocality is removed by interlocked behavioral cycles (i.e., by sequences of double interacts; Weick, 1969b, p. 33), we mean that members negotiate over specific issues of punctuation (e.g., "I don't think that the temperature of this room is important, but you seem to think it is") and issues of connection (e.g., "We seem to agree that temperature is crucial to our performane, but I think we play better when we are warmer and you think we play better when we are cooler"). Once members can reach some agreement as to what is consequential and what is trivial in their elapsed experience, and once they can get some kind of agreement as to the nature and direction of the connections among these consequential elements, then the elapsed experience becomes more sensible. That is, there is more overlap in the separate maps that are stored in the minds of the musicians when they leave the rehearsal and there is a greater likelihood that they will interlock their activities of music making more tightly when they confront new music at subsequent rehearsals.

The crucial point is that equivocality removal is both a social and a solitary process. What we are trying to specify is precisely what in that social process is crucial for what is basically a private, singular, and solitary activity. Sensemaking is largely solitary in the sense that structures contained within *individual* minds are imposed on streams of *individual* elapsed experience that are capable of an infinite number of *individual* reconstructions.

As we said in the *The Social Psychology of Organizing* (Weick, 1969b), behaviors rather than people constitute groups. That being the case, a substantial portion of the variance associated with "group" activities can be explained if we concentrate on those behaviors that are interlocked and on those occasions when individual maps prove to be too idiosyncratic for coordinated activity to occur. While we want to be sure that we stay attentive to crucial determinants at both the group and individual level, we also do not want to have the proverbial "tie that binds" be a tie that blinds us to the ways in which individuals impose the organization that organizes the imposer.

To recapitulate, musicians *enact an environment* when they first play a piece of music and the outcome of this first play-through is an *equivocal display*. Based on previous experiences in processing new music, the musicians impose a *figure-ground structure* on this undifferentiated enacted display. This *imposed structure*, which is in the form of a *causal map*, *punctuates* the display into a set of variables that are *connected* by means of *reasonable causal* linkages. The act of superimposing a causal map involves *retrospecting* elapsed experience. Although an imposed causal map makes the equivocal display more sensible for an individual musician, there remains the problem that the punctuations and connections are both uncertain within individuals and different between individuals. Causal maps are approximations and deal with likelihoods, not certainties. Since residual equivocality remains after individual causal maps are superimposed, it is necessary to gain some consensus among musicians as to what the orchestra is confronted with and how it is to be handled. Members activate *sets of interlocked behavior cycles* to deal with this residual equivocality. Initially, they try to *negotiate* a consensus on which portions of the display are figure and which are ground. When people collectively try to shrink the possible meanings attached to an equivocal input, they essentially are negotiating issues of punctuation and connection (e.g., "What did we or the composer do that caused that horrible chord?). Having consensually made the enacted environment more sensible, the members then store their revised and presumably more homogeneous causal maps for imposition on future similar circumstances.

Conclusion

Oliver Wendell Holmes has written a charming fable that summarizes the intent of this chapter. He writes:

> When we are as yet small children . . . there comes up to us a youthful angel, holding in his right hand cubes like dice, and in his left spheres like marbles. The cubes are of stainless ivory, and on each is written in letters of gold – *Truth*. The spheres are veined and streaked and spotted beneath, with a dark crimson flush above, where the light falls on them and in a certain aspect you can make out upon every one of them the three letters, *L, I, E*. The child to whom they are offered very probably clutches at both. The spheres are the most convenient things in the world; they roll with the least possible impulse just where the child would have them. The cubes will not roll at all; they have a great talent for standing still, and always keep right side up. But very soon the young philosopher finds that things that roll so easily are very apt to roll into the wrong corner, and to get out of his way when he most wants them, while he always knows where to find the others which stay where they are left. Thus he learns – to drop the streaked and speckled globes of falsehood and to hold fast the white angular blocks of truth. But then comes Timidity, and after her Good-nature, and last of all Polite-behavior, all insisting that truth must *roll*, or nobody can do anything with it; and so the first with her coarse rasp and the second with her broad file, and the third with her silken sleeve, do so round off and smooth and polish the snow-white cubes of truth, that, when they get a little dingy by use, it becomes hard to tell them from the rolling spheres of falsehood. (1901, pp. 98–99)

I like that fable because it warns against glibness. Investigators who study organization–environment relations sometimes lean toward separatist imagery. Environments are separated from organizations and things happen between these distinct entities. This way of carving up the problem of organizational analysis effectively rules out certain kinds of questions. Talk about bounded environments and organizations, for example, compels the investigator to ask questions such as how does an organization *discover* the *underlying* structure in *the* environment? Having separated the "two" entities and given them independent existence, investigators have to make elaborate speculations concerning the ways in which one entity becomes disclosed to and known by the other. But the firm partitioning of the world into the environment and the organization excludes the possibility that people *invent* rather than discover what they think they see. We have tried to provide an alternative to "discovery" formulations of organizational knowing.

What this essay supplies, then, is a way to talk about organizations. It contains a set of punctuations and connections that can be superimposed on streams of happenings viewed by organizational watchers. As is true of any enacted environent, the proposed punctuations and connections are arbitrary though possibly useful. As people begin to become comfortable with talking about enactment, they will undoubtedly find the ideas sketched in this chapter more fallible and less reasonable. That's fine, because when present concepts are improved, we should then be in a good position to understand a final example of enactment at its finest hour.

Truck drivers have a running feud with ICC inspectors who check for overweight loads. Truckers lose few opportunities to make their sentiments known to the people who man the scales. A driver nicknamed Ole Red was a past master at enacting environments for inspectors.

> He'd pull into entry points when he was carrying nothing, just to drive those guys crazy. He'd pull up to the scales, get out of his truck, and start pounding all over his trailer with a little hammer. The operator would come out and ask him what the hell he was doing. Red would start at him real good and tell him that he was overloaded, but was carrying a load of canaries and he wanted to get them all into the air before he got weighed. (Krueger, 1975, p. 118)

Notes

1. I have learned much about enactment from discussions with Michel Bougon, discussions which I acknowledge with gratitude. The National Science Foundation provided support for this work through Grant SOC 75–09864.
2. Since a tacit message of this chapter is that nouns like "organization" and "environment" are dormitive, we encounter some genuine problems of exposition. The theory on which this work is based views organizations as flows of experience. As members enact and punctuate in parallel their individual flows of experience, they develop inferences about their experiences. These inferences are arranged cognitively in causal maps which in turn predispose future behavior. Individual member's causal maps are altered and developed through experience. This development produces some cognitive and behavioral correspondence which defines, for them, an organization.

    When it is asserted that "an organization" acts, believes, soliloquizes, and so forth, reification is avoided because we mean that at least one member enacts on behalf of others some experience, punctuates that experience using in part a retained and superimposed causal map, some of whose variables have been jointly parsed, and produces an enacted enviornment which occasionally has vicarious relevance.
3. This passage translated into English by Michel Bougon from the following: ". . . l'univers initial n'est pas un reseau de séquences causales, mais une simple collection d'envénéments surgissant en prolongement de l'activé propre."
4. This example was inspired by James Fixx (1972, p. 29) and by Karen Weick's solution of the Fixx puzzle.

References

Archibald, W. P. Alternative explanations for self-fullfilling prophecy. *Psychological Bulletin,* 1974, *31,* 74–84.

Bateson, G. W. Conventions of communications: Where validity depends on belief. In J. Reusch and G. Bateson (eds.), *Communication, the Social Matrix of Society.* New York: Norton, 1951, pp. 212–27.

Bateson, G. W. *Steps to an Ecology of Mind.* New York: Ballantine, 1972.

Campbell, D. T. Unjustified variation and selective retention in scientific discovery. In F J. Ayala and T. Dobzhansky (eds.), *Studies In the Philosophy of Biology.* New York: Macmillan, 1974, pp. 139–61.

Campbell, D. T. On the conflicts between biological and social evolution and between psychology and moral tradition. *American Psychologist,* 1975, *30,* 1103–26.

Faris, R. E. L. Graduate education in sociai psychology. In S. Lundstedt (ed.), *Higher Education in Social Psychology.* Cleveland: Case Western Reserve University, 1968, pp. 53–72.

Filley, A. C., House, R. J., and Kerr, S. *Managerial Process and Organizational Behavior* (2nd ed.), Glenview, Ill.: Scott, Foresman, 1976.

Fixx, J. *Games for the Superintelligent.* New York: Doubleday, 1972.

Garfinkel, H. *Studies in Enthnomethodology.* Englewood Cliffs, N. J.: Prentice-Hall, 1967.

Henshel, R. L. and Kennedy, L. W. Self-altering prophecies: Consequences for the feasibility of social prediction. *General Systems Yearbook,* 1973, *18,* 119–26.

Holmes, O. W. *The Autocrat of the Breakfast Table.* London: Walter Scott, 1901.

Hume, D. *An Inquiry Concerning Human Understanding.* New York: Bobbs-Merrill, 1955.

James, W. *Is life worth living?* In W. James, *The Will to Believe,* New York Dover,1956. pp. 32–62.

Jencks, C. and Silver, N. *Adhocism.* Garden City, New York: Anchor, 1973.

Katz, D. and Kahn, D. L. *The Social Psychology of Organizations.* New York: Wiley,1966.

Kelley, H. H. and Stahelski, A. J. Social interaction basis of cooperators and competitors' beliefs about others. *Journal of Personality and Social Psychology,* 1970, *16,* 66–91.

Krueger, R. *Gypsy on 18 Wheels.* New York: Praeger, 1975.

Mailer, N. *Of a Fire on the Moon.* Boston: Little, Brown, 1970.

McHugh, P. *Defining the Situation.* New York: Bobbs-Merrill, 1968.

Merton, R. K. The self-fulfilling prophecy. *Antioch Review,* 1948, *8,* 193–210.

Meyer, L. B. *Emotion and Meaning In Music.* Chicago: University of Chicago, 1956.

Miller, D. W., and Starr, M. K. *Executive Decisions and Operations Research.* Englewood Cliffs, N.J.: Prentice-Hall, 1960.

Miller, S. Ends, means, galumphing: Some leitmotifs of play. *American Anthropologist,* 1973, *75,* 87–98.

Piaget, J. *La construction du reel ches l'enfant.* 2 éme éd. Neuchátel: Delachaux and Niestlé, 1962.

Popper, K. R. *Conjecture and Refutation.* New York: Basic, 1962.

Powers, W. *Behavior: The Control of Perception.* Chicago: Aldine, 1973.

Rogers, C. R. *Client-centered Therapy.* Boston: Houghton Mifflin, 1951.

Rottenberg, D. The moneyweight champion. *New York Times Magazine,* Feb. 22, 1976. pp. 16–26.

Russell, B. *Introduction to Mathematical Philosophy* (2nd ed.). London: Allen and Unwin, 1948.

Scheff, T. J. Decision rules, types of error, and their consequences in medical diagnosis. In F.

Massarik and P. Ratoosh (eds.), *Mathematical Explorations in Behavioral Science*. Homewood, Ill.: Dorsey, 1965, pp. 66–83.

Thayer, L. Communication and organization theory. In F. E. X. Dance (ed.), *Human Communication Theory*. New York: Holt, Rinehart, and Winston, 1967.

Watzlawick, P., Beavin, J. H., and Jackson, D. D. *Pragmatics of Human Communication*. New York: Norton, 1967.

Weick, K. E. Social psychology in an era of social change. *American Psychologist*, 1969a, *24*, 990–98

Weick, K. E. *The Social Psychology of Organizing*. Reading, Mass.: Addison-Wesley, 1969b.

Weick, K. E. Organizations as enacted settings. Paper presented at Massachussetts Institute of Technology, Cambridge, May 1975.

Weick, K. E. Careers as eccentric predicates. *Executive*, 1976, *2*, 6–10.

Weick, K. E., and Gilfillan, D. P. Fate of arbitrary traditions in a laboratory microculture. *Journal of Personality and Social Psychology*, 1971, *17*, 179–91.

Weick, K. E., Gilfillan, D. P., and Keith, T. The effect of composer credibility on orchestra performance. *Sociometry*, 1973, *36*, 435–62.

8

Enactment and the Boundaryless Career: Organizing as We Work

Mary Catherine Bateson captures the theme of this chapter in her comments about deviant resumes:

> Resumes full of change show resiliency and creativity, the strength to welcome new learning; yet personnel directors often discriminate against anyone whose resume does not show a clear progression. Quite a common question in job interviews is, 'What do you want to be doing in five years?' 'Something I cannot now imagine' is not yet a winning answer. Accepting that logic, young people worry about getting 'on track' yet their years of experimentation and short-term jobs are becoming longer. If only to offer an alternative, we need to tell other stories, the stories of shifting identities and interrupted paths, and to celebrate the triumphs of adaptation. (1994: 83)

This chapter is a story of shifting identities. Its message is that interrupted career paths can be opportunities. When people make sense of these interruptions and use them as occasions for improvisation and learning, "triumphs of adaptation" occur. The vehicle for converting shifts and interruptions into adaptations is the boundaryless career, which I view as improvised work experiences that rise prospectively into fragments and fall retrospectively into patterns – a mixture of continuity and discontinuity.

A crucial shift in traditional careers is the disappearance of external guides for sequences of work experience, such as advancement in a hierarchy. In their place, we find more reliance on internal, self-generated guides, such as growth, learning, and integration. As a result of this shift, more of the influence over organizing devolves to the level of interaction and small groups, since the boundaries of organizations have become more permeable, more fluid, more dynamic, and less distinct. Nowadays, an organization is known by its organizing, just as the organizing effort is known by the interactions that comprise it. This emerging pattern of continuing collective experiments, short-term jobs, and retrospective acts of improvisation (Gioia,

1988) constitutes one meaning of the term *self-designing systems*. The continuous updating inherent in such systems is a significant source of the adaptation that Bateson wants to celebrate.

The patterns that comprise the boundaryless career are seen to start on a smaller scale, and are more local, more tentative, and more subtle, than are the patterns associated with traditional, externally defined careers. But the fact that these newer patterns start small does not mean that they are trivial. On the contrary, precisely because they are patterns in a world of fragments, they can influence the expectations that distal stakeholders use when they define what constitutes work. A career system begins to form when stakeholders take the logic that was handed to them by the people who first enacted it, and redirect it to the enactors in the form of expectations, requests, meanings, and images that define what their enactment meant. As these relations between enactors and stakeholders continue to unfold and recycle, they generate histories, movements from novices to experts, older and newer participants, increasing explication of tacit understandings, more integration, and more internalization, all of which are changes that mimic a career system. What is different now is that work experience is more decoupled from specific organizations, more proactive and enactive, more indistinguishable from organizing, more portable, more discontinuous, less predictable, and more reliant on improvisation.

This map of boundaryless careers in boundaryless organizations is an extension of the map that Lisa Berlinger and I first drew in 1989 when we suggested that the growing importance of self-designing systems, such as entrepreneurial start-ups in Silicon Valley (Delbecq and Weiss, 1988), was likely to reshape the meaning of career systems and career development. We argued that images of career planning and advancement would be replaced by images of improvisation and learning. We argued further that as hierarchies became less available to mark progress in objective careers, this void would be filled by greater reliance on milestones in subjective careers, such as an increase in competence. These subjective milestones would serve as proxies for advancement, development, and upward movement. Thus, a change in competence would substitute for a change in job title. More significant, this shift from a position-based career system to a system based more on skill, competence, and experience should place more control over the design of the organization in the hands of the people who are building subjective careers. Organizations that incorporate this experience in an ongoing redesign program should themselves have more adaptability than those that ignore it. In a quiet, subtle inversion, the boundaryless career enacts the boundaryless organization.

The suggestion that career development can have a significant effect on the structure and processes of organization is relatively rare in career literature. For example, Nystrom and MacArthur (1989) categorized the 155 propositions they culled from the *Handbook of Career Theory* (Arthur, Hall, and Lawrence, 1989), and found that 135 of them treated the organization as the independent variable and careers as the dependent variable. Of the remaining 20 propositions suggesting that causation ran in the other direction, 25% of them appeared in the chapter on self-designing systems that Berlinger and I wrote in the *Handbook of Career Theory*. As Nystrom and MacArthur noted, the organizational properties that are highlighted when causation flows from careers to organizations differ from those highlighted when causation flows the other way. In our chapter, for example, the independent variable of careers had an effect on the organizational variables of self-design, adaptability, innovation, rigidity, and change, whereas organizations had an effect on careers through the independent variables of self-design, incompleteness of design, idea overload, and professionalization.

I conclude four things from this discussion. First, the literature on careers is relatively silent about the ways in which career development affects the form and functioning of organizations. Second, boundaryless careers in boundaryless organizations shape one another. Third, to capture how career development shapes organizational form requires that one pay attention to organizational properties that are often invisible when people examine organizations as independent variables. And fourth, the very fact that boundaries are in flux means that whatever structuring does come to define career systems may originate in unexpected places and have unexpected effects.

The rest of this chapter is organized in the following way: After a brief look at examples of boundaryless careers and organizations, I suggest, following Bell and Staw (1989), that as organizations become less bounded, they function more like weak situations. One result is that micro-level phenomena such as personality dispositions, tightly coupled interpersonal routines, and cohesive alliances have greater effects on outcomes and structure. To describe more systematically the way in which these effects are achieved, I then introduce the concept of enactment and show how it can give form to weak situations. A crucial point in my discussion builds on Barley's (1989) suggestion that career scripts mediate this structuring. Having suggested that boundaryless careers can be understood as moments of enactment that leave defining traces in social systems, I then suggest several ways to refine this basic theme.

Images of Boundaryless Life

Recent descriptions of boundaryless organizations and careers have taken a variety of forms: They are described as an increased outsourcing of activities and as distributed boundary spanning (DeFillippi and Arthur, 1994); as having greater reliance on just-in-time employees (Barner, 1994); as stemming from the growing influence of informal divisions of labor, information networks, adhocracies, flat structures, structural chaos, strong cultures, professional autonomy, self-regulation, decentralization, and trust (Thompson, 1993); as a movement to career systems that resemble those associated with baseball teams (Sonnenfeld, 1989); and as the creation of such diverse forms as the community, the federation, the octopus, the mobile, the tangled web, and the skyscraper (Power, 1988: 72). Behind most of these depictions is the assumption that organizations will increasingly need to leverage diverse knowledge resources, and that to do so, they will need to lose some of their bureaucratic form and discipline.

The weakening of boundaries in careers has also been described with evocative images. Bateson (1994: 82) describes the growing number of people who live with multiple discontinuities and make multiple fresh starts as the "zigzag people." Among such people, she numbers immigrants, refugees, displaced housewives, foreclosed farmers, bankrupt entrepreneurs, and people with obsolete skills. To think of oneself as a perennial consultant (Peters, 1992: 218), or as a business of one, or as a person "who has learned to acquire additional specialties rapidly in order to move from one kind of job to another" (Drucker, 1994: 68), is to edge toward a mindset appropriate for boundaryless careers. Mirvis and Hall (1994: 377), quoting the indelicate imagery of people who are more attached to their work than to organizations, suggest that the boundaryless career is "just sex, not marriage." Nicholson and West (1989: 190) make the important empirical point that even though boundaryless careers seem novel, in fact, conventional career moves have been rare for a long time (for example, data from the 1970s and 1980s suggest that 10% of moves were lateral or simple promotions; 50% involved a change in status and function; and 50% occurred between organizations). In the context of these examples, it seems reasonable to define boundaryless careers as "sequences of job opportunities that go beyond the boundaries of single employment settings" (Defillippi and Arthur, 1994).

Boundaryless Organizations as Weak Situations

One way to understand the growing influence of career development on organizational form is to argue that the loosening of organizational boundaries has transformed strong situations, which used to be well defined by structured, salient cues, into weaker situations that are now ambiguous, with fewer salient guides for action. When situations weaken, behavior tends to be guided by more tightly coupled structures, such as enduring personality dispositions (Bell and Staw, 1989; see Carson, 1989; 228–229, for a contrasting perspective). I suggest that the set of structuring mechanisms includes more than individual dispositions. It is this larger set of possibilities that includes mechanisms by which career development shapes social systems.

The distinction between strong and weak situations was proposed by Mischel (1968) and is generally understood in terms of the following elaboration:

> Psychological 'situations' (stimuli, treatment) are powerful to the degree that they lead everyone to construe the particular events in the same way, induce *uniform* expectancies regarding the most appropriate response pattern and require skills that everyone has to the same extent. ... Conversely, situations are weak to the degree that they are not uniformly encoded, do not generate uniform expectancies concerning the desired behavior, do not offer sufficient incentives for its performance, or fail to provide the learning conditions required for successful genesis of behavior. (Mischel, 1977: 347)

Some commentators, such as Thompson (1993) and Perrow (1993), argue that organizations have always generated strong situations and continue to do so. They note that, whereas centralized organizations once exerted top-down control, local and lower management increasingly exercise operational autonomy, but still within a more tightly controlled framework. Observers who see organizations as generating weaker situations refer to other trends. Knowledge creation as a newer route to adaptability (e.g. Bird, 1996, Nonaka, and Takeuchi, 1995) is neither well understood nor consistently implemented. Thus, organizations moving toward this goal should be less well structured. Efforts to downsize have removed knowledgeable people, which has resulted in "an erosion of company knowledge stores over time" (Bird, 1996). With less knowledge, but more demand for knowledge creation, organizations moving toward this goal should indeed be less well structured. With greater demand for updating of knowledge, organizations now need knowledge workers more than knowledge workers need them (Drucker, 1994: 71). This reversal of dependency, if recognized, should heighten uncertainty.

While organizations may seem to create strong situations, especially in the face of control over job security and centralized information processing, they also create more conflicting practices (e.g., airline cost-cutting threatens safety); these encourage a greater variety of interpretations, diverse expectations, contradictory incentives, and shifting definitions of competencies that are needed. Organizational situations may not be weak, but they are weakening. And guides for action may lie elsewhere.

Guides for action may in fact lie in personality disposition and in collective improvisation. People make sense of uncertainty on a small scale by a stable process of collective trial and error that resembles an evolutionary system (Weick, 1979). And it is this small and tight learning process that imposes structure on larger and looser situations. Both stable personality dispositions and the stable collective improvisation of local evolution are sources of structure when situations weaken and work experience comes in fragments. The restructuring originates from the bottom up. Starting with more intense assertion of personality and collective improvisation, the restructuring first strengthens situations and then redraws organizational boundaries. As people work, they organize within weak situations. As they organize, they organize the weak situations into stronger ones. And stronger situations lay down traces of larger organizations. These traces are formed out of work and organizing and reflect both influences. Local coping and local scripting of that coping into careers constrain and define coping and scripting on a larger scale. People enact the stronger situation, which then constrains them.

Whether the shaping is driven by individual or collective action is less crucial than the fact that microstrength shapes macroweakness. Such reversals of causation should not be read as triumphs of the individual spirit in a crass capitalistic world of coercive organizations. Nor should they be read as humanistic wishful thinking. They should be read instead as straightforward extrapolations of responses to uncertainty that locate an important source of organizational design in the attempts of interdependent actors to make sense of recurring work transitions.

Collective enactment can create enduring changes in social systems, including broad-scale institutions. As I have noted, people enact and sustain images of a wider reality that justify what they are doing collectively (Weick, 1993: 16). When boundaries begin to dissolve, traditions become less prescriptive and institutions become less structured. Traditional career scripts (e.g., internal labor markets) become less suitable as guides for action and interaction. Nonetheless, interactions become more patterned as people collectively pursue learning in order to cope with ambiguity (e.g., by forming local alliances and obtaining work using regional networks). These patterns come to exert more influence over career scripts and institutions. That is the theoretical significance of a shift from bounded to boundaryless careers. Significant structuring originates in more micro levels and modifies more macro levels.

Institutions imply that there is some sort of logic to the boundaryless organization. What is significant is that this is not a logic that awaits discovery, even though it often seems that way. Instead, it is a logic waiting to be constructed retrospectively out of the organizational traces laid down during action and interaction. Selective retention of adaptive enactments (Weick, 1979) provides the pattern that enacts a career script that in turn becomes institutionalized as a boundaryless career. Thus, a boundaryless career comes to mean organizing rather than organization; small projects rather than large divisions; enaction rather than reaction; transience rather than permanence; self-design rather than bureaucratic control; and struggles for continuity rather than struggles for discontinuity. I do not mean to imply that organizations and institutions are simply passive containers in these developments. I do mean that they are not as monolithic as others contend and that enactment shapes both career scripts and institutions.

Refinements of Enactment

To think more clearly about boundaryless careers by using the themes of enactment and organizing, one must be alert to subtleties in what is already a moderately complex set of ideas. For example, the concept of enactment suggests that individuals are agents of their own development, but not simply because they are active, controlling, and independent. People also organize cooperatively in order to learn. This continual mixing of agency and communion (Bakan, 1966; Marshall, 1989) manifests itself in the reciprocity between individual and organizational needs (Arthur & Kram, 1989); between personal change and role development (Nicholson and West, 1989: 188); between strategic choices and market cues (Porac, Thomas, and Baden-Fuller, 1989: 399); and between imposed and evolved jobs (Miner, 1987).

While the relations are reciprocal in the sense of codetermination, this codetermination is also asymmetrical. The basic asymmetry is one in which microdynamics shapes macrostructures. As the situations they confront weaken, people increasingly enact their social constraints, including career systems. What I have added to Bell and Staw's (1989) argument is a larger set of processes that potentially is capable of structuring the void left by weakness. I have also added the more important possibility that these newly influential processes come to dominate and define the weak situations, thereby strengthening them. Once strengthened, these situations now create conformity as well as deviation, which means that people live careers partly in response to their own constructions.

Implicit in the story of boundaryless careers are subtleties of acceptance, organizing, and identity, which I now want to introduce. These refinements suggest some of the conditions under which the story I propose is more or less likely to unfold. These refinements provide leads for research. But they also illustrate ways of talking that can be used by people trying to make sense of the boundaryless careers they are living.

Enactment and communion

Although I described enactment as a mixture of agentlike control and communionlike, cooperative learning, the idea of enactment tends to evoke images of unmitigated agency. Such images include having expectations of self-assertion, wanting to be judged by concrete achievement, changing the environment to match preconceived images, showing independence, doing, having feelings of outer rather than inner development, and of separation rather than affiliation.

To develop a richer sense of enactment, organizing, and boundaryless careers, I need to pursue an intriguing footnote in Bailyn's (1989) attempt to summarize major themes in the *Handbook of Career Theory*. Her note 10 reads:

> There are a number of interesting commonalities between certain of the chapters in this handbook. One of the more intriguing is that between the Weick and Berlinger chapter on the self-designing career and the ones by Gallos and Marshall on women. Is an organization based on principles of communion – of "being" and "caring" – a self-designing organization? Is it possible that people whose dominant mode is communion will fit more easily into such organizations than do those whose behavior is guided more by agency? (p. 487)

Communion is about tolerance, trust, being oriented to the present, and noncontractual cooperation. What is striking is the way in which career plans influenced by communion differ from the future-oriented and goal-dominated plans of an agent perspective. In the following description of communion, notice the extent to which it is synonymous with organizing to learn:

> [The keynotes of communion are] flexibility, openness to opportunities and right timing as the person and appropriate environment meet. This process is not usually change seeking but change accepting. Individuals must be prepared for transformation, to lose and gain definitions of self. . . . Communion is essentially present oriented, concerned with the next appropriate step when choices are made rather than looking beyond. People may have "dreams" but hold them lightly, using them as visions of possibility rather than as aspirations that have to be realized. (Marshall, 1989: 287–288)

Communion is about readiness and adaptability just as agency is about initiative and adaptation. Both are invaluable to a boundaryless career and, in tandem, complement each other. Marshall suggests that a powerful means to integrate both sets of values is to practice "communion enhanced by agency." By this, Marshall means that "communion can draw on agency to supplement, protect, support, aid, focus, and arm it" (p. 280). Essentially, one says, "I choose to go with the flow." The agency of choosing is integrated with the communion of accepting "flows." As the act of organizing controls and enacts changes into scripts, situations, organizations, and institutions, agency dominates and is mitigated by communion. But, when these enacted changes then shape the meaning of growth, learning, and development, communion once more dominates and is enhanced by agency. Thus, an unfolding boundaryless career combines the communion of organized learning, the agency of environmental control, the communal acceptance of the environments and scripts thus created, and the agency of further structuring of initiatives driven by new recognition of what remains to be known and done.

There are several implications of using the concept of communion to enrich our understanding of careers and enactment. First, if weak situations evoke overlearned dispositions, and if overlearned dispositions tend to be pure rather than mixed, then career systems built to cope with boundaryless careers should be stronger on agency than on communion if they are enacted by men rather than women. Changes in the demographics of projects organized around learning should change the nature of the career system. Second, individual experiences organized around learning may themselves vary in the ratio of agency to communion. As the ratio of communion to agency increases, so, too, should the incidence of learning. What remains unclear is the extent to which that learning will then diffuse and become structured into scripts, situations, and institutions. Third, the recurrent suggestion that "people skills" are an asset in boundaryless careers reflects a reality in which the communion that enables organizing, learning, and trust also supplies the continuities that span the discontinuities created by shifting boundaries. The problem here is that, even though these skills play a major role in knowledge creation, they tend to be overlooked. Marshall puts it this way:

> Communion sees itself, including its actions, as part of a wider context of interacting influences. It tends not to assume personal accomplishment when events turn out favorably and is certainly less likely to be able to identify its contribution. This may be significant but largely invisible and difficult to disentangle because work has been largely pursued through influence, by shaping environments for others or in mutually empowering relationships. Action based in communion may therefore go unrewarded by formal organizational systems. (1989: 285)

A fourth implication of an enriched view of enactment is that one's capability for learning is dependent on the adequacy with which one can alternate between and integrate assertion and acceptance. To notice what has changed is to be attentive and accepting; to change what is noticed is to be focused and assertive; and to notice what has been changed by one's actions is to return to attentive acceptance. If continuous learning is the hallmark of a boundaryless career, then those who can integrate communion and agency should develop faster than those who can't. They develop faster because they learn more.

Fifth, people who face the loss of boundaries and value communion would not necessarily create new structure immediately to reverse these losses. What they might do instead is come to terms with uncertainty and recast it as a realm of possibilities. In fact, action might unfold with a minimum of conceptual premeditation, in the interest of heightened sensitivity to whatever the loss of boundaries might hold. People might be less likely to reconstruct hierarchies and more likely to construct heterarchies. "A heterarchy has no one person or principle in command. Rather, temporary pyramids of authority form as and when appropriate in a system of mutual constraints and influences. The childhood game of paper, stone, and scissors provides a simple illustration: paper wraps stone, stone blunts scissors, scissors cut paper. There is no fixed hierarchy, but each is effective, and recognized, in its own realm. In this way different values can take primacy in an individual's career pattern at different stages" (Marshall, 1989: 289). Organizing for learning that is structured heterarchically should legitimate a greater variety of perspectives, should blend agency with communion, and should mean more rapid adaptation.

A sixth implication is that people with strong dispositions, favoring agency, control, and predictability, should be bothered sooner by the loss of boundaries and situational structure than would people disposed toward communion. Those with an agency mind-set should persist longer in treating boundaryless organizations as if they still had traditional boundaries, and boundaryless careers as if they still were about hierarchical advancement. The admonition to get closer to the customer should be especially galling to people with an agency mind-set, who are more inclined to enact customers who want whatever the enactor has to offer.

Finally – and with a touch of irony – organizations and careers with fewer boundaries should favor either agency or communion. Either value, when pursued intensely, creates new boundaries, either those of the entrepreneur or those of the community. Framed in this way, efforts to cope with boundaryless careers could create even more intense conflicts over themes of independence versus the community, since either one can restore some of the structure that was lost. Integration may become more difficult and seem less necessary unless continuous learning becomes a dominant value. Continuous learning requires both agency and communion. To learn is to accept in order to change; to enact in order to be guided; to say in order to see; to organize in order to differentiate. To define boundaryless careers as a chance to fuse agency and communion is to turn a threat and a male response of control into an opportunity and a female response of integration.

Enactment and Organizing

I have repeatedly described the process of organizing (to learn) as a stable, bounded process in a boundaryless world. Organizing consists of self-designing cycles of enactment–selection–retention, in which retained outcomes partially shape subsequent action. Interaction is the feedstock for organizing, and learning is often the outcome. When situations weaken, people revert to the relative stabilities of organizing. This means that in a boundaryless world, organizing should be more common, more influential, and more visibly embodied in both career systems and organizations. The purpose of this section is to refine the understanding of organizing in ways that tie it more closely to careers. Specifically, I will briefly explore three ideas: expectation enactment, the institutionalization of projects, and reciprocity during development.

Expectation enactment

The idea of role occurs repeatedly in the careers literature and was central in Barley's discussion of career scripts. Barley (1989: 50) distinguishes between role and identity, defining the former as the interaction structure of a setting, and the latter as stable definitions of self that enable people to enact roles. Fondas and Stewart (1994) have elaborated the idea of roles by citing the concept of expectation enactment, suggesting that under certain conditions, people teach others how to interact with them. A manager enacts expectations by defining criteria for successful job performance or by shaping the expectations others hold about acceptable behavior or career prospects.

Expectation enactment is central to organizing and boundaryless careers, for at least two reasons. First, the process of teaching–learning that is involved in expectation enactment seems to follow roughly the sequence of enactment–selection–retention that is associated with organizing. Thus, when people organize to learn, they may organize to enact expectations and learn from feedback. Expectation enactment done locally on a small scale may be the template for related processes on a larger scale. Second, the variables assumed by Fondas and Stewart (1994: 92, figure 2) to influence expectation enactment share an interesting property: Virtually all of them strengthen as boundaries weaken, which should mean that as organizations become less bounded, there is more expectation enactment. For example, with fewer boundaries and weaker boundaries, distances between people, in terms of authority, decrease: role-set diversity increases; focal managers take more risks and, of necessity, adopt a more internal locus of control; focal managers and people in the role-set interact more and are more interdependent; and the organization itself displays more change in size, more mission ambiguity, and more variability in job definitions. All of these influences move in the direction of producing greater expectation enactment.

Projects

Organizing lies behind expectation enactment and gives it shape, just as it may also give shape to projects. Projects are relatively pure occasions of organizing. And one way to view boundaryless careers is as a "project-based game as in a checkerboard" (Peters, 1992: 220). Boundaryless careers consist of the repeated reaccomplishment of organizing in order to learn. And the reaccomplishment takes the form of a series of projects. People gain experience from both the content of what they do and the way they organize to do it. These experiences enlarge the repository of ideas that Alan Bird describes, and the knowledge of why, how, and whom, as described by Arthur and DeFillippi. Boundaryless careers become defined in terms of movements among projects and within projects.

While projects may be a dominant organizational form and may best be understood by closer attention to organizing than to organization, it remains possible to stratify projects and the assignments within them. I mention this because it is easy to confuse a loss of boundaries with a loss of differential authority and to forget that small differences in influence can amplify. The principle of hierarchy dies slowly – if ever – which means that organizing to learn may retain vestiges of advancement, upward movement, and tournaments. The hierarchies being "ascended" in a boundaryless career, however, become project based rather than organization based. Even successful replacement of hierarchies by heterarchies does not preclude informal ranking of required expertise and differential influence over the process.

The point is that in boundaryless organizations, the meaning of a boundaryless career shifts from advancement to learning and knowledge acquisition – but not entirely. Substitutes for hierarchical advancement can still be discerned. If a boundaryless career is a checkerboard career, there are stronger and weaker pieces, positions, and configurations, and there are moves that gain power and moves that lose it. To remove boundaries is to mobilize more primitive, more overlearned sources of structure, including personality and basic forms of organizing. Implicit in organizing is differentiation (Sherif and Sherif, 1964: chap. 7); and implicit in differentiation is the potential for advancement, plateauing, and descent.

Reciprocity during development

If projects are an important medium through which organizing is expressed, if projects take a more conspicuous social form in boundaryless careers, and if life in projects comes to define career scripts, then we may understand boundaryless careers better if we translate organization-level formulations into project-level formulations. Arthur and Kram's (1989) discussion of individual-organizational reciprocity provides an example of how to do this.

Arthur and Kram (1989) argue that as adults develop, their dominant needs change from needs to explore to needs to advance, ending with needs to protect. If each of these needs are met when they are salient, the person will offer the organization exuberance, directedness, and stewardship, respectively. These offerings, when aggregated, enable the organization to adapt, achieve objectives, and maintain the internal structure (pp. 294–296). Tensions arise when individual needs are ahead or behind of organizational stages. For example, the individual has progressed to the advancement need, but the organization needs adaptation, and so the poor fit is expressed by the individual as boredom at the prospect of movement to an earlier stage, and by the organization as worry and a paralyzing thought that it will be drawn to a more advanced stage for which it is ill-prepared.

I suggest that in a boundaryless world, Arthur and Kram's development sequence continues to unfold, but it does so more quickly, with more intensity, in smaller gatherings. A lifetime of development is compressed into the lifetime of a project, just as the "seasons" of an organization become compressed into the seasons of a project.

One implication is that life in a boundaryless career is likely to be volatile. The volatility arises because timing now assumes more importance. Short projects pass through stages rapidly, and the chances that project stages will match individual stages are lower because the length of time during which a match can occur is shorter. With shorter intervals for a reciprocal fit to occur, more of the time may be filled with the mismatches and the attendant anxiety produced by boredom and worry. Whether individual development leads or is behind the development of projects will be influenced by a host of factors, the discussion of which is beyond the scope of the point I want to make: My point here is that projects are the medium through which organizing is expressed.

As a boundaryless career unfolds and experience accumulates, individuals may steadily outdistance the start-up needs of new projects for adaptation, unless these new projects are so novel that individuals have no choice except to explore. It is also possible, however, that when people shuffle in and out of a project, but the project itself continues, then advanced project needs for achievement and maintenance may be thwarted by newcomers who explore rather than implement, and who offer diffuse exuberance in a setting that needs focused attention. In either case, mismatches persist and produce strong feelings and weak learning.

If we play by the rules sketched by Arthur and Kram, the "remedy" would seem to be greater discontinuity from project to project. With greater discontinuities, it is more likely that individual and collective needs will coincide (that is, exploration, advancement, and adaptation line up); that reciprocity will be established, and that learning will occur.

Enactment and Continuity

Two descriptions frame the issue discussed in this final section, on refinements:

> The transfer of learning relies on some recognizable element of continuity – a woman describing her patchwork of careers for me recently remarked wryly on a continuity between work as a kindergarten teacher, a teacher of the deaf, and dean for "Greek life" (fraternities) on a university campus! (Bateson, 1994: 86)

> Salman Rushdie, in discussing that quest [for coherence in self], describes personal meaning as a "shaky edifice we build out of scraps, dogmas, childhood injuries, newspaper articles, chance remarks, old films, small victories, people hated, people loved"; and then adds that "perhaps it is because our sense [of that meaning] is constructed from such inadequate materials that we defend it so fiercely, even to the death." (Lifton, 1993: 88)

The concept of a career has at least two sides to it, a personal side and a public side (Barley, 1989: 46). The personal (internal) side is characterized by a felt identity or an image of self, whereas the public (external) side is characterized more by official position, the institutional complex, and styles of life. The issue addressed in this section is: What happens to the personal side when the public side consists of fragments (Mirvis and Hall, 1994: 369), and when a person is tempted to say, "I'm not quite anything" (Lifton, 1993: 52)? Boundaryless careers generate fragments in search of continuity.

The importance of continuity in boundaryless careers arises for several reasons. First, people without any sense of continuity whatsoever should experience substantial ongoing states of arousal that interfere with learning. The same should hold true for organizations whose identity is up for grabs (e.g., see Dutton and Dukerich, 1991).

Themes of continuity are also crucial because learning itself is a process that builds on similarities and differences between the present and the past (e.g., stimulus generalization). With no continuity, there is no learning. Instead, in the interest of economy, there is simply reaction without either cumulation or repetition.

A third reason that we need to think carefully about continuity is that if organizing is enacted into enduring career scripts and institutions, then these newer career systems create novel continuities with which people have little familiarity. When people enact new continuities, the necessity to learn increases, rather than decreasing. If people enact a self-designing system, they are able to spot a "recognizable element of continuity" only with the passage of time and action.

If the construction of continuity is crucial for a boundaryless career, how do people accomplish it? There are several possibilities, some of which I will discuss briefly. To begin with, no single experience provides a pure case of continuity or discontinuity. As Michael puts it, "There are many pasts" (1985: 95). Bateson (1994) has capitalized on the fact that continuity lies partly in the eyes of the beholder, by having people interpret their own life history twice, focusing first on continuity ("Everything I have ever done has been heading me for where I am today"), and then on discontinuity ("It is only after many surprises and choices, interruptions and disappointments, that I have arrived somewhere I could never have anticipated"). She finds that tales of continuity and discontinuity can be constructed from the same facts (e.g., "Sure, I've had the same job for thirty years, but meanwhile consider the turnover in my body's cells"); that the tales are not mutually exclusive (e.g., "I have always enjoyed tackling the unknown"); and that some tales focus on different aspects of the person's life (e.g., the person keeps the same spouse but has different jobs), while some show a preference for continuity but recognize discontinuity (e.g., "I have always been a writer, but I shifted from being a poet to being a journalist"). Thus, one way to deal with the apparent fragments of a boundaryless career is to look more closely for sources of continuity.

Continuities also can be highlighted if one recasts the nature of a boundaryless career itself. Consider Defillippi and Arthur's description:

> The ideal-typical boundaryless career is characterized by a career identity that is employer-independent (e.g., "I am a software engineer"), the accumulation of employment-flexible know-how (e.g., how to do work in an innovative, efficient, and/or quality enhancing way), and the development of networks that are interorganizational (e.g., occupational or industry-based), non-hierarchic (e.g., communities of practice) and worker enacted. (1994: 320)

Adoption of this mind-set should enable people to span specific settings and to derive continuity from self-descriptions that are more like those of professionals with their core beliefs, values, and skills that are not organization-specific. Those who view their boundaryless life in ways that simulate the work of a professional see themselves as people who "have technical skills transferable across organizations, recognized apart from hierarchical status, and with opportunity decoupled from promotion within a single organization" (Kanter, 1989: 510).

As I noted earlier, boundaryless careers may have their own unique continuities. Probably the most obvious new continuity is learning: "Learning is the new continuity for individuals, innovation the new continuity for business" (Bateson, 1994: 83). There is a hitch in this seemingly seamless picture of learning as the new continuity. The problem is that organizations are often poor places to learn.

Norms of compassion encourage the vulnerability that is a precondition for learning; yet, organizations are often unsafe and devoid of compassion. Organizations violate these norms in order to be lean and mean, but thereby increasing the odds of their becoming dumb and dated. Michael (1985: 101) makes this very clear when he talks about a challenge that has been repeatedly ignored by those (e.g., Huber, 1991) who attempt to specify the nature of organizational learning – namely, the role of compassion in learning. Michael suggests that acknowledging and experiencing the personal and organizational life of the learner depend on being open to unfamiliar ideas and experiences and on being increasingly interdependent. Both requirements demand exceptional degrees of vulnerability. But being vulnerable can lead to a humane world only if the norms of compassion are observed. Otherwise, those willing to risk a learning stance will be destroyed by the power-hungry and hostile people. He suggests that everyone needs all the clarity they can muster, regarding their ignorance and finiteness, and all the support they can obtain in order to face the upsetting implications of what their clarity reveals to them. "A compassionate person is one who, by virtue of accepting this situation, can provide others as well as self with such support. Learning how to establish such norms will be as difficult as it is unavoidable" (Michael, 1985: 101).

Just as communion is crucial to collective learning, as I have noted here, pure agency isn't sufficient for boundaryless organizations. Pure agency tends to encourage raw assertions of power as well as an unwillingness to become vulnerable in order to learn (remember, Karl Deutsch defined power as "the ability not to have to learn"). Both tendencies reduce the knowledge creation that Drucker feels will become commonplace. Drucker is wrong in this prediction, unless much more fundamental changes occur than simply those associated with the rational recognition that knowledge and learning are sources of competitive advantage. Organizational and career advantage, in the face of fewer boundaries, is more likely to favor those who shift to a more complicated sense of themselves and their capabilities, including their capability for compassion.

As a final source of continuity, I want to reiterate that continuity may lie in higher-order, more-abstract capabilities such as mutability itself (e.g., see Zurcher, 1977), adaptability, improvisation, or being a generalist. What endures across varying experiences is a constancy of being a quick study, of fitting in, of making do in ways that add value. The constancy is continuous swift adaptation made possible by ongoing enhancements of adaptability. These enhancements of adaptability occur as people articulate and make explicit their tacit knowledge, and transform explicit knowledge into tacit knowledge that enlarges their understanding (Bird, 1996). The tension here, again, involves trade-offs. To be an adaptable generalist may be to sacrifice an in-depth specialty and a higher degree of temporary adaptation. In some industries, it may be possible to specialize in being a generalist, especially if problems routinely are nonroutine (e.g., see Pacanowsky, 1995). What seems to be true of boundaryless careers is that either orientation seems to be adaptive: There seem to be opportunities for the adaptability of the generalist and for the adaptation by the specialist. Where the opportunities seem to disappear is for people who blend the two orientations, rather than alternating between purer expressions of the two. As is often the case in complex environments, evolution favors treating ambivalence as the optimal compromise (Campbell, 1965: 304–306).

Conclusion

Boundaryless organizations seem more and more to generate discontinuous episodes of growth, during which people organize to learn. This macrochange is reflected in career scripts that increasingly focus on organizing, learning, enactment, projects, self-design, tools for continuity, cycles, knowledge acquisition, networks, reputations, self-management, benchmarking of skills, and self-reliance. Careers still mean journeys, but the destinations are no longer fixed levels in a hierarchy, but fluid positions of expertise in a heterarchy organized around collective learning. While all of this sounds minimally structured, what I have tried to show is that the structure of boundaryless careers comes from moments during which people organize in order to learn. When people do this, they enact both the learning process, and its outcomes, into the scripts, organizations, and institutions that subsequently constrain them. Macrocareer systems come to resemble microorganizing.

Career success comes to be defined in terms of things like amount of learning accumulated; meaningfulness of continuities constructed; ability to create and manage organizing; comfort in returning to the novice role over and over; ability to explicate what had previously been known only tacitly; tolerance for fragmentary experience; skill in making sense of fragments retrospectively in ways that help others make sense of their fragments; willingness to improvise, and skill at doing so; persistence; compassion for others struggling with the uncertainty of a boundaryless life; and durable faith that actions will have made sense, even though that sense is currently not evident. People skilled in these ways are likely to find a series of challenging projects that, when strung together, simulate traditional advancement. The difference is that the transitions from project to project are more dramatic and more discontinuous.

There is basically no substitute for trial and error in dealing with surprise. When large organizations are surprised, smaller groups organize for improvisation and experimentation, to deal with the surprise. In doing so, these smaller groups essentially replace organization with organizing. This change provides the infrastructure that shapes boundaryless organizations so that they look and function more like the self-designing systems that dealt with the surprise in the first place. This shift to self-design becomes embodied in scripts and institutions that become the hallmark of life in the boundaryless organization. Thus, coming full circle, people adapt to the life of continuous learning that they implanted in the first place to cope with the loss of boundaries.

References

Arthur, M. B.; Hall, D. T.; and Lawrence, B. S. (eds.). (1989). *Handbook of Career Theory*. New York: Cambridge University Press.

Arthur, M. B., and Kram, K. E. (1989). Reciprocity at work: The separate yet inseparable possibilities for individual and organizational development. In M. B. Arthur; D. T. Hall; and B. S. Lawrence (eds.), *Handbook of Career Theory* (pp. 292–312). New York: Cambridge University Press.

Bailyn, L (1989). Understanding individual experience at work: Comments on the theory and practice of careers. In M. B. Arthur; D. T. Hall; and B. S. Lawrence (eds.), *Handbook of Career Theory* (pp. 477–489). New York: Cambridge University Press.

Bakan, D. (1966). *The Duality of Human Existence*. Boston: Beacon.

Barley, S. R (1989). Careers, identities, and institutions: The legacy of the Chicago School of Sociology. In M. B. Arthur; D. T. Hall; & B. S. Lawrence (eds.), *Handbook of Career Theory* (pp. 41–65). New York: Cambridge University Press.

Barner, R (1994). The new career strategist: Career management for the year 2000 and beyond. *The Futurist, 28* (5), 8–14.

Bateson, M. C. (1994). *Peripheral Visions: Learning along the Way*. New York: HarperCollins.

Bell N. E, and Staw, B. M. (1989). People as sculptors versus sculpture: The roles of personality and personal control in organizations. In M. B. Arthur; D. T. Hall; and B. S. Lawrence (eds.), *Handbook of Career Theory* (pp. 232–251). New York: Cambridge University Press.

Bird, A. (1996). Careers as repositories of knowledge: Considerations for boundaryless careers. In M. B. Arthur and D. Rousseau (eds.), *The Boundaryless Career: A New Employment Principle for a New Organizational Era*, (pp. 150–168). Oxford, UK: Oxford University Press.

Campbell, D. T. (1965). Ethnocentric and other altruistic motives. In D. Levine (ed.), *Nebraska Symposium on Motivation* (pp. 283–311). Lincoln: University of Nebraska Press.

Carson, R C. (1989). Personality. *Annual Review of Psychology, 40,* 227–248.

DeFillippi, R., and Arthur, M. B. (1996). Boundaryless contexts and careers: A competency-based perspective. In M. B. Arthur and D. Rousseau (eds.), *The Boundaryless Career: A New Employment Principle for a New Organizational Era*, (pp. 116–131). Oxford, UK: Oxford University Press.

Delbecq, A. L, and Weiss, J. (1988). The business culture of Silicon Valley: Is it a model for the future? In J. Hage (ed.), *Futures of Organizations* (pp. 123–141). Lexington, Mass.: Lexington Books.

Drucker, P. F. (1994). The age of social transformation. *Atlantic Monthly*, November, pp. 53–80.

Dutton, J. E, and Dukerich, J. M. (1991). Keeping an eye on the mirror: Image and identity in organizational adaptation. *Academy of Management Journal, 34,* 517–554.

Fondas, N., and Stewart, T. (1994). Enactment in managerial jobs: A role analysis. *Journal of Management Studies, 31* (1), 83–103.

Gioia, T. (1988). *The Imperfect Art*. New York: Oxford University Press.

Huber, G. P. (1991). Organizational learning: The contributing processes and the literature. *Organization Science, 2* (1), 88–115.

Kanter, R. M. (1989). Careers and the wealth of nations: A macro-perspective on the structure and implications of career forms. In M. B. Arthur; D. T. Hall; and B. S. Lawrence (eds.), *Handbook of Career Theory* (pp. 506–522). New York: Cambridge University Press.

Lifton, R. J. (1993). *The Protean Self*. New York: Basic Books.

Marshall, J. (1989). Re-visioning career concepts: A feminist invitation. In M. B. Arthur; D. T. Hall; and B. S. Lawrence (eds.), *Handbook of Career Theory* (pp. 275–291). New York: Cambridge University Press.

Michael D. N. (1985). With both feet planted firmly in mid-air: Reflections on thinking about the future. *Futures*, April, pp. 94–103.

Miner, A. S. (1987). Idiosyncratic jobs in formalized organizations. *Administrative Science Quarterly, 32,* 327–351.

Miner, A. S. (1990). Structural evolution through idiosyncratic jobs: The potential for un-planned learning. *Organization Science, 1* (2), 195–210.

Mirvis, P. H., and Hall, D. T. (1994). Psychological success and the boundaryless career. *Journal of Organizational Behavior*, 15, 365–380.

Mischel, W. (1968). *Personality and Assessment*. New York: Wiley.

Mischel, W. (1977). The interaction of person and situation. In D. Magnuson and N. S. Endler (eds.), *Personality at the Crossroads*. Hillsdale, N.J.: Erlbaum.

Nicholson, N., and West, M. (1989). Transitions, work histories, and careers. In M. B. Arthur; D. T. Hall; and B. S. Lawrence (eds.), *Handbook of Career Theory* (pp. 181–201). New York: Cambridge University Press.

Nonaka, I., and Takeuchi, H. (1995). *The Knowledge-creating Company*. New York: Oxford University Press.

Nystrom, P. C., and MacArthur, A. W. (1989). Propositions linking organizations and careers. In M. B. Arthur; D. T. Hall; and B. S. Lawrence (eds.), Handbook of Career Theory (pp. 490–505). New York: Cambridge University Press.

Pacanowsky, M. (1995). Team tools for wicked problems. *Organizational Dynamics*, 23(3), 36–51.

Perrow, C. (1993). *"Dartmouth Speech."* Mimeographed. Yale University, Department of Sociology.

Peters, T. (1992). *Liberation Management*. New York: Knopf.

Porac, J. F., Thomas, H., and Baden-Fuller, C. (1989). Competitive groups as cognitive communities: The case of Scottish knitwear manufacturers. *Journal of Management Studies*, 26, 397–416.

Power, D. J. (1988). Anticipating organization structures. In J. Hage (ed.), *Futures of Organizations* (pp. 67–79). Lexington, Mass.: Lexington Books.

Quinn, J. B. (1992). *Intelligent Enterprise*. New York: Free Press.

Sherif, M., and Sherif, C. W. (1964). *Reference Groups: Exploration into Conformity and Deviation of Adolescents*. New York: Harper and Row.

Sonnenfeld, J. A. (1989). Career system profiles and strategic staffing. In M. B. Arthur; D. T. Hall; and B. S. Lawrence (eds.), *Handbook of Career Theory* (pp. 202–226). New York: Cambridge University Press.

Thompson, P. (1993). Postmodernism: Fatal distraction. In J. Hassard and M. Parker (eds.), *Postmodernism and Organizations* (pp. 183–203). Newbury Park, Calif.: Sage.

Weick, R E. (1979). *The Social Psychology of Organizing*, 2nd ed. Reading, Mass.: Addison-Wesley.

Weick, K. E. (1987). Substitutes for corporate strategy. In D. J. Teece (ed.), *The Competitive Challenge* (pp. 221–233). Cambridge, Mass.: Ballinger.

Weick, K. E. (1993). Sensemaking in organizations: Small structures with large consequences. In J. K Murnighan (ed.), *Social Psychology in Organizations: Advances in Theory and Research* (pp. 10–37). Englewood Cliffs, N.J.: Prentice Hall.

Weick, K. E., and Berlinger, L. (1989). Career improvisation in self-designing organizations. In M. B. Arthur; D. T. Hall; and B. S. Lawrence (eds.), *Handbook of Career Theory* (pp. 313–328). New York: Cambridge University Press.

Zurcher, L. A., Jr. (1977). *The Mutable Self*. Beverly Hills: Sage.

9

Enacted Sensemaking in Crisis Situations

Introduction

Crises are characterized by low probability/high consequence events that threaten the most fundamental goals of an organization. Because of their low probability, these events defy interpretations and impose severe demands on sensemaking. The less adequate the sensemaking process directed at a crisis, the more likely it is that the crisis will get out of control. That straightforward proposition conceals a difficult dilemma because people think by acting. To sort out a crisis as it unfolds often requires action which simultaneously generates the raw material that is used for sensemaking and affects the unfolding crisis itself. There is a delicate tradeoff between dangerous action which produces understanding and safe inaction which produces confusion. The purpose of this article is to explore the complications of that tension.

Two exhibits highlight the central issue. The first involves explorers, the second involves the last paragraph of Union Carbide's procedure for dealing with gas leaks.

(1) An explorer can never know what he is exploring until it has been explored (Bateson, 1972, p. xvi).

(2) The [Bhopal] plant's operating manual for methyl isocyanate offered little guidance in the event of a large leak. After telling the operators to dump the gas into a spare tank if a leak in a storage tank cannot be stopped or isolated, the manual says: There may be other situations not covered above. The situation will determine the appropriate action. We will learn more and more as we gain actual experience (Diamond, 28 January 1985, p. 7).

Bateson's description of exploring illustrates the key point about sensemaking. The explorer cannot know what he is facing until he faces it, and then looks back over the episode to sort out what happened, a sequence that involves retrospective sensemaking But the act of exploring itself has an impact on what is being explored, which means that parts of what the explorer discovers retrospectively are consequences of his own making. Furthermore, the exploring itself is guided by preconceptions of some kind, even though they may be generic preconceptions such as "this will have made sense once I explore it although right now it seems senseless" (Weick, Gilfillan and Keith, 1973).

The explorer who enacts a sensible environment is no different from the operator of a console in a chemical plant control room who confronts a puzzling assortment of dials, lights and sounds and discovers, through action, what the problem is, but in doing so, shapes the problem itself (see McHugh, 1968, for an analogue). Both the explorer and the control room operator understand the problem they face only after they have faced it and only after their actions have become inextricably wound into it.

Imagine that the control room operator faces a gas leak and the admonition from the Union Carbide procedure cited above. Carbide is right when it says experience is the source of learning, but it is wrong when it says, "The situation will determine the appropriate action". People often don't know what the "appropriate action" is until they take some action and see what happens. Thus, actions determine the situation. Furthermore, it is less often true that "situations" determine appropriate action than that "preconceptions" determine appropriate action. Finally, the judgement of "appropriateness" is likely to be a motivated assessment constructed partially to validate earlier reasoning. These corrections show not so much that Carbide's statement is in error, as that Carbide's assessment is incomplete because it misrepresents the contribution of action to human understanding.

Understanding is facilitated by action, but action affects events and can make things worse. Action during crisis is not just an issue of control, it is an epistemological issue. If action is a means to get feedback, learn, and build an understanding of unknown environments, then a reluctance to act could be associated with less understanding and more errors.

In the remainder of this article I will enlarge these introductory ideas in three ways. First, I will describe the concept of enactment that drives this analysis. Second, I will discuss how cognition and understanding are affected by commitment, capacity, and expectations during crises. I conclude with a brief survey of implications for crisis management.

The Enactment Perspective

Assumptions of the enactment perspective

The concept of enactment is a synthesis, tailored for organizational settings, of four lines of scholarship: self-fulfilling prophecies (E. E. Jones, 1986; R. A. Jones, 1977; Snyder, 1984); retrospective sensemaking (Staw, 1980; Weick, 1979); commitment (Salancik, 1977; Staw, 1982); and social information processing (Salancik and Pfeffer, 1978). The term "enactment" is used to preserve the central point that when people act, they bring events and structures into existence and set them in motion. People who act in organizations often produce structures, constraints, and opportunities that were not there before they took action.

Enactment involves both a process, enactment, and a product, an enacted environment.

Enactment is the social process by which a "material and symbolic record of action" (Smircich and Stubbart, 1985, p. 726) is laid down. The process occurs in two steps. First, portions of the field of experience are bracketed and singled out for closer attention on the basis of preconceptions. Second, people act within the context of these bracketed elements, under the guidance of preconceptions, and often shape these elements in the direction of preconceptions (Powers, 1973). Thus, action tends to confirm preconceptions.

An enacted environment is the residuum of changes produced by enactment. The word "residuum" is preferred to the word "residue" because residuum emphasizes that what is left after a process cannot be ignored or left out of account because it has potential significance (*Webster's Dictionary of Synonyms*, 1951, p. 694). The product of enactment is not an accident, an afterthought, or a byproduct. Instead, it is an orderly, material, social construction that is subject to multiple interpretations. Enacted environments contain real objects such as reactors, pipes and valves. The existence of these objects is not questioned, but their significance, meaning, and content is. These objects are inconsequential until they are acted upon and then incorporated retrospectively into events, situations, and explanations.

The external residuum of enacted changes is summarized internally by people in the form of a plausible map by which observed, actions produced observed consequences. Since the summary map contains if–then assertions, it is called a cause map (Weick and Bougon, 1986) and is the source of expectations for future action. When we assert that the organization and the environment are in the mind of the actor, this means two things. It means that cause maps affect the construction of new experience through the mechanism of expectations and it means that cause maps affect the interpretation of old experience through the mechanism of labeling.

Thus, an enacted environment has both a public and a private face. Publicly, it is a construction that is usually visible to observers other than the actor. Privately, it is a map of if–then assertions in which actions are related to outcomes. These assertions serve as expectations about what will happen in the future.

At the heart of enactment is the idea that cognition lies in the path of the action. Action precedes cognition and focuses cognition. The sensemaking sequence implied in the phrase, "How can I know what I think until I see what I say?" involves the action of talking, which lays down traces that are examined so that cognitions can be inferred. These inferred cognitions then become preconceptions which partially affect the next episode of talk, which means the next set of traces deposited by talk is affected partially by previous labels and partially by current context. These earlier inferences also affect how the next episode of talk is examined and what is seen. This sensemaking sequence has the potential to become closed and detached from the context in which it occurs. However, that potential is seldom realized because preconceptions are usually weak, actions are usually novel, and memories are usually flawed.

Relationship of enactment perspective to crisis literature

The enactment perspective is applied to crisis situations in this chapter in an attempt to address Shrivastava's (1987, p. 118) observation that we do not yet understand much about how individual actions can cause an industrial crisis. The analysis of enactment suggests that individual actions involved in sensemaking can cause a crisis, but also manage it to lower levels of danger. Actions often construct the reasons for their occurrence as they unfold, which means their consequences are difficult to forecast in advance. Our actions are always a little further along than is our understanding of those actions, which means we can intensify crises literally before we know what we are doing. Unwitting escalation of crises is especially likely when technologies are complex, highly interactive, non-routine, and poorly understood. The very action which enables people to gain some understanding of these complex technologies can also cause those technologies to escalate and kill.

To learn more about how sensemaking can be decoupled from escalation, we focus on triggered events: "a specific event that is identifiable in time and place and traceable to specific man-made causes" (Shrivastava, 1987, p. 8). Triggered events are places where interventions can have an effect, these events involve judgment which can deteriorate when pressure increases (Staw, Sandelands, and Dutton, 1981), and these events can escalate into a crisis.

The enactment perspective is about both crisis prevention and crisis management. We share with Ayres and Rohatgi (1987, p. 41) the assumption that "while the probability of operator error can often be reduced, there is no evidence whatever that it can be eliminated altogether. ... Human errors are fundamentally 'caused' by human variability, which cannot be designed away". This assumption suggests to us that errors are inevitable, so the key issue is how to keep errors from enlarging. Errors are less likely to enlarge if they are understood more fully, more quickly. If we can understand the process of sensemaking during a crisis, then we can help people to prevent larger crises by smarter management of small crises. It is this sense in which enactment blurs the line between crisis prevention and crisis management. By understanding triggering events and the ways in which small sensemaking actions can grow into large senseless disasters, we hope to develop a better understanding of how crises can be isolated and contained.

The enactment approach shares an interest with Billings, Milburn, and Schaalman (1980) in triggering events, and complements their analysis by emphasizing that action is instrumental to crisis perception. The enactment perspective focuses on "proactive crisis management" in Mitroff, Shrivastava, and Udwadia (1987) and develops specifically the activities of pre-assessment, prevention, preparation, and coping. The threat-rigidity cycle (Staw, Sandelands, and Dutton, 1981) is in the background throughout our analysis since we assume that action often manages threat toward lower levels of intensity thereby reducing the tendency toward rigid problem solving.

Crises obviously are overdetermined and human sensemaking may play only a small part in their development. Nevertheless, crises engage human action, human action can amplify small deviations into major crises, and in any search for causes, we invariably can find some human act which may have set the crisis in motion. It is our contention that actions devoted to sensemaking play a central role in the genesis of crises and therefore need to be understood if we are to manage and prevent crises.

The Enacted Quality of Crises

Shrivastava's (1987) analysis of Bhopal can be read for themes of enactment, as when he observes that "the initial response to the crisis sets the tone for the rest of the effort" (p. 134). From the standpoint of enactment, initial responses do more than set the tone; they determine the trajectory of the crisis. Since people know what they have done only after they do it, people and their actions rapidly become part of the crisis. That is unavoidable. To become part of the problem means that people enact some of the environment they face. Had they not acted or had they acted differently, they would face a different set of problems, opportunities, and constraints.

All crises have an enacted quality once a person takes the first action. Suppose that a gauge shows an unexpected increase in temperature. That is not enactment. Suppose further that in response to the unexpected temperature increase people tap the gauge or call the supervisor or proceed with a tea break or walk out to look at the tank whose temperature is being measured. That still is not enactment, because all that exists so far is a simple stimulus and response. But the response of tapping, calling, drinking, or walking produces a new stimulus that would not have been there had the first been ignored. The "second stimulus" is now a partial human construction. The assumptions that underlie the choice of that first response contribute to enactment and the second stimulus. As action continues through more cycles, the human responses which stimulate further action become increasingly important components of the crisis. "When a triggering event occurs, spontaneous reactions by different stakeholders solve some of the immediate problems, but they also create new problems – thus prolonging the crisis and making it worse" (Shrivastava, 1987, p. 24).

Thus, from the perspective of enactment, what is striking is that crises can have small, volitional beginnings in human action. Small events are carried forward, cumulate with other events, and over time systematically construct an environment that is a rare combination of unexpected simultaneous failures.

Shrivastava (1987, p. 42) identified "the leakage of toxic gas" as the triggering event at Bhopal, but my choice would be the failure to insert a slip blind into a pipe being cleaned, which allowed water to back up and enter the MIC tank and catalyze a complex chemical interaction (Ayres and Rohatgi, 1987, p. 32; Shrivastava, 1987, p. 46). The slip blind oversight occurred in close proximity to the "leakage of toxic gas"; it was a small deviation that amplified because MIC was stored in 60 ton tanks rather than 55 gallon drums, and it resulted from a proximate combination of preconceptions about a job and its safety, inadequate supervision, and inadequate training.

It is not sufficient to deal with the enacted quality of crises by striving to make the technology operator proof. All that does is move the dynamics of enactment to an earlier point in time where incomplete designs are enacted into unreliable technology by fallible designers who believe they can bypass the very human variability that has already been exhibited by their design process.

The enacted quality of crises is especially visible when we apply the concepts of commitment, capacity, and expectations to crisis conditions.

Enactment and commitment

The importance of commitment (Salancik, 1977) for enactment is straightforward. Normally, when people act, their reasons for doing things are either self-evident or uninteresting, especially when the actions themselves can be undone, minimized, or disowned. Actions that are neither visible nor permanent can be explained with casual, transient explanations. As those actions become more public and irrevocable, however, they become harder to undo; and when those same actions are also volitional, they become harder to disown. When action is irrevocable, public, and volitional, the search for explanations becomes less casual because more is at stake. Explanations that are developed retrospectively to justify committed actions are often stronger than beliefs developed under other, less involving, conditions. A tenacious justification can produce selective attention, confident action, and self-confirmation. Tenacious justifications prefigure both perception and action, which means they are often self-confirming.

Tenacious justifications can be forces for good or evil in crises. They are forces for good because they generate meaning in times of ambiguity, surprise, and confusion (Staw, 1980). Justifications provide sufficient structure for people to get their bearings and then create fuller, more accurate views of what is happening and what their options are.

The dark side of commitment is that it produces blind spots. Once a person becomes committed to an action, and then builds an explanation that justifies that action, the explanation tends to persist and become transformed into an assumption that is taken for granted. Once this transformation has occurred it is unlikely that the assumption will be readily viewed as a potential contributor to a crisis.

For example, the public, irrevocable choice at Bhopal to keep the dangerous process of MIC production secret, was justified in terms of competitive advantage and the prevention of "unnecessary" alarm. As a result, the commitment to secrecy was one of the last assumptions workers considered as a contributor to the crisis. To minimize alarm, the warning siren at Bhopal was not turned on until gas actually started to leak into the atmosphere, the siren was turned off after 5 minutes, and it was not restarted until gas had been escaping for 90 minutes. The commitment to secrecy induced a blind spot toward a partial solution, necessary alarm.

As another example, the public, irrevocable decision by Bhopal management to announce that all safety violations reported to them in a September 1982 report, had been corrected (Ayres and Rohatgi, 1987, p. 36), was justified by actions which took safety for granted and inadvertently allowed it to deteriorate steadily in several different places. Thus, the eventual public, irrevocable choice to disconnect the refrigeration equipment that kept MIC temperature under control, was justified as a relatively safe means to save electricity, reduce costs, and recover freon which could be used elsewhere in the plant. It was the uncontrolled heating of MIC in Tank 610 that led to rupture of the safety valves and venting of the gas.

When people make a public commitment that an operating gauge is inoperative, the last thing they will consider during a crisis is that the gauge is operating. Had they not made the commitment, the blind spot would not be so persistent. When a person becomes committed to the view that fluctuations in electricity cause 90 per cent of the variances that are seen in gauges, the possibility that a much different percentage is more accurate will not be entertained until the crisis is at an advanced stage.

Given the effects of commitments on attention, practitioners and researchers alike might learn more about crisis potential (Mitroff, Shrivastava and Udwadia, 1987 p. 290) if they see which people are "on record" as making irreversible assertions about technology, operators, and capabilities. Those assertions, and their associated justifications, will have been shielded from scrutiny more than other assertions in which less is at stake. The practices and assumptions that those justifications shield may be significant contributors to crisis.

Enactment and capacity

Action in the form of capacity can affect crisis management through perception, distribution of competence and control within a hierarchy, and number and diversity of actors.

Capacity and response repertoire affect crisis perception, because people see those events they feel they have the capacity to do something about. As capacities change, so too do perceptions and actions. This relationship is one of the crucial leverage points to improve crisis management.

The rationale for these relationships has been described by Jervis (1976, pp. 374–5): "(T)he predisposition to perceive a threat varies with the person's beliefs about his ability to take effective counteraction if he perceives the danger. . . . Whether they are vigilant or defensive depends in large part on whether they think they can act effectively on the undesired information".

If people think they can do lots of things, then they can afford to pay attention to a wider variety of inputs because, whatever they see, they will have some way to cope with it. The more a person sees of any situation, the higher the probability that the person will see the specific change that needs to be made to dampen the crisis. Accuracy in perception comes from an expanded response capacity. Perrow (1984) argues that operators who have specialized expertise do not see the "big picture" as crises develop and therefore miss key events. That scenario is consistent with the proposition that capacity affects perception. Specialists can do a few things well, which means that they search the world to see if it needs what they can do. If it doesn't, they do nothing else because they see nothing else.

If people are aware that volitional action may enact conditions that intensify or deescalate crises, and if they are also aware of their actions and capacities, this heightened awareness could allow them to see more of a developing crisis. Seeing more of the developing crisis, people should then be able to see more places where they could intervene and make an actual difference in what is developing. The joint beliefs, "I have capacity" and "capacity makes a difference", should reduce defensive perception and allow people to see more. As they see more, there is a greater probability that they will see some place where their intervention can make a difference.

Capacity can also affect crisis management by the way in which it is distributed in a hierarchy. Perrow (1984, p. 10) notes that "operators need to be able to take independent and creative action because they are closest to the system, yet centralization tight coupling, and prescribed steps prevent decentralized action".

Action of any kind may be prevented or slowed in a centralized system. Hermann (1963) has noted when crises occur, authority becomes contracted in one of three ways: it moves to higher levels of the hierarchy, fewer people exercise authority, or there is an increase in the number of occasions when authority is exercised even though the number of units exercising it remains constant (p. 70).

The danger in centralization and contraction of authority is that there may be a reduction in the level of competence directed at the problem as well as an overall reduction in the use of action to develop meaning. For example, Bhopal had relatively unsophisticated sensing devices and had to rely on workers to sense problems by means of the "tear gas effect of the vapor" (Diamond, 28 January, 1985, p. 6). But the presence of that vivid indicator was still not enough because the tearing was given little attention by authorities. Furthermore, if people had moved around at Bhopal, they would have heard gurgling and rumbling in the MIC tank, seen drops of water near the tank, and felt tearing in their eyes.

The person in authority is not necessarily the most competent person to deal with a crisis, so a contraction of authority leads either to less action or more confusion. Career ladders in crisis-prone organizations are crucial antecedents for coping. People who come up through the technical ranks have hands-on experience and the requisite knowledge to sense variations in the technological environment they face. Those who administer without a technical background have less requisite expertise and miss more.

Diamond (30 January, 1985, p. 6), in his account of Bhopal, noted that during the crisis, "K. V. Shetty, the plant superintendent for the shift, had come racing over from the main gate on a bicycle, workers said. 'He came in pretty much in a panic', Mr Day said. 'He said, "what should we do?"' Mr Shetty, who declined to be interviewed, was on the administrative and not the technical side of the factory, the workers said".

Capacity can also affect crisis potential through staffing decisions that affect the diversity of acts that are available. Enactment is labour-intensive, which means understaffing has serious effects. Even though the Bhopal plant had few automated controls, high manual control over processes, and a potentially large amount of action data from which understanding could be built, these potential assets were neutralized because operating staffs had been cut from 12 to 6 people per shift. Thus, knowledge was reduced, not because of automation, but because of understaffing. If action is the means to understanding, then the number and quality of actors available to do that acting and interpretation become crucial variables.

Turnover is as much a threat to capacity as is understaffing, but for a different reason. Institutional memory is an important component of crisis management. People can see only those categories and assumptions that they store in cause maps built up from previous experience. If those cause maps are varied and rich, people should see more, and good institutional memory would be an asset. However, if cause maps are filled with only a handful of overworked justifications, then perception should be limited and inaccurate, and a good memory would be a liability.

Shrivastava (1987, p. 52) reported that there was no institutional memory at

Bhopal because turnover in top management was high and Smith (1984, p. 908) made the same observation about crisis management in the US government. In both cases, there are few beliefs that control seeing. It might seem desirable for few preconceptions to be carried in institutional memory because then people will perceive more of what is "really there". Perception, however, is never free of preconceptions, and when people perceive without institutional memories, they are likely to be influenced by salient distractions (e.g. Kirwan, 1987) or by experience gained in settings that are irrelevant to present problems.

If more people are in constant touch with the system, this will make it easier to detect and correct anomalies and also to implant more reliable environments. These outcomes should be especially likely when the people doing the enactment have diverse experience, novel categories and justifications, and diverse activities at which they are skilled and in terms of which they perceive the world. We are not talking about specialists isolated from one another. Instead, we are talking about heterogeneous teams of diverse people with sufficient mutual respect that they maintain dense interaction with one another. Teams able to meet these demands are scarce, do not come cheap, and may be most likely to form if high levels of professionalism are associated with them.

Enactment and expectations

The assumptions that top management make about components within the firm often influence enactment in a manner similar to the mechanism of self-fulfilling prophecy. Many of these assumptions can increase or decrease the likelihood that small errors will escalate into major crises. Thus, assumptions are an important source of crisis prevention.

This mechanism is clearly visible in Bhopal where top management assumed that the Bhopal plant was unimportant and therefore allocated limited resources to maintain it. That assumption of unimportance set in motion a self-confirming vicious circle in which worker indifference and management cost-cutting became mutually reinforcing and resulted in deteriorating conditions that became more dangerous. " 'The whole industrial culture of Union Carbide at Bhopal went down the drain', said Mr Pareek, the former project engineer. 'The plant was losing money, and top management decided that saving money was more important than safety. Maintenance practices became poor, and things generally got sloppy. The plant didn't seem to have a future, and a lot of skilled people became depressed and left as a result' " (Diamond, 28 January, 1985, p. 6).

A plant perceived as unimportant proceeds to act out, through turnover, sloppy procedures, inattention to details, and lower standards, the prophecy implied in top management's expectations. A vicious circle is created and conditions become increasingly dangerous. Notice that the most crucial assumption does not involve safety directly. Instead, the crucial assumptions focus on themes of competence, importance, and value. Susceptibility to crisis varies as a function of top management assumptions about which units are important.

When cost cutting is focused on less important units, it is not just decreased maintenance which raises susceptibility to crisis. Instead, it is all of the indirect effects on workers of the perception that their unit doesn't matter. This perception results in increased inattention, indifference, turnover, low cost improvisation, and working-to-rule, all of which remove slack, lower the threshold at which a crisis will escalate, and increase the number of separate places at which a crisis could start. As slack decreases, the technology becomes more interactively complex (Perrow, 1984), which means there are more places where a minor lapse can escalate just when there are more minor lapses occurring.

The point is, this scenario starts with top management perceptions that set in motion enactments that confirm the perceptions. Furthermore, the initial perceptions were concerned with strategy, not safety. Strategy became an inadvertent source of crisis through its effects on realities constructed by disheartened workers. The realities they enacted removed buffers, dampers, and controls between steps in the technology, made it harder for errors to be contained, and easier for errors to get started.

Implications for Crisis Management

Crisis management is often portrayed as reactive activity directed at problems that are already escalating. That portrait is too narrow and I have tried to show why.

Perrow (1984) captured the core issue in crisis management, but did so in a way that exhibited rather than remedied the blind spot that concerns us. He observed that "our ability to organize does not match the inherent hazards of some of our organized activities" (p. 10). The potential blindspot in that otherwise tight description is the reference to "inherent hazard".

Hazards are not given nor do they necessarily inhere in organized activity. Instead, they are often constructed and put into place by human actors. Their development is indeterminant rather than fixed, and crisis management can mean quick action that deflects a triggering event as it unfolds rather than delayed action that mops up after the triggering event has run its course. These possibilities are more likely to be seen if we think of large crises as the outcome of smaller scale enactments.

When the enactment perspective is applied to crisis situations, several aspects stand out that are normally overlooked.

To look for enactment themes in crises, for example, is to listen for verbs of enactment, words like manual control, intervene, cope, probe, alter, design, solve, decouple, try, peek and poke (Perrow, 1984, p. 333), talk, disregard, and improvise. These verbs may signify actions that have the potential to construct or limit later stages in an unfolding crisis.

To look for enactment themes in crises is also to assess the forcefulness of actions and the ambiguity of the situation (Perrow, 1984, p. 83) in which those actions occur. As forcefulness and ambiguity increase, enactment is more consequential, and more of the unfolding crisis is under the direct control of human action. Conversely, as action becomes more tentative and situations become more clearly structured, enactment processes will play a smaller role in crisis development and management. Enactment, therefore, will have most effect on those portions of a crisis which are loosely coupled. If pipe cleaning procedures are not standardized, if supervision is intermittent, if job specifications are vague, or if warning devices are activated capriciously, then these loosely coupled activities will be susceptible to alteration through enactment. Human action will produce environments involving pipes, supervision, specifications, and alarms, either in dangerous or safe combinations, because these are the most influencible elements. Loose coupling does not guarantee safety. Instead, it guarantees susceptibility to human action, and those actions can either reduce or increase hazards.

Enactment affects crisis management through several means such as the psychology of control, effects of action on stress levels, speed of interactions, and ideology.

An enactment perspective suggests that crisis events are more controllable than was first thought. That suggestion, by itself, can be self-affirming because as perceptions of control increase, stress decreases, and as stress decreases perceptual narrowing also decreases which means people see more when they inspect any display (George, 1986). As people see more, they are more likely to notice things they can do something about, which confirms the perception of control and also reduces crisis intensity to lower levels by virtue of early intervention in its development.

Enactment can also reduce the perceptual narrowing produced by stress in another way. When people take some action, they often transform a more complex task into a simpler task. This occurs because action clarifies what the problem may be, specific action renders many cues and options irrelevant, and action consolidates an otherwise unorganized set of environmental elements. All of these simplifications gain significance in the context of stress because there is good evidence that stress has less adverse effects on performance of simple tasks than on performance of complex tasks (Eysenck, 1982). Since stress is an accompaniment of all crises, and since many crises escalate because of the secondary effects of crisis-induced stress, the beneficial effect of action in the form of task simplification is important.

Not only does action simplify tasks, it also often slows down the effects of one variable on another. Perrow (1984) has shown tight coupling, in the presence of interactive complexity, leads to rapid escalation of crisis events. Action, such as rearrangements of traffic patterns by air traffic controllers (Weick, 1987), often dampens the tight coupling between variables and reduces both the speed and magnitude with which connected variables affect one another. Especially if a controller becomes a step in a process (Perrow, 1984, p. 331), the actions of that controller can slow the speed with which the process unfolds and can also slow the speed with which unanticipated interactions occur.

Perhaps the most important implication of enactment is that it might serve as the basis for an ideology of crisis prevention and management. By ideology, we mean a "relatively coherent set of beliefs that bind people together and explain their worlds in terms of cause-and-effect relations" (Beyer, 1981, p. 166). Enactment leverages human involvement in systems and, as a coherent set of beliefs about the form and outcomes of such involvement, could elicit self-control and voluntary co-operation similar to that elicited by more formal structures designed to do the same thing (Meyer, 1982, p. 55).

An ideology built around the preceding ideas would mean that people have a fuller idea of how individuals generate their own environments including crisis environments, have an appreciation that the strength of commitments is a manipulable variable that has tangible environment effects, see the importance of expertise in action and the value of multiple small actions, understand how structures can accelerate or decelerate responsive action, and see more potential causes of crises and more places where interventions are possible, while maintaining an awareness of the necessity to balance dangerous action with safe inaction in the interest of diagnosis.

If these beliefs were adopted as a component of crisis management, people could think about crises in ways that highlight their own actions and decisions as determinants of the conditions they want to prevent.

The activity of crisis management, viewed through the lens of enactment involves such things as managing crises to lower levels of intensity, increasing skill levels and heightening the awareness of existing skill levels in the interest of expanded perception, appreciation of the ways in which small interventions can amplify, and being exquisitely aware of commitments that may bias diagnoses.

Perrow (1984) has, I think, correctly identified a new cause of human-made catastrophes, "interactive complexity in the presence of tight coupling, producing a system accident" (p. 11). Recent benchmark catastrophes such as Chernobyl, Bhopal, and Challenger all fit this recipe. The way to counteract catastrophes, therefore, is to reduce tight coupling and interactive complexity. To do this it seems important not to blame technology, but rather to look for and exaggerate all possible human contributions to crises in the hope that we can spot some previously unnoticed contributions where we can exert leverage. Therefore, even if the relative importance of enactment is exaggerated and borders on hyperbole, the important outcome of such exaggeration could be discovery of unexpected places to gain control over crises. The enactment perspective urges people to include their own actions more prominently in the mental experiments they run to discover potential crises of which they may be the chief agents.

Note

I acknowledge with appreciation the comments of Barbara Kelly, Reuben McDaniel, and Douglas Orton on an early version of this manuscript.

References

Ayres, R. U. and Rohatgi, P. K. (1987). "Bhopal: lessons for technological decision-makers". *Technology in Society*, **9**, 19–45.

Bateson, G. (1972). *Steps to an Ecology of Mind*. New York: Ballantine.

Beyer, J. M. (1981). "Ideologies, values, and decision-making in organizations". In Nystrom, P. C. and Starbuck, W. H. (Eds.), *Handbook of Organizational Design. Vol 2*, 166–202. New York: Oxford University Press.

Billings, R. S., Milburn, T. W. and Schaalman, M. L. (1980). "A model of crisis perception: a theoretical analysis". *Administrative Science Quarterly*, **25**, 300–16.

Diamond, S. (1985). "The Bhopal disaster: how it happened". *New York Times*, 28 January, 1, 6, 7.

Diamond, S. (1985). "The disaster in Bhopal: workers recall horror". *New York Times*, 30 January, 1, 6.

Eysenck, M. S. (1982). *Attention and Arousal*. New York: Springer-Verlag.

George, A. L. (1986). "The impact of crisis-induced stress on decision-making". In Solomon, F. and Marston, R. Q. (Eds.), *The Medical Implications of Nuclear War*. Washington, DC: National Academy of Sciences Press.

Hermann, C. F. (1963). "Some consequences of crisis which limit the viability of organizations". *Administrative Science Quarterly*, **8**, 61–82.

Jervis, R. (1976). *Perception and Misperception in International Politics*. Princeton, NJ: Princeton University Press.

Jones, E. E. (1986). "Interpreting interpersonal behavior: The effects of expectancies". *Science*, **234**, 41–6.

Jones, R. A. (1977). Self-Fulfilling Prophecies. Hillside, NJ: Erlbaum.

Kirwan, B. (1987). "Human reliability analysis of an offshore emergency blowdown system". *Applied Ergonomics*, **18**, 23–33.

McHugh, P (1968). *Defining the Situation*. Indianapolis: Bobbs-Merrill.

Meyer, A. D. (1982). "How ideologies supplant formal structures and shape responses to environment". *Journal of Management Studies*, **19**, 45–61.

Mitroff, I. I., Shrivastava, P. and Udwadia, F. (1987). "Effective crisis management". *Executive*, **1**, 283–92.

Perrow, C. (1984) *Normal Accidents*. New York: Basic Books.

Powers, W. T. (1973). *Behavior: The Control of Perception*. Chicago: Aldine.

Salancik, G. R. (1977). "Commitment and the control of organizational behavior and belief". In Staw, B. M. and Salancik, G. R. (Eds.), *New Directions in Organizational Behavior*, 1–54. Chicago: St. Clair.

Salancik, G, R, and Pfeffer, J. (1978). "A social information processing approach to job attitude and task design". *Administrative Science Quarterly*, **23**, 224–53.

Shrivastava, P. (1987). *Bhopal: Anatomy of a Crisis*. Cambridge MA: Ballinger.

Smircich, L. and Stubbart, C. (1985). "Strategic management in an enacted world". *Academy of Management Review*, **10**, 724–36.

Smith, R. J. (1984). "Crisis management under strain". *Science*, **225**, 907–9.

Snyder, M. (1984). When belief creates reality". In Berkowitz, L. (Ed.), *Advances in Experimental Social Psychology*. Vol. 18, 247–305. New York: Academic Press.

Staw, B. M. (1980). "Rationality and justification in organizational life". In Cummings, L. and Staw, B. (Eds.), *Research in Organizational Behavior: Vol 2*, 45–80. Greenwich, CT: JAI Press.

Staw, B. M. (1982). "Counterforces to change". In Goodman, P. S. and Associates (Eds.), *Change in Organizations: New Perspectives on Theory, Research, and Practice*, 87–121. San Fransisco: Jossey-Bass.

Staw, B. M., Sandelands, L. E. and Dutton, J. E. (1981). "Threat-rigidity effects in organizational behavior: a multi-level analysis". *Administrative Science Quarterly*, **26**, 501–24.

Webster's Dictionary of Synonyms. First Ed. (1951). Springfield, MA: Merriam.

Weick, K. E. (1979). *The Social Psychology of Organizing*, 2nd ed. Reading, MA: Addison-Wesley.

Weick, K. E. (1987). "Organizational culture as a source of high reliability". *California Management Review*, **29**, 2, 112–27.

Weick, K. E. and Bougon, M. G. (1986). "Organizations as cause maps". In Sims, H. P. Jr. and Gioia, D. A. (Eds.), *Social Cognition in Organizations*, 102–35. San Francisco: Jossey-Bass.

Weick, K. E., Gilfillan, D. P. and Keith, T. (1973). "The effect of composer credibility on orchestra performance". *Sociometry*, **36**, 435–62.

Selection

In sensemaking as well as organizing, it is often tough to separate enactment from selection. Interpretation, embellishment, variation, and improvisation, all of which are forms of enactment that vary in their reliance on scripts, are also all activities associated with labeling retrospectively whatever actions and artifacts are noticed. Campbell (1965) described enactment as "unjustified variation," which leads naturally to the suggestion that selection involves "justified variation." Justifications were the means to resolve and make sense of the dissonant compliance in the dissertation study. Justifications of behavioral commitments were the source of values and organizational culture in Chapter 1. And here, in the present discussion of selection, we see further development of the idea that selective retrospective elaboration of cues made salient during enactment justifies and makes sense of prior actions. Selection is about generating an answer to the ever-present question, "what's the story here?" To answer that question, individuals and groups sort through prior cues, label them, and connect them, which often results in plausible stories that are good enough to keep going and enlarge the circle of interested parties.

There is a twist here in how we are using the idea of "selection" that needs to be made clear. Normally, when macro theories of organization invoke evolutionary models, selection occurs when an external environment of financial resources and competitors sorts among variations in organizational forms and retains those that make more efficient use of resources. In sensemaking, selection occurs when an enacted environment of plausible stories from the past sorts among variations in current accounts of enactment and retains those that best fit with prior understandings of plausibility. Some variations in organizational forms make better use of financial resources and survive, but most die. Some variations in accounts of enactment make better use of pre-existing understandings of plausibility and survive, but most die. In both cases, selection involves editing, pruning, winnowing. In both cases, there is an editor in the form of scarce resources, the scarcity being either financial resources or meanings judged to be plausible. And in both cases there are variations that lay claim to scarce resources, these claimants being either variations in organizational forms or variations in organizational accounts. The only thing that differs is the environment doing the selecting. It is crucial that these environments be described in terms that are commensurable with the phenomenon of interest. Thus, resources of money are the environment for novel organizational forms. And resources of meaning are the environment for novel organizational accounts.

The following three chapters focus on selection as the retrospective interpretation of enacted cues. We begin with a close look at the role of interpretation in organizational systems. Next we look at the complex environment of meaning that is created by interactions during flight operations on an aircraft carrier. And we conclude with an in-depth look at how people create and revise interpretations, moment by moment, in ways that parallel those associated with jazz improvisation.

Chapter 10, "Toward a Model of Organizations as Interpretation Systems", co-authored with Richard Daft, focuses less on the variability of connections among organizational components featured in Chapter 2 (sources) and more on the way people interpret this variability. Daft and I tried to describe interpretation processes at the organizational level of analysis, and to argue that the main product of an organization is interpretations rather than decisions. Once strategic-level managers produce an interpretation, people at other levels make their own customized use of it. The interpretation becomes an environment within which they then make decisions and act. Thus, interpretations precede and constrain decision making and serve as the environment that shapes and is shaped by the decision.

The style of argument used in this chapter is similar to the style in Thompson and Tuden (1959). They were concerned with decision-making styles and said that agreements on preferences and means-ends relations determine the appropriate style. In analogous manner, we are concerned with interpretation styles and argue that assumptions made about the environment and the vigor of environmental scanning determine how one organizes for interpretation. Interpretation is not treated as a homogenous activity, and this chapter is one of the few places where boundary conditions for enactment are specified. This chapter is also one of the few places where the notions of assembly rules and equivocality reduction, first introduced in 1969 (Weick, 1969), are taken seriously. And this is one of the earlier papers where organizational learning is treated as a significant outcome of interpretation.

Chapter 11, "Collective Mind in Organizations: Heedful Interrelating on Flight Decks," co-authored with Karlene Roberts, is a serious effort to ground the mischievous yet useful concept of "group mind." Two important sets of ideas, those of Gilbert Ryle on thinking as an adverbial verb (see Weick, 1983) and those of Solomon Asch (1952) on the defining properties of a group, are adapted and merged to suggest that the ways in which people interconnect their actions are the medium through which mindful operations occur at the organizational level of analysis. When individuals have an ongoing concern with contributing to, representing, and subordinating to an emerging social system they produce interpretations with sufficient commonality to allow for coordinated sensemaking. These interpretations are based not so much on shared mental models as they are on equivalent mental models. Even though the models differ, their focus on the common means of contributing, representing, and subordinating as the way to get work done is sufficient to grasp complex environments that none of the actors individually could comprehend. Each system member has part of the picture. Depending on the heedfulness of their ties, these equivalent models form a whole and the system acts as if it knows more than any of its members can say. The example of flight operations on an aircraft carrier is a good vehicle to illustrate these operations of mind. The mind of a carrier deck is distributed among a variety of actors each of whom understands his or her specific assignment in ways that are more or less mindful of the way that assignment contributes to, represents, and is subordinate to the system which gives that assignment meaning. With more heedful individual interrelating the emerging system is more intelligent and is capable of knowing more complex circumstances. The range of what is sensed in enactments is enlarged with heedful interrelating as is the range of plausible explanations for what those enactments might mean. It is this enlarged set of interpretations that enables a well-formed collective mind to manage a high-risk technology, safely (e.g. Schulman, 1993).

Chapter 12, "Improvisation as a Mindset for Organizational Analysis," deepens our understanding of selection by drawing out the activity of enacting and knowing. In Chapter 10, "Interpretation Systems" it was shown that when managers judge an environment to be unanalyzable, they rework precomposed material by means of strategies that are less linear, more ad hoc, and more improvisational. As nonroutine enacting unfolds in the moment, we see that minimal structures such as the melody and chord changes available to a jazz musician or the core values available to an applied energy systems powerplant operator (Waterman, 1995), are sufficient to encourage continuing action, attentiveness, novel interpretation, and the creation of unexpected artifacts. Mangham and Pye (1991, p. 36) observe in their data on managers that "much of the doing of organizing is either a matter of running through a script or an instance of improvisation." Tilly (1997) more recently has argued that organizing has both some degree of scriptedness and some degree of improvisation. While there is "ad hoc adroitness" present in most enactment, this adroitness can range from minor changes in precomposed scripts enacted through interpretation and embellishment, to more substantial changes reflected in acts of variation, and improvisation. Radical changes such as reframing, second-order change, or deutero-learning are more likely when enactment takes the form of variation and improvisation, whereas incremental change may be more likely when enactment takes the form of interpretation and embellishment. Questions such as "what does it mean to get better at improvisation" or "what constitutes an error in improvisation" or "how does one practice improvisation" hint at puzzles of enactment that await thoughtful scholars. The portrait of jazz music and everyday life as both consisting of moments of rare beauty, failures of reach, and aimless passages, gives some substance to the existence that precedes essence, the enactment that precedes selection, and adds even more of an edge to Mailer's observation that jazz is "American existentialism."

References

Asch, Solomon (1952). *Social Psychology*, Englewood Cliffs, NJ: Prentice-Hall.

Campbell, D. T. (1965). Variation and selective retention in socio-cultural evolution. In H. R. Barringer, G. I. Blanksten, and R. Mack (eds.), *Social Change in Developing Areas*, Cambridge, MS: Schenkman, pp. 19–49.

Mangham, Iain, and Pye, Annie (1991). *The Doing of Managing*, Oxford, UK: Blackwell.

Schulman, P. R. (1993). The analysis of high reliability organizations: A comparative framework. In K. H. Roberts (ed.), *New Challenges to Understanding Organizations*, New York: Macmillan, pp. 33–54.

Thompson, James D., and Tuden, Arthur (1959). Strategies, structures, and processes of organizational decision. In J. D. Thompson (ed.), *Comparative Studies in Organization*, Pittsburgh: University of Pittsburgh, pp. 197–216.

Tilly, Charles (1997). Social itineraries. In C. Tilly, *Roads from Past to Future*, Lanham, MD: Rowham & Littlefield, pp. 1–13.

Waterman, Robert H. Jr. (1995). *What America Does Right*, New York: Penguin.

Weick, Karl E. (1969). *Social Psychology of Organizing*. Reading, MA: Addison-Wesley.

Weick, Karl E. (1983). Managerial thought in the context of action. In S. Srivastava (ed.), *The Executive Mind*, San Francisco, CA: Jossey-Bass, pp. 221–42.

10

Toward a Model of Organizations as Interpretation Systems[1]

Richard L. Daft and Karl E. Weick

Consider the game of 20 questions. Normally in this game one person leaves the room, the remaining people select a word that the person is to guess when he/she returns, and the only clue given about the word is whether it signifies an animal, vegetable, or mineral. The person trying to guess the word asks up to 20 question that can be answered yes or no in an effort to guess what the word is. Each question is designed to provide new information about the correct word. Together, the questions and answers are the process by which an interpretation is built up by the person who is "it."

Organizations play 20 questions. Organizations have limited time and questions, and they strive for the answer. The answer is discovering what consumers want that other organizations do not provide. The answer is finding that there is a market for pet rocks, roller skates, encounter groups, erasable ballpoint pens, or zero population growth. Many organizations presume that there is a correct answer to the puzzle of 20 questions. They query the environment with samples, market surveys, and test markets. They may establish specialized scanning departments that use trend analysis, media content analysis, and econometric modeling to obtain answers about the external environment. These organizations try to find an acceptable answer before their resources run out, before competitors corner the market, before people's interests change, or before more compelling opportunities in other environmental sectors dominate the search.

All of these activities, whether in organizations or in 20 questions, represent a form of interpretation. People are trying to interpret what they have done, define what they have learned, solve the problem of what they should do next. Building up interpretations about the environment is a basic requirement of individuals and organizations. The process of building the interpretation may be influenced by such things as the nature of the answer sought, the characteristics of the environment, the previous experience of the questioner, and the method used to acquire it.

Why Interpretation?

Pondy and Mitroff (1979) have reminded organizational scientists that organizations have characteristics typical of level 8 on Boulding's (1956) 9-level scale of system complexity. Boulding concluded that organizations are among the most complex systems imaginable. Organizations are vast, fragmented, and multidimensional. Pondy and Mitroff argue that most empirical research is at Boulding's level 1 to 3, which assumes that organizations behave as static frameworks or mechanical systems.

One purpose of this chapter is to propose a conceptualization of organizations that is at a higher level of system complexity and incorporates organizational activities and variables that have not been captured in other approaches (Weick & Daft, 1983). The critical issue for interpretation systems is to differentiate into highly specialized information receptors that interact with the environment. Information about the external world must be obtained, filtered, and processed into a central nervous system of sorts, in which choices are made. The organization must find ways to know the environment. Interpretation is a critical element that distinguishes human organizations from lower level systems.

A second purpose of this chapter is to integrate diverse ideas and empirical facts that pertain to organizational interpretation of the environment. Pfeffer and Salancik (1978) reviewed the literature on organization and environment relationships. They concluded that scanning is a key topic for explaining organizational behavior, yet practically no research had been reported on environmental scanning processes. There also is little understanding of the interpretation process and the organizational configurations that may enhance interpretation. The scarcity of empirical studies remains, although a few findings have been reported in diverse areas, such as organization theory, policy and strategy, futures research, and planning. The consolidation of these ideas and the organization of them into a model of interpretation system characteristics may provide a stimulus for future research into scanning and interpretation processes.

Working Assumptions

Any approach to the study of organizations is built on specific assumptions about the nature of organizations and how they are designed and function. Four specific assumptions underlie the model presented in this chapter and clarify the logic and rationale on which the interpretation system approach is based.

The most basic assumption, consistent with Boulding's scale of system complexity, is that organizations are open social systems that process information from the environment. The environment contains some level of uncertainty, so the organization must seek information and then base organizational action on that information. Organizations must develop information processing mechanisms capable of detecting trends, events, competitors, markets, and technological developments relevant to their survival.

The second assumption concerns individual versus organizational interpretations. Individual human beings send and receive information and in other ways carry out the interpretation process. Organization theorists realize that organizations do not have mechanisms separate from individuals to set goals, process information, or perceive the environment. People do these things. Yet in this chapter it is assumed that the organizational interpretation process is something more than what occurs by individuals. Organizations have cognitive systems and memories (Hedberg, 1981). Individuals come and go, but organizations preserve knowledge, behaviors, mental maps, norms, and values over time. The distinctive feature of organization level information activity is sharing. A piece of data, a perception, a cognitive map is shared among managers who constitute the interpretation system. Passing a startling observation among members, or discussing a puzzling development, enables managers to converge on an approximate interpretation. Managers may not agree fully about their perceptions (Starbuck, 1976), but the thread of coherence among managers is what characterizes organizational interpretations. Reaching convergence among members characterizes the act of organizing (Weick, 1979) and enables organization to interpret as a system.

The third assumption is that strategic-level managers formulate the organization's interpretation. When one speaks of organizational interpretation one really means interpretation by a relatively small group at the top of the organizational hierarchy. A large number of people may span the boundary with the external environment (Aldrich & Herker, 1977; Leifer & Delbecq, 1978), and this information is channeled into the organization. Organizations can be conceptualized as a series of nested systems, and each subsystem may deal with a different external sector. Upper managers bring together and interpret information for the system as a whole. Many participants may play some part in scanning or data processing, but the point at which information converges and is interpreted for organization level action is assumed to be at the top manager level. This assumption is consistent with Aguilar's (1967) observation that below the vice presidential level, participants are not informed on issues pertaining to the organization as a whole.

The fourth assumption is that organizations differ systematically in the mode or process by which they interpret the environment. Organizations develop specific ways to know the environment. Interpretation processes are not random. Systematic variations occur based on organization and environmental characteristics, and the interpretation process may in turn influence organizational outcomes such as strategy, structure, and decision making. For example, Aguilar (1967) interviewed managers about their sources of environmental information. He concluded that scanning behavior might vary according to the breadth or narrowness of the organization's viewing and also by the extent of formal search. Other authors have suggested that institutional scanning can be classified as regular or irregular (Fahey & King, 1977; Leifer & Delbecq, 1978) or by the extent to which organizations passively perceive the environment versus creating or enacting external reality (Weick, 1979; Weick & Daft, 1983).

Definition of Interpretation

Organizations must make interpretations. Managers literally must wade into the ocean of events that surround the organization and actively try to make sense of them. Organization participants physically act on these events, attending to some of them, ignoring most of them, and talking to other people to see what they are doing (Braybrooke, 1964). Interpretation is the process of translating these events, of developing models for understanding, of bringing out meaning, and of assembling conceptual schemes among key managers.

The interpretation process in organizations is neither simple nor well understood. There are many interpretation images in the literature, including scanning, monitoring, sensemaking, interpretation, understanding, and learning (Duncan & Weiss, 1979; Hedberg, 1981; Weick, 1979; Pfeffer & Salancik, 1978). These concepts can be roughly organized into three stages that constitute the overall learning process, as reflected in Figure 10.1. The first stage is *scanning*, which is defined as the process of monitoring the environment and providing environmental data to managers. Scanning is concerned with data collection. The organization may use formal data collection systems, or managers may acquire data about the environment through personal contacts.

Interpretation occurs in the second stage in Figure 10.1. Data are given meaning. Here the human mind is engaged. Perceptions are shared and cognitive maps are constructed. An information coalition of sorts is formed. The organization experiences interpretation when a new construct is introduced into the collective cognitive map of the organization. Organizational *interpretation* is formally defined as the process of translating events and developing shared understanding and conceptual schemes among members of upper management. Interpretation gives meaning to data, but it occurs before organizational learning and action.

Learning, the third stage, is distinguished from interpretation by the concept of action. Learning involves a new response or action based on the interpretation (Argyris & Schon, 1978). Organizational *learning* is defined as the process by which knowledge about action outcome relationships between the organization and the environment is developed (Duncan & Weiss, 1979). Learning is a process of putting cognitive theories into action (Argyris & Schon, 1978; Hedberg, 1981). Organizational interpretation is analogous to learning a new skill by an individual. The act of learning

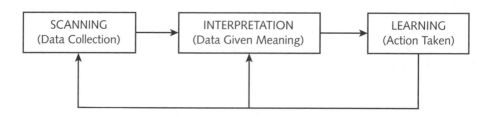

Figure 10.1   Relationships among organizational scanning, interpretation, and learning

also provides new data for interpretation. Feedback from organizational actions may provide new collective insights for coalition members. Thus, the three stages are interconnected through a feedback loop in Figure 10.1.

Figure 10.1 and the definitions of scanning, interpretation, and learning oversimplify complex processes. Factors such as beliefs, politics, goals, and perceptions may complicate the organizational learning cycle (Staw, 1980). The purpose of Figure 10.1 is to illustrate the relationship of interpretation to scanning and learning as the basis for a model of organizational interpretation.

Toward a Model of Organizational Interpretation

Two key dimensions are used here to explain organizational interpretation differences. They are: (1) management's beliefs about the analyzability of the external environment and (2) the extent to which the organization intrudes into the environment to understand it. The proposed model provides a way to describe and explain the diverse ways organizations may obtain knowledge about the environment.

Assumptions about the environment

Many organizations undoubtedly play the interpretation game with the goal of finding the correct answer, just as in the game of 20 questions. The game of 20 questions, however, is of limited value as a metaphor because there is one way in which it mocks many organizational worlds. Many organizations have nothing that corresponds to "the answer." In everyday life the act of questioning may be much more influential in determining the correct answer than is the case with the clear-cut roles of asking and answering and the fixed answer present in the conventional version of 20 questions.

The game, 20 questions, becomes more typical with a variation suggested by the physicist John Wheeler. Once the player leaves the room so that those remaining can choose the word, the game unfolds in a different fashion.

> While he is gone the other players decide to alter the rules. They will select no word at all; instead each of them will answer "yes" or "no" as he pleases – provided he has a word in mind that fits both his own reply and all the previous replies. The outsider returns and, unsuspecting, begins asking questions. At last he makes a guess: "Is the word 'clouds'?" Yes, comes the answer, and the players explain the game. (*Newsweek*, 1979, p. 62)

When the questioner began, he assumed the answer already existed. Yet the answer was created through the questions raised. If the player asked different questions, a different answer would emerge.

If some organizations play 20 questions in the traditional way, seeking the correct answer already in the environment, and if others play 20 questions John Wheeler's way, constructing an answer, then there is an interesting difference in interpretation behavior. This difference reflects the organization's assumption about the analyzability of its environment.

If an organization assumes that the external environment is concrete, that events and processes are hard, measurable, and determinant, then it will play the traditional game to discover the "correct" interpretation. The key for this organization is discovery through intelligence gathering, rational analysis, vigilance, and accurate measurement. This organization will utilize linear thinking and logic and will seek clear data and solutions.

When an organization assumes that the external environment is unanalyzable, an entirely different strategy will apply. The organization to some extent may create the external environment. The key is to construct, coerce, or enact a reasonable interpretation that makes previous action sensible and suggests some next steps. The interpretation may shape the environment more than the environment shapes the interpretation. The interpretation process is more personal, less linear, more ad hoc and improvisational than for other organizations. The outcome of this process may include the ability to deal with equivocality, to coerce an answer useful to the organization, to invent an environment and be part of the invention.

What factors explain differences in organizational beliefs about the environment? The answer is hypothesized to be characteristics of the environment combined with management's previous interpretation experience. When the environment is subjective, difficult to penetrate, or changing (Duncan, 1972), managers will see it as less analyzable (Perrow, 1967; Tung, 1979). Wilensky's (1967) work on intelligence gathering in government organizations detected major differences in the extent to which environments were seen as rationalized, that is subject to discernible, predictable uniformities in relationships among significant objects. In one organization studied by Aguilar (1967), managers assumed an analyzable environment because of previous experience. Accurate forecasts were possible because product demand was directly correlated to petroleum demand, which in turn was correlated to well-defined trends such as population growth, auto sales, and gasoline consumption. However, for a similar organization in another industry, systematic data collection and analysis were not used. Statistical trends had no correlation with product demand or capital spending. Facts and figures were not consistent with the unanalyzable assumptions about the environment. Soft, qualitative data, along with judgment and intuition, had a larger role in the interpretation process.

Organizational intrusiveness

The second major difference among interpretation systems is the extent to which organizations actively intrude into the environment. Some organizations actively search the environment for an answer. They allocate resources to search activities. They hire technically oriented MBAs; build planning, forecasting, or special research departments; or even subscribe to monitoring services (Thomas, 1980). In extreme cases, organizations may send agents into the field (Wilensky, 1967). Organizational research may also include testing or manipulating the environment. These organizations may leap before they look, perform trials in order to learn what an error is, and discover what is feasible by testing presumed constraints. Forceful organizations may break presumed rules, try to change the rules, or try to manipulate critical factors in the environment (Kotter, 1979; Pfeffer, 1976). A survey of major corporations found that many of them established departments and mechanisms for searching and/or creating environments (Thomas, 1980). These organizations might be called test makers (Weick & Daft, 1983), and they will develop interpretations quite different from organizations that behave in a passive way.

Passive organizations accept whatever information the environment gives them. These organizations do not engage in trial and error. They do not actively search for the answer in the environment. They do not have departments assigned to discover or manipulate the environment. They may set up receptors to sense whatever data happen to flow by the organization. By accepting the environment as given, these organizations become test avoiders (Weick, 1979). They interpret the environment within accepted limits.

Research evidence suggests that many organizations are informal and unsystematic in their interpretation of the environment (Fahey & King, 1977). These organizations tend to accept the environment as given and respond actively only when a crisis occurs. For a crisis, the organization might search out new information or consciously try to influence external events. Other organizations actively search the environment on a continuous basis (Aguilar, 1967; Wilensky, 1967). Organizations thus differ widely in the active versus passive approach toward interpretation.

One explanation of differential intrusion into the environment is conflict between organization and environment. Wilensky (1967) argued that when the environment is perceived as hostile or threatening, or when the organization depends heavily on the environment, more resources are allocated to the intelligence gathering function. Organizations attempt to develop multiple lines of inquiry into the environment. In the corporate world, intense competition or resource scarcity will lead to allocation of more resources into interpretation-related functions. Organizations in benevolent environments have weaker incentives to be intrusive (Child, 1974; Hedberg, 1981). Only rarely do organizations in benevolent environments use their slack resources for trial and error experimentation or formal search. A hostile environment generates increased search because of new problems and a perceived need to develop new opportunities and niches. More exhaustive information is needed.

Another explanation of different levels of intrusion is organizational age and size (Kimberly & Miles 1980). New, young organizations typically begin their existence as test makers. They try new things and actively seek information about their limited environment. Gradually, over time, the organization interpretation system begins to accept the environment rather than searching or testing its boundaries. New organizations are disbelievers, are unindoctrinated, and have less history to rely on. They are more likely to dive in and develop a niche that established organizations have failed to see. But as the organization grows and as time passes, the environment may be perceived as less threatening, so search will decrease.

The model

Based on the idea that organizations may vary in their beliefs about the environment and in their intrusiveness into the environment, organizations can be categorized according to interpretation modes. The two underlying dimensions are used as the basis for an interpretation system model, presented in Figure 10.2, which describes four categories of interpretation behavior.

The *enacting* mode reflects both an active, intrusive strategy and the assumption that the environment is unanalyzable. These organizations construct their own environments. They gather information by trying new behaviors and seeing what happens. They experiment, test, and stimulate, and they ignore precedent, rules, and traditional expectations. This organization is highly activated, perhaps under the belief that it must be so in order to succeed. This type of organization tends to develop and market a product, such as polaroid cameras, based on what it thinks it can sell. An organization in this mode tends to construct markets rather than waiting for an assessment of demand to tell it what to produce. These organizations, more than others, tend to display the enactment behavior described by Weick (1979).

The *discovering* mode also represents an intrusive organization, but the emphasis is on detecting the correct answer already in an analyzable environment rather than on shaping the answer. Carefully devised measurement probes are sent into the environment to relay information back to the organization. This organization uses market research, trend analysis, and forecasting to predict problems and opportunities. Formal data determine organizational interpretations about environmental characteristics and expectations. Discovering organizations are similar to organizations that rely on formal search procedures for information (Aguilar, 1967) and in which staff analysts are used extensively to gather and analyze data (Wilensky, 1967).

Organizations characterized as *conditioned viewing* (Aguilar, 1967) assume an

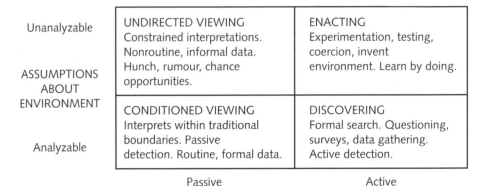

Figure 10.2 Model of organizational interpretation modes

analyzable environment and are not intrusive They tend to rely on established data collection procedures, and the interpretations are developed within traditional boundaries. The environment is perceived as objective and benevolent, so the organization does not take unusual steps to learn about the environment. The viewing is conditioned in the sense that it is limited to the routine documents, reports, publications, and information systems that have grown up through the years. The view of the environment is limited to these traditional sources. At some time historically, these data were perceived as important, and the organization is now conditioned to them. Organizations in this category use procedures similar to the regular scanning of limited sectors described by Fahey and King (1977).

Undirected Viewing (Aguilar, 1967) reflects a similar passive approach, but these organizations do not rely on hard, objective data because the environment is assumed to be unalyzable. Managers act on limited, soft information to create their perceived environment. These organizations are not conditioned by formal management systems within the organization, and they are open to a variety of cues about the environment from many sources. Managers in these organizations are like the ones Aguilar (1967) found that relied on information obtained through personal contacts and casual information encounters. Fahey and King (1977) also found some organizational information gatherings to be irregular and based on chance opportunities.

Examples of conditioned and undirected viewing modes have been illustrated by clothing companies in England (Daft & Macintosh, 1978). These companies developed different interpretation systems over time, although they were in a similar industry. Top management in the conditioned viewing organization used a data collection system to record routinely such things as economic conditions, past sales, and weather forecasts. These data were used to predict sales and to schedule production. These systems had grown up over the years and were used routinely to interpret problems that occurred. The other company gathered information from personal contacts with a few store buyers, salespeople, and informants in other companies. Managers also visited a few stores to observe and discuss in a casual manner what seemed to be selling. This company used undirected viewing. Interpretation was based on a variety of subjective cues that happened to be available.

Another example of interpretation styles is illustrated by the relationship between corporations and their shareholders (Keim, 1981), A few corporations actively influence and shape shareholder attitudes. The enacting organization may try to manipulate shareholder perceptions toward itself, environmental issues, or political candidates by sending information to shareholders through various media. Discovery-oriented corporations actively stay in touch with shareholders to learn what they are thinking, and they conduct surveys or use other devices to discover attitudes. A few corporations handle the shareholder relationships through routine data transactions (stockholder voting, mailing out dividend checks), which is typical of conditioned viewing. Finally, some corporations rely on informal, personal contact with shareholders (undirected viewing). Managers use whatever opportunities arise (annual meetings, telephone contact about complaints and questions) to learn shareholders' opinions and to adapt to those opinions.

Other Organizational Characteristics

The model can be completed by making predictions about other organizational characteristics associated with interpretation modes. The predictions pertain to: (1) scanning and data characteristics; (2) the interpretation process within the organization; and (3) the strategy and decision processes that characterize each mode. The predicted relationships with interpretation modes are shown in Figure 10.3.

Scanning Characteristics

Scanning characteristics pertain to the nature and acquisition of data for top management about the environment. The data may vary by source and acquisition, depending on the interpretation mode of the organization.

1. *Data sources.* Data about the environment can come to managers from external or internal sources, and from personal or impersonal sources (Aquilar, 1967; Daft & Lengel 1984; Keegan, 1974). Sources are external when managers have direct contact with information outside the organization. Internal sources pertain to data collected about the environment by other people in the organization and then provided to managers through internal channels. Per-

Unanalyzable	UNDIRECTED VIEWING Scanning Characteristics: 1. Data sources: external, personal. 2. Acquisition: no scanning department, irregular contacts and reports, casual information. Interpretation Process: 1. Much equivocality reduction. 2. Few rules, many cycles. Strategy and Decision Making: 1. Strategy: reactor. 2. Decision process: coalition building.	ENACTING Scanning Characteristics: 1. Data sources: external, personal. 2. Acquisition: no department, irregular reports and feedback from environment, selective information. Interpretation Process: 1. Some equivocality reduction. 2. Moderate rules and cycles. Strategy and Decision Making: 1. Strategy: prospector. 2. Decision process: incremental trial and error.
ASSUMPTIONS ABOUT ENVIRONMENT	CONDITIONED VIEWING Scanning Characteristics: 1. Data sources: internal, impersonal. 2. Acquisition: no department, although regular record keeping and information systems, routine information. Interpretation Process: 1. Little equivocality reduction. 2. Many rules, few cycles Strategy and Decision Making: 1. Strategy: defender. 2. Decision process: programmed, problemistic search.	DISCOVERING Scanning Characteristics: 1. Data sources: internal, impersonal. 2. Acquisition: Separate departments, special studies and reports, extensive information. Interpreation Process: 1. Little equivocality reduction. 2. Many rules, moderate cycles. Strategy and Decision Making: 1. Strategy: analyzer. 2. Decision process: systems analysis, computation.
Analyzable		

Passive   Active

ORGANIZATIONAL INTRUSIVENESS

Figure 10.3 Relationship between interpretation modes and organizational processes

sonal sources involve direct contact with other individuals. Impersonal sources pertain to written documentation such as newspapers and magazines or reports from the organization's information system.

Generally, the less analyzable the perceived external environment the greater the tendency for managers to use external information gained from personal contact with other managers. Organizations characterized as undirected viewing will obtain most of their information from the relationship of senior managers with colleagues in the environment (Keegan, 1974). Managers in enacting organizations also will use personal observations to a large extent, although this information often will be obtained through experimentation and from trying to impose ideas on the environment. When the environment is analyzable, a larger percentage of the data will be conveyed through the management information system. The discovering organization also will use internal, formal reports, although these reports are the outcome of specialized inquiries rather than a routine, periodic reporting system.

2. *Data acquisition.* Organizational mechanisms for acquiring information and the regularity of acquisition are other distinguishing characteristics of organizational scanning (Fahey & King, 1977). Discovering organizations will allocate many resources to data acquisition. Special departments typically will be used to survey and study the environment. Regular reports and special studies will go to top managers. Conditioned viewing organizations will have regular reports available through the formal information system of the organization. These organizations will devote few resources to external scanning.

    Undirected viewing organizations will make little use of formal management information. Data will tend to be irregular and casual. Scanning departments are not needed; formal reports will be ad hoc and irregular. The enacting organization also will use data that are somewhat irregular and will reflect feedback about selected environmental initiatives. The general pattern across organizations is that environmental information is more regular when the environment is analyzable, and more studies and information are available when the organization is active in information acquisition.

Interpretation process

Interpretation pertains to the process by which managers translate data into knowledge and understanding about the environment. This process will vary according to the means for equivocality reduction and the assembly rules that govern information processing behavior among managers.

1. *Equivocality reduction.* Equivocality is the extent to which data are unclear and suggest multiple interpretations about the environment (Daft & Macintosh, 1981; Weick, 1979). Managers in all organizations will experience some equivocality in their data. Equivocality reduction will be greatest in organizations characterized as undirected viewing. External cues of a personal nature are subject to multiple interpretations. Managers will discuss these cues exten-

sively to arrive at a common interpretation. Equivocality is reduced through shared observations and discussion until a common grammar and course of action can be agreed on (Weick, 1979). The enacting organization also will experience high equivocality, which will be reduced more on the basis of taking action to see what works than by interpreting events in the environment. Information equivocality generally is lower in the conditioned viewing and discovering organizations. Some equivocality reduction takes place before the data reach managers. Specialists will routinize the data for periodic reports and perform systematic analyses and special studies. The data thus provide a more uniform stimulus to managers, and less discussion is needed to reach a common interpretation.

2.   *Assembly rules.* Assembly rules are the procedures or guides that organizations use to process data into a collective interpretation. The content of these rules and the extent to which they are enforced depend on the organization. Generally, the greater the equivocality in the data, the fewer the number of rules used to arrive at an interpretation. Conversely, the smaller the perceived equivocality of data entering the organization, the greater the number of rules used to assemble the interpretation (Weick, 1979).

Fewer rules are used for equivocal information inputs because there is uncertainty as to exactly what the information means. Only a small number of rather general rules can be used to assemble the process. If the input is less equivocal, there is more certainty as to what the item is and how it should be handled. Hence a greater number of rules can be assigned to handle the data and assemble an interpretation (Putnam & Sorenson, 1982).

The number of information cycles among top management follows a similar logic. The greater the equivocality, the more times the data may be cycled among members before a common interpretation is reached. The lower the equivocality, the fewer cycles needed. The number of assembly rules and cycles tends to be inversely related.

Undirected viewing organizations, which receive equivocal information, will have few rules but will use many internal cycles during the course of assembling an interpretation. By contrast, managers within a directed viewing organization receive unequivocal information that will be handled according to numerous rules, but few cycles are needed to reach a common understanding. The discovering organization also will use many rules, although a moderate number of cycles may be needed because of some equivocality in the reports and data presented to managers. The equivocality in interpreting the success of initiatives in the enacting organization will be associated with the moderate number of assembly rules and information cycles.

Strategy formulation and decision making

The variables described above are directly related to the scanning and interpretation behaviors through which organizations learn about and make sense of the external environment. Two additional variables – strategy formulation and decision making –

may be associated with interpretation modes. The hypothesized relationships with interpretation modes also are shown in Figure 10.3

1. *Strategy formulation.* Miles and Snow (1978) proposed that corporations can be organized according to four types of strategies: prospector, analyzer, defender, and reactor. Strategy formulation is the responsibility of top management and thus may be related to environmental conditions that are similar to interpretation modes. The prospector strategy reflects a high level of initiative with regard to the environment. The environment is seen as changing and as containing opportunities. The organization develops new products and undertakes new initiatives. This is consistent with the enacting mode of interpretation. The analyzer organization is more careful. It is concerned with maintaining a stable core of activities but with occasional innovations on the periphery if the environment permits. This strategy is consistent with the discovering orientation, in which the organization studies the environment and moves ahead only in a careful constrained way.

   The defender strategy is one in which top management perceives the environment as analyzable and stable and the management is determined to protect what it has. This organization is concerned with maintaining traditional markets and is focused on internal efficiency rather than on external relationships. The defender strategy will tend to be related to the conditioned viewing mode of interpretation. Finally, the reactor strategy is not really a strategy at all. The organization moves along, more or less accepting what comes. This organization will react to seemingly random changes in the environment. Scanning behavior in this organization is based on casual data from personal contact rather than from specialized information systems. The reactor strategy will be associated with the interpretation mode classified as undirected viewing.

2. *Decision making.* The organizational literature suggests that organizations make decisions in various ways. Organizational decisions may be influenced by coalition building and political processing (Cyert & March, 1963); by incremental decision steps (Lindblom, 1959; Mintzberg, Raisinghani, & Théoret, 1976); by systems analysis and rational procedures (Leavitt, 1975); and by programmed responses to routine problems (March & Simon, 1958; Simon, 1960). Decision making generally is part of the information and interpretation processes in organizations; it thus is posed that decision processes may be associated with interpretation modes

   In undirected viewing organizations, the environment is not analyzable. Factors cannot be rationalized to the point of using rational decision models. Managers respond to divergent, personal cues and extensive discussion and coalition building are required to agree on a single interpretation and course of action. Managers will spend time making sense of what happened and reaching agreements about problems before proceeding to a solution.

   In enacting organizations, by contrast, a more assertive decision style will appear. The enacting organization does not have precedent to follow. A good idea, arrived at subjectively, may be implemented to see if it works. Enacting organizations utilize the trial and error incremental process described by Mintzberg et al. (1976). When organizations decide on a course of action, they design a custom solution and try it. If the solution does not work, they have to recycle and try again. Enacting organizations move ahead incrementally and gain information about the environment by trying behaviors and seeing what works.

Discovering organizations also take an active approach, but they assume that the environment is analyzable. Here the emphasis is on rational understanding. Systems analysis will be an important decision tool. Operational researchers and other staff personnel will perform computations on environmental data and weigh alternatives before proceeding. This organization's decision process will be characterized by logic and analysis. Solutions will be tried until alternatives have been carefully weighed.

Finally, directed viewing organizations may be considered the easiest situation for decision makers. The organization is passive and operates in an analyzable environment. Decision making by managers is programmed. Programs are built into the organization to describe reactions to external events based on previous experience. Rules and regulations cover most activities and are applied unless a genuine crisis erupts. Crises will be rare, but if one occurs, managers will respond with problemistic search (March & Simon, 1958). Problemistic search means that the organization performs a local search through its immediate memory bank for a solution. Only after exhausting traditional responses will the organization move toward a new response of some sort.

Implications

The purpose of this chapter is to present a model of organizations as interpretation systems and to bring together a number of ideas that are related to interpretation behavior. The two variables underlying the model are (1) management's beliefs about the analyzability of the external environment and (2) organizational intrusiveness. These variables are consistent with empirical investigations of interpretation behavior (Aguilar, 1967; Wilensky, 1967), and they are the basis for four modes of interpretation – enacting, discovering, undirected viewing, and conditioned viewing. The model explains interpretation behaviors ranging from environmental enactment to passive observation. The model also makes predictions about scanning characteristics, interpretation processes, and top management strategy and decision behavior.

The model is proposed as a set of tentative hypotheses for future test. Evidence in the literature does support the general framework, but the specific predictions remain to be tested. The model might best be characterized as an initial organization of ideas about scanning and interpretation behavior, and it has implications for research and the practice of management.

Organizational research

The implications of the interpretation system model for organizational research are two-fold. First, the interpretation system perspective is concerned with high level processes on Boulding's system hierarchy (Daft, 1980; Pondy and Mitroff, 1978). An organization might be viewed as a framework, control system, or open system by organization scholars. The interpretation system view is concerned with specialized information reception, equivocality reduction, and sensemaking. This perspective represents a move away from mechanical and biological metaphors of organizations. Organizations are more than transformation processes or control systems. To survive, organizations must have mechanisms to interpret ambiguous events and to provide meaning and direction for participants. Organizations are meaning systems, and this distinguishes them from lower level systems.

Perhaps the process of interpretation is so familiar that it is taken for granted, which may be why little research on this topic has been reported. But interpretation may be one of the most important functions organizations perform. Indeed, the second research implication of the interpretation system perspective is that scanning and sensemaking activities are at the center of things. Almost every other organizational activity or outcome is in some way contingent on interpretation. For example, one of the widely held tenets in organization theory is that the external environment will influence organization structure and design (Duncan, 1972; Pfeffer & Salancik, 1978; Tung, 1979). But that relationship can be manifested only if participants within the organization sense and interpret the environment and respond to it. Almost all outcomes in terms of organization structure and design, whether caused by the environment, technology, or size, depend on the interpretation of problems or opportunities by key decision makers. Once interpretation occurs, the organization can formulate a response. Many activities in organizations, whether under the heading of structure, decision making, strategy formulation, organizational learning, goal setting, or innovation and change, may be connected to the mode of interpreting the external environment.

The paradox is that research into environment-structure relationships gives scant attention to interpretation. An issue that seems crucial for explaining the why of organizational form has produced little systematic research. One value of the model proposed here, then, is the introduction of an interpretation model and set of relationships as candidates for empirical research in the future.

Management

The interpretation system model has two implications for managers. First, it says that the job of management is to interpret, not to do the operational work of the organization. The model calls attention to the need in organizations to make sense of things, to be aware of external events, and to translate cues into meaning for organizational participants. Managers, especially top managers, are responsible for this process and are actively involved in it. Managers may do interpretations spontaneously and intuitively, without realizing their role in defining the environment for other participants. One implication is for managers to think of organizations as interpretation systems and to take seriously their roles as interpreters.

The other implication of the model is that it provides a comparative perspective for managers. The model calls attention to interpretation modes managers may not have thought of before. If managers have spent their organizational lives in a discovery-oriented interpretation system, using relatively sophisticated monitoring systems, they might want to consider modifying these activities toward a more subjective approach. The external environment may not be as analyzable as they assume. Discovery-oriented managers could consider intuition and hunch in some situations and decide to launch test markets instead of market surveys. On the other hand, passive, conditioned viewers might be encouraged to try breaking established rules and patterns to see what happens. The value of any comparative model is that it provides new alternatives. Managers can understand where they are as opposed to where they would like to be. Managers may find that they can create a new and valuable display of the environment by adopting new interpretation assumptions and modes.

Conclusion

Any model is itself a somewhat arbitrary interpretation imposed on organized activity. Any model involves trade-offs and unavoidable weaknesses. The greatest weakness in the model presented in this paper is reflected in Thorngate's (1976) postulate of commensurate complexity. His postulate states that a theory of social behavior cannot be simultaneously general, accurate, and simple. Two of the three characteristics are possible, but only at a loss to the third. The model in this chapter has attempted to be general and simple, and the trade-off is a model that is not very accurate at specifying details. The loss in precision may not be all bad, however. An interpretation system is an awesomely complex human social activity that may not be amenable to precise measurement at this point in development (Daft & Wiginton, 1979). To design a model that is precise and accurate may be to lose the phenomenon of interest.

Interpretation is the process through which information is given meaning and actions are chosen. Even in the most objective environments, the interpretation process may not be easy. People in organizations are talented at normalizing deviant events, at reconciling outliers to a central tendency, at producing plausible displays, at making do with scraps of information, at translating equivocality into feasible alternatives, and at treating as sufficient whatever information is at hand (Weick & Daft, 1983). The result of these human tendencies is that the organization can build up workable interpretations from scraps that consolidate and inform other bits and pieces of data. The process and the outcomes are a good deal less tidy than many have come to appreciate with current models and assumptions about organizations. The ideas proposed in this chapter suggest a new viewpoint – perhaps a starting point of sorts – from which to interpret the richness and complexity of organizational activity.

Note

1. This paper is an extension of Weick and Daft (1983). The preparation of this manuscript was supported by the Office of Naval Research grant N00014-83-C-0025.

References

Aguilar, F. *Scanning the business environment*. New York: Macmillan, 1967.

Aldrich, H., & Herker, D. Boundary spanning roles and organization structure. *Academy of Management Review*, 1977, 2, 217–230.

Arygris, C., & Schon, D. A. *Organizational learning: A theory of action perspective*. Reading, Mass.: Addison-Wesley, 1978.

Boulding, K. E. General systems theory: The skeleton of a science. *Management Science*, 1956, 2, 197–207.

Braybrooke, D. The mystery of executive success re-examined. *Administrative Science Quarterly*, 1964, 8, 533–560.

Child, J. Organization, management and adaptiveness. Working paper, University of Aston, 1974.

Cyert, R. M. & March, J. G. *A behavioral theory of the firm*. Englewood Cliffs, N.J.: Prentice-Hall, 1963.

Daft, R. L. The evolution of organization analysis in *ASQ: 1959–1979*. *Administrative Science Quarterly*, 1980. 25, 623–636.

Daft, R. L., & Lengel, R. H. Information richness: A new approach to manager behavior and organization design. In B. Staw & L. L. Cummings (Eds.), *Research in organizational behavior* (Vol. 6). Greenwich, Conn.: JAI Press, 1984, 191–233.

Daft, R. L., & Macintosh, N. B. A new approach to design and use of management information. *California Management Review*, 1978, 21(1), 82–92.

Daft, R. L., & Macintosh, N. B. A tentative exploration into the amount and equivocality of information processing in organizational work units. *Administrative Science Quarterly*, 1981, 26, 207–224.

Daft, R. L., & Wiginton, J. C. Language and organization. *Academy of Management Review*, 1979, 4, 179–192.

Duncan, R. B. Characteristics of organizational environments and perceived environmental uncertainty. *Administrative Science Quarterly*, 1972, 17, 313–327

Duncan, R. B. & Weis, A. Organizational learning: Implications for organizational design. In B. Staw (Ed.) *Research in organizational behavior* (Vol. 1). Greenwich, Conn.: JAI Press, 1979, 75–123.

Fahey, L., & King, W. R. Environmental scanning for corporate planning. *Business Horizons*, 1977, 20(4), 61–71.

Hedberg, B. How organizations learn and unlearn. In P. Nystrom & W. Starbuck (Eds.), *Handbook of organizational design*. New York: Oxford University Press, 1981, 1–27.

Keegan, W. J. Multinational scanning: A study of information sources utilized by headquarters executives in multinational companies. *Administrative Science Quarterly*, 1974, 19, 411–421.

Keim, G. D. Foundations of a political strategy for business. *California Management Review*, 1981, 23, 41–48.

Kimberly, J. R., & Miles, R. H. *The organizational life cycle.* San Francisco: Jossey-Bass, 1980.

Kotter, J. P. Managing external dependence. *Academy of Management Review,* 1979, 4, 87–92.

Leavitt, H. J. Beyond the analytic manager: 1. *California Management Review,* 1975, 17(3), 5–12.

Leifer, R. T., & Delbecq, A. Organizational/environmental interchange: A model of boundaries spanning activity. *Academy of Management Review,* 1978, 3, 40–50.

Lindblom, C. The science of "muddling through." *Public Administration Review,* 1959, 19(2), 79–88.

March, J. G., & Simon, H. A. *Organizations.* New York: Wiley, 1958.

Miles, R. E., & Snow, C. C. *Organizational strategy, structure and process.* New York: McGraw-Hill, 1978.

Mintzberg, H., Raisinghani, D., & Théoret, A. The structure of "unstructured" decision processes. *Administrative Science Quarterly,* 1976, 21, 246–275.

Newsweek, March 12, 1979, 62.

Perrow, C. A framework for the comparative analysis of organizations. *American Sociological Review,* 1967, 32, 194–208.

Pfeffer, J. Beyond management and the worker: The institutional function of management. *Academy of Management Review,* 1976, 1(2), 36–46.

Pfeffer, J. & Salancik, G. R. *The external control of organizations: A Resource dependence perspective.* New York: Harper & Row, 1978.

Pondy, L. R., & Mitroff, I. I., Beyond open systems models of organizations. In B. M. Staw (Ed.), *Research in organizational behavior.* Greenwich, Conn.: JAI Press, 1979, 3–39.

Putnam, L. L., & Sorenson, R. L. Equivocal messages in organizations. *Human Communication Research,* 1982, 8(2), 114–132.

Simon, H. A. *The new science of management decision,* Englewood Cliffs, N.J.: Prentice-Hall, 1960.

Starbuck, W. H. Organizations and their environments. In M. D. Dunnette (Ed.), *Handbook of industrial and organizational psychology.* New York: Rand McNally, 1976, 1069–1123.

Staw, B. M. Rationality and justification in organizational life. In B. M. Staw & L. L. Cummings (Eds.), *Research in organizational behavior* (Vol. 2). Greenwich, Conn.: JAI Press, 1980, 45–80.

Thomas, T. S. Environmental scanning – The state of the art. *Long Range Planning,* 1980, 13(1), 20–28.

Thorngate, W. "In general" vs. "it depends": Some comments on the Gergen-Schlenker debate. *Personality and Social Psychology Bulletin,* 1976, 2, 404–410.

Tung, R. L. Dimensions or organizational environment: An exploratory study of their impact on organization structure. *Academy of Management Journal,* 1979, 22, 672–693.

Weick, K. *The social psychology of organizing.* Reading, Mass.: Addison-Wesley, 1979.

Weick, K. E. & Daft, R. L. The effectiveness of interpretation systems. In K. S. Cameron & D. A. Whetten (Eds.), *Organizational effectiveness: A comparison of multiple models.* New York: Academic Press, 1983, 71–93.

Wilensky, H. L. *Organizational intelligence.* New York: Basic Books, 1967.

11

Collective Mind in Organizations: Heedful Interrelating on Flight Decks

Karl E. Weick and Karlene H. Roberts[1]

Some organizations require nearly error-free operations all the time because otherwise they are capable of experiencing catastrophes. One such organization is an aircraft carrier, which an informant in Rochlin, LaPorte, and Roberts' (1987: 78) study described as follows:

> . . . imagine that it's a busy day, and you shrink San Francisco Airport to only one short runway and one ramp and one gate. Make planes take off and land at the same time, at half the present time interval, rock the runway from side to side, and require that everyone who leaves in the morning returns that same day. Make sure the equipment is so close to the edge of the envelope that it's fragile. Then turn off the radar to avoid detection, impose strict controls on radios, fuel the aircraft in place with their engines running, put an enemy in the air, and scatter live bombs and rockets around. Now wet the whole thing down with sea water and oil, and man it with 20-year-olds, half of whom have never seen an airplane close-up. Oh and by the way, try not to kill anyone.

Even though carriers represent "a million accidents waiting to happen" (Wilson, 1986: 21), almost none of them do. Here, we examine why not. The explanation we wish to explore is that organizations concerned with reliability enact aggregate mental processes that are more fully developed than those found in organizations concerned with efficiency. By fully developed mental processes, we mean that organizations preoccupied with reliability may spend more time and effort organizing for controlled information processing (Schneider and Schiffrin, 1977), mindful attention (Langer, 1989), and heedful action (Ryle, 1949). These intensified efforts enable people to understand more of the complexity they face, which then enables them to respond with fewer errors. Reliable systems are smart systems.

Before we can test this line of reasoning we need to develop a language of organizational mind that enables us to describe collective mental processes in organizations. In developing it, we move back and forth between concepts of mind and details of reliable performance in flight operations on a modern super carrier.[2] We use flight operations to illustrate organizational mind for a number of reasons: The technology is relatively simple, the coordination among activities is explicit and visible, the socialization is continuous, agents working alone have less grasp of the entire system than they do when working together, the system is constructed of interdependent know-how, teams of people think on their feet and do the "right thing" in novel situations, and the consequences of any lapse in attention are swift and disabling. Because our efforts to understand deck operations got us thinking about the possibility that performance is mediated by collective mental processes, we use these operations to illustrate that thinking, but the processes of mind we discuss are presumed to be inherent in all organizations. What may vary across organizations is the felt need to develop these processes to more advanced levels.

The Idea of Group Mind

Discussions of collective mental processes have been rare, despite the fact that people claim to be studying "social" cognition (e.g., Schneider, 1991). The preoccupation with individual cognition has left organizational theorists ill-equipped to do much more with the so-called cognitive revolution than apply it to organizational concerns, one brain at a time. There are a few exceptions, however, and we introduce our own discussion of collective mind with a brief review of three recent attempts to engage the topic of group mind.

Wegner and his associates (Wegner, Giuliano, and Hertel, 1985; Wegner, 1987; Wegner, Erber, and Raymond, 1991) suggested that group mind may take the form of cognitive interdependence focused around memory processes. They argued that people in close relationships enact a single transactive memory system, complete with differentiated responsibility for remembering different portions of common experience. People know the locations rather than the details of common events and rely on one another to contribute missing details that cue their own retrieval. Transactive memory systems are integrated and differentiated structures in the sense that connected individuals often hold related information in different locations. When people trade lower-order, detailed, disparate information, they often discover higher-order themes, generalizations, and ideas that subsume these details. It is these integrations of disparate inputs that seem to embody the "magical transformation" that group mind theorists sought to understand (Wegner, Giuliano, and Hertel, 1985: 268). The important point Wegner contributes to our understanding of collective mental processes is that group mind is *not* indexed by within-group similarity of attitudes, understanding, or language, nor can it be understood without close attention to communications processes among group members (Wegner, Giuliano, and Hertel, 1985: 254–255). Both of these lessons will be evident in our reformulation.

Work in artificial intelligence provides the backdrop for two additional attempts to conceptualize group mind: Sandelands and Stablein's (1987) description of organizations as mental entities capable of thought and Hutchins' (1990, 1991) description of organizations as distributed information-processing systems. The relevant ideas are associated with theories of "connectionism," embodied in so-called "neural networks." Despite claims that their work is grounded in the brain's microanatomy, connectionists repeatedly refer to "neurological plausibility" (Quinlan, 1991: 41), "neuron-like units" (Churchland, 1992: 32), "brain-style processing" (Rumelhart, 1992: 69), or "neural inspiration" (Boden, 1990: 18). This qualification is warranted because the "neural" networks examined by connectionists are simply computational models that involve synchronous parallel processing among many interrelated unreliable and/or simple processing units (Quinlan, 1991: 40). The basic idea is that knowledge in very large networks of very simple processing units resides in patterns of connections, not in individuated local symbols. As Boden (1990: 14) explained, any "unit's activity is regulated by the activity of neighboring units, connected to it by inhibitory or excitatory links whose strength can vary according to design and/or learning." Thus, any one unit can represent several different concepts, and the same concept in a different context may activate a slightly different network of units.

Connectionism by itself, however, is a shaky basis on which to erect a theory of organizational mind. The framework remains grounded in a device that models a single, relatively tightly coupled actor as opposed to a loosely coupled system of multiple actors, such as an organization. Connectionists have difficulty simulating emotion and motivation (Dreyfus and Dreyfus, 1990), as well as everyday thought and reasoning (Rumelhart, 1992). In computational models there is no turnover of units akin to that found in organizations, where units are replaced or moved to other locations. And the inputs connectionists investigate are relatively simple items such as numerals, words, or phrases, with the outputs being more or less accurate renderings of these inputs (e.g., Elman, 1992). This contrasts with organizational researchers who pay more attention to complex inputs, such as traditional competitors who make overtures to cooperate, and to outputs that consist of action as well as thought.

What connectionism contributes to organizational theory is the insight that complex patterns can be encoded by patterns of activation and inhibition among simple units, if those units are richly connected. This means that relatively simple actors may be able to apprehend complex inputs if they are organized in ways that resemble neural networks. Connectionists also raise the possibility that mind is "located" in connections and the weights put on them rather than in entities. Thus, to understand mind is to be attentive to process, relating, and method, as well as to structures and content.

Sandelands and Stablein (1987: 139–141) found parallels between the organization of neurons in the brain and the organization of activities in organizations. They used this parallel to argue that connected activities encode concepts and ideas in organizations much like connected neurons encode concepts and ideas in brains. Ideas encoded in behaviors appear to interact in ways that suggest operations of intelligent processing. These parallels are consistent with the idea that organizations are minds. The important lessons from Sandelands and Stablein's analysis are that connections between behaviors, rather than people, may be the crucial "locus" for mind and that intelligence is to be found in patterns of behavior rather than in individual knowledge.

Hutchins (1990, 1991: 289) has used connectionist networks, such as the "constraint satisfaction network," to model how interpretations based on distributed cognitions are formed. These simulations are part of a larger inquiry into how teams coordinate action (Hutchins, 1990) and the extent to which distributed processing amplifies or counteracts errors that form in individual units. Hutchins' analysis suggests that systems maintain the flexible, robust action associated with mindful performance if individuals have overlapping rather than mutually exclusive task knowledge. Overlapping knowledge allows for redundant representation that enables people to take responsibility for all parts of the process to which they can make a contribution (Hutchins, 1990: 210).

The potential fit between connectionist imagery and organizational concepts can be inferred from Hutchins' (1990: 209) description of coordination by mutual constraint in naval navigation teams:

> [The] sequence of action to be taken [in group performance] need not be explicitly represented anywhere in the system. If participants know how to coordinate their activities with the technologies and people with which they interact, the global structure of the task performance will emerge from the local interactions of the members. The structure of the activities of the group is determined by a set of local computations rather than by the implementation of the sort of global plan that appears in the solo performer's procedure. In the team situation, a set of behavioral dependencies are set up. These dependencies shape the behavior pattern of the group.

The lessons we use from Hutchins' work include the importance of redundant representation, the emergence of global structure from local interactions, and behavioral dependencies as the substrate of distributed processing.

Our own attempt to describe group mind has been informed by these three sources but is based on a different set of assumptions. We pay more attention to the form of connections than to the strength of connections and more attention to mind as activity than to mind as entity. To make this shift in emphasis clear, we avoid the phrases "group mind" and "organizational mind" in favor of the phrase "collective mind." The word "collective," unlike the words "group" or "organization," refers to individuals who act as if they are a group. People who act as if they are a group interrelate their actions with more or less care, and focusing on the way this interrelating is done reveals collective mental processes that differ in their degree of development. Our focus is at once on individuals and the collective, since only individuals can contribute to a collective mind, but a collective mind is distinct from an individual mind because it inheres in the pattern of interrelated activities among many people.

We begin the discussion of collective mind by following the lead of Ryle (1949) and developing the concept of mind as a disposition to act with heed. We then follow the lead of Asch (1952) and develop the concept of collective interrelating as contributing, representing, and subordinating, and illustrate these activities with examples from carrier operations. We next combine the notions of heed and interrelating into the concept of collective mind as heedful interrelating and suggest social processes that may account for variations in heedful interrelating. Finally, we describe three examples of heedful interrelating, two from carrier operations and one from the laboratory, and present an extended example of heedless interrelating that resulted in a $38-million accident.

Mind as Disposition to Heed

"Mind" is a noun similar to nouns like faith, hope, charity, role, and culture. "Mind" is not the name of a person, place, or thing but, rather, is a dispositional term that denotes a propensity to act in a certain manner or style. As Ryle (1949: 51) said,

> The statement "the mind is its own place," as theorists might construe it, is not true, for the mind is not even a metaphorical "place." On the contrary, the chessboard, the platform, the scholar's desk, the judge's bench, the lorry-driver's seat, the studio and the football field are among its places. These are where people work and play stupidly or intelligently.

That mind is actualized in patterns of behavior that can range from stupid to intelligent can be seen in the example Ryle (1949: 33) used of a clown who trips and stumbles just as clumsy people do. What's different is that "he trips and stumbles on purpose and after much rehearsal and at the golden moment and where the children can see him and so as not to hurt himself." When a clown trips artfully, people applaud the style of the action, the fact that tripping is done with care, judgment, wit, and appreciation of the mood of the spectators. In short, the tripping is done with heed. Heed is not itself a behavior but it refers to the way behaviors such as tripping, falling, and recovering are assembled. Artful tripping is called heedful, not so much because the tripping involves action preceded by thought but because the behaviors patterned into the action of tripping suggest to the observer qualities such as "noticing, taking care, attending, applying one's mind, concentrating, putting one's heart into something, thinking what one is doing, alertness, interest, intentness, studying, and trying" (Ryle, 1949: 136). These inferences, based on the style of the action, are called "heed concepts" and support the conclusion that the behaviors were combined intelligently rather than stupidly.

The word "heed" captures an important set of qualities of mind that elude the more stark vocabulary of cognition. These nuances of heed are especially appropriate to our interest in systems preoccupied with failure-free performance. People act heedfully when they act more or less carefully, critically, consistently, purposefully, attentively, studiously, vigilantly, conscientiously, pertinaciously (Ryle, 1949: 151). Heed adverbs attach qualities of mind directly to performances, as in the description, "the airboss monitored the pilot's growing load of tasks attentively." Notice that the statement does not say that the airboss was doing two things, monitoring and also checking to be sure that the monitoring was done carefully. Instead, the statement asserts that, having been coached to monitor carefully, his present monitoring reflects this style. Mind is in the monitoring itself, not in some separate episode of theorizing about monitoring.

Heedful performance is not the same thing as habitual performance. In habitual action, each performance is a replica of its predecessor, whereas in heedful performance, each action is modified by its predecessor (Ryle, 1949: 42). In heedful performance, the agent is still learning. Furthermore, heedful performance is the outcome of training and experience that weave together thinking, feeling, and willing. Habitual performance is the outcome of drill and repetition.

When heed declines, performance is said to be heedless, careless, unmindful, thoughtless, unconcerned, indifferent. Heedless performance suggests a failure of intelligence rather than a failure of knowledge. It is a failure to see, to take note of, to be attentive to. Heedless performance is not about ignorance, cognition (Lyons, 1980: 57), and facts. It is about stupidity, competence, and know-how. Thus, mind refers to stretches of human behavior that exhibit qualities of intellect and character (Ryle, 1949: 126).

Group as interrelated activity

Ryle's ideas focus on individual mind. To extend his ideas to groups, we first have to specify the crucial performances in groups that could reflect a disposition to heed. To pinpoint these crucial performances, we derive four defining properties of group performance from Asch's (1952: 251–255) discussion of "mutually shared fields" and illustrate these properties with carrier examples.[3]

The first defining property of group performance is that individuals create the social forces of group life when they act as if there were such forces. As Asch (1952: 251) explained it,

> We must see group phenomena as both *the product and condition* of actions of individuals. . . . There are no forces between individuals as organisms; yet to all intents and purposes they act as if there were, and they actually create social forces. Group action achieves the kind of result that would be understandable if all participants were acting under the direction of a single organizing center. No such center exists; between individuals is a hiatus, which nevertheless, they succeed in overcoming with surprising effectiveness.

An example from carriers occurs during flight operations. The men in the tower (Air Department) monitor and give instructions to incoming and departing aircraft. Simultaneously, the men on the landing signal officers' platform do the same thing. They are backed up by the men in Air Operations who monitor and instruct aircraft at some distance from the ship. From the aviator's viewpoint, he receives integrated information about his current status and future behavior from an integrated source when, in reality, the several sources are relatively independent of one another and located in different parts of the ship.

The second defining property of group performance is that when people act as if there are social forces, they construct their actions (contribute) while envisaging a social system of joint actions (represent), and interrelate that constructed action with the system that is envisaged (subordinate). Asch (1952: 251–252) explained this as follows:

There are group actions that are possible only when each participant has a representation that includes the actions of others and their relations. The respective actions converge relevantly, assist and supplement each other only when the joint situation is represented in each and when the representations are structurally similar. Only when these conditions are given can individuals subordinate themselves to the requirements of joint action. These representations and the actions that they initiate bring group facts into existence and produce the phenomenal solidity of group process.

The simultaneous envisaging and interrelating that create a system occur when a pilot taxies onto the catapult for launching, is attached to it, and advances his engines to full power. Even though pilots have to rely on the catapult crew, they remain vigilant to see if representations are similar. Pilots keep asking themselves questions like, "Does it feel right?" or "Is the rhythm wrong?" The referent for the question, "Does *it* feel right?" however, is not the aircraft but the joint situation to which he has subordinated himself. If a person on the deck signals the pilot to reduce his engines from full power, he won't do so until someone stands in front of the plane, directly over the catapult, and signals for a reduction in power. Only then is the pilot reasonably certain that the joint situation has changed. He now trusts that the catapult won't be triggered suddenly and fling his underpowered aircraft into a person and then into the ocean.

The third defining property of group performance is that contributing, representing, and subordinating create a joint situation of interrelations among activities, which Asch (1952: 252) referred to as a system:

> When these conditions are given we have a social system or a process of a definite form that embraces the actions of a number of individuals. Such a system does not reside in the individuals taken separately, though each individual contributes to it; nor does it reside outside them; it is present in the interrelations between the activities of individuals.

An example from carriers is a pilot landing an aircraft on a deck. This is not a solitary act. A pilot doesn't really land; he is "recovered." And recovery is a set of interrelated activities among air traffic controllers, landing signal officers, the control tower, navigators, deck hands, the helmsman driving the ship, etc. As the recovery of a single aircraft nears completion in the form of a successful trap, nine to ten people on the landing signal offices' platform, up to 15 more people in the tower, and two to three more people on the bridge observe the recovery and can wave the aircraft off if there is a problem. While this can be understood as an example of redundancy, it can also be interpreted as activities that can be interrelated more or less adequately, depending on the care with which contributing, representing, and subordinating are done.

The fourth and final defining property of group performance suggested by Asch is that the effects produced by a pattern of interrelated activities vary as a function of the style (e.g., heedful–heedless) as well as the strength (e.g., loose–tight) with which the activities are tied together. This is suggested by the statement that, in a system of interrelated activities, individuals can work with, for, or against each other:

> The form the interrelated actions take – on a team or in an office – is a datum of precisely the same kind as any other fact. One could say that all the facts of the system

266   COMPONENTS OF SENSEMAKING

can be expressed as the sum of the actions of individuals. The statement is misleading, however, if one fails to add that the individuals would not be capable of these particular actions unless they were responding to (or envisaging the possibility of) the system. Once the process described is in motion it is no longer the individual "as such" who determines its direction, nor the group acting upon the individual as an external force, but individuals working with, for, or against each other. (Asch, 1952: 252)

It is these varying forms of interrelation that embody collective mind. An example of interrelating on carriers can be seen when ordnance is loaded onto an aircraft and its safety mechanisms are removed. If there is a sudden change of mission, the live ordnance must be disarmed, removed, and replaced by other ordnance that is now activated, all of this under enormous time pressure. These interrelated activities, even though tightly coupled, can become more or less dangerous depending on how the interrelating is done.

In one incident observed, senior officers kept changing the schedule of the next day's flight events through the night, which necessitated a repeated change in ordnance up to the moment the day launches began. A petty officer changing bombs underneath an aircraft, where the pilot couldn't see him, lost a leg when the pilot moved the 36,000-pound aircraft over him. The petty officer should have tied the plane down before going underneath to change the load but failed to do so because there was insufficient time, a situation created by continual indecision at the top. Thus, the senior officers share the blame for this accident because they should have resolved their indecision in ways that were more mindful of the demands it placed on the system.

Although Asch argued that interrelated activities are the essence of groups, he said little about how these interrelations occur or how they vary over time. Instead, he treated interrelations as a variable and interrelating as a constant. If we treat interrelations as a variable and interrelating as a process, this suggests a way to conceptualize collective mind.

Heedful Interrelating as Collective Mind

The insights of Ryle and Asch can be combined into a concept of collective mind if we argue that dispositions toward heed are expressed in actions that construct interrelating. Contributing, representing, and subordinating, actions that form a distinct pattern external to any given individual, become the medium through which collective mind is manifest. Variations in heedful interrelating correspond to variations in collective mind and comprehension.

We assume, as Follett (1924: 146–153) did, that mind begins with actions, which we refer to here as contributions. The contributions of any one individual begin to actualize collective mind to the degree that heedful representation and heedful subordination define those contributions. A heedful contribution enacts collective mind as it begins to converge with, supplement, assist, and become defined in relation to the imagined requirements of joint action presumed to flow from some social activity system.

Similar conduct flows from other contributing individuals in the activity system toward others imagined to be in that system. These separate efforts vary in the heedfulness with which they interrelate, and these variations form a pattern. Since the object of these activities ("the envisaged system," to use Asch's phrase) is itself being constituted as these activities become more or less interrelated, the emergent properties of this object are not contained fully in the representation of any one person nor are they finalized at any moment in time. A single emergent property may appear in more than one representation, but seldom in all. And different properties are shared in common by different subsets of people. Asch seems to have had this distributed representation of the envisaged system in mind when he referred to "structurally similar representations." This pattern of distributed representation explains the transindividual quality of collective mind. Portions of the envisaged system are known to all, but all of it is known to none.

The collective mind is "located" in the process of interrelating just as the individual mind for Ryle was "located" in the activities of lorry driving, chess playing, or article writing. Collective mind exists potentially as a kind of capacity in an ongoing activity stream and emerges in the style with which activities are interrelated. These patterns of interrelating are as close to a physical substrate for collective mind as we are likely to find. There is nothing mystical about all this. Collective mind is manifest when individuals construct mutually shared fields. The collective mind that emerges during the interrelating of an activity system is more developed and more capable of intelligent action the more heedfully that interrelating is done.

A crude way to represent the development of a collective mind is by means of a matrix in which the rows are people and the columns are either the larger activities of contributing, representing, and subordinating, or their component behaviors (e.g., converging with, assisting, or supplementing). Initially, the cell entries can be a simple "yes" or "no." "Yes" means a person performs that action heedfully; "no" means the action is done heedlessly. The more "yeses" in the matrix, the more developed the collective mind.

We portray collective mind in terms of method rather than content, structuring rather than structure, connecting rather than connections. Interrelations are not given but are constructed and reconstructed continually by individuals (Blumer, 1969: 110) through the ongoing activities of contributing, representing, and subordinating. Although these activities are done by individuals, their referent is a socially structured field. Individual activities are shaped by this envisioned field and are meaningless apart from it. When people make efforts to interrelate, these efforts can range from heedful to heedless. The more heed reflected in a pattern of interrelations, the more developed the collective mind and the greater the capability to comprehend unexpected events that evolve rapidly in unexpected ways. When we say that a collective mind "comprehends" unexpected events, we mean that heedful interrelating connects sufficient individual know-how to meet situational demands. For organizations concerned with reliability, those demands often consist of unexpected, nonsequential interactions among small failures that are hard to see and hard to believe. These incomprehensible failures often build quickly into catastrophes (Perrow, 1984: 7–12, 22, 78, 88).

An increase in heedful interrelating can prevent or correct these failures of comprehension in at least three ways. First, longer stretches of time can be connected, as when more know-how is brought forward from the past and is elaborated into new contributions and representations that extrapolate farther into the future. Second, comprehension can be improved if more activities are connected, such as when interrelations span earlier and later stages of task sequences. And third, comprehension can be increased if more levels of experience are connected, as when newcomers who take nothing for granted interrelate more often with old-timers who think they have seen it all. Each of these three changes makes the pattern of interrelations more complex and better able to sense and regulate the complexity created by unexpected events. A system that is tied together more densely across time, activities, and experience comprehends more of what is occurring because the scope of heedful action reaches into more places. When heed is spread across more activities and more connections, there should be more understanding and fewer errors. A collective mind that becomes more comprehensive, comprehends more.

Variations in heed

If collective mind is embodied in the interrelating of social activities, and if collective mind is developed more or less fully depending on the amount of heedfulness with which that interrelating is done, we must address the issue of what accounts for variations in heed. We suspect the answer lies in Mead's (1934: 186) insight that mind is "the individual importation of social process." We understand the phrase "social process" to mean a set of ongoing interactions in a social activity system from which participants continually extract a changing sense of self-interrelation and then re-enact that sense back into the system. This ongoing interaction process is recapitulated in individual lives and continues despite the replacement of people.

Mead stressed the reality of recapitulation, as did others. Ryle (1949: 27), for example, observed that "this trick of talking to oneself in silence is acquired neither quickly nor without effort; and it is a necessary condition to our acquiring it that we should have previously learned to talk intelligently aloud and have heard and understood other people doing so. Keeping our thoughts to ourselves is a sophisticated accomplishment." Asch (1952: 257) described the relationship between the individual and the group as the only part-whole relation in nature "that depends on recapitulation of the structure of the whole in the part." The same point is made by Morgan (1986) and Hutchins (1990: 211), using the more recent imagery of holograms: System capacities that are relevant for the functioning of the whole are built into its parts. In each of these renderings, social processes are the prior resources from which individual mind, self, and action are fashioned (Mead, 1934: 191–192). This means that collective mind precedes the individual mind and that heedful interrelating foreshadows heedful contributing.

Patterns of heedful interrelating in ongoing social processes may be internalized and recapitulated by individuals more or less adequately as they move in and out of the system. If heedful interrelating is visible, rewarded, modeled, discussed, and preserved in vivid stories, there is a good chance that newcomers will learn this style of responding, will incorporate it into their definition of who they are in the system, and will reaffirm and perhaps even augment this style as they act. To illustrate, Walsh and Ungson (1991: 60) defined organization as a "network of intersubjectively shared meanings that are sustained through the development and use of a common language and everyday social interactions." Among the shared meanings and language on carriers we heard these four assertions: (1) If it's not written down you can do it; (2) Look for clouds in every silver lining; (3) Most positions on this deck were bought in blood; and (4) Never get into something you can't get out of. Each of these guidelines, if practiced openly, represents an image of heedful interrelating that can be internalized and acted back into the system. If such guidelines are neglected, ignored, or mocked, however, interrelating still goes on, but it is done with indifference and carelessness.

Whether heedful images survive or die depends importantly on interactions among those who differ in their experience with the system. While these interactions have been the focus of preliminary discussions of communities of practice (e.g., Lave and Wenger, 1991: 98–100) involving apprentices and experts, we highlight a neglected portion of the process, namely, the effects of socialization on the insiders doing the socializing (Sutton and Louis, 1987).

When experienced insiders answer the questions of inexperienced newcomers, the insiders themselves are often resocialized. This is significant because it may remind insiders how to act heedfully and how to talk about heedful action. Newcomers are often a pretext for insiders to reconstruct what they knew but forgot. Heedful know-how becomes more salient and more differentiated when insiders see what they say to newcomers and discover that they thought more thoughts than they thought they did.

Whether collective mind gets renewed during resocialization may be determined largely by the candor and narrative skills of insiders and the attentiveness of newcomers. Candid insiders who use memorable stories to describe failures as well as successes, their doubts as well as their certainties, and what works as well as what fails, help newcomers infer dispositions of heed and carelessness. Insiders who narrate richly also often remind themselves of forgotten details when they reconstruct a previous event. And these reminders increase the substance of mind because they increase the number of examples of heed in work.

Narrative skills (Bruner, 1986; Weick and Browning, 1986; Orr, 1990) are important for collective mind because stories organize know-how, tacit knowledge, nuance, sequence, multiple causation, means-end relations, and consequences into a memorable plot. The ease with which a single story integrates diverse themes of heed in action foreshadows the capability of individuals to do the same. A coherent story of heed is mind writ small. And a repertoire of war stories, which grows larger through the memorable exercise of heed in novel settings, is mind writ large.

The quality of collective mind is heavily dependent on the way insiders interact with newcomers (e.g., Van Maanen, 1976). If insiders are taciturn, indifferent, preoccupied, available only in stylized performances, less than candid, or simply not available at all, newcomers are in danger of acting without heed because they have only banal conversations to internalize. They have learned little about heedful interdependence. When these newcomers act and try to anticipate the contributions of others, their actions will be stupid, and mistakes will happen. These mistakes may represent small failures that produce learning (Sitkin, 1992). More ominous is the possibility that these mistakes may also represent a weakening of system capacity for heedful responding. When there is a loss of particulars about how heed can be expressed in representation and subordination, reliable performance suffers. As seasoned people become more peripheral to socialization, there should be a higher incidence of serious accidents.

We have dwelt on insider participation simply because this participation is a conspicuous phenomenon that allows us to describe collective mind, but anything that changes the ongoing interaction (e.g., preoccupation with personalities rather than with the task) can also change the capability of that interaction to preserve and convey dispositions of heed. Those changes in turn should affect the quality of mind, the likelihood of comprehension, and the incidence of error.

Illustrations of Heed in Interrelating

The concepts of heed, interrelating, contributing, representing, subordinating, intelligent action, comprehension, recapitulation, and resocialization come together in the concept of collective mind as heedful interrelating. Applying the language of collective mind to four examples of complex systems, we illustrate the adequate comprehension produced by heedful interrelating and the problematic comprehension produced by heedless interrelating.

Heedful interrelating

The first example of interrelating that is heedful involves a laboratory analogue of collective mind (Weick and Gilfillan, 1971). Three people who can neither see nor talk with one another are given target numbers between 1 and 30. Whenever a target number is announced, each person is to contribute some number between 0 and 10 such that, when all three contributions are added together, they sum to the target number.

There are many ways to solve this problem (e.g., a target number of 13 can be achieved with a 3s strategy, 4-4-5, or a 10s strategy, 10-3-0). Once a group evolves a strategy, people are removed one at a time, and strangers, who know nothing of the strategy in use, enter. The questions are, how do old-timers interrelate with newcomers, what strategy emerges, how soon does it emerge, and how stable is it?

Austere as these operations are, they have the rudiments of a collective mind. A newcomer knows a number of things: (1) There are others in the activity system but they must be envisioned, since it is impossible to communicate with them (representation); (2) the two other people have had some experience with the system and with the game (there are imagined requirements to which one must subordinate); (3) each contribution is important and must interrelate with the others (contributions must converge, supplement, assist, and be defined in relation to one another); (4) to learn the existing system or to create a new one requires attention, careful calculations, and clear signals of intent (heedful contribution, representation, and subordination);

and, (5) casual, indifferent interrelating will not be punished severely, because people are anonymous, and the rewards for participation are trivial (heedless responding is an option).

Just as the newcomers know these things, so do the old-timers. When these three people try to work out and maintain a system that hits each target on the first try, they are attempting to interrelate. They contribute, represent, and subordinate with varying amounts of heed. Their interrelating is better able to distinguish a mistake from an intentional effort to change strategy the more heedfully it was assembled. Likewise, heedful interrelating can "read" a newcomer's intentions quickly, whereas heedless interrelating cannot. These discriminations are not accomplished by single individuals but are accomplished by interrelated activities and the heedfulness with which those activities are defined in relation to one another. Heedful action at any one of these three positions can be undermined if it is not reciprocated at the other two. What is undermined, however, is a pattern of interrelations, not a person. A pattern of nonreciprocated heedfulness represents a loss of intelligence that is reflected in missed targets and slow change.

Heedful interrelating on carriers looks a lot like the pattern of interrelating seen in the common target game. A vivid example of this similarity is Gillcrist's (1990: 287–288) account of what it feels like to land and taxi on a carrier deck at night. Having successfully trapped onto the deck, Gillcrist watched the flight director's two amber wands:

> I raised the hook handle with my right hand and simultaneously added a lot of power to get the Crusader moving forward. There was an urgency in the taxi signal movement of the wands, telling me that there must be another plane close behind me in the groove. They wanted to get my airplane completely across the foul line as quickly as possible. Taxiing at night was more carefully done than in the light of day, however. We'd had enough airplanes taxi over the side at night to learn that lesson. . . . The wands pointed to another set of wands further up the flight deck and I began to follow their direction as my F-8 was taxied all the way to the first spot on the bow. "God, how I hate this," I muttered to myself. "Do they really have to do this or are they just trying to scare me?" In spotting me in the first taxi spot on the bow, the taxi director was turning the F-8 so close to the edge of the flight deck that the cockpit actually swung in an arc over the deck's edge. All I could see was black rushing water eighty feet below. "Jesus" I said to myself, "I hope that guy knows what he is doing."

The taxi director does know what he is doing, as does the pilot, but that alone does not keep the plane from dropping off the deck. The interrelating of their know-how keeps the plane on the deck. A command from the director that is not executed by the pilot or a pilot deviation that is not corrected by the director are equally dangerous and not controllable by either party alone. The activities of taxiing and directing remain failure-free to the extent that they are interrelated heedfully.

A third example of heedful interrelating is of special interest because so much of it appears to involve the mind of one individual, in this case, the person responsible for deck operations (the bos'n). One of the people in this position who was interviewed had 23 years of experience on 16 carriers. At the time he joined this carrier's crew, it took six hours to spot 45 aircraft on the deck. He reduced that time to two hours and 45 minutes, which gave his crew more time to relax and maintain their alertness.

This person tries constantly to prevent the four worst things that can happen on a deck: It catches fire, becomes fouled, locked (nothing can move), or a plane is immobilized in the landing area. The more times a plane is moved to prevent any of these conditions, the higher the probability that it will brush against another plane ("crunch"), be damaged, and be out of service until repaired.

This bos'n, who is responsible for the smooth functioning of deck operations, gets up an hour early each day just to think about the kind of environment he will create on the deck that day, given the schedule of operations. This thinking is individual mind at work, but it also illustrates how collective mind is represented in the head of one person. The bos'n is dealing with collective mind when he represents the capabilities and weaknesses of imagined crewmembers' responses in his thinking, when he tailors sequences of activities so that improvisation and flexible response are activated as an expected part of the day's adaptive response, and when he counts on the interrelations among crewmembers themselves to "mind" the day's activities.

The bos'n does not plan specific step-by-step operations but, rather, plans which crews will do the planning and deciding, when, and with what resources at hand. The system will decide the operations, and the bos'n sets up the system that will do this. The bos'n does this by attempting to recognize the strengths and weaknesses of the various crews working for him. The pieces of the system he sets up may interrelate stupidly or intelligently, in large part because they will either duplicate or undermine the heedful contributing, representing, and subordinating he anticipates.

Heedless interrelating

When interrelating breaks down, individuals represent others in the system in less detail, contributions are shaped less by anticipated responses, and the boundaries of the envisaged system are drawn more narrowly, with the result that subordination becomes meaningless. Attention is focused on the local situation rather than the joint situation. People still may act heedfully, but not with respect to others. Interrelating becomes careless. Key people and activities are overlooked. As interrelating deteriorates and becomes more primitive, there is less comprehension of the implications of unfolding events, slower correction of errors, and more opportunities for small errors to combine and amplify. When these events are set in motion and sustained through heedless interrelating, there is a greater chance that small lapses can enlarge into disasters.

An incident that happened during a nighttime launch and recovery, which was described to us in interviews and correspondence, illustrates the steady loss of collective mind as interrelating became less heedful. This incident began to unfold during a night launch in which one-third of the planes in the mission were still on deck waiting to be launched, even though other planes were already beginning to be recovered.

Aircraft A, which was in the air and the fourth plane in line to land, had an apparent hydraulic failure, although the pilot was able to get his gear and tail hook down. This failure meant that if the plane were landed, its wings could not be folded, and it would take up twice the space normally allotted to it. This complicates the landing of all planes behind it.

While the pilot of plane A was trying to get help for his problem on a radio channel, plane B, an F-14, which was number three in order of landing, had a compound hydraulic failure, and none of his back-up hydraulic systems appeared to work, something that was unheard of. Plane C, which was fifth in line to land, then developed a control problem. Thus, the airboss was faced, first, with several A-7 aircraft that still had to be launched. This is not a trivial complication, because the only catapult available for these aircraft was the one whose blast-deflector panel extends part way into the area where planes land. Second, the airboss had a string of planes about to land that included (1) a normally operating A-7, (2) a normally operating A-7, (3) plane B with a compound hydraulic failure, (4) plane A with a hydraulic failure but gear and tail hook down, and (5) plane C with an apparent control problem.

The first plane was taken out of the landing pattern and the second was landed. Plane B, the one with the most severe problems, was told to land and then had to be waved off because the person operating the deflector panel for launches lowered the panel one second too late to allow B to land. The deflector operator had not been informed that an emergency existed. Plane B and its increasingly frightened pilot were reinserted into the landing pattern behind plane C for a second pass at the deck. Plane B then experienced an additional hydraulic failure. Plane A landed without incident, as did plane C. Plane C had corrected its control problem, but no one was informed. Thus, plane B's second pass was delayed longer than necessary because he had to wait for C to land in the mistaken belief that C still had a problem. The pilot of plane B became increasingly agitated and less and less able to help diagnose what might be wrong with his aircraft. The decision was made to send plane B to a land base, but it ran out of fuel on the way and the pilot and his RIO (radar intercept officer) had to eject. Both were rescued, but a $38-million aircraft was lost. If aircraft B had not been waved off the first time it tried to land, it would have been safely recovered. If we analyze this incident as a loss of collective mind produced by heedless interrelating, we look for two things: events that became incomprehensible, signifying a loss of mind, and increasingly heedless interrelating.

There were several events that became harder to comprehend. The failure of the hydraulic system in aircraft B was puzzling. The triggering of additional hydraulic failures was even more so. To have three of five aircraft on final approach declare emergencies was itself something that was hard to comprehend, as was the problem of how to recover three disabled planes while launching three more immediately.

Incomprehensible events made interrelating more difficult, which then made the events even harder to comprehend. The loss of heed in interrelating was spread among contributions, representations, and subordinations. The squadron representative who tried to deal with the stressed pilot in plane B was not himself a pilot (he was an RIO), and he did not scan systematically for possible sources of the problem. Instead, he simply told the pilot assorted things to try, not realizing that, in the pilot's doing so, additional systems on the plane began to fail. He didn't realize these growing complications because the pilot was both imprecise in his reports of trouble and slow to describe what happened when he tested some hypothesis proposed by the representative. And the representative did nothing to change the pilot's style of contributing.

But heedless interrelating was not confined to exchanges between pilot and representative. The RIO in plane B made no effort to calm the pilot or help him diagnose. The deflector operator was not treated as a person in the *recovery* system. Three different problems were discussed on two radio frequencies, which made it difficult to sort out which plane had which problem. No one seemed to register that the squadron representative was himself getting farther behind and making increasingly heedless contributions. The airboss in command of the tower was an F-14 pilot, but he was preoccupied with the five incoming and the three outgoing aircraft and could not be pulled completely into the activity system that was dealing with the F-14 problem. As heed began to be withdrawn from the system, activities and people became isolated, the system began to pull apart, the problems became more incomprehensible, and it became harder for individuals to interrelate with a system of activities that was rapidly losing its form. The pattern of interrelated activities lost intelligence and mind as contributions became more thoughtless and less interdependent.

Had the pattern of interrelations been more heedful, it might have detected what was subsequently said to be the most likely cause of the failures in plane B. Although the aircraft was never recovered, the navy's investigation of the incident concluded that too many demands were placed on the emergency back-up systems, and the plane became less and less flyable. Sustained heedful interrelating might well have registered that the growing number of attempted solutions had in fact created a new problem that was worse than any problem that was present to begin with.[4]

It is important to realize that our analysis, using the concepts of collective mind and heedful interrelating, implies something more than the simple advice, "be careful." People can't be careful unless they take account of others and unless others do the same. Being careful is a social rather than a solitary act. To act with care, people have to envision their contributions in the context of requirements for joint action. Furthermore, to act with care does not mean that one plans how to do this and then applies the plan to the action. Care is not cultivated apart from action. It is expressed in action and through action. Thus people can't *be* careful, they *are* careful (or careless). The care is in the action.

The preceding analysis also suggests that it is crucial to pay attention to mind, because accidents are not just issues of ignorance and cognition, they are issues of inattention and conduct as well. The examples of incomprehension mentioned above are not simply issues of fact and thinking. Facts by themselves are of no help if they cannot be communicated or heard or applied or interpreted or incorporated into activities or placed in contexts, in short, if they are not addressed mindfully. One "fact" of this incident is that plane B could have landed had it not been waved off because of the extended deflector. Furthermore, individuals within the system were not ignorant of crucial details (e.g., the pilot of plane C knew he no longer had a problem).

One interpretation of this incident is that individuals were smarter than the system, but the problem was more complex than any one individual could understand.

Heedful interrelating of activities constructs a substrate that is more complex and, therefore, better able to comprehend complex events than is true for smart but isolated individuals. The F-14 may have been lost because heedful interrelating was lost. Heightened attentiveness to social process might have prevented both losses.

Discussion

We conclude from our analysis that carrier operations are a struggle for alertness and that the concept of heedful interrelating helps capture this struggle. We began with the question, How can we analyze a complex social activity system in which fluctuations in comprehension seem to be consequential? We focused on heed (understood as dispositions to act with attentiveness, alertness, and care), conduct (understood as behavior that takes into account the expectations of others), and mind (understood as integration of feeling, thinking, and willing).

We were able to talk about group mind without reification, because we grounded our ideas in individual actions and then treated those actions as the means by which a distinct higher-order pattern of interrelated activities emerged. This pattern shaped the actions that produced it, persisted despite changes in personnel, and changed despite unchanging personnel. Thus, we did not reify social entities, because we argued that they emerge from individual actions that construct interrelations. But neither did we reify individual entities, because we argued that they emerge through selective importation, interpretation, and re-enactment of the social order that they constitute.

In broadening our focus, we conceptualized mind as action that constructs mental processes rather than as mental processes that construct action. We proposed that variations in contributing, representing, and subordinating produce collective mind. Common hallmarks of mind such as alertness, attentiveness, understanding, and relating to the world were treated as coincident with and immanent in the connecting activities. To connect *is* to mind.

For the collective mind, the connections that matter are those that link distributed activities, and the ways those connections are accomplished embody much of what we have come to mean by the word "mind." The ways people connect their activities make conduct mindful. Mindless actions ignore interrelating or accomplish it haphazardly and with indifference (Bellah et al., 1991).

As a result of our analysis, we now see the importance of disentangling the development of mind from the development of a group. In Asch's description of the essence of group life, as well as in other discussions of group cognition, the development of mind is confounded with the development of the group. As a group matures and moves from inclusion through control to affection (Schutz, 1958), or as it moves from forming through storming, norming, and performing (Tuckman, 1965), both interrelating and intimacy develop jointly. If a mature group has few accidents or an immature group has many, it is difficult to see what role, if any, mind may play in this. An immature group of relative strangers with few shared norms, minimal disclosure, and formal relationships might well find it hard to cope with nonroutine events. But this has nothing to do with mind.

In our analysis we have assumed that there is something like a two-by-two matrix in which a group can be developed or undeveloped and a collective mind can be developed or undeveloped. And we assume that the combinations of developed-group–undeveloped mind and undeveloped-group–developed mind are possible. These two combinations are crucial to any proposal that collective mind is a distinct process in social life.

The combination of developed-group–undeveloped mind is found in the phenomenon of groupthink (Janis, 1982), as well as in cults (Galanter, 1989), interactions at NASA prior to the Challenger disaster (Starbuck and Milliken, 1988), and ethnocentric research groups (Weick, 1983). Common among these examples is subordination to a system that is envisaged carelessly, or, as Janis (1982: 174) put it, there is an overestimation of the group's power, morality, and invulnerability. Furthermore, contributions are made thoughtlessly; as Janis (1982: 175) put it, there is self-censorship of deviations, doubts, and counterarguments. And, finally, representations are careless; members maintain the false assumption that silence means consent (Janis, 1982: 175). In the presence of heedless interrelating, comprehension declines, regardless of how long the group has been together, and disasters result.

The combination of undeveloped-group–developed mind is found in ad hoc project teams, such as those that produce television specials (e.g., Peters, 1992: 189–200) or motion pictures (Faulkner and Anderson, 1987), and in temporary systems such as those that form in aircraft cockpits (Ginnett, 1990), around jazz improvisation (Eisenberg, 1990), in response to crises (Rochlin, 1989), or in high-velocity environments (Eisenhardt, 1993). The common feature shared among these diverse settings is best captured by Eisenberg (1990: 160), who characterized them as built from nondisclosive intimacy that "stresses coordination of action over alignment of cognitions, mutual respect over agreement, trust over empathy, diversity over homogeneity, loose over tight coupling, and strategic communication over unrestricted candor."

Translated into the language of heedful interrelating, what Eisenberg depicted were relationships in which shared values, openness, and disclosure, all hallmarks of a developed group, were *not* fully developed, but in which collective mind was developed. Nondisclosive intimacy is characterized by heedful contributing (e.g., loose coupling, diversity, strategic communication), heedful representing (e.g., mutual respect, coordination of action), and heedful subordinating (e.g., trust).

If heedful interrelating can occur in an undeveloped group, this changes the way we think about the well-known stages of group development. If people are observed to contribute, represent, and subordinate with heed, these actions can be interpreted as operations that construct a well-developed collective mind; however, those same actions can also be seen as the orienting, clarifying, and testing associated with the early stages of a new group just beginning to form (McGrath, 1984: 152–162). By one set of criteria, that associated with group formation, people engaged in forming are immature. By another set of criteria, that associated with collective mind, these acts of forming represent well-developed mental processes.

These opposed criteria suggest that groups may be smartest in their early stages. As they grow older, they lose mind when interrelating becomes more routine, more casual, more automatic. This line of reasoning is consistent with Gersick's (1988) demonstration that groups tend to re-form halfway through their history. In our language, this midcourse reshuffling can be understood as redoing the pattern of interrelations that constitute mind, thereby renewing mind itself. If groups steadily lose mind and comprehension as they age, their capability for comprehension may show a dramatic increase halfway through their history. If that is plausible, the sudden surge in comprehension should be accompanied by a sudden decrease in the number of accidents they produce.

The conceptualization of topics in organizational theory

Our analysis of collective mind and heedful interrelating throws new light on several topics in organizational theory, including organizational types, the measurement of performance, and normal accidents.

The concept of mind may be an important tool in comparative analysis. LaPorte and Consolini (1991) argued that high-reliability organizations such as aircraft carriers differ in many ways from organizations usually portrayed in organizational theory as (for convenience) high-efficiency organizations. Typical efficiency organizations practice incremental decision making, their errors do not have a lethal edge, they use simple low-hazard technologies, they are governed by single rather than multilayered authority systems, they are more often in the private than the public sector, they are not preoccupied with perfection, their operations are carried on at one level of intensity, they experience few nasty surprises, and they can rely on computation or judgment as decision strategies (Thompson and Tuden, 1959) but seldom need to employ both at the same time. LaPorte and Consolini (1991: 19) concluded that existing organizational theory is inadequate to understand systems in which the "consequences and costs associated with major failures in some technical operations are greater than the value of the lessons learned from them."

Our analysis suggests that most of these differences can be subsumed under the generalization that high-efficiency organizations have simpler minds than do high-reliability organizations. If dispositions toward individual and collective heed were increased in most organizations in conjunction with increases in task-related interdependence and flexibility in the sequencing of tasks, then we would expect these organizations to act more like high-reliability systems. Changes of precisely this kind seem to be inherent in recent interventions to improve total quality management (e.g., U.S. General Accounting Office, 1991).

Our point is simply that confounded in many comparisons among organizations that differ on conspicuous grounds, such as structure and technology, are less conspicuous but potentially more powerful differences in the capability for collective mind. A smart system does the right thing regardless of its structure and regardless of whether the environment is stable or turbulent. We suspect that organic systems, because of their capacity to reconfigure themselves temporarily into more mechanistic structures, have more fully developed minds than do mechanistic systems.

We also suspect that newer organizational forms, such as networks (Powell, 1990), self-designing systems (Hedberg, Nystrom, and Starbuck, 1976), cognitive oligopolies (Porac, Thomas, and Baden-Fuller, 1989: 413), and interpretation systems (Daft and

Weick, 1984) have more capacity for mind than do M forms, U forms, and matrix forms. But all of these conjectures, which flow from the idea of collective mind, require that we pay as much attention to social processes and microdynamics as we now pay to the statics of structure, strategy, and demographics.

The concept of mind also suggests a view of performance that complements concepts such as activities (Homans, 1950), the active task (Dornbusch and Scott, 1975), task structure (Hackman, 1990: 10), group task design (Hackman, 1987), and production functions (McGrath, 1990). It adds to all of these a concern with the style or manner of performance. Not only can performance be high or low, productive or unproductive, or adequate or inadequate, it can also be heedful or heedless. Heedful performance might or might not be judged productive, depending on how productivity is defined.

Most important, the concept of mind allows us to talk about careful versus careless performance, not just performance that is productive or unproductive. This shift makes it easier to talk about performance in systems in which the next careless error may be the last trial. The language of care is more suited to systems concerned with reliability than is the language of efficiency.

Much of the interest in organizations that are vulnerable to catastrophic accidents can be traced to Perrow's (1981) initial analysis of Three Mile Island, followed by his expansion of this analysis into other industries (Perrow, 1984). In the expanded analysis, Perrow suggested that technologies that are both tightly coupled and interactively complex are the most dangerous, because small events can escalate rapidly into a catastrophe. Nuclear aircraft carriers such as those we have studied are especially prone to normal accidents (see Perrow, 1984: 97) because they comprise not one but several tightly coupled, interactively complex technologies. These include jet aircraft, nuclear weapons carried on aircraft, nuclear weapons stored on board the ship, and nuclear reactors used to power the ship. Furthermore, the marine navigation system and the air traffic control system on a ship are tightly coupled technologies, although they are slightly less complex than the nuclear technologies.

Despite their high potential for normal accidents, carriers are relatively safe. Our analysis suggests that one of the reasons carriers are safe is because of, not in spite of, tight coupling. Our analysis raises the possibility that technological tight coupling is dangerous in the presence of interactive complexity, unless it is mediated by a mutually shared field that is well developed. This mutually shared field, built from heedful interrelating, is itself tightly coupled, but this tight coupling is social rather than technical. We suspect that normal accidents represent a breakdown of social processes and comprehension rather than a failure of technology. Inadequate comprehension can be traced to flawed mind rather than flawed equipment.

The conceptualization of practice

The mindset for practice implicit in the preceding analysis has little room for heroic, autonomous individuals. A well-developed organization mind, capable of reliable performance is thoroughly social. It is built of ongoing interrelating and dense interrelations. Thus, interpersonal skills are not a luxury in high-reliability systems. They are a necessity. These skills enable people to represent and subordinate themselves to communities of practice. As people move toward individualism and fewer interconnections, organization mind is simplified and soon becomes indistinguishable from individual mind. With this change comes heightened vulnerability to accidents. Cockpit crews that function as individuals rather than teams show this rapid breakdown in ability to understand what is happening (Orlady and Foushee, 1987). Sustained success in coping with emergency conditions seems to occur when the activities of the crew are more fully interrelated and when members' contributions, representations, and subordination create a pattern of joint action. The chronic fear in high-reliability systems that events will prove to be incomprehensible (Perrow, 1984) may be a realistic fear only when social skills are underdeveloped. With more development of social skills goes more development of organization mind and heightened understanding of environments.

A different way to state the point that mind is dependent on social skills is to argue that it is easier for systems to lose mind than to gain it. A culture that encourages individualism, survival of the fittest, macho heroics, and can-do reactions will often neglect heedful practice of representation and subordination. Without representation and subordination, comprehension reverts to one brain at a time. No matter how visionary or smart or forward-looking or aggressive that one brain may be, it is no match for conditions of interactive complexity. Cooperation is imperative for the development of mind.

Reliable performance may require a well-developed collective mind in the form of a complex, attentive system tied together by trust. That prescription sounds simple enough. Nevertheless, conventional understanding seems to favor a different configuration: a simple, automatic system tied together by suspicion and redundancy. The latter scenario makes sense in a world in which individuals can comprehend what is going on. But when individual comprehension proves inadequate, one of the few remaining sources of comprehension is social entities. Variation in the development of these entities may spell the difference between prosperity and disaster.

Notes

1. We acknowledge with deep gratitude, generous and extensive help with previous versions of this manuscript from Sue Ashford, Michael Cohen, Dan Denison, Jane Dutton, Les Gasser, Joel Kahn, Rod Kramer, Peter Manning, Dave Meader, Debra Meyerson, Walter Nord, Linda Pike, Joe Porac, Bob Quinn, Lance Sandelands, Paul Schaffner, Howard Schwartz, Kathie Sutcliffe, Bob Sutton, Diane Vaughan, Jim Walsh, Rod White, Mayer Zald, and the anonymous reviewers for *Administrative Science Quarterly*.

2. Unless otherwise cited, aircraft carrier examples are drawn from field observation notes of air operations and interviews aboard Nimitz class carriers made by the second author and others over a five-year period. Researchers spent from four days to three weeks aboard the carriers at any one time. They usually made observations from different vantage points during the evolutions of various events. Observations were entered into computer systems and later compared across observers and across organizational members for clarity of meaning. Examples are also drawn from quarterly workshop discussions with senior officers from those carriers over the two years. The primary observational research methodol-

ogy was to triangulate observations made by three faculty researchers, as suggested by Glaser and Strauss (1967) and Eisenhardt (1989). The methodology is more fully discussed in Roberts, Stout, and Halpern (1993). Paper-and-pencil data were also collected and are discussed elsewhere (Roberts, Rousseau, and LaPorte, 1993). That research was supported by Office of Naval Research contract #N-00014-86-k-0312 and National Science Foundation grant #F7-08046.

3. We could just as easily have used Blumer's (1969: 78–79) discussion of "the mutual alignment of action."

4. There is a limit to heedfulness, given the number and skill of participants, and on this night this ship was at that iimit. The system was overloaded, and the situation was one that managers of high-technology weapons systems worry about all the time. They call it OBE (overcome by events). Given perhaps only minor differences in the situation, the outcomes might have been different. In this situation, for example, had the carrier air group commander come to the tower (which he often does), he would have added yet another set of eyes and ears, with their attendant skills. Perhaps he could have monitored one aspect of the situation while the boss and mini boss took charge of others, and the situation would have been a more heedful one. Had the squadron representative in the tower been a pilot, he might have searched through his own repertoire of things that can go wrong and helped the F-14's pilot calm down and solve his problem, increasing the heedfulness of the situation.

References

Asch, Solomon E. (1952). *Social Psychology*. Englewood Cliffs, NJ: Prentice-Hall.

Bellah, Robert N., Richard Madsen, William M. Sullivan, Ann Swidler, and Steven M. Tipton (1991). *The Good Society*. New York: Knopf.

Blumer, Herbert (1969). *Symbolic Interaction*. Berkeley: University of California Press.

Boden, Margaret A. (1990). "Introduction." In Margaret A. Boden (ed.), *The Philosophy of Artificial Intelligence*: 1–21. New York: Oxford University Press.

Bruner, Jerome (1986). *Actual Minds. Possible Worlds*. Cambridge, MA: Harvard University Press.

Churchland, Paul M. (1992). "A deeper unity: Some Feyerabendian themes in neurocomputational form." In Steven Davis (ed.), *Connectionism: Theory and Practice*: 30–50. New York: Oxford University Press.

Daft, Richard, and Karl E. Weick (1984). "Toward a model of organizations as interpretation systems." *Academy of Management Review*, 9: 284–295.

Dornbusch, Sandford M., and W. Richard Scott (1975). *Evaluation and the Exercise of Authority*. San Francisco: Jossey-Bass.

Dreyfus, Hubert L., and Stuart E. Dreyfus (1990). "Making a mind versus modeling the brain: Artificial intelligence back at a branch point." In Margaret A. Boden (ed.), *The Philosophy of Artificial Intelligence*: 309–333. New York: Oxford University Press.

Eisenberg, Eric (1990). "Jamming: Transcendence through organizing." *Communication Research*, 17: 139–164.

Eisenhardt, Kathleen M. (1989). "Building theories from case study research." *Academy of Management Review*, 14: 532–550.

Eisenhardt, K. M. (1993). "High reliability organizations meet high velocity environments: Common dilemmas in nuclear power plants, aircraft carriers, and microcomputer firms." In

Karlene Roberts (ed.), *New Challenges to Understanding Organizations*: 117–135. New York: Macmillan.

Elman, Jeffrey L. (1992). "Grammatical structure and distributed representations." In Steven Davis (ed.), *Connectionism: Theory and Practice*: 138–178. New York: Oxford University Press.

Faulkner, Robert R., and A. B. Anderson (1987). "Short-term projects and emergent careers: Evidence from Hollywood." *American Journal of Sociology*, 92: 879–909.

Follett, Mary Parker (1924). *Creative Experience*. New York: Longmans, Green.

Galanter, Marc (1989). *Cults*. New York: Oxford University Press.

Gersick, Connie G. (1988). "Time and transition in work teams: Toward a new model of group development." *Academy of Management Journal*, 31: 9–41.

Gillcrist, P. T. (1990). *Feet Wet Reflections of a Carrier*. Novato, CA: Presidio Press.

Ginnett, Robert C. (1990). "Airline cockpit crew." In J. Richard Hackman (ed.), *Groups That Work (and Those That Don't)*: 427–448. San Francisco: Jossey-Bass.

Glaser, Barney, and Anselm L. Strauss (1967). *The Discovery of Grounded Theory: Strategies for Qualitative Research*. Chicago: Aldine.

Hackman, J. Richard (1987). "The design of work teams." In Jay Lorsch (ed.). *Handbook of Organizational Behavior*: 315–342. Englewood Cliffs, NJ: Prentice-Hall.

Hackman, J. Richard (ed.) (1990). *Groups That Work (and Those That Don't)*. San Francisco: Jossey-Bass.

Hedberg, Bo L. T., Paul C. Nystrom, and William H. Starbuck (1976). "Camping on seesaws: Prescriptions for a self-designing organization." *Administrative Science Quarterly*, 21: 41 65.

Homans, George C. (1950). *The Human Group*. New York: Harcourt.

Hutchins, Edwin (1990). "The technology of team navigation." In Jolene Galegher, Robert E. Kraut, and Carmen Egido (eds.), *Intellectual Teamwork*: 191–220. Hillsdale. NJ: Erlbaum.

Hutchins, Edwin (1991). "The social organization of distributed cognition." In Lauren B. Resnick, John M. Levine, and Stephanie D. Teasley (eds.). *Perspectives on Socially Shared Cognition*: 283–307. Washington. DC: American Psychological Association.

Janis, Irving (1982). *Groupthink*, 2nd ed. Boston: Houghton-Mifflin.

Langer, Eleanor J. (1989). "Minding matters: The consequences of mindlessness-mindfulness." In Leonard Berkowitz (ed.), *Advances in Experimental Social Psychology*, 22: 137–173. New York: Academic Press.

LaPorte, Todd R., and Paula M. Consolini (1991). "Working in practice but not in theory: Theoretical challenges of high-reliability organizations." *Journal of Public Administration Research and Theory*, 1: 19–47.

Lave, Jean, and Etienne Wenger (1991). *Situated Learning: Legitimate Peripheral Participation*. New York: Cambridge University Press.

Lyons, William (1980). *Gilbert Ryle: An Introduction to His Philosophy*. Atlantic Highlands, NJ: Humanities Press.

McGrath, Joseph E. (1984). *Groups: Interaction and Performance*. Englewood Cliffs, NJ: Prentice-Hall.

McGrath, Joseph E. (1990). "Time matters in groups." In Jolene Galegher, Robert E. Kraut, and Carmen Egido (eds.), *Intellectual Teamwork*: 23–61. Hillsdale, NJ: Erlbaum.

Mead, George Herbert (1934). *Mind, Self, and Society*. Chicago: University of Chicago Press.

Morgan, Gareth (1986). *Images of Organization*. Beverly Hills, CA: Sage.

Orlady, Harry W., and H. Clayton Foushee (1987). *Cockpit Resource Management Training*. Springfield, VA: National Technical Information Service (N87-22634).

Orr, Julian E. (1990). "Sharing knowledge, celebrating identity: Community memory in a service culture." In David Middleton and Derek Edwards (eds.), *Collective Remembering*: 169–

189. Newbury Park, CA: Sage.

Perrow, Charles (1981). "The President's Commission and the normal accident." In D. Sills, C. Wolf, and V. Shelanski (eds.), *The Accident at Three Mile Island: The Human Dimensions*: 173–184. Boulder, CO: Westview Press.

Perrow, Charles (1984). *Normal Accidents*. New York: Basic Books.

Peters, Tom (1992). *Liberation Management*. New York: Knopf.

Porac, Joseph F., Howard Thomas, and Charles Baden-Fuller (1989). "Competitive groups as cognitive communities: The case of Scottish knitwear manufacturers." *Journal of Management Studies, 26*: 397–416.

Powell, Walter W. (1990). "Neither market nor hierarchy: Network forms of organization." In Barry M. Staw and Larry L. Cummings (eds.), *Research in Organizational Behavior, 12*: 295–336. Greenwich, CT: JAI Press.

Quinlan, Phillip (1991). *Connectionism and Psychology*. Chicago: University of Chicago Press.

Roberts, Karlene H., Denise M. Rousseau, and Todd R. LaPorte (1993). "The culture of high reliability: Quantitative and qualitative assessment aboard nuclear powered aircraft carriers." *Journal of High Technology Management Research, 5*(1): 141–161.

Roberts, Karlene H., Susan Stout, and Jennifer J. Halpern (1993). "Decision dynamics in two high reliability military organizations." *Management Science, 40*(5): 614–624.

Rochlin, Gene (1989). "Organizational self-design is a crisis-avoidance strategy: U.S. naval flight operations as a case study." *Industrial Crisis Quarterly, 3*: 159–176.

Rochlin, Gene I., Todd R. LaPorte and Karlene H. Roberts (1987). "The self-designing high-reliability organization: Aircraft carrier flight operations at sea." *Naval War College Review, 40*(4): 76–90.

Rumelhart, David E. (1992). "Towards a microstructural account of human reasoning." In Steven Davis (ed.), *Connectionism: Theory and Practice*: 69–83. New York: Oxford University Press.

Ryle, Gilbert (1949). *The Concept of Mind*. Chicago: University of Chicago Press.

Sandelands, Lloyd E., and Ralph E. Stablein (1987). "The concept of organization mind." In Samuel Bacharach and Nancy DiTomaso (eds.), *Research in the Sociology of Organizations, 5*: 135–161. Greenwich, CT: JAI Press.

Schneider, David J. (1991). "Social cognition." In Lyman W. Porter and Mark R. Rosenzweig (eds.), *Annual Review of Psychology, 42*: 527–561. Palo Alto, CA: Annual Reviews.

Schneider, W., and R. M. Shiffrin (1977). "Controlled and automatic human information processing: I. Detection, search and attention." *Psychological Review, 84*: 1–66.

Schutz, William C. (1958). *FIRO: A Three-Dimensional Theory of Interpersonal Behavior*. New York: Holt, Rinehart, and Winston.

Sitkin, Sim (1992). "Learning through failure: The strategy of small losses." In Barry Staw and Larry Cummings (eds.). *Research in Organizational Behavior, 14*: 231–266. Greenwich, CT: JAI Press.

Starbuck, William H., and Francis J. Milliken (1988). "Challenger: Fine-tuning the odds until something breaks." *Journal of Management Studies, 25*: 319–340.

Sutton, Robert I., and Meryl R. Louis (1987). "How selecting and socializing newcomers influences insiders." *Human Resource Management, 26*: 347–361.

Thompson, James D., and Arthur Tuden (1959). "Strategies, structures, and processes of organizational decision." In James D. Thompson (ed.), *Comparative Studies in Organization*: 195–216. Pittsburgh: University of Pittsburgh Press.

Tuckman, Bruce W. (1965). "Developmental sequence in small groups." *Psychological Bulletin, 63*: 384–399.

U.S. General Accounting Office (1991). *Management Practices: U.S. Companies Improve Perform-ance through Quality Efforts*. Document GAO/NSIAD-91-190. Washington, DC: U.S. Government Printing Office.

Van Maanen, John (1976). "Breaking in: Socialization to work." In Robert Dubin (ed.). *Handbook of Work, Organization and Society*: 67–130. Chicago: Rand McNally.

Walsh, James P., and Gerardo R. Ungson (1991). "Organizational memory." *Academy of Management Review*, 16: 57–91.

Wegner, Daniel M. (1987). "Transactive memory: A contemporary analysis of the group mind." In Brian Mullen and George R. Goethals (eds.), *Theories of Group Behavior*: 185–208. New York: Springer-Verlag.

Wegner, Daniel M., Ralph Erber, and Paula Raymond (1991). "Transactive memory in close relationships." *Journal of Personality and Social Psychology*, 61: 923–929.

Wegner, Daniel M., Toni Giuliano, and Paula T. Hertel (1985). "Cognitive interdependence in close relationships." In William J. Ickes (ed.), *Compatible and Incompatible Relationships*: 253–276. New York: Springer-Verlag.

Weick, Karl E. (1983). "Contradictions in a community of scholars: The cohesion-accuracy tradeoff." *Review of Higher Education*, 6(4): 253–267.

Weick, Karl E., and Larry Browning (1986). "Arguments and narration in organizational communication." *Journal of Management*, 12: 243–259.

Weick, Karl E., and David P. Gilfillan (1971). "Fate of arbitrary traditions in a laboratory microculture." *Journal of Personality and Social Psychology*, 17: 179–191.

Wilson, G. C. (1986). *Supercarrier*. New York: Macmillan.

12

Improvisation as a Mindset for Organizational Analysis

The emphasis in organizational theory on order and control often handicaps theorists when they want to understand the processes of creativity and innovation. Symptoms of the handicap are discussions of innovation that include the undifferentiated use of concepts like flexibility, risk, and novelty; forced either-or distinctions between exploration and exploitation; focus on activities such as planning, visioning, and strategizing as sites where improvements are converted into intentions that await implementation; and reliance on routine, reliability, repetition, automatic processing, and memory as the glue that holds organization in place. Since the term "organization" itself denotes orderly arrangements for cooperation, it is not surprising that mechanisms for rearranging these orders in the interest of adaptation, have not been developed as fully. (See Eisenberg (1990) for an important exception.) That liability can be corrected if we learn how to talk about the process of improvisation.

Thus, the purpose of this essay is to improve the way we talk about organizational improvisation, using the vehicle of jazz improvisation as the source of orienting ideas. I start with two brief descriptions of the complexity involved when musicians compose in the moment. Then I review several definitions intended to capture holistically what is happening when people improvise. Next, I take a closer look at selected details in improvisation, namely, degrees of improvisation, forms for improvisation, and cognition in improvisation. These understandings are then generalized from jazz to other settings such as conversation, therapy, and relationships of command. I conclude with implications for theory and practice.

Descriptions of Jazz Improvisation

Here are two accounts of what happens when order and control are breached extemporaneously in jazz performances, and a new order created.

The sense of exhilaration that characterizes the artist's experiences under such circumstances is heightened for jazz musicians as storytellers by the activity's physical, intellectual, and emotional exertion and by the intensity of struggling with creative processes under the pressure of a steady beat. From the outset of each performance, improvisers enter an artificial world of time in which reactions to the unfolding events of their tales must be immediate. Furthermore, the consequences of their actions are irreversible. Amid the dynamic display of imagined fleeting images and impulses – entrancing sounds and vibrant feelings, dancing shapes and kinetic gestures, theoretical symbols and perceptive commentaries – improvisers extend the logic of previous phrases, as ever-emerging figures on the periphery of their vision encroach upon and supplant those in performance. Soloists reflect on past events with breathtaking speed, while constantly pushing forward to explore the implications of new outgrowths of ideas that demand their attention. Ultimately, to journey over musical avenues of one's own design, thinking in motion and creating art on the edge of certainty and surprise, is to be "very alive, absolutely caught up in the moment." (Berliner 1994, p. 220)

While they are performing their ideas, artists must learn to juggle short- and intermediate-range goals simultaneously. To lead an improvised melodic line back to its initial pitch requires the ability to hold a layered image of the pitch in mind and hand while, at the same time, selecting and performing other pitches. The requirements of this combined mental and physical feat become all the more taxing if, after improvising an extended phrase, soloists decide to manipulate more complex material, developing, perhaps, its middle segment as a theme. In all such cases, they must not only rely on their memory of its contour, but their muscular memory must be flexible enough to locate the segment's precise finger pattern instantly within their motor model of the phrase. (Berliner 1994, p 200)

Attempts to capture definitionally what is common among these examples have taken a variety of forms.

The word improvisation itself is rooted in the word "proviso" which means to make a stipulation beforehand, to provide for something in advance, or to do something that is premeditated. By adding the prefix "im" to the word proviso, as when the prefix "im" is added to the word mobile to create immobile, improvise means the *opposite* of proviso. Thus improvisation deals with the unforeseen, it works without a prior stipulation, it works with the unexpected. As Tyler and Tyler (1990) put it, improvisation is about the un-for-seen and unprovided-for which means it "is the negation of foresight, of planned-for, of doing provided for by knowing, and of the control of the past over the present and future" (p. x).

Some descriptions of improvisation, often those associated with jazz, describe this lack of prior stipulation and lack of planning as composing extemporaneously, producing something on the spur of the moment. Thus, we have Schuller's (1968, p. 378) influential definition that jazz involves "playing extemporaneously, i.e., without the benefit of written music ... (C)omposing on the spur of the moment." Schön describes this extemporaneous composing in more detail as "on-the-spot surfacing, criticizing, restructuring, and testing of intuitive understandings of experienced phenomena" while the ongoing action can still make a difference (1987, pp. 26–27).

I have found it hard to improve on the following definition, which is the one that guides this chapter: "Improvisation involves reworking precomposed material and designs in relation to unanticipated ideas conceived, shaped, and transformed under the special conditions of performance, thereby adding unique features to every creation" (Berliner 1994, p. 241).

It is also possible to highlight definitionally, subthemes in improvisation. Thus, one can focus on order and describe improvisation as "flexible treatment of preplanned material" (Berliner 1994, p. 400). Or one can focus on the extemporaneous quality of the activity and describe improvisation as "intuition guiding action in a spontaneous way" (Crossan and Sorrenti 1996, p. 1) where intuition is viewed as rapid processing of experienced information (p. 14). Attempts to situate improvisation in organization lead to definitions such as the Miner et al. (1996) suggestion that improvisation consists of deliberately chosen activities that are spontaneous, novel, and involve the creation of something while it is being performed (pp. 3–4).

While it is tempting to adopt these compressed themes in the interest of economy, we may be better served as theorists if we retain the larger and more complex set of options and see which subsets are most useful to explain which outcroppings. For example, spontaneity and intuition are important dimensions of improvisation. Yet, in a rare outspoken passage, Berliner argues as follows.

> [T]he popular definitions of improvisation that emphasize only its spontaneous, intuitive nature – characterizing it as the 'making of something out of nothing' – are astonishingly incomplete. This simplistic understanding of improvisation belies the discipline and experience on which improvisers depend, and it obscures the actual practices and processes that engage them. Improvisation depends, in fact, on thinkers having absorbed a broad base of musical knowledge, including myriad conventions that contribute to formulating ideas logically, cogently, and expressively. It is not surprising, therefore, that improvisers use metaphors of language in discussing their art form. The same complex mix of elements and processes coexists for improvisers as for skilled language practitioners; the learning, the absorption, and utilization of linguistic conventions conspire in the mind of the writer or utilization of linguistic conventions conspire in the mind of the writer or speaker – or, in the case of jazz improvisation, the player – to create a living work. (Berliner 1994, p. 492)

What Berliner makes clear is that the compression of experience into the single word "intuition" desperately needs to be unpacked because it is the very nature of this process that makes improvisation possible and separates good from bad improvisation.

Similarly, Berliner is worried lest, in our fascination with the label "spontaneous," we overlook the major investment in practice, listening, and study that precedes a stunning performance. A jazz musician is more accurately described as a highly disciplined "practicer" (Berliner 1994, p. 494) than as a practitioner.

Reminders that we should take little for granted in initial studies of improvisation seem best conveyed by more complex definitions that spell out what might be taken for granted. In the following section, I will suggest three properties of improvisation that may be especially sensitive to changes in other organizational variables. The implied logic is that changes in these variables affect the adequacy of improvisation which in turn affects adaptation, learning, and renewal.

Degrees of Improvisation

To understand improvisation more fully, we first need to see that it lies on a continuum that ranges from "interpretation," through "embellishment" and "variation" ending in "improvisation" (Lee Konitz cited in Berliner 1994, pp. 66–71). The progression implied is one of increased demands on imagination and concentration. "Interpretation" occurs when people take minor liberties with a melody as when they choose novel accents or dynamics while performing it basically as written. "Embellishment" involves greater use of imagination, this time with whole phrases in the original being anticipated or delayed beyond their usual placements. The melody is rephrased but recognizable. "Variation" occurs when clusters of notes not in the original melody are inserted, but their relationship to that original melody is made clear. "Improvisation" on a melody means "transforming the melody into patterns bearing little or no resemblance to the original model or using models altogether alternative to the melody as the basis for inventing new phrases" (Berliner 1994, p. 70). When musicians improvise, they "radically alter portions of the melody or replace its segments with new creations bearing little, if any, relationship to the melody's shape" (Berliner 1994, p. 77). To improvise, therefore, is to engage in more than paraphrase or ornamentation or modification.

With these gradations in mind it is instructive to re-examine existing examples of improvisation to see whether they consist of radical alterations, and new creations. Miner et al. (1996, pp. 9–4) describe several instances of organizational improvisation and the verbs they use suggest that their examples fit all four points on the continuum. Thus, they describe improvisations during new product development that consists of a "shift" in a light assembly (interpretation); a "switch" in a product definition or "adding" a light beam source (embellishment); "altering" the content of a prior routine or "revising" a test schedule (variation); and "creating" an internal focus group or "discovering" a way to do a 22-second information search in 2 seconds (improvisation). If my attempt to assign the Miner et al. (1996) verbs to Konitz's four categories is plausible, then it suggests several things. First, activities that alter, revise, create, and discover are purer instances of improvisation than are activities that shift, switch, or add. Second, activities toward the "interpretation" end of the continuum are more dependent on the models they start with than are activities toward the improvisation end. As dependency on initial models increases, adaptation to more radical environmental change should decrease. Third, as modifications become more like improvisations and less like interpretations, their content is more heavily influenced by past experience, dispositions, and local conditions. When people increasingly forego guidance from a common melody, they resort to more idiosyncratic guidance. It is here where differentials in prior experience, practice, and knowledge are most visible and have the most effect. Fourth, the stipulation that people deliberately act extempore should be easier to execute if they stick closer to a guideline than if they depart radically from it. Thus, interpretation and embellishment should be initiated more quickly under time pressure than is true for variation and improvisation. Deliberate injunctions to be radically different may falter if they fail to specify precisely what the original model is, in what sense it is to remain a constraint, and which of its properties are constants and which are variables. These questions don't arise in the three approximations to improvisation represented by interpretation, embellishment, and variation. The point is, deliberate improvisation is much tougher, much more time consuming, and places higher demands on resources, than does deliberate interpretation. If deliberateness is a key requirement for something to qualify as organizational improvisation, and if we construe improvisation in the sense used by Konitz, then full-scale improvisation should be rare in time-pressured settings. But, if it could be accomplished despite these hurdles, then it should be a substantial, sustainable, competitive advantage.

Fifth, and finally, any one activity may contain all four gradations, as sometimes happens in jazz.

> Over a solo's course, players typically deal with the entire spectrum of possibilities embodied by these separable but related applications of improvisation. At one moment, soloists may play radical, precomposed variations on a composition's melody as rehearsed and memorized before the event. The very next moment, they may spontaneously be embellishing the melody's shape, or inventing a new melodic phrase. There is a perpetual cycle between improvised and precomposed components of the artists knowledge as it pertains to the entire body of construction materials. . . . The proportion of precomposition to improvising is likewise subject to continual change throughout a performance. (Berliner 1994, p. 222)

Re-examination of the Miner et al. (1996) examples suggests that some involve the entire spectrum of improvisation and others do not. For example, when design engineers tackled the problem of flawed filters at Fast Track, they improvised a new feature, reworked the assemblies, shifted how lights were to stand, changed the formal technical features, and added a light beam source. The intriguing possibility is that full spectrum improvisation like this has different properties than simple stand-alone improvisation. Full spectrum improvisation makes fuller use of memory and past experience, can build on the competencies of a more diverse population, is more focused by a melody, and may be more coherent. If this is plausible then it should be more persuasive, diffuse faster, and be more acceptable since a greater variety of people within the firm can understand how it has developed. Furthermore, they are able to recognize some of its pre-existing components. It is also possible that the smooth versus sudden changes celebrated by those who invoke the concept of punctuated equilibrium are simply manifestations of full spectrum (smooth) or solitary (sudden) improvisation.

The point of all this is that we may want to be stingy in our use of the label improvisation and generous in our use of other labels that suggest approximations to improvisation. When we focus on approximations, we focus both on connections to the past and on the original model that is being embellished. The spectrum from interpretation to improvisation mirrors the spectrum from incremental to transformational change. It becomes less common in organizations than we anticipated, but its antecedents become clearer as do its connections with themes of order and control.

Forms of Improvisation

These connected themes of order and improvisation become even clearer when we look more closely at the object to which the process of improvisation is applied. As bassist-composer, Charles Mingus, insisted, "you can't improvise on nothing; you've gotta improvise on something" (Kernfeld 1995, p. 119). This is the same Mingus who once actually reduced a promising young saxophonist to tears before an audience, with his running commentary of "Play something different, man; play something different. This is jazz, man. You played that last night and the night before" (Berliner 1994, p. 271). The ongoing tension to "improvise on something" but to keep the improvisations fresh is the essence of jazz. That tension may be weaker in non-musical organizations where routine embellishment of routines is sufficient and expected and where surprise is unwelcome. But, whether embellishment is major or minor, improvisation involves the embellishment of something.

In jazz, that "something" usually is a melody such as originated in African-American blues and gospel songs, popular songs, ragtime piano and brass-band marches, Latin American dances, or rock and soul music (Kernfeld 1995, p. 40). What is common to these melodies is form imposed by a sequence of harmonic chords and a scheme of rhythm. Other objects available for embellishment that are more common to organizations range from routines and strategic intent (Perry 1991), to a set of core values, a credo, a mission statement, rules of engagement, or basic know-how. Gilbert Ryle (1979) argued that virtually all behavior has an ad hoc adroitness akin to improvisation because it mixes together a partly fresh contingency with general lessons previously learned. Ryle describes this mixture as paying heed. Improvisation enters in the following way.

> (T)o be thinking what he is here and now up against, he must both be trying to adjust himself to just this present once-only situation *and* in doing this to be applying lessons already learned. There must be in his response a union of some Ad Hockery with some know-how. If he is not at once *improvising* and improvising *warily*, he is not engaging his somewhat trained wits in a partly fresh situation. It is the pitting of an acquired competence or skill against unprogrammed opportunity, obstacle or hazard. It is a bit like putting some *new* wine into *old* bottles. (Ryle 1979, p. 129)

Thus, improvisation shares an important property with phenomena encompassed by chaos theory (e.g., McDaniel 1996, Stacey 1992), namely, origins are crucial small forms that can have large consequences [e.g., cracks in shoulder bones determine hunting success among Naskapi Indians (Weick 1979, pp. 262–263.)] Melodies vary in the ease with which they evoke prior experience and trigger generative embellishments. Some melodies set up a greater number of interesting possibilities than do other melodies. The same holds true for organizational "melodies" such as mission statements, which range from the banal to the ingenious and invite well-practiced or novel actions on their behalf.

While improvisation is affected by one's associates, past experiences, and current setting, it is also determined by the kernel that provides the pretext for assembling these elements in the first place. These pretexts are not neutral. They encourage some lines of development and exclude other ones. And this holds true regardless of the improviser. While it is true that a masterful musician like tenor saxophonist, Sonny Rollins, can find incredible richness in mundane melodies such as "Tennessee Waltz" and "Home on the Range," it is equally true that these melodies themselves unfold with unusual progressions relative to the standard jazz repertory (e.g., "I Got Rhythm"). It is the capability of these progressions to challenge and evoke, as well as the competence of the performer, that contribute to improvisation. It is easy to overlook the substantive contribution of a melody because it is so small and simple. It's important to remember that a melody is also an early and continuing influence.

The important point is that improvisation does not materialize out of thin air. Instead, it materializes around a simple melody that provides the pretext for real-time composing. Some of that composing is built from precomposed phrases that become meaningful retrospectively as embellishments of that melody. And some comes from elaboration of the embellishments themselves. The use of precomposed fragments in the emerging composition is an example of Ryle's (1979) "wary improvisation" anchored in past experience. The further elaboration of these emerging embellishments is an example of Ryle's opportunistic improvisation in which one's wits engage a fresh, once-only situation. Considered as a noun, an improvisation is a transformation of some original model. Considered as a verb, improvisation is composing in real time that begins with embellishments of a simple model, but increasingly feeds on these embellishments themselves to move farther from the original melody and closer to a new composition. Whether treated as a noun or a verb, improvisation is guided activity whose guidance comes from elapsed patterns discovered retrospectively. Retrospect may range back as far as solos heard long before or back only as far as notes played just this moment. Wherever the notes come from, their value is determined by the pattern they make *relative to* a continuing set of constraints formed by melody. The trick in improvisation is, as Paul Desmond put it, to aim for "clarity, emotional communication on a not-too-obvious level, form in a chorus that doesn't hit you over the head but is there if you look for it, humor, and construction that sounds logical in an unexpected way" (Gioia 1988, p. 89).

Cognition in Improvisation

As this more detailed picture of improvisation begins to emerge, there is a recurring implication that retrospect is significant in its production. In jazz improvisation people act in order to think, which imparts a flavor of retrospective sensemaking to improvisation. Ted Gioia puts it this way: unlike an architect who works from plans and looks ahead, a jazz musician cannot "look ahead at what he is going to play, but he can look behind at what he has just played; thus each new musical phrase can be shaped with relation to what has gone before. He creates his form retrospectively" (Gioia 1988, p. 61). The jazz musician, who creates form retrospectively, builds something that is recognizable from whatever is at hand, contributes to an emerging structure being built by the group in which he or she is playing, and creates possibilities for the other players. Gioia's description suggests that intention is loosely coupled to execution, that creation and interpretation need not be separated in time, and that sensemaking rather than decision making is embodied in improvisation. All three of these byproducts of retrospect create a different understanding of organized action than the one we are more accustomed to where we commonly look for the implementation of intentions, the interpretation of prior creations, and for decisions that presume prior sensemaking.

When musicians describe their craft, the importance of retrospect becomes clear, as these excerpts make clear.

> After you initiate the solo, one phrase determines what the next is going to be. From the first note that you hear, you are responding to what you've just played: you just said this on your instrument, and now that's a constant. What follows from that? And then the next phrase is a constant. What follows from that? And so on and so forth. And finally, let's wrap it up so that everybody understands that that's what you're doing. It's like language: you're talking, you're speaking, you're responding to yourself. When I play, it's like having a conversation with myself. (Max Roach cited in Berliner 1994, p. 192)

> If you're not affected and influenced by your own notes when you improvise, then you're missing the whole essential point. (Lee Konitz cited in Berliner 1994, p. 193)

> When I start off, I don't know what the punch line is going to be. (Buster Williams cited in Berliner 1994, p. 218)

The importance of retrospect for improvisation imposes new demands that suggest why organizational improvisation may be rare. To add to a store of ironies that are beginning to accumulate, not only is improvisation grounded in forms, but it is also grounded in memory. Forms and memory and practice are all key determinants of success in improvisation that are easy to miss if analysts become preoccupied with spontaneous composition. Implied in each musician's account is the relationship that "the larger and more complex the musical ideas artists initially conceive, the greater the power of musical memory and mental agility required to transform it" (Berliner 1994, p. 194).

To improve improvisation is to improve memory, whether it be organizational (Walsh and Ungson 1991), small group (Wegner 1987), or individual (Neisser and Winograd 1988). To improve memory is to gain retrospective access to a greater range of resources. Also implied here is the importance of listening *to oneself* as well as to other people. Prescriptions in organizational studies tout the importance of listening to others (e.g., the big news at GE is that Jack Welch discovered ears) but miss the fact that good improvisation also requires listening to one's own comments and building on them.

The reader is referred back to the description of composing in the moment on p. 285 that starts "while they are performing," to see again how important memory is to improvisation. This importance is reflected in formal jazz study.

> In one class, a teacher arbitrarily stopped the solos of students and requested that they perform their last phrase again. When they could not manage this, he chastised them

for being "like people who don't listen to themselves while they speak." Aspiring impro-visers must cultivate impressive musical recall in both aural and physical terms if they are to incorporate within their ongoing conversation new ideas conceived in perform-ance. (Berliner 1994, p. 200)

Viewed through the lens of retrospect, jazz looks like this.

The artist can start his work with almost random maneuver – a brush stroke on a canvas, an opening line, a musical motif – and then adapt his later moves to this initial gambit. A jazz improviser, for example, might begin his solo with a descending five-note phrase and then see, as he proceeds, that he can use this same five-note phrase in other contexts in the course of his improvisation.

This is, in fact, what happens in Charlie Parker's much analyzed improvisation on Gershwin's "Embraceable You." Parker begins with a five-note phrase (melodically simi-lar to "you must remember this" phrase in the song "As Time Goes By") which he employs in a variety of ingenious contexts throughout the course of his improvisation. Parker obviously created his solo on the spot (only a few minutes later he recorded a second take with a completely different solo, almost as brilliant as the first), yet this should not lead us to make the foolish claim that his improvisation is formless. (Gioia 1988, p. 60)

Viewed through the lens of retrospect, larger issues look like this. If events are im-provised and intention is loosely coupled to execution, the musician has little choice but to wade in and see what happens. What will actually happen won't be known until it is too late to do anything directly about it. All the person can do is justify and make sensible, after the fact, whatever is visible in hindsight. Since that residue is irrevoca-ble, and since all of this sensemaking activity occurs in public, and since the person has a continuing choice as to what to do with that residual, this entire scenario seems to contain a microcosm of the committing forces that affect creative coping with the human condition (Weick 1989). Small wonder that Norman Mailer, in his famous essay "The White Negro," described jazz as "American existentialism."

This simple exposition of degrees of improvisation, forms for improvisation, and cognition in improvisation does not begin to exhaust the dimensions of jazz improvi-sation that are relevant for organizational theory. Other potential themes of interest might include the ways in which "mistakes" provide the platform for musical "saves" that create innovations (e.g., Berliner 1994, p. 191, 209, 210–216; Weick, 1995); skills of bricolage that enable people to make do with whatever resources are at hand (Harper 1987, Levi-Strauss 1966, Weick 1993); and social conventions that comple-ment structures imposed by tunes (Bastien and Hostager, 1992).

Non-jazz Settings for Improvisation

What I have tried to show so far is that descriptions of composing on the spur of the moment, and attempts to portray this process definitionally and dimensionally, com-prise a language that allows analysts to maintain the images of order and control that are central to organizational theory and simultaneously introduce images of innovation and autonomy. The ease with which improvisation mixes together these disparate images of control and innovation (Nemeth and Staw 1989) becomes even clearer if we look at other settings where improvisation seems to occur.

A swift way to see the potential richness of improvisation as a metaphor is simply to look in the index of Berliner's (1994) authoritative volume under the heading, "Metaphors for aspects of improvisation" (p. 869). In his analyses Berliner finds that jazz improvisation is likened to cuisine, dance, foundation building, a game of chess, a journey, landing an airplane, language, love, marriage, preparing for acting, painting, singing, sports, and acting like a tape recorder (some drummers "are like tape recorders. You play something and then they imitate it"; p. 427). By a process of backward diagnosis, we therefore expect to find improvisation where people cook, move, construct, compete, travel, etc.

Perhaps the setting that most resembles jazz improvisation, at least judging from its frequency of mention, is language acquisition and use (e.g., Ramos 1978, Suhor 1986). Jazz musician Stan Getz describes improvisation as a way of conversing.

> It's like a language. You learn the alphabet, which are the scales. You learn sentences, which are the chords. And then you talk extemporaneously with the horn. It's a wonderful thing to speak extemporaneously, which is something I've never gotten the hang of. But musically I love to talk just off the top of my head. And that's what jazz music is all about. (Maggin 1996, p. 21)

An example of the easy movement that is possible between the two domains is Berliner's equating of improvisation with rethinking.

> The activity [of jazz improvisation] is much like creative thinking in language, in which the routine process is largely devoted to rethinking. By ruminating over formerly held ideas, isolating particular aspects, examining their relationships to the features of other ideas, and, perhaps, struggling to extend ideas in modest steps and refine them, thinkers typically have the sense of delving more deeply into the possibilities of their ideas. There are, of course, also the rarer moments when they experience discoveries as unexpected flashes of insight and revelation.

> Similarly, a soloist's most salient experiences in the heat of performance involve poetic leaps of imagination to phrases that are unrelated, or only minimally related, to the storehouse, as when the identities of formerly mastered patterns melt away entirely within new recombinant shapes. (Berliner 1994, pp. 216–217)

Discussions of improvisation in groups are built on images of call and response, give and take (Wilson 1992), transitions, exchange, complementing, negotiating a shared sense of the beat (see Barrett's (1998) discussion of groove), offering harmonic possibilities to someone else, preserving continuity of mood, and cross-fertilization. In jazz, as in conversation, self-absorption is a problem. Wynton Marsalis observed that in playing, as in conversation, the worst people to talk to and play with are those who, "when you're talking, they're thinking about what they are going to tell you next, instead of listening to what you're saying" (Berliner 1994, p. 401). What is also striking about jazz conversation, as with conversations in other settings, is the many levels at which they function simultaneously. Thus, jazz improvisation involves conversation between an emerging pattern and such things as formal features of the underlying composition, previous interpretations, the player's own logic, responsiveness of the instrument, other musicians, and the audience.

Managerial activities, which are dominated by language and conversation, often become synonymous with improvisation. Thus, we find Mangham and Pye (1991) proposing close parallels between improvisation and organizing. Here is what they observe in top management teams.

> Our respondents assert that they learn what they are about in talking to and trusting their colleagues, that they often recognize and develop their own views in the very process of seeking consensus, that talking to others heightens their awareness, sharpens their focus. But they also assert that they are in command, that they do plan and shape the future with clear intent, that they know where it is they are heading. (p. 77)

Like jazz musicians, managers simultaneously discover targets and aim at them, create rules and follow rules, and engage in directed activity often by being clearer about which directions are not right than about specified final results. Their activity is controlled but not predetermined (Mangham and Pye 1991, p. 79).

Here is how Mangham and Pye make sense of what they observe.

> What we are proposing is that in their daily interactions our managers, no less than managers elsewhere, sustain appreciative systems or improvise readinesses which reflect their values and beliefs which, in turn, are likely to be influenced by and to influence received ideas about the doing of organizing. We hold that much of the doing of organizing is either a matter of running through a script or an instance of improvisation, and that both of these activities relate to readings which have reference to appreciative systems which are, in turn, reflections of deeply held beliefs and values. (Mangham and Pye 1991, p. 36)

What Mangham and Pye (1991) make clear is that managing shares with jazz improvisation such features as simultaneous reflection and action (p. 79), simultaneous rule creation and rule following (p. 78), patterns of mutually expected responses akin to musicians moving through a melody together (p. 45), action informed by melodies in the form of codes (p. 40), continuous mixing of the expected with the novel (p. 24), and the feature of a heavy reliance on intuitive grasp and imagination (p. 18). These managers are not just Herbert Simon's (1989) chess grandmasters who solve problems by recognizing patterns. And neither are jazz musicians. They are that, but more. The more is that they are also able to use their experience of "having been there" to recognize "that one is now somewhere else, and that that 'somewhere else' is novel and may be valuable, notwithstanding the 'rules' which declare that one cannot get here from there" (Mangham and Pye 1991, p. 83).

Daft and Weick (1984) suggest that when managers deem an environment to be unanalyzable, they seek information by means of strategies that are "more personal, less linear, more ad hoc and improvisational" (p. 287). Sutcliffe and Sitkin (1996) have argued that total quality interventions basically involve what they call a "redistribution of improvisation rights." [See also Wruck and Jensen (1994, p. 264) on allocation of decision rights to initiation, ratification, implementation, and monitoring.] Successful quality management occurs when people are newly authorized to paraphrase, embellish, and reassemble their prevailing routines, extemporaneously. Furthermore, they are encouraged to think while doing rather than be guided solely by plans. Thus, when a firm "disseminates improvisation rights" it tends to encourage the "flexible treatment of preplanned material," which means that quality improvement and jazz improvisation are closely aligned.

Improvisation is common in public-sector organizations and occurs often on the front-line, as Weiss (1980, p. 401) suggests.

> Many moves are improvisations. Faced with an event that calls for response, officials use their experience, judgment, and intuition to fashion the response for the issue at hand. That response becomes a precedent, and when similar questions come up, the response is uncritically repeated. Consider the federal agency that receives a call from a local program asking how to deal with requests for enrollment in excess of the available number of slots. A staff member responds with off-the-cuff advice. Within the next few weeks, programs in three more cities call with similar questions, and staff repeat the advice. Soon what began as improvisation has hardened into policy. (p. 401)

Improvisation also occurs in settings as disparate as psychotherapy, medical diagnosis, and combat.

Improvisation is the heart of psychotherapy. Thus, it is not surprising to find that one of the most prominent and original jazz pianists, Denny Zeitlin, is also a practicing psychiatrist who sees patients approximately 30 hours per week (Herrington 1989). Keeney (1990, p. 1) describes the parallels between therapy and improvisation.

> Given the unpredictable nature of a client's communication, the therapist's participation in the theatrics of a session becomes an invitation to improvise. In other words, since the therapist never knows exactly what the client will say at any given moment, he or she cannot rely exclusively upon previously designed lines, pattern, or scripts. Although some orientations to therapy attempt to shape both the client and therapist into a predetermined form of conversation and story, every particular utterance in a session offers a unique opportunity for improvisation, invention, innovation, or more simply, change. (Keeney 1990, p. 1)

If therapy is viewed as improvisation, then therapies are viewed as songs. The song can be played exactly as scored or with improvisation, but one would not expect an improvisational therapist to play only one song over and over anymore than one would expect a jazz musician to play only one song throughout a lifetime.

Improvisation sometimes lies at the heart of medical diagnosis as well, but only when practitioners jettison narrow versions of decision rationality in favor of improvisation. Starbuck (1993) suggests that good doctors do not base their treatments on diagnosis. They leave diagnosis out of the chain between symptoms and treatment because it discards too much information and injects random errors. There are many more combinations of symptoms than there are diagnoses, just as there are many more treatments than diagnoses.

(T)he links between symptoms and treatments are not the most important keys to find-ing effective treatments. Good doctors pay careful attention to how patients respond to treatments. If a patient gets better, current treatments are heading in the right direction. But, current treatments often do not work, or they produce side-effects that require correction. The model of symptoms-diagnoses-treatments ignores the feedback loop from treatments to symptoms, whereas this feedback loop is the most important factor. (Starbuck 1993, p. 87)

The logic can be applied to academic research.

Academic research is trying to follow a model like that taught in medical schools. Scientists are translating data into theories, and promising to develop prescriptions from the theories. Data are like symptoms, theories like diagnoses, and prescriptions like treatments. Are not organizations as dynamic as human bodies and similarly complex? Theories do not capture all the information in data, and they do not determine prescrip-tions uniquely. Perhaps scientists could establish stronger links between data and pre-scriptions if they did not introduce theories between them. Indeed, should not data be results of prescriptions? Should not theories come from observing relations between prescriptions and subsequent data? (Starbuck 1993)

Starbuck reminds us that, when faced with incomprehensible events, there is often no substitute for acting your way into an eventual understanding of them. How can I know what I am treating until I see how it responds? To organize for diagnosis is to design a setting that generates rich records of symptoms, a plausible initial treatment, alertness to effects of treatments, and the capability to improvise from there on. Theories, diagnoses, strategies, and plans serve mostly as plausible interim stories that mix ignorance and knowledge in different patterns.

Isenberg (1985, pp. 178–179), following the work of Bursztjahn et al. (1981), has also discussed what he calls treating a patient empirically. Like Starbuck, he notes that a diagnosis, if it is inferred at all, occurs retrospectively after the patient is cured. Isenberg then generalizes this medical scenario to battlefield situations. This applica-tion fleshes out a much earlier statement by Janowitz (1959, p. 481) that a combat soldier is not a rule-following bureaucrat who is "detached, routinized, self-contained; rather his role is one of constant improvisation. . . . The impact of battle destroys men, equipment, and organization, which need constantly and continually to be brought back into some form of unity through on-the-spot improvisation." For Isenberg, the parallel between empirical medicine and empirical fighting is that in both cases

tactical maneuvers (treatment) will be undertaken with the primary purpose of learning more about (diagnosing) the enemy's position, weaponry, and strength, as well as one's own strength, mobility, and understanding of the battlefield situation. . . . Sometimes the officer will need to implement his or her solution with little or no problem definition and problem solving. Only after taking action and seeing the results will the officer be able to better define the problem that he or she may have already solved! (pp. 178–179)

The steady progression from jazz to other sites where improvisation is plausible culminates in the idea that living itself is an exercise in improvisation. People compose their lives, as Mary Catherine Bateson (1989) suggests in this composite description.

> I have been interested in the arts of improvisation, which involve recombining partly familiar materials in new ways, often in ways especially sensitive to context, interaction, and response. . . . (The idea of life as an improvisatory art) started from a disgruntled reflection on my own life as a sort of desperate improvisation in which I was constantly trying to make something coherent from conflicting elements to fit rapidly changing settings . . . Improvisation can be either a last resort or an established way of evoking creativity. Sometimes a pattern chosen by default can become a path of preference. . . . Much biography of exceptional people is built around the image of a quest, a journey through a timeless landscape toward an end that is specific, even though it is not fully known. . . . (These assumptions are increasingly inappropriate today because) fluidity and discontinuity are central to the reality in which we live. Women have always lived discontinuous and contingent lives, but men today are newly vulnerable, which turns women's traditional adaptations into a resource. . . . The physical rhythms of reproduction and maturation create sharper discontinuities in women's lives than in men's, the shifts of puberty and menopause, of pregnancy, birth, and lactation, the mirroring adaptations to the unfolding lives of children, their departures and returns, the ebb and flow of dependency, the birth of grandchildren, the probability of widowhood. As a result, the ability to shift from one preoccupation to another, to divide one's attention, to improvise in new circumstances, has always been important to women. (pp. 2, 3, 4, 5, 6, 13)

The newfound urgency in organizational studies to understand improvisation and learning is symptomatic of growing societal concerns about how to cope with discontinuity, multiple commitments, interruptions, and transient purposes that dissolve without warning. To understand more about improvisation undoubtedly will help us get a better grasp on innovation in organizations. That's important. But it is not nearly as important as is understanding how people in general "combine familiar and unfamiliar components in response to new situations, following an underlying grammar and an evolving aesthetic" (Bateson 1989, p. 3). To watch jazz improvisation unfold is to have palpable contact with the human condition. Awe, at such moments, is understandable.

Implications for Theory

While several implications for organizational theory have already been mentioned, I want to suggest some of the richness implicit in improvising by brief mention of its relation to postmodern organizational theory and to paradox.

The idea of improvisation is important for organizational theory because it gathers together compactly and vividly a set of explanations suggesting that to understand organization is to understand organizing or, as Whitehead (1929) put it, to understand "being" as constituted by its "becoming." This perspective, found in previous work by people such as Allport (1962), Buckley (1968), Follett (1924), Mangham and Pye (1991), Maruyama (1963), Mintzberg and McHugh (1985), and Weick (1969, 1979) has been newly repackaged as the "unique intellectual preoccupation of 'postmodern' organizational theorists" (Chia 1996. p. 44). Thus, we find people talking once more about the ontology of becoming, using images already familiar to process theorists and musicians alike, images such as emergence, fragments, micropractices that enact order, reaccomplishment, punctuation, recursion, reification, relations, transcience, flux, and "a sociology of verbs rather than a sociology of nouns" (Chia 1996, p. 49). If theorists take improvisation seriously, they may be able to give form to the idea of "becoming realism" (Chia 1996) and add to what we already know.

They may, for example, be able to do more with the simultaneous presence of seeming opposites in organizations than simply label them as paradoxes. There is currently an abundance of conceptual dichotomies that tempt analysts to choose between things like control and innovation, exploitation and exploration, routine and nonroutine, and automatic and controlled, when the issue in most organizations is one of proportion and simultaneity rather than choice. Improvisation is a mixture of the precomposed and the spontaneous, just as organizational action mixes together some proportion of control with innovation, exploitation with exploration, routine with nonroutine, automatic with controlled. The normally useful concepts of routine (Gersick and Hackman 1990, Cohen and Bacdayan 1994) and innovation (Amabile 1988, Dougherty 1992) have become less powerful as they have been stretched informally to include improvisation. Thus, a routine becomes something both repetitious and novel, and the same is true for innovation. A similar loss of precision [Reed (1991) refers to it as a "rout"] has occurred in the case of decision making where presumptions of classical rationality are increasingly altered to incorporate tendencies toward spontaneous revision. Neither decisions nor rationality can be recognized in the resulting hodgepodge. What is common among all of these instances of lost precision is that they attempt to acknowledge the existence of improvisation, but do so without giving up the prior commitment to stability and order in the form of habit, repetition, automatic thinking, rational constraints, formalization, culture, and standardization. The result, when theorists graft mechanisms for improvisation onto concepts that basically are built to explain order, is a caricature of improvisation that ignores nuances highlighted in previous sections. These caricatures leave out properties of organizational improvisation such as the tension involved in mixing the intended and the emergent and the strong temptation to simplify in favor of one or the other; the possibility that order can be accomplished by means of ongoing ambivalent mixtures of variation and retention that permit adaptation to dynamic situations; the chronic temptation to fall back on wellrehearsed fragments to cope with current problems even though these problems don't exactly match those present at the time of the earlier rehearsal; the use of emergent structures as sources for embellishment which enables quick distancing from previous solutions; the close resemblance between improvising and editing; the sensitivity of improvisation to originating conditions; and the extensive amount of practice necessary to pull off successful improvisation. The remedy would seem to lie in a variety of directions such as positing routines, innovation, and decision making as inputs to improvisation akin to melodies (e.g., people improvised on this routine); treating improvisation as a distinct form of each (e.g., this routine was executed improvisationally); treating each of the three as a distinct way to engage in organizational improvisation (e.g., routinizing of improvisation); and, treating improvisation as a stand-alone process like the other three consisting of a fixed sequence of conceiving, articulating, and remembering.

Implications for Practice

The concept of improvisation also engages several concepts in mainstream organizational practice and likewise suggests ways to strengthen them. For example, if time is a competitive advantage then people gain speed if they do more things spontaneously without lengthy prior planning exercises (Crossan and Sorrenti 1996, p. 4). To do more things spontaneously is to become more skilled at thinking on your feet, a skill that is central in improvisation even though it is not given much attention in accounts of managerial action. Improvisation has implications for staffing. Young musicians who are laden with technique often tend to be poor at improvisation because they lack voices, melodies, and feeling (Berliner 1994, p. 792, ftn. 17; Davis 1986, p. 87), which sounds a lot like the liability that corporations associate with newly minted MBAs. The remedy for students is to mix listening with history, practice, modeling, and learning the fundamentals, which can be tough if they are driven, instrumental, in a hurry, and have little sense of what they need to know. The irony is that it is this very haste which dooms them to be a minor player who sounds like every other technique-laden minor player, none of whom have much to say.

If we treat the preceding description of improvisation as if it contained the shell of a set of prescriptions for adaptive organizing, then here are some possible characteristics of groups with a high capability for improvisation:

1. Willingness to forego planning and rehearsing in favor of acting in real time;
2. Well-developed understanding of internal resources and the materials that are at hand;
3. Proficient without blueprints and diagnosis;
4. Able to identify or agree on minimal structures for embellishing;
5. Open to reassembly of and departures from routines;
6. Rich and meaningful set of themes, fragments, or phrases on which to draw for ongoing lines of action;
7. Predisposed to recognize partial relevance of previous experience to present novelty;
8. High confidence in skill to deal with nonroutine events;
9. Presence of associates similarly committed to and competent at impromptu making do;
10. Skillful at paying attention to performance of others and building on it in order to keep the interaction going and to set up interesting possibilities for one another.
11. Able to maintain the pace and tempo at which others are extemporizing;
12. Focused on coordination here and now and not distracted by memories or anticipation;
13. Preference for and comfort with process rather than structure, which makes

it easier to work with ongoing development, restructuring, and realization of outcomes, and easier to postpone the question, what will it have amounted to?

Limits to Improvisation

If theorists conceptualize organizations as sites where the activity of improvisation occurs, this may offset their tendency to dwell on themes of control, formalization, and routine. It may also help them differentiate the idea of "flexibility," which tends to be used as a catchall for the innovative remainder. Nevertheless, there are good reasons why the idea of improvisation may have limited relevance for organizations. If organizations change incrementally – punctuations of an equilibrium seldom materialize out of thin air without prior anticipations – then those incremental changes are more like interpretation and embellishment than variation or improvisation. Thus, even if organizations wanted to improvise, they would find it hard to do so, and probably unnecessary. Improvisation in one unit can also compound the problems faced by other units to which it is tightly coupled. Furthermore, bursts of improvisation can leave a firm with too many new products and processes to support (Miner et al. 1996, p. 26).

The intention of a jazz musician is to produce something that comes out *differently* than it did before, whereas organizations typically pride themselves on the opposite, namely, reliable performance that produces something that is standardized and comes out the same way it did before. It is hard to imagine the typical manager feeling "guilty" when he or she plays things worked out before. Yet most jazz musicians perform with the intention of "limiting the predictable use of formerly mastered vocabulary" (Berliner 1994, p. 268). Parenthetically, it is interesting to note that the faster the tempo at which a musician plays, the more likely he or she is to fall back on the predictable use of a formerly mastered vocabulary. It is difficult to be affected by one's own newly created notes when musical ideas have to be conceived and executed at 8½ eighth notes per second (tempo of one quarter note = 310). At extremely fast tempos there is no choice but to use preplanned, repetitive material to keep the performance going. This suggests that there are upper limits to improvisation. If this is true then high-velocity organizations (Eisenhardt 1989) – which resemble jazz ensembles in many ways – become especially interesting as sites where the increasing tempo of activity may encourage, not improvisation, but a sudden reversion back to old ideas that have no competitive edge. A key issue in high-velocity organizations is just how much of a constraint velocity really is. Recall that in the case of jazz improvisation, creative processes continually struggle under the unrelenting demands of a steady beat. In jazz improvisation, deadlines are reckoned in seconds and minutes whereas high-velocity organizations deal with deadlines reckoned in hours and days. While it is true that pressure is pressure, it is also true that at some speeds memory plays an increasingly large role in the product produced. This suggests that high-velocity organizations may have more latitude for improvisation than do jazz ensembles, but only up to a point. High-velocity organizations may be vulnerable in ways similar to those described by Starbuck and Milliken (1988) and

Miller (1993). Success encourages simplification, more risk taking, less slack, and accelerated production, all of which shrink the time available for adaptive improvisation and force people back on older ideas and away from the very innovating that made them successful in the first place.

Even if organizations are capable of improvisation, it is not clear they need to do it. One of the realities in jazz performance is that the typical audience is none the wiser if a musician makes a mistake and buries it, plays a memorized solo, solves a tough problem, inserts a clever reference to a predecessor, or is playing with a broken instrument and working around its limits. If composing in real time is difficult and risky, and if the customer is unable to appreciate risk taking anyway, then the only incentives to take those risks lie with one's own standards and with fellow musicians. Those incentives may be sufficient to hold sustained improvisation in place. However, most organizations may not reward originality under the assumption that customers don't either. If we add to these characteristics the fact that the musical consequences in a jazz performance are irreversible whereas managers try never to get into anything without a way out, and the fact that musicians love surprises but managers hate them, then we begin to see that improvisation may be absent from the organizational literature, not because we haven't looked for it, but because it isn't there.

My bet is that improvising is close to the root process in organizing and that organizing itself consists largely of the embellishment of small structures. Improvising may be a tacit, taken-for-granted quality in all organizing that we fail to see because we are distracted by more conspicuous artifacts such as structure, control, authority, planning, charters, and standard operating procedures. The process that animates these artifacts may well consist of ongoing efforts to rework and reenact them in relation to unanticipated ideas and conditions encountered in the moment. In organizing as in jazz, artifacts and fragments cohere because improvised storylines impose modest order among them in ways that accommodate to their peculiarities. Order through improvisation may benefit some organizations under some conditions and be a liability under other conditions. These contingencies need to be spelled out. But so too does the sense in which improvisation may be part of the infrastructure present in all organizing.

Conclusion

A final sense in which jazz improvisation mirrors life is captured in an entry from Norman Mailer's journal dated December 17, 1954 (source of this quotation is unknown).

> Jazz is easy to understand once one has the key, something which is constantly triumphing and failing. Particularly in modern jazz, one notices how Brubeck and Desmond, off entirely on their own with nothing but their nervous system to sustain them, wander through jungles of invention with society continually ambushing them. So the excitement comes not from victory but from the effort merely to keep musically alive. So, Brubeck, for example will to his horror discover that he has wandered into a musical cliché, and it is thrilling to see how he attempts to come out of it, how he takes the

cliché, plays with it, investigates it, pulls it apart, attempts to put it together into some-thing new and sometimes succeeds, and sometimes fails, and can only go on, having left his record of defeat at that particular moment. That is why modern jazz despite its apparent lyricalness is truly cold, cold like important conversations or Henry James. It is cold and it is nervous and it is under tension, just as in a lunch between an editor and an author, each makes mistakes and successes, and when it is done one hardly knows what has happened and whether it has been for one's good or for one's bad, but an "experience," has taken place. It is also why I find classical music less exciting for that merely evokes the echo of a past "experience" – it is a part of society, one of the noblest parts, perhaps, but still not of the soul. Only the echo of the composer's soul remains. And besides it consists too entirely of triumphs rather than of life.

Life in organizations is filled with potential inventions that get ambushed when people slide into old clichés. Pulling oneself out is tense work. It can be cold work. Occasionally there is triumph. Usually, however, as people at Honda put it, "A 1 per cent success rate is supported by mistakes made 99 per cent of the time" (Nonaka and Takeuchi 1995, p. 232). Jazz improvisation, itself built of "moments of rare beauty intermixed with technical mistakes and aimless passages" (Gioia 1988, p. 66), teaches us that there is life beyond routines, formalization, and success. To see the beauty in failures of reach is to learn an important lesson that jazz improvisation can teach.[1]

Note

1. This chapter expands on themes mentioned in my brief remarks in Vancouver on August 8, 1995 (e.g., "defining characteristics of improvisation," "examples of improvisation in non-musical settings") and it retains all specifics used to ground those themes (e.g.. Ryle and Gioia on adroit ad hoc action. Mingus on melodies, Keeney on psychotherapy, and Mailer on society's proneness to ambush invention). These expansions are a perfect example of "re-working precomposed material in relation to unanticipated ideas" conceived during the writing itself, which is simply another way of saying, it is an exhibit of improvisation.

References

Allport, F. H. 1962. A structuronomic conception of behavior: Individual and collective. *Journal of Abnormal and Social Psychology*. **64** 3–30.

Amabile, T. M. 1988. A model of creativity and innovation in organizations. *Research in Organizational Behavior*. **10** 123-167. JAI, Greenwich, CT.

Barrett. Frank. 1998. Creativity and Improvisation in Jazz and Organizations: Implications for Organizational Learning. *Organization Science*. **9** 5 605–622.

Bastien, D. T., T. J. Hostager. 1992. Cooperation as communicative accomplishment: A symbolic interaction analysis of an improvised jazz concert. *Communication Studies*. **43** 92–104.

Bateson. M. C. 1989. *Composing a Life*. Atlantic Monthly, New York.

Berliner. Paul F. 1994. *Thinking in Jazz: The Infinite Art of Improvisation*. Univ. of Chicago, Chicago, IL.

Buckley. W. 1968. Society as a complex adoptive system. W. Buckley, ed. *Modern Systems Research for the Behavioral Scientist*. Aldine, Chicago. IL. 490–513.

Bursztjahn. H., A. Feinbloom, R. Hamm, A. Brodsky 1981. *Medical Choices, Medical Chances*. Dell, New York.

Chia. R. 1996. The problem of reflexivity in organizational research: Towards a postmodern science of organization. *Organization*. 3 31–59.

Cohen. M. D., P. Bacdayan. 1994. Organizational routines are stored as procedural memory: Evidence from a laboratory study. *Organization Science*. 5 554–568.

Crossan, M., M. Sorrenti. 1996. Making sense of improvisation. Unpublished manuscript. Univ. of Western Ontario.

Daft, R., K. Weick. 1984. Toward a model of organizations as interpretation systems. *Academy of Management Review*. 9 284–295.

Davis, F. 1986. *In the Moment*. Oxford, New York.

Dougherty, D. 1992. Interpretive barriers to successful product innovation in large firms. *Organization Science*. 3 179–202.

Eisenberg, E. 1990. Jamming! Transcendence through organizing. *Communication Research*. 17 2 139–164.

Eisenhardt, K. M. 1989. Making fast strategic decisions in high-velocity environments. *Academy of Management Journal*. 32 543–576.

Follett, M. P. 1924. *Creative Experience*. Longmans, Green, New York.

Gersick, C. J. G., J. R. Hackman. 1990. Habitual routines in task-performing groups. *Organizational Behavior and Human Decision Processes*. 47 65–97.

Gioia, T. 1988. *The Imperfect Art*. Oxford. New York.

Harper, D. 1987. *Working Knowledge*. Univ. of Chicago Press, Chicago, IL.

Herrington, B. S. 1989. Merging of music, psychiatry yields richly composed life. *Psychiatric News*. April 7, 16+.

Isenberg, D. J. 1985. Some hows and whats of managerial thinking: Implications for future army leaders. J. G. Hunt and J. D. Blair, eds., *Leadership on the Future Battlefield*. Pergamon-Brassey's, Washington, DC. 168–181.

Janowitz, M. 1959. Changing patterns of organizational authority: The military establishment. *Administrative Science Quarterly*. 3 473–493.

Keeney, B. P. 1990. *Improvisational Therapy*. Guilford, New York.

Kernfeld, B. 1995. *What to Listen for in Jazz*. Yale Univ., New Haven, CT.

Levi-Strauss, C. 1966. *The Savage Mind*. Univ. of Chicago, Chicago, IL.

Maggin, D. L. 1996. *Stan Getz: A Life in Jazz*. Morrow, New York.

Mangham, I., A. Pye. 1991. *The Doing of Managing*. Blackwell, Oxford, UK.

Maruyama, M. 1963. The second cybernetics: Deviation-amplifying mutual causal processes. *American Scientist*. 51 164–179.

McDaniel, Reuben R., Jr. 1996. Strategic leadership: A view from quantum and chaos theories. W. J. Duncan, P. Ginter, L. Swayne, eds., *Handbook of Health Care Management*. Blackwell, Oxford, UK.

Miller, D. 1993. The architecture of simplicity. *Academy of Management Review*. 18 116–138.

Miner, A. J., C. Moorman, C. Bassoff. 1996. Organizational improvisation in new product development. Unpublished manuscript. University of Wisconsin, Madison, WI.

Mintzberg, H., A. McHugh. 1985. Strategy formation in an adhocracy. *Administrative Science Quarterly*. 30 160–197.

Neisser, U., E. Winograd, eds. 1988. *Remembering Reconsidered: Ecological and Traditional Approaches to the Study of Memory*. Cambridge University, Cambridge, UK.

Nemeth. C. J.. B. M. Staw. 1989. The tradeoffs of social control and innovation in groups and organizations. L. Berkowitz, ed. *Advances in Experimental Social Psychology*. **22** 175–210. Academic, San Diego, CA.

Nonaka, l., H. Takeuchi. 1995. *The Knowledge-creating Company*. Oxford, New York.

Perry, L. T 1991. Strategic improvising: How to formulate and implement competitive strategies in concert. *Organizational Dynamics*. **19** 4, 51–64.

Ramos, R. 1978. The use of improvisation and modulation in natural talk: An alternative approach to conversational analysis. N. K. Denzin, ed. *Studies in Symbolic Interaction*. **1** 319–337. JAI, Greenwich, CT.

Reed, M. 1991. Organizations and rationality: The odd couple. *Journal of Management Studies*. **28** 559–567.

Ryle, G. 1979. Improvisation. G. Ryle, ed. *On Thinking*. Blackwell, London, UK, 121–130.

Schön, D. A. 1987. *Educating the Reflective Practitioner*. Jossey-Bass, San Francisco, CA.

Schuller, G. 1968. *Early Jazz*. Oxford. New York.

Simon, H. A. 1989. Making management decisions: The role of intuition and emotion. W. H. Agor, ed. *Intuition in Organizations*. Sage, Newbury Park, CA. 23–39.

Stacey, R. D. 1992. *Managing the Unknowable*. Jossey-Bass, San Francisco, CA.

Starbuck, W. H. 1993. "Watch where you step!" or Indiana Starbuck amid the perils of academe (Rated PG). A. G. Bedeion, ed. *Management Laureates*. **3** 65–110. JAI, Greenwich, CT.

Starbuck, W. H., F. Milliken. 1988. Challenger: Fine tuning the odds until something breaks. *Journal of Management Studies*. **25** 319–340.

Suhor. C. 1986. Jazz improvisation and language performance: parallel competitiveness. *ETC*. **43** 4, 133–140.

Sutcliffe, K. M., S. Sitkin. 1996. New perspectives on process management: Implications for 21st century organizations. C. Cooper, S. Jackson, eds. *Handbook of Organizational Behavior*. Wiley, New York.

Tyler. S. A., M. G. Tyler. 1990. Foreword. B. P. Keeney, ed. *Improvisational Therapy*. ix–xi. Guilford, New York.

Walsh, J. P., G. R. Ungson. 1991. Organizational memory. *Academy of Management Review*. **16** 57–91.

Wegner, D. M. 1987. Transactive memory: A contemporary analysis of the group mind. B. Mullen, G. R. Goethals, eds. *Theories of Group Behavior*. 185–208. Springer-Verlag, New York.

Weick, K. E. 1969. *The Social Psychology of Organizing*. Addison-Wesley, Reading, MA.

Weick, K. E. 1979. *The Social Psychology of Organizing*. 2d ed. Addison-Wesley, Reading, MA.

Weick, K. E. 1989. Organized improvisation: 20 years of organizing. *Communication Studies*. **40** 241-248.

Weick, K. E. 1993. Organizational redesign as improvisation. G. P. Huber, W. H. Glick, eds. *Organization Change and Redesign*. Oxford, New York, 346–379.

Weick, K. E. 1995. Creativity and the aesthetics of imperfection. C. M. Ford, D. A. Gioia, eds. *Creative Action in Organizations*. 187–192. Sage, Thousand Oaks, CA.

Weiss, C. H. 1980. Knowledge creep and decision accretion. *Knowledge: Creation, Diffusion, Utilization*. **1** 381–404.

Whitehead, A. N. 1929. *Process and Reality*. Macmillan. New York.

Wilson, R. C. 1992. Jazz: A metaphor for high-performance teams. J. A. Heim, D. Compton, eds. *Manufacturing Systems*. 238–244. National Academy Press, Washington, D.C.

Wruck, K. H., M. C. Jensen. 1994. Science, specific knowledge, and total quality management. *Journal of Accounting and Economics*. **18** 247–287.

Retention

Meanings of enactment, selected for their fit with previous interpretations, are preserved as organizational memory. These meanings, often in the form of cause maps, are the source of culture and strategy in the case of organizations, and of identities and continuities in the case of individuals. Episodes of successful sensemaking culminate in meanings that fit present moments into the context of past moments. Because plausibility rather than accuracy is the prevailing criterion that guides retention, ecological changes that filter through enactment and selection, have numerous features that are overlooked and forgotten. The process of learning occurs when people notice some of what was previously overlooked and overlook some of what was previously noticed (Weick and Westley, 1996). These shifts in apprehension that we call learning occur when enactment and selection are loosely coupled to retention. Retention is crucial for sensemaking because it articulates plausible maps, often in narrative form, that summarize a sense of the situation. What people and organizations retain are the meaningful results of a process where enactment is mixed with ecological change and this mixture is untangled by means of biased hindsight. As I mentioned in the analysis of Bhopal, the enacted environment is as much an outcome of sensemaking stored in retention, as it is an input to enactment and selection. When I learn what I think by seeing what I say, the thoughts I wind up with are a meaningful environment of my own making and thus an outcome. But, since those thoughts also affect what I say and see subsequently, they comprise a meaningful enacted environment that serves as an input to subsequent sensemaking. There is immense slippage in this whole sequence. I say more things than I see, I see more things than I say, I think more things than I see, I forget more things than I remember, and I imagine more things than I see. In these slippages lie the ongoing surprises in everyday life that necessitate ongoing sensemaking.

We get a sense of the summarization associated with retention in the following three chapters that focus on cognitive maps, culture, and strategy as retained narratives.

Chapter 13, "Organizations as Cognitive Maps," co-authored with Michel Bougon, differentiates cause maps that connect events spread across time, from the larger class of cognitive maps that connect personal experience using all kinds of relationships. When interpretations are cast in terms of relations of influence among events (e.g. as the quality of my performance increases my satisfaction with the occasion increases), the connected events suggest a plausible story that supplies a sense of what is happening. Causality is a tool of sensemaking, not necessarily a deep commitment to positivism. It is an inference that reduces equivocality. And it is a plausible inference in a world where the activity of enactment is experienced as trials that sometimes produce consequences that sometimes produce feelings of efficacy and control. Maps have become a common metaphor for the content of cognition, partly because they lend themselves to methods and graphics associated with cartography. What is missing in many cases is much theory about why maps matter or how they weave together with action. This chapter fills some of that void. A good example is the discussion suggesting that cause maps develop in a manner that parallels the four forms of interpretation systems mentioned in Chapter 10. People who organize interpretation systems in which there is high activity but low analyzability, tend to see causality between pairs of events. As analyzability increases, stories should contain more cause chains. As organizations resort less to exploration and more to exploitation (i.e. shift from active to passive search) the stories that make sense to them should contain more cause loops and more themes of tragedy and being the author of one's fate (e.g. the Icarus paradox) which then give way to themes of an unanalyzable world of chaos and unconnected elements where sense is fleeting. Retention is much more than just a repository. It is a site of summaries that matter.

Chapter 14, "Organizational Culture as a Source of High Reliability," shows that retention is about culture as well as maps. Culture is an enacted environment that results from retrospective interpretation of recurrent patterns in enactment. These recurrent patterns are "how we do things around here." The specific pattern of interest in this chapter is the continuous use of stories to enlarge the pool of experience when actual trial and error is too dangerous. When the next error could be the last trial, people need substitute routes for learning. In this chapter I argue that the more fully an organizational culture values storytelling, the more effective that organization will be. Effectiveness here means reliable performance of high-risk operations under conditions where unexpected threats to continuation can erupt without much warning. This essay is one of the earlier attempts to understand what allows some organizations to perform reliably even though they embody thousands of accidents waiting to happen. Not surprisingly the answer is found partly in capabilities for making sense of the unexpected. That answer complements Perrow's (1984) earlier proposal that organizational structure influences reliability and susceptibility to normal accidents. The theme of requisite variety is the glue that holds the culture chapter together. To make sense of complex ecological change people can try either to simplify the changes or to complicate themselves. Given the degree of complexity people face, it makes sense to do everything possible to keep up. Thus, to make sense of complex change people need to intervene and enact in the interest of simplification; they need to tell stories, value imagination, and use rich communication media in the interest of complication; and they need to encourage collective mindfulness through teams and networks in the interest of both simplification and complication. This complex adaptation is stored in retention in the form of narratives with a moral.

The moral is that lapses in mindfulness can be fatal. That moral is less obvious than it sounds if you remember that reliability is a dynamic non-event. To remain mindful of the non-existent is a major exercise in sensemaking.

Chapter 15, "Substitutes for Strategy," argues that strategy is a retained outcome that is formed and affirmed through action. It is hard to ignore strategy in any discussion of sensemaking when strategy is defined as "good luck rationalized in hindsight." Or when realized strategy is treated as an emergent outcome of action that has undergone minimal guidance from a plan. Two favorite stories of sensemaking bracket this chapter. Soldiers lost in the alps in a snowstorm and hungry Naskapi Indians searching for game both find what they are looking for by means of just enough strategy, just in time, to get them moving and acting mindfully. In both cases an important cultural expectation, the presumption of logic, instills confidence and motivates improvised self-validating action. The retained presumption plus a handful of retained symbols such as a core value, are sufficient to provide a direction. Action that moves in this direction churns up data from which meaning can be constructed. Thus, execution becomes analysis and implementation becomes formulation. If confidence and improvisation are important determinants of just-in-time strategy making, then this suggests that people will benefit from a larger repertoire of interpretations, labels, and capabilities that enables them to sense richly the variations they enact. And this in turn suggests that generalists and those with varied experience are in the better position to impose meanings that include more of the sensed data. It is easy to think of sensemaking as the province of specialists and experts, people who are accustomed to nuance, subtle cues, and deep readings. But in a world tied together by forceful actions and presumptions of logic, meaning may come more quickly and remain more stable for those whose capabilities are more varied, whose logics are more diverse, and whose presumptions are more robust. Fewer things should surprise generalists than surprise specialists. If any old map will do when you're lost, then generalists, with their varied experience, may have more maps lying around than do specialists.

References

Perrow, Charles (1984). *Normal Accidents*, New York: Basic Books.

Weick, Karl E., and Westley, Frances (1996). Organizational learning: Affirming an oxymoron. In S. R. Clegg, C. Hardy, and W. Nord (eds.), *Handbook of Organization Studies*, London: Sage, pp. 440–58.

13

Organizations as Cognitive Maps: Charting Ways to Success and Failure

Karl E. Weick and Michel G. Bougon

> Managers basically possess only ideas. Hierarchy, organization, control – these reside primarily in the mind. In fact, management exists only because the manager and managed believe it exists.
>
> *Joseph McGuire*

> VISA is highly structured conceptually, philosophically, and ethically. What we do and why we do it is carefully planned. How we do it is not. We give it just enough procedural structure to make it respectable to those who are enamored of forms, job descriptions, reports, consultants' presentations, statistics, and other such impediments.
>
> *Dee Hock, chief executive officer, VISA*

Organizations exist largely in the mind, and their existence takes the form of cognitive maps. Thus, what ties an organization together is what ties thoughts together. People who study cognitive maps take those assertions seriously and literally. This chapter shows why.

Background

To see that what ties an organization together is what ties thoughts together, first, we must consider how we think of organizations in terms of causes and effects, and second, we must examine how we assemble personal cognitive maps from such primitive cause-effect relations.

Causality as an epistemological primitive

There are only four possible things that can happen among events in an organization. The events can be either similar or different, and they can occur either at the same or at different times. That is it. These four combinations are the primitives of all organizing. This chapter is about the most relevant combination in organization theory: the combination of different events at different times. It is this combination that generates the inferences of causality that are stored in the sets of related causality beliefs we call *cause maps*.

The relationship between the four epistemological primitives and causality can be seen in Figure 13.1, Cell A, which stands for the same events occurring at the same time, is exemplified by two whistles blowing at the same time; this combination of events is called coincidence or *identity*. Cell B, which represents the same event happening at different times, is labeled *seriality* and would be exemplified by a series of explosions occurring over a period of time. Cell C, which stands for different events occurring at the same time, is characterized as *correlation* and is exemplified by a whistle and an explosion occurring at the same time. Cell D, which exhibits different events occurring at different times, is the situation on which patterns of *causality* are imposed. An example of this combination would be a whistle followed by an explosion. It is conceivable that a person observing these two different events spread over time might conclude that the whistle caused the explosion. It is important to empha-

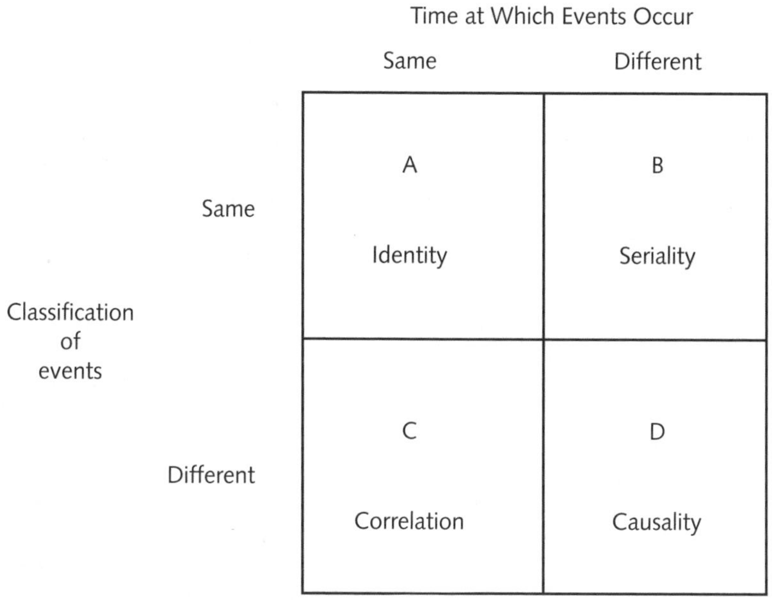

Time at Which Events Occur

		Same	Different
Classification of events	Same	A Identity	B Seriality
	Different	C Correlation	D Causality

Figure 13.1   Epistemological primitives

size that linking an earlier event to some later event is a reasonable connection, but it is also arbitrary and speculative (see Hume, [1748] 1955).

As Figure 13.1 indicates, causality is one of only four cognitive archetypes, and it is one of only two archetypes that are rich enough to incorporate the dimension of time. The relevance of causality to organizational issues is evident if we recall the basic way organizations are usually described. Selznick (1957, p. 5) is representative: "The term *organization* thus suggests a certain barrenness, a lean, no-nonsense system of consciously coordinated activities. It refers to an expendable tool, a rational instrument engineered to do a job."

This description emphasizes that the organization is an instrument to do things, a means, a consciously constructed tool. Thus an organization is often valued literally because it embodies causality. Organizations institutionalize means-ends relationships and if-then assertions and transform earlier inputs into very different later outcomes, all of which invite inferences of causality.

Maps as epistemological structures

In the most general sense, a map "is an aggregate of interrelated information" (O'Keefe and Nadel, 1978, p. 62). Maps help people perceive large-scale environments beyond the range of immediate perception. Since maps focus beyond the range of immediate perception, they deal with phenomena that cannot be observed but rather must be explored. Thus, maps are intimately tied to action. O'Keefe and Nadel use an early position paper by Ittelson (1973) to highlight the close ties between action and maps. " 'Most perception research has been carried out in the context of object perception, rather than environment perception. The distinction between object and environment is crucial, because objects require subjects. . . . In contrast, one cannot be a subject of an environment, one can only be a participant. The very distinction between self and non-self breaks down cold. The environment surrounds, enfolds, engulfs, and no thing and no one can be isolated and identified as standing outside of, and apart from it. . . .' The fact that they surround means that one cannot observe an environment; rather the organism explores it" (pp. 74–75).

Thus, action and mapping have a close relationship. When people build cognitive maps, they start with outcomes, small experiments, and consequences that are produced either by one's own action or by that of someone else. These perceived regularities form the raw materials for cognitive maps.

The key nuance that is preserved when the metaphor of a map is used to describe cognitive structures is the nuance of flexibility. Tolman (1948) is credited with the label *cognitive map*, but what is mentioned less frequently is that Tolman contrasted cognitive maps with something that he called a *strip map*. A strip map develops when a person learns a specific path by rote learning and has a simple stimulus-response memory of how to get from one place to another. A strip map might take the following form: at this point turn left, at the next choice turn right, and then turn right at each of the next six choices. What is distinctive about a strip map is that each choice point calls up the appropriate response, which means that a structural component is unnecessary. All you need to do is learn a sequence of turns;

neither do you need to measure distance, nor do you need very precise directions.

This relatively mindless strip map contrasts with a cognitive map, which tells routes, environmental relationships, and alternative ways to get from one position to another. The important point about Tolman's distinction between cognitive maps and strip maps is his feeling that you need to invoke the concept of a cognitive map when there is some evidence of flexible behavior, or when, in other words, we find that people can deal with alternative starting positions and alternative routes to a goal.

Cognitive maps as epistemological structures

The concept of maps in organization theory dates back at least to Paul Goodman's attempt (1968) to operationalize Lewin's concept of life-space by applying it to regions unique to organizations (such as the authority region, reward region, salary region, promotion region, organizational problem region, financial region). Goodman's interest was in the extent to which managers differentiated regions that were closer and farther from them personally (salary and promotion regions were seen to be closer to the personality than were financial or authority regions) and whether the degree of differentiation was related to hierarchal level, level of aspiration, job involvement, or cognitive complexity. The issue of variations in differentiation has remained a staple in cognitive approaches, and it remains a relatively neglected property of cause maps.

A cognitive map approach to organizations begins with the recognition that participants edit their own organizational experience into patterns of personal knowledge. A representation of that knowledge is called a *cognitive map*. A cognitive map consists of the concepts and the relations a participant uses to understand organizational situations. When we consider all possible types of relations among concepts, such as contiguity, proximity, continuity, resemblance, and implication, then an exhaustive mapping of these relations can be called a cognitive map. If we limit ourselves to mapping only causality relations, as we do in this chapter, then we talk about a more specific form of cognitive map called a *cause map*. Thus, a cause map is a form of cognitive map that incorporates concepts tied together by causality relations.

Other people have described cognitive maps and cause maps in roughly similar ways. For example, Eden, Jones, Sims, and Smithin (1981) state that a cognitive map "consists of concepts (idiomatically expressed in the client's own phrasing) linked by arrows representing a causal link between the concepts of the form 'concept A has consequences for or can be explained by concept B'" (p. 40). Hart (1977, pp. 115–116) says: "I will define cognitive maps as sets of causal beliefs or assertions though some scholars use the term to stand for general beliefs about the fundamental characteristics of some aspect of a physical or social environment, whether or not such beliefs are causal. . . . Other scholars are interested in sets of causal assertions as they are used in discussions and arguments among groups of policymakers. Such sets are more correctly called rhetorical maps, because they do not assume that the individuals believe the causal assertions that they make in order to persuade others to go along with a particular policy."

Cause maps as epistemological structures

A cause map develops as the mind reflects on experience, constructs concepts in the form of variables, and imposes connections among these variables. When variables are connected, they become meaningful since meaning flows from relationships. Thus, the more equivocality the individual can remove from experience by means of concept-structures, the more the world will make sense to that person, and the more productive that person can be. Structures such as cause maps remove equivocality, both because they place concepts in relation to one another, and because they impose structure on vague situations. Since structures are simpler than the qualities on which they are imposed, they reduce equivocality. These are the basic mechanisms by which a cause map operates, and these mechanisms define the basic properties of a cause map: namely, variables and cause ties.

The concepts contained in cause maps are variables. "A concept variable is something like 'the amount of security in Persia'; something that can take on different values such as 'a great amount of security' or 'a small amount of security.' A cognitive map allows great flexibility in the variables. They may be continuous variables, such as more or less of something; or they may be dichotomous variables, such as the existence or nonexistence of something. But whatever type of concept is represented, it is always regarded as a variable that can take on more than one value" (Axelrod, 1976, p. 59).

Since leaders establish organizations to serve their needs, we expect the language used by the participants in organizations to be rich in variables. We also expect the language and models of analysts of organizations to be rich in those variables. Assume, for example, that an orchestra musician already possesses the higher-level concept "performance." That noun can be elaborated into the variables "quality of performance," "number of performances," "satisfactoriness of performance." Eventually the attributes "quality," "number," and "satisfactoriness" become qualifiers that can be attached to practically any noun to transform it into a variable.

Once people have formed concepts or variables, they begin to tie them together to make sense of them. Concepts can be tied by causality relations based on logic, observed matters of fact, or beliefs when evidence is not available (Hall, 1984, p. 908). In most representations of the causality relations between concepts, the simple notations of plus (+), meaning a direct relationship, minus (−), meaning an inverse relationship, and zero (0), meaning no relationship, are sufficient. These notations are sufficient because decision makers typically do not use a more refined set of gradations than this (Axelrod, 1976, p. 69).

In the cause map procedure called the *Self-Q* technique (Bougon, 1983), a more refined description of the strength of causality ties is used. These Self-Q measures are based on both theoretical considerations (Weick, 1979, p. 227) and empirical findings that indicate experience is *curvilinear*. That is, experience is not just either "+" *or* "−" (as assumed, for example, in the studies of Axelrod and associates) but is "+" *and* "−." This represents the fact that some amount of a variable is good, but too much of the same variable is bad (or vice versa). For example, many studies have demonstrated that as stress increases, task performance improves, yet beyond some optimal level, as stress keeps increasing, performance then degrades.

Even though all experience has this curvilinear quality, specific experiences sample relatively small portions of the complete curvilinear function. In a single experience, people seldom see the whole range of values as well as the shape of the whole function. What people do experience is relationships that differ, depending on which portion of the curve they operate in. Thus, in the previous example, some of the time more stress leads to more task performance, some of the time more stress leads to less performance, and some of the time (in the vicinity of the optimal level of stress – at the near-flat top of the curve) a change in stress has no effect on performance.

Such partial observations that reveal only portions of the whole curvilinear function are the stuff of which individual reflections on experience are made. For purpose of cause-effect inference, the most accurate way to portray these opposing reflections on the same experience is to say that the experience is *equivocal*. Equivocal does not mean unclear or uncertain; rather, it means that there are two or more clear, distinct meanings for several related variables because the relationships among them differ. Thus, the cause-effect relation between stress and task performance is both more/ more (+) *and* more/less (−). A sensitive mapping technique will capture the fact that for a person an experience often means both one thing and its opposite and that what varies is the proportion of time each relation occurs.

Cause maps as collective structures

Cause maps are relevant to groups as well as individuals. When people try to make sense of their joint experiences, they must guide each other through three levels of agreement: (1) agreement on which concepts capture and abstract their joint experience (for example, "This is a grievance, but this is humorous"); (2) consensus on relations among these concepts (for example, "Smaller groups lead to higher-quality work"); and (3) similarity of view on how these related concepts affect each party (for example, "I feel ignored in large groups") and on how they themselves can affect the concepts (for example, "In small groups I can make things happen").

Cause maps can be coordinated with relatively little shared understanding (Weick, 1979, p. 91), a characteristic that is important to emphasize given the current emphasis on shared beliefs in organizational culture. Concerted action is possible where there is common relevance of two concepts in two cause maps and a *double interact* (Weick, 1979) to link the maps.

The following example illustrates how two concepts become linked by a double interact: Two actors, A and B, both with quite different cause maps, may become organized when person B wants X and person A has the capacity to fulfill X. To make this example more concrete, assume that A is President Reagan, and he wants person B, Senator Bill Bradley, to vote for his tax program. Concept Y, a vote for the tax program, is an element in both maps but the meaning of that element differs in each map because it is connected to different ideas. Reagan's question is "How do I get Bradley's vote?"

Reagan has to create some object X that Bradley might desire, and then he has to create a desire on Bradley's part for that object. Reagan has to define an X in his own map that he can deliver, and he then has to create a desire for X in Bradley's map.

We now have two concepts that are salient to two people, and that is all we need for an initial collective exchange and the possibility for subsequent coordinated action.

In order to coordinate the two maps, three things must happen. First, objects (Xs) for wants need to be identified or created. Second, wants need to be identified or created. And third, wants and objects need to be linked. This process is not easy, since it requires that one person reconstruct someone else's definition of who he or she is. This is difficult to pull off because people often define who they are by what they want ("I want influence"), or by what they have ("I have a Rolls Royce"), or by what they know ("I know software"), or by what they believe ("I am a Buddhist").

The important point is that the basic condition for starting a collective structure is a situation in which A needs B's Y, and this can occur when B is persuaded to want A's X. What was originally an *interact* (A wanted B's Y, and B's Y could fulfill what A wanted) has become a double interact because for A to get Y, A has to give or create some valued X to B in return.

The core of a double interact is the cause map, since concepts and relationships are what are being negotiated. A double interact forms when we discover that I can be a cause of your X, you can be a cause of my Y, and momentarily we have no better source for these concepts and relationships.

The concepts of interact, double interact, and *assemblage* are illustrated by Hall's (1984, p. 915) description of five separate cause maps for five key departments at the *Saturday Evening Post* (circulation, publisher, editorial, production, and President and Board). The maps constitute a single organization because there are inter-map inter-acts across the maps. Specific goals in one department become policy variables in other departments. This common relevance of concepts is what ties these departments together into an organization (although their relevance is different in each department).

The important point is that one way to describe collective structure is to identify common elements in diverse cause maps that are linked across maps.

There are two other forms that collective cause maps can take. One form is a *composite cause map*, which is represented in the extensive work done by Eden and his associates (for example, Eden, Jones, and Sims, 1979 and 1983). These consultants-scientists strive to develop a common appreciation of a group situation by first having individuals describe their own idiosyncratic cause maps. Then individuals see both the cause maps constructed by others and a composite map that contains all the concepts and relations found in all the individuals' maps. Using these complex data as a point of departure, people discuss, edit, and reaffirm views in an attempt to build a team map that is both accurate and acceptable. The final team map is developed by a process that resembles the nominal group technique. The resulting composite cause map represents what the group thinks, is likely to perceive, and how it defines itself.

The third form of collective cause map is an *average map* (Bougon, Weick, and Binkhorst, 1977; Ford and Hegarty, 1984; Komocar, 1985, pp. 143–170). To illustrate, in the individual cause maps constructed by the nineteen musicians in the Utrecht Jazz Orchestra, each cell entry was either a −1 (indicating an inverse causality relationship between the column and row variables), a 0 (indicating no causality relationship), or a +1 (indicating a direct relationship). When these entries are added across musicians, the cell entries in the average map could range from −19/19 to

+19/19, depending on the number of people who thought a relationship existed and the direction of the relationship. The average map, therefore, is the algebraic mean of the signed links reported by the nineteen participants.

Causality relationships mentioned by a significant number of orchestra members (see p. 610 in Bougon, Weick, and Binkhorst, 1977, for a summary of significant relationships) can then be treated as a consensual view of what the orchestra is. As with any average, no one cause map may coincide exactly with the average map. However, all nineteen musicians share at least two variables in common, so minimal structures are present among all possible pairs. Since these musicians interacted at least four hours every week, they developed common understanding of many variables and similar definitions of new variables that were added to the map.

In summary, collective cause maps can take the form of an assemblage (Hall, 1984), a composite (Eden, Jones, Sims, and Smithin, 1981), or an average (Bougon, Weick, and Binkhorst, 1977). In each case, dependencies between people involve concepts and potential exchanges. The importance of exchange is clearest in the case of an assemblage and least clear in the case of an average map. In an average map, people can share beliefs but not have the mutual dependencies implied by an exchange. However, since most concepts have dependencies built into them (for example, "quality of orchestra performance" involves mutual dependence), average maps usually involve exchange.

Methods for Gathering Cause Maps

The root of the cause map perspective lies in subjective reality; thus, the closer one gets to the subject, the closer one gets to what he or she thinks and means, and the closer one remains to the language of the subject, the greater the validity of the resulting map. Cognitive maps can be gathered through several different means, but the main ones used so far are

1. Systematic coding of documents representing the writings or statements of an individual.
2. Coding of verbatim transcripts of private meetings in which the individual participates.
3. Eliciting causality beliefs through questionnaires and interviews.

Hart (1977, p. 117) makes the following observations about these three methods. The advantage of documents is that they represent an individual's beliefs and are easy to find. Since they are plentiful, documents allow one to trace changes in beliefs over time. Furthermore, since the individual is usually writing for a general audience, the causality assertions are likely to represent defensible beliefs, although they may not always represent sincere beliefs.

Precisely because of the sincerity problem, many believe that participants are more likely to reveal their beliefs in private decision-making contexts (see, for example, Levi and Tetlock, 1980), which means that verbatim transcripts of private meetings may be more valid sources of cognitive maps than are public documents. However, not only are transcripts rarer but they may also have problems of sincerity. Insincerity also may be a drawback in questionnaires and interviews, although such dissembling can sometimes be assessed by items inserted to detect it. Also, face-to-face interviews may provide crucial nonverbal information that suggests deception.

Insincerity is not the only problem when cause maps are collected. A more stubborn problem is the fact that meaning does not reside in the labels attached to concepts. Instead, meaning lies in the map itself – that is, in the larger pattern among the other labels to which a specific label is linked and between these other labels and the specific label. Only the speaker can know for sure what any concept means, and investigators impute meaning at the risk of misrepresentation.

Researchers should remember that in any cause map "nodes are codes." When participants mention a specific concept (for example, "the home"), the observer cannot know for sure what lies behind that phrase. In order to guard against arrogance, observers need to treat phrases as coded buzzwords that imply a coherent set of meanings in a cause map. Precisely because nodes are codes, it is more defensible to do content-free analyses that examine structures and the placement of concepts than to puzzle over the meanings of the words themselves. Thus, the Utrecht Jazz Orchestra analysis focuses on associations between the placement of concepts in a flow of causality and on other properties, such as controllability, goal stability, and coalitions.

Problems that can occur when observers presume that their own meanings are identical with those a participant would develop are illustrated by a study forecasting energy use. Diffenbach (1982) constructed cause maps to understand which elements were involved in peak-load pricing of electricity, and he developed a composite map on the basis of judgments by three members of a research team (p. 143). Diffenbach's work is exemplary because he makes explicit the reasoning used by his research team to develop the links and concepts they used (see pp. 144–145). Nevertheless, a weakness of the Diffenbach work is that what you really want to know in peak-load pricing is how the electricity users see the situation, since they are the ones who are going to have to choose, for example, between taking a shower at night when the rates are cheap and taking a shower in the morning when they are not. Those are the mundane decisions that will nullify or affirm a peak-load pricing mechanism, yet those are the very data that are unavailable.

In the literature, there are several gradations in the extent to which researchers move closer to the participants and give them greater control over what they insert in their cause maps. For example, Roos and Hall (1980) interviewed and observed people over a three-year period and then drew a cause map for them. That is an improvement over Axelrod (1976) because there is fuller information available than is found in single documents stripped of their context of delivery and intention.

Ford and Hegarty (1984) move one step closer to participants' thoughts and meanings than Roos and Hall. They extracted contingency variables from the research literature, but rather than connect these variables as they thought participants would, they had managers and MBA students connect them. Somewhat troublesome is that these variables are abstract and not anchored in any specific organization, which makes it difficult to tell what referent the subjects had in mind when they, for example, connected size with formalization and division of work. The fact that similar connections were made by MBAs and the managers suggests either common socialization, common ignorance, or equivalent stereotypes. But what we cannot be sure of is precisely what it means when people take labels used by academics and connect them the way academics connect them.

To move even closer, researchers can have participants both create the variables and connect them. This is what happened in the study of the Utrecht Jazz Orchestra (UJO). Musicians generated a single list of seventeen variables, which they then causally connected.

There still is the possibility that even though the seventeen UJO variables codify statements made by specific musicians, the labels we have used have more meaning for some musicians than for others. To move even closer to the natural language of participants, Bougon (1983, 1986) developed the self-questioning (Self-Q) technique (see also Baird, 1984a, 1984b). As its name implies, people ask themselves questions about whatever topic is being mapped, and concepts are then extracted from the questions. This format is fruitful because people are not practiced in defending against questions that they ask themselves and over which they have control. Furthermore, since the person is asking questions rather than making assertions, the questions themselves seem harmless.

Once the causality assertions have been collected, they need to be displayed systematically for purposes of analysis.

The general aim of analyses conducted on cause maps is to discover universal structural regularities in these maps. Specific aims include the study of universal relationships between these structural regularities and a person's values, means, goals, emotions, influence, power, expertise, inconsistencies, sense of self, and formation of double interacts leading to the creation of organizations. Another major aim of the analyses is to simplify and clarify individual cause maps to reveal the dominant flow of causality that people impose on their experience.

In the pursuit of these aims, most cause map analyses start with an *adjacency* matrix in which causes are listed at the West side of the matrix and effects are listed at the North side (see Figure 13.2). Thus, the matrix summarizes causality flowing from the concepts listed on the left to the concepts listed on the top.

In this matrix, if we sum absolute cell values in each North–South column, we learn how many causes terminate in each effect. We write these sums at the South margin of the matrix. These South marginal values are labeled *indegrees* because they summarize the relative density of relationships flowing into a particular variable. Dense flows into a variable correspond to a person's tacit inference of a goal, or end, or outcome (Bougon, Weick, and Binkhorst, 1977; Komocar, 1985).

If we sum absolute cell values in each West–East row, we learn how many effects each cause has created. We write these sums at the East margin of the matrix. These East marginal values are labeled *outdegrees* because they summarize the relative density of relationships flowing out of a particular variable. Theory and data suggest that dense flows out of a variable correspond to a person's tacit inference of a value, or reason, or imperative (Bougon, 1985; Komocar, 1985). More is known about the pattern of South marginals (hence about tacit goals, ends, or outcomes), but the interesting question lies in the degree to which a rank ordering of the East marginals reveals tacit values, reasons, or imperatives imposed on a situation.

The important point about working with marginals in a cause-effect matrix is that

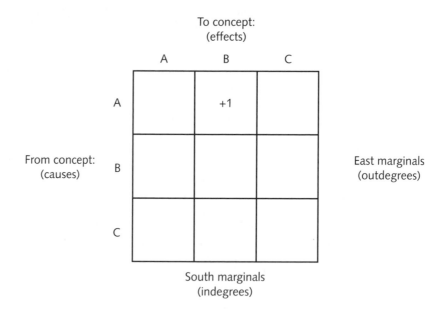

Figure 13.2   The adjacency matrix for summarizing cause ties[1]

they untangle causality relations and reveal order in the information contained in the map. For example, if the flow into a variable is more dense than the flow from that variable, then the North–East portion of the ordered cause matrix will have more or stronger or both more and stronger cell entries than the South–West portion. The ratio of one portion to another tells us both how much structure exists and whether there is a dominant direction in which causality flows. Thus, we are able to specify both a vectorial and a scalar measure of order in a social system.

Cause maps usually contain dense patterns of relations among variables and we need to know which relations are dominant. Each variable in a cause map can have an effect on every other variable, either directly or indirectly through paths involving other variables. Indirect paths can be calculated by using adjacency matrices and then raising the adjacency matrix to successive powers. Squaring an adjacency matrix, for example, will give paths of length 2 (for example, the effect of B on D through C), while raising the matrix to the third power would indicate how many indirect effects there are of B on D through paths that contain three links. Reachability matrices have been used by Axelrod (1976, pp. 350–53), Ford and Hegarty (1984, p. 283), and Bougon, Weick, and Binkhorst (1977), and are the basis on which Bougon (1986) extracts the dominant linkages in a cause map using the Self-Q technique. Two variables that are linked by a large number of strong direct and indirect paths are assumed to be more influential in determining what a person does and sees than are two variables that are linked by fewer, weak paths. The more ways one variable can affect another variable, the more robust and dominant that linkage is assumed to be.

Cause Map Findings

Since much cause map research consists of tool development and atheoretical description, the preceding sections already contain much of what has been found in cause map research.

The two most complete, self-contained organizational analyses of cause maps are Bougon, Weick, and Binkhorst (1977) and Hall (1984). These two works, each devoted to a single organization, provide models for cause map investigations because they are theory driven, explore collective maps, incorporate both lineal and reciprocal causation, and generate new theory and methodology.

Bougon, Weick, and Binkhorst (1977) develop ways to untangle raw cause data and show how causality flows in an orderly manner that can be highly hierarchal. The study demonstrates that the orderliness of a social structure can be assessed by the structure of causality generated by the members of that structure.

Hall's (1984) longitudinal study of the *Saturday Evening Post* is noteworthy because he shows that in the early stages, the pattern of cause maps led to growth of the firm, but as the pattern among maps changed, these same maps destroyed the firm. Thus, there is clear evidence that maps can have a tangible effect. Hall analyzes cause maps among coalitions, and shows that it is the balance of cause map logics among these coalitions that determines whether the organization survives or disappears. Since all of this is interpreted in the context of strategy and policy, Hall shows the tight fit between cause maps and strategic thinking.

Several specific cause map findings also seem worth pursuing here. We have seen that there are dominant links in any cause map and that they show a distinct pattern, with causality flowing only or almost only from left to right along a causality continuum. Although this finding is content-free, positions along this flow of causation are sensible. Ford and Hegarty (1984, p. 286) found that variables toward the left-hand end of the causality continuum contain context factors, that the middle variables correspond to structure, and that the right-hand end corresponds to performance variables. In the Utrecht Jazz Orchestra, variables at the left were givens (for example, difficulty of number played), variables in the middle were means (for example, time spent rehearsing), and variables at the right were ends (for example, quality of the band's performance). Roos and Hall (1980) describe policy variables as being at the left, intervening variables as being in the middle, and utilities (that is, ultimate pragmatic values) as being at the right-hand end, sorted more finely into utilities for the director and utilities for the sponsoring agency.

Variables at the right that terminate activity sequences have a distinctive character not found in variables at the left that initiate causality sequences. Ends contain significantly fewer logical inconsistencies than do origins, due to a greater abundance of deviation-amplifying loops at the right end of the causality continuum. Thus, ends are more sensible but also more unstable and subject to change because they are nested in positive feedback loops (Bougon, Weick, and Binkhorst, 1977, p. 624).

Not only are different positions along the causality continuum sensible, but different positions also seem to have different degrees of controllability. As we found in the Utrecht Jazz Orchestra, if a variable is controlled by other variables (it has a high indegree value), people tend to say they have control over that variable. Apparently, if a variable is controlled by several other variables, then people feel that they too can control that variable because they too are causal agents. These findings support what we have called the *confluence model*. If there are lots of paths to a variable, then there is a better chance that an individual can affect one of those paths and the variable itself.

Notice, however, that the degree of personal influence is dependent on where the individual tacitly places himself or herself in that flow of causation. If self as a concept is placed at the right, then many variables affect it, and the self has relatively little effect on any other variables. This would correspond to a situation often described as *external locus of control*. If the position of self moves more toward the left-hand end of a causality continuum, then this is more consistent with an interpretation of an internal locus of control, high self-efficacy, or being an origin rather than a pawn.

Cause maps contain the two basic components of cognitive complexity: differentiation and integration. *Integration* is measured by the number of connections among differentiated concepts. *Differentiation*, the number of characteristics or dimensions of a problem that are included, is often fixed by the observer, but when it is not, complexity can be assessed. For example, in Self-Q assessments, degree of differentiation is measured by the number of concept variables in a question relative to the logarithm of the number of words in a question (the logarithm reduces the influence of variations in the length of the questions). Levi and Tetlock (1980) found that cognitive complexity, coded from transcripts using Schroder, Driver, and Streufert's (1967) content rules, correlated significantly (0.57) with complexity in cognitive maps developed to portray the same events. Thus, maps may provide a means to examine requisite variety and the development of complicated thinking (Bartunek, Gordon, and Weathersby, 1983).

One of the more durable findings in studies of cognitive process is that crisis-produced stress leads to low-quality information processing. This finding has received modest support in work on cause maps (for example, Hall, 1984, p. 922), although it is not clear that the proposition has yet been tested adequately. Levi and Tetlock (1980) studied transcripts of conferences in 1941 among Japanese policy makers who were discussing whether to go to war against the United States. It was found that from June 15, 1941, to December 7, 1941, there was a slight tendency for cause maps to become simpler, this effect being most pronounced for the navy chief of staff, Nagano. Levi and Tetlock question whether this is a strong test of the disruptive stress hypothesis since a key aspect of crisis – namely, surprise – was missing, and since the Japanese had relatively high control over their environment and could do unilateral planning rather than face an escalation of mutual antagonism and hostility (spirals of mutual hostility seem to force simplification).

Since there is good evidence that decision makers in crisis consider less information, focus on shorter term consequences, and stereotype more, it seems likely that cause maps would not be shielded from these effects. Specifically, as stress increases, dominant links should exert relatively stronger effects over what is perceived. Concepts that are more complex and more recently learned would be likely to disappear from maps sooner than older, simpler concepts. Cause loops, which are hard enough to understand in times of quiescence, would be likely to seem especially baffling in crisis and to be ignored (see Hall 1984, for data supporting this deduction). If a crisis lowers perceived control over events, then the more severe the crisis, the more "self" would be shifted toward the right end of the causaliity continuum. A shift of self toward the right might even induce the perception that an event is a crisis, since less seems to be under one's personal control. If stress simplifies cognition, variables with extreme indegree and outdegree values (that is, variables at the Ends and Values extremities of the causality continuum) should remain salient, but variables with intermediate values should become merged, indistinguishable, and of relatively little value in sensemaking.

A puzzling finding, especially considering the origin of cause map technique (Maruyama, 1963), is that feedback loops are relatively rare in cause maps. This finding takes on added importance because executives of the *Saturday Evening Post* neglected the one prominent cause loop that existed in their cause maps: namely, having more readers leads to a lower advertising rate per reader, more advertising pages, and more magazine pages, which in turn attracts yet more readers. Neglect of this prominent cause loop eventually led to the demise of their organization (Hall, 1984, pp. 916, 923).

When cognitive maps are coded from documents, it is rare to find loops (for example, Hart, 1977; Levi and Tetlock, 1980). When Hall simulated the *Saturday Evening Post* on a computer, subjects were unable to detect any of the six feedback loops that were built into the model. Even more important, when the loops were pointed out to them, they could not interpret them (p. 915). This pattern of no significant strong loops was found in the Utrecht Jazz Orchestra data, although numerous weak loops were found.

Axelrod (1976) and Porac (1981) found two-step cause loops when people responded to concepts two at a time, which is the format used in the Utrecht Jazz Orchestra. When people generate their cause maps spontaneously, loops are less likely to be found. Diffenbach's (1982, pp. 140–141) cause map had several loops, but recall that three persons experienced in electrical engineering produced that map. Roos and Hall (1980) found important loops in their study of an extended-care hospital.

Given the potential importance of loops for survival and change (Maruyama, 1963; Ashton, 1976; Masuch, 1985), how are we to interpret the fact the loops seldom appear in cause maps (Axelrod, 1976, pp. 231–239) or appear under unusual conditions? One answer is that loops do not appear because they are not there when people act. Despite the fact that we talk about feedback all the time, there is evidence that people who normally perceive loops ignore them and impose a clear, categorical, lineal structure on their experience when there is uncertainty (Steinbruner, 1974). Hall (1984, p. 919) argues that when there is indeterminacy, executives often pick the simplest and most direct arguments that offer immediate, tangible results, and favor the dominant coalition. These preferences effectively rule out loops. Levi and Tetlock (1980) find that maps tend to be simplified under stress. Since uncertainty produces stress and since organizations operate under uncertainty much of the time, we might expect to find relatively simple, nonrecursive structures in dominant cause maps.

It could also be argued that lineal relationships are sufficient to get things done in a world where there is so much turnover that the effects of an action seldom affect the originator, who has left by the time the consequences become clearer. A lineal view of causality may also be an appropriate perception, especially in the early stages of organizing. When people explore situations, they take several actions, only some of which have consequences. In the early stages of exploration, simple stimulus-response connections are sufficient to portray what is happening.

Dominant loops also may be absent from cause maps either because loops are relatively weak (weak loops can still produce regularity if they cycle often enough) or because it takes parts of several different individual maps to form a dominant loop. The connected variables that form loops in Maruyama's (1963) description of how cities deal with refuse are connected only because several actors acted interdependently. The assemblage of their maps made one dominant loop and that loop is what provided stability for the larger social systems (see also Axelrod, 1976, p. 242).

In summary, cautioned by the reminder that nodes are codes and that inferences need to be triangulated (that is, verified by multiple independent measurements), there are several things we can learn from cause maps. We can look for the degree to which the relationships are structured, the degree to which tacit goals are singular or plural, and what the content of those goals might be. We can also ask whether the tacit values that drive activities are singular or plural, what the content of those values might be, and what the dominant linkages are. It is important to assess the degree to which the self is seen as an origin (is it far to the left?) or a pawn (is it far to the right?) in the flow of causality, the extent of equivocality present in the cause relations, and the degree to which the Values or Ends extremities of the causality continuum contain relatively more or fewer logical inconsistencies. Finally, cause maps can reveal the extent to which loops either stabilize or destabilize that portion of the causality continuum where the loops cluster; for example, in the UJO, destabilizing loops clustered around the indegree pole and therefore tended to destabilize goals. We can also learn what concepts exist that may enable one person to be linked with another person and thus create an organization.

Implications

Cause mapping is attractive because it lends substance to phenomenology, is an alternative to case studies as a means to analyze social construction of reality (Pfeffer, 1985, p. 385), and is a means to move higher in Boulding's (1956) hierarchy of systems levels. A cause map starts where people actually are in their understanding of issues and preserves the natural language of their understanding. Respect for understanding, however, does not occur at the expense of analysis, since structure is analyzed while content is left in the subject's own words.

Cause maps also represent a blend of the rational and the nonrational (Shweder, 1984). Maps contain inconsistencies, equivocal relations, tacit values, and concepts originating in metaphors, yet they also contain the more rational components of means-ends relations – that is, observed regularities, consensually validated relationships, changes in response to experience, and sensible inconsistencies.

Implications for research

Axelrod's data suggest that people do act rationally within the limits of the map they build, but the map is simplified because loops and inconsistent pathways are ignored.

People are both rational (they make correct explanations, predictions, and deductions) and irrational (by ignoring data, they form a map from which it is easy to make deductions). "The picture of a decision maker that emerges from the analysis of cognitive maps is of one who has more beliefs than he can handle, who employs a simplified image of the policy environment that is structurally easy to operate with, and who then acts rationally within the context of his simplified image" (Axelrod, 1976, p. 244).

The research question implied is "under what conditions can people build, maintain, and apply more complex maps so that a wider range of problems is represented appropriately?" As we are better able to assess differentiation and integration in cause maps, and as we are better able to state the conditions under which people can complicate their understanding, the attention bottleneck implied by maps with no loops and inconsistencies will be removed and appropriateness should improve.

Against this background, it becomes crucial to see how the cause maps of experts differ from those of novices. We need to know such things as whether experts differentiate more, integrate more, have less hierarchy and more loops or whether the reverse is the case. We also need to know whether experts change their maps less often or more often, and whether they change only those links that are minor and preserve those links that are strong links or whether the opposite is the case. Do experts consistently place "self" in positions with greater control over causality flows, or do they place "self" at different positions depending on their expertise concerning the issue being addressed? Questions such as these are variations on the theme that structure, rather than competencies in making inferences, predicts when decision makers will make better policy choices.

Aside from the issue of the ratio of rational to nonrational components in a cause map and the relevance of these ratios to appropriate perception, there are several other research implications of what has been reviewed.

The level of analysis appropriate for a cause map is the individual. Thus, psychological processes suggest conditions under which cause maps should be especially influential (Levi and Tetlock, 1980, p. 196; Holsti, 1976). Cause maps should exert influence when the situation is nonroutine and requires something more than standard operating procedures. Maps will have more effect when key actors are relatively free of organizational constraints, when overload necessitates simplifying strategies, when stress impairs the performance of cognitively complex tasks, and when ambiguity is high.

Hall's (1984) examination of changes in cause maps over twenty years at the *Saturday Evening Post* raises the important issue of how maps develop. Documentation of the development of maps is crucial because of primacy effects, the regression under crisis conditions to first-learned concepts, and the likelihood that assimilation is less cognitively effortful than is accommodation (meaning that older meanings dominate and incorporate newer information). Study of the development of cause maps is also important because groups and collectivities form around concepts and because concepts that are shared early should exert disproportionate effects on who is judged to be similar and thus available for future interaction.

A plausible sequence for the development of cause maps is suggested by the dimensions of presumed analyzability of the external environment (high/low) and intensity of search processes within the environment (active/passive) (Daft and Weick, 1984). The presumption of high analyzability occurs when people assume that the environment is measurable, determinant, logical, and that correct interpretations can be discovered. The presumption of low analyzability occurs when people assume that the environment is indeterminant and subjective, and that interpretations are created and imposed. Active search occurs when people move around in the environment and act to see what responds and with what consequences. Active searchers perform trials in order to learn what an error is and are often described as proactive. Passive search occurs when people accept whatever information the environment gives them, and try to discover the pattern in those data. This style is often labeled reactive.

When the dimensions of active and passive search and analyzable and unanalyzable environment are combined, the sequence shown in Figure 13.3 is suggested. When people face an unknown environment, they act to see what happens (Cell 1). If some action is repeatedly followed by the same effect, this leads to an isolated if-then proposition (for example, "If I talk about money, then more people pay attention to what I say"). A series of separate actions coupled with separate consequences generates pairs of related concepts that are not linked among the pairs.

As the person continues to act and believes he or she knows the environment more fully (Cell 2), pairs of causally connected concepts become linked into chains, and more remote effects are seen because the person now knows what to look for.

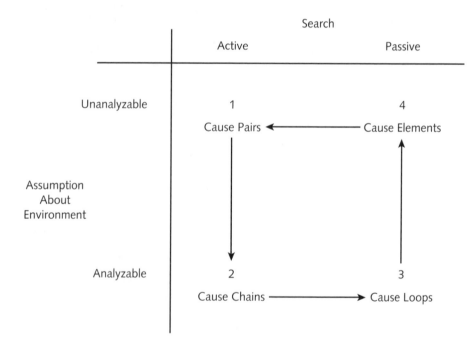

Figure 13.3 Development of cause maps

As more chains and more data accumulate, the person spends less time acting and more time analyzing connections that spread among more variables (Cell 3). As a result, some effects are now seen to be causal for earlier events that influenced these effects. When loops are added to pairs and chains, the complexity of a cause map increases dramatically and the map may become an armchair cosmology, disconnected and no longer edited by firsthand experience in the world it supposedly represents.

It is this very lack of connection with experience and of updating that now causes the map to disintegrate into arbitrary pairs and chains (Cell 4), none of which correspond to events that can be discovered or created. When a map disintegrates, the person has little choice but to wade back into the world again, act, and see what now happens (Cell 1).

This model suggests several possibilities. Pairs and chains are compatible with action, while loops and elements are not. The maps of active people should have fewer loops than the maps of passive people. If newcomers are socialized by being presented with chains and loops, their sensemaking should be accelerated since chains and loops represent cause maps at a more advanced stage of development. As an organization disintegrates, the maps of its chief actors should move in a reverse direction – namely, from loops to chains to pairs. In this situation, it becomes crucial to distinguish Cell 2 maps from Cell 4 maps. Movement from loops to chains to pairs would signal disintegration, while movement from loops to elements to pairs means ironically, further development and an attempt to find the simple structures and pairs that are crucial for adaptation to changed circumstances. In short, the life cycle of organizing should be traceable through changes in the maps that reflect and constrain that organizing.

Greater attention has been paid to the South marginals or the Ends region of a cause map than to the East marginals or the Values region of a map Variables with high outdegrees (East marginals) would be treated as values within the context of the UJO analyses, but this would not be true in other cause map formulations. Levi and Tetlock (1980, p. 201), for example, define a value as a variable that affects utility without affecting other concepts. However, a variable characterized in this way would have low outdegrees, would appear toward the right end of a causality continuum, and would be of questionable meaning since utility is an observer concept, not a participant concept. Since rankings by indegree are not a mirror image of rankings by outdegree, each ranking seems to be tapping something unique. What is being tapped differentially is not yet clear, especially in the case of variables that cluster toward the left end of a causality continuum.

Future research should also spell out the links between cause maps and other organizational concepts. For example, the developmental sequence proposed earlier might parallel the way organizational culture develops (for example, initial agreement on causal pairs followed by agreement on chains and then on loops). Cultural evolution might also follow the stages implicit in the design of Eden, Jones, Sims, and Smithin (1981) – namely, people articulate their own maps, then view other maps, and finally build composite maps.

A cause map is also an ideology (Beyer, 1981) and a basis for a presumption of logic (Weick, 1983). A script (Gioia and Poole, 1984) can be viewed as a strip map

– that is, as a frozen deduction from a cause map. Placement of a concept in a map would allow a sharper distinction between causes (at left) and objectives (at right) than has been found in much causal attribution work (Buss, 1978). Hall's (1984) successful prediction of preferred policies from cause maps suggests that policy decisions across time are not a random walk (p. 918). The amount of differentiation and integration in a cause map can be treated as a proxy for requisite variety, which would enable tests of the proposition that it takes variety to destroy variety.

A cause map can represent a motivational structure (House, 1971) if we argue that *expectancies* equal *values*, *instrumentality* equals *means*, and *valence* equals *goals*. Thus, to put an expectancy theory of motivation in motion, the leader picks means from the middle of an individual's causality continuum and a goal from the right end, shows that high effort will produce a significant change in the means, and that this significant change will cause a desired outcome to occur. Since the leader is working with the employees' own map, rather than with contingencies that are externally imposed and subject to suspicion, linkages should be tighter and motivation higher.

Locus of control is an important variable used by people who study social cognition. Perceptions of control fit neatly into cause maps since the placement of variables toward the right end of a continuum of causality is associated with perceptions of controllability, regardless of the content of the variables. This suggests that future research should explore the effect of placement of variables on perceptions of control, and the effects of controllability on placement. For example, the perception that a variable is a goal might be induced by demonstrating the apparently unrelated idea that the individual is able to control the variable. Conversely, people with an external locus of control might be induced to take more responsibility for a variable if that variable is moved from left to right on the causality continuum and is seen as more controllable.

While there are many more implications for research than we have suggested here, it is important also to discuss implications for practice, since cause maps have several such implications.

Implications for practice

Cause maps are evocative. They lay bare personal cause-effect logic, which in turn forces the individual to confront the reasonableness and validity of tacit cause-effect assumptions. A cause map provides an occasion to think carefully, deeply, and deliberately about an issue.

A decision maker can become a more sophisticated thinker by externalizing and studying a previously implicit map. Particularly attractive is the fact that this externalization does not require dependence on an outside expert and can be done in private.

Axelrod (1976, p. 246) identifies several advantages of "do-it-yourself" mapping. First, the person can be honest in stating beliefs and connections, since no one else will see the map. Second, since the person uses concepts that are personally meaningful, larger maps can be comprehended. Third, the person is not influenced by the preferences and values of an outsider but instead has control over the values that are included. And fourth, "The decision maker will not become overconfident in the methodology . . . since everything is explicit and easy to understand. To the extent that the beliefs are oversimplified so that they can be represented in the format of a cognitive map, the decision maker himself is in a position to evaluate the nature of the oversimplifications, since he made them himself" (p. 246).

When we move from private to public use of cause maps, there is agreement that maps allow groups to diagnose disagreements and manage those disagreements (Pfeffer, 1982, p. 217; Diffenbach, 1982, p. 144). Eden, Jones, Sims, and Smithin (1981), for example, find that a result of negotiations over individual maps among team members is that there is a "careful and gradual change of mutual understanding which is evidenced as each individual map absorbs more concepts from the team maps and, conversely, the team map absorbs more individuality" (p. 43).

Discussions of concepts, relations, and meanings are focused by a cause map graph in ways that are not possible with brainstorming. It is interesting that this focus is accomplished sometimes with less than complete data. Eden, Jones, Sims, and Smithin (1981) emphasize that they do not assign weights to causality relationships so that people have some latitude for movement during discussion (p. 42). In private, weights are informative, but in public, they may necessitate justification and preclude change. Managers need to develop maps that are easily updateable.

Cause maps have the potential to be used prescriptively and normatively, but this application has yet to be explored. Hart (1977, p. 139) has suggested some standards against which a person's cause map could be judged. First, does the person fail to make distinctions that are commonly made by others? (Hart labels this "conflation of concepts.") Second, do the assertions made agree with those made by people of similar experience and expertise? Third, are the assertions consistent over time? And fourth, do changes in the assertions represent an ability to learn?

Hart summarizes his position about criticizing the cause maps of other people this way: "Perhaps the most important application of cognitive mapping, therefore, would be to provide the user with a list of concepts which he himself distinguished but which others did not, and vice versa Similarly, one could provide the user with a list of assertions made by others which do not agree with those that he himself would make. The purpose of such an application would be to prevent the sort of talking at cross-purposes that often takes place at political negotiating sessions" (p. 139).

Conclusion

Maps are guides as well as products. They are guides in the sense that they assimilate uncertain events into an existing structure. Because maps relate an uncertain event to existing concepts, they generate meaning for the event. Maps are also products in the sense that concepts change in order to accommodate new experience.

People often build meaning in novel situations when they impose a structure on those situations and assimilate them. An equivocal situation becomes more sensible when it is assimilated in an existing cause map. Seldom, however, is the fit perfect. Reorganization of concepts often occurs, which means that accommodation is an eventual outcome with cognitive maps. Since cause maps determine what a person will perceive and do in situations, they have a substantial effect on what people call "real."

The important thing to remember about a cause map is that it *is* the organization

(Weick, 1979, p. 141). The cause map contains the structure, the process, and the raw materials from which agreements and conflicts are built when people coordinate action.

Note

1. Example: IF variable A is "people in the group" and variable B is "I feel ignored" AND the person reported the cause–effect relation. "The more people in the group, the more I feel ignored" THEN entry in cell AB will be +1, indicating a direct (more/more) relation between A and B (from A to B).

References

Ashton, R. H. "Deviation-Amplifying Feedback and Unintended Consequences of Management Accounting Systems." *Accounting, Organizations, and Society,* 1976, *1,* 289–300.

Axelrod, R. (ed.). *Structure of Decision: The Cognitive Maps of Political Elites.* Princeton, N.J.: Princeton University Press, 1976.

Baird, N. "The Use of Cause Maps To Explore an Organizational Question." Unpublished manuscript, Pennsylvania State University, 1984a.

Baird, N. "Procedures for Using the Self-Q Interview for Data Collection." Unpublished manuscript, Pennsylvania State University, 1984b.

Bartunek, J. M., Gordon, J. R., and Weathersby, R. P. "Developing 'Complicated' Understanding in Administrators." *Academy of Management Review,* 1983, *8,* 273–284.

Beyer, J. M. "Ideologies, Values, and Decision Making in Organizations." In P. C. Nystrom and W. H. Starbuck (eds.), *Handbook of Organizational Design.* Vol. 2. New York: Oxford University Press, 1981.

Bougon, M. G. "Uncovering Cognitive Maps: The Self-Q Technique." In G. Morgan (ed.), *Beyond Method: Strategies for Social Research.* Beverly Hills, Calif.: Sage, 1983.

Bougon, M. G. *Uncovering Cognitive Maps: The Self-Q Handbook.* (5th ed.) Privately printed handbook, Pennsylvania State University, 1986.

Bougon, M. G., Weick, K. E., and Binkhorst, D. "Cognition in Organizations: An Analysis of the Utrecht Jazz Orchestra." *Administrative Science Quarterly,* 1977, *22,* 606–639.

Boulding, K. E. "General Systems Theory – The Skeleton of Science." *Management Science,* 1956, *2,* 197–208.

Buss, A. R. "Causes and Reasons in Attribution Theory: A Conceptual Critique." *Journal of Personality and Social Psychology,* 1978, 36, 1311–1321.

Daft, R. L., and Weick, K. E. "Toward a Model of Organizations as Interpretation Systems." *Academy of Management Review,* 1984, *9,* 284–295.

Diffenbach, J. "Influence Diagrams for Complex Strategic Issues." *Strategic Management Journal,* 1982, *3,* 133–146.

Eden, C., Jones, S., and Sims, D. *Thinking in Organizations.* London: Macmillan, 1979.

Eden, C., Jones, S., and Sims, D. *Messing About in Problems.* Elmsford, N.Y.: Pergamon, 1983.

Eden, C., Jones, S., Sims, D., and Smithin, T. "The Intersubjectivity of Issues and Issues of Intersubjectivity." *Journal of Management Studies,* 1981, *18,* 37–47.

Ford, J. D., and Hegarty, W. H. "Decision Makers' Beliefs About the Causes and Effects of Structure: An Exploratory Study." *Academy of Management Journal,* 1984, *27,* 271–291.

Gioia, D. A., and Poole, P. P. "Scripts in Organizational Behavior." *Academy of Management Review,* 1984, *9,* 449–459.

Goodman, P. S. "The Measurement of an Individual's Organization Map." *Administrative Science Quarterly*, 1968, *13*, 246–265.

Hall, R. I. "The Natural Logic of Management Policy Making: Its Implications for the Survival of an Organization." *Management Science*, 1984, *30*, 905–927.

Hart, J. A. "Cognitive Maps of Three Latin American Policy Makers." *World Politics*, 1977, *30*, 115–140.

Holsti, O. "Foreign Policy Formation Viewed Cognitively." In R. Axelrod (ed.), *Structure of Decision*. Princeton, NJ.: Princeton University Press, 1976.

House, R. J. "A Path Goal Theory of Leader Effectiveness." *Administrative Science Quarterly*, 1971, 16, 321–338.

Hume, D. *An Inquiry Concerning Human Understanding*. New York: Bobbs-Merrill, 1955. (Originally published 1748.)

Ittelson, W. H. (ed.). *Environmental Cognition*. New York: Seminar Press, 1973.

Komocar, J. M. "Participant Cause Maps of a Work Setting: An Approach to Cognition and Behavior in Organizations." Unpublished doctoral dissertation, University of Illinois at Champaign-Urbana, 1985.

Levi, A., and Tetlock, P. E. "A Cognitive Analysis of Japan's 1941 Decision for War." *Journal of Conflict Resolution*, 1980, *24*, 195–211.

Maruyama, M. "The Second Cybernetics: Deviation-Amplifying Mutual Causal Processes." *American Scientist*, 1963, *51*, 164–179.

Masuch, M. "Vicious Circles in Organizations." *Administrative Science Quarterly*, 1985, 30, 14–33.

O'Keefe, J., and Nadel, L. *The Hippocampus as a Cognitive Map*. Oxford: Clarendon Press, 1978.

Pfeffer, J. *Organizations and Organization Theory*. Marshfield, Mass.: Pitman, 1982.

Pfeffer, J. "Organizations and Organization Theory." In G. Lindzey and E. Aronson (eds.), *Handbook of Social Psychology*. (3rd ed.) Vol. 1. New York: Random House, 1985.

Porac, J. E. "Causal Loops and Other Intercausal Perceptions in Attributions for Exam Performance." *Journal of Educational Psychology*, 1981, *73*, 587–601.

Roos, L. L., and Hall, R. I. "Influence Diagrams and Organizational Power." *Administrative Science Quarterly*, 1980, *25*, 57–71.

Schroder, H. M., Driver, M., and Streutert, S. *Human Information Processing*. New York: Holt, Rinehart, and Winston, 1967.

Selznick, P. *Leadership in Administration*. New York: Harper & Row, 1957.

Shweder, R. A. "Anthropology's Romantic Rebellion Against the Enlightenment, or There's More to Thinking than Reason and Evidence." In R. A. Shweder and R. A. LeVine (eds.), *Culture Theory: Essays on Mind, Self, and Emotion*. Cambridge: Cambridge University Press, 1984.

Steinbruner, J. D. *The Cybernetic Theory of Decision*. Princeton, N.J.: Princeton University Press, 1974.

Tolman, E. C. "Cognitive Maps in Rats and Men." *Psychological Review*, 1948, 55, 189–208.

Weick, K. E. *The Social Psychology of Organizing*, (2nd ed.). Reading, Mass.: Addison-Wesley, 1979.

Weick, K. E. "Managerial Thought in the Context of Action." In S. Srivastva and Associates, *The Executive Mind: New Insights on Managerial Thought and Action*. San Francisco: Jossey-Bass, 1983.

14

Organizational Culture as a Source of High Reliability

As organizations and their technologies have become more complex, they have also become susceptible to accidents that result from unforeseen consequences of misunderstood interventions.[1] Recent examples include Bhopal, the *Challenger*, and Three Mile Island.

What is interesting about these examples is that they involve issues of reliability, not the conventional organizational issues of efficiency. Organizations in which reliability is a more pressing issue than efficiency often have unique problems in learning and understanding, which, if unresolved, affect their performance adversely.

One unique problem is that a major learning strategy, trial and error, is not available to them because errors cannot be contained. The more likely an error is to propogate, the less willing a system is to use trial and error to understand that source of error firsthand. Because of this limitation, systems potentially know least about those very events that can be most damaging because they can propogate widely and rapidly. This chapter will explore an unconventional means by which organizations achieve error-free performance despite limited use of trial and error.

The point is that accidents occur because the humans who operate and manage complex systems are themselves not sufficiently complex to sense and anticipate the problems generated by those systems. This is a problem of "requisite variety,"[2] because the variety that exists in the system to be managed exceeds the variety in the people who must regulate it. When people have less variety than is requisite to cope with the system, they miss important information, their diagnoses are incomplete, and their remedies are short-sighted and can magnify rather than reduce a problem.

If the issue of accidents is posed this way, then there should be fewer accidents when there is a better match between system complexity and human complexity. A better match can occur basically in one of two ways: either the system becomes less complex or the human more complex. This chapter has more to say about the latter alternative than about the former.

Since learning and reliable performance are difficult when trial and error are precluded, this means that reliable performance depends on the development of substitutes for trial and error. Substitutes for trial and error come in the form of imagination, vicarious experiences, stories, simulations, and other symbolic representations of technology and its effects. The accuracy and reasonableness of these representations, as well as the value people place on constructing them, should have a significant effect on the reliability of performance.

The basic idea is that a system which values stories, storytellers, and storytelling will be more reliable than a system that derogates these substitutes for trial and error. A system that values stories and storytelling is potentially more reliable because people know more about their system, know more of the potential errors that might occur, and they are more confident that they can handle those errors that do occur because they know that other people have already handled similar errors.

Training as a Source of Accidents

Training is often used to prevent errors, but in fact can create them.

Training for the operation of high reliability systems is often tough and demanding so that the faint of heart and the incompetent are weeded out. People training to be air traffic controllers, for example, are targets of frequent verbal abuse in the belief that this will better prepare them to deal with pilots who are hostile, stubborn, and unresponsive. As one trainer said, "When you are training to be an air traffic controller, you only walk away from your screen once in anger and you're out." The trainer assumes that people who walk away from training screens under instructor abuse would walk away from real screens under pilot abuse. The problem with that assumption is that its validity never gets tested.

Furthermore, trainees who are unable to handle trainer hostility may be good controllers because they are more likely to sense emotions conveyed by pilots and be better able to predict impending problems. Thus, a person who walks away from a training screen may be better able to deal with the more frequent problem of emotional communications than with the less frequent problem of pilot abuse. The other side of the argument, however, is that in situations where there is the possibility of catastrophic failure, the marginal gain made by keeping controllers who are more sensitive to emotions is less important than the possibility that the price of this sensitivity is occasional inadequate response.

Training settings themselves often have modest validity, as is shown by the widespread agreement that much that is learned during training for air traffic control has to be unlearned once the controller starts to work traffic. For example, simulators used in training do not accurately simulate change of speed in an airplane. When a plane on the simulator changes speed, the new speed takes effect immediately, whereas in real life the change in speed is gradual. That discrepancy could become consequential because people under pressure revert to their first-learned ways of behaving.[3] Under pressure, controllers who first learned to control planes that changed speed swiftly might systematically underestimate the time it actually takes for planes to execute the speed changes that are ordered. Thus, a controller will assume that developing problems can be resolved more quickly than in fact is the case.

When people are trained for high reliability, the first tendencies they learn are crucial because those may be the ones that reappear when pressure increases. If trainers are more concerned with weeding out than with the adequacy of initial responses, then training could again become the source of a breakdown in reliability which it was designed to prevent.

Even when training works, there are problems. If training is successful, there is usually no pattern to the errors trainees make once they actually operate the system. But if operational errors are randomly distributed because the training is good, then it is not clear how operators can reduce those errors that still occur, since there is no way to predict them.

In each of these examples, the benefits of training are either diluted or reversed due to unanticipated effects of emotional, social, and interpretive processes. Closer attention to these processes may uncover new ways to cope with conditions that set accidents in motion. To illustrate this possibility, following is an examination of three ways in which variations in the social construction of reality can affect the likelihood of error-free operations.

Reliability and requisite variety

As noted, to regulate variety, sensors must be as complex as the system which they intend to regulate. An interesting example of less complicated humans who try to manage more complicated systems is found in the repeated observation that the first action of many senior airline captains, when they enter the cockpit and sit down, is to turn up the volume control on the radio equipment to a level which the junior officers regard as unnecessarily high.[4] Data show that the number of aircraft system errors is inversely related to pilots acknowledging the information they receive from controllers. More errors are associated with fewer acknowledgements.[5] When pilots acknowledge a message, they are supposed to repeat the message to verify that they have received it correctly, but busy pilots often acknowledge a transmission by saying simply "Roger," and at other times, they make no acknowledgement at all.

While aircraft errors are often attributed to communication deficiencies, the observation that senior officers turn up the volume on the radio suggests that one source of error may be a hearing deficiency. Older commercial pilots often learned to fly in older, noisier aircraft; and chronic exposure to these conditions may cause current messages to be missed or heard incorrectly. (The hypothesis of a hearing deficiency was not ruled out in the Tenerife disaster on March 27, 1977, and is consistent with all the data assembled about that accident.)

Problems with hearing deficiency are not confined to the airways. Before people are licensed to operate the reactor at Diablo Canyon, they spend up to five years as Auxiliary Operators, which means they work on the floor servicing pipes and valves before they ever set foot inside a control room. As is true with most power generation plants, Diablo Canyon is noisy. This creates the same possible history for reactor operators as is created for senior pilots: they develop less sensory variety than is present in the systems of signals, alarms, voices, and strange noises that are symptoms of changes in the system they are trying to control.

Humans gain as well as lose the variety that is requisite for reliability in several ways. Daft and Lengel, for example, propose that the ways in which people receive information provide varying amounts of requisite variety.[6] Information richness is highest when people work face to face, and informational richness declines steadily as people move from face-to-face interaction to interaction by telephone, written personal communiques (letters and memos), written formal communiques (bulletins, documents), and numeric formal communiques (computer printouts). Effectiveness is postulated to vary as a function of the degree to which informational richness matches the complexity of organizational phenomena. Rich media provide multiple cues and quick feedback which are essential for complex issues but less essential for routine problems. Too much richness introduces the inefficiencies of overcomplication, too little media richness introduces the inaccuracy of oversimplification.

In the context of the Daft and Lengel argument, it becomes potentially important that communication between Morton Thiokol and NASA about the wisdom of launching *Challenger* in unusually cold temperatures was made by a conference telephone call,[7] a medium with less variety than a face-to-face conversation. With only voice cues, NASA did not have visual data of facial expressions and body cues which might have given them more vivid information about the intensity of Thiokol's concerns.

Face-to-face communication in high reliability systems is interesting in the context of the large number of engineers typically found in such systems. One way to describe (and admittedly stereotype) engineers is as smart people who don't talk. Since we know that people tend to devalue what they don't do well, if high reliability systems need rich, dense talk to maintain complexity, then they may find it hard to generate this richness if talk is devalued or if people are unable to find substitutes for talk (e.g., electronic mail may be a substitute).

Up to this point, we have been talking largely about the development of requisite variety in individuals, but in high reliability organizations, requisite variety is often gained or lost by larger groups. When technical systems have more variety than a single individual can comprehend, one of the few ways humans can match this variety is by networks and teams of divergent individuals. A team of divergent individuals has more requisite variety than a team of homogeneous individuals. In problems of high reliability, the fact of divergence may be more crucial than the substance of divergence. Whether team members differ in occupational specialities, past experience, gender, conceptual skills, or personality may be less crucial than the fact that they do differ and look for different things when they size up a problem. If people look for different things, when their observations are pooled they collectively see more than any one of them alone would see. However, as team members become more alike, their pooled observations cannot be distinguished from their individual observations, which means collectively they know little more about a problem than they know individually. And since individuals have severe limits on what they can comprehend, a homogeneous team does little to offset these limits. This line of argument, which suggests that collective diversity increases requisite variety which in turn improves reliability, may conflict with the common prescription that redundancy and parallel systems are an important source of reliability. That prescription is certainly true. But a redundant system is also a homogeneous system and homogenous systems often have less variety than the environments they are trying to manage and less variety than heterogeneous systems that try to manage those same environments.

The issues with collective requisite variety are fascinating as well as complex.

As an example of collective requisite variety, the operating team in the control room at Diablo Canyon has five people who stay together as a team when they change shifts. The lead person on the team is the Shift Foreman whose responsibility is to maintain the "big picture" and not to get into details. There is a Shift Technical Advisor who has engineering expertise and a Senior Control Room Operator who is the most senior union person in the control room. Under the Senior Operator are the Control Room Operator and the Assistant Control Room Operator, the latter being the person who has the newest operating license and who most recently has worked outside the control room. What is striking about this team is the spread of attention among several issues induced by diverse roles.[8]

The issue of effective delegation of responsibility is crucial in high reliability systems. The most effective means for airline pilots to handle crisis, for example, is for the captain to delegate the task of flying the plane and then make decisions about how to handle the crisis without worrying about the details of flying. Obvious as this solution may seem, a failure to delegate positive responsibility for flying the plane has often meant that a crisis absorbed everyone's attention, no one flew the plane, and it crashed.[9]

The importance of collective requisite variety as a means to enhance reliability is one reason people are increasingly concerned about the reduction of flight crews from three to two people, and are especially concerned when that two-person crew is mixed gender. A female co-pilot adds considerable requisite variety, but if it is hard for a male to trust a woman communicating in an environment that has culturally always been a "man's world," then the two-person crew quickly loses variety and errors become more likely.

Collective requisite variety is higher when people both trust others, which enlarges the pool of inputs that are considered before action occurs, and themselves act as trustworthy reporters of their own observations to enlarge that same pool of inputs. Trust, however, is often difficult when diversity increases, because as people become more diverse they also become harder to trust and it is harder to be trusted by them.

Social psychologists have studied these issues in the context of the Asch conformity experiments. Collective requisite variety "is maximized when each person so behaves as to be in his turn a valid dependable model for the others. Each acts as both model and observer."[10] Translated to the Asch situation, this means that the best response for the sake of requisite variety is for the naive subject exposed to discrepant reports to say, "'You fellows are probably right, but I definitely see line B as longer,' i.e., both rationally respecting others as a source of information about the world, and so reporting that others can rationally depend on his report in turn. It is failure in this latter respect that instigates our moral indignation at the conformant chameleon character who parasitically depends upon the competence of others but adds no valid information, no clarifying triangulation, to the social pool."[11]

Requisite variety is enhanced by face-to-face communications for two reasons. First, face-to-face contact makes it easier to assess and build trust and trustworthiness. Second, face-to-face contact makes it easier to get more complete data once trust and trustworthiness have been established. Since people are the medium through which reliability is accomplished, signals relevant to reliability flow through them. When those people are both trusted and dealt with face to face, more information is conveyed, which should produce earlier detection of potential errors.

Building trust in high reliability systems is difficult because so much is at stake. People want to delegate responsibility, but not too soon and not without continued surveillance to see that continued delegation is warranted. A neat resolution of this dilemma is found in the comment of a Navy nuclear propulsion expert who parries a complaint from a second-class petty officer. The complaint goes, "Sir, I'm not stupid or incompetent. I've had over a year of specialized training and two years of experience, but no one trusts me. Everything I do is checked and double-checked." The engineer replies, "It's not a matter of trust. Your ability, training, and experience allow me to trust completely that in an emergency you will do the right thing – or at least a survivable thing. In a non-emergency situation, however, . . . we all make mistakes. . . . That is why your work is checked."[12]

This particular system builds reliability by institutionalizing an important bit of evolutionary wisdom: "Ambivalence is the optimal compromise."[13] The answer to the question "Don't you trust me?" is both yes and no: "Yes, I trust you if it's an emergency; no, I don't trust you if it's practice." Application of this rule presumably builds confidence, competence, and trustworthiness so that trust takes care of itself when the stakes rise dramatically.

Reliability is a dynamic non-event

Reliability is both dynamic and invisible, and this creates problems. Reliability is dynamic in the sense that it is an ongoing condition in which problems are momentarily under control due to compensating changes in components. Reliability is invisible in at least two ways. First, people often don't know how many mistakes they could have made but didn't, which means they have at best only a crude idea of what produces reliability and how reliable they are. For example, if a telephone switching unit normally loses dial tone for 12 minutes out of 72 hours, but could have potentially lost it for 15 minutes, that suggests very different information about its reliability than if it could have lost dial tone for 120 minutes during that same period. Reliability is also invisible in the sense that reliable outcomes are constant, which means there is nothing to pay attention to. Operators see nothing and seeing nothing, presume that nothing is happening. If nothing is happening and if they continue to act the way they have been, nothing will continue to happen. This diagnosis is deceptive and misleading because dynamic inputs create stable outcomes.

A nuclear power plant operator: "I'll tell you what dull is. Dull is operating the power plant." Another operator describing his plight: "I have total concentration, for five hours, on nothing happening." A senior officer on a nuclear carrier: "When planes are missing the arresting wire, and can't find the tanker where they are to refuel, and the wind is at 40 knots and the ship is turning, there are no errors." This latter experience is confirmed in studies of air traffic controllers. There tend to be more errors in air traffic control under light traffic load than under heavy load because, under high load, controllers visually sweep the entire radar screen whereas in low load they don't. When they fail to sweep the screen, problems can build to more extreme levels at the edges.

When there are non-events, attention not only flags, it is often discouraged. Consider the homespun advice: if it ain't broke, don't fix it. The danger in that advice is that something that isn't broken today, may be tomorrow. Just because a two-engine Boeing 767 airplane hasn't crashed yet while crossing the Atlantic Ocean doesn't mean that a system with two rather than three pilots having two rather than three engines is a reliable system. What it means is that there hasn't been any trial and error on two-engine transatlantic flights, which means people don't yet have any idea of what they know about such flying. That uncertainty can give way to an illusion that since there have been no errors, there must be nothing to learn, which must mean we know what there is to know.

More attentiveness and more reliability might be induced if we were able to shift the homespun advice from its static form to a more dynamic form: if it isn't breaking, don't fix it. Such a modification might alert observers to the dynamic properties of reliable situations, to the fact that small errors can enlarge, to the possibility that complacency is dangerous, to the more active search for incipient errors rather than the more passive wait for developed errors. Both the early explosions of the de Haviland Comet jet airliners as well as the capsizing of the newly designed Alexander L. Keilland oil rig were traced to small cracks that enlarged gradually and then catastrophically under high stress.[14] The Comet aircraft exploded when a crack, which started at the edge of one cabin window after repeated pressurization and depressurization, suddenly enlarged and ripped open the skin of the aircraft.[15] The oil rig collapsed when a 3-inch crack in the frame, which was painted over rather than re-welded, enlarged during a North Sea gale.[16]

Part of the mindset for reliability requires chronic suspicion that small deviations may enlarge, a sensitivity that may be encouraged by a more dynamic view of reliability. People need to see that inertia is a complex state, that forcefield diagrams have multiple forces operating in opposed directions, and that reliability is an ongoing accomplishment. Once situations are made reliable, they will unravel if they are left unattended.

While it is a subtle point, most situations that have constant outcomes – situations such as a marriage, or social drinking, or an alcohol rehabilitation program – collapse when people stop doing whatever produced the stable outcome. And often what produced the stable outcome was continuous change, not continuous repetition. We all smile when we hear the phrase, "the more things change, the more they stay the same." The lesson in that truism for problems of reliability is that sameness is a function of change. For a relationship to stay constant, a change of one element must be compensated for by a change in other elements.

When people think they have a problem solved, they often let up, which means they stop making continuous adjustments. When the shuttle flights continued to depart and return successfully, the criterion for a launch – "Convince me that I should send the *Challenger*" – was dropped. Underestimating the dynamic nature of reliability, managers inserted a new criterion – "Convince me that I shouldn't send the *Challenger*."

Reward structures need to be changed so that when a controller says, "By God, I did it again . . . not a single plane collided in my sector today," that is not treated as a silly remark. If a controller can produce a dull, normal day, that should earn recognition and praise because the controller had to change to achieve that outcome.

People aren't used to giving praise for reliability. Since they see nothing when reliability is accomplished, they assume that it is easier to achieve reliability than in fact is true. As a result, the public ignores those who are most successful at achieving reliability and gives them few incentives to continue in their uneventful ways.

Reliability as enactment

A peculiar problem of systems is that people in them do not do what the system says they are doing. John Gall illustrates this problem with the example of shipbuilding: "If you go down to Hampton Roads or any other shipyard and look around for a ship-builder you will be disappointed. You will find – in abundance – welders, carpenters, foremen, engineers, and many other specialists, but no shipbuilders. True, the company executives may call themselves shipbuilders, but if you observe them at their work, you will see that it really consists of writing contracts, planning budgets, and other administrative activities. Clearly, they are not in any concrete sense building ships. In cold fact, a system is building ships, and the *system* is the shipbuilder."[17]

If people are not doing what the system says they are doing, then they know less about what is dangerous and how their own activities might create or undermine reliability. Just as nurses commit medical errors when they forget that the chart is not the patient, operators commit reactor errors when they forget that the dial is not the technology.

These misunderstandings, however, are not inevitable. There are systems which achieve high reliability because, for them, the chart is the patient. They provide one model of ways to restructure other systems which have reliability problems.

The system that will illustrate the argument is the air traffic control system. One striking property of air traffic control is that controllers are the technology, they don't watch the technology. Controllers build their own system in the sense that they build the pattern of aircraft they manage by interacting with pilots, using standard phraseology, and allocating space. The instructions that controllers issue are the system and hold the system together. Controllers do not suffer the same isolation from the world they work with as do people in other systems. For example, air traffic controllers on the carrier *Carl Vinson* make an effort to learn more about the quirks of their carrier pilots. As a result, they are able to separate quick responders from slow responders. This knowledge enables controllers to build a more stable environment when they line up pilots to land on a carrier under conditions where high reliability performance is threatened. Because controllers also use voice cues, they often are able to build a more complete picture of the environment they "face" because they are able to detect fear in voices and give a fearful pilot more airspace than is given to a confident pilot.

The ability of controllers to enact their environments can be interpreted as the use of slack as a means of increase reliability. Controllers can add slack to the system by standardizing their customers so that they expect more delays. Overload comes not so much from the number of planes that a controller is working as from the complexity of the interactions with the pilot that occur. A complicated reroute can monopolize so much time that a nearly empty sky can become dangerous when the few remaining planes are totally neglected. If controllers can reduce the number of times they talk to a pilot and the length of time they talk to a pilot, they can add slack to their system.

Controllers can also hold planes on the ground, slow them, accelerate them, turn them sooner, line them up sooner, stack them, or refuse to accept them, to build an environment in which reliability is higher. Airplanes stacked into holding patterns provide a perfect example of an enacted environment. Space which had previously been formless and empty now is structured to have layers 1000 feet apart, a shape, and a pattern in which planes enter at the top and exit from the bottom. An environment has been created by the controller which then constrains what he or she does.

While a stack is a good example of an enacted environment, it also illustrates that when people construct their own environments, they create problems as well as solutions. When a controller creates slack by stacking airplanes, this solution creates at least two problems. First, stacks "get loose," which means that planes drift outside the circular pattern as well as up or down from their assigned altitude. Second, a stack, when viewed on a radar screen, creates lots of clutter in a small space so it is harder for the controller to keep track of all the players.

As if discretion and looseness were not enough heresy to introduce into a discussion of high reliability, it is also important to make the point that the air traffic control system works partly because it is an exercise in faith. Unless pilots and controllers each anticipate what the other is going to say, the clipped phraseology they use would never work. Their communiques usually ratify expectations rather than inform, which means that if an unexpected remark is made, then people begin to listen to one another.

For example, foreign national pilots (e.g., China Air) who fly into San Francisco International Airport, and for whom English is a distant second language, are hard to understand. Controllers are unsure what those pilots have heard or what their intentions are. In cluttered skies, this uncertainty increases the probability of error. The system around San Francisco is held together by faith in the sense that the pilots and controllers each anticipate what they will be told to do and each tries to meet these anticipations as much as possible. The elegant solution adopted when the language problem is especially severe is that the foreign pilot is directed to fly straight to the airport and land, and all other aircraft, piloted by people who have better command of English, are routed around the straight-in flight.

The importance of faith in holding a system together in ways that reduce errors has been discussed for some time as "The Right Stuff." The right stuff often creates reliability, and the way it does so is important to identify, partly because that process is currently in jeopardy at NASA.

No system can completely avoid errors. Any discussion of reliability must start with that as axiomatic. Actors frequently underestimate the number of errors that can occur. But if these same actors are dedicated people who work hard, live by their wits, take risks, and improvise, then their intense efforts to make things work can prevent some errors. Because they are able to make do and improvise, they essentially create the error-free situation they expected to find. What they fail to see is that their own committed efforts, driven by faith in the system, knit that system together and create the reliability which up to that point existed only in their imaginations.

While this mechanism is sometimes interpreted as macho bravado,[18] it is important to remember that confidence is just as important in the production of reliability as is doubt. The mutually exclusive character of these two determinants can be seen in the growing doubt among astronauts that they have been flying the safe system they thought they were. Notice that the system itself has not suddenly changed character. What has changed is the faith that may have brought forth a level of commitment that created some of the safety that was anticipated. Obviously, there are limits to faith. The *Challenger* did explode. But whatever increments to safety the process of faith may have added are no longer there as astronauts see more clearly the shortcuts, problems, and uncertainties which their committed efforts had previously transformed into a temporarily functioning system.

While the activity of air traffic control can be viewed in many ways, I have chosen to emphasize that qualities such as discretion, latitude, looseness, enactment, slack, improvisation, and faith work through human beings to increase reliability. The air traffic control system seems to keep the human more actively in the loop of technology than is true for other systems in which reliability is a bigger problem. It is not immediately clear what the lesson in design is for a nuclear power generation facility, but neither is it self-evident that such a design question is nonsensical. The air traffic control system, because it has not been taken over by technology, accommodates to human limitations rather than automates them away.

But there are threats to the enacted quality of air traffic control and they come from plans to automate more control functions so that the system can be speeded up. Any automated system that controls traffic can go down without warning, which forces controllers to intervene and pick up the pieces.[19] If automated control allows planes to fly closer together (e.g., separated by 10 seconds), the problem is that then when the control fails, humans will not be able to pick up the pieces because they are not smart enough or fast enough. A system in which looseness, discretion, enactment, and slack once made reliability possible will have become a system in which reliability is uncontrollable.

Automation, however, is not at fault. Automation makes a 10-second separation possible. But just because such separation is possible, doesn't mean it has to be implemented. That remains a human decision. The heightened capacity isn't dumb, but the decision to heighten capacity may be.

Cultures of Reliability

In many of the problems we've looked at, the recurring question is, "What's going on here?" That's not so much a question of what decision to make as it is a question of what meaning is appropriate so we can then figure out what decision we need to make. It is important to underscore that difference because more attention is paid to organizations as decision makers than to organizations as interpretation systems that generate meaning. That's one reason why the recent interest in organizational culture is important, because it has redistributed the amount of attention that is given to issues of meaning and deciding. That shift in emphasis is summarized in Cohen, March, and Olsen's observation that "an organization is a set of procedures for argumentation and interpretations as well as for solving problems and making decisions."[20]

One reason organizational theorists have had trouble trying to think clearly about issues of reliability is that they have made a fundamental error when they think about meaning and decisions. A discussion by Tushman and Romanelli illustrates the problem.[21] In their presentation of an evolutionary model of organization, they argue that managers are concerned both with making decisions and with managing meaning. They accommodate these two rather different activities by arguing that managers make decisions when environments are turbulent and make meanings when environments are stable. I think they've got it backwards, and that's symptomatic of the problems people have when they think about reliability and how to achieve it.

To make decisions, you need a stable environment where prediction is possible, so that the value of different options can be estimated. The rational model works best in a stable environment. When environments become unstable, then people need first to make meaning in order to see what, if anything, there is to decide. When there is swift change, you either label the change to see what you should be paying attention to, or you take action in an effort to slow the change so that you can then make a rational decision. Stabilization and enactment make meaning possible, which means they necessarily precede decision making.

Making meaning is an issue of culture, which is one reason culture is important in high reliability systems. But culture is important for another reason. Throughout the preceding analysis, I have highlighted the importance of discretion and have played down the necessity for centralization. But the real trick in high reliability systems is somehow to achieve simultaneous centralization and decentralization. People need to benefit from the lessons of previous operators and to profit from whatever trials and errors they have been able to accumulate. And when errors happen, people need a clear chain of command to deal with the situation. These are requirements of centralization. There has to be enough centralization that no one objects when the airline captain delegates authority for flying the plane while he tries to focus his full attention on the crisis. A control room full of people all shouting contradictory diagnoses and directions, as was the case at Three Mile Island, does little to clarify thinking.

But a system in which both centralization and decentralization occur simultaneously is difficult to design. And this is where culture comes in. Either culture or standard operating procedures can impose order and serve as substitutes for centralization. But only culture also adds in latitude for interpretation, improvisation, and unique action.

Before you can decentralize, you first have to centralize so that people are socialized to use similar decision premises and assumptions so that when they operate their own units, those decentralized operations are equivalent and coordinated.[22] This is precisely what culture does. It creates a homogeneous set of assumptions and decision premises which, when they are invoked on a local and decentralized basis, preserve coordination and centralization. Most important, when centralization oc-curs via decision premises and assumptions, compliance occurs without surveillance. This is in sharp contrast to centralization by rules and regulations or centralization by standardization and hierarchy, both of which require high surveillance. Further-more, neither rules nor standardization are well equipped to deal with emergencies for which there is no precedent.

The best example of simultaneous centralization and decentralization remains Herbert Kaufman's marvelous study of the Forest Ranger[23] which shows, as do many of Philip Selznick's analyses,[24] that whenever you have what appears to be successful decentralization, if you look more closely, you will discover that it was always pre-ceded by a period of intense centralization where a set of core values were hammered out and socialized into people before the people were turned loose to go their own "independent," "autonomous" ways.

It is potentially relevant that operators and managers in many nuclear power reactors (those with fewest errors?) have had prior Navy nuclear experiences and that many FAA controllers are former military controllers. In both cases, there are previously shared values concerning reliability which then allow for coordinated, decentralized action. The magnitude of shared values varies among power stations as does the content of the values which are shared. A research question that may predict the likelihood of errors is the extent of sharing and the content that is shared on operating teams.

Culture coordinates action at a distance by several symbolic means, and one that seems of particular importance is the use of stories. Stories remind people of key values on which they are centralized. When people share the same stories, those stories provide general guidelines within which they can customize diagnoses and solutions to local problems.

Stories are important, not just because they coordinate, but also because they register, summarize, and allow reconstruction of scenarios that are too complex for logical linear summaries to preserve. Stories hold the potential to enhance requisite variety among human actors, and that's why high reliability systems may handicap themselves when they become preoccupied with traditional rationality and fail to recognize the power of narrative rationality.[25]

Daft and Wiginton have argued that natural language, metaphors, and patterns that connect have more requisite variety than do notation, argumentative rational-ity, or models.[26] Models are unable to connect as many facts as stories, they preserve fewer interactions, and they are unable to put these interactions in motion so that outcomes can be anticipated.

Richard Feynman tells a story about the *Challenger* disaster when he dips O-ring material from the booster into a glass of ice water and discovers that it becomes brittle. Rudolph Pick, a chemical engineer writing to the *New York Times* on January 14, 1986, observed that the only way he could impress people with the danger of overfilling vessels with chemicals was to use what he called the psychological ap-proach. "After I immersed a piece of chicken meat for several minutes in the toxic and corrosive liquid, only the bone remained. Nobody took any short cuts to estab-lished procedures after this demonstration and there were no injuries." Pick tells this story about hydrofluoric acid and the message remains with people once they scatter to their various assignments. Thus, the story coordinates them by instilling a similar set of decision premises. But the story also works because, from this small incident, people are able to remember and reconstruct a complicated set of chemical interactions that would be forgotten were some other medium, such as a set of regulations, used.

When people do troubleshooting, they try to tell stories that might have, as their punch lines, the particular problem that now confronts them.[27] When stories cannot be invented, troubleshooting and reliability become more difficult. For example, Diablo Canyon has a poor memory for some past decisions and relatively few stories. This creates trouble when people find that a problem can be traced to an odd configuration of pipes. When this happens, they face the disturbing possibility that the odd configuration may solve some larger, more serious problem that no one can remember. Rerouting may solve the immediate problem, but it might also set in motion an unexpected set of interactions that were once anticipated and blocked, though no one now can recall them. Stories about infrastructure are not trivial.

What all of this leads to is an unusual reconstruction of the events of the night of January 27, 1986, when NASA was arguing with Morton Thiokol about whether freezing weather would disable the booster rocket. That conversation apparently took the traditional course of people arguing in linear, sequential fashion about the pros and cons of a launch. If, somewhere in those discussions, someone had said, "That reminds me of a story,"[28] a different rationality might have been applied and a different set of implications might have been drawn. Those, in turn, might well have led to a different outcome. There are precedents in history. The solution of the Cuban Missile crisis by a surgical airstrike was dropped when Robert Kennedy recalled the story of Pearl Harbor, and portrayed a U. S. attack on Cuba as Pearl Harbor in reverse.[29]

We have thought about reliability in conventional ways using ideas of structure, training, and redundancy, and seem to be up against some limits in where those ideas can take us. Re-examination of the issue of reliability using a less traditional set of categories associated with an interpretive point of view seems to suggest some new places to attack the problem.

Acknowledgment

I am grateful to Lisa Berlinger, Larry Browning, George Huber, Todd LaPorte, Reuben McDaniel, Karlene Roberts, and Sim Sitkin for comments on an initial draft of this manuscript.

The analyses in this chapter represent work in progress and are derived from interaction with a group at Berkeley that is concerned with hypercomplex organizations and a group at Texas that is concerned with narrative rationality. The key people in the Berkeley group include Karlene Roberts, Todd LaPorte, and Gene Rochlin. Key people at Texas include Larry Browning, George Huber, Reuben McDaniel, Sim Sitkin, and Rich Cherwitz. The data with which I am working come from observations and interviews with people who operate the Diablo Canyon nuclear reactor, the Nuclear Carrier *U.S.S. Carl Vinson*, and the air traffic control center at Fremont, California, as well as workshops, literature reviews, and discussions.

References

1. C. Perrow, *Normal Accidents* (New York, NY: Basic Books, 1984).
2. See, for example, W. Buckley, "Society as a Complex Adaptive System," in W. Buckley, ed., *Modern Systems Research for the Behavioral Scientist* (Chicago, IL: Aldine, 1968), pp. 490–513.
3. K. E. Weick, "A Stress Analysis of Future Battlefields," in J. G. Hunt and J. D. Blair, eds., *Leadership on the Future Battlefield* (Washington, D.C.: Pergamon, 1985), pp. 32–46.
4. R. Hurst, "Portents and Challenges," in R. Hurst and L. R. Hurst, eds., *Pilot Error: The Human Factors*, 2nd Ed. (New York, NY: Aronson, 1982), p. 175.
5. Ibid., p. 176.
6. R. L. Daft and R. H. Lengel, "Information Richness: A New Approach to Manager Information Processing and Organization Design," in B. Staw and L. L. Cummings, eds., *Research in Organizational Behavior: Vol. 6* (Greenwich, CT: JAI Press, 1984), pp. 191–233.
7. R. J. Smith, "Shuttle Inquiry Focuses on Weather, Rubber Seals, and Unheeded Advice," *Science*, 231 (1986): 909.
8. N. W. Biggart and G. G. Hamilton, "The Power of Obedience," *Administrative Science Quarterly*, 28 (1984): 540–549.
9. See, for example, E. L. Wiener, "Mid-Air Collisions: The Accidents, the Systems, and the Realpolitik," in R. Hurst and L. R. Hurst, eds., *Pilot Error: The Human Factors*, 2nd Ed. (New York, NY: Aronson, 1982), pp. 101–117.
10. D. T. Campbell, "Conformity in Psychology's Theories of Acquired Behavioral Dispositions," in I. A. Berg and B. M. Bass, eds., *Conformity and Deviation* (New York, NY: Harper, 1961), p. 123.
11. Ibid.
12. J. D. Jones, "Nobody Asked Me, But . . . ," *United States Naval Institute Proceedings*, November 1977, p. 87.
13. D. T. Campbell, "Ethnocentric and Other Altruistic Motives," in D. Levine, ed., *Nebraska Symposium on Motivation, 1965* (Lincoln, NE: University of Nebraska), pp. 2283–2311.
14. H. Petroski, *To Engineer is Human* (New York, NY: St. Martin's Press, 1985).
15. Ibid., p. 178.
16. Ibid., p. 174.
17. J. Gall, *Systematics: How Systems Work and Especially How They Fail* (New York, NY: New York Times Book Co., 1977), pp. 32–33.
18. M. Allnutt, "Human Factors: Basic Principles," in R. Hurst and L. R. Hurst, eds., *Pilot Errors: The Human Factors*, 2nd Ed. (New York, NY: Aronson, 1982), pp. 14–15.
19. J. M. Finkelman and C. Kirschner, "An Information-Processing Interpretation of Air Traffic Control Stress," *Human Factors*, 22 (1980): 561.
20. M. D. Cohen, J. G. March, and J. P. Olsen, "People, Problems, Solutions, and the Ambiguity of Relevance," in J. G. March and J. P. Olsen, eds., *Ambiguity and Choice in Organizations* (Bergen, Norway: Universitetsforlaget, 1976), p. 25.
21. M. L. Tushman and E. Romanelli, "Organizational Evolution: A Metamorphosis Model of Convergence and Reorientation," in L. L. Cummings and B. M. Staw, eds., *Research in Organizational Behavior: Vol. 7* (Greenwich, CT: JAI Press, 1985), pp. 196, 209–212.
22. C. Perrow, "The Bureaucratic Paradox: The Efficient Organization Centralizes in Order to Decentralize," *Organizational Dynamics*, 5/4 (1977): 3–14.

23. H. Kaufman, *The Forest Ranger* (Baltimore, MD: Johns Hopkins, 1967).

24. P. Selznick, *Leadership in Administration* (New York, NY: Harper & Row, 1957).

25. K. E. Weick and L. B. Browning, "Argument and Narration in Organizational Communication," *Journal of Management*, 12 (1986): 243–259.

26. R. L. Daft and J. Wiginton, "Language and Organizations," *Academy of Management Review*, 4 (1979): 179–191.

27. N. M. Morris and W. B. Rouse, "Review and Evaluation of Empirical Research in Troubleshooting," *Human Factors*, 27 (1985): 503-530.

28. M. H. Brown, "That Reminds Me of a Story: Speech Action in Organizational socialization," *Western Journal of Speech Communication*, 49 (1985): 27–42.

29. P. A. Anderson, "Decision Making by Objection and the Cuban Missile Crisis," *Administrative Science Quarterly*, 28 (1983): 211–212.

15

Substitutes for Strategy

A little strategy goes a long way. Too much can paralyze or splinter an organization. That conclusion derives from the possibility that strategy-like outcomes originate from sources other than strategy. Adding explicit strategy to these other tacit sources of strategy can be self-defeating and reduce effectiveness (Bresser and Bishop 1983). Thus, the focus of this chapter is substitutes for strategy.

The model for this exercise is the concept in the leadership literature of substitutes for leadership (Kerr and Jermier 1978). Substitutes are conditions that either neutralize what leaders do or perform many of the same functions they would. Substitutes include characteristics of subordinates (ability, knowledge, experience, training, professional orientation, indifference toward organizational rewards), characteristics of the task (unambiguous, routine, provides its own feedback, intrinsically satisfying), and characteristics of the organization (high formalization, highly specified staff functions, closely knit cohesive groups, organizational rewards not controlled by leaders, spatial distance between subordinates and superiors). Leadership has less impact when one or more of these conditions obtains. It is not that the situation is devoid of leadership; rather, the leadership is done by something else.

It seems reasonable to work analogically and investigate the extent to which it is possible to create substitutes for strategies.

If pressed to define *strategy*, I am tempted to adopt de Bono's (1984: 143) statement that "strategy is good luck rationalized in hindsight," but I am also comfortable with a definition much like Robert Burgelman's (1983) – namely, "strategy is a theory about the reasons for past and current success of the firm." Both of my definitional preferences differ sharply from Chandler's (1962) classic definition of *strategy* – "The determination of the basic long-term goals and objectives of an enterprise, and the adoption of courses of action and the allocation of resources necessary for carrying out these goals."

Definitions notwithstanding, I can best show what I think strategy is by describing an incident that happened during military maneuvers in Switzerland. The young lieutenant of a small Hungarian detachment in the Alps sent a reconnaissance unit into the icy wilderness. It began to snow immediately, snowed for two days, and the unit did not return. The lieutenant suffered, fearing that he had dispatched his own people to death. But the third day the unit came back. Where had they been? How had they made their way? Yes, they said, we considered ourselves lost and waited for the end. And then one of us found a map in his pocket. That calmed us down. We pitched camp, lasted out the snowstorm, and then with the map we discovered our bearings. And here we are. The lieutenant borrowed this remarkable map and had a good look at it. He discovered to his astonishment that it was not a map of the Alps, but a map of the Pyrenees.

This incident raises the intriguing possibility that when you are lost, any old map will do. Extended to the issue of strategy, maybe when you are confused, any old strategic plan will do.

Strategic plans are a lot like maps. They animate people and they orient people. Once people begin to act, they generate tangible outcomes in some context, and this helps them discover what is occurring, what needs to be explained, and what should be done next. Managers keep forgetting that it is what they do, not what they plan that explains their success. They keep giving credit to the wrong thing – namely, the plan – and having made this error, they then spend more time planning and less time acting. They are astonished when more planning improves nothing.

Kirk Downey has suggested that the Alps example is a success story for two quite specific reasons. First, the troops found a specific map that was relevant to their problem. Had they found a map of Disneyland rather than a map of the Pyrenees their problem would have deepened materially. Second, the troops had a purpose – that is, they wanted to go back to their base camp – and it was in the context of this purpose that the map took on meaning as a means to get them back. These conditions, however, do not negate the basic theme that meaning lies in the path of the action. A map of Disneyland makes it harder to develop a shared understanding of what has happened and where we have been, but if it does not inhibit action and observation, some clearer sense of the situation may emerge as action proceeds.

When I described the incident of using a map of the Pyrenees to find a way out of the Alps to Bob Engel, the executive vice president and treasurer of Morgan Guaranty, he said, "Now, that story would have been really neat if the leader out with the lost troops had known it was the wrong map and still been able to lead them back."

What is interesting about Engel's twist to the story is that he has described the basic situation that most leaders face. Followers are often lost and even the leader is not sure where to go. All the leader knows is that the plan or the map he has in front of him is not sufficient by itself to get them out. What he has to do, when faced with this situation, is instill some confidence in people, get them moving in some general direction, and be sure they look closely at what actually happens, so that they learn where they were and get some better idea of where they are and where they want to be.

If you get people moving, thinking clearly, and watching closely, events often become more meaningful. For one thing, a map of the Pyrenees can still be a plausible map of the Alps because in a very general sense, if you have seen one mountain range, you have seen them all (readers can test this assertion for themselves by examining "A Traveler's Map of the Alps" in the April 1985 issue of *National Geographic Magazine*). The Pyrenees share some features with the Alps, and if people pay attention to these common features, they may find their way out. For example, most mountain ranges are wet on one side and dry on the other. Water flows down rather than up. There is a prevailing wind. There are peaks and valleys. There is a highest point, and then the peaks get lower and lower until there are foothills.

Just as it is true that if you have seen one mountain range you have seen them all, it also is true that if you have seen one organization you have seen them all. Any old plan will work in an organization because people usually learn by trial and error, some people listen and some people talk, people want to get somewhere and have some general sense of where they now are, 20 percent of the people will do 80 percent of the work (and vice versa), and if you do something for somebody, they are more likely to do something for you. Given these general features of most organizations, any old plan is often sufficient to get this whole mechanism moving, which then makes it possible to learn what is going on and what needs to be done next.

The generic process involved is that meaning is produced because the leader treats a vague map or plan as if it had some meaning, even though he knows full well that the real meaning will come only when people respond to the map and do something. The secret of leading with a bad map is to create a self-fulfilling prophecy. Having predicted that the group will find its way out, the leader creates the combination of optimism and action that allows people to turn their confusion into meaning and find their way home.

There are plenty of examples in industry where vague plans and projects provide an excuse for people to act, learn, and create meaning.

The founders of Banana Republic, the successful mail order clothier, started their business by acting in an improbable manner. They bought uniforms from over-thrown armies in South America and advertised these items in a catalog, using drawings rather than photographs. All of these actions were labeled poor strategy by other mail order firms. When these three actions were set in motion, however, they generated responses that no one expected (because no one had tested them) and created a belated strategy as well as a distinct niche for Banana Republic.

Tuesday Morning, an off-price retailing chain that sells household and gift items, opens its stores when they have enough merchandise to sell and then closes them until they get the next batch. As managers followed this pattern, they discovered that customers love grand openings and that anticipation would build between closings over when the store would open again and what it would contain. These anticipations were sufficiently energizing that stores that opened intermittently for four to eight weeks sold more than equivalent stores that were open year round.

The Microelectronics and Computer Technology Corporation (MCC) consortium in Austin, Texas, is a clear example of the sequence in which vague projects trigger sufficient action that vagueness gets removed. A key Texas state official described MCC as "an event, not a company." Bidding for MCC to locate in Texas became a vehicle to pull competing Texas cities together. It also became a vehicle to tell out-of-state people, "We are a national and an international force, not just a regional force, and not just a land of cowboys and rednecks." MCC became a tangible indication that Texas was growing, maturing, and on its way up. MCC's criteria for a good site became defining characteristics of what Austin was as a city, though Austinites did not realize they had this identity before. MCC said in its specifications that it did not want to locate where everyone thinks they know how high-tech R&D should be done. Texas thus "discovered" that its backwardness was in fact one of its biggest assets.

Acquiring MCC became a strategy to strengthen Texas, but only quite late, when more and more problems were seen to be solved if it landed in Austin. The action of bidding for MCC fanned out in ways that people had not anticipated. The point is, if action is decoupled from strategy, then people have a better chance to be opportunistic, to discover missions and resources they had no idea existed.

So far three themes have been introduced: (1) that action clarifies meaning; (2) that the pretext for the action is of secondary importance; (3) and that strategic planning is only one of many pretexts for meaning-generation in organizations. To clarify some ways in which action can substitute for strategy, we will look more closely at the dynamics of confidence and improvisation.

Confidence as Strategy

In managerial work, thought precedes action, but the kind of thought that often occurs is not detailed analytical thought addressed to imagined scenarios in which actions are tried and options chosen. Instead, thought precedes action in the form of much more general expectations about the orderliness of what will occur.

Order is present, not because extended prior analysis revealed it but because the manager anticipates sufficient order that she wades into the situation, imposes order among events, and then "discovers" what she had imposed. The manager "knew" all along that the situation would make sense. This was treated as a given. Having presumed that it would be sensible, the manager then acts confidently and implants the order that was anticipated.

Most managerial situations contain gaps, discontinuities, loose ties among people and events, indeterminacies, and uncertainties. These are the gaps that managers have to bridge. It is the contention of this argument that managers first think their way across these gaps and then, having tied the elements together cognitively, actually tie them together when they act and impose covariation. This sequence is similar to sequences associated with self-fulfilling prophecies (see Snyder, Tanke, and Berscheid 1977).

Thus presumptions of logic are forms of thought that are crucial for their evocative qualities. The presumption leads people to act more forcefully, the more certain the presumption. Strong presumptions (such as, "I know that these are the Pyrenees") lead to strong actions that impose considerable order. Weaker presumptions lead to more hesitant actions, which means either that the person will be more influenced by the circumstances that are already present or that only weak order will be created.

Presumptions of logic are evident in the chronic optimism often associated with managerial activity. This optimism is conspicuous in the case of companies that are in trouble, but it is also evident in more run-of-the-mill managing. Optimism is one manifestation of the belief that situations will have made sense. William James (1956) described the faith that life is worth living that generates the action that then makes life worth living. Optimism is not necessarily a denial of reality. Instead it may be the belief that makes reality possible.

Presumptions of logic should be prominent among managers because of the climate of rationality in organizations (Staw 1980). Presumptions should be especially prominent when beliefs about cause and effect linkages are unclear (Thompson 1964: 336). Thompson labels the kind of managing that occurs when there are unclear preferences and unclear cause/effect beliefs *inspiration*. It is precisely in the face of massive uncertainty that beliefs of some sort are necessary to evoke some action, which can then begin to consolidate the situations. To inspire is to affirm realities, which then are more likely to materialize if they are sought vigorously. That sequence may be the essence of managing.

Examples of the effect of presumptions are plentiful. A male who believes he is telephoning an attractive female speaks more warmly, which evokes a warm response from her, which confirms the original stereotype that attractive women are sociable (Snyder, Tanke, and Berscheid 1977). A new administrator, suspecting that old-timers are traditional, seeks ideas from other sources, which increases the suspicion of old-timers and confirms the administrator's original presumption (Warwick, 1975). People who presume that no one likes them approach a new gathering in a stiff, distrustful manner, which evokes the unsympathetic behavior they presumed would be there (Watzlawick, Beavin, and Jackson 1967: 98–99). A musician who doubts the competence of a composer plays his music lethargically and produces the ugly sound that confirms the original suspicion (Weick, Gilfillan, and Keith 1973).

In each case, an initial presumption (she is sociable, they are uncreative, people are hostile, he is incompetent) leads people to act forcibly (talk warmly, seek ideas elsewhere, behave defensively, ignore written music), which causes a situation to become more orderly (warmth is exchanged, ideas emerge, hostility is focused, music becomes simplistic), which then makes the situation easier to interpret, thereby confirming the original presumption that it will have been logical.

This sequence is common among managers because managerial actions are almost ideally suited to sustain self-fulfilling prophecies (Eden 1984). Managerial actions are primarily oral, face to face, symbolic, presumptive, brief, and spontaneous (McCall and Kaplan 1985). These actions have a deterministic effect on many organizational situations because those situations are less tightly coupled than are the confident actions directed at them. The situations are loosely coupled, subject to multiple interpretations, monitored regularly by only a handful of people, and deficient in structure.

Thus a situation of basic disorder becomes more orderly when people overlook the disorder and presume orderliness, then act on this presumption, and finally rearrange its elements into a more meaningful arrangement that confirms the original presumption. It is suggested that typical managerial behavior is more likely to create rather than disrupt this sequence. Thus, a manager's preoccupation with rationality may be significant less for its power as an analytic problem-solving tool than for its power to induce action that eventually implants the rationality that was presumed when the sequence started.

The lesson of self-fulfilling prophecies for students of strategy is that strong beliefs that single out and intensify consistent action can bring events into existence (see Snyder 1984). Whether people are called fanatics, true believers, or the currently popular phrase *idea champions*, they all embody what looks like strategy in their persistent behavior. Their persistence carries the strategy; the persistence is the strategy. True believers impose their view on the world and fulfill their own prophecies. Note that this makes strategy more of a motivational problem than a cognitive forecasting problem.

An argument can be made that the so-called computer revolution is an ideal exhibit of confidence as strategy. The revolution is as much vendor-driven as it is need-driven. The revolution can be viewed as solutions in search of problems people never knew they had. Vendors had more forcefulness, confidence, and focus than did their customers, who had only a vague sense that things were not running right, although they could not say why. Vendors defined the unease as a clear problem in control and information distribution, a definition that was no worse than any other diagnosis that was available.

To say that it was IBM's strategy to be forceful is to miss the core of what actually happened. The key point is that IBM's strategy worked after it became self-confirming, when it put an environment in place. A common error is that the strategic plan is valued because it looks like it correctly forecast a pent-up demand for computers. Actually, it did no such thing. Instead, the plan served as a pretext for people to act forcefully and impose their view of the world. Once they imposed, enacted, and stabilized that view and once it was accepted, then more traditional procedures of strategic planning could be made to work because they were directed at more predictable problems in a more stable environment. What gets missed by strategy analysts is that proaction precedes reaction. Strategic planning works only after forceful action has hammered the environment into shape so that it is less variable and so that conventional planning tools can now be made to work. Because the constrained environment contains demands, opportunities, and problems that were imposed during proaction, proaction, not planning, predicts what the organization has to contend with.

To see how self-fulfilling prophecies can mimic strategy and affect the direction of behavior, consider the problem of regulation. Although companies groan about the weight of regulation, data (McCaffrey 1982) suggest that regulators do not have their act together and are loosely coupled relative to the tightly coupled organizations and lawyers they try to regulate. Thus, many organizations ironically create the regulators who control them. The way they do this is a microcosm of the point being made here about confidence.

If a firm treats regulators as if they are unified and have their act together, then the firm gets its own act together to cope with the focused demands that are anticipated from the regulators. As the firm gets its act together it becomes a clearer target that is easier for the regulators to monitor and control. Concerted action undertaken by the firm to meet anticipated action from regulators now makes it possible for regulators to do something they could not have done when the firms were more diffuse targets.

A confident definition of regulatory power, confidently imposed, stabilizes the regulation problem for a firm. The irony is that the faulty prophecy brings the problem into existence more sharply than it ever was before confident behavior was initiated. The firm has become easier to regulate by virtue of its efforts to prevent regulation.

Environments are more malleable than planners realize. Environments often crystallize around prophecies, presumptions, and actions that unfold while planners deliberate. Guidance by strategy often is secondary to guidance by prophecies. These prophecies are more likely to fulfill themselves when they are in the heads of fanatics who work in environments where the definition of what is occurring can be influenced by confident assertions.

Thus, presumptions can substitute for strategy. We assume co-workers know where they are going, they assume the same for us, and both of us presume that the directions in which we both are going are roughly similar. A presumption does not necessarily mean that whatever is presumed actually exists. We often assume that people agree with us without ever testing that assumption. Vague strategic plans help because we never have to confront the reality of our disagreements. And the fact that those disagreements persist undetected is not necessarily a problem because those very differences provide a repertoire of beliefs and skills that allow us to cope with changing environments. When environmental change is rapid, diverse skills and beliefs are the solution, not the problem.

Improvisation as Strategy

Much of my thinking about organizations (such as Weick 1979) uses the imagery of social evolution, but there is a consistent bias in the way I use that idea. I consistently argue that the likelihood of survival goes up when variation increases, when possibilities multiply, when trial and error becomes more diverse and less stylized, when people become less repetitive, and when creativity becomes supported. Notice that variation, trial and error, and doing things differently all imply that what you already know, including your strategic plan, is not sufficient to deal with present circumstances.

When it is assumed that survival depends on variation, then a strategic plan becomes a threat because it restricts experimentation and the chance to learn that old assumptions no longer work. Furthermore, I assume that whatever direction strategy gives can be achieved just as easily by improvisation.

Improvisation is a form of strategy that is misunderstood. When people use jazz or improvisational theater to illustrate improvising, they usually forget that jazz consists of variations on a theme and improvisational theater starts with a situation. Neither jazz nor improvisational theater are anarchic. Both contain some order, but it is underspecified.

To understand improvisation as strategy is to understand the order within it. And what we usually miss is the fact that a little order can go a long way.

For example, we keep underestimating the power of corporate culture because it seems improbable that something as small as a logo, a slogan, a preference (Harold Geneen's famous obsession to find the 'one unshakeable fact' in reports from divisions in ITT), a meeting agenda, or a Christmas party could have such a large effect. The reason these symbols are so powerful is that they give a general direction and a frame of reference that are sufficient. In the hands of bright, ambitious, confident people who have strong needs to control their destinies, general guidelines are sufficient to sustain and shape improvisation without reducing perceived control.

If improvisation is treated as a natural form of organizational life, then we become interested in a different form of strategy than we have seen before. This newer form I will call a *just-in-time strategy*. Just-in-time strategies are distinguished by less investment in front-end loading (try to anticipate everything that will happen or that you will need) and more investment in general knowledge, a large skill repertoire, the ability to do a quick study, trust in intuitions, and sophistication in cutting losses.

Like improvisation, a just-in-time strategy glosses, interprets, and enlarges some current event, gives it meaning, treats it as if it were sensible, and brings it to a conclusion. This form of activity looks very much like creating a stable small win (Weick 1984). And once an assortment of small wins is available, then these can be gathered together retrospectively and packaged as any one of several different directions, strategies, or policies.

Strategies are less accurately portrayed as episodes where people convene at one time to make a decision and more accurately portrayed as small steps (writing a memo, answering an inquiry) that gradually foreclose alternative courses of action and limit what is possible. The strategy is made without anyone realizing it. The crucial activities for strategy making are not separate episodes of analysis. Instead they are actions, the controlled execution of which consolidate fragments of policy that are lying around, give them direction, and close off other possible arrangements. The strategy making *is* the memo writing, *is* the answering, *is* the editing of drafts. These actions are not precursors to strategy; they *are* the strategy.

Strategies that are tied more closely to action are more likely to contain improvisations (Weiss 1980: 401):

> Many moves are improvisations. Faced with an event that calls for response, officials use their experience, judgment, and intuition to fashion the response for the issue at hand. That response becomes a precedent, and when similar – or not so similar – questions come up, the response is uncritically repeated. Consider the federal agency that receives a call from a local program asking how to deal with requests for enrollment in excess of the available number of slots. A staff member responds with off-the-cuff advice. Within the next few weeks, programs in three more cities call with similar questions, and staff repeat the advice. Soon what began as improvisation has hardened into policy.

Managers are said to avoid uncertainty, but one of the ironies implicit in the preceding analysis is that managers often create the very uncertainty they abhor. When they cannot presume order they hesitate, and this very hesitancy often creates events that are disordered and unfocused. This disorder confirms the initial doubts concerning order. What often is missed is that the failure to act, rather than the nature of the external world itself, creates the lack of order. When people act, they absorb uncertainty, they rearrange things, and they impose contingencies that might not have been there before. The presence of these contingencies is what is treated as evidence that the situation is orderly and certain.

Conclusion

The thread that runs through this chapter is that execution *is* analysis and implementation *is* formulation. The argument is an attempt to combine elements from a linear and adaptive view of strategy, with a largely interpretive view (Chaffee 1985: 95). Any old explanation, map, or plan is often sufficient because it stimulates focused, intense action that both creates meaning and stabilizes an environment so that conventional analysis now becomes more relevant. Organizational culture becomes influential in this scenario because it affects what people expect will be orderly. These expectations, in turn, often become self-fulfilling. Thus the adequacy of any explanation is determined in part by the intensity and structure it adds to potentially self-validating actions. More forcefulness leads to more validation. Accuracy becomes secondary to intensity. Because situations can support a variety of meanings, their actual content and meaning is dependent on the degree to which they are arranged into sensible, coherent configurations. More forcefulness imposes more coherence. Thus, those explanations that induce greater forcefulness often become more valid, not because they are more accurate but because they have a higher potential for self-validation.

Applied to managerial activity, substitutes for strategy are more likely among executives because their actions are capable of a considerable range of intensity, the situations they deal with are loosely connected and capable of considerable rearrangement, and the underlying explanations that managers invoke (such as, "This is a cola war") have great potential to intensify whatever action is underway. All of these factors combine to produce self-validating situations in which managers are sure their diagnoses are correct. What they underestimate is the extent to which their own actions have implanted the correctness they discover.

What managers fail to see is that solid facts are an ongoing accomplishment sustained as much by intense action as by accurate diagnosis. If managers reduce the intensity of their own action or if another actor directs a more intense action at the malleable elements, the meaning of the situation will change. What managers seldom realize is that their inaction is as much responsible for the disappearance of facts as their action was for the appearance of those facts.

Gene Webb often quotes Edwin Boring's epigram "Enthusiasm is the friend of action, the enemy of wisdom." Given the preceding arguments we can see reasons to question that statement. Enthusiasm can produce wisdom because action creates experience and meaning. Furthermore, enthusiasm can actually create wisdom when prophecies become self-fulfilling and factual.

One final example of a vague plan that leads to success when people respond to it and pay close attention to their response involves a religious ritual used by the Naskapi Indians in Labrador. Every day they ask the question, "Where should we hunt today?" That question is no different from, "Where is the base camp?" or "What should we do with these uniforms?" or "Should we open today?" or "Could this conceivably be the Silicon prairie?"

The Naskapi use an unusual procedure to learn where they should hunt. They take the shoulder bone of a caribou, hold it over a fire until the bone begins to crack, and then they hunt wherever the cracks point. The surprising thing is that this procedure works. The Naskapi almost always find game, which is rare among hunting bands.

Although there are several reasons why this procedure works, one is of special interest to us: The Naskapi spend most of each day actually hunting. Once the cracks appear, they go where the cracks point. What they do not do is sit around the campfire debating where the game are today based on where they were yesterday. If the Naskapi fail to find any game, which is rare, they have no one in the group to blame for the outcome. Instead, they simply say that the gods must be testing their faith.

The cracks in the bone get the Naskapi moving, just as the mountain paths drawn on the map get the soldiers moving, and just as high-tech backwardness gets Texans moving. In each case, movement multiplies the data available from which meaning can be constructed.

Because strategy is often a retrospective summary that lags behind action, and because the apparent coherence and rationality of strategy are often inflated by hindsight bias, strategic conclusions can be misleading summaries of what we can do right now and what we need to do in the future.

I do not suggest doing away with strategic plans altogether, but people can take a scarce resource, time, and allocate it between the activities of planning and acting. The combination of staffs looking for work, high-powered analytic MBAs, unused computer capability, the myth of quantitative superiority, and public pressure to account for everything in rational terms tempts managers to spend a great deal of time at their terminals doing analysis and a great deal less time anyplace else (see Chapter 20, this volume). It seems astonishing that one of the hottest managerial precepts to come along in some time (MBWA, management by walking around) simply urges managers to pull the plug on the terminal, go for a walk, and act like champions. One reason those recommendations receive such a sympathetic reception is that they legitimize key aspects of sensemaking that got lost when we thought we could plan meanings into existence. As we lost sight of the importance of action in sensemaking, we saw situations become senseless because the wrong tools were directed at them.

Strategic planning is today's pretext under which people act and generate meanings and so is the idea of organizational culture. Each one is beneficial as long as it encourages action. It is the action that is responsible for meaning, even though planning and symbols mistakenly get the credit. The moment that either pretext begins to stifle action meaning will suffer, and these two concepts will be replaced by some newer management tool that will work, not for the reasons claimed but because it restores the fundamental sensemaking process of motion and meaning.

References

Bresser, R. K., and R. C. Bishop. 1983. "Dysfunctional Effects of Formal Planning: Two Theoretical Explanations." *Academy of Management Review* 8: 588–99.

Burgelman, R. A. 1983. "A Model of the Interaction of Strategic Behavior, Corporate Context, and the Concept of Strategy." *Academy of Management Review* 8: 61–70.

Chaffee, E. E. 1985. "Three Models of Strategy." *Academy of Management Review* 10: 89–98.

Chandler, A. D. 1962. *Strategy and Structure.* Cambridge, Mass.: MIT Press.

de Bono, E. 1984. *Tactics: The Art and Science of Success.* Boston: Little, Brown.

Eden, D. 1984. "Self-Fulfilling Prophecy as a Management Tool: Harnessing Pygmalion." *Academy of Management Review* 9: 64–73.

James, W. 1956. "Is Life Worth Living?" In *The Will to Believe,* edited by W. James, pp. 32–62. New York: Dover.

Kerr, S., and J. M. Jermier. 1978. "Substitutes for Leadership: Their Meaning and Measurement." *Organizational Behavior and Human Performance* 22: 375–403.

McCaffrey, D. P. 1982. "Corporate Resources and Regulatory Pressures: Toward Explaining a Discrepancy." *Administrative Science Quarterly* 27 398–419.

McCall, M. W., Jr., and R. W. Kaplan. 1985. *Whatever It Takes: Decision Makers at Work.* Englewood Cliffs, N.J.: Prentice Hall.

Snyder, M. 1984. "When Belief Creates Reality." In *Advances in Experimental Social Psychology, Vol. 18,* edited by L. Berkowitz, pp. 247–305. New York: Academic Press.

Snyder, M., E. D. Tanke, and E. Berscheid. 1977. "Social Perception and Interpersonal Behavior: On the Self-Fulfilling Nature of Social Stereotypes." *Journal of Personality and Social Psychology* 35: 656–66.

Staw, B. M. 1980. "Rationality and Justification in Organizational Life." In *Research in Organizational Behavior, Vol. 2,* edited by B. M. Staw and L. L. Cummings, pp. 45–80. Greenwich, Conn.: JAI.

Thompson, J. D. 1964. "Decision-making, the Firm, and the Market." In *New Perspectives in Organization Research,* edited by W. W. Cooper, H. J. Leavitt, and M. W. Sheely II, pp. 334–48. New York: Wiley.

Warwick, Donald P. 1975. *A Theory of Public Bureaucracy: Politics, Personality, and Organization in the State Department.* Cambridge, Mass.: Harvard University Press.

Watzlawick, P., J. H. Beavin, and D. D. Jackson. 1967. *Pragmatics of Human Communication.* New York: Norton.

Weick, K. E. 1979. *The Social Psychology of Organizing,* 2d ed. Reading, Mass. Addison-Wesley.

Weick, K. E. 1984. "Small Wins Redefining the Scale of Social Problems." *American Psychologist* 39: 40–49.

Weick, K. E., 1985. "Cosmos vs. Chaos; Sense and Nonsense in Electronic Contexts." *Organizational Dynamics* 14 (Autumn) 50–64.

Weick, K. E., D. P. Gilfillan, and T. Keith. 1973. "The Effect of Composer Credibility on Orchestra Performance." *Sociometry* 36: 435–62.

Weiss, C. H. 1980. "Knowledge Creep and Decision Accretion." *Knowledge: Creation, Diffusion, Utilization* 1(3): 381–404.

Remembering

No sooner do people make some sense of the world than that sense is out of date. The sense is out of date for at least two reasons. First, retrospect lags action. When people "see what they say" in order to learn what they think, the saying is already history by the time it is understood. Second, once people retain what they think after they see what they say, those retained thoughts become dated because events have continued to unfold and the thoughts may be less plausible than they were before. But retained knowledge is certainly not worthless. Events usually don't change that much, that fast. Therein lies the tension. Retained knowledge is partly a useful guide to the future and partly a misleading guide. For effective sensemaking, people need to both believe and doubt what they know. In Donald Campbell and William James's provocative imagery, people need to act as if "ambivalence is the optimal compromise." Whether people do this or not, and how they do it, are key questions for students of sensemaking.

Here is an example of how ambivalence works in the interest of sensemaking. Caroline Paul is one of the first women firefighters to join the militantly male San Francisco Fire Department. She recounts what happened the first time she was allowed to take the nozzle of a fire hose and lead a crew into a burning building. In this case the smoke was so thick that she could not even see her own hand when she pressed it against the face plate of her air mask. As she works her way into the building, with zero visibility, here's what happens:

> Intent on finding the seat of the fire by myself, I run into something that hits my knees. For some reason, I decide that this must be a stairway, and I step up onto it. I try to step up again but I hit something ahead of me. Sure that this must be a small attic space, I step up and lunge forward as if to squeeze into a hole. Again I hit something and my foot finds no step. Insistent, I lunge again, and perhaps again, rapping my head, hard, each time. All this happens quickly, and then I feel a hand on my coat pulling. Someone is behind me. The hand, all-knowing and seemingly all-seeing (or more likely, adjusted to non-seeing), guides me to the left and we crawl down what must (it must!) be a hallway. The heat heightens. Shafts of lightning streak out in front of us. (Paul, 1998, p. 86)

Not long thereafter the alarm on Paul's air bottle goes off which means her air supply is getting low. She hands the hose to the person behind her, follows the hoseline back out of the building, and gets a new air bottle. By the time she re-enters the building, the smoke has cleared out and the rooms have taken form. As she retraces her steps she finds the stairway that caused her so much trouble. Here's how she describes the discovery:

> One glance tells me that it is no attic staircase that I was on. Instead, in a far corner, a single chair is propped against the wall. A sharp breath escapes me. *Jesus, no.* I was there, *on the chair.* I was not getting into an attic, I was butting the wall. Momentarily, I was a disoriented cow. I was Quixote, mistaking a windmill for a knight; I was from the Middle Ages, sure that the line of the horizon was the edge of the flat world. A portrait of prejudgment, I think. Thank God for the pitch black. No one else, not even The Hand, could see me. (Paul, 1998, p. 87)

The moral that Caroline Paul draws from this experience is the following:

> In the coming years I will realize that the experienced firefighter must shed all precon- ceived images; they will only play tricks on her in the dark. Instead, her mind and body should remain supple and pliable. When she runs into something, it does not have to be named (table? chair? bed?) so much as gotten around—a small point but an important one. If you think that you have bumped into a table, you will try to get around it as a table. But if instead it is a bed, you will be thwarted by this bigger, less movable object. Trying to circle it or push it over will not work. Every fire is a new experience. (Paul, 1998, p. 85)

What Caroline Paul has stumbled into and stumbled onto is the realization that what she "knows" can trip her up. Meaning is a composite of language, imagination, and action that has worked in the past but may not work in the future. The language of "table," "chair," "bed," and "attic staircase" worked in the past for Paul when her sight was unobstructed and when the consequences of mistakes were not life threat- ening. But in the present world of urban firefighting, where strange dwellings and objects obscured by smoke can entrap, and where flames can flash over the heads of incoming firefighters, a "better" language for imagination and action is the language of "something to be gotten around." The mind and body stay more flexible when people, at least those people suppressing fire, deal with general directions rather than with the specifics of mistakenly named objects.

The point here for sensemaking is tricky. It is not true that the past is an enemy of the future, since some guidance is necessary for a line of action to get started. This is the circumstance of the jazz musician whose improvisation is guided by a melody line that is being embellished. What is noteworthy in continuous sensemaking is that guidance from the past needs to be mixed with alertness to the nonroutine in the present. Flexible use of retained knowledge occurs when previous meanings are treated as binding *either* on selection (I use interpretations that have worked before) *or* on enactment (I act in ways that have worked before), but *not* on both. In a changing world that is difficult to know and difficult to predict, it is important to hold retained meanings lightly. To hold one's meanings lightly means that one of the two processes of enactment or selection is tied to meanings that have worked in the past, but the other process isn't. You don't want to ignore past experience in both processes because then there is no guidance. But you also don't want to act as if nothing has changed because that too is probably incorrect. Instead, you have to act as if what you retain is both true and false, both plausible and implausible, a combination of knowledge and ignorance. The more you know, the more you discover that you don't know. You do know more because experience is cumulative and coheres because patterns are recognized over time. And you should use this knowledge as you continue to act and interpret. But, increments in pattern recognition always leave an unexplained remainder. That residual represents a limitation in the adequacy of retention. To deal with that residual means accepting the limits of what is known. Pragmatically, that occurs when lessons from the past are set aside in the present.

It is these complex remembering processes that often make sensemaking "a struggle for alertness." The struggle is with the temptation to normalize unusual events, the temptation to search for confirmation rather than disconfirmation, the temptation to feel that one has experienced it all and that there are no surprises left. The premium in business organizations on "aggressive confidence" tends to dull alertness and to encourage imposing the same old sense on a changing world. It's tough to discount hard-won lessons of experience. Tough, but necessary. The next three chapters show why.

Chapter 16, "The Attitude of Wisdom: Ambivalence as the Optimal Compromise," is an extended reflection on how people hold their knowledge. The argument comes to grips with a key puzzle of sensemaking, namely, how do people simultaneously know and doubt yet mobilize sufficient confidence to act rather than deliberate? It is suggested that this complex integration is made possible by the capability for improvisation. As the capability for improvisation is increased, people with the attitude of wisdom come to see that even though their existing knowledge is fallible, it can be recombined to meet novel circumstances. This means that the person has wisdom in the sense that what is known is seen as only a portion of what is knowable. But the prospect of recombination through improvisation to meet the unforeseen, raises the ratio of the amount known relative to the amount knowable. Thus, knowledge is treated as both fallible and substantial, which is the ambivalent compromise that is "optimal" for sensemaking and action. If one chapter had to stand for the principal arguments in this book, this would be the one. A recurring theme in sensemaking is visible in the idea that wisdom is an attitude rather than a body of thought. The nature of that attitude is captured in Meacham's (1990) statement that "the essence of wisdom is in knowing that one does not know, in the appreciation that knowledge is fallible, in the balance between knowing and doubting" (p. 210). What recurs in discussions of sensemaking is the idea that action incorporates qualities of thought. Thus, here we have the idea that people can act more or less wisely. In other chapters we have seen that people can act more or less respectfully (Mann Gulch), heedfully (aircraft carriers), or thinkingly (managerial action in Weick, 1983). In each case the action of remembering or interacting or coordinating or managing is done with more or less mindfulness, alertness, care. Thus sensemaking is affected both by the content of the interpretations that are imposed and by the manner in which they are imposed. To portray sensemaking as action followed by interpretation followed by retention is to miss the reality of configurations and mutual influences. Observation of that intertwining makes for scientific headaches. But as we will see in the following chapter, those headaches are of our own making.

Chapter 17, "Management of Organizational Change Among Loosely Coupled Elements," argues that remembering has a structural component as well as a content component. Ambivalence in this chapter takes the form of a dynamic balance between the flexibility of loose ties between retention and current enactment, and the stability of tighter ties between these two processes. This is the venerable issue that is summarized in the warning "adaptation precludes adaptability." Actions selected for their fit with current environments may be detrimental for fit with future environments. Adaptation represented as tight coupling between retention and enactment vies with adaptability represented as loose coupling between retention and enactment. And, as in Chapter 16, reconciliation is possible only when opposites function simultaneously. In Chapter 16, the presumed baseline condition was a tendency to trust past experience, to credit it, to normalize toward it, to treat it as sufficient, in short, to believe rather than doubt it. Under these conditions the danger is that adaptation precludes adaptability. We persist too long with ways of acting that no longer work. Balance is restored when capabilities for improvisation are developed more fully. In Chapter 17, we move to a more macro level of analysis where the presumed baseline condition is one of loose coupling, multiple realities, and indeterminate relationships that are activated suddenly, occasionally, negligibly, indirectly, and eventually. Here, the danger is that adaptability precludes adaptation. We discard too quickly ways of acting that are working quite well. Balance is restored when people are tied together more tightly on a handful of core values. The task in organizational change is to maintain or restore the complex balance between adaptation and adaptability. In a change intervention, loose ties need to be tightened to disseminate the homogeneous change. But this tightening threatens both structural and substantive variety, which are sources of adaptability. Likewise, a change intervention also means that tight ties among elements in a self-contained frame of reference need to be disconfirmed and loosened to make way for a different frame of reference. But this disconfirmation and loosening threaten the attention to details that is a source of adaptation. From the standpoint of sensemaking, adaptation is achieved by minimizing surprise whereas adaptability is achieved by dwelling on surprise. Adaptation favors strong abrupt sensemaking that confirms the past and achieves closure. Adaptability favors weak sustained sensemaking that questions the past and postpones closure. And change favors disrupting both of these well-honed processes. The good news in all of this is that a system in which adaptation and adaptability operate simultaneously and effectively will never face the episodic upheavals of revolutionary change. Effective continuous functioning in the context of sensemaking means restraint in normalizing, zeal for improvisation, restraint in autonomy, and zeal for common affirmations. But if it becomes necessary to intervene in a loosely coupled system, then ambivalence may still remain the optimal compromise.

Chapter 18, "Organization Design: Organizations as Self-designing Systems," shows in greater detail what a system looks like when adaptation and adaptability occur simultaneously. The theme of remembering is still uppermost because this chapter argues that effectiveness is achieved when new designs are "underdetermined" by old designs. Familiar themes of ambivalence, wisdom, recombination, improvisation and recipes are stirred into the suggestion that more responsibility for ongoing redesign should be lodged closer to the front line and placed in the hands of insiders. They are closer to the scene of the action where lousy designs for assigned tasks become all too clear. The Skylab examples are a vivid illustration of this mismatch. There are several interesting undertones in this chapter. One is the quiet "boosterism" for the idea that less is more when it comes to organizational structure. References to loose coupling, organized anarchies, self-organizing, and improvisation all suggest the adaptive value of departures from a tighter top-down influence. What holds these looser structures together is not hierarchical authority but collective sensemaking. If capabilities for joint sensemaking are underdeveloped then attempts at self-design are likely to prove disastrous. There is also the undertone that when an analyst imposes a consistent process perspective on organization, the resulting picture of organizing will reveal that change is continuous rather than episodic (Weick and Quinn, 1999). That revelation is important because continuous change requires freezing, labeling, and then unfreezing if it is to be redirected. The better known sequence, unfreeze–change–refreeze is the language of episodic change applied to static, inertial structures, and is less well suited for self-designing structures. There is also the undertone that borrowing solutions to novel problems is not much help, an observation that raises questions about the value of benchmarking and institutional mimesis. If borrowing is to occur, what needs to be borrowed are ideas and directions that can be embellished in the context of idiosyncratic local particulars. The "villains" in this chapter are detached analysts whose acts of hubris produce routines, procedure manuals, and plans that are senseless.

References

Meacham, John A. (1990). The loss of wisdom. In R. Sternberg (ed.), *Wisdom*, New York: Cambridge University Press, pp. 181–211.

Paul, Caroline (1998). *Fighting Fire*, New York: St Martin's Press.

Weick, Karl E. (1983). Managerial thought in the context of action. In S. Srivastava (ed.), *The Executive Mind*, San Francisco, CA: Jossey-Bass, pp. 221–42.

Weick, Karl E., and Quinn, Robert E. (1999). Organizational change and development. *Annual Review of Psychology*, 50, 361–86.

16

The Attitude of Wisdom: Ambivalence as the Optimal Compromise

When people create maps of an unknowable, unpredictable world, they face strong temptations toward either overconfident knowing or overly cautious doubt. Wisdom consists of an attitude toward one's beliefs, values, knowledge, and information that resists these temptations through an ongoing balance between knowing and doubt (Meacham, 1983, 1990). In an earlier article (Weick, 1993b) I used this view of wisdom to reanalyze the Mann Gulch wildfire disaster, made famous in Norman Maclean's book (1992) *Young Men and Fire*. I suggested that the firefighters became trapped by the fire partly because of overconfidence that they would have it extinguished by 10:00 the next morning. Failure to treat this belief as fallible led the firefighters to ignore growing signs that the fire was about to explode. Although my discussion in that article of the attitude of wisdom was a mere sketch (it originally covered forty-one lines of text in a specialized academic journal), the idea struck sufficient resonance among wildland firefighters that it has since been incorporated into some of their training programs.

The purpose of this chapter is to explore the idea of an attitude of wisdom in greater detail. I intend to focus on issues related to action, information processing, and thought in complex social systems and to argue that adopting an attitude of wisdom is one way complex systems function reliably and heedfully even though they work with fallible knowledge. Before moving to these issues, I first sample the wisdom literature and connect some of its themes to a piece of wisdom in wildland firefighting.

The Wisdom Literature and Firefighting

People in charge of wildland firefighting crews have begun to follow the maxim, "Never hand over a fire in the heat of the day." What this maxim means is that when a departing crew hands over a fire to an incoming crew, they should do so when it is easiest for the incoming crew to understand what is happening and step in and continue the strategy used by the departing crew. The easiest transitions normally take place at night, when the combination of low winds, high humidity, and cool temperatures will stabilize a fire and render it the most predictable. In the heat of the day, by contrast, the fire is at its most dynamic and most volatile, which makes it harder for the incoming crew to catch up with its rapidly changing character. When there is an attempted handoff in the heat of the day, the incoming crew is always behind. The crew's understanding of what is happening lags behind what is actually happening, making it difficult to properly adjust their actions to a rapidly developing situation. As a result, the level of danger increases dramatically.

The firefighters' heat-of-the-day maxim is a good example of wisdom because it reflects several ways in which wisdom has been described. For example, it is consist-ent with Blanshard's all-purpose description (1967) of wisdom as "sound and serene judgment regarding the conduct of life" (p. 322). The maxim represents sound judg-ment because it is based on an actual wildland fire tragedy, the Dude Fire in Payson, Arizona (see Johns, 1996). Six firefighters burned to death when a change of com-mand was botched at 1:00 P.M., on a hot, windy day with temperatures in the high nineties, while the fire was making spectacular runs. The maxim represents serene judgment because it counsels against brash, impulsive action, because it is based on distance and detachment from the Dude Fire tragedy itself, and because it is conveyed to crew chiefs in training settings, where reflection is possible. Furthermore, it is a recipe for preserving control and stability without making a situation worse, and it is a calming edict intended to provide firm guidance in chaotic moments. The heat-of-the-day maxim is also relevant to two properties of wisdom that are often mentioned: reflection and judgment.

The theme of reflection

Reflection, understood as "the habit of considering events and beliefs in the light of their grounds and consequences" (Blanshard, 1967, p. 323), is synonymous with wisdom when wisdom is considered a "mode of knowledge that tries to understand the ultimate consequences of events in a holistic, systemic way" (Csikszentmihalyi and Rathunde, 1990, p. 32). "Whether a belief is warranted must be decided by the evidence it rests on and the implications to which it leads, and one can become aware of these only by reflection" (Blanshard, 1967, p. 323). The reflection associ-ated with wisdom consists of "a well-ordered and controllable series of symbolic links in a train of thought, to the exclusion of the more 'natural' meandering of the stream of consciousness" (Csikszentmihalyi and Rathunde, 1990, p. 39). Reflection also involves the articulation of the "big picture" that results from a grasp of multiple connections. The reflective component of wisdom may be thought of as the substan-tive side of wisdom. It is implicit in current discussions of cause maps (Huff, 1990), interactive complexity (Perrow, 1984), causal interdependence (Maruyama, 1963), and systems (Roberts, 1991).

Reflection on the tendency of the diverse, interrelated components of systems – for example, weather forecasting, the necessary conditions for fire (the "fire triangle," consisting of flammable material, a temperature above the point of ignition, and oxygen), shared meanings based on briefings, experience levels, and availability of air reconnaissance – to generate conflicting cues about unstable events led to the wisdom of the heat-of-the-day maxim. To be wise, in this case, is to be aware of the systemic quality of firefighting, to envision longer causal chains among the components within that system, and to appreciate what happens when these complex interdependencies are allowed to unfold in the absence of clear communication.

The theme of judgment

If reflection is about substantive wisdom, then judgment can be said to be about process wisdom. This second component of wisdom is found in descriptions such as these: "Wisdom is the capacity of judging rightly in matters relating to life and conduct" (Simpson and Weiner, 1989, p. 3,794), and wisdom is "informed judgment based on a comparison of situations" (Sakaiya, 1991, p. 233). Blanshard (1967, p. 323) describes judgment as the "wisdom of ends," by which he means the appraisal and choice of values, intrinsic goods, and ends.

While many scholars are eager to equate wisdom with judgment, few of them seem willing to say what they mean by judgment. One is tempted to fill this void by adopting William James's (1963, p. 75) description: "In practical talk, a man's common sense means his good judgment, his freedom from eccentricity, his *gumption*." "Gumption" is a colloquial expression that means resourcefulness, enterprise, and a quality of mind that enables one to make intelligent choices. As a potential descriptor of wisdom, *gumption* implies sense, "but in addition it suggests a capacity to estimate shrewdly or cleverly the possibilities of success or failure, of change for the better or worse, or the like; as, an investor without *gumption* is bound to lose money; he is a dreamer and, what is worse, he hasn't the slightest bit of *gumption*; if the voters have *gumption* they will re-elect the mayor" (Webster, 1951, p. 737). Thus, when judgment is incorporated into wisdom, it contributes the relatively rare quality of "discernment of facts or conditions that are not obvious as well as knowledge of those that are ascertainable, an ability to comprehend the significance of those facts and conditions" (p. 737). To process the data of reflection with special attention directed to that which is nonobvious, significant, clever, shrewd, and a harbinger of possibilities is to engage in activities that simultaneously know and doubt.

Judgment, understood as the appraisal of ends, is evident in the heat-of-the-day maxim in that it places higher value on informed transitions than on uninformed ones. Judgment is also understood as the prudent use of knowledge, and this is evident in the presumption that knowledge of a fire should be used not just to fight it but also to decide how and when to walk away from it. Consistent with Sakaiya's description (1991) of judgment as making comparisons, the maxim suggests that compared to making the transition in cool temperatures, hot transitions are more dangerous. Even the old-fashioned, commonsense aspect of judgment connoted by the word *gumption* figures in the maxim. The advice to avoid handoffs in the heat of the day reflects a shrewd awareness that even a relatively small event in the complex mobilization of resources to suppress a large fire will have an important bearing on the success or failure of the mission. It is *not* obvious that when a tired crew leaves a fire and is replaced by fresh crew, things will get worse. The addition of fresh resources normally would be expected to produce a redoubled effort and faster success. The maxim alerts people that precisely the opposite could occur. That forewarning is a mark of wisdom, facilitated by good judgment that comprehends significance in unexpected places.

The theme of metaphysical commitments

While various treatments of wisdom share the themes of soundness, serenity, reflection, and judgment, one crucial theme they don't share turns on the question, "What is the 'it' that wisdom understands better?" This is shorthand for Robinson's concern (1990, p. 22) with metaphysical commitments in discussions of wisdom:

> The concept of wisdom is perforce dependent upon a prior metaphysical commitment, taking metaphysics to be composed of ontological and epistemological elements. To regard one as *wise*, after all, is to ascribe a deeper understanding of reality, but this assumes that a more or less settled (ontological) position has been reached on the question of what is *real*. And this very position can be reached only after taking a stand (epistemologically) on the question of *how one can know anything*. Thus, to regard one as "wise" for knowing an absolute, universal, and nonempirical ("transcendent") truth is at once to accept that there is such a truth and that it *can* be known through, for example, contemplation, revelation, logic, intuition, or genius. If, instead, the official ontology leaves room only for the reality of physical things, then "wisdom" can be nothing but a scientific understanding of the laws governing matter in motion. The greater the inclination toward a materialistic ontology, therefore, the greater will be the degree of synonymy among *sophia*, *phronesis*, and *episteme*. In the end, "wisdom" would then refer to no more than a technical knowledge of how things work, its claims exhausted by purely pragmatic modes of evaluation.

To specify the ontology and epistemology behind the view of wisdom described here would take us too far afield, if in fact it could even be accomplished. In lieu of that, one is tempted either to invoke Robin Williams's exclamation – "Reality. What a concept!" (Davis, 1993, p. 74) – or to argue that "ontological oscillation" is a constant in everyday sensemaking (Weick, 1995, pp. 34–37) and let it go at that. Actually, both of those shortcuts are close to the presumptions that lie behind the present argument. The argument presumes, along with James (1963, p. 85), that "profusion, not economy, may after all be reality's key-note." It presumes, following lessons from chaos theory and quantum theory (McDaniel, 1996), that the world is largely unknowable and unpredictable, which means that sensemaking is all we have. And it also presumes that the maps people form to deal with unknowable territories are influenced by generic categories (such as "thing," "the same or different," "kind," and so on; James, 1963, p. 76) handed down by fallible predecessors: "Reality is an accumulation of our intellectual inventions, and the struggle for 'truth' in our progressive dealings with it is always a struggle to work in new nouns and adjectives while altering as little as possible the old" (p. 169).

The "reality" that wisdom more deeply understands consists of tenacious categories, constructed and validated consensually by both contemporaries and predecessors. Mere empirical technical knowledge plays a relatively minor part in this validation. The larger part – the part contributed by wisdom – lies in awareness of influences like legacies, predecessors, contingencies, and relationships as the object of wisdom (Follett, 1924, pp. 62–63); interpersonal relations as the vehicle for wisdom (Gergen, 1994); and questions as the output from wisdom. The reality behind wisdom is prefigured by symbolic systems that people have invented and imposed on one another because they seem to make a difference in practice (James, 1963, p. 75). People see and are bound by the constraints and categories they enact. Thus it is the task of wisdom to remain mindful of this ongoing fallible knowing and to witness both for its fallibility, through acts of doubt, and for its knowing, through acts of affirmation.

Returning to the heat-of-the-day maxim and the metaphysical commitments that drive it, the maxim's claim to wisdom is that it understands better than do formal models of fire behavior (Rothermel, 1993) the unknowable, unpredictable profusion of interdependencies associated with dynamic events such as uncontained wildland fires. The maxim, in other words, embodies an appreciation of ignorance and of the fact that actions such as crew transitions and fire suppression often occur in the midst of such ignorance. The maxim represents a consensus among the people who investigated the Dude Fire incident, including the crew chiefs involved in the incident. The maxim introduces new nouns, adjectives, and categories (for example, handoffs in the face of dynamic uncertainty) that supplement older understandings inherited from predecessors. Finally, this maxim, considered as a product of wisdom, is as much a question as it is an answer: "How knowable and predictable is this fire that I am about to inherit [or hand over]?" No matter how the crew chiefs answer this question, their answer will be flawed and incomplete. To be wise is to proceed anyway, knowing that your knowing is fallible and that whatever you do will shape what you face.

The theme of wisdom as an attitude

To conclude this introduction to the literature on wisdom, I want to return to Meacham's formulation (1990). Meacham argued that "the essence of wisdom . . . lies not in what is known but rather in the manner in which that knowledge is held and in how that knowledge is put to use. To be wise is not to know particular facts but to know without excessive confidence or excessive cautiousness. . . . To both accumulate knowledge while remaining suspicious of it, and recognizing that much remains unknown, is to be wise" (pp. 185, 187). Thus "the essence of wisdom is in knowing that one does not know, in the appreciation that knowledge is fallible, in the balance between knowing and doubting" (p. 210). Wisdom is a quality of thought that is animated by a dialectic in which the more one knows, the more one realizes the extent of what one does not know. Defined algebraically, wisdom equals the ratio of knowledge one has acquired and not lost (k) to the knowledge one believes might be accumulated or acquired (K), expressed as one's confidence in what one knows ($p = k/K$) and one's doubts ($u = K-k$).

These four variables interact to form a context of knowledge that describes what one knows in relation to what is not yet known. If one presumes that there is a fixed upper boundary on knowledge to be acquired, then the closer one comes to that limit, the greater one's confidence. This gain in confidence is at the expense of wisdom, because new questions, doubts, and uncertainties are ignored. People are lured away from wisdom and toward more extreme confidence by pressures to "accumulate" knowledge, power that deters other people from challenging one's apparent knowledge, and an intellectual climate that forces premature foreclosure of possible conceptual positions (Meacham, 1990). Movements in the opposite direction, from wisdom toward overcautiousness, involve forgetting or dismissing what one knows and inflating the amount of potential knowledge that remains to be known. People are lured toward excessive caution when they get overwhelmed by rapid technological change, doubt what they have come to know, or suffer personal tragedies that dissolve the intellectual frameworks that had previously given meaning to their actions.

Wisdom, defined conceptually as a balance between knowing and doubting, or behaviorally as a balance between too much confidence and too much caution, is set at $k/K = .5$ to capture the dialectical assumption that an increment in what one knows is matched by an equal increment in one's realization of what one does not know but could know. Deviations above this value are associated with confidence, purchased at the expense of ignoring questions and uncertainties. Deviations below this value represent insufficient confidence, due to the ignoring of answers and certainties. These patterns form a "knowledge context" that shapes the meaning of incoming data. The same piece of information could add to or dissolve what one thought one already knew and enlarge or shrink the perceived size of what one does not know but could potentially know.

If we reexamine the firefighting maxim in light of Meacham's argument, we see that it is about the deployment of fallible knowledge. The maxim reminds firefighters that fires in the heat of the day are least knowable, which means that this is when the firefighters' knowledge of the fire will be most fallible. The maxim reminds firefighters that they do not (and cannot) know midday fires as well as they know midnight fires. They are perfectly free to ignore their ignorance, of course, and they may be tempted to do so if they *have* to accept a midday fire and do their best to continue the effort to suppress it. But even if the handoff must proceed at midday, the fire can still be fought with either more or less wisdom.

Wise firefighting is indexed by how firefighters hold and use the knowledge they do have about a fire they are fighting. If they engage the fire warily, having first located escape routes, safety zones, lookouts, and communication links (Gleason, 1991), then they perceive their knowledge about the fire without either excessive confidence or excessive caution. They hedge their confidence by having a way out in case they are wrong or conditions change. But they also hedge their caution when they engage the midday fire believing that their crew chief knows what the previous crew chief knew and that their chief would not have let the other chief leave the scene until a satisfactory picture of the fire had been conveyed. There are several presumptions in those beliefs (for example, questions of trust and trustworthiness are central). Those presumptions are things that are *not* known for sure. They are the ambiguities that one is tempted to ignore in the name of boldness or magnify in the name of caution. Those are the same ambiguities that are neither ignored nor magnified but are balanced during wise moments when people act with full attention. That is Meacham's point. And that is the lesson of the Dude Fire.

Refinements in the Attitude of Wisdom

I chose Meacham's ideas about wisdom as the basis for this chapter because they are relevant to organizational learning and knowledge creation (for example, see Nonaka and Takeuchi, 1995). The ideas also provide a platform to fold action and knowledge together, which fits my ongoing interest in adaptation (Weick, 1969) through actions that incorporate qualities of thought, as in "heedful interrelating" (Weick and Roberts, 1993), "acting thinkingly" (Weick, 1983), and "committed interpretation" (Weick, 1993a). The idea that wisdom may be an attitude rather than a body of thought also has a certain appeal because it implies that people can improve their capability for wise action. Furthermore, once wisdom is decoupled from specific knowledge, we expect to find it expressed by more people more often, in more diverse settings. That very pluralism could strip the idea of its nuance, but not if the nature of the attitude is specified with some precision. There is also a certain attractiveness to the notion that wise people recognize the limits of their knowledge.

These attractions notwithstanding, one does encounter limits when trying to work with Meacham's ideas. As it stands, Meacham's definition is a bit too cool in its heavy dependence on cognition, a bit too solitary in its focus mainly on a single actor (although Meacham, 1990, pp. 207–208 does discuss wisdom communities), a bit too passive in its focus on deliberation rather than action, a bit too structural in its failure to describe processes that move toward wisdom, a bit too silent about doubt and caution, and a bit too preoccupied with overconfident knowing. Take, for example, the case of wildland firefighting that we started with. People who do that kind of work need to see what they don't know, because it can kill them. But they also need to remain confident if they are to muster the courage to face fire and knock it down. To doubt and to hesitate is to let events get irretrievably beyond control. People responsible for wildland firefighting need both to keep asking questions and to act like they have most of the answers. The same holds true for people in any other high-tempo setting where complex interdependencies can swiftly unfold, out of sight and out of mind, with irrevocable, possibly catastrophic consequences. Thus the question is, how do people in any of these settings simultaneously know and doubt? The answer I am pursuing is the possibility that successful simultaneity lies in how people deploy the attitude of wisdom. This possibility makes more sense, however, if we develop Meacham's ideas further. That is the task to which we now turn. We take a closer look at overconfidence, overcaution, and balance and conclude that the attitude of wisdom makes action more intelligent and adaptive because it recapitulates the wisdom inherent in all evolutionary processes.

Confidence and its Excesses

The attitude of wisdom is relatively rare, because people find it hard to doubt what they know or to admit to themselves that the knowledge they possess is only a small portion of what could be known. At first that sounds absurd. Everyone knows that there is much they don't know. But people often judge what they don't know to be unimportant, absurd, irrelevant, of little use, or lacking in credibility. Judgments of importance tend to be negatively correlated with judgments of ignorance. If I don't know it, it's probably not important, or even likely to be true. People feel attached to old ideas and tend to modify new inputs to fit them. These tendencies have been recognized for a long time, as in this eloquent description from William James (1963):

> The individual has a stock of old opinions already, but he meets a new experience that puts them to a strain. Somebody contradicts them; or in a reflective moment he discovers that they contradict each other; or he hears of facts with which they are incompatible; or desires arise in him which they cease to satisfy. The result is an inward trouble to which his mind till then had been a stranger, and from which he seeks to escape by modifying his previous mass of opinions. He saves as much of it as he can, for in this matter of belief we are all extreme conservatives. So he tries to change first this opinion, and then that (for they resist change very variously), until at last some new idea comes up which he can graft upon the ancient stock with a minimum of disturbance of the latter, some idea that mediates between the stock and the new experience and runs them into one another most felicitously and expediently.
>
> This new idea is then adopted as the true one. It preserves the older stock of truths with a minimum of modification, stretching them just enough to make them admit the novelty, but conceiving that in ways as familiar as the case leaves possible. . . .
>
> New truth is always a go-between, a smoother-over of transitions. It marries old opinion to new fact so as ever to show a minimum of jolt, a maximum of continuity [pp. 29–30].

The combination of tenacious older "truths" and the tendency to assimilate the novel into one's existing stock of knowledge often results in the belief that what one knows is what is true. And if it is true, why doubt it? Remember, we are talking about an attitude toward knowledge, not the substance of knowledge itself. Tendencies toward "extreme conservatism," exemplified by the assimilation of new information into old understandings, systematically remove grounds for doubt. Therefore, to increase wisdom we need to sharpen our ability to distinguish the bases on which we judge events to be the same or different. It is this distinction that is blurred during assimilation. We also need to be more stingy in our use of *same* and more generous in our use of *different*.

If this is plausible, then it raises interesting questions about the role of metaphor in making wise judgments. While the use of metaphor may promote one form of wisdom – holistic, systemic awareness (for example, the Gaia hypothesis) – it may undermine the attitude of wisdom. Metaphors obscure difference in favor of sameness, which should encourage assimilation, more confidence in one's stock of knowledge, and a heightened reluctance to doubt oneself. Even though metaphors hold the potential to increase doubt when they uncover neglected dimensions and differences, assimilation masks those differences, and the metaphor appears to confirm this masking. Instead of new questions, there is strengthened conservatism.

If doubt is made difficult because people seldom add new facts raw but instead embed them in their thoughts "cooked, as one might say, or stewed down in the sauce of the old" (James, 1963, p. 75), then doubt is made doubly difficult by tendencies toward selective perception in the service of justification. When people take actions that are visible (the act clearly occurred), irrevocable (the act cannot be undone), and volitional (the act is the responsibility of the person who did it), they often feel pressure to justify those actions, especially if their self-esteem is shaky. The felt need to justify committed action is the antithesis of doubt. Justification is about mobilizing good reasons that show, beyond a doubt, that one knows what one is doing. Thus commitment, like metaphor, can be an enemy of wisdom. Both of them minimize doubt and doubting.

If it is the case that once people begin to act they become attached to their choices and defend them, then adjustments toward wisdom should occur when people become more aware of their attachments and of reasons that favor other attachments. (A prominent theme in wisdom literatures, such as Buddhist texts, is the avoidance of attachments.) With respect to attachment per se, one might expect to find an attitude of wisdom expressed in receptiveness to beliefs that minimize the visibility of action (for example, "people are so wrapped up in their own world that they fail to notice anything that anyone else does"), in beliefs that downplay the irrevocability of action ("the world has changed, so the act no longer means what it once did"), and in beliefs that discount the responsibility for action ("at the time it seemed like the right thing to do, I had no choice"). Oddly enough, an attitude of wisdom may he expressed in the form of worldviews that emphasize narcissism, relativity, and fatalism, not because these views are "true" but because they weaken commitments, arrest the tendency to justify, and sustain doubt in contexts that might otherwise trigger commitment and overconfidence. Again, reluctance to engage in committed action may be too big a price to pay for wisdom, which could explain why wisdom is hard to find.

The commitment scenario can be taken one step further. One could choose to become committed, knowing full well that commitment encourages things like blind spots, overconfidence, and inattention to questions and alternatives. This is equivalent to *doubting* the merits of committed action itself, which introduces the attitude of wisdom at a meta-level. One doubts the commitment to commitment. If one doubts a commitment to commitment, then this should at least weaken the property of irrevocability. If the commitment to commitment is potentially revocable because it is doubted, then the strength of the commitment itself should be weakened. That, in turn, should produce more openness to information suggesting the merits of alternative actions.

Both assimilation and justification can weaken doubt and put wisdom out of reach. These two mechanisms reduce the occasions for surprise, which means people have more confidence in what they know and are less willing to doubt it. The problem, of course, is that people badly underestimate how much they overlook to keep surprise at arm's length.

Overconfidence may be an impediment to wisdom, but it persists because structures and cultures support it. In an unknowable, unpredictable world, bold actions can shape events and enact realities that favor capabilities people already possess. For example, hubris (insolent presumption) shapes markets, which can make it a virtue in many organizations. The liabilities (for the individual) normally associated with hubris get attenuated in organizations because the executives who act with hubris are located higher in the hierarchy, where their informational inputs are filtered more heavily to support their perspectives. People in high places are able to ignore their ignorance because organizational designs make this possible. Central placement of executives in networks encourages the fallacy of centrality (if this existed I surely would have known about it, but since I don't know about it it doesn't exist: Westrum, 1982; Weick, 1995). Furthermore, their success at shaping events, their continual receipt of supportive information, and their search for confirming instances under the pressure of speed (Fiske, 1992) reinforce the notion that they know most of what there is to know. Thus there's no reason for them to doubt their knowledge. If we add to these organizational dynamics that of anticipatory socialization (by which people lower in a hierarchy imitate those higher up), culture that mirrors the values of top management, and constant pressure for results rather than reflection, it is not surprising that overconfidence in the form of hubris is common in organizations and that the attitude of wisdom is rare. Not only is wisdom rare, but there is no incentive to introduce it.

Thus the achievement of ignorance is harder than it looks because there are strong incentives for bold action that can blur into overconfidence. Furthermore, organizational designs can shape information in ways that minimize doubt. Organizations are action generators (Starbuck, 1983), and anything that gets in the way of action, including wisdom, is discouraged. Thus it becomes important to look more closely at ways in which an attitude of wisdom and action can coexist. I explore two options here and additional ones later. The first option is to accept ignorance as an inevitable accompaniment of acting, but to act anyway. The second option is to use action to shift the domain and size of ignorance.

To be aware that one is ignorant but to act anyway is made possible when people trust that a combination of attentiveness, resilience (Wildavsky, 1988), and improvisation can substitute for omniscience. The social version of this option is to spread ignorance around but ensure that different people are ignorant in different ways and that they are trustworthy reporters of what they know and trust those who know what they do not. Schulmann (1993) describes this strategy as the creation of "conceptual slack," which he equates with requisite variety. Conceptual slack represents the attitude of wisdom embodied in an organizational design. The resulting design may look a lot like distributed information processing. What's significant about this design, from the standpoint of wisdom, however, is not that it increases the amount that people know but that it reminds individuals of what they don't know. Distributed information processing, by this line of reasoning, is effective not because it makes knowing less fallible but because it makes it more so. The fact that knowing is distributed makes people more aware of what they don't know, which heightens their attentiveness to the limits of what they do know. As a result, all of them act with more wisdom and update their knowledge more often with greater attention to larger systemic consequences.

A second way to act without ignoring one's ignorance is to use action to shift the timing, domain, and size of that ignorance. Here the focus is less on accepting the inevitability of one's ignorance and more on shifting it from one set of concerns to another. An example of this form of wise action is found in the way some physicians modify the traditional sequence symptom–diagnosis–treatment to symptom–treatment–diagnosis. In the modified approach they treat the symptoms in order to be able to make the diagnosis. This is not as irrational as it might sound. Since any diagnosis will ignore some presenting symptoms, to refrain from making a diagnosis is to remain attentive to more symptoms. To do this, physicians start with a plausible treatment and observe its effects on the presenting symptoms. Obviously the tricky phrase here is "plausible treatment," since "arriving at a plausible treatment" could simply be another way of saying "making a diagnosis." The nuance I want to accentuate is not that a bundle of symptoms is either explained (that is, a diagnosis is made) or not. Instead I want to preserve the quality of understanding that is associated with an attitude of wisdom. When physicians make a formal diagnosis under time pressure, their rush to label the disease, begin treatment, and achieve closure leads them to overlook and then forget the symptoms that don't fit the diagnosis. This forgetting encourages more confidence in their diagnosis than may be warranted. Doubt, correction, and revision of the diagnosis do not occur, because they are deemed unnecessary. One way around this is to postpone making a diagnosis. If doctors substitute modest hunches for full-blown diagnoses, modest treatments for "cures," and frequent monitoring for occasional monitoring, then they are likely to ignore fewer symptoms. A hunch held lightly (that is, without commitment) is a direction to be followed, not a decision to be defended. It is easier to change directions than to reverse a decision, simply because less is at stake. Similar flexibility has been demonstrated on battlefields where commanders "fight empirically" in order to discover what kind of enemy they are up against (Isenberg, 1985).

Whether one accepts one's ignorance and acts anyway while trusting to one's resilience, improvisation, and attentiveness, or one accepts one's ignorance and acts in order to shift it to another domain, the result represents an application of the attitude of wisdom. Fallible knowing replaces overconfidence. The important point is that, in both cases, action does not grind to a halt. Instead the action becomes infused with learning, and adaptation improves. The one problem associated with both of these scenarios is that they may occur mostly near the bottom of the organization, where information is filtered less fully. As we move higher up, more filtering leads to more overconfident knowing. With overconfidence comes blind spots, crises, and face-saving downsizing that diverts attention from the effects of hubris in high places. When organizations ignore their ignorance, they mistake arrogance for good management. If this happens, wisdom could become the ultimate source of competitive advantage, since it is so hard to duplicate.

Caution and its Excesses

There is an imbalance in the wisdom literature that is reflected in Meacham's discussions – namely, excess confidence is treated as more of a threat to wisdom than is excess caution. As a result we know less about what it means to apply an attitude of wisdom to doubts than about what it means to apply it to certainties. Consider, for example, this account from Plato, quoted by Meacham (1983, p. 127): "Socrates questioned a man with a reputation for being knowledgeable and seeming to be wise both to others and to himself. *Plato* reports *Socrates'* conclusion: 'I went away thinking to myself that I was wiser than this man; the fact is that neither of us knows anything beautiful and good, but he thinks he does know when he doesn't, and I don't know and don't think I do: so I am wiser than he is by only this trifle, that what I do not know I don't think I do.'" And consider this bit of doggerel from R. D. Laing, quoted by Mangham and Pye (1991, p. 31): "The range of what we think and do is limited by what we fail to notice. And because we fail to notice *that* we fail to notice there is little we can do to change until we notice how failing to notice shapes our thoughts and deeds."

If I admit what I don't know, or if I notice that I fail to notice, then my knowledge declines, my doubt increases, and I move toward wisdom, *if* I had too much confidence to begin with. But I move even farther away from wisdom if I make these same changes from a prior position of caution. In the case of excess caution, I need to ignore what I don't know rather than admit it, if I want to increase wisdom. When I adopt the attitude of wisdom under conditions of excess caution, I need to doubt my doubts and learn more of what there is to know. I need to repunctuate my state, from *fallible* knowledge to fallible *knowledge*. If I can make this shift, then I should move toward a more balanced state of knowing and doubting. Shifts from more caution to less caution can occur in many ways. In terms of the variables specified by Meacham, I can increase confidence if I eliminate a potential area of knowledge (reduce K), acquire information at a faster rate than the rate at which new questions develop, or lose information that I have acquired at a slower rate than the rate at which potential questions disappear.

The nature of these moves can be illustrated using the example of wildland firefighters facing a fire that defies categorization. Suppose they believe initially that the fire could be anything from a minor fire that will be out by 10:00 the next morning to a fire that is just about to explode (K is high, k is low, p is low, u is high). The firefighters face a knowledge context characterized by excess caution. The amount of information they have acquired relative to the amount that could be known is small, possibly too small. There may be pieces of information that they have already acquired even though they do not yet realize it, or there may be pieces they could easily acquire.

Suppose the firefighters observe that small pieces of burning wood (firebrands) are being thrown out ahead of the flames. This information suggests that the fire is at least volatile enough to throw spots. If the fire is capable of doing that, then it is less likely to be a minor fire at 10:00 the next morning. They now have a reason to decrease their doubts about what kind of fire they face. Furthermore, their reason for decreasing their doubts is a good reason, backed by their prior experience in firefighting. When this piece of information is interpreted in a knowledge context of caution, it raises doubts about their doubts and increases their confidence. Expressed in Meacham's notation, caution gives way to more confidence when there is an increase in k (knowledge already acquired) and a decrease in both K (knowledge potentially acquirable) and u (size of one's doubts).

All of this may sound like much ado about traditional information processing. It is more than that. It is about the deployment of an attitude that creates a knowledge context that then affects how information is interpreted. The meaning of any informational input is determined by whether it flows into a condition of excess confidence or one of excess caution. The very same input could either (1) invalidate other acquired information without necessarily suggesting what is correct, (2) raise new questions and possibilities, (3) be a newly acquired piece of knowledge, or (4) eliminate a potential area of knowledge. Any one of these results is possible. Which meaning actually sticks will depend on the importance of an attitude of wisdom, the value placed on a balance between knowing and doubting, and the state of the knowledge system prior to the input.

So far we have remained within Meacham's system in our efforts to develop a fuller picture of excess caution as a knowledge context. To adopt an attitude of wisdom toward deep doubt and to reduce some of that doubt, one can either learn something new while holding new uncertainties constant, or eliminate potential domains of questions and uncertainties.

There are other options, however. Some of these simply reverse prescriptions discussed earlier in discussions of overconfidence. For example, excess caution may be reduced if people are encouraged to assimilate new inputs into old understandings. When assimilation is encouraged, acquired knowledge should climb faster than new questions, which means that both confidence and tendencies toward wisdom increase. The same conversion of caution into wisdom should occur when new inputs are interpreted to justify old behavioral commitments.

Other options, not yet discussed, introduce some unexpected themes. Postmodernism, normally thought to epitomize relativity and doubt, actually can also be viewed as a source of confidence, belief, and certainty when it is incorporated into an attitude of wisdom. Postmodern doubt can apply just as readily to one's doubts as to what one knows. If the world is unknowable – a possibility implicit in quantum theory, chaos theory, and postmodern thought – then the amount of potential knowledge that could be known (the denominator K in the attitude of wisdom) *shrinks* relative to what is known, which means confidence and wisdom should increase. If, in addition, multiple readings of any "text" are equally plausible, then the knowledge that comes from any one reading is a credible acquisition. If one makes a credible acquisition in a domain where there is *less* to be acquired, then this is equivalent to a simultaneous increase in k and decrease in K. Caution should change into wisdom.

Tendencies to discard complexities, to increase knowing through an increase in requisite variety, or to make meaningful connections can all be viewed as efforts to deploy an attitude of wisdom toward doubts and to weaken doubts by eliminating potential areas of knowledge (K). The strategy of small wins could have a powerful impact on doubt. When people create controllable opportunities of modest size that produce visible and tangible outcomes (Peters, 1977; Weick, 1984), they increase what is known, thus raising k. Since this learning derives from a modest intervention that produces a tangible, incremental result, the learning tends *not* to raise new questions. Instead, since the small win is basically a self-contained episode, learning reaffirms rather than reopens issues previously settled. Furthermore, since the intervention is also controllable, it remains completely knowable and within the intellectual grasp of the person performing it. This means that once the knowledge attendant to it is acquired, there is little residual uncertainty to raise new questions and doubts. Encoded into Meacham's notation, a small win adds learning (k) but does not enlarge the size of the domain to be known (K). Previous doubts about the malleable world are successfully doubted and replaced by something known, with more certainty than before. Because the win is so small, it raises few questions while supplying a clearer understanding of what the world may be like.

Balance and Improvisation

To portray wisdom as an attitude is to suggest that it is a dynamic process in which people make sense of information differently depending on which side of the knowing–doubting scale they find themselves. If they are above the scale, the input is used to raise questions and move downward, toward wisdom. If they are below the scale, the input is treated more like new learning or as information that reduces what there is to know. The choice of interpretation is affected not just by its relationship to a balance point, however, but also by the implications for action. And therein lies the rub. Action benefits from *higher* levels of confidence. Thus demands for wisdom and demands for confidence to strengthen action can work at odds, especially when confidence is already high. The ways in which people balance interpretations, confidence, knowing, and doubting to sustain action have not been given much attention. Instead, "balance" is usually invoked in discussions of wisdom as a kind of mantra and left at that.

I want to argue that one way out of this dilemma is to conceptualize balance as confidence in one's skills of improvisation. Improvisation can be defined as "reworking precomposed material and designs in relation to unanticipated ideas conceived, shaped, and transformed under the special conditions of performance, thereby adding unique features to every creation" (Berliner, 1994, p. 241). Since improvisation involves the flexible treatment of preplanned material, it is an ideal means to stretch existing knowledge in the interest of confident action and still preserve an attitude of wisdom.

Improvisation is not "making something out of nothing." Instead, it is making something out of previous experience, practice, and knowledge during those moments when one surfaces and tests intuitive understandings of experienced phenomena – while the ongoing action can still make a difference (Schön, 1990). Jazz musician Stan Getz described the preplanning of improvisation using the metaphor of language: Jazz is "like a language. You learn the alphabet, which are the scales. You learn sentences, which are the chords. And then you talk extemporaneously with the horn. It's a wonderful thing to *speak* extemporaneously, which is something I've never gotten the hang of. But musically I love to talk just off the top of my head. And that's what jazz music is all about" (Maggin, 1996, p. 21).

Gilbert Ryle (1979) discussed improvisation as one means to convert knowledge and doubt into adaptive action. He argued that virtually all behavior has an ad hoc adroitness akin to improvisation, because it mixes together a partly fresh contingency with general lessons previously learned. Ryle (1979) describes this mixture as paying heed. Improvisation enters in the following way: "To be thinking what he is here and now up against, he must both be trying to adjust himself to just this present once-only situation *and* in doing this to be applying lessons already learned. There must be in his response a union of some Ad Hockery with some know-how. If he is not at once *improvising* and improvising *warily*, he is not engaging his somewhat trained wits in a partly fresh situation. It is the pitting of an acquired competence or skill against unprogrammed opportunity, obstacle or hazard. It is a bit like putting some *new* wine into *old* bottles" (p. 129).

These ideas about improvisation can be spliced into the emerging picture of an attitude of wisdom in the following way. So far we have seen that to adopt the attitude of wisdom is to treat one's "beliefs, values, knowledge, information, abilities, and skills as fallible" (Meacham, p. 187). This fallible knowledge may represent a wise blend of knowledge and uncertainties, but this blend holds down confidence ($k/K = .5$). However, higher levels of confidence necessary for bold action can be achieved if the wise person also believes that what is already known can be combined in novel ways to deal with previously unmapped uncertainties. Faith in one's ability to recombine items already in one's repertoire in effect raises the amount of information already acquired and lowers the amount that is potentially knowable. Faith in improvisation, in other words, creates a shadow equation that has a much higher level of confidence than does the equation that represents a wise balance between knowing and doubting.

Both equations are plausible. The wisdom equation is a plausible representation of the ratio of what one knows to what one does not know. What the wisdom equation does not capture are the potential ways in which novel combinations of what is already known can create new knowledge that reduces old domains of uncertainty. Faith in this possibility creates a higher level of confidence than does the simple ratio of acquired to potential knowledge.

Once we define balance as a capability for improvisation, then we can keep the idea that to deploy an attitude of wisdom is to doubt that what is known and done is necessarily true, valid, or an exhaustive set of those things that could be known (Ryle, 1979). Knowing and doubt remain balanced, and confidence remains modest. What we add with the idea of improvisation is the possibility that what people know is sufficient to move ahead. Modest as their knowledge may be relative to what they could know, it is nevertheless sufficient because of the possibility of recombination. Belief in the power of improvisation animates an attitude of wisdom. The inability to juxtapose wisdom and improvisation may lie behind arrogant boldness that backfires (for example, the "dynamic entry" of first the Bureau of Alcohol, Tobacco, and Firearms and then the FBI at Waco failed to generate a peaceful resolution of the Branch Davidian standoff). If people are unable to decouple wisdom from confidence and pursue both, then they tend to act with dogmatic overconfidence and suppress their doubts. However, if they balance knowing and doubt around the belief that their fallible knowledge can be recombined to deal with the unexpected, and if they remain attentive, wary, and willing to explore, then they tend to remain wise and retain sufficient confidence to act. Improvisation enables people to wade into situations with fallible knowledge, secure in the belief that they can recombine that knowledge by shifting their fallibilities around. Faith in their ability to "make do" infuses confidence into their balance of knowledge and doubt.

Conclusion

An attitude of wisdom may be one way people in complex systems deal with the fallibility of their knowledge and remain adaptive. To maintain an attitude of wisdom, people can introduce doubt into a state of overconfidence by emphasizing differences and contrasts among events, minimizing connections between new facts and old facts, reducing their tendency to overjustify their actions, uncovering unexpected surprises, raising new questions, removing filters on informational inputs, recognizing the fallacy of centrality, increasing conceptual slack to show that there is more than one way to interpret data, and distributing different portions of what is known among several people. People can introduce confidence into a state of doubt by focusing on what they do know, shrinking their estimates of the size of what is not known but could be known, raising doubts about their doubts, generating experiences that answer larger sets of basic questions, enlarging the relevance of what is already known to new areas of potential information, assimilating new inputs to old understandings, and originating small wins. The balance point toward which these operations move can itself encourage these adjustments, even when there is continuing pressure for bold action. These conflicting pressures can be accommodated if the balance point consists of an attitude of improvisation that supplements an attitude of wisdom. Improvisation does not deny that knowing is fallible. Instead, it overlays that fallibility with the confidence-restoring prospect of adaptive recombination. Adaptive recombination of fallible knowledge produces wise action.

I want to conclude by suggesting that wisdom, conceived as an attitude that balances knowing and doubt, mirrors an even more basic principle of adaptation – namely, that ambivalence is the optimal compromise. The idea is Donald Campbell's (1965); the inspiration for it comes from William James (1890). First, the inspiration:

> The whole story of our dealings with the lower wild animals is the history of our taking advantage of the way in which they judge of everything by its mere label, as it were, so as to ensnare or kill them. Nature, in them, has left matters in this rough way, and made them act *always* in the manner which would be *oftenest* right. There are more worms unattached to hooks than impaled upon them; therefore, on the whole, says Nature to her fishy children, bite at *every* worm and take your chances. But as her children get higher and their lives more precious, she reduces the risks. Since what seems to be the same object may be now a genuine food and now a bait; since in gregarious species each individual may prove to be either the friend or the rival, according to the circumstances, of another; since any entirely unknown object may be fraught with weal or woe, *Nature implants contrary impulses to act on many classes of things*, and leaves it to slight alterations in the conditions of the individual case to decide which impulse shall carry the day. Thus, greediness and suspicion, curiosity and timidity, coyness and desire, bashfulness and vanity, sociability and pugnacity, seem to shoot over into each other as quickly, and to remain in as unstable equilibrium, in the higher birds and mammals as in man. . . . We may confidently say that however uncertain man's reactions upon his environment may sometimes seem in comparison with those of lower creatures, the uncertainty is probably not due to their possession of any principles of action which he lacks. *On the contrary, man possesses all the impulses that they have, and a great many more besides.* In

other words, there is no material antagonism between instinct and reason. Reason, *per se*, can inhibit no impulses; the only thing that can neutralize an impulse is an impulse the other way. Reason may, however, make an *inference which will excite the imagination so as to set loose* the impulse the other way; and thus, though the animal richest in reason might be also the animal richest in instinctive impulses too, he would never seem the fatal automaton which a *merely* instinctive animal would be. . . .

Curiosity and fear form a couple of antagonistic emotions liable to be awakened by the same outward thing, and manifestly both useful to their possessor. The spectacle of their alternation is often amusing enough, as in the timid approaches and scared wheelings which sheep or cattle will make in the presence of some new object they are investigating. I have seen alligators in the water act in precisely the same way towards a man seated on the beach in front of them – gradually drawing near as long as he kept still, frantically careering back as soon as he made a movement. Inasmuch as new objects *may* always be advantageous, it is better that an animal should not *absolutely* fear them. But, inasmuch as they may also possibly be harmful, it is better that he should not be quite indifferent to them either, but on the whole remaining on the *qui vive*, ascertain as much about them, and what they may be likely to bring forth, as he can, before settling down to rest in their presence. Some such susceptibility for being excited and irritated by the mere novelty, as such, of any movable feature of the environment must form the instinctive basis of all human curiosity; though, of course, the superstructure absorbs contributions from so many other factors of the emotional life that the original root may be hard to find [James, 1890, vol. 2, pp. 392–393, 429].

Here, now, is Campbell's distillation (1965, p. 305) of the key point he draws from James: "The presence in moral codes, proverb sets, and motivational systems of opposing values is often interpreted as discrediting the value system by showing its logical inconsistency. This is a misapplication of logic, and in multiple-contingency environments, the joint presence of opposing tendencies has a functional survival value. Where each of two opposing tendencies has survival relevance, the biological solution seems to be an ambivalent alternation of expressions of each rather than the consistent expression of an intermediate motivational state. Ambivalence, rather than averaging, seems the optimal compromise."

If we return once more to the world of wildland firefighting, ambivalence in assessing the dynamic Mann Gulch fire might have taken the form, "We believe this is a fire we'll extinguish by 10:00 tomorrow morning, but we can't say for sure. We will fight it as if we're right, but we will remain attentive as if we were wrong." As Carl Wilson's later analysis (1977) showed, attentiveness was warranted because the small Mann Gulch fire had all four of the signs that suggest that a minor fire is just about to explode.

We can illustrate ambivalence as the optimal compromise in a different aspect of wildland firefighting, designs for organizing fire crews. There is growing use of Paul Gleason's LCES system (1991), which prescribes that a crew should not attack a fire until the crew's lookouts, communication links, escape routes (at least two), and safety zones are in place and known to everyone. What's interesting about an LCES design is that it is a blend of knowledge and doubt. The lookouts and communication capabilities imply that the crew knows what is going on and how the local conditions are related to the big picture. The attention to escape routes and safety zones, however, implies that what the crew knows may be incomplete and that this potential ignorance needs to be recognized and hedged. The crew is simultaneously confident and cautious. This is made possible because they trust that their ability to pool and recombine what they know, should the unexpected occur, will enable them to keep acting. The escape routes and safety zones preclude hubris on the part of the crew, and the lookouts and communication links preclude timidity. The combination of these four LCES components encourage an attitude of wisdom in the face of danger, without paralyzing action. Knowledge and ignorance balance on the pivot of improvisation. This configuration exhibits the ambivalence of wisdom and celebrates the wisdom of ambivalence.

References

Berliner, P. F. *Thinking in Jazz: The Infinite Art of Improvisation*. Chicago: University of Chicago Press, 1994.

Blanshard, B. "Wisdom." In P. Edwards (ed.), *The Encyclopedia of Philosophy*. New York: Free Press, 1967.

Campbell, D. T. "Ethnocentric and Other Altruistic Motives." In D. Levine (ed.), *Nebraska Symposium on Motivation*. Lincoln: University of Nebraska Press, 1965.

Csikszentmihalyi, M., and Rathunde, K. "The Psychology of Interpretation: On Evolutionary Interpretation." In R. J. Sternberg (ed.), *Wisdom*. New York: Cambridge University Press, 1990.

Davis, M. S. *What's So Funny?* Chicago: University of Chicago Press, 1993.

Fiske, S. T. "Thinking Is for Doing: Portraits of Social Cognition from Daguerreotype to Laserphoto." *Journal of Personality and Social Psychology*, 1992, 63, 877–889.

Follett, M. P. *Creative Experience*. New York: Longmans, Green, 1924.

Gergen, K. J. *Realities and Relationships*. Cambridge, Mass.: Harvard University Press, 1994.

Gleason, P. "LCES – A Key to Safety in the Wildland Fire Environment." *Fire Management Notes*, 1991, 52(4), 9.

Huff, A. (ed.). *Mapping Strategic Thought*. New York: Wiley, 1990.

Isenberg, D. J. "Some Hows and Whats of Managerial Thinking: Implications for Future Army Leaders." In J. G. Hunt and J. D. Blair (eds.), *Leadership on the Future Battlefield*. New York: Pergamon Press, 1985.

James, W. *The Principles of Psychology*. New York: Dover, 1890.

James, W. *Pragmatism and Other Essays*. New York: Washington Square Press, 1963.

Johns, M. "Dude Fire Still Smokin'." *Wildfire*, 1996, 5(2), 39–42.

Maclean, N. *Young Men and Fire*. Chicago: University of Chicago Press, 1992.

Maggin, D. C. *Stan Getz: A Life in Jazz*. New York: Marrow, 1996.

Mangham, I., and Pye, A. *The Doing of Managing*. Oxford, England: Blackwell, 1991.

Maruyama, M. "The Second Cybernetics: Deviation Amplifying Mutual Causal Processes." *American Scientist*, 1963, 51, 164–179.

McDaniel, R. R., Jr. "Strategic Leadership: A View from Quantum and Chaos Theories." In W. J. Duncan, P. Ginter, and L. Swayne (eds.), *Handbook of Health Care Management*. Cambridge, Mass.: Blackwell, 1996.

Meacham, J. A. "Wisdom and the Context of Knowledge: Knowing That One Doesn't Know." In D. Kuhn and J. A. Meacham (eds.), *On the Development of Developmental Psychology*. Basel, Switzerland: Karger, 1983.

Meacham, J. A. "The Loss of Wisdom." In R. J. Sternberg (ed.), *Wisdom*. New York: Cambridge University Press, 1990.

Nonaka, I., and Takeuchi, H. *The Knowledge-Creating Company*. New York: Oxford University Press, 1995.

Perrow, C. *Normal Accidents*. New York: Basic Books, 1984.

Peters, T. J. "Patterns of Winning and Losing: Effects on Approach and Avoidance by Friends and Enemies." Unpublished doctoral dissertation, Stanford University, 1977.

Roberts, K. H. "Structuring to Facilitate Migrating Decisions in Reliability Enhancing Organizations." In L. Gomez-Meija and M. W. Lawless (eds.), *Top Managerial and Effective Leadership in High Technology Firms*. Greenwich, Conn.: JAI Press, 1991.

Robinson, D. N. "Wisdom Through the Ages." In R. J. Sternberg (ed.), *Wisdom*. New York: Cambridge University Press, 1990.

Rothermel, R. C. *Mann Gulch Fire: A Race That Couldn't Be Won*. [General Technical Report INT-299.] Ogden, Utah: Intermountain Research Station, U.S. Forest Service, 1993.

Ryle, G. "Improvisation." In G. Ryle (ed.), *On Thinking*. Cambridge, Mass.: Blackwell, 1979.

Sakaiya, T. *The Knowledge-Value Revolution*. Tokyo: Kodansha International, 1991.

Schön, D. A. *Educating the Reflective Practitioner: Toward a New Design for Teaching and Learning in the Professions*. San Francisco: Jossey-Bass, 1990.

Schulmann, P. R. "The Negotiated Order of Organizational Reliability." *Administration and Society*, 1993, *25*, 353–372.

Simpson, J. A., and Weiner, E. S. C. (eds.). *The Compact Edition of the Oxford English Dictionary*. (2nd ed.) New York: Oxford University Press, 1989.

Starbuck, W. H. "Organizations as Action Generators." *American Sociological Review*, 1983, *48*, 91–102.

Webster, N. (ed.). *Webster's Dictionary of Synonyms*. (1st ed.) Springfield, Mass.: Merriam-Webster, 1951.

Weick, K. E. *The Social Psychology of Organizing*. Reading, Mass.: Addison-Wesley, 1969.

Weick, K. E "Managerial Thought in the Context of Action." In S. Srivastva (ed.), *The Executive Mind: New Insights on Managerial Thought and Action*. San Francisco: Jossey-Bass, 1983.

Weick, K. E. "Small Wins: Redefining the Scale of Social Problems." *American Psychologist*, 1984, *39*, 40–49.

Weick, K. E. "Sensemaking in Organizations: Small Structures with Large Consequences." In J. K. Murnighan (ed.), *Social Psychology in Organizations: Advances in Theory and Research*. Englewood Cliffs, N.J.: Prentice Hall, 1993a.

Weick, K. E. "The Collapse of Sensemaking in Organizations: The Mann Gulch Disaster." *Administrative Science Quarterly*, 1993b, 38, 628–652.

Weick, K. E. *Sensemaking in Organizations*. Thousand Oaks, Calif.: Sage, 1995.

Weick, K. E., and Roberts, K. H. "Collective Mind in Organizations: Heedful Interrelating on Flight Decks." *Administrative Science Quarterly*, 1993, *38*, 357–381.

Westrum, R. "Social Intelligence About Hidden Events." *Knowledge*, 1982, *3*(3), 381–400.

Wildavsky, A. *Searching for Safety*. New Brunswick, N.J.: Transaction, 1988.

Wilson, C. C. "Fatal and Near-Fatal Forest Fires: The Common Denominator." *The International Fire Chief*, 1977, *43*(9), 9–15.

17

Management of Organizational Change Among Loosely Coupled Elements

Organizational theory is beginning to move away from a preoccupation with rational systems toward equivalent development of ideas about natural systems and open systems (Scott, 1981). I suggest how traditional ideas about organizational change, many of them grounded in theories of rational systems, may need to be altered when they are fitted to one distinctive property of open systems, loose coupling among their elements (Weick, 1976).

The image of rational systems contains assumptions such as the following: "In the rational system perspective, structural arrangements within organizations are conceived as tools deliberately designed for the efficient realization of ends. . . . Rationality resides in the structure itself, not in the individual participants – in rules that assure participants will behave in ways calculated to achieve desired objectives, in control arrangements that evaluate performance and detect deviance, in reward systems that motivate participants to carry out prescribed tasks, and in the set of criteria by which participants are selected, replaced, or promoted. . . . We have noted the great emphasis placed in the rational system perspective on control – the determination of the behavior of one subset of participants by the other. Decision making tends to be centralized, and most participants are excluded from discretion or from exercising control over their own behavior. Most rational system theorists justify these arrangements as being in the service of rationality: control is the means of channeling and coordinating behavior so as to achieve specified goals" (Scott, 1981, pp. 77–78).

To manage change in a rational system "is to find goals and or means that can be evaluated easily and to which the participants can commit themselves. It is assumed that if relevant information is gathered to define the problem properly and if the resistance of recalcitrant parties is overcome, then a decision can be made that will correct any problems. In this view, a fairly stable group of decision makers who agree on goals and technology is managing change" (Berger, 1981, p. 135).

The image of organizations as open systems contains assumptions that differ substantially from rational assumptions. "The open systems view of organizational structure stresses the complexity and variability of the individual component parts – both individual participants and subgroups – as well as the looseness of connections among them. Parts are viewed as capable of semiautonomous action; many parts are viewed as, at best, loosely coupled to other parts. Further, in human organizations, the system is multicephalous: many heads are present to receive information, make decisions, direct performance. Individuals and subgroups form and leave coalitions. Coordination and control become problematic. Also system boundaries are seen as amorphous; the assignment of actors or actions to either the organization or the environment often seems arbitrary and varies depending on what aspect of system functioning is under consideration. Open systems imagery does not simply blur the more conventional views of the structural features of organizations: it shifts attention from structure to process" (Scott, 1981, p. 119).

To manage change in an open system is to adopt strategies such as these:

1. Concentrate efforts on one or two critical problems.
2. Learn the history of an issue, including when it came up, who took what positions, who won, and who lost.
3. Build coalitions to mobilize support.
4. Use the formal system of committee memberships and the informal system of discussions and mediation (Berger, 1981, p. 136).

These four guidelines for change are cryptic, incomplete, and tentative, as are March's (1981) five footnotes to change, Cohen and March's (1974) eight administrative tactics, and Peters's (1980) signals, phases, and tools by which attention of organizational members can be redirected. All these sources do little more than hint at subtleties and complications that follow when assumptions about rationality are relaxed and assumptions about indeterminacy are substituted for them. The purpose of this chapter is to add substance to the few commentaries available concerning change and loosely coupled systems. The discussion focuses on characteristics of loosely coupled systems, characteristics of change in loosely coupled systems, and targets for change in loosely coupled systems.

A microcosm of the themes to be developed in all three sections is contained in the following demonstration.

> If you place in a bottle half a dozen bees and the same number of flies, and lay the bottle down horizontally, with its base to the window, you will find that the bees will persist, till they die of exhaustion or hunger, in their endeavor to discover an issue through the glass; while the flies, in less than two minutes, will all have sallied forth through the neck on the opposite side. . . . It is their (the bees') love of light, it is their very intelligence, that is their undoing in this experiment. They evidently imagine that the issue from every prison must be there where the light shines clearest; and they act in accordance, and persist in too logical action. To them glass is a supernatural mystery they never have met in nature; they have had no experience of this suddenly impenetrable

atmosphere; and the greater their intelligence, the more inadmissible, more incomprehensible, will the strange obstacle appear. Whereas the feather-brained flies, careless of
logic as of the enigma of crystal, disregarding the call of the light, flutter wildly hither
and thither, and meeting here the good fortune that often waits on the simple, who find
salvation there where the wiser will perish, necessarily end by discovering the friendly
opening that restores their liberty to them. (Maurice Maeterlinck, Belgian, 1862–1949)
[Siu, 1968, p. 189].

This episode speaks of experimentation, persistence, trial and error, risks, improvisation, the one best way, detours, confusion, rigidity, and randomness all in the
service of coping with change. Among the most striking contrasts are those between
tightness and looseness. There are differences in the degree to which means are tied
to ends, actions are controlled by intentions, solutions are guided by imitation of
one's neighbor, feedback controls search, prior acts determine subsequent acts, past
experience constrains present activity, logic dominates exploration, and wisdom and
intelligence affect coping behavior.

In this example loose ties provide the means for some actors to cope successfully
with a serious change in their environment. Each individual fly, being loosely tied to
its neighbor and its own past, makes numerous idiosyncratic adaptations that eventually solve the problem of escape. Looseness is an asset in this particular instance,
but precisely how and when looseness contributes to successful change and how
change interventions must be modified to cope with the reality of looseness is not
obvious.

Our understanding of change against the backdrop of loose ties is underdeveloped
because most models people use to think about change rely heavily on connections,
networks, support systems, diffusion, imitation, and social comparison, none of which
are plentiful in loosely coupled systems.

The Nature of Loosely Coupled Systems

Here is an example of a loosely coupled system:

> A bizarre case of segregation of parts of an organization concerns the Butterfield Division
> of UTD Corporation, which makes precision cutting instruments. This factory straddles
> the international border between Vermont and Quebec, with its front door in Canada
> and its back door in the United States. As a result of a treaty made in 1842, the
> Canadian-American border was fixed through a number of existing communities, some-
> times even dividing buildings. One of these was this precision instrument factory. Both
> matter-energy and information processes are affected by this split. An imaginary line,
> which only top executives cross, is drawn through the plant. On the American side the
> plant buys raw steel from producers in the United States, maintains a separate stock
> room and machine shop, and hires citizens of the United States, who are paid in United
> States dollars. On the Canadian side the plant buys from Canadian producers, also
> maintains a separate stock room and machine shop, and hires workers from Canada,
> who are paid in the currency of that country. Since moving steel from one side of the
> shop to the other would constitute smuggling, steel on one side of the factory is "ex-

ported," driven across the international border, and "imported" through customs, where forms are filled out and duty is paid. At regular intervals taxes are paid to each government based upon the profit made on that part of the operation which is inside its borders [Miller, 1978, p. 702].

Here is an example of a tightly coupled system: "Martin Coyle, the head of Chevrolet, always preached with great unction. Once when I [Peter Drucker] was sitting in his office listening to his favorite sermon on the beatitudes of decentralization, the tele-printer in the corner of the office next to a big brass spitoon began to yammer. 'Pay no attention,' Coyle said. 'It's only the Kansas City plant manager letting me know he's going out to lunch,' and continued the sermon on complete freedom by local managers" (Peters, 1979, p. 54). The contrasts implicit in these two examples will be discussed in terms of their differences in determinacy, system integration, levels of analysis, and bounded rationality.

Loose coupling and indeterminacy

Miller's (1978, p. 16) description of systems provides the context within which I can specify the property of organizations on which this chapter is focused: "A *system* is a set of interacting units with relationships among them. The word 'set' implies that the units have some common properties. These common properties are essential if the units are to interact or have relationships. The state of each unit is constrained by, conditioned by, or dependent on the state of other units. The units are coupled." When people make theoretical verbal statements about the units and relationships in systems, "nouns, pronouns, and their modifiers typically refer to concrete systems, subsystems, or components; verbs and their modifiers usually refer to the relationships among them" (Miller, 1978, p. 17).

This chapter is grounded in five adverbs that modify the relationship between any two components in a system. Loose coupling exists if A affects B (1) suddenly (rather than continuously), (2) occasionally (rather than constantly), (3) negligibly (rather than significantly), (4) indirectly (rather than directly), and (5) eventually (rather than immediately). Connections may appear *suddenly*, as in the case of a threshold function; may occur *occasionally*, as in the case of partial reinforcement; may be *negligible*, as when there is a damping down of response between A and B due to a constant variable; may be *indirect*, as when a superintendent can affect a teacher only by first affecting a principal; and may occur *eventually*, as when there is a lag between legislator voting behavior and response by his or her electorate.

The Canadian side of the Butterfield Division affects the American side occasionally, negligibly, and often indirectly. Relations *among* the Canadian components are more continuous, constant, significant, direct, and immediate. The plant manager in Kansas City is in fact tied to Martin Coyle constantly, directly, and immediately, even though Coyle prefers to see these ties as occasional, indirect, and slow.

The five adverbs provide a guideline for inquiry because they advise investigators to pool all organizational episodes of the variety "if A, then B, maybe" and see what they have in common. These episodes are not treated as errors, as testimonials to poor measurement, as sloppiness, or as randomness. Instead, they are episodes from which we induce a picture of normal functioning in the face of indeterminate relationships.

The adverbs index loose coupling in terms of the reliability with which B can be predicted given the behavior of A (Glassman, 1973). The concept of loose coupling indicates why people cannot predict much of what happens in organizations. In this sense, the concept has some parallel with meteorology. The science of meteorology often explains conditions under which it is impossible to forecast the weather. To gain a better understanding of weather is to understand more clearly why accurate forecasting is sometimes impossible. Understanding does not necessarily lead to more accurate predictions; rather, it leads to better predictions about those times when predicting will not work. Loose coupling operates the same way. To understand a loosely coupled system is to understand more clearly why predictions about that system may fail. To talk about a loosely coupled system is not to talk about structural looseness, but about process looseness. The image is that of a sequence of events that unfolds unevenly, discontinuously, sporadically, or unpredictably, if it unfolds at all.

The concept of a loosely coupled system is an attempt to reintroduce some indeterminacy into conventional portraits of systems. To describe an organization as a system is to imply that connections are tight and responsive and that effects are large and ramify swiftly.

To affirm that systems in organizations also have delays, lags, unpredictability, erratic guidance by feedback, unstable equilibria, and untrustworthy feedback, one can highlight the fact that components within the system are loosely coupled.

Loose coupling and system integration

Phenomena related to loose coupling in organizations appear most often in discussions of "integration." Lawrence and Lorsch (1969), for example, argue that greater differentiation among components is necessary to cope with complex environments, and this creates added problems of coordination. To cope with these problems, tighter coupling among units is required, and this is often accomplished through devices such as liaison roles. Thus, Lawrence and Lorsch are most interested in cases of high differentiation – high integration. My interest is in cases of high differentiation – low integration and in the possible ways in which such cases may trade off short-term adaptation for longer term adaptability. Systems with high differentiation – low integration may appear ineffective when assessed by criteria tied to efficiency, but may be more effective when assessed against criteria that index flexibility, ability to improvise, and capability for self-design (Weick, 1977).

Miller's (1978) discussion of integration provides an additional contrast to highlight the nature of loosely coupled systems. Miller argues that as size, number of units, and complexity increase, organizations reorganize into semiautonomous, decentralized components acting on information that is partly segregated. "As a system grows and adds more components, the components in general become increasingly independent in decision making" (Miller, 1978, p. 109). The point at which my interest diverges from Miller's is a proposition that resembles Lawrence and Lorsch's.

Miller (1978, p. 109) predicts that, "As a system's components become more numerous, they become more specialized, with resulting increased interdependence for critical processes among them." My disagreement is with "more specialized" and "increased interdependence." Differentiation can produce generalists as well as specialists, independence as well as interdependence. Differentiated systems can be self-contained and can carry out critical subsystem processes. If there is an emphasis on general competence rather than specific skills, people can replace one another and the unit can survive even if its ties to other units are infrequent and weak.

Decentralization, differentiation, segregation, and division of labor often are confounded with specialization. As a result, differentiation seems to increase dependence on those whose skills lie outside one's own specialty and special efforts must be made to tighten the relationships among the specialists. Differentiation, however, can produce either general, self-organizing, independent units that can remain loosely coupled to other units and still adapt or specialist, reactive-organizing, dependent units that maintain tight couplings with other units in order to adapt. A loosely coupled system need not be a vulnerable system.

Loose coupling and levels of analysis

The property of loose coupling is pervasive, and all organizational theorists and change agents are affected by it, even if they choose to ignore it. The property is pervasive in at least two decisions: (1) the level of analysis used to conceptualize phenomena and (2) the choice of target at which change efforts are directed.

Simon's (1962) empty world hypothesis and concept of the nearly decomposable system asserts that in any set of systems ties *within* a subsystem are stronger than are ties *between* subsystems.

Investigators often say that the concept of loose coupling applies only to "higher" levels of analysis. What sometimes gets missed is that, pragmatically, a higher level of analysis is *anything* above the level at which the investigator concentrates. For example, if as a psychologist I study individuals, then dyads and small groups – both higher levels of analysis – will seem to be loosely coupled systems. Ties are stronger within individual actors than they are between actors. Notice that the small group, which seems like a loosely coupled system to me, may seem tightly coupled to the investigator who *starts* with that level of analysis. Notice also that all of us who study small sized units – individual, dyad, triad, small group, set of small groups – will agree that an organization is loosely coupled because organizations are a higher level of analysis than any of us works with. We will encounter disagreement from those people who talk about firms, industries, communities, occupations, societies, professions, and interorganizational networks. For these people, individual organizations are relatively tightly coupled.

It is not obvious what an investigator concludes about units of analysis *smaller* than the one being examined. For example, as a person who works with the individual level of analysis, I find it inconceivable to talk about systems of loosely coupled organs or loosely coupled cells; yet physiologists argue that indeed that is possible.

The moral is that you first have to specify what elements you are examining and then look *among* these elements to find instances of loose coupling. Disagreement about the presence or absence of loose coupling may reflect a confounding of different levels of analysis.

The choice of targets for change and the success of change efforts should also be affected by the pattern of tight within, loose between. The general rule is that it is easier to produce change within than change between. Change interventions within are more likely to diffuse quickly with less modification than is true for change interventions between. If I focus on individuals, then individuals are tight within and loose between. Thus, I should have more success changing one individual and less success changing a couple or a family. If I concentrate on the small group, then the group is tight within and there are loose ties among groups. Thus, I should have more success changing a nuclear family than an extended family. Between change will always be harder than within change, even though there is a certain amount of arbitrariness involved in the decision of where to draw the boundaries that separate units. To draw boundaries around people is to direct their attention and energy *inside* the box. Change efforts within are more successful simply because they capitalize on that occurrence.

Loose coupling and bounded rationality

Systems may become more loosely coupled as organizational size increases or as environments become more complex, but cognitive processes on a much more micro level may also produce loose coupling.

Loosely coupled systems are often characterized as systems in which there is low agreement about preferences and cause–effect linkages (Thompson and Tuden, 1959). When people see things differently, their efforts will be only loosely coordinated and they will share few variables in their individual cause maps (Bougon, Weick, and Binkhorst, 1977) of the organization and its environment. Furthermore, those variables they do share will often be unimportant.

Disagreements about preferences and cause–effect linkages occur not simply because people have different perceptions, but also because they act and modify the environments they perceive. People wade into settings that puzzle them, rearrange those settings (often inadvertently), and when they finally ask the question, "what's up here" they *already* have had an effect on the answer (for example, Jones, 1977). When people examine environments, they often see the effects of their own actions emitted while positioning themselves for a better view. People implant a sizable portion of what they reify into *the* external reality but underestimate the extent to which different people implant different things.

The sequence of activity and sensemaking that produces loose coupling begins when individual actions produce individual realities that have only modest overlap. Having acted toward chaos differently, people arrange that chaos in different ways and, as a result, see different things when they inspect it. These unique "things" are the raw material from which multiple realities are built. Multiple realities, in turn, cause loosely coupled systems because individuals share few variables, share weak variables, and differ in their perceptions of covariation among these variables.

The existence of multiple realities is not just a byproduct of enactment; it is the major consequence of bounded rationality. People with limited information processing capabilities, memories that are loosely coupled to detail and uniqueness, and attention spans that are short, individually will notice different things, will reflect at different times, and will process different segments at different speeds.

Steinbrunner (1974) suggests the potential for loosely coupled systems that is implicit in bounded rationality. He argues that many cognitive processes, such as the search for cognitive consistency, simplify complex inputs. Cognitive processes transform problems into simple replicas that can be monitored by simple cybernetic processes. The important outcome of this process for students of loosely coupled systems is that massive typification and editing leave a great deal of variance unaccounted for. Even though it is unrecognized, this variance *does* influence processes, overdetermine phenomena, and introduce slippage between intention and outcome. What simplification procedures ignore remains to undo plans built on incomplete versions of "what's up."

A loosely coupled system is one consequence of bounded rationality, but the constraints on rationality *differ* across people and groups. Bounded rationality is not homogeneous. For example, when people search in the vicinity of the problem, it has been presumed that they will search in the same ways and in the same places. However, because people differ in their definitions of what a problem is, what constitutes search, and how much information they can store before they have to process it, they differ in what they find.

We have mistakenly thought that bounded rationality meant that people use similar simplifications. Similar simplifications are easy to coordinate because everybody sees the "same" world even though each is seeing very little of it. However, people bound rationality in different ways. They focus on small portions, but they focus on different small portions. As a result, the best they can do is have vague understandings of what to do next. They find it hard to agree either on explicit definitions of ends or on clear statements of what will lead to what. As a result, their actions are only moderately contingent on those of their neighbors or on their own personal intentions.

The propositions implicit in this analysis are the following: To the extent that rationality becomes less bounded, pressures toward cognitive consistency decline, attention spans lengthen, and cognitive complexity increases, people should share a greater number of important variables and become more tightly coupled. Furthermore, when enactment becomes less prominent as an input to the environment – a circumstance that is possible when tasks are specified, supervision is close, and sanctions for deviance are swift and harsh – there should be fewer realities, more shared variables, and tighter coupling among people.

The Nature of Change in Loosely Coupled Systems

A key dilemma in organizations involves the trade-off between adaptation to exploit present opportunities and adaptability to exploit future opportunities. Future opportunities may appear suddenly when the environment changes and may require a repertoire of responses that have been neglected because of their irrelevance to present demands. The trade-off between adaptation and adaptability is often described in the context of flexibility and stability.

Flexibility is required to modify current practices so that nontransient changes in the environment can be adapted to. This means that the organization must detect changes and retain a sufficient pool of novel responses to accommodate to these changes. But total flexibility makes it impossible for the organization to retain a sense of identity and continuity. Any social unit is defined in part by its history, by what it has done repeatedly and chosen repeatedly. Stability also provides an economical means to handle new contingencies; there are regularities that an organization can exploit if it has a memory and the capacity for repetition. But total adherence to past wisdom would be as disruptive as total flexibility because more economical ways of responding would never be discovered and new environmental features would seldom be noticed.

An organization can reconcile the need for flexibility with the need for stability in several ways: by some form of compromise response (a solution tried too often with much too disastrous results), by alternation between stability and flexibility, or by simultaneous expression of the two necessities in different portions of the system. Only in the last two cases is continued existence possible. A compromise response often accomplishes neither flexibility nor stability.

Adaptability in loosely coupled systems

The dilemma involving adaptation and adaptability threads through loosely coupled systems in several ways. First, loose coupling is the source of adaptability in most organizations, whereas tight coupling is the source of most adaptation. Second, in a loosely coupled system there is less necessity for major change because change is continuous. Frequent local adjustments, unconstrained by centralized policy, keep small problems from amplifying. If major change becomes necessary, however, it is much harder to diffuse it among systems that are loosely coupled. Loosely coupled systems reduce the necessity for large-scale change but also make it more difficult to achieve if it is needed. Third, tight coupling can facilitate adaptability under certain conditions, and loose coupling may also produce adaptation under specific circumstances.

The ways in which loose coupling preserves adaptability and flexibility are straightforward. Loose coupling of structural elements "may be highly adaptive for the organization, particularly when confronting a diverse, segmented environment. To the extent that departmental units are free to vary independently, they may provide a more sensitive mechanism to detect environmental variation. Loose coupling also encourages opportunistic adaptation to local circumstances, and it allows simultaneous adaptation to conflicting demands. Should problems develop with one departmental unit, it can be more easily sealed off or severed from the rest of the system. Moreover, adjustment by individual departments to environmental perturbations allows the rest of the system to function with greater stability. Finally, allowing local units to adapt to local conditions without requiring changes in the larger system reduces coordination costs for the system as a whole" (Scott, 1981, p. 248). A loosely coupled system reduces the costs of trial and error, preserves variety because it allows innovations to be retained and cumulate (Ashby, 1960), and can improve the accuracy with which situations are diagnosed.

The suggestion that loosened couplings improve the accuracy of perception (Campbell, 1979; Heider, 1959; Weick, 1978) introduces a productive tension into theorizing about change. When things are loosely coupled, sensing is improved, small deviations are sensed more quickly, and corrective actions are directed at those small deviations sooner. The result of this swifter response to smaller deviations is that potentially big problems are anticipated and solved before they become unmanageable and before they attract the attention of lots of other people. With loose coupling, diagnosis is more accurate, but interventions on the basis of this diagnosis have only minor, local effects. With tight couplings, diagnosis is less accurate, but interventions on the basis of the misdiagnosis have large effects.

The tidiness of the proposition that loosely coupled systems improve adaptability and tightly coupled systems improve adaptation is weakened by the possibility that tightly coupled organizations can sometimes communicate quickly that an environmental change has occurred and can retool with it. This sequence is not common because information about all changes, spurious as well as serious, flows through a tightly coupled system and overloads participants (for example, see Perrow, 1981a, 1981b). To cope with this overload, people ignore indiscriminately most data signifying environmental change and therefore miss the necessity for organizational change. Because they also have to do a more significant retooling to adapt to what may prove to be a spurious event, lags persist and escalation of current commitments is likely.

Nevertheless, a tightly coupled system may be slow to innovate yet retain "the privilege of historic backwardness" that allows it to benefit from the lessons of the more loosely coupled systems that made the first innovation. The efficiencies that accompany tight coupling may then allow those organizations that are second on the scene to grind up those who were first.

Problems with local adaptations

Lustick (1980), in an important critique of the strategy of disjointed incrementalism, suggests four conditions under which local adjustments, such as occur in loosely coupled systems, could lead to outcomes that are inferior to those that could be achieved by more synoptic, rational, centralized planning. Three of these conditions are relevant in the present context.

First, if the values of variables in the environment generate smooth continuous changes in values of causally connected variables, then local remedial actions are less harmful than if there are sharp discontinuities or thresholds in the values of the variables. Diverse local attempts to manage levels of sulphur dioxide pollution are plausible, but local experiments to manage radiation pollution by nuclear power plants are not. In the case of radiation, there are sharp discontinuities in the levels of damage that can be produced by incremental errors.

Second, if the complexity of an organization's environment can be decomposed into short causal chains so that consequences can be contained and monitored, then local remedial actions are less harmful than if causal chains were elongated. A society with many separate watersheds can experiment with diverse strategies to use and protect water resources because errors do not ramify the way they would if a society's watershed was a single large river with all pollution experiments being conducted upstream. Elongated causal chains are relatively nondecomposable and they conceal the significant consequences of discrete actions. This means that dependence on immediate feedback, a common feature of adjustments in loosely coupled systems, is misleading in complex environments where effects are delayed.

Lustick (1980, p. 347) summarizes the proposition concerning complexity and causal chains this way: "Complexity is commonly defined as some combination of differentiation, rate of change, and interdependence. Complex task environments are relatively more resistant to incrementalist coping techniques to the extent that their complexity derives from the interdependence of changing and differentiated components, rather than from the rate of change or extent of differentiation per se."

Third, incremental, local, disjointed accommodations are less harmful when an organization has redundant resources than when it lacks such redundancy. "For an organization with minimal slack in its budget, the sacrifice of some resources now for a little knowledge later may prevent it from surviving long enough to apply the knowledge gained" (Lustick, 1980, p. 349). A rich family can use its food budget to experiment with nutrition in food purchases and can discard the failures, but poor families cannot afford this hit-or-miss strategy. As resources diminish, a series of expensive partial successes from incremental changes made to collect insights may ensure total failure.

The relatively swift, relatively frequent adjustments to environmental changes made by loosely coupled systems may be detrimental when the variables affected are of different orders of magnitude or embedded in long causal chains or when scarce resources are used up so that the system dies. Organizational change should be centralized when subunit adjustments can have discontinuous, long-term effects at considerable expense and decentralized when adjustments have continuous, abbreviated, inexpensive effects.

One reason schools may persist as loosely coupled systems is that their local experiments with curricula, staffing, parent relations, and special programs have small, linear effects that do not ramify across time in obvious ways (for example, at age forty-five, I cannot see how I am better or worse off because I went to Lincoln Elementary School in Findlay, Ohio) and do not cost much. However, as resources become less plentiful, adult lethargy is traced to malnutrition in school lunches, and curricular decisions about creationism have discontinuous effects on the number of people who now monitor a school, loose coupling should be less satisfactory as a structure for adaptation and efforts should be made to recentralize strategy to avoid actions or commitments that become amplified.

In summary, change in loosely coupled systems is continuous rather than episodic, small scale rather than large, improvisational rather than planned, accommodative rather than constrained, and local rather than cosmopolitan. Furthermore, loosely coupled systems may store innovations that are not presently useful. Change diffuses slowly, if at all, through such systems, which means that components either invent their own solutions – which may be inefficient compared with other solutions available in the system – or they die. To construct a loosely coupled system is to design a system that updates itself and may never need the formal change interventions that sometimes are necessary to alter the hard-wired routines in tightly coupled systems.

Adaptability requires loosening; adaptation requires tightening. How a person manages this opposition over time will determine how well a component can both exploit an explicit niche and adapt to change in the niche. Simultaneous loose and tight coupling could represent "ambivalence as the optimal compromise." Simultaneous loose and tight coupling occurs, for example, when people simultaneously credit and discredit their past experience. Crediting of past experience is the equivalent of tight coupling in the sense that experience is used as a direct guide to future action. Discrediting is equivalent to loose coupling in the sense that people treat past knowledge as dated and no longer relevant to the environment that exists. Both conclusions are partially true in most settings. There has been some change but there has also been some continuity.

Targets for Change in Loosely Coupled Systems

There are several properties of loosely coupled systems that are crucial for their functioning and thus important objects of change. It is important to begin an inventory of such targets because they differ from targets such as goals, procedures, rules, controls, and design, which are targets in rational systems. The targets to be reviewed here include the following:

1. Presumptions of logic that tie loose events together (doubt produces change)
2. Socialization processes where common premises for dispersed decision making are implanted (resocialization produces change)
3. Differential participation rates that accelerate processes of loosening (equalization produces change)
4. Constant variables that disconnect parts of systems (distraction produces change)
5. Corruptions of feedback that obstruct contingent action (dependability produces change)

Presumptions of logic

The introduction of doubt into a loosely coupled system is a much more severe change intervention than most people realize. Core beliefs, such as the presumption of logic and the logic of confidence, are crucial underpinnings that hold loose events together. If these beliefs are questioned, action stops, uncertainty is substantial, and receptiveness to change is high. The rationale for these expectations is this: Prevailing thinking about organizations places a disproportionate emphasis on interaction, interpersonal relations, and being together. Loose coupling imagery suggests that people can get by far longer, on less thick socializing, with less pathology, and more energy and creativity than we presumed. The loose coupling image has also suggested that people can be tied together by less tangible relationships than face-to-face contact. Meyer and Rowan (1977, p. 358) argue that weak ties can be sustained by a "*logic of confidence*. . . . Confidence in structural elements (in loosely coupled systems) is maintained through three practices – avoidance, discretion, and overlooking. . . . Assuring that individual participants maintain face sustains confidence in the organization, and ultimately reinforces confidence in the myths that rationalize the organization's existence. . . . The assumption that things are as they seem, that employees and managers are performing their roles properly, allows an organization to perform its daily routines with a decoupled structure."

In my own work the concept of the *presumption of logic* (Weick, 1979; Weick, Gilfillan, and Keith, 1973) has served the same purpose as the concept of logic of confidence. The presumption of logic resembles a self-fulfilling prophecy. A person about to confront an event presumes in advance that the event *will have* made sense. Sensibleness is treated as a closed issue a priori. Having made this presumption, the person then tries to make the event sensible as it unfolds, postpones premature judgments on whether it makes sense or not, and thereby makes his or her own contribution toward inventing a sensible, complete experience. Other persons are not central in this sensemaking.

The presumption of logic is a way to bridge weak connections among events. A cause map (Weick, 1979) can be thought of as a summary of the presumptions one makes about a structure that hold that structure together. People do not actually see causes and effects; they infer them. With that cause map in mind, people examine events and act as if those events are tied together in the ways displayed in the map. Acting toward those events as if they were tied together causally in fact makes those events cohere more tightly than they would if a person without those assumptions had encountered them.

A member of the Utrecht Jazz Orchestra (Bougon, Weick, and Binkhorst, 1977) basically says that this rehearsal will have made sense because the events here are all organized so as to produce more satisfaction for me with my performance. Having presumed that order in a rehearsal, the musician treats it as a sensible event and *transforms* the assortment of happenings into an orderly, predictable evening.

Presumptions fill in the gaps that are created when a loosely coupled system is built. People create loosely coupled systems so they can sense and adapt to changes in the environment. In the face of that loose structure, which is finely tuned to accomplish adaptability, people simultaneously improve their present adaptation by presuming that any present niche in which they find themselves *does* make sense. To presume that it makes sense is to create that sense.

The question for change agents is how local perceptions of order break down. The answer would seem to be that the presumptions simply do not work. People make presumptions and act; yet nothing makes sense.

To change the presumption of logic is to weaken all presumptions by inducing the role of stranger, introduce novel logic systems either as presumptions or into the event being comprehended (Shapiro, 1978), make people self-conscious about their presumptions so that it is harder for them to invoke them, demonstrate that events are related randomly, discredit the rationality of the event to be observed, lower the self-esteem of the presumer, evoke contradictory sets of presumptions, demonstrate how much data are overlooked by the presumptions the observer is using and that the overlooked data contradict the presumption in force, and so forth. All these actions are nothing but variants on what happens when change agents try to unfreeze people. The difference is that all these variants share a common relevance to the "glue" presumed to hold loosely coupled systems together. To insert change into a loosely coupled system is to pay special attention to the nature and quality of those ties that do exist, namely, ties fashioned out of presumptions.

Socialization processes

"An anecdote comes to mind. A friend recently said to me, 'You're damn right we're autonomous; for example, last year corporate didn't modify any of my 17 top management salary/bonus recommendations.' I responded, 'It sounds to me like the height of "centralization"; *you* didn't make any recommendations that were out of bounds.' We agreed that there was truth in both statements" (Peters, 1979, p. 22).

One way to explain the persistence and functioning of loosely coupled systems is to argue that some form of integration overlays the systems and binds members together. Two suggestions of such an integrative overlay have already been discussed: the logic of confidence and the presumption of logic. Explicit internal controls, which are the essence of tight coupling, can be relaxed if organizational members are homogeneous at the time they assume their jobs or if they mingle and know one another sufficiently so that they can anticipate the moves of one another and coordinate actions at a distance.

Prior homogeneity that constrains subsequent variability can occur through rigorous selection and training procedures, anticipatory socialization, recruitment from a common source, or socialization into independent functioning. In each case, individuals are stand-ins for one another and explicit tight coupling is unnecessary. Issues are defined in a similar fashion because alternative sets of premises simply are not recognized. District school administrators who have come up through the ranks "know" the small latitude of discretion present in local schools and turn this into a self-fulfilling prophecy by not making proposals to the principals that presumably would be rejected anyway. Patterns of succession serve to homogenize the premises, presumptions, and ideology of administrators and to allow for their coordination at a distance.

Thus, loosely coupled systems may have pseudolooseness because members are tightly coupled to a limited set of decision premises determined by top management and implanted during socialization experiences. If we assume that more intense indoctrination leads to tighter coupling of people and premises, then, using Van Maanen's (1978) eight strategies for socialization, we would predict that newcomers who were socialized formally, collectively, sequentially, in a closed manner, with divestiture rituals would be more tightly coupled, more interchangeable with their peers, better able to coordinate at a distance, and better able to predict one another's behavior than newcomers who were socialized informally, individually, nonsequentially, in an open manner, with investiture rituals.

However, loosely coupled systems of people, decision premises, and procedures may be much less integrated than the preceding case suggests, if socialization practices encourage individuality, independence, and improvisation and expose newcomers to inaccurate or incomplete versions of organizational practice. This happens when newcomers encounter unique training, develop restricted loyalties, gain experience in being self-contained, and see the organization in ways that are shared by few other people. These outcomes can result from socialization strategies that are informal, individual, nonsequential, variable, disjunctive, and open.

Consider the contrast between formal and informal processes. Formality refers to the degree to which the setting in which training takes place is set apart from the ongoing work context and to the degree to which the individual's role as recruit is specified (Van Maanen, 1978). When the recruit's role is segregated and specified, the formal training processes focus on attitudes, rather than acts. (This happens of necessity because of the separation from the everyday work place.) As a result, there is inconsistency between what the person is taught and the realities of the job situation. The greater the separation of the newcomer from the work-a-day reality of the organization, the less the newcomer will be able to carry over or generalize any abilities or skills learned in the socialization setting.

Informal socialization also encourages loosely coupled systems, but through a different mechanism. Informal socialization increases the influence upon the individual of the specific group doing the socializing, a circumstance that is almost ideal to create stronger ties within than between groups. Left to their own devices, recruits drift toward those veterans who are most attractive. Whatever controls this attraction also restricts the range of training and exposure recruits will get from the informal training.

Perhaps the most crucial contributor to loose coupling in informal socialization is the shielding of the recruit from mistakes. Mistakes happen, but learning on the job can be dangerous in the case, for example, of interdependent police work. The recruit's need and desire for real experiences may be ignored on the grounds that veterans cannot afford to take the chance of giving the new person sufficient discretion to put their own assignments and reputations in jeopardy.

In both formal and informal socialization, the causal linkages between A and B become more tenuous, but for different reasons. Formal socialization, with its cultural island, does produce homogeneity in attitudes and, to the extent that similar attitudes facilitate coordination at a distance, produces a tightly coupled system that may appear loose. Ironically, formality also can produce loose coupling directly because this very emphasis on attitudes ill prepares the similar recruits for what they will encounter once they graduate. When this discrepancy becomes apparent, the recruits begin to resocialize themselves in ways that are more idiosyncratic and more attuned to the specific situation in which they find themselves. The similar attitudes with which they have been prepared become less valuable as guides for action and are dropped in favor of more pragmatic beliefs that are locally appropriate.

Informal socialization promotes loose coupling because recruits align themselves with veterans who themselves have had a skewed sample of experience and who also are wary of allowing the recruit to make instructive errors in serious activities. The recruit gets exposed to a novel set of moderately safe aspects of the ongoing organization and is ill prepared to cope with worlds other than the one to which he or she was initiated.

Having considered just one of Van Maanen's eight distinctions, we find ourselves in the unusual position of arguing that no matter what happens during socialization, individuals will develop a loose coupling between their own beliefs and actions, between themselves and rules and procedures, and between themselves and both peers and predecessors. The socialized newcomer is unlike everyone else and therefore shares few variables and unimportant variables with them. The recruit is also like everyone else in the training cohort, and to the extent that recruits function among themselves after training as a separate organization, the recruits can coordinate actions through accurate anticipation of others' responses and assumptions. If people are trained similarly but then dispersed, there is still slippage between training and practice when each individual discovers different ways in which formal instruction is dated and idealized and tries to remedy the misinformation.

The preceding line of argument suggests a curvilinear relationship. Both relatively pure formal socialization and relatively pure informal socialization have identical outcomes, namely, predispositions to create loosely coupled systems between headquarters and the field. The mixed case of part formal and part informal socialization avoids the unreality of an idealized view of the world (it has accuracy) and the unreality of one mentor's skewed view of the world (it has generality). In producing valid experience among likeminded peers, it might set the stage for tight couling both with these peers and with other veterans who are actually doing what the socialization experiences portray them as doing. A mixture of formality and informality leads to tighter coupling than does either component when pursued by itself.

To change a loosely coupled system is to resocialize people away from provincial views adopted during the "second" socialization toward more comprehensive, more accurate views of different segments of the organization. This "third" socialization in effect suggests different practices adopted independently by similar loosely coupled systems elsewhere that might be of help to people who improvised their own current procedures without the benefit of much consultation. This third socialization also informs individual systems of the context within which their activities occur and of possible tacit interdependencies that exist among systems. Presumably, this information allows for more mutual adjustment and more coordination without a serious loss of adaptability.

To change a loosely coupled system is also to influence the original socialization processes so that their content is both more general and more accurate than is common when relatively pure socialization strategies are used. A mixture of indoctrination in key values plus training in the management of discretion and improvisation seems most appropriate to preserve the flexibility of a loosely coupled system but to stabilize that flexibility in terms of a handful of central values. To produce a blend of formality and flexibility seems to require that oppositions in socialization strategies, such as individual–collective or formal–informal, themselves be blended. The presence of relatively pure socialization strategies of the kind analyzed earlier should alert change agents that either generality (for example, informal practices) or accuracy (for example, formal practices) is being sacrificed in training. Either sacrifice loosens ties between people and ideology to such an extent that crucial functions may no longer be performed adequately when the newcomers are put in the field.

Centralized change seldom reaches the components of loosely coupled systems and routinely is undone when people are socialized, first, and then dispersed. The impact of change interventions addressed to loosely coupled systems increases when they are tailored to the realities that loosely coupled systems face (socialization content is accurate) and when they equip people to improvise in constructive, low-cost ways when these local realities change (socialization content is general).

Differential participation

Equalization of participation has been a major tool in organizational change, but little attention has been paid to *differential* participation as a mechanism for change. Differential participation is more common in loosely coupled systems, less common in tightly coupled systems. As Pfeffer (1978, p. 31) notes, "organizations are loosely coupled, in part because few participants are constantly involved or care about every dimension of the organization's operation."

The mechanism for change implicit in differential participation is straightforward and has been analyzed most fully by Weiner (1976) in his discussion of the competence multiplier.

Change is possible in a loosely coupled system when one person becomes more closely coupled with issues and analysis and in doing so makes it harder for others to gain access to the decision-making process. Loose coupling among people in their rates of attendance and tight coupling among attendance, competence, and experience allow for differential amplification of individual efforts.

Participants who show up repeatedly at meetings produce an environment of sophisticated analyses that requires more participation from them, which makes them even more informed to deal with the issues that are presented. A vicious circle is created in which the regular participants of an advisory council enact the very set of sophisticated and subtle issues that their newfound competence enables only them to deal with. People who attend less often feel less informed, increasingly unable to catch up, and more reluctant to enter the conversation at the level of sophistication voiced by the persistent participants. The relatively less informed people select themselves out of the decision-making process, and this elevates the level of planning to an even more detailed and complicated level, where even fewer people can comprehend it. Over time the combination of high and low participation rates, a minor deviation in the beginning, changes the issues, plans, and environment that confront committees.

To change a loosely coupled system is to pay special attention to absentee members, latecomers, and regular attendees and then to alter attendance patterns, give thorough briefings to those who attend less frequently, change agendas without notice, thereby handicapping everyone equally, introduce topics on which infrequent participants have unique and visible expertise, change meeting times, or any other devices that introduce a new pattern of differential participation and a new pattern of concerns and expertise.

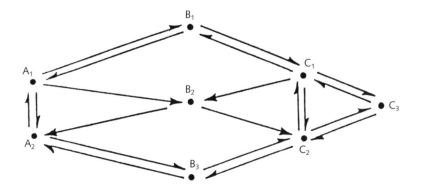

Figure 17.1 Hypothetical system vulnerable to constant variables

Constant variables

Loose coupling may occur because variables in a system lose most of their variation and become constant. In Ashby's (1960, p. 169) words, "constancies can cut a system to pieces." To see this point, imagine a hammock that is narrow at the right and lefthand ends and broad in the middle. Imagine that there are two variables at the lefthand end labeled A_1 and A_2, three variables in the center of the hammock labeled $B_{1,2,3}$, and three variables at the righthand end labeled $C_{1,2,3}$. Imagine that A and C are connected by relationships that pass through B (see Figure 17.1).

If the variables in B become constant, they construct a "wall of constancies" between subsystem A and subsystem C, and those two systems become severed and loosely coupled. If the constancies dissolve, the subsystems once again become fully jointed. As Ashby (1960, p. 169) notes, "if some variables or subsystems are constant for a time, then during that time the connections through them are reduced functionally to zero, and the effect is as if the connections had been severed in some material way during that time."

Secrets can sever systems. Jackson (1977) argues that educational administrators know more than they can say or use in their dealings with constituencies. They hear all kinds of secrets that they cannot pass along or invoke to rationalize and justify action. For our purposes, the administrator acts as a damper, as a constant variable, as a person who absorbs but does *not* pass along variation. A "quiet" administrator personifies the adverb "negligibly" in the statement, if A then B, negligibly. Superintendents are often praised as people who do not raise their voice (for example, McCleery, 1979), but what this means is that they are disconnecting portions of the system that are bound together by that voice. Administrators who make decisions by indecision effectively hold variables constant.

Bateson (1972, pp. 496–497) describes constant variables, although he prefers to call them uptight variables:

When, under stress, a variable must take the value close to its upper or lower limit of tolerance, we shall say, borrowing a phrase from the youth culture, that the system is "uptight" in respect to this variable, or lacks "flexibility" in this respect. But, because the variables are interlinked, to be uptight in respect to one variable commonly means that other variables cannot be changed without pushing the uptight variable. The loss of flexibility thus spreads throughout the system. In extreme cases, the system will only accept those changes which *change the tolerance limits* for the uptight variable. For example, an overpopulated society looks for those changes (increased food, new roads, more houses, etc.) which will make the pathological and pathogenic conditions of over-population more comfortable. But these *ad hoc* changes are precisely those which in longer time can lead to more fundamental ecological pathology. The pathologies of our time may broadly be said to be the accumulated results of this process – the eating up of flexibility in response to stresses of one sort or another (especially the stress of population pressure) and the refusal to bear with those byproducts of stress (e.g., epidemic and famine) which are the age old correctives for population excess.

Notice a crucial analytic subtlety that is associated with constant variables. In many organizational studies, the presence of variation and discretion is treated as an indicator of loose coupling. As discretion and variation decrease, the system is said to be more tightly coupled. Constant variables alter this reasoning. Evidence of low variation and low discretion can be interpreted to mean that variables are tightly coupled *or* that variables cannot move and may soon tear a system apart if they mediate crucial relationships. Variables with restricted variation do not tighten systems; they loosen them. Only when variation is restored do interactions increase and systems become more tightly coupled. To change a loosely coupled system is to restore variation to variables that have become constant and have frozen other variables that are dependent on them for variation. Variation can be restored by widening the tolerance limits of the constant variable, introducing lower standards of performance, circumventing the constant variable by introducing new linkages into the system, reversing the direction in which either the constant variable or related variables have been moving, institutionalizing and legitimatizing the separate severed systems while ignoring the original system, stressing the constant variable even more until the whole system explodes and forms new systems, and declaring a moratorium in the hope that relief from pressure will restore variation.

Change tactics that are useful for de-escalation and conflict resolution often are effective because they restore variation to variables that have become unresponsive. Changes of this sort are especially important in loosely coupled systems.

Corruptions of feedback

Conventional strategies for inducing change rely heavily on feedback (for example, Block, 1981). In loosely coupled systems, flawed feedback is often a major source of looseness. Consequently, feedback is often suspect when it is introduced, and some-times people are not even clear how to use it. Loosely coupled systems often learn to make do with minimal feedback because feedback is unavailable, meaningless, or discredited. When feedback is offered by a change agent, people wonder why they should believe it and how they should use it.

Feedback becomes suspect in loosely coupled systems for a variety of reasons. For a tight coupling to form between actions and consequences, there must be swift, accurate feedback of those consequences to the action. As the speed and accuracy of feedback diminishes, there are looser couplings formed between actions and consequences and between actors. Loosely coupled systems show stability in the presence of environmental change. One way to understand this is to argue that organizations seldom benefit from trial-and-error learning because all they generate are trials. Data indicating errors are too noisy to coordinate with a specific action or too late for anyone to remember the precise trial that generated them.

When people in organizations take action and generate some consequences, these consequences may not inform subsequent actions because information about the consequences is (1) delayed, (2) neutralized (Millman, 1977), (3) confounded, (4) composed of lies, or (5) forgotten.

In each of these cases, it is predicted that the incidence of superstitious behavior will increase. Faced with imprecise information about what actions produce what outcomes, individuals on future occasions typically do more than is necessary to make specific outcomes happen. The individual overdetermines his or her own future responses when acting on the basis of ambiguous feedback. The important point is that action becomes even less finely tuned to the environment and to what other individuals are doing, and this is the prototypic situation for loose coupling.

Even though educational organizations produce feedback in large quantities, molecular analyses suggest that it is often not coupled to relevant actions. For example, professional norms among teachers often discourage offering assistance to faltering instructors unless it is asked for. Thus, faltering teachers get imprecise feedback about what they are doing wrong. As a result they are likely both to develop more elaborate teaching techniques and to find that these elaborated techniques are even more resistant to change because they are under the control of aperiodic reinforcement. In educational organizations, mistakes are often neutralized. As a result, actors in these systems are left with mere trials, an outcome that decouples action from environmental consequences and from the actions of other individuals.

Organizational actions are guided less often by their consequences fed back as an input than mechanistic metaphors would lead us to expect. Furthermore, despite abundant pronouncements about the value and importance of interpersonal feedback, organizational realities such as distance, diverse roles, infrequent inspection, professional norms respecting autonomy, limited vocabularies, and collective action the individual effects of which cannot be untangled, all blur feedback that people may try to give. As feedback becomes less credible and less frequent, actions become less tightly coupled to consequences and more difficult to coordinate. Continued neutralization of feedback can cut a system to pieces quite as handily as can constant variables.

To change a loosely coupled system requires either avoidance of feedback, at least initially, or "overkill" to avoid the discrediting of feedback that is given.

To change people without using feedback is to use modeling, role playing, case method, lectures, self-monitoring, guided imagery, audiovisual presentations, alone time, reading, projects, and field experiences (Walter and Marks, 1981). Each of these techniques is only moderately dependent on feedback for its impact or can be conducted so that feedback is incidental.

To change people by presenting convincing feedback is to be concerned with explicitness, immediacy, accuracy, and relevance and to have material presented by an expert source as an issue of fact rather than an issue of taste, dispassionately, and on an issue where the target person has no preconceptions (McGuire, 1968). These conditions make it harder to discredit and dismiss feedback, but they are also a harder set of conditions to create.

Loosely coupled systems can perceive their environments and themselves accurately because of their mediumlike quality noted earlier. As a result, feedback can be redundant and of little consequence as a vehicle for change. What a loosely coupled system often does not know is what other loosely coupled systems experience and how they cope with it. This ignorance is a result of minimal diffusion. Feedback may have more impact when it provides more information about *other* systems and less information about the target system.

Conclusion

A loosely coupled system is a problem in causal inference. For actors and observers alike, the prediction and activation of cause-effect relations is made more difficult because relations are intermittent, lagged, dampened, slow, abrupt, and mediated. Microchanges predominate in loosely coupled systems. The crucial links in a loosely coupled system occur among small groups of people, including dyads, triads, and small groups. That being the case, change models appropriate for small groups (for example, Herr and Weakland, 1979) seem most useful.

My own thinking about how to apply psychological findings to issues of change places a strong emphasis on language and communication. The main reason for this is that I use therapy as my model of application (Weick, 1981). My image is that of a conceptual therapist, a person who provides conceptual frameworks that individuals may not have previously imposed on their activities. A conceptual therapist articulates confusion and acts like a grammarian who gives people rules for tying together and labeling parts of their experiences. People provide a description in common language (Mandler and Kessen, 1959); the conceptual therapist consolidates, edits, and repunctuates the language and gives it back in somewhat different form. Having received back a somewhat novel version of what is going on, people may then monitor and do something different than before. Notice that the interventions of the person providing the gloss are innocuous. That person is directing attention, providing signals, asking questions, managing language, telling stories, and not much else. This way of acting is basically an elaboration of the following prototype: An individual says "I need a sounding board." Another individual says "I'll provide it." The two people meet regularly, and the sounding board provides feedback that is helpful to the degree that "(1) it provides information, (2) the learner is motivated to improve, (3) the learner has better response alternatives available" (McKeachie, 1976, p. 824).

Thus, one of the realities in loosely coupled systems is the reality that a person doing change can be no more or less effective than a therapist who builds conceptual frameworks and has only modest control over whether the feedback implicit in the communication provides information, induces motivation, and creates or elicits better response alternatives.

Actors in a loosely coupled system rely on trust and presumptions, persist, are often isolated, find social comparison difficult, have no one to borrow from, seldom imitate, suffer pluralistic ignorance, maintain discretion, improvise, and have less hubris because they know they cannot change the universe because it is not sufficiently connected to make this possible.

A loosely coupled system is not a flawed system. It is a social and cognitive solution to constant environmental change, to the impossibility of knowing another mind, and to limited information processing capacities. It is ethnocentrism writ small, and it is the ultimate neutralizer of managerial hubris. It is our recognition in our own language that delegation remains the primordial organizational act Selznick said it was and that it still remains the precarious venture he saw it to be. Loose coupling is to social systems as compartmentalization is to individuals, a means to achieve cognitive economy and a little peace.

Note

I am grateful to Lee Sproull, Charles Perrow, Barry Staw, David Clark, Randy Bobbitt, and Paul Goodman for comments on a preliminary draft of this chapter.

References

Ashby, W. R. *Design for a Brain*. (2nd ed.) London: Chapman and Hall, 1960.

Bateson, G. *Steps to an Ecology of Mind*. New York: Ballantine, 1972.

Berger, M. A. "Coping with Anarchy in Organizations." In J. E. Jones and J. W. Pfeiffer (Eds.), *The 1981 Annual Handbook for Group Facilitators*. San Diego, Calif.: University Associates, 1981.

Block, P. *Flawless Consulting*. Austin, Tex.: Learning Concepts, 1981.

Bougon, M., Weick, K. E., and Binkhorst, D. "Cognition in Organizations: An Analysis of the Utrecht Jazz Orchestra." *Administrative Science Quarterly*, 1977, *22*, 606–639.

Campbell, D. T. "A Tribal Model of the Social System Vehicle Carrying Scientific Knowledge." *Knowledge: Creation, Diffusion, Utilization*, 1979, *1*, 141–201.

Cohen, M. D., and March, J. G. *Leadership and Ambiguity*. New York: McGraw-Hill, 1974.

Glassman, R. B. "Persistence and Loose Coupling in Living Systems." *Behavioral Science*, 1973, *18*, 83–98.

Heider, F. "Thing and Medium." *Psychological Isuues*, 1959, *1*(3), 1–34.

Herr, H. H., and Weakland, J. H. *Counseling Elders and Their Families*. New York: Springer, 1979.

Jackson, P. W. "Lonely at the Top: Observations on the Genesis of Administrative Isolation." *School Review*, May 1977, pp. 425–432.

Jones, R. A. *Self-Fulfilling Prophecies*. Hillsdale, N.J.: Erlbaum, 1977.

Lawrence, P. R., and Lorsch, J. W. *Organization and Environment*. Homewood, Ill.: Irwin, 1969.

402 COMPONENTS OF SENSEMAKING

Lustick, I. "Explaining the Variable Utility of Disjointed Incrementalism: Four Propositions." *American Political Science Review*, 1980, *74*(2), 342–353.

McCleery, M. "Stranger in Paradise: Process and Product of a District Office." Unpublished manuscript, NIE, June 1979.

McGuire, W. J. "Personality and Susceptibility to Social Influence." In E. F. Borgatta and W. W. Lambert (Eds.), *Handbook of Personality Theory and Research*. Chicago: Rand McNally, 1968.

McKeachie, W. J. "Psychology in America's Bicentennial Year." *American Psychologist*, 1976, *31*, 819–833.

Mandler, G., and Kessen, W. *The Language of Psychology*. New York: Wiley, 1959.

March, J. G. "Footnotes to Organizational Change." *Administrative Science Quarterly*, 1981, *26*, 563–577.

Meyer, J. W., and Rowan, B. "Institutionalized Organizations: Formal Structure as Myth and Ceremony." *American Journal of Sociology*, 1977, *83*, 340–363.

Miller, J. G. *Living Systems*. New York: McGraw-Hill, 1978.

Millman, M. *The Unkindest Cut*. New York: Morrow, 1977.

Perrow, C., "Disintegrating Social Sciences." *New York University Education Quarterly*, 1981a, *12*(2), 2–9.

Perrow, C. "Normal Accident at Three Mile Island." *Society*, 1981b, *18*(5), 17–26.

Peters, T. J. "Structure as a Reorganizing Device: Shifting Attention and Altering the Flow of Biases." Unpublished manuscript, McKinsey & Co., 1979.

Peters, T. J. "Management Systems: The Language of Organizational Character and Competence." *Organizational Dynamics*, Summer 1980, pp. 3–26.

Pfeffer, J. "The Micropolitics of Organizations." In M. W. Meyer and Associates, *Environments and Organizations: Theoretical and Empirical Perspectives*. San Francisco: Jossey-Bass, 1978.

Scott, W. R. *Organizations: Rational, Natural, and Open Systems*. Englewood Cliffs, N.J.: Prentice-Hall, 1981.

Shapiro, D. H., Jr. *Precision Nirvana*. Englewood Cliffs, N.J.: Prentice-Hall, 1978.

Simon, H. A. "The Architecture of Complexity." *Proceedings of the American Philosophical Society*, 1962, *106*(6), 467–482.

Siu, R. G. K. *The Man of Many Qualities: A Legacy of the I Ching*. Cambridge, Mass.: M.I.T. Press, 1968.

Steinbruner, J. D. *The Cybernetic Theory of Decision*. Princeton, N.J.: Princeton University Press, 1974.

Thompson, J. D., and Tuden, A. "Strategies, Structures, and Processes of Organizational Decision." In J. D. Thompson, P. B. Hammond, R. W. Hawkes, B. H. Junker, and A. Tuden (Eds.), *Comparative Studies in Administration*. Pittsburgh: University of Pittsburgh Press, 1959.

Van Maanen, J. "People Processing: Strategies of Organizational Socialization." *Journal of Organizational Dynamics*, 1978, *7*(1), 19–36.

Walter, G. A., and Marks, S. E. *Experiential Learning and Change*. New York: Wiley, 1981.

Weick, K. E. "Educational Organizations as Loosely Coupled Systems." *Administrative Science Quarterly*, 1976, *21*, 1–19.

Weick, K. E. "Organization Design: Organizations as Self-Designing Systems." *Organizational Dynamics*, 1977, *6*(2), 30–46.

Weick, K. E. "The Spines of Leaders." In M. W. McCall, Jr., and M. M. Lombardo (Eds.), *Leadership: Where Else Can We Go?* Durham, N.C.: Duke University Press, 1978.

Weick, K. E. *The Social Psychology of Organizing*. (2nd ed.) Reading, Mass.: Addison-Wesley, 1979.

Weick, K. E. "Psychology as Gloss." In R. A. Kasschau and C. N. Cofer (Eds.), *Psychology's Second Century*. New York: Praeger, 1981.

Weick, K. E., Gilfillan, D. P., and Keith, T. A. "The Effect of Composer Credibility on Orchestra Performance." *Sociometry*, 1973, *36*, 435–462.

Weiner, S. S. "Participation, Deadlines, and Choice." In J. G. March and J. P. Olsen (Eds.), *Ambiguity and Choice in Organizations*. Bergen, Norway: Universitetsforlaget, 1976.

18

Organization Design: Organizations as Self-Designing Systems

On Friday, December 27, 1973, the Apollo 3 astronauts conducted the first daylong sit-down strike in outer space. Their grievance concerned a problem of self-design.

To get the most information from this final trip in the Apollo program, ground control in Houston had removed virtually all the slack from the astronauts' schedule of activities and had treated the men as if they were robots. To get everything in, ground control shortened meal times, reduced setup times for experiments, and made no allowance for the fact that previous crews aboard Skylab had stowed equipment in an unsystematic manner. The astronauts' favorite pastimes – watching the sun and earth – were forbidden.

As Neal Hutchinson, flight director of the mission said, "We send up about six feet of instructions to the astronauts' teleprinter in the docking adapter every day – at least 42 separate sets of instructions – telling them where to point the solar telescope, which scientific instruments to use, and which corollaries to do. We lay out the whole day for them, and the astronauts normally follow it to a 'T.' What we've done is we've learned how to maximize what you can get out of a man in one day."

Not quite. Here's where the issue of self-design entered the picture. Edward Gibson, the civilian physicist in the Apollo 3 crew, made the following plea to ground control shortly before the strike: "I think in the future the ground should give the astronauts the bare framework of a schedule, together with a shopping list of things for them to do, and then let the guys on board figure out the best way of doing them."

This had already been done with one activity – making solar observations. Shopping lists had been designed "to allow the crewmen to work independently of ground advice in selecting targets and objectives for solar observations. These lists were originally devised to suggest to the crewmen a variety of short objectives that could be met if an extra five or ten minutes of observing time should become available. The data collected in these intervals were found to be so useful that soon the ground team was requesting specific allotments of time to be used entirely at crewmen option. Because the crewmen had the current sensor outputs ... [they were] in the best position to select the most interesting features and programs for study. In this activity the crewmen truly performed as the alter ego of the science community." (Cooper, 1976)

Despite the reasonableness of general frameworks and shopping lists, mission control saw things differently. "So many jobs interfere with one another!" Hutchinson said, after the third crew had returned to earth. "What if a guy gets an instrument focused on a star and just then his buddies in the docking adapter maneuver the vehicle around to look at the earth? Or what if a guy starts riding the bicycle ergometer, jiggling the space station, while another guy is taking a long film of the solar flare? Now, say that I gave the crew a rough framework of a schedule that said, for example, 'Do five orbits of solar work followed by two orbits of earth resources passes over Africa.' They might get so superinterested in the sun that they didn't get ready in time for the earth resources passes and miss an important target on the ground! With so many constraints, I'd say they're bound to screw something up!"

The problem of distributing authority for the Skylab activities between the ground and the sky has classical overtones. We can analyze the situation using such concepts as autonomy, discretion, perceived control, self-determination, job enrichment, delegation, power, time span of discretion, or role conflict. To this already lengthy list I want to add the proposition that there are features of Skylab that the preceding concepts overlook, and these oversights require us to invent still another way of thinking – namely, the concept of a self-designing system.

Skylab as a Problem in Self-Design

Several nuances of the Skylab situation are thrown into relief when we think about it as a problem in self-design:

- If the astronauts *had* received a bare framework and a shopping list, and if they did screw up and miss the earth resources pass as Hutchinson feared, *the three-man Skylab crew, acting alone,* might still have been capable of restructuring their ways of combining the framework and the shopping list. One means of restructuring potentially available to the Skylab crew would be for them, not ground control, to decide that frameworks and laundry lists were not useful and then to request that a greater portion of their activities be suggested by mission control.
- In response to missed experiments, space station jiggles, or pure fascination, the astronauts might redefine the mission and alter the priorities of assignments. This is not as heretical as it may sound; it happened anyway. The original mission of Apollo 3 was to see if men could really live in space for long periods of time, and living meant to live decently with regular shifts and time off for relaxation. Given the somewhat precarious position of the NASA program and of this series of flights, this aim disappeared and relaxation time became the occasion for just one more experiment.
- If they had a self-designing system, the astronauts could have modified their resources by lengthening or shortening the mission, asking for other persons to

join them, or starting a Skylab-to-earth rest and relaxation cycle with people shuttling back and forth. They could have shut off the teleprinter while they were doing a set of tasks and restarted it only when they were ready for a new batch. They could have requested that a second crew be sent aloft and treated this second crew as robots; or the original crew could have built actual robots out of junk on board so that commands from the ground that assumed robots at the other end could in fact have been assigned to robots.

- There apparently had been detailed advance planning about what to do in space, but less attention had been paid to planning how to plan what to do, a second-order issue that pervades the issue of self-design and is not covered in the other concepts I mentioned.

- The astronauts didn't seem to have any solution-generating process on board except trial and error and working to the limits of human energy. The idea of self-design suggests that they might have been better prepared with processes that would generate solutions. It is interesting that Gerald Carr's diatribe, blasting mission control and announcing the strike, does not contain an alternative design. Instead, Carr says in essence, "You have given us too much to do. We're not going to do a thing until you get your act in better order."

- Thinking about self-design also leads us to examine what actually happened *after* the astronauts revolted. Their one-day strike, plus Commander Carr's blast at mission control, did get results – but results of the most unimaginative sort. Ground control gave the astronauts fewer experiments and more time in which to complete them. Quantities were altered but patterns were not. There was no discrediting of the previous design and no rearrangement of activities and responsibilities.

- Conspicuously absent from the zealous scheduling by ground personnel – "We knew how long it took to screw in each screw up there" – was any sense of the astronauts' "selves" and of their needs to reflect, to observe, to find their place amid these baffling, fascinating, unprecedented experiences.

Sensitivity to this range of concerns is what is preserved by *self*-design. The phrase literally suggests that you integrate yourself into the design. This is what mission control failed to allow the astronauts to do until halfway through the mission. As Hutchinson said later, somewhat grudgingly, "Those guys know how valuable their time up there is! Then I saw we'd done a bad thing by forcing them. I saw they needed time to think about what they were doing and to reestablish themselves. They were not asking for time to read beddy-bye stories." The likelihood is that sensitive self-design would have taken astronaut needs into account more consistently over a much greater portion of the mission.

NASA did not seem to be sensitive to the quality of the relationships between ground control and Skylab or to the fact that it was steadily deteriorating. The flight surgeons, however, suspected as early as the second week that the relationships were being mismanaged (the strike occurred in the sixth week), but when they conveyed these observations to the flight planners, the surgeons were told, "The flight schedule is a nonmedical duty."

The flight planners lacked the detachment to perceive a design that said, essentially, "If there's a spare minute, fill it." And while they viewed the flight surgeons as people with the necessary detachment, the latter were considered too uninformed to make observations of consequence. If the capability for self-design was weak in Skylab, it was virtually nonexistent on the ground.

The design used initially – assuming that the astronauts could go flat out until bedtime – suggests that NASA got convinced by its own rhetoric that astronauts were supermen. These design assumptions proved faulty. Despite the inflated imagery, some of which was warranted given the extraordinary care used in selecting and training the astronauts, they encountered normal, natural troubles. For example, they had an initial interlude of sickness on entering Skylab, tried to suppress the evidence of this sickness, and received a severe reprimand for doing so the very first day in space. Furthermore, based on their experience with the Apollo 1 and 2 crews, ground controllers had come to expect the astronauts to be chronically enthusiastic. What they had failed to realize was that those earlier crews were enthusiastic partly because they had fewer things to do and stayed up for shorter periods of time.

Thus, those people who tried to control the design actually had a somewhat faulty understanding of what the elements in the design were really like.

Focusing on the designs envisioned and imposed by ground control suggests that pursuit of rational means and easily measured performance criteria (for example, number of rolls of film exposed) took precedence over pursuit of nonrational but more important goals (for example, allowing the astronauts plenty of time to stare out the windows).

It seems likely that the Apollo 3 mission was trying to optimize an unknown criterion. Everyone tried to get an extra experiment into this final mission – including the flight surgeons who went to bat for the astronauts – making the most visible criterion simply the number of experiments completed.

At the same time, there was strong pressure on the astronauts to observe and film spontaneous and unplanned phenomena such as sun flares; of course, time observing flares is time taken away from unpacking and running canned experiments. And as if these conflicting criteria weren't confusing enough, NASA was also looking for ways to justify the cost of space stations. As a consequence, NASA was interested in whether the astronauts could form such things as perfect lenses, perfect crystals, or perfect ball bearings under gravity-free conditions, all of which, if they could be done, would be profitable enterprises that would require NASA space expertise.

Last, as we noted earlier, some NASA people were interested in "quality of life" aboard a space station. Getting this information clearly detracts from the claims of *all* other criteria. If to these aims we add the fact that some physical decay and bodily deformation is inevitable in space so that astronauts have to spend time counteracting the physical effects of weightlessness (for example, the blood flows from the legs to the chest and the legs deteriorate), it becomes evident that what is to be optimized is unclear. The design problems, as a result, become more ambiguous.

Two other missions had preceded Apollo 3. In using the equipment aboard Skylab, they had not stowed the equipment where they were supposed to store it. By the time the Apollo 3 crew arrived, storage was completely out of hand.

The magnitude of the problem can be inferred from the following description: "There were some forty thousand items stashed away in over a hundred cabinets in the space station, and Pogue bitched that none of them was ever stowed where a person might logically expect to find them. Although there were six men and a computer in Houston whose sole purpose was to help the astronauts keep track of items in the space station, the system, which had been breaking down since the beginning of the second mission because of the progressive failure of crews to report where they put things, had now collapsed altogether. To confuse Pogue more, all the cabinets looked alike, and although they were numbered and their contents were sometimes written on the outside, the writing was small and the labels were difficult to read, particularly if Pogue approached them sideways or upside down. He had a stowage list, but he found it useless. 'The stowage list refers to numbers that are not even here!' he griped."

Thus we have the space-age equivalent of the problems of interdependence associated with long-wall coal mining. The conspicuous issue of designing stowage is visible in this example, but so too is the issue of an intricate interweaving of design and technology and the prospect that self-designing systems may need to rearrange and edit their tools and trappings as well as their time and territory. There is also in this example the hint that prior "designs" restrict freedom of design of subsequent occupants severely.

Throughout Henry Cooper's (1976) analysis of Skylab, and in the material quoted here, there is the suggestion that ground control defined itself as *the* planners and defined the astronauts as *the* implementers. While planning, designing, and implementing are distinct activities, frequently the implementation undertaken before the designs have been formed serves to create the design. After implementing the first steps of the "design," the designers discover what that design was in the first place. Similarly, as the design unfolds, this development actually amounts to implementation in progress. Although seemingly separate activities, design and implementation provided the opportunity to improve and learn more about their counterparts. Implementation clarifies design; design clarifies implementation.

The thinking involved in coming up with a design is not completely guided by evaluations of probable success or failure. To say "it was done by design" is to indicate that there was some order, some arrangement, some unity by which resources were coupled. It does not imply that this coupling was done solely in the name of efficiency, speed, or any other utilitarian criterion. While self-design often occurs in times of crisis to improve conditions, design in the pure sense of the word means ordering, arranging, or making less equivocal. Designs are important, not only because they increase productivity or meet some other specific criterion, but also because they clarify circumstances.

In the case of the Apollo 3 astronauts, self-design was an issue because the overrationalized order imposed by the ground controllers turned out to be unworkable. It is also true, however, that constraining as the six-foot printout was, it *did* impose some kind of order on the uncertainties housed in those 100 lockers and it *was* an orderly arrangement of time, men, and activities that by at least one standard – number of items accomplished – was reasonable. The problem in Skylab was to devise alternate ways of arranging materials, activities, and time so that other criteria, such as the astronauts' willingness to work, were also satisfied.

Designs are simply patterns that integrate diverse elements. Self-designing systems are able to incorporate the current design, the needs for alternative designs, and alternatives that will produce a different set of consequences from the current design.

Some people who talk about self-design equate it with designing a system so that it is a machine for teaching itself. That requires the right flow of information to the right places, with these places interconnected and able to develop their own feedback loops.

From this viewpoint, the Apollo 3 astronauts may have been incapable of redesign because they had the wrong kind of information. Furthermore, one could argue that the ground controllers' worries about the astronauts screwing up was based on the assumption that the astronauts had different information than the controllers did – and less of it. If, however, the information were distributed more equally or distributed with the idea that the three astronauts would have the capability to redesign, the presumed inferior scheduling of the astronauts might never had happened.

The Concept of Self-Designing Systems

The astronauts' world may appear specialized. In fact, it mirrors design problems that are found in all kinds of organized relationships that span long distances or large differences: headquarters and branches, ships controlled partly from the shore, superiors and subordinates, control towers and pilots, sales managers and salesmen, teachers and pupils, superintendents and teachers.

The concept of self-design is so new that concrete illustrations of it in business organizations are rare. Furthermore, since self-design is as much a strategy as it is an object, it's not obvious what it would look like or where it would be visible.

Nevertheless, it's easy to spot organizations that are incapable of self-design and therefore vulnerable. They value forecasts more than improvisation, they dwell on constraints rather than opportunities, they borrow solutions rather than invent them, they defend past actions rather than devise new ones, they cultivate permanence rather than impermanence, they value serenity more highly than argument, they rely on accounting systems as their sole means to assess performance rather than use more diverse measures, they remove doubt rather than encourage it, they search for final solutions rather than continuously experimenting, and they discourage contradictions rather than seek them.

Any organization that shows this pattern will make the same mistakes mission control did and will show the same inability to devise and insert new ways of acting. In the face of swift changes in the environment, such organizations will do too little, too late – and will fail.

To become more self-designing, organizations must reverse many of the patterns and preferences we have just listed. People must look at their organization in a different way and begin to value features of it that they used to disparage. The remainder of this chapter suggests some ways to initiate that rethinking and revaluing.

The essential problem in self-design is to make a teacher out of the learner – that is, to have the same people performing both functions. When an organization finds a present design inadequate, it avoids having someone from the outside come in to rewire the organization; it does the rewiring itself.

At the most elementary level, self-design involves generating alternatives and testing them against the requirements and constraints perceived by people in the organization. The old design may provide some of the pieces for the new design or be used as one criterion to select among various alternatives, but unless it serves in this subsidiary role, the organization is merely introducing variations on the old theme. In self-design, the new design is underdetermined by the old design. It is underdetermined in the sense that fortuitous, arbitrary, sometimes even random elements are added to portions of old designs and in the interaction between them new forms are generated.

General Characteristics of Self-Design

The Skylab particulars described in the introduction suggest a set of general characteristics associated with organizations as self-designing systems. The concept of self-design is a way for an organization watcher to prime himself with images and problems so that when he examines his own organization, he can diagnose the places at which it is capable of self-design and what might be done to improve these capabilities.

In examining the following half-dozen characteristics, it would be well to remember an unfortunate connotation of the word "design." The word brings to mind artifacts such as blueprints, pictures, graphs, and displays. These images direct our attention away from a potentially richer set of images, namely, that of designing as an ongoing process and that of designs as recipes rather than blueprints, recipes that may require varying amounts of improvisation. Recipes trigger actions, sometimes in ways that even the cooks don't understand. This analogy gives a more realistic picture of what happens in self-design.

With that qualification behind us, we can examine six general characteristics of self-design.

1. Self-design involves arranging and patterning, linking and decoupling sets of elements to change the consequences from those currently occurring.
2. Self-designing systems must contain provisions for and support of the continuous evaluation of ongoing designs.
3. Issues of self-design typically focus, not on the designs themselves, but on the processes responsible for the designs. Emphasis is on processes that reflect the need for and create alternative arrangements of people and activities. The qualifier *self* identifies the location of these processes; they are in the hands of insiders (the people who will do the work) rather than outsiders (for example, consultants).

    The Apollo 3 crew constitutes a self-designing system if it contains the norms, resources, willingness, and mandate to monitor and evaluate its ongoing design, generate alternative designs, and implement the alternatives that are expected to generate a different set of reasonable consequences. Thus the idea that the astronauts could serve as "alter egos of the principal investigators" is a design, a way of arranging people, activities, discretion, and responsibilities. The alter-ego design would be a self-design if it were a self-generated replacement for an existing design that was imposing a degree of orderliness on the group's activities.

The act of *designing* self-designing systems would be exemplified if the astronauts generated their alter-ego solution by following some general maxim for design that had been planted earlier, such as, "Act as if you're someone else."

A pervasive assumption in creating any alternative design is that occupants can rearrange their activities and responsibilities but not their identities. (In the case of the Apollo 3 crew, the original identities were scientist-pilot, physician-pilot, commander in chief.) If the prescription "be someone else" is used as a general framework for redesign, it relaxes the constraints imposed by fixed identities. The participants in the self-designing system can take liberties with self-definition and can try to construct a set of selves that they find more engaging, interesting, or efficient. This is a higher-order prescription, a way, if you will, to design designs.

Thus a designer of self-designing systems might decide to have members practice shuffling between identities so that they become comfortable with this kind of process. The designer uses, in effect, the myth of Proteus as his text for designing a self-designing process. On the basis of this text, he implants in that system both a process – "Experiment with who you are" – and possible examples – "Imagine you're the experimenter who built your apparatus" or "Imagine that you people in Skylab are actually mission control and that those people on the ground in Houston are to be guided through their tasks by a teleprinter that you control from outer space."

Having implanted both a general process and some concrete examples, the designer gives the system enough practice so that it knows how to run the process and when it might be appropriate to activate it. Then the designer exits. He has rendered himself obsolete. His design expertise has been shifted to the participants themselves.

As another example of the changeability of self-design issues, a self-designing system might well conclude that the trouble with its current design is that it is a design and that what those involved need to do is engage in a design-free interlude of improvisation.

4. A self-designing system wrestles chronically with the stubborn reality that specific adaptations often restrict subsequent adaptability. In accomplishing good group-environment fit in one setting, the group may inadvertently reduce its chances of fitting well in some other setting. This curtailment of adaptability can occur for such reasons as trained incapacity, lethargy, inattention, changed desires, or specialization. Students of self-designing systems thus are often interested in the question, "What forms of adaptation preclude what forms of adaptability?" If astronauts cope with 42 pages of instructions every day and perform them perfectly without complaint, what happens if radio contact is lost and their environment no longer contains a printed script for their day?

5. Designs must often be fabricated in the absence of specific performance criteria. Frequently performance criteria are determined after the fact. Having carried out a design, the group *then* discovers what it was trying to accomplish

and what its performance criteria *were*. As we noted earlier, designs are not necessarily constructed with an eye to their probable success.

Thus a durable design problem is how to maximize unknown performance criteria. The problem can theoretically be solved either by *homogeneity designs* where you bet on what the criterion *is* and then concentrate all your resources on maximizing the function you have bet on or by *heterogeneity designs* where you act as if several different performance criteria are operating and portions of the system are trying to achieve satisfactory performance on all of them.

6. Self-design is often hard to separate from implementation. Efforts to carry out a partially formed design often create the design retrospectively just as efforts to design turn into implementations. Self-design should not be portrayed as a rigid, linear sequence of steps proceeding from designs to outcomes. More commonly, the so-called steps in designing appear in illogical sequences (for example, symptoms are treated and, when they disappear, a diagnosis is made) or some steps are omitted altogether (for example, symptoms are treated without any diagnosis ever being made).

Principles of Self-Design

Self-design involves a different way of thinking about what is valuable and what is worthless in organizations. Four principles will illustrate some of the ways in which a preoccupation with self-design alters what you notice about organizations. These principles, not intended to exhaust the possibilities of self-design, deal with how to generate and select alternative designs and what it takes for an organization to make itself capable of implementing them.

Self-design is more than unfreezing

Most organization watchers have encountered what they assume to be design issues when they interact with organizational development specialists or change agents who believe in the formula "unfreeze, change, refreeze." That litany has its merits, but it glosses over several issues of self-design.

Failures of self-design occur quite as often because too little is frozen as because too much is frozen. A designer should not automatically assume that he's got to build in a capacity for systems to unfreeze themselves in order for them to be self-designing. The incipient model of a self-designing system that we're beginning to develop in this chapter is one in which there is considerable fluidity and modest amounts of anarchy. The last thing organized anarchy needs is unfreezing.

The designer of self-designing systems considers freezing in at least two distinct ways. He designs either chronically frozen or chronically unfrozen entities.

With a *chronically frozen system* the designer freezes the system initially into a set of job descriptions, assigned tasks, rules, structures, and so on. Having done this, he knows that self-design invokes orchestrating how to loosen and modify the elements he originally built into this system. The designer needs to put into the system both respect for and suspicion about implanted structures. This sanctioned ambivalence is not easy to create on a sustained basis, but it is a necessity when freezing is used as a design principle. Essentially, the trick is to educate system participants in the art of decommitting themselves from concepts in which they have made considerable investments.

The designer says basically, "I'll build a system and spend most of my design time educating participants in ways to unfreeze what I gave them." Notice that this form of indoctrination can weaken the initial commitments – "If he's spending all this time lecturing me about the virtues of unfreezing, why did he implant this in the first place?" – so building chronically frozen systems is not as simple as it may sound. The designer has the tough task of saying to people, "Take this system seriously enough to operate it with gusto, but don't take it so seriously that you can't imagine any other way of running it or even the prospect of not running it any more." With this strategy the designer can create belief and solidity by building a substantial structure, by freezing some portion of a process, and by trying to lengthen the life of the system by simultaneously incorporating doubts about its solidity.

The opposite strategy, building a *chronically unfrozen system*, involves cultivating enthusiasm for improvisation, fluidity, minimal constraints, and a chronically Protean existence. Self-design under these conditions requires members to be trained to trust structures and distrust anarchies, since self-design will require unfrozen systems to engage in selective freezing.

In the chronically unfrozen system, people may coalesce temporarily when some crisis occurs so that they can resolve the problem successfully. But once they have agreed on what changes are necessary, people can continue to go about their autonomous ways secure in the knowledge that they have workably consistent views about the organization and the directions in which it should be going. In the chronically unfrozen system, people negotiate less often about less consequential events because their continuing improvisation and short memories make them update themselves more often. They make a habit of self-design.

It's probably easier in the short run to build structures and instill irreverence for them than it is to foster pattern-free improvisation and qualify it by inserting the occasional need for collective action and constraints. Improvisation and anarchies are costly in time, costly in coordination costs, expensive in dollars, and costly in terms of the demands they make on people's attention. In an organized anarchy, people have to watch more things for longer periods to make any sense out of them. If we assume that people prefer certainty to uncertainty and programmed tasks to unprogrammed ones, then the strategy of starting with tangible structures makes immediate sense. The problem with this strategy is that we have merely postponed our troubles with design.

Chronically unfrozen systems are deceptive. They cause immediate problems because of their uncertainty, fluid job descriptions, occasional overlapping assignments, and healthy amounts of improvisation, but their redesign problems are relatively minor since this redesign can take the form of imposing some minor constraints, a relatively easy exercise given the comforts conferred by orderliness. The real subtlety in a chronically unfrozen system is that it may never have to redesign itself. With its steady diet of improvisation, its continual rearrangements of structure, its continual updating to meet changing realities, it may never need a major redesign.

Chronically unfrozen systems may appear to use more energy than frozen systems because everything is treated as problematic, past learning doesn't count for much, and the efficiencies produced by memory are sacrificed. However, if we compare this large expenditure of energy with the amount of energy consumed by structures that organize specific activities plus the energy needed to dismantle former structures, cut old loyalties, formulate new structures, and develop new loyalties, then the drains on energy called for by the two systems might in fact be similar.

In summary, if a designer of self-designing systems used the metaphor of "freezing" to guide his design efforts, he does considerably more with it than a typical change agent does. He either unfreezes the chronically frozen system or freezes the chronically unfrozen system. The designer has to implant the idea that structures are to be trusted or mistrusted depending on what the participants in the system start with.

Beginning a system with structure brings about a smoother start but rougher ending – when the structure in which people have a substantial investment needs to be dissolved and replaced. Unfrozen systems start roughly. Things never settle down, but they seldom get worse either. Self-design becomes less of a problem in the unfrozen system because it subsists on a steady diet of self-design. When the unfrozen system does find a problem requiring self-design, it can meet this problem by the relatively easier solution of imposing structure than the more difficult task of dissolving the structure. And the structure momentarily imposed by the unfrozen systems may be more readily dissolved at any time, since it consists of shared meanings rather than altered patterns of interdependence or more substantial structural arrangements.

Quantities don't generate designs; discrediting does

Psychologists have established that as stress and arousal increase, people pay less attention to what is going on around them. As stress increases and our vision narrows, our views of the world become more simplified and more impoverished. We neglect more and more important variables. We see the same old things even less imaginatively than we did before. Whenever this happens, managers respond by urging people to continue doing what they have done before but to do it with more vigor.

Whenever managers tell people to solve their problems by redoubling their efforts, they make a fatal mistake. They assume that quantities can *change* patterns. They can't. If, for example, you pour money into a system that's defective, all you're doing is reinforcing the defects. Pouring money, which is a quantity, into a system that has a shape will not generate a new shape.

All quantities can do is to help you discover the pattern that already exists. For example, if you increase the tension on a chain you can break it at its weakest link, and you then know which the weakest link was. But the tension didn't create the weakest link. If you want to change something, pouring money into it won't do it. Something *else* will have to change the pattern first. *Then* you can use an infusion of money to lock the new pattern into place.

The demise of the *Saturday Evening Post* is a perfect example of pouring money into a defective system and merely reinforcing the defects. For years the *Saturday Evening Post* used the rule of thumb in the publishing industry that the number of editorial pages should match the number of advertising pages. The tight coupling between these two elements means that when advertising shrinks, the magazine's editorial coverage also shrinks. A thinner magazine that attracts fewer readers is generated making advertisers even more reluctant to purchase ads. Eventually profits vanish. But when the ads and editorial pages increase, printing expenses also increase. In fact, the costs of the enlarged magazine rise faster than the revenues, and profits again disappear. Whether publishers try to cope with this vicious circle by increasing promotional expenditures, cutting advertising costs, or buying more high-priced, sensational articles, the outcome is the same.

One way to break this pattern and to insert a *qualitative* change is by controlling the number of pages in the magazine. And one way to accomplish this, of course, is to control the price of advertising. In the old days, advertising was priced on a per-page basis. When the readership increased, the advertiser got more people for the same price. Consequently, the cost per reader went down for him. Changing this pricing method so that the advertising rate per 1,000 readers is kept constant removes the lethal linkage and publishing becomes more stable.

The important point is that the *Saturday Evening Post* could have returned to prosperity not from a quantitative change, not from doing more of the same, not from putting more money in or directing the money to different places, but by acting in a different way.

Hypocrisy often makes sense in self-design. The *Saturday Evening Post* failed to raise questions about a publisher's rule of thumb. They failed to realize that frequently "ambivalence is the optimal compromise." Doing what you have always done is necessary in short-term adaptations. Doing what you have never done is necessary in longer-term adaptations, and both need to be done simultaneously.

If words and deeds are contradictory, if one of them perpetuates past wisdom while the other discredits that past wisdom, then our current functioning should be effective and we should be able to preserve our ability to adapt to future contingencies. It is not simply that an organization should doubt what it knows for certain. It should also treat as certain the very things it doubts. If to doubt is to discredit clear information, then to act decisively is to discredit ambiguous information. Therefore, if you want to act on the point that ambivalence is the optimal compromise, when things are clear, you should doubt those things; when they are unclear, you should treat them as if they're clear. That's the meaning of discrediting.

We can observe discrediting in numerous organizational problems. The failure of watchmakers to entertain the possibility that watches could be made without gears left many of them close to bankruptcy when digital watches caught on. Banks "know" that it is good for people to save money, but unless they discredit that knowledge and successfully get people to borrow money, they fail. Albert Speer noted, ironically, that Allied bombing raids frequently helped the cause of the Third Reich during World War II. The raids destroyed files that contained information about past procedures used to run bureaucracies, and this automatic discrediting led to developing newer, more streamlined administrative procedures. Many city libraries are in trouble, for example, because they have failed to discredit procedures that are geared to service a white, middle-class population that has fled to the suburbs. The center city now contains groups who have neither a tradition of book learning nor a strong desire to adopt the values of the white majority, which are the values librarians are well suited to inculcate. Another example: The failure of *The New York Times* to doubt its skill at investigative reporting led it to overlook clues that, if noticed, would have enabled it to break the Watergate story two months before *The Washington Post*.

Discrediting the hard-won lessons of experience may seem silly in generating designs. However, we have to remember that the lessons from experience are always dated. The world in which they were learned changes chronically and discontinuously. Discrediting means that all past experience has lots of surplus meanings and there is no reason to think that we have exhausted the meanings of that experience by how we currently process it. So if we look back at that experience and alter it by new kinds of crediting and discrediting, if we rewrite portions of our history, new designs should be generated and the selections among them should be more intelligent.

Self-design requires inefficient acting

Many people argue that design isn't much of a problem because when an old design falters or fails we can always borrow a new design. I think that's naive. If responses become standardized when organizations merge, if people show strong tendencies to praise their own groups and downgrade other groups, and if people are less willing to run the risk of appearing frivolous, from whom are we going to borrow these elegant designs? We seem to have plenty of parasites, but where's the host?

If borrowing is not all it's cracked up to be, we must look elsewhere for alternative designs. The main alternative is to look inside the organization. We should invent some organizational equivalents of an off-off-Broadway experimental theater and try to describe the conditions under which these theaters thrive and produce acceptable designs. Off-off-Broadway experimental theater groups are in the forefront of producing new designs for Broadway.

One way to sponsor experimental designs inside an organization is to encourage "galumphing." Galumphing is the "patterned voluntary elaboration or complication of process, where the pattern is not under the dominant control of goals." Stephen Miller argues that play or galumphing preserves adaptability because it provides a way to develop novel designs. Play "makes us flexible and gives us exercise in the control of means that we are capable of using which are superfluous right now. . . . [When people play] they are using their capacity to combine pieces of behavior that would have no basis for juxtaposition in a utilitarian framework."

From this standpoint, play is not a direct means to an end; instead it is a crooked line to the end. It gets around obstacles put there by the player in order to complicate his life. Deliberate complication, if it gives a person experience in combining elements in novel ways, could be potentially important in generating new design. Notice that in the case of galumphing, means activities are given much more leeway to unfold. No longer are they dominated by goals. What play basically does is "unhook behavior from the demands of real goals." The person gains experience in combining pieces of behavior that he would never have thought of combining given the practical problems that confront him.

Several possibilities are implicit in this line of analysis. Less efficient organizations could retain more adaptability than more efficient organizations. The assumption would be that less efficient organizations, which use more complicated means to achieve ends, might actually learn to recombine their repertoire. This would hold true only if they continually reshuffled their ways of being inefficient.

A further benefit of galumphing might be that people would discover capabilities they had overlooked before. When people build new activities and recombine acts, they may learn more about what's being recombined. Therefore, one of the possible benefits when people deliberately complicate themselves is that they learn more about the elements in their repertoire as well as the way in which these elements can be recombined.

The activity of recombining the elements in a repertoire can be illustrated in several ways. Analysts typically act according to this sequence: symptoms, diagnosis, treatment. However, questions have been raised about the importance, accuracy, and necessity of diagnosis. It has been suggested that closely monitored treatment of symptoms without diagnosis may be just as successful in producing cures as when diagnosis precedes treatment. This revised repertoire means that diagnosis can be the last rather than the first step in organizational change. Most organizations have standard operating procedures. Those organizations whose procedures are stored in loose-leaf notebooks so they can be shuffled and recombined into novel sequences should be more adaptive than those organizations whose procedures are filed in bound volumes. The profitable business of shipping containerized floating cargo was developed when Malcolm McLean combined the elements of trucks, boxes, and old tankers into the idea of a floating bridge between two land masses that could serve as a floating warehouse.

In each case a complication is introduced: treatment is undertaken without the security of a diagnosis, operating procedures are rendered nonstandard, and trucks drive on water. None of these is a conspicuously efficient way to do business. Yet out of these seeming inefficiencies have come novel designs for adaptation.

The idea that inefficient organizations preserve adaptability suggests an alternative interpretation of the unique phenomenon called "the privilege of historic backwardness." It has been argued that backward nations and inefficient organizations sometimes have an advantage over advanced organizations because they can profit from their mistakes. For example, the Wankel engine was developed by an organization that had no previous experience with engines. But backward organizations may also cultivate (perhaps unwittingly) a flexibility in emphasizing combinations that are unknown in so-called advanced organizations.

Many contemporary organizations should find self-design next to impossible because they live in a climate of accountability. Within such climates, variability is treated as noise, significant changes are a nuisance, and unjustified variation is prohibited. The unfortunate effects of these practices may be reversed if people learn more about the activity of combining elements.

Self-design benefits from superstitious acting

As we have just seen, intentionally complicated action through galumphing can provide a means of generating alternative designs. Alternative designs can also be generated through superstitious acts that unwittingly complicate the life of the actor and his designs. We can outline the argument by analyzing divination as practiced by a group of hunters in Labrador called the Naskapi Indians.

Every day the Naskapi face the question: "What direction should the hunters take to locate game?" They answer this question by holding dried caribou shoulder bones over a fire. As the bones become heated they develop cracks and smudges that are then "read" by an expert. These cracks indicate the direction in which the hunter should go to look for game. The Naskapi believe that this practice involves the gods in their hunting decisions.

The interesting feature of these practices is that they work. To realize why they work, think about the characteristics of this decision process. First, the final decision about where to hunt is not a purely personal or group choice. If no game is found, the gods, not the group, are to blame. Second, the final decision is not affected by the outcomes of past hunts. If the Indians were influenced by the outcomes of past hunts, they would run the definite risk of depleting the stock of animals. Prior success would induce subsequent failure. Third, the final decision is not influenced by the inevitable patterning of choice and preferences that holds true for all human beings. These very patterns enable the hunted animals to take evasive action and to develop sensitivity to the presence of human beings.

Given these general characteristics of bone reading, we can say something about the utility of the practice. The use of scapulla (bones) is a very crude way of randomizing human behavior under conditions in which fixed patterns of behavior could be used advantageously by adversaries. Thus, if people want to avoid regularities that can be exploited, they need something like a table of random numbers to generate their behavior.

My impression is that using tables of random numbers to make decisions may be effective in a broader range of settings than those involving adversaries. For example, one reason adaptation may preclude adaptability is that people remember only those practices that are currently useful. Memory may preclude innovation.

It's conceivable that if groups used randomizing devices more frequently, they would forget what enables them to function in the here and now and would be positioned to generate better designs. For example, if an executive burned caribou bones to decide how to tackle his in-basket, where to relocate his factory, what territory to move into, or what product to market next, it's not clear to me that his organization would be any worse off than if he used a highly rational approach as his basis for decision making. The use of randomizing is equivalent to discrediting retained wisdom and treating memory as an enemy, and there are occasions when this type of intentional forgetting makes sense.

Conclusion

Self-design involves some difficult managerial actions, including the management of anarchy, the encouragement of doubt, the fostering of inefficiency, and the cultivation of superstition. If an organization wants to take control of its own destiny and designs, the changes necessary to pull this off are substantial. But those changes aren't impossible. The likelihood of pulling them off, however, depends heavily on the attitudes of the managers committed to self-design.

The best example I can find of the proper attitude for engaging in successful self-design was the poet W. H. Auden's speculations about what he would like his last words to be before he passed away. "In these days when it has become the medical convention, firstly, to keep the dying people in ignorance of their condition and, secondly, to keep them under sedation, how are any of us to utter what could be legitimately called our 'last' words? Still, it's fun to imagine what one would like them to be. The best proposed comment I know of is that of my friend Chester Kalman who said: 'Well, I've never done this before.'"

Now that's self-design!

Selected Bibliography

Henry Cooper's *A House in Space* (Holt, Rinehart, and Winston, 1976) is a vivid, illustrated description of the Apollo 3 mission, from which illustrative material in this chapter was taken. Roger Hall's "A System Pathology of an Organization: The Rise and Fall of the Old *Saturday Evening Post*" (*Administrative Science Quarterly*, 1976, Volume 21, pp. 185–211) contains a detailed analysis of the reasons why the *Saturday Evening Post* went out of existence. Stephen Miller's "Ends, Means, Galumphing: Some Leitmotifs of Play" (*American Anthropologist*, 1973, Volume 75, pp. 87–98) expands the argument that play enhances the capacity for survival in the face of change.

Ralph Kilmann, Louis R. Pondy, and Dennis Slevin's *The Management of Organization Design* (2 volumes, North-Holland, 1976) constitutes a definitive collection of academic research and theory on organizational design, with selected items on self-design. Aaron Wildavsky's "The Self-Evaluating Organization" (*Public Administration Review*, 1972, Volume 32, pp. 509–520) focuses on the thought-provoking argument that organizations can't afford to evaluate themselves. Karl E. Weick's *The Social Psychology of Organizing* (Addison-Wesley, 1969) argues that organizational processes and designs unfold in ways that parallel the processes of evolution and natural selection.

Applications of
Sensemaking

Introduction

To take sensemaking more seriously is to take some explanations of change less seriously. As these three final chapters show, a sensemaking perspective can induce muted enthusiasm for the hype of transformational change, electronic information processing, and globalization. The enthusiasm is muted because, in Goffman's (1974, p. 30) apt turn of phrase, "we tolerate the unexplained but not the inexplicable." Transformational change, electronic information processing, and globalization often run roughshod over the mechanisms of sensemaking and can turn the unexplained into the inexplicable. To ignore sensemaking is to encourage severe unanticipated consequences. Sensemaking doesn't prevent unanticipated consequences. But it does slow their development. And it allows people to sense unanticipated consequences at an earlier stage before they have incubated into irreversible trouble. People tend to remain alert when they punctuate flows of experience into events that are jointly meaningful. And joint meaning is more likely when people do such things as learn through small experiments, understand by using the full array of sensory modalities, and explain the inexplicable by starting with the plausible. It is small structures such as these that forestall larger problems. It is small sensemaking structures such as these that precede and pave the way for transformation, cyberspace, and globalization. And it is these same sensemaking operations that mop up after the visionaries have left and make the "revolution" work. To explain change by means of charisma, vision, and conversion is to overlook the more mundane change engines of sensemaking. To overlook those engines is to render change inexplicable.

Chapter 19, "Small Wins: Redefining the Scale of Social Problems," discusses how people make sense of large problems. If problems are defined as crises, this may drive arousal levels so high that details go unnoticed, old habits resurface, and consultation contracts, all of which curtail the invention of solutions. To treat problems instead as "mere" problems is to reduce many of these detrimental effects. Once again we see a difficult balancing act in sensemaking. People need sufficient optimism to keep arousal at manageable levels and sufficient pessimism to remain wary in the face of all the details they have chosen to ignore. This chapter is about sensemaking and change on a human scale. People have dreams. But they also have limits. Small wins reconcile this disparity. Small wins are not simply about breaking a big task down into small subtasks. Instead, small wins tend to be separate opportunistic improvements that move in the same general direction. They are effective because they recruit allies, disarm opponents, and suggest further improvements that no one had envisioned. This trajectory is visible in the KOR social movement that is described in Chapter 21. I remain fascinated with the "lineage" of the small wins idea which "began" with Tom Peters' doctoral dissertation at Stanford. The thread that connects small wins with subsequent topics such as an action bias, enactment, thinking while doing, knowing as doing, acting thinkingly, informed opportunism, and searching for excellence, is a thread which assumes that people act their way into meaning. In the language of the small wins chapter, " small wins are like miniature experiments that test implicit theories about resistance and opportunity and uncover both resources and barriers that were invisible before the situation was stirred up."

Chapter 20, "Cosmos vs. Chaos: Sense and Nonsense in Electronic Contexts," takes the mechanism of sensemaking seriously and argues that those enamored with cyberspace often put significant barriers in the way of sensemaking. When this happens people are faced with cryptic, incomplete, inexplicable displays and experience the same "cosmology episodes" that we saw at Mann Gulch. E-commerce may be the new frontier, but if people try to get a piece of that action solely through reliance on electronic information processing, they are doomed to failure. The failure arises from information overload created by insufficient variety in input. Overload occurs when people try to process too much of the same kind of information. Flaws built into the homogeneous source remain undetected and, as more information is gathered, more questions crop up and remain unresolved. Thus, a vicious circle often results when people process the same kind of information. They face uncertainty, gather information to reduce it, the more they gather the less certain they become, and overload and stress creep upwards. As stress increases attention narrows, out-of-date interpretations intrude, and fewer people are consulted, which thwarts sensemaking even more. To break this vicious circle, people need to pull the plug and walk around. "When people walk around they generate outcomes (effectuate), compare sources of information (triangulate), meet people and discover what they think (affiliate), slow down the pace of input (deliberate), and get a more global view of what is happening (consolidate)." Computers look like powerful engines that operate in the service of sensemaking. That appearance is deceptive. Sensemaking at a terminal creates *a* plausible story. But unless that story is treated as a dispensable starting point for sensemaking, unless it is treated as a map that is important mostly because it animates, then terminal impressions sans updating will be terminal. In Gene Rochlin's phrase, "people get trapped in the net." Entrapment is a sign of deficient sensemaking.

Chapter 21, "Sensemaking as an Organizational Dimension of Global Change," is also the final one in this volume. Appropriately it pulls together several themes. It speaks to the "context" issues that we first saw at the beginning of this book by suggesting that organizational forms vary in their capability to support sensemaking. As support decreases the likelihood of tragedy increases. This chapter recasts enactment–selection–retention into the more differentiated seven categories of sensemaking, these seven being captured by the acronym SIR COPE. This chapter also revisits the Mann Gulch disaster that was first examined as an unexpected ecological change. In the present chapter Mann Gulch is shown to be a situation where people lost sight of what was happening when sensemaking resources were in short supply. And this chapter supplies an especially good illustration of enactment, remembering, and the strategy of small wins, by means of an analysis of the Worker Defense Committee in Poland (KOR). KOR, in sharp contrast to Mann Gulch, enacts an organizational design that is well suited to support sensemaking. Vivid sense created by KOR proves to be persuasive sense.

The chapter ends by connecting the small world of Mann Gulch to the much larger world of social life in a new century. The story of Mann Gulch is a story of thrownness, of the struggle for alertness, and of old sense that persists a little too long without updating. Nevertheless, three people in Mann Gulch survived through reframing. And in the case of KOR, many more people survived, again through acts of reframing. In both cases, attentive sensemaking was at work. What that work consists of has been the object of this book.

References

Goffman, Erving (1974). *Frame Analysis*, Cambridge, MA: Harvard University Press.

19

Small Wins: Redefining the Scale of Social Problems

There is widespread agreement that social science research has done relatively little to solve social problems (Berger, 1976; Cook, 1979; Kohn, 1976). Common to these assessments is the assumption that social science is best suited to generate solutions, when in fact it may be better-equipped to address how problems get defined in the first place.

A shift of attention away from outcomes toward inputs is not trivial, because the content of appropriate solutions is often implied by the definition of what needs to be solved. To focus on the process of problem definition is to incorporate a more substantial portion of psychology, specifically, its understanding of processes of appraisal, social construction of reality, problem finding, and definition of the situation.

Whether social problems are perceived as phenomena that have a serious negative impact on sizable segments of society (Kohn, 1976, p. 94), as substantial discrepancies between widely shared social standards and actual conditions of life (Merton, 1971), or as assertions of grievances or claims with respect to alleged conditions (Spector & Kitsuse, 1977, p. 75), there is agreement that they are big problems. And that's the problem.

The massive scale on which social problems are conceived often precludes innovative action because the limits of bounded rationality are exceeded and arousal is raised to dysfunctionally high levels. People often define social problems in ways that overwhelm their ability to do anything about them.

To understand this phenomenon, consider the following descriptions of the problems of hunger, crime, heart disease, traffic congestion, and pollution.

To reduce domestic hunger we grow more food, which requires greater use of energy for farm equipment, fertilizers, and transportation, adding to the price of energy, which raises the cost of food, putting it out of the price range of the needy.

To solve the problem of soaring crime rates, cities expand the enforcement establishment, which draws funds away from other services such as schools, welfare, and job training, which leads to more poverty, addiction, prostitution, and more crime.

To ward off coronary heart disease, people who live in cities spend more time jogging and cycling, which exposes their lungs to more air pollution than normal, increasing the risk of coronary illness.

To ease traffic congestion, multilane highways are built, which draws people away from mass transit so that the new road soon becomes as overcrowded as the old road.

To reduce energy use and pollution, cities invest in mass transit, which raises municipal debt, leading to a reduction in frequency and quality of service and an increase in fares, which reduces ridership, which further raises the municipal debt (Sale, 1980).

When social problems are described this way, efforts to convey their gravity disable the very resources of thought and action necessary to change them. When the magnitude of problems is scaled upward in the interest of mobilizing action, the quality of thought and action declines, because processes such as frustration, arousal, and helplessness are activated.

Ironically, people often can't solve problems unless they think they aren't problems. If heightened arousal interferes with diagnosis and action, then attacking a less arousing "mere problem" should allow attention to be broader and action to be more complex. Responses that are more complex, more recently learned, and more responsive to more stimuli in changing situations usually have a better chance of producing a lasting change in dynamic problems.

To recast larger problems into smaller, less arousing problems, people can identify a series of controllable opportunities of modest size that produce visible results and that can be gathered into synoptic solutions. This strategy of small wins addresses social problems by working directly on their construction and indirectly on their resolution. Problems are constructed to stabilize arousal at moderate intensities where its contribution to performance of complex tasks is most beneficial.

Arousal and Social Problems

The following analysis of small wins assumes that arousal varies among people concerned with social problems, but tends to be relatively high, which affects the quality of performance directed at these problems. Arousal is treated as a generic concept under which is assembled a variety of findings that cohere because of their mutual relevance to the Yerkes–Dodson Law (Broadhurst, 1959). Although arousal mechanisms are neither simple nor unidimensional, they do seem to be localized in at least two physiological sites (reticular formation, limbic system), are visible under conditions of sensory deprivation, produce differences in the quality of learning and performance, and have observable physiological effects.

The specific effects of arousal on performance associated with the Yerkes–Dodson Law are that (a) there is an inverted-U relationship between arousal and the efficiency of performance with increasing levels of arousal, first improving and then impairing performance and (b) the optimal level of arousal for performance varies inversely with task difficulty. Even though these coarse propositions have been amended, tuned more finely, and differentiated, they remain basic principles in which an analysis of social-problem solving can be anchored.

Key assertions for the present analysis culled from previous investigations of arousal and performance include the following:

1. Arousal coincides with variation in degrees of activation and varies along at least two dimensions, energy–sleep and tension–placidity (Eysenck, 1982; Thayer, 1978a, 1978b).

2. As arousal increases, attention to cues becomes more selective and this editing is especially detrimental to performance of difficult tasks (Easterbrook, 1959, although this generalization has received mixed support. See Baddeley, 1972; Pearson & Lane, 1983; Weltman, Smith, & Egstrom, 1971, for representative work).

3. At relatively high levels of arousal, coping responses become more primitive in at least three ways (Staw, Sandelands, & Dutton, 1981): (a) people who try to cope with problems often revert to more dominant, first learned actions; (b) patterns of responding that have been learned recently are the first ones to disappear, which means that those responses that are most finely tuned to the current environment are the first ones to go; and (c) people treat novel stimuli as if they are more similar to older stimuli than in fact they are, so that clues indicating change are missed.

To invert this list, highly aroused people find it difficult to learn a novel response, to brainstorm, to concentrate, to resist old categories, to perform complex responses, to delegate, and to resist information that supports positions they have taken (Holsti, 1978).

When these findings are focused on problem solving, they suggest that to call a problem serious is to raise arousal, which is appropriate if people know what to do and have a well-developed response to deal with the problem. This is analogous to the situation of a simple task, the performance of which improves over a considerable range of activation because selective attention does not delete the few cues that are essential for performance. High arousal can improve performance if it occurs after a person has decided what to do and after she or he has overlearned how to do it.

To call a problem minor rather than serious is to lower arousal, which is also appropriate if people don't know what to do or are unable to do it. If we assume that most people overlook the fine-grain detail of problems, think only in terms of force as a response (Nettler, 1980), and overlook minor leverage points from which the problem might be attacked, then it is clear they have neither the diagnoses nor the responses to cope. This means that people need lower arousal to keep diagnostic interference at a minimum and to allow for the practice of relatively complex skills. To keep problem-related arousal at modest intensities, people need to work for small wins.

Sometimes problem solving suffers from too little arousal. When people think too much or feel too powerless, issues become depersonalized. This lowers arousal, leading to inactivity or apathetic performance. The prospect of a small win has an immediacy, tangibility, and controllability that could reverse these effects. Alinsky (1972, pp. 114–115) persuaded a demoralized neighborhood group to picket for reinstatement of Infant Medical Care, which he knew would be granted if they merely asked. Organizing for the protest, making the demand, and then receiving what they asked for energized people who had basically given up.

Examples of Small Wins

Small wins have been designed and implemented in a variety of settings. For example, the Pittsburgh Steelers in the National Football League have won 88 games and lost 27 under their coach Chuck Noll (as of February 4, 1980). Those statistics become more interesting if they are partitioned on the basis of whether the Steelers were playing against teams with winning records or teams with losing records ("Superbowls," 1980). Against opponents who won more than half of their games, the Steelers won 29 and lost 26, or slightly more than half of these games (53%). However, against opponents with winning percentages below .500, the Steelers' record was 59–1, meaning they won 98% of these games.

Thus a professional team renowned for its power got that way by consistently and frequently doing the easy stuff. The Steelers did not become great by winning the big one. Against tough opponents, they did no better than anyone else. These data suggest that winning teams distinguish themselves by more consistent behavior in games in which their skill advantage should make a difference, a condition that is part of the prototype for a small win. Thus, the best indication of good coaching may be the ability to induce consistent high performance against weak opponents rather than against strong opponents (Peters, 1977, p. 286).

The successful effort by the Task Force on Gay Liberation to change the way in which the Library of Congress classified books on the gay liberation movement is another example of a small win. Prior to 1972, books on this topic were assigned numbers reserved for books on abnormal sexual relations, sexual crimes, and sexual perversions (HQ 71-471). After 1972, the classifications were changed so that homosexuality was no longer a subcategory of abnormal relations, and all entries formerly described as "abnormal sex relations" were now described as varieties of sexual life (Spector & Kitsuse, 1977, pp. 13–14). Labels and technical classifications, the mundane work of catalogers, have become the turf on which claims are staked, wins are frequent, and seemingly small changes attract attention, recruit allies, and give opponents second thoughts.

The feminist campaign against sexism has been more successful with the smaller win of desexing English than with the larger win of desexing legislation (ERA – Equal Rights Amendment). The success of attempts to make people more self-conscious about words implying sex bias is somewhat surprising, because it represents an imposition of taboos at a time when taboos in general are being removed. "For even as books, periodicals and dictionaries (not all, to be sure) are liberally opening their pages to obscenities and vulgarisms, they are unliberally leaning over backward to ostracize all usage deemed offensive to the sexes" (Steinmetz, 1982, p. 8). This hypocrisy notwithstanding, the reforms have been adopted with little objection, due in part to their size, specificity, visibility, and completeness. As one commentator on Steinmetz's essay put it, "winning equality in the language was necessary; and while the winning shouldn't be overestimated, it will work – the drops of water on the rock – to change consciousness, and in time, unconsciousness" (Williams, 1982, p. 46).

When William Ruckelshaus became the first administrator of the U.S. Environmental Protection Agency in the early 1970s, he laid aside his mandate to clean up all aspects of the environment and went instead for a small win.

> He discovered some obscure 80-year-old legislation that permitted him to go after some cities on water pollution. He took advantage of the legislation, effectively narrowing his practical agenda for the first year or two to "getting started on water pollution." On day one of the agency's formal existence, Ruckelshaus announced five major lawsuits against major American cities. The impact was electrifying. The homework had been meticulously done. Noticeable progress was made quickly. It formed the beachhead for a long series of successes and distinguished EPA from most of its sister agencies. (Peters, 1979, p. 5)

Ruckelshaus did not tackle everything nor did he even tackle the most visible source of pollution, which is air pollution. Ruckelshaus identified quick, opportunistic, tangible first steps only modestly related to a final outcome. The first steps were driven less by logical decision trees, grand strategy, or noble rhetoric than by action that could be built upon, action that signaled intent as well as competence.

Alcoholics Anonymous has been successful in helping alcoholics, partly because it does not insist that they become totally abstinent for the rest of their lives. Although this is the goal of the program, alcoholics are told to stay sober one day at a time, or one hour at a time if temptation is severe. The impossibility of lifetime abstinence is scaled down to the more workable task of not taking a drink for the next 24 hours, drastically reducing the size of a win necessary to maintain sobriety. Actually gaining that small win is then aided by several other small measures such as phone calls, one-hour meetings, slogans, pamphlets, and meditations, which themselves are easy to acquire and implement.

Several studies of microinnovation are also compatible with the idea of small wins. For example Hollander's (1965) closely documented microeconomic study of decreases in production costs of viscose rayon yarn manufacturing at five DuPont plants between 1929 and 1960 demonstrates that minor technical changes – rather than major changes – accounted for over two thirds of the reductions. A technical change is a change "in the technique of production of given commodities by specific plants, designed to reduce unit production costs" (p. 23). Major technical changes (e.g., introduction of compensation spinning) differ from minor changes (e.g., introduction of forklift trucks) in time, skill, effort, and expense required to produce them.

Analyses showed that the cost reductions were substantial (e.g., from 53.51 to 17.55 cents per pound of rayon from 1929 to 1951 at the Old Hickory plant). Technical changes, as opposed to changes in quality of pulp input, management practices, quality of labor, and plant size, accounted for approximately 75% of the reductions, and most of these technical changes were minor (specific percentage of reduction attributable to minor changes in the five plants was 83%, 80%, 79%, 100%, and 46%, the last being a new plant making a new product, tire cord yarn).

The minor technical changes were small improvement inventions, rather than major inventions, made by people familiar with current operations (p. 205). Experience with the process was crucial, since the very acts of production that created the problems in the first place were also the sources of the minor improvements that could solve the problem. People learned by doing.

Left for further research is the interesting possibility in this study that minor innovations were dependent on preceding major innovations. Ten to fifteen years after a major change, the number of minor changes that were improvements was close to zero (pp. 205–206). Small alterations in technique can improve productivity for some time after a major change, but these improvements may not go on indefinitely.

Implied in Hollander's analysis is the possibility that older plants can produce almost as efficiently as newly built plants if technical changes are identified and funds are invested in them. Thus, contemporary fascination with quality circles may be appropriate if it aids in identifying needed minor technical changes.

The point to be drawn from Hollander's analysis is summarized by Machlup (1962):

> A technological invention is a big step forward in the useful arts. Small steps forward are not given this designation; they are just "minor improvements" in technology. But a succession of many minor improvements add up to a big advance in technology. It is natural that we hail the big, single step forward, while leaving the many small steps all but unnoticed. It is understandable, therefore, that we eulogize the great inventor, while overlooking the small improvers. Looking backward, however, it is by no means certain that the increase in productivity over a longer period of time is chiefly due to the great inventors and their inventions. It may well be true that the sum total of all minor improvements, each too small to be called an invention has contributed to the increase in productivity more than the great inventions have. (p. 164)

Characteristics of Small Wins

A small win is a concrete, complete, implemented outcome of moderate importance. By itself, one small win may seem unimportant. A series of wins at small but significant tasks, however, reveals a pattern that may attract allies, deter opponents, and lower resistance to subsequent proposals. Small wins are controllable opportunities that produce visible results.

The size of wins can be arranged along a continuum from small to large. Lindblom's (1979) example of monetary control makes this point. Raising or lowering the discount rate is a smaller win than is the decision to use the discount rate as a method of monetary control. Both of those actions are smaller than introducing the Federal Reserve system, which is smaller than a change that eliminates the use of money entirely. Lindblom summarizes the example by drawing the generalization that a small change is either a change in a relatively unimportant variable (people tend to agree on what is an important change) or a relatively unimportant change in an important variable (Braybrooke & Lindblom, 1963, p. 64).

Small wins often originate as solutions that single out and define as problems those specific, limited conditions for which they can serve as the complete remedy. I emphasize the importance of *limits* for both the solution and the problem to distinguish the solutions of small wins from the larger, more open-ended solutions that define problems more diffusely (e.g., "burn the system down").

Once a small win has been accomplished, forces are set in motion that favor another small win. When a solution is put in place, the next solvable problem often becomes more visible. This occurs because new allies bring new solutions with them and old opponents change their habits. Additional resources also flow toward winners, which means that slightly larger wins can be attempted.

It is important to realize that the next solvable problem seldom coincides with the next "logical" step as judged by a detached observer. Small wins do not combine in a neat, linear, serial form, with each step being a demonstrable step closer to some predetermined goal. More common is the circumstance where small wins are scattered and cohere only in the sense that they move in the same general direction or all move away from some deplorable condition. Ideals, broad abstract ends, and lasting ambitions are less influential in defining a means–ends structure for a series of small wins than they are in articulating the specific trade-offs that occur when each win improves something at the expense of something else (Lindblom, 1979, p. 519).

A series of small wins can be gathered into a retrospective summary that imputes a consistent line of development, but this post hoc construction should not be mistaken for orderly implementation. Small wins have a fragmentary character driven by opportunism and dynamically changing situations. Small wins stir up settings, which means that each subsequent attempt at another win occurs in a different context. Careful plotting of a series of wins to achieve a major change is impossible because conditions do not remain constant. Much of the artfulness in working with small wins lies in identifying, gathering, and labeling several small changes that are present but unnoticed (e.g., the Aquarian conspiracy, megatrends, back to basics), changes that in actuality could be gathered under a variety of labels.

Small wins provide information that facilitates learning and adaptation. Small wins are like miniature experiments that test implicit theories about resistance and opportunity and uncover both resources and barriers that were invisible before the situation was stirred up. Attempts to induce self-consciousness about sex references in speech revealed that language was more susceptible to change than had been thought earlier (e.g., Basic English never took hold); that opponents to language change were more dispersed, more stuffy, and less formidable than anticipated; that sex-biased language was more pervasive and therefore a stronger leverage point than people realized; and that language reform could be incorporated into a wide variety of agendas (e.g., APA *Publication Manual* revision). Language experiments uncovered entrenched sexism that had been invisible and created a more differentiated picture of allies, opponents, bystanders, and issues.

A series of small wins is also more structurally sound than a large win because small wins are stable building blocks. This characteristic is implicit in Simon's (1962) analysis of nearly decomposable systems and is illustrated by a fable (Kuhn & Beam, 1982):

> Your task is to count out a thousand sheets of paper, while you are subject to periodic interruptions. Each interruption causes you to lose track of the count and forces you to

start over. If you count the thousand as a single sequence, then an interruption could cause you, at worst, to lose a count of as many as 999. If the sheets are put into stacks of 100, however, and each stack remains undisturbed by interruptions, then the worst possible count loss from interruption is 108. That number represents the recounting of the nine stacks of 100 each plus the 99 single sheets. Further, if sheets are first put into stacks of ten, which are then joined into stacks of 100, the worst possible loss from interruption would be 27. That number represents nine stacks of 100 plus nine stacks of ten plus nine single sheets. Not only is far less recounting time lost by putting the paper into "subsystems" of tens and hundreds, but the chances of completing the count are vastly higher. (pp. 249–250)

Small wins are like short stacks. They preserve gains, they cannot unravel, each one requires less coordination to execute, interruptions such as might occur when there is a change in political administration have limited effects, and subparts can be assembled into different configurations. To execute a large win such as ratification of the Equal Rights Amendment requires much greater coordination because inter-dependencies are more dense, timing is more crucial, and defections are a greater threat. If one crucial piece is missing, the attempted solution fails and has to be restarted.

Parts of Saul Alinsky's (1972) model for building community organization parallel the notion of small wins. Alinsky's three criteria for working goals are that the goals be highly specific, realizable, and immediate (Peabody, 1971, p. 525). If people work for something concrete, if people have an opportunity for visible success from which they draw confidence, and if people can translate their excitement and optimism into immediate action, then a small win is probable, as is their heightened interest in attempting a second win.

As an example of how these goals might be directed toward solving the problem of pollution, Alinsky suggests that people try to influence polluters by influencing the polluters' bankers. To do this, the normal time-consuming process of opening and closing a savings account is turned to advantage by having 1000 people enter the bank, each with $5, to open a savings account. Although this volume of business may paralyze the bank, it is not illegal and no bank is eager to be known as an institution that forcibly ejects depositors. Once the deposits have been made, the people come back a day later, close their accounts – again a time-consuming activity – and the process continues until this secondary target, being punished for someone else's sins, brings pressure to bear on the offender. Making mass changes in savings accounts is a specific, realizable, immediate, small, and controllable opportunity. It is just like defeating a second-rate team, changing the card catalog, finding a chairperson, suing five cities, staying sober for an hour, or introducing a forklift into a work procedure.

The Psychology of Small Wins

From a psychological perspective, small wins make good sense. This is evident if we review what is known about cognitive limitations, affective limitations, stress, and the enactment of environments.

Cognitive limitations

Given the reality of bounded rationality (March, 1978; Perrow, 1981), small wins may be effective as much because they are "small" as because they are "wins." The growing documentation of ways in which people take cognitive shortcuts on larger problems (e.g., Kahneman, Slovic, & Tversky, 1982; Kiesler & Sproull, 1982; Miller & Cantor, 1982) suggests that smaller wins may suffer less distortion from these heuristics. People with limited rationality have sufficient variety to visualize, manage, and monitor the smaller amount of variety present in scaled-down problem environments. When people initiate small-scale projects there is less play between cause and effect; local regularities can be created, observed, and trusted; and feedback is immediate and can be used to revise theories. Events cohere and can be observed in their entirety when their scale is reduced.

An example of scaling down problems to more manageable size is an incident that occurred during the Apollo 3 mission when the astronauts staged what some regard as the first strike in space on December 27, 1973. Mission control had been sending more and more directions, corrections, and orders to the astronauts until finally Commander Gerald Carr said, "You have given us too much to do. We're not going to do a thing until you get your act in better order." He then shut off communications for 12 hours and the astronauts spent their day catching up and looking out the windows. They regained control over their circumstance. They did so partly by complicating themselves – an astronaut who both disobeys and obeys mission control is a more complicated individual than one who merely obeys, and partly by simplifying their system – they cut off one whole set of demands and reduced their problems simply to dealing with their own preferences. Their system became simpler because they had fewer demands to accommodate and simpler schedules to follow.

To gain some control over interdependent problems, people can disconnect the parts so they don't affect each other. Problems escalate only because they are tied together in a circular fashion and become vicious circles. A system with fewer interdependent events is a simpler system. It is easier to comprehend, easier to control, easier to improve.

Small wins disconnect incomprehensible systems such as the Library of Congress, a DuPont factory, EPA, or NASA. Once the system is disconnected, people then focus their attention on specific events that have been stripped out of their context, specific events such as the HQ portion of the Library classification system or a sequence of space experiments. What is common in instances such as these is that the "mere problem" that people finally end up with becomes manageable, understandable, and controllable by fallible individuals and stays that way until the larger system is reconnected. Arousal is reduced because control and predictability increase. The mere problem is also seen more clearly, which improves the chances that a small, specific solution that fits it will be invented. The resulting small win becomes a visible change in a highly inertial world. The change was made possible because the bounds of rationality were not exceeded. The change also becomes more visible to other people because its size is compatible with their own bounded rationality.

Affective limitations

Repeatedly, psychologists have demonstrated that small changes are preferred to large changes. The small scale of small wins is important affectively as well as cognitively. Examples are plentiful.

Successive small requests are more likely to produce compliance (Freedman & Fraser, 1966). Changes in level of aspiration are most satisfying when they occur in small increments. Positions advocated within the latitude of acceptance modify opinions more often than does advocacy that exceeds these limits. Orders within the zone of indifference are followed more quickly and reliably. The central measure of perception is the *just noticeable* difference. Theories are judged interesting when they disconfirm assumptions held with moderate intensity (Davis, 1971). People whose positions are close to one's own are the targets of intensive persuasion, while those whose positions are farther away are dismissed, isolated, or derogated. Social comparison is more stable the more similar the comparison other is. Small discrepancies from an adaptation level are experienced as more pleasurable than are larger discrepancies. Brief therapy is most successful when the client is persuaded to do just one thing differently that interdicts the pattern of attempted solutions up to that point. Extremely easy or extremely difficult goals are less compelling than are goals set closer to perceived capabilities. Learning tends to occur in small increments rather than in an all-or-none fashion (this generalization is highly sensitive to the size of the building blocks that are postulated in all-or-none positions such as stimulus sampling theory). Programmed learning works best when there is a gradual progression to complex repertoires and a gradual fading out of stimulus prompts for answers. Retention is better when people are in the same emotional state in which they learned the original material (Bower, Monteiro, & Gilligan, 1978). Numerous other examples could be given. The point is that incremental phenomena such as small wins have a basic compatibility with human preferences for learning, perception, and motivation.

Small wins are not only easier to comprehend but more pleasurable to experience. While no one would deny that winning big is a thrill, big wins can also be disorienting and can lead to unexpected negative consequences. The disruptiveness of big wins is evident in the high stress scores associated with positive changes in Life Events Scales (e.g., Dohrenwend, Krasnoff, Askenasy, & Dohrenwend, 1978). Big wins evoke big countermeasures and altered expectations, both of which make it more difficult to gain the next win (e.g., attention paid to Nobel prize winners often makes it impossible for them to do any further significant work).

Stress

Since arousal is a central construct in stress research, the soundness of small wins should be evident when stress formulations are examined. Work by McGrath (1976) and Kobasa (1979) reveals just such a fit. McGrath argued that there is a potential for stress when people perceive that demands exceed capabilities under conditions where it would be extremely costly to ignore the issue (p. 1352). The severity of perceived stress becomes stronger as uncertainty about the outcome increases. Uncertainty intensifies the closer the perceived demand is to the perceived ability. Large demand–capability discrepancies in either direction virtually assure successful or unsuccessful outcomes compared with situations of smaller discrepancy in which the outcome could go either way.

When people scale up the gravity of social problems, they raise at least the importance of the issue and the magnitude of the demand. The crucial question then becomes: What happens to the third variable of perceived capability to cope with demands?

Although numerous assumptions about perceived ability are possible, it would seem that the generic statement, "This problem affects you, and you can make a difference," reduces the perceived discrepancy between demands and abilities. If people respond to "you can make a difference" with the retort, "that's nonsense," then larger discrepancies will be created and stress will be minimal. If, however, people respond with a different reaction such as "that might just be true," then the demand–capability discrepancy is narrowed, which makes the outcome more uncertain and the stress more intense. As stress increases, the disruptive effects of arousal on problem solving increase. Just when people feel most encouraged to do something about a problem, they become least capable of translating that growing optimism into detailed diagnoses and complex responses. They become disabled by their own optimism, because it intensifies the perceived uncertainty of outcomes.

Once the gap between ability and demand begins to narrow, it becomes crucial that people see how their abilities can unequivocally *exceed* demands in order to remove some uncertainty. This assurance of success is precisely what people begin to feel when they define their situation as one of working for a small win. When a large problem is broken down into a series of small wins, three things happen. First, the importance of any single win is reduced in the sense that the costs of failure are small and the rewards of success considerable. Second, the size of the demand itself is reduced (e.g., all we need to do is get one city to discipline local polluters). And third, existing skills are perceived as sufficient to deal with the modest demands that will be confronted.

A small win reduces importance ("this is no big deal"), reduces demands ("that's all that needs to be done"), and raises perceived skill levels ("I can do at least that"). When reappraisals of problems take this form, arousal becomes less of a deterrent to solving them.

The potential attractiveness of a small win is that it operates simultaneously on importance, demands, and resources and defines situations away from the "close calls" where higher uncertainty and higher stress reduce problem-solving performance. Small wins induce a degree of certainty that allows greater access to the very resources that can insure more positive outcomes.

Additional recent research on resistance to stress, especially Kobasa's work with hardiness (Kobasa, 1979, 1982; Kobasa, Maddi, & Kahn, 1982), suggests the psychological soundness of the strategy of small wins. While Kobasa has interpreted hardiness as a personality disposition, pursuit of a small wins strategy could induce more generally the perceptions associated with this disposition.

Hardiness is composed of commitment, control, and challenge. Commitment refers to involvement and a generalized sense of purpose that allows people to impose meaning on things, events, and persons. Control is the tendency to act and feel as if one can have a definite influence (not *the* influence) on situations through the exercise of imagination, knowledge, skill, and choice. People with a sense of control tend to experience events as natural outgrowths of their actions rather than as foreign, overwhelming events. Challenge is the belief that change is an incentive to grow rather than a threat to security. Thus, incongruent events are opportunities rather than disasters.

Deliberate cultivation of a strategy of small wins infuses situations with comprehensible and specific meaning (commitment), reinforces the perception that people can exert some influence over what happens to them (control), and produces changes of manageable size that serve as incentives to expand the repertory of skills (challenge). Continued pursuit of small wins could build increasing resistance to stress in people not originally predisposed toward hardiness.

Enactment of environments

Small wins build order into unpredictable environments, which should reduce agitation and improve performance. Most "reality" surrounding social problems is disorganized, fragmented, piecemeal. When people confront situations that contain gaps and uncertainties, they first think their way across these gaps. Having tied the elements together cognitively, they then actually tie partial events together when they act toward them and impose contingencies. This sequence is similar to sequences associated with self-fulfilling prophecies (Snyder, Tanke, & Berscheid, 1977).

A crucial element in thoughtful action consists of "presumptions of logic" (Weick, 1979, p. 138,) about situations that will be confronted. These presumptions draw people into situations in anticipation that the situations will make sense. This anticipation sets the stage for the second half of the process where, finding themselves in a presumably sensible situation, people take action. In doing so, they create patterns and consolidate scattered elements, both of which create the sensible situation that was anticipated.

This sequence of events is especially probable in the case of small wins. A small win is a bounded, comprehensible, plausible scenario that coheres sufficiently that people presume in advance that a forthcoming situation will be orderly. Having imposed the logic of small wins on a situation cognitively, the person then wades into the situation and acts with persistence, confidence, and forcefulness (Moscovic, 1980). Such decisive action is appropriate for an ostensibly orderly situation which, of course, has actually become more orderly precisely because forceful action consolidated it. Forceful action monopolizes the attention of other actors and becomes a causal variable in their construction of the situation. As a result, their actions become more interdependent and more orderly than they were before the intervention occurred.

Even though the actions associated with small wins are brief, specific, and localized, they can have a deterministic effect on many problem situations, because those situations are often even less coherent than the actions directed at them. The situations are loosely coupled, subject to multiple interpretations, and monitored regularly by only a handful of people. The confidence that flows from a pursuit of small wins frequently enacts environments in which the original problem becomes less severe and the next improvement more clear.

The Politics of Small Wins

Small wins can penetrate the main occupational hazard in Washington – information overload. The pace of work in Washington is fast, incessant, and unavoidable. The Obey Commission in 1977 found that in an average 11-hour day, a House member has only 11 minutes for discretionary reading (O'Donnell, 1981). That is where small wins have power. Small wins are compact, tangible, upbeat, noncontroversial, and relatively rare. They catch the attention of people with short time perspectives who have only 11 minutes to read.

Small wins also attract the attention of the opposition, though this is not inevitable. Opponents often assume that big effects require big causes, which means that they discount the importance of small wins. Opponents also often assume that attempted solutions cluster. Since small wins are dispersed, they are harder to find and attack than is one big win that is noticed by everyone who wants to win big somewhere else and who defines the world as a zero-sum game.

Because someone's small win is someone else's small loss, the stakes are reduced, which encourages the losers to bear their loss without disrupting the social system. A vague consensus is preserved by small wins because basic values are not challenged. People can accept a specific outcome even if they disagree on the values that drive it or the goals toward which it is instrumental.

The fact that small wins attract attention is not their only political virtue. In the world of policy, there are seldom clear decisions or clear problems (Weiss, 1980). Outcomes are built from bits and pieces of action, policy, and advice that are lying about. Since small wins are of a size that lets them supplement rather than dominate policy, they are more likely to be incorporated than are other more conspicuous solutions (McNaugher, 1980; Redman, 1973).

Despite their apparent political advantages, however, small wins may sound hopelessly naive, since they rely heavily on resources such as hope, faith, prophecies, presumptions, optimism, and positive reappraisals. Authors of many of the policy articles that have appeared in the *American Psychologist* have criticized psychologists for being naive and knowing relatively little about playing "hardball" with constituencies that have serious resources and know the game (e.g., Bazelon, 1982; Dörken, 1981; Hager, 1982; Sarason, 1978). Psychologists have responded by deprecating the game (e.g., March, 1979), making efforts to learn hardball (e.g., DeLeon et al., 1982), or by defining new games (e.g., Fishman & Neigher, 1982). The thrust of the present analysis, however, is that we need to be less apologetic for our apparent naivete than we have been.

First, being naive simply means that we reject received wisdom that something *is* a problem. Being naive means nothing more than that. We are always naive relative to some definition of the situation, and if we try to become less so, we may accept a definition that confines the definition of small wins to narrower issues than is necessary.

Second, being naive probably does have a grain of denial embedded in it. But denial can lower arousal to more optimal levels, so that more complex actions can be developed and more detailed analyses can be made.

Third, to be naive is to start with fewer preconceptions. Since it's usually true that believing is seeing, strong a priori beliefs narrow what is noticed (e.g., concern with sexism leads people to ignore threats that could annihilate both sexes). People with naive preconceptions will see a different set of features and are less likely to become fixated on specific features.

Fourth, naive beliefs favor optimism. Many of the central action mechanisms for small wins, such as self-fulfilling prophecies, affirmation, self-confirming faith that life is worth living (as first described by William James), the presumption of logic, trust, the belief in personal control, and positive self-statements, all gain their energy from the initial belief that people can make a difference. That belief is not naive when the world is tied together loosely. Firm actions couple events. And firm actions are more likely to occur when belief is strongly positive than when it is hesitant, doubtful, or cynical.

Optimism is also not naive if we can deny the relevance of hopelessness for the spirit of optimism. We justify what we do, not by belief in its efficacy but by an acceptance of its necessity. That is the basis on which Don Quixote survives.

> Don Quixote embraces the foolishness of obligatory action. Justification for knight-errantry lies not in anticipation of effectiveness but in an enthusiasm for the pointless heroics of a good life. The celebration of life lies in the pleasures of pursuing the demands of duty. (March, 1975, p. 14)

One can argue that it is our duty as psychologists to be optimistic. To view optimism as a duty rather than as something tied to unsteady expectations of success is to position oneself in a sufficient variety of places with sufficient confidence that events may be set in motion that provide substance for that hope. Small wins may amount to little, but they are after all wins, and wins encourage us to put the most favorable construction on actions and events.

Naivete can be a problem when optimistic expectations are disconfirmed (small flops), for although it increases the likelihood that good things will happen, it does not guarantee they will. Disconfirmation often leads people to abandon their expectations and adopt skepticism and inaction as inoculation against future setbacks. The important tactic for dealing with the flops implicit in trying for small wins is to localize the disconfirmation of expectations. Cognitive theories of depression (e.g., Beck et al., 1979) suggest that people often generalize disconfirmed expectations far beyond the incident in which they originated. The faith that makes life worth living can suffer setbacks, but these setbacks are specific and, in the case of small flops, limited. Highly aroused people who have flopped attempting a large win can't see those specifics, so they abandon all faith and all possible scenarios for how life might unfold. That is the generalizing that needs to be contained and often is contained by trying for smaller wins, with smaller stakes.

Conclusion

The preceding analysis leaves several questions unanswered. For example, is the concept of arousal really necessary to understand why attempts to cope with large problems are self-defeating? Cognitive explanations (e.g., "I simply can't cure cancer so I'll work to make terminally ill patients more comfortable") may make it unnecessary to resort to motivational explanations. I favor motivational explanations under the assumption that social problems are emotional issues argued under emotionally charged conditions.

What is the natural distribution of arousal around social problems? The preceding analyses assume that most people feel intensely about social problems most of the time, or at least at those crucial times when they try to diagnose what is wrong and rehearse what to do about it. That assumption is a simplification, because it is clear that participation is uneven, unpredictable, and easily distracted (Weiner, 1976). Furthermore, interest in a given issue soon diminishes and bored people wander off to other problems (Koestler, 1970). Nevertheless, there are problem elites, opinion leaders, and hubs in networks. These people are central because they feel strongly about issues. Those strong feelings can affect their thought and action directly, and others who model this thought and action indirectly.

What role do individual differences in arousability or sensation seeking (Zuckerman, 1979) play in strategies to cope with social problems? Implicit in the preceding argument is a rule of thumb: If you can tolerate high levels of arousal, go for big wins; if you can't, go for small wins.

Questions such as this notwithstanding, it seems useful to consider the possibility that social problems seldom get solved, because people define these problems in ways that overwhelm their ability to do anything about them. Changing the scale of a problem can change the quality of resources that are directed at it. Calling a situation a mere problem that necessitates a small win moderates arousal, improves diagnosis, preserves gains, and encourages innovation. Calling a situation a serious problem that necessitates a larger win may be when the problem starts.

Note

Tom Peters's (1977) original description of small wins was a crucial point of departure for this formulation. Subsequent discussions with Peters, as well as with Linda Pike, Richard Thaler, Joseph McGrath, Sharon McCarthy, David Anderson, Marianne LaFrance, and students and faculty of the Psychology Department at Rice University contributed to my understanding of this phenomenon and I am grateful to all of them for their help.

References

Alinsky, S. D. (1972). *Rules for radicals*. New York: Vintage.
Baddeley, A. D. (1972). Selective attention and performance in dangerous environments. *British Journal of Psychology, 63,* 537–546.

Bazelon, D. L. (1982). Veils, values, and social responsibility. *American Psychologist, 37,* 115–121.

Beck, A. T., Rush, A. J., Shaw, B. F., & Emery, G. (1979). *Cognitive theory of depression.* New York: Guilford.

Berger, B. M. (1976). Comments on Mel Kohn's paper. *Social Problems, 24,* 115–120.

Bower, G. H., Monteiro, K. P., & Gilligan, S. G. (1978). Emotional mood as a context for learning and recall. *Journal of Verbal Learning and Verbal Behavior, 17,* 573–585.

Braybrooke, D., & Lindblom, C. E. (1963). *A strategy of decision.* Glencoe, IL: Free Press.

Broadhurst, P. L. (1959). The interaction of task difficulty and motivation: The Yerkes-Dodson Law revived. *Acta Psychologica, 16,* 321–338.

Cook, S. W. (1979). Social science and school desegregation: Did we mislead the Supreme Court? *Personality and Social Psychology Bulletin, 5,* 420–437.

Davis, M. S. (1971). That's interesting: Towards a phenomenology of sociology and a sociology of phenomenology. *Philosophy of Social Science, 1,* 309–344.

DeLeon, P. H., O'Keefe, A. M., VandenBos, G. R., & Kraut, A. G. (1982). How to influence public policy: A blueprint for activism. *American Psychologist, 37,* 476–485.

Dohrenwend, B. S., Krasnoff, L., Askenasy, A. R., & Dohrenwend, B. P. (1978). Exemplification of a method for scaling life events: The PERI life events scale. *Journal of Health and Social Behavior, 19,* 205–229.

Dörken, H. (1981). Coming of age legislatively: In 21 steps. *American Psychologist, 36,* 165–173.

Easterbrook, J. A. (1959). The effect of emotion on cue utilization and the organization of behavior. *Psychological Review, 66,* 183–201.

Eysenck, M. W. (1982). *Attention and arousal: Cognition and performance.* New York: Springer.

Fishman, D. B., & Neigher, W. (1982). American psychology in the eighties: Who will buy? *American Psychologist, 37,* 533–546.

Freedman, J. L., & Fraser, S. C. (1966). Compliance without pressure: The foot-in-the-door technique. *Journal of Personality and Social Psychology, 4,* 195–202.

Hager, M. G. (1982). The myth of objectivity. *American Psychologist, 37,* 576–579.

Hollander, S. (1965). *The sources of increased efficiency: A study of DuPont rayon plants.* Cambridge, MA: MIT Press.

Holsti, O. R. (1978). Limitations of cognitive abilities in the face of crisis. In C. F. Smart & W. T. Stanbury (Eds.), *Studies on crisis management* (pp. 35–55). Toronto: Butterworth.

Kahneman, D., Slovic, P., & Tversky, A. (Eds.). (1982). *Judgement under uncertainty: Heuristics and biases.* Cambridge, England: Cambridge University Press.

Kiesler, S., & Sproull, L. (1982). Managerial response to changing environments: Perspectives on problem sensing from social cognition. *Administrative Science Quarterly, 27,* 548–570.

Kobasa, S. C. (1979). Stressful life events, personality, and health: An inquiry into hardiness. *Journal of Personality and Social Psychology, 37,* 1–11.

Kobasa, S. C. (1982). Commitment and coping in stress resistance among lawyers. *Journal of Personality and Social Psychology, 42,* 707–717.

Kobasa, S. C., Maddi, S. R., & Kahn, S. (1982). Hardiness and health: A prospective study. *Journal of Personality and Social Psychology, 42,* 168–177.

Koestler, A. (1970). Literature and the law of diminishing returns. *Encounter, 34,* 39–45.

Kohn, M. L. (1976). Looking back – A 25-year review and appraisal of social problems research. *Social Problems, 24,* 94–112.

Kuhn, A., & Beam, R. D. (1982). *The logic of organizations.* San Francisco: Jossey-Bass.

Lindblom, C. E. (1979). Still muddling, not yet through. *Public Administration Review, 39,* 517–526.

Machlup, F. (1962). *The production and distribution of knowledge in the United States*. Princeton, NJ: Princeton University Press.

March, J. G. (1975). Education and the pursuit of optimism. *Texas Tech Journal of Education, 2*, 5–17.

March, J. G. (1978). Bounded rationality, ambiguity, and the engineering of choice. *The Bell Journal of Economics, 9*, 587–608.

March, J. G. (1979). Science, politics, and Mrs. Gruenberg. In *The National Research Council in 1979* (pp. 27–36). Washington, DC: National Academy of Sciences.

McGrath, J. E. (1976). Stress and behavior in organizations. In M. D. Dunnette (Ed.), *Handbook of industrial and organizational psychology* (pp. 1351–1395). Chicago: Rand McNally.

McNaugher, T. L. (1980). Marksmanship, McNamara, and the M16 rifle: Innovation in military organizations. *Public Policy, 28*, 1–37.

Merton, R. K. (1971). Epilogue: Social problems and sociological theory. In R. Merton & R. Nisbet (Eds.), *Contemporary social problems* (pp. 793–846). New York: Harcourt Brace Jovanovich.

Miller, G. A., & Cantor, N. (1982). Book review of Nisbett and Ross, "Human Inference." *Social Cognition, 1*, 83–93.

Moscovici, S. (1980). Toward a theory of conversion behavior. In L. Berkowitz (Ed.), *Advances in experimental social psychology* (Vol. 13, pp. 209–239). New York: Academic Press.

Nettler, G. (1980). Notes on society; sociologist as advocate. *Canadian Journal of Sociology, 5*, 31–53.

O'Donnell, T. J. (1981). Controlling legislative time. In J. Cooper & G. C. Mackenzie (Eds.), *The house at work* (pp. 127–150). Austin: University of Texas Press.

Peabody, G. L. (1971). Power, Alinsky, and other thoughts. In H. A. Hornstein, B. B. Bunker, W. W. Burke, M. Gindes, & R. J. Lewicki (Eds.), *Social intervention: A behavioral science approach* (pp. 521–532). New York: Free Press.

Pearson, D. A., & Lane, D. M. (1983). *The effect of arousal on attention*. Unpublished manuscript, Rice University.

Perrow, C. (1981). Disintegrating social sciences. *New York University Educational Quarterly, 12*, 2–9.

Peters, T. J. (1977). *Patterns of winning and losing: Effects on approach and avoidance by friends and enemies*. Unpublished doctoral dissertation, Stanford University.

Peters, T. J. (1979). *Designing and executing "real" tasks*. Unpublished manuscript, Stanford University.

Redman, E. (1973). *The dance of legislation*. New York: Simon & Schuster.

Sale, K. (1980). *Human scale*. New York: Putnam.

Sarason, S. B. (1978). The nature of problem solving in social action. *American Psychologist, 33*, 370–380.

Simon, H. A. (1962). The architecture of complexity. *Proceedings of the American Philosophical Society, 106*, 467–482.

Snyder, M., Tanke, E. D., & Berscheid, E. (1977). Social perception and interpersonal behavior: On the self-fulfilling nature of social stereotypes. *Journal of Personality and Social Psychology, 35*, 656–666.

Spector, M., & Kitsuse, J. I. (1977). *Constructing social problems*. Menlo Park, CA: Cummings.

Staw, B. M., Sandelands, L. E., & Dutton, J. E. (1981). Threat-rigidity effects in organizational behavior: A multi-level analysis. *Administrative Science Quarterly, 26*, 501–524.

Steinmetz, S. (1982, August 1). The desexing of English. *The New York Times Magazine*, pp. 6, 8.

Superbowls super coach. (1980, February 4). *Time Magazine*, p. 58.

Thayer, R. E. (1978a). Factor analytic and reliability studies on the activation–deactivation adjective check list. *Psychological Reports, 42,* 747–756.

Thayer, R. E. (1978b). Toward a psychological theory of multidimensional activation (arousal). *Motivation and Emotion, 2,* 1-34.

Weick, K. W. (1979). *The social psychology of organizing* (2nd ed.). Reading, MA: Addison-Wesley.

Weiner, S. S. (1976). Participation, deadlines, and choice. In J. G. March & J. P. Olsen (Eds.), *Ambiguity and choice in organizations* (pp. 225–250). Bergen, Norway: Universitetsforlaget.

Weiss, C. H. (1980). Knowledge creep and decision accretion. *Knowledge: Creation, Diffusion, Utilization, 1,* 381–404.

Weltman, G., Smith, J. E., & Egstrom, G. H. (1971). Perceptual narrowing during simulated pressure-chamber exposure. *Human Factors, 13,* 99–107.

Williams, C. T. (1982, September 5). Letter to the editor about "Desexing the English language." *The New York Times Magazine*, p. 46.

Zuckerman M. (1979). Sensation seeking: Beyond the optimal level of arousal. Hillsdale, NJ: Erlbaum.

20

Cosmos vs. Chaos: Sense and Nonsense in Electronic Contexts

The growth of electronic information processing has changed organizations in profound ways. One unexpected change is that electronic processing has made it harder, not easier, to understand events that are represented on screens. As a result, job dissatisfaction in the next decade may not center on issues of human relations. It may involve the even more fundamental issue of meaning: Employees can tolerate people problems longer than they can tolerate uncertainty about what's going on and what it means.

Representations of events normally hang together sensibly within the set of assumptions that give them life and constitute a "cosmos" rather than its opposite, a "chaos." Sudden losses of meaning that can occur when an event is represented electronically in an incomplete, cryptic form are what I call a "cosmology episode."

Representations in the electronic world can become chaotic for at least two reasons: The data in these representations are flawed, and the people who manage those flawed data have limited processing capacity. These two problems interact in a potentially deadly vicious circle. The data are flawed because they are incomplete; they contain only what can be collected and processed through machines. That excludes sensory information, feelings, intuitions, and context – all of which are necessary for an accurate perception of what is happening. Feelings, context, and sensory information are not soft-headed luxuries. They are ways of knowing that preserve properties of events not captured by machine-compatible information. To withhold these incompatible data is to handicap the observer. And therein lies the problem.

When people are forced to make judgments based on cryptic data, they can't resolve their puzzlement by comparing different versions of the event registered in different media. When comparison is not possible, people try to clear up their puzzlement by asking for more data. More data of the same kind clarify nothing, but what does happen is that more and more human-processing capacity is used up to keep track of the unconnected details.

As details build up and capacity is exceeded, the person is left with the question, "What's going on here?" That emotional question is often so disconcerting that perception narrows, and even less of a potential pattern is seen. This leads people to seek more information and to have less understanding, more emotional arousal, less complete perception and, finally, a cosmology episode.

When a person is able to connect the details and see what they might mean, processing capacity is restored. Meanings that can impose some sense on detail typically come from sources outside the electronic cosmos – sources such as metaphors, corporate culture, archetypes, myths, history. The electronic world makes sense only when people are able to reach outside that world for qualitatively different images that can flesh out cryptic representations. Managers who fail to cultivate and respect these added sources of meaning, and bring them to terminals, will make it impossible for people who work at screens to accurately diagnose the problems they are expected to solve.

This chapter provides a groundwork for this conclusion. After a brief discussion of how people make sense of the world when they are away from terminals, I will show how those same sensemaking processes are disrupted when people return to the terminal. The problem at the terminal is that people no longer have access to data and actions by which they usually validate their observations. When confined to inputs that make invalidity inevitable, people understandably feel anxious. That's when cosmology episodes occur. I will conclude by suggesting what steps organizations can take to avoid such episodes.

Sensemaking Away from Terminals

People use a variety of procedures to make sense of what happens around them, five of which are the focus of this analysis. To understand events, people (1) effectuate, (2) triangulate, (3) affiliate, (4) deliberate, and (5) consolidate.

Effectuating

People learn about events when they prod them to see what happens. To learn our way around a new job we try things to see what gets praised and what gets punished. To see what physical problem a patient has, a physician often starts a treatment, observes the response, and then make a diagnosis. To discover what their foreign policy consists of, diplomats sometimes give speeches in which a variety of assertions are made. They then read editorial comments to learn what reporters think they "said," how the reporters reacted, and what should be preserved in subsequent speeches and policy statements.

People often say, "How can I know what I think until I see what I say?" People find out what's going on by first making something happen. Doing something is the key. Until I say something – anything – I can't be sure what I think or what is important or what my preferences are. I can't be sure what my goals are until I can observe the choices I made when I had some discretion over how to spend my time.

Action is a major tool through which we perceive and develop intuitions. Machines perform many operations that used to call for professional judgment – operations like reasoning, analyzing, gathering data, and remembering. Now perception and intuition are the major inputs that human beings can contribute when solving a problem with a computer. Since action is the major source of human perceptions and intuition, any assessment of the potential for sensemaking must pay close attention to action.

Triangulating

People learn about an event when they apply several different measures to it, each of which has a different set of flaws. When perceptions are confirmed by a series of measures whose imperfections vary, people have increased confidence in those perceptions or their conclusions about them. For example, committee reports, financial statements, and computer printouts are not sufficient by themselves to provide unequivocal data about the efficiency of operations. The conclusions from these data need to be checked against qualitatively different sources such as formal and informal field visits, exit interviews, mealtime conversations in the company cafeteria, complaints phoned to an 800 number, conversations with clients, and the speed with which internal memos are answered. These various "barometers," each of which presents its own unique problem of measurement, begin to converge on an interpretation. The key point is that the convergence involves qualitatively different measures, not simply increasingly detailed refinements, ratios, and comparisons within one set of measures. What survives in common among the several measures is something that is sensible rather than fanciful.

Affiliating

People learn about events when they compare what they see with what someone else sees and then negotiate some mutually acceptable version of what really happened. The highly symbolic character of most organizational life makes the construction of social reality necessary for stabilizing some version of "what is really happening."

People also affiliate when they want answers to specific questions. Herbert Simon explained how affiliation works by using this question as an example: "Do whales have spleens?" Suppose someone asked you that, what would you answer? Simon's reply was that he'd make five calls and by the time he got to the fifth one he'd know the answer. In each phone call he'd ask, "Who do you know who's the closest to being an expert on this topic?" He would call whoever was mentioned and would rapidly converge on the answer.

Deliberating

People learn about events through slow and careful reasoning during which they formulate ideas and reach conclusions. When the reasoning process is drawn out, partially formed connections are allowed to incubate and become clarified, irrelevancies are forgotten, later events are used to reinterpret earlier ones, and all of these processes are used to edit and simplify the initial mass of input. This reduction of input, or deliberation, takes time.

The activity of comprehending a speech is an example of how time can affect deliberation. If a speaker talks to an audience instead of reading a speech, then the speaker's mind works at the same speed as the listener's mind. Both are equally handicapped, and comprehension is high. If, however, a speaker reads a prepared text, the substance is more densely packed and is delivered at a speed that is faster than the listener's mind can work. The listener deliberates while the speaker accelerates, and comprehension decreases. Of course, we are talking about the speed of the mind, not the speed of the nervous system. Nervous systems can accelerate in response to environmental input from displays such as television or video-game screens. The only way to cope with this acceleration of activity in the nervous system is to stop thinking, because ideas cannot form, dissolve, and combine as fast as eye-hand coordination can make adjustments in response to computer displays. Mindless activity takes less time than mindful activity, and this difference can affect the kind and depth of sense one is able to construct within information systems.

Consolidating

People learn about events when they can put them in a context. The statement, "It is 30 degrees," is senseless until we know whether the context is Centigrade or Fahrenheit. An event means quite a different thing when it is seen as part of a cycle, part of a developmental sequence, random, predetermined, or in transition from one steady state to another.

The power of a context to synthesize and give meaning to scattered details can be seen in the current fascination with the "back to basics" movement. The diverse, unexplainable troubles people have right now are lumped into the diagnosis, "We've strayed from the basics." People think that if they go back to the basics (for example, Kenneth Blanchard's *The One Minute Manager*), their fortunes will improve. It is interesting that John Naisbitt's *Megatrends* has a more disorienting, less soothing message. According to Naisbitt, the basics themselves are changing. Naisbitt's view holds the prospect that events will become even more senseless.

To consolidate bits and pieces into a compact, sensible pattern frequently requires that one look beyond those bits and pieces to understand what they might mean. The pieces themselves generate only a limited context, frequently inadequate to understanding what is happening in the system, what its limitations are, or how to change it. That diagnosis has to be made outside the system and frequently involves a different order of logic. It is often the inability to move outside an information system, and see it as a self-contained but limited context, that makes it difficult to diagnose, improve, and supplement what is happening inside that system.

The famous paradox of Epimenides is an example of a problem in context. "Epimenides was a Cretan who said, 'Cretans always lie.'" The larger quotation becomes a classifier for the smaller, until the smaller quotation takes over and reclassifies the larger one to create contradiction. Gregory Bateson explains that when we ask:

> "Could Epimenides be telling the truth?" The answer is: "If yes, then no," and "If no, then yes." . . . If you present the Epimenides paradox to a computer, the answer will come out YES . . . NO . . . YES . . . NO . . . until the computer runs out of ink or energy or encounters some other ceiling.

To avoid the paradox, you have to realize that a context in which classification used to be appropriate has become senseless. It is our inability to step outside, and invoke some context other than classification, that makes the situation senseless.

Consider a different problem. A dog is trained to bark whenever a circle appears and to paw the ground whenever an ellipse appears. If the correct response is made, the dog gets a reward. Now, begin to flatten the circle and fatten the ellipse, and watch what happens. As the two figures become more indistinguishable, the animal gets more agitated, makes more errors, and gets fewer rewards. Why? The animal persists in treating the context as one in which it is supposed to discriminate. When discrimination becomes impossible, the situation becomes senseless – but only because it continues to be treated as a problem requiring discrimination. If the animal moved to a different level of reasoning outside the system and saw that discrimination was only one of several contexts within which it could try to distinguish the lookalike ellipses and circles, then sense might be restored. If, for example, the context were seen instead as one that required guesswork, then there would be no problem. Reframing the situation as guesswork is possible only if you realize that many contexts are possible, not just the one in which your life is lived.

It is the very self-contained character of the electronic cosmos that tempts people, when data make less and less sense, to retain assumptions rather than move to different orders of reasoning. This error is especially apt to be made when information is defined only as that which can be collected and processed by machines. Different orders of meaning, those meanings that can impose new sense, can't be collected and processed by machines. The big danger is that these meanings will then be dismissed rather than seen as vehicles for resolving some of the senseless episodes generated by the assumptions inherent in machine processing.

Sensemaking in Front of Terminals

People using information technologies are susceptible to cosmology episodes because they act less, compare less, socialize less, pause less, and consolidate less when they work at terminals than when they are away from them. As a result, the incidence of senselessness increases when they work with computer representations of events.

Action deficiencies

The electronic cottage is a more difficult site for sensemaking than people may realize, because events are never confronted, prodded, or examined directly. People's knowledge of events is limited to the ways they are represented by machine and by the ways in which they can alter those machine representations. A crucial source of data – feedback generated by direct, personal action – is absent.

For example, Shoshana Zuboff describes what happens when a centralized "information interface," based on microprocessors, is placed between operators and machinery in a pulp mill. Operators no longer see directly what happens in pulp operations. They leave a world "in which things were immediately known, comprehensively sensed, and able to be acted upon directly" for a more distant world that requires a different response and different skills. What is surprising is the extent to which managers underestimate what is lost when action is restricted to one place. Zuboff quotes one manager as saying:

> The workers have an intuitive feel of what the process needs to be. Someone in the process will listen to things and that is their information. All of their senses are supplying data. But once they are in the control room, all they have to do is look at the screen. Things are concentrated right in front of you. You don't have sensory feedback. You have to draw inferences by watching the data, so you must understand the theory behind it. In the long run you would like people who can take data, trust them, and draw broad conclusions from them. They [workers] must be more scientific.

This manager makes several errors. "Things" are not in front of operators in the control room – symbols are. And symbols carry only partial information that needs to be verified by other means. Operators "don't have sensory feedback," but that's a problem, not a virtue, of technology. The display will substitute indirect for direct experience, because operators will have to "draw inferences" based on "the theory behind" the data. However, theories are just theories, and conjectures and inferences are shaky when based on partial data, tentative regularities, and flawed human induction. Operators are told to "take data ... and draw broad conclusions from them," but the data are not of the operators' own choosing nor are they in a form that allows intuition to be part of the inferential process.

In the words of another of Zuboff's managers, "We are saying your intuition is no longer valuable. Now you must understand the whole process and the theory behind it." The irony is that intuition is the very means by which a person is able to know a whole process, because intuition incorporates action, thought, and feeling; automated controls do not.

An additional problem with terminal work is the fact that trial and error, perhaps the most reliable tool for learning, is stripped of much of its power. Trials within an information system are homogeneous and correlated. What is tried next depends on what was done before and is a slight variation of the last trial. For example, spreadsheets are the very essence of trial and error, or so it seems. People vary quantities that are acceptable within the spreadsheet program, but they do not vary programs, hardware, algorithms, databases, or the truthfulness of inputs. People vary what the program lets them vary and ignore everything else. Since programs do not have provisions to switch logics or abandon logics or selectively combine different logics, trials are correlated and they sample a restricted range of choices.

The more general point is that trial and error is most effective with a greater number of heterogeneous trials. That is why brainstorming groups often come up with solutions that no individual would have thought of before the discussion started. In these groups, suggestions are idiosyncratic and unconnected, but they sample a broader range of possibilities and improve the odds that someone will stumble onto a solution that lies outside traditional lines of thought.

Spreadsheets do not let people introduce whatever comes to mind or follow lines of thought that have arisen from previous comments or inputs to whatever conclusions these thoughts may lead. These constraints are action deficiencies, because they restrict the ways in which the target can be manipulated, which restricts what can be known about the target.

Comparison deficiencies

Action is a major source of comparative data, which is one reason that the sedentary quality of information systems is so deadly. Moreover information systems do not give access to much of the data about a phenomenon, or treat those data as noise. Not enough different perspectives are compared to improve accuracy. The illusion of accuracy can be created if people avoid comparison (triangulation), but in a dynamic, competitive, changing environment, illusions of accuracy are short-lived, and they fall apart without warning. Reliance on a single, uncontradicted data source can give people a feeling of omniscience, but because these data are flawed in unrecognized ways, they lead to nonadaptive action.

Visual illusions such as those depicted in Figure 20.1 are a metaphor for what happens when triangulation is ignored. The point of a visual illusion is that the eye can be tricked. But that is true only if you maintain a fixed eye position and do nothing but stare. If you tilt the illusion, view it along an edge, measure it, look at it from a different angle, or manipulate it, the illusion vanishes. As you manipulate the object, you add to the number of sensory impressions you initially had and therefore should run the risk of overload. Actually, however, you get clarity, because the several active operations give you a better sense of what is common among the several different kinds of information. One thing you discover is that the specific illusion that you saw when you did nothing disappears when you do something. Moving around an illusion is an exercise in triangulation because different perspectives are compared. Moving around is also an exercise in action that tells us about an object.

It is difficult to triangulate within a computer world because it's highly probable that the blindspots in the various alterations tried on a representation will be similar. For example, consider a simulated, three-dimensional computer design that represents bone fractures. The object is seen from several vantage points, but the program's assumptions are carried along with each view and are neither detected by the observer nor canceled by perspectives that make a different set of assumptions. Thus the system will keep making the same errors.

If you take a computer printout into the field and hold it alongside the event it is supposed to represent (for example, the behavior of a purchasing agent), the chances

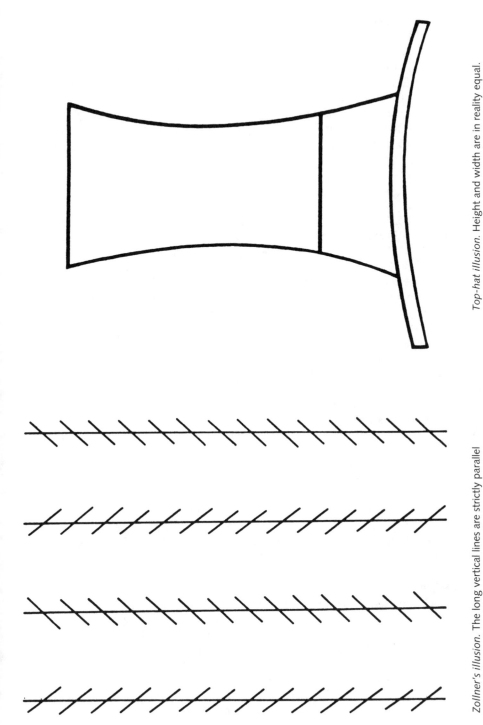

Zollner's illusion. The long vertical lines are strictly parallel although they appear to converge and diverge.

Top-hat illusion. Height and width are in reality equal.

Figure 20.1   Two optical illusions

are good that the actual event will be noisier, less orderly, and more unique than is evidenced by the smoothed representation on the printout. Even though different kinds of potential error are inherent in a printout reading and a face-to-face observation, some similarities will be found when comparing these two perceptual modes. Those similarities are stable features of the observed phenomenon and are worth responding to. The differences between the two are the illusions (errors) inherent in any specific view of the world. What's important to remember is that if people stick to one view, their lives may be momentarily more soothing, but they also become more susceptible to sudden jolts of disconfirmation.

Affiliation deficiencies

Terminals are basically solitary settings. Christopher Lehmann-Haupt described computing as "quantified narcissism disguised as productive activity." Of course, computing is not always solitary; FAA air traffic control systems assign two controllers to each "scope." But when the face-to-face, social character of sensemaking in information systems decreases, several problems can arise.

First, less opportunity exists to build a social reality, some consensus version of events as they unfold. Different people viewing the terminal display see different things, because they are influenced by different beliefs. There is a grain of truth in each of the different things that are "seen." As people work to build an interpretation they all can agree on, these grains of truth find their way into the final account and make that account more objective.

Cut off from this diversity and the negotiation process itself, the solitary person sees less of what there is to see. Even more troublesome, when a situation is ambiguous, is that invention of some version of reality is the only way to cope. When uncertainty is high, it's especially important to know what other people think, and what their analyses have in common with one's own.

A more subtle social issue in sensemaking is pointed out by Marion Kester's striking question: "If children are separated from their parents by hours of TV, from their playmates by video games, and from their teachers by teaching machines, where are they supposed to learn to be human?" A recent study of electronic mail in an open office found that people used terminals to communicate with the person in the next cubicle even when they could stand up, lean over the cubicle, and ask the person the same question face to face. Thus it would seem Kester's worry is not an idle one.

Extensive nonsocial interaction with a terminal can atrophy social skills. That becomes a problem when people confront an uncertain situation in which they have to construct a jointly acceptable version of reality. If they participate in such discussions with minimal social skills, the interaction may not last long enough or probe deeply enough to build a decent model that people can work with. If clumsy interactions distort social realities, then failure is inevitable. Working agreements about what is going on can make even the most incomplete electronic representations look coherent. This is so because consensual information fills in the gaps in electronic representations. However, when social skills are in short supply, those gaps may remain unfilled. That's when people begin asking, "What's going on here?"

Deliberation deficiencies

Mander raises the interesting point that in an age of computers and information flow, the operative phrase may not be "small is beautiful," but rather "slow is beautiful." Deliberation takes time, yet that's the very thing that disappears when the velocity of information flow intensifies in information systems.

A more subtle problem with this acceleration is that computers operate close to the speed at which the stream of consciousness flows. This means that the whims and mixtures of feeling, thought, and images that flow through consciousness can be dumped into the analyzing process continuously. Not only does this increase demands on the person coming in afterward, who must deal with this kind of input; it also makes it harder to see priorities, preferences, and hierarchical structure and to separate the trivial from the important. The run-on sentences that have become a trademark of people writing with word processors exemplify this problem. As fast as images and possibilities bubble up, they are typed in and strung together with the conjunction *and*, which renders all images equally important. Most of what is typed is junk. But without discipline, self-editing, and deliberation, junk is left for someone else to wade through. The sheer volume and variety in an externalized stream of consciousness make it harder to separate figure from ground, which sets the stage for a cosmology episode.

Consolidation deficiencies

When spontaneous material from stream of consciousness replaces deliberated thoughts and images based on data outside the information system, understanding becomes a problem. It is the very self-contained character of information systems that can undercut their value. Users fail to see that they need to reach outside the system for a different set of assumptions to understand what is happening inside the system. Herbert Simon explains that:

> Whether a computer will contribute to the solution of an information-overload problem, or instead compound it, depends on the distribution of its own attention among four classes of activities: listening, storing, thinking, and speaking. A general design principle can be put as follows: An information processing subsystem (a computer or new organization unit) will reduce the net demand on the rest of the organization's attention only if it absorbs more information previously received by others than it produces – that is, if it listens and thinks more than it speaks.

But to register and absorb information (to listen and think), the sensor must be at least as complex as the information it is receiving and, often, information systems fall short. The sensor must go beyond mere enumeration if it is to synthesize detail. To go beyond detail is to move to higher levels of abstraction and to invoke alternative realities. At these higher levels, feeling informs thinking, imagination informs logic, and intuition informs sensation. Feeling, imagination, and intuition use vivid, compact images to order the details in a way that the system cannot. This is why meta-phors that draw on our common culture, fairy tales, or archetypes ("This place is like a cathouse"; "Our agency is like the tale of Rumplestiltskin"; "Each quarter we live through the four seasons.") and novel labels or idioms (greenmail, golden para-chutes, fast trackers), have such evocative power in linear systems. Each of these summarizing devices does three things: presents a compact summary of details, predi-cates characteristics that are difficult to name, and conveys a more vivid, multilevel image. All of these devices represent ways to absorb detail using logics that are qualitatively different from those contained within information systems.

Ways to Improve Sensemaking

What is surprising is how many of the problems described here can be solved if people simply push back from their terminals and walk around. When people walk around they generate outcomes (effectuate), compare sources of information (trian-gulate), meet people and discover what they think (affiliate), slow down the pace of input (deliberate), and get a more global view of what is happening (consolidate).

Recent jokes about the invention of a new tool for word processing, which turns out to be a pencil, may be replaced by another joke about the new tool for managing called, "Pull the plug and go for a walk." The swiftness with which the idea of management-by-walking-around spread and the intensity with which people tout its benefits may be explained by the fact that many things that look like problems when they are viewed from a fixed position vanish when one changes position. Just as illusions disappear when you move them around or move around them, so too do problems disappear when they no longer are confined to one medium and one set of assumptions.

People who carry terminals into the field should be better problem solvers than are people who leave terminals at home, because people with terminals in the field are able to use different forms of data and test their hunches with triangulation.

A computer program can have action steps that ask people to leave the terminal, walk around, and come back, after which the program can ask them some questions. Imagine, for example, that a manager is trying to figure out whether there is a market for brand-name vegetables. He or she examines demographics and buying patterns and extrapolates trends; then the screen says, "Go walk through a super-market for two hours and come back." (That same action step is appropriate for all kinds of related problems, from the question of whether you should purchase Conrail to what level inventories should be held at.)

The reason that the supermarket tour is appropriate for such diverse agendas is that it generates data that differ from those on the screen. The problem is seen in a different setting and thus is viewed differently: The supermarket is a place where people handle vegetables in distinctive ways, which might suggest what kinds of vegetable wrappers are appealing. The supermarket is a place stocked with items that could be shipped by rail, or perhaps these items could be handled efficiently only by other modes of transportation. Or perhaps the supermarket is seen as a place where stock moves directly from trucks to shelves, and just-in-time strategies are being used more widely than the person doing this exercise realized, so his or her own distribution needs to get more attention. With these vivid, nonmachine images in mind, the person returns to the terminal and sees its displays in a different light. The same notations take on different meanings, and more is seen.

While augmentation of sensemaking can occur if people become more mobile, other actions need to be taken as well. When any reorganization or change in information systems is contemplated, companies should systematically examine what those changes will do to action (effectuation), comparison (triangulation), interaction (affiliation), deliberation, and consolidation. A significant, permanent decrease in any of those five raises the likelihood that employees will know less about phenomena and will make more mistakes in managing them.

If any one of these five decline, local remedies are possible. If the potential for action drops, insert more breaks, longer breaks, or more interactive displays that allow for a wider variety of personal experiment or encourage the use of portable computing equipment. If the potential for comparison drops, make greater use of tie-ins between terminals and visual simulations of the phenomena being monitored, locate terminals closer to the events they control, or add other sensory modalities to the output from terminals. When interaction is lessened, assign two people to one terminal, have one person tell another what is being observed, set up teleconferencing and have operators' pictures continually visible in the corner of the display, or allow more intermixing of solitary work with group work.

When deliberation drops off, more time can be allocated for summarizing and thinking about information away from terminals, several people can be assigned to the same terminal so they are forced to spend some of their time thinking somewhere else, or processing can be slowed down to allow time to ponder what is displayed. Finally, when consolidation tapers off, people can read poetry, look at art, question assumptions, or engage in whatever activities will expose them to syntheses, theories, or generalizations that can put the inputs being considered into a new context.

The preceding analysis implies that overload is not really the problem with information systems. And indeed, confinement to a terminal is the problem, because it limits the variety of inputs, precludes comparison, and thus makes sensemaking more difficult. Overload occurs when you get too much of the same kind of information; ironically, if you increase the kinds of information you get, overload declines. In changing the quality of information about a phenomenon, one is able to see what stays constant and what changes. Impressions that change are method specific. Impressions that don't are likely to be stable features that need to be dealt with. Since the common elements are fewer in number and better organized, they also make fewer demands on processing capacity. The key point is that overload can be reduced by moving around and thus getting a variety of inputs. As the number of vantage points increases, the amount of overload decreases.

A second implication of my analysis is that people and groups need to listen more and talk less. The value of an information system lies in what it withholds, as much as in what it gives. Listening and withholding require editing and categorizing – and these, in turn, require typologies, concepts, and ideas. The detail, specificity, and concreteness that can be achieved by information systems are worthless until patterns are imposed on them. Some of these patterns are inherent in the system itself, but most are found outside of it. People must listen for these patterns and, when they hear them in detail, transmit the pattern rather than the detail.

Third, not only do people need to listen – they need to edit. Job descriptions in the information organization need to specify each person's responsibility to absorb uncertainty and to transmit less than they receive. While there is always danger that people will edit out the wrong things, an even greater danger is that they will leave in too much, and thus paralyze themselves or those who come in after with too much detail. While electronic processing has the potential for everyone to check up on everyone else all the time, that kind of scrutiny will probably be infrequent because of the sheer quantity of work involved. It is more likely that faith and trust will become increasingly important as people become more dispersed, delegation is practiced more fully, and people come to depend on others to fill in their own limited, obsolete knowledge.

Finally, corporate culture takes on added importance in the context of the preceding arguments. Culture provides the framework within which cryptic data become meaningful. Current efforts to articulate culture may represent efforts to cope with intensified commitments to electronic processing, because it takes the former to understand the latter. Electronic organizations need to develop new respect for generalists, philosophers, and artists, because all three work with frameworks that provide context and meaning for the programs already in place.

Conclusion

Managers need to be just as attentive to meaning as they are to money. As organizations move more and more vigorously into electronic information processing, they will increasingly bump up against the limits of human processing capacity. The key to overcoming these limits is meaning, because it increases processing capacity.

And meanings that free up capacity usually originate outside the information-processing system in the form of different assumptions and contexts. Unless these qualitatively different kinds of logic are developed, disseminated, and valued by the organization, people will find themselves increasingly unable to make sense of the products of information technology.

Selected Bibliography

For further reading about sensemaking, see *The Social Psychology of Organizing*, by Karl E. Weick (Addison-Wesley, 1979). Gregory Bateson's work on logical types is *Mind and Nature* (E. P. Dutton, 1979).

Marion Kester's and Gerry Mander's comments about computers appear in the December 1984 issue of the *Whole Earth Review*. Another work that discusses the limitations of computers is *The Network Revolution*, by Jacques Vallee (And/Or Press, 1982).

For more on corporate culture as a source of meaning, see the September 1983 issue of *Administrative Science Quarterly*.

Herbert Simon's discussion of overload appears in M. Greenberger's book titled *Computers,*

Communications, and the Public Interest (Johns Hopkins Press, 1971).

Christopher Lehmann-Haupt's view of computing may be found in his book review that appeared in the *New York Times* (October 3, 1984).

Finally, Shoshana Zuboff discusses human adaptation to automated factories in "Technologies That Informate" (in *Human Resource Management: Trends and Challenges*, edited by R. Walton and P. Lawrence, Harvard Business School Press, 1985).

21

Sensemaking as an Organizational Dimension of Global Change

Global issues that involve organizing on a massive scale have been described as contested, nonlinear metaproblems with long lead times, unintended side effects, unclear cause-effect structures, and consequences that are often irreversible (Cooperrider & Bilimoria, 1993, p. 110). Issues demanding change on a global scale are like an onrushing wall of fire and are just as tricky to manage. Normally, managing complexity on a global scale, especially when it is framed in a strategic framework, as Cooperrider and Bilimoria have done, means that the primary organizational issue is one of strategies for decision making. Decision making is certainly involved in managing complexity in global change, and this is evident when people refer to transboundary relations, development of environmentally sound technologies, translation of complex global realities into decisive action, environmental governance, establishment of international norms, and the management of strategic global social change organizations (GSCOs).

But I want to argue that to organize for global change is also a problem in sensemaking, a problem that partly subsumes Cooperrider and Bilimoria's interest in the management of meaning, vision, and relationships (p. 126).

Precisely because global change is so difficult to comprehend, organizations designed to deal with it must be organizations designed as much to develop a coherent story of what is going on as to decide what should be done given that unfolding story. Thus, a potentially crucial organizational dimension of global change is the effect of organizational form on the kind of sense that people are able to make of what they face. I want to argue that at least seven resources affect sensemaking, and that organizational designs used in global organizations can strengthen or weaken these resources. These effects of design on resources for sensemaking, in turn, make it easier or harder to build a common idea of what is happening and what decisions need to be made.

I will contrast a system whose design weakens the resources for sensemaking (the firefighting crew at Mann Gulch) with a system in which the design strengthens the resources for sensemaking (the Worker's Defense Committee in Poland). In the case of the weak sensemaking system, the outcome was tragedy. In the case of the strong sensemaking system, the outcome was success against overwhelming odds.

Before I discuss sensemaking and two examples of how it unfolds differently in response to different designs, I should say a word about the two systems I will describe, because they have little obvious resemblance to GSCOs such as World Vision. By this I mean that, compared with global organizations, my two examples involve fewer people who are more homogeneous, who span fewer boundaries, whose contacts are more transient, and who are less dominated by visionary missions, although this may be a matter of degree. The firefighters and the defense committee are not, however, irrelevant to organizing on a global scale. They resemble GSCOs in the sense that they have singular focus on a relatively clear issue (a fire that is consuming wildland, a totalitarian regime that is eroding liberty); they are complex in their own ways; they each contain subsets of players that frame issues differently; they are more cooperative than competitive; and collaboration is essential for their success.

Aside from debates about whether firefighters and opposition movements are organized in ways that resemble organizing for global social change, the more important point is that my purpose here is to present a perspective rather than a model organization to be imitated. Given the way that global change has been depicted, it appears that variations in the ease with which potential participants can make sense of their own participation, the participation of others, and the referent problem itself affect both their willingness to expend energy and their decision about how to deploy that energy. I want to introduce the image of organizational sensemaking as a language to describe part of what determines the enthusiasm, improvisation, and persistence of people who organize for global change. I introduce the sensemaking perspective by contrasting two systems, chosen not for their involvement in global change but for their ability to make the notion of sensemaking vividly visible.

The Phenomenon of Sensemaking

Imagine an EMS technician arriving at the scene of an accident; a representative of World Vision walking into a newly discovered "Home for the Deficient and Unsalvageable" in Romania; a firefighter crew chief sizing up a fire, part of which is burning downhill and part of which is burning uphill (see picture on page 38 of Thoele, 1995, for an illustration of this situation); a United Airlines pilot turning the control wheel after a sudden loud noise and finding that none of the control surfaces on the DC-10 aircraft respond (the experience of Captain Al Heyns on UA flight 232); or finding a pocket of smallpox cases in a remote village in 1996 after the World Health Assembly has declared smallpox eradicated. What these circumstances all share, aside from their possible dramatic overkill, is that they all consist of a pile of cues in need of some frame to organize them. There is also an imperative to act. In each case, small, familiar cues can have a disproportionate influence in framing what one feels one is dealing with. Sensemaking is about sizing up a situation, about trying to discover what you have while you simultaneously act and have some effect on what you discover. Sensemaking, in other words, is seldom an occasion for passive diagnosis. Instead, it is usually an attempt to grasp a developing situation in which the observer affects the trajectory of that development. Object and subject are hard to separate in sensemaking, as when a physician starts several different treatments with a patient who is slow to respond and soon finds that he or she is treating the treatments rather than the presenting symptom.

Although size-ups may seem short-lived, their influence is enduring because once a hypothesis is formed, people tend to look for evidence that confirms it. This tendency is especially strong if people are under pressure to act quickly and if it is hard for them to find time to question their initial beliefs (Gilbert, 1991). Furthermore, initial actions are often publicly chosen and hard to revoke (Salancik, 1977), which means that people are bound to those actions and search for reasons that justify the actions as rational.

Thus, sensemaking involves the ongoing retrospective development of plausible images that rationalize what people are doing. When people engage in acts of sensemaking, it is more precise to think of them as accomplishing reality rather than discovering it. Discovery is a less appropriate description because in order for people to make sense of something, they often have to *ignore* much that others might notice. Reality is not so much discovered as buried in the interest of sensemaking. To make sense is to focus on a limited set of cues, and to elaborate those few cues into a plausible, pragmatic, momentarily useful guide for actions that themselves are partially defining the guide that they follow. Once a sense of the situation begins to develop, that sense can be terribly seductive and can resist updating and revision. The feeling of relief one gets the moment there is some idea of what might be happening makes it that much harder to remain attentive and willing to alter one's sense of what is happening and one's own position in that altered scenario.

These considerations seem relevant to global social change because there, too, people develop some sort of sense regarding what they are up against, what their own position is relative to what they sense, and what they need to do, including walking away from the scene. In discussions of organizational dimensions of global change, I feel it is important to separate sensemaking from decision making because sensemaking sets the frame within which decisions are made. In many cases, sensemaking may even do the bulk of the "deciding" that is present in any organized activity. So-called decision making may simply ratify what was made inevitable much earlier when an innocent appearing set of judgments mapped an issue out of a much larger set of possibilities that has now been forgotten.

Sensemaking is such a sprawling topic that it seems arbitrary to choose some portion of it as being especially relevant to global social change. That danger notwithstanding, I want to discuss seven properties that have an important effect on sensemaking. These seven are (a) social context, (b) personal identity, (c) retrospect, (d) salient cues, (e) ongoing projects, (f) plausibility, and (g) enactment. These seven can be remembered by means of the acronym SIR COPE. They are important in any discussion of organizing for global social change for at least two reasons. First, these seven properties affect not only the initial sense one develops of a situation – this initial sense is often overdetermined by one's own personal history – but more importantly, the extent to which people will update and develop their sense of the situation.

In other words, these properties have an effect on the willingness of people to disengage from, discard, or "walk away" from their initial story and adopt a newer story that is more sensitive to the particulars of the present context. Second, these seven properties are affected by organizational designs, as will be clear in the examples I contrast. There appear to be organizational conditions that facilitate sensemaking and conditions that thwart sensemaking. Given the complexity of global change issues and of the structures needed to manage that change, any adjustments that increase the collective capability to grasp this complexity should be given serious consideration. Obviously, there is far more to organizing for global change than the process of sensemaking. All I want to argue is that, given a choice between organizational forms, all of which seem to manage other issues equally well, the choice should favor a form that allows for more conversations, clearer identities, more use of elapsed action as a guide, unobstructed access to a wider range of cues, more focused attention on interruptions whenever projects are disrupted, wider dissemination of stories, and deeper acceptance of the reality that people face in situations that are of their own making.

The Seven Properties of Sensemaking

When people talk about sensemaking in an organizational setting, they discuss at least seven properties of that setting that have an effect on their efforts to size up what they face. These seven are discussed in detail in Weick (1995, pp. 17–62), and the interested reader is referred to that source.

For the sake of the present discussion, the seven are summarized in a highly minimalist form that relies heavily on a commonsense understanding of the terms employed.

1. *Social context*: Sensemaking is influenced by the actual, implied, or imagined presence of others. Sensible meanings tend to be those for which there is social support, consensual validation, and shared relevance. To change meaning is to change the social context. When social anchors disappear and one feels isolated from a social reality of some sort, one's grasp of what is happening begins to loosen.

2. *Personal identity*: A person's sense of who he or she is in a setting; what threats to this sense of self the setting contains; and what is available to enhance, continue, and render efficacious that sense of who one is all provide a center from which judgments of relevance and sense fan out. When identity is threatened or diffused, as when one loses a job without warning, one's grasp of what is happening begins to loosen.

3. *Retrospect*: The perceived world is actually a past world in the sense that things are visualized and seen *before* they are conceptualized. Even if the delay is measured in microseconds, people know what they have done only after they do it. Thus, sensemaking is influenced by what people notice in elapsed events, how far back they look, and how well they remember what they were doing. When people refuse to appreciate the past and instead use it casually, and when they put their faith in anticipation rather than resilience, then their acts of retrospect are shallow, misleading, and halfhearted, and their grasp of what is happening begins to loosen.

4. *Salient cues*: If sensemaking is about nothing else, it is about the resourcefulness with which people elaborate tiny indicators into full-blown stories, typically in ways that selectively shore up an initial hunch. The prototype here is a self-fulfilling prophecy or an application of the documentary method. Both elaborate an initial linkage between a particular and a category into a confident diagnosis through successive rounds of selective search for confirming evidence. Thus, both individual preferences for certain cues as well as environmental conditions that make certain cues figural and salient affect one's sense of what is up. When cues become equivocal, contradictory, or unstable, either because individual preferences are changing or because situations are dynamic, people begin to lose their grasp of what is happening.

5. *Ongoing projects*: Experience is a continuous flow, and it becomes an event only when efforts are made to put boundaries around some portion of the flow, or when some interruption occurs. Thus, sensemaking is constrained not only by past events, but also by the speed with which events flow into the past and interpretations become outdated. The experience of sensemaking is one in which people are thrown into the middle of things and forced to act without the benefit of a stable sense of what is happening. These handicaps are not attributable to personal shortcomings but rather to the stubborn, ongoing character of experience. When people lose their ability to bound ongoing events, to keep pace with them by means of continuous updating of actions and interpretations, or to focus on interrupting conditions, they begin to lose their grasp.

6. *Plausibility*: To make sense is to answer the question "What's the story here?" To answer this question, people usually ask a slightly different question: "What's a story here?" Sensemaking is about coherence, how events hang together, certainty that is sufficient for present purposes, and credibility. Plausibility should not be mistaken for fantasy, however, because a sense that survives has been influenced by the other six properties. Thus, plausible sense is constrained by agreements with others, consistency with one's own stake in events, the recent past, visible cues, projects that are demonstrably under way, scenarios that are familiar, and actions that have tangible effects. When one or more of these sources of grounding disappears, stories may strain credibility, leave too many cues unaddressed, or be impossible to compose, in which case people begin to lose their grasp.

7. *Enactment*: Action is a means to gain some sense of what one is up against, as when one asks questions, tries a negotiating gambit, builds a prototype to

evoke reactions, makes a declaration to see what response it pulls, or probes something to see how it reacts.

Having done any of these interventions in the interest of sensemaking, one will never know for sure what might have happened had no intervention been made. It is that sense in which, part of what one sees in any moment of sensemaking is a partial reflection of oneself. But to stay detached and passive is not to improve one's grasp, because much of what any situation means lies in the manner of its response. When probing actions are precluded, or avoided, or unduly narrow, it becomes more difficult to grasp what one might be facing.

These seven properties can be arrayed into a sensemaking process in at least two ways. First, sensemaking seems to follow roughly a sequence in which people concerned with identity in the social context of other actors engage ongoing events from which they extract cues and make plausible sense retrospectively while enacting more or less order into those ongoing events. This sequence breaks down as identity and the social context and cues become more ambiguous, retrospect becomes more difficult, ongoing events become more resistant to bounding, plausibility becomes more tenuous, and action becomes more constrained. A second way to animate these seven properties of sensemaking into a process is by means of the familiar recipe, "How can I know what I think or feel until I see what I say and do?" When people enact this recipe, they are affected by social context (what I say and do is affected by the audience that I anticipate will audit the conclusions I reach); identity (the recipe is focused on the question of who I am, the answer to which lies partly in what my words and deeds reveal about what I think and feel); retrospect (to learn what I think and feel, I look back over what I said and did); cues (what I single out from what I say and do is only a small portion of all possible things I might notice); ongoing flows (my talk and action are spread across time, which means my interests early in the scanning may change by the time the scanning concludes); plausibility (I need to know only enough about what I think to keep my project going); and enactment (the whole recipe works only if I produce some object in the first place that can be scrutinized for possible thoughts and feelings).

Organizing for Sensemaking

Given those seven properties of sensemaking and their potential sequencing, it remains to link them with issues of organizational design. The linkage is straightforward. The operative question is, "What happens to these seven resources for sensemaking when people organize to accomplish tasks that cannot be done alone?" If the design maintains or strengthens these seven resources, then people will be able to continue making sense of what they face. If the design undermines or weakens these resources, then people will tend to lose their grasp of what may be occurring. For each resource, there is a corresponding question about the organizational form that coordinates their activities. These questions are crude, more suited for practice than theory, and are currently being refined. Nevertheless, they are an initial means to raise issues related to sensemaking in the context of organizing for global social change. The initial questions are these:

1. Social context: Does the form encourage conversation?
2. Identity: Does the form give people a distinct, stable sense of who they are and what they represent?
3. Retrospect: Does the form preserve elapsed data and legitimate the use of those data?
4. Salient cues: Does the form enhance the visibility of cues?
5. Ongoing projects: Does the form enable people to be resilient in the face of interruptions?
6. Plausibility: Does the form encourage people to accumulate and exchange plausible accounts?
7. Enactment: Does the form encourage action or hesitation?

As I will now show, the organizational form associated with the crew that fought the Mann Gulch fire made it difficult for them to access many resources for sensemaking. As a result, they were unable to grasp what was happening to them, and most of these young men lost their lives as a result. The contrasting case of the KOR opposition movement in Poland is one in which access to sensemaking resources is not as difficult. As a result, people were able to make sense of their actions and could sustain them under oppressive conditions.

The Mann Gulch Disaster as Problematic Sensemaking

The Mann Gulch disaster, made famous in Norman Maclean's (1992) book *Young Men and Fire*, unfolded in the following sequence, which is a composite of Maclean (1992), Weick (1993), and Rothermel (1993).

On August 5, 1949, at about 4 p.m., 15 smoke jumpers – trained firefighters but new to one another as a group – parachuted into Mann Gulch. The crew's leaders originally believed that the blaze was a basic "ten o'clock fire," meaning that the crew would have it under control by 10 a.m. the next morning. Instead, the fire exploded and forced the men into a race for their lives.

The fire at Mann Gulch probably began on August 4 when lightning set a small fire in a dead tree. The temperature reached 97°F the next day and produced a fire danger rating of 74 out of a possible 100, indicating the potential for the fire to spread uncontrollably. When the fire was spotted by a lookout on a mountain 30 miles away, 16 smoke jumpers were sent at 2:30 p.m. from Missoula, Montana in a C-47 transport plane. (One man became ill and did not make the jump.) A forest ranger posted in the next canyon, Jim Harrison, was already on the scene trying to fight the fire on his own.

Wind conditions that day were turbulent, so the smoke jumpers and their cargo were dropped from 2,000 feet rather than the usual 1,200. The parachute connected to their radio failed to open, and the radio was pulverized as it hit the ground. But the remaining crew and supplies landed safely in Mann Gulch by 4:10 p.m. The smoke jumpers then collected their supplies, which had scattered widely, and grabbed a quick bite to eat.

While the crew ate, foreman Wagner Dodge met up with ranger Harrison. They scouted the fire and came back concerned that the thick forest near which they had landed could become a "death trap." Dodge told the second-in-command, William Hellman, to take the crew across to the north side of the gulch, away from the fire, and march along its flank toward the river at the bottom of the gulch. While Hellman did this, Dodge and Harrison ate a quick meal. Dodge rejoined the crew at 5:40 p.m. and took his position at the head of the line moving toward the river.

He could see flames flapping back and forth on the south slope as he looked to his left. Then, Dodge saw that the fire had suddenly crossed the gulch about 200 yards ahead and was moving toward them. He yelled at the crew to run from the fire and began angling up the steep hill toward the bare ridge of rock.

The crew was soon moving through slippery grasses two-and-a-half feet high but was quickly losing ground to the flames – eventually towering at a height of 30 feet – rushing toward them at a rate that probably reached a speed of 660 feet per minute. Sensing that the crew was in serious danger, Dodge yelled at them to drop their tools. Two minutes later, to everyone's astonishment, he lit a fire in front of the men and motioned to them to lie down in the area it had burned. No one did. Instead, they ran for the ridge and what they hoped would be safety.

Two firefighters, Robert Sallee and Walter Rumsey, made it through a crevice in the ridge unburned. Dodge survived by lying down in the ashes of his escape fire. The other 13 perished. The fire caught up with them at 5:56 p.m. – the time at which the hands on Harrison's watch melted in place.

We see the collapse of sensemaking when firefighters persist in calling the exploding fire a ten o'clock fire even though their senses tell them it is something more than this. We also see the collapse of the relating that is so crucial for sensemaking when individuals are torn between leaders, forget about their buddies, disobey orders, fail to share information, and ignore the solution that would have saved them. Access to resources for sensemaking was made difficult by the way the firefighters were organized.

Firefighters in Mann Gulch lost their *social anchors* when they found it hard to communicate, when they were uncertain how much trust they could put in their leader, and when they remained strangers to one another. The form and the environment discouraged conversation.

Firefighters in Mann Gulch found their *identity* threatened when they were told to drop their tools, which was the reason they were in Mann Gulch in the first place. It became increasingly unclear whether they were smoke jumpers or victims, and whether they were fighting or fleeing the fire.

Firefighters in Mann Gulch found it hard to resort to *retrospective sensemaking* because they did not know what was going on, their actions were unclear, and there was no explanation of why their foreman was adding a new fire when they already had all the fire they could deal with.

Firefighters in Mann Gulch faced *cues* that were difficult to interpret. They did not know whether they were retreating from the fire or flanking it, whether it was big or small, whether their foreman was scared or not, whether the grass they were walking in burned the same way as the trees where the fire was now located, and whether this was a fire they should flee or face.

Firefighters in Mann Gulch faced an *ongoing* dynamic fire that was becoming more intense and moving faster, and which they could neither stop nor avoid.

Firefighters in Mann Gulch, having spent all their lives fighting small fires, did not find it *plausible* that the small fire they expected to find had grown monstrous. The question "What's the story here?" remained fatally unanswerable.

Firefighters in Mann Gulch were unclear where and when they would take a stand to suppress the fire, what their actions were accomplishing, and whether they might even be making things worse by *enacting* a new fire.

Firefighters in Mann Gulch may have experienced a crisis in sensemaking that was due in part to the way in which they were organized. Their organization cut off access to crucial resources for sensemaking, which meant they persisted too long with the definition they carried into Mann Gulch when they first sized it up. It is this fate that global change organizations should take seriously.

There are alternative ways of organizing, as we will now see in the case of the opposition movement in Poland.

The Worker's Defense Committee as Successful Sensemaking

The democratic opposition movement in Poland, which started with the Worker's Defense Committee (KOR) in September 1976, is a dramatic example of heedful interrelating on a local scale that results in large changes on a national scale. Jonathan Schell (1987) has described the unfolding of these relationships in sufficient detail that we are able to encode them into resources for sensemaking.

The KOR movement started in Adam Michnik's clear thinking about what could and could not be changed in Poland. The Polish people said that it was impossible to defeat the threat of nuclear weapons, the 200 divisions of the Russian army, and General Jaruzelski's totalitarian rule; therefore, resistance was hopeless and doomed to fail. "It was Michnik's genius to separate the two halves of the propositions and to accept the first (the impossibility of defeating the armies and police forces) and reject the second (the hopelessness of all resistance)" (Schell, 1987, p. xxiii). Michnik rejected the idea that resistance was hopeless and defined areas of permissible maneuver in the "minutiae of their local environment" (p. xxiii).

The reasoning went like this. What if 10 people gathered in an apartment and listened to an uncensored lecture on Polish history? "What if a group of workers began to publish a newsletter in which factory conditions were truthfully described?" (Schell, 1987, p. xxiv). What if people did social work and gave direct medical, financial, and legal aid to those who needed it? Would this not set up an alternative set of institutions that the government would eventually accept? The important theme was direct local activity done independent of government that would "restore social bonds outside official institutions" (p. xxix). Rather than seize power and then use that power to do the good things in which they believed, KOR did the opposite: They did the good things first and worried about the state later (p. xxx).

The beauty of their actions was that each one both exemplified a democratic value they thought was important and, at the same time, accomplished something. For example, when KOR wrote their declaration of purpose, people signed the document and listed their addresses and phone numbers, a small action that both exemplified the value of open public action and allowed networking. The group made autonomy (the capacity to act freely) a principle for their own actions and encouraged people to do anything that was not contrary to the principles of the movement (Schell, 1987, p. xxviii). People were encouraged to *act* freely within small local areas even though their right to act freely (liberty) was supposedly constrained. Notice that every act proved to be a test of just how much liberty they might have, and in these tests were valuable learnings. When people put autonomy into practice, they formed associations around whatever issues they thought were important (e.g., pollution, trade, working conditions), which created diversity, contagion, and enthusiasm in many different areas of the country.

Schell (1987) describes this combination of open, truthful, autonomous, trusting local action as "militant decency" (p. xxix). The strength of the movement came from peaceful activities in a normal civic life, which set a new tone for that life. The guiding principle was simple but radical:

> Start doing the things you think should be done, and . . . start being what you think society should become. Do you believe in freedom of speech? Then speak freely. Do you love the truth? Then tell it. Do you believe in a decent and humane society? Then behave decently and humanely. (p. xxx)

What is radical and revolutionary is that when all of this is put in motion, it is not one more hollow promissory note from the government that says that if you are loyal and comply today, we will guarantee you a better tomorrow. Polish people had heard these lies for years and years. What KOR did was use multiple, parallel, small wins to reverse the Polish political experience. Their program created an immediate, visible, day-to-day community of free people. KOR did not promise a better tomorrow. It delivered a better today. It did not try to seize power from the government. Instead, it created new power by building up society and enacting new order and organization.

KOR did not get carried away by its success nor lose sight of its aims, nor did it finally come to resemble the bureaucratic nightmare it resisted. In its final, and perhaps most dramatic, act exemplifying democracy and the subordination of ego, pride, and vanity, KOR voted itself out of existence in September 1981 when people decided that their role was being filled by Solidarity (Schell, 1987, p. xxix). KOR had carved out a sphere of compromise within the totalitarian, violent Polish system without themselves resorting to domination and violence. Having demonstrated that it was possible to do this, KOR dissolved, symbolizing that the people themselves had learned how to act locally and enact a just society.

The lessons are clear. Large consequences can be produced by small actions when people change the only thing they can change: their own actions. In the case of Poland, the actions were controllable opportunities that generated tangible accomplishments (e.g., signatures, discussions, documents, medical aid, networks). The actions uncovered latitude within the totalitarian system, attracted allies and deferred government intervention, and lowered the necessity to confront the government head-on. The demands for strategizing, planning, calculation, and suspicion were made manageable when people were encouraged to behave in whatever truthful, trusting, open, autonomous, nonviolent way made sense in their local community. They improvised, and they acquired details of how the system worked. Thousands of uncorrelated variations sprang up all over Poland, some of which proved adaptive and were retained and circulated. Evolution was discovered to be a powerful form of revolution when it combined nonviolence, rehearsal of important values in immediate action, a social order based on small acts of decency, and patience and persistence. KOR demonstrated that control and freedom are to be found in the microaction of sensemaking even when macro structures appeared confining and coercive.

KOR did not plan all of this in advance. Instead, direct local acts of decency, undertaken wherever an opportunity presented itself, created tangible outcomes that attracted attention, uncovered new opportunities, built confidence, enlarged the number of people who tried to improve civic life, and built a bandwagon from small beginnings. Adam Michnik gave voice and substance to changes. He spotted the patterns and portrayed what was happening in stirring rhetoric. KOR changed the words, actions, sensitivities, and images with which the Polish people had to work. KOR changed what people saw when they looked back at the indeterminate flow of events that was the Poland of the 1970s. KOR did *not* change the realities of indeterminacy, flow, and thrownness. Instead, what KOR *did* change were actions and words that were added to that flow (e.g., this is a self-limiting revolution that will not attempt to overthrow the government). They changed the interpretations that were imposed retrospectively on those flows (e.g., we have enough faith in the people of Poland to dissolve KOR). And KOR encouraged people to enact reliable periods of determinacy in an otherwise indeterminate set of events (e.g., the government may renege on its promises of a better tomorrow, but here is a better today; our promises come later). KOR knew that just as indeterminacy, flow, and thrownness constrained them, they also constrained the government's response. KOR knew that there were seams in a totalitarian world, and so did Jaruzelski. Large retaliation against small acts of decency was as unthinkable for Jaruzelski as were small acts of violence to overthrow a vast army for Michnik. In the space between these two versions of the unthinkable, there is room to maneuver. The maneuvering room is small, but it is not trivial.

And the room to maneuver consists of nothing more or less than the power of local interaction to create a new sense of what is possible. What could be more local than yourself, and what could be more immediate than your own action? The Polish people demonstrated the power of this lesson in the context of much more oppressive organizational structures than many of those in global change.

This account of KOR's strategy and mode of organizing can be coded into the seven resources for sensemaking introduced earlier. When we do so, we find that KOR is as rich in these resources as Mann Gulch was bereft of them. Before we do this coding, we need to review key aspects of the organizational design evolved by KOR that affected sensemaking. The following seem relevant:

1. There are just a few guiding principles, and they provide wide latitude, for autonomy, and to locate interpretation of the meaning of those principles.

People are urged to follow their own enthusiasms and initiatives and to create new centers of autonomous activity. This configuration resembles tight coupling on a handful of core values and loose coupling on everything else (Peters & Waterman, 1982).

2. There is a clear adversary whose power could squash any direct effort at overthrow.

3. There are seams created by the fact that neither overthrow by the opposition movement nor military oppression by the group in power will be politically successful. These common interests create small but tangible spaces for compromise.

4. There is ongoing articulation by intellectuals such as Michnik of what is happening and what it means. These accounts are not filled with stirring, visionary rhetoric or simplistic accounts of good and evil. Instead, there is a calming tone of "angerless wisdom" (Schell, 1987, p. xi), reaffirmation of the importance of living one's beliefs, discussion of being ready to die but unwilling to kill, and renewed emphasis on scrutinizing the local scene for opportunities to build an alternative society.

5. There are highly diverse activities done simultaneously across the country that amount to independent experiments from which people learn that totalitarianism has variable resistance to change.

6. Acts of militant decency create an alternative society, which means that people become less dependent on the totalitarian society and effectively ignore it in more and more of their dealings.

7. There is an ongoing effort to act "as if" Poland were already a free country, which, in Schell's (1987) words, enables the "as if to melt away" (p. xxx), with substance replacing pretense.

Minimal as this organizational design may seem, it does foster sensemaking even if it also might well make decision making more difficult. Specific examples in KOR of access to sensemaking resources include the following:

1. *Social context*: There are gatherings, groups that publish newsletters, attempts to restore social bonds, networking by means of signed documents, trust in local action, the formation of associations, and an ongoing focus on "independent public opinion" rather than on totalitarian power (Schell, 1987, p. xxvi). The form encourages conversation.

2. *Identity*: People see themselves as agents who do what they think needs to be done to exemplify democratic values. They see themselves as engaged in a new form of revolution, as a community of free people, as rehearsing values that matter, and as helping a self-limiting revolution. The form provides a distinct, stable, workable sense of who the participants are as individuals.

3. *Retrospect*: People act in order to discover how much liberty they actually have. There is ongoing discovery of what the revolution is about based on seeing what works and what does not. The form thrives on elapsed data and uses those data to form an emerging definition of what the opposition stands for.

4. *Salient cues*: Close attention is directed to local activities to find spaces of permissible maneuver. People are urged to pay attention to things they can improve using only the skills and sensitivities they now possess. The counsel is to "scrutinize the minutiae of their local environment" (Schell, 1987, p. xxiii), which means that the form enhances the visibility of cues from which sense can be made.

5. *Ongoing projects*: The "revolution" consists basically of peaceful activities in a normal, ongoing civic life that sets a new tone. There is a day-to-day community of people acting as if they are free and carving out small areas of compromise as they do so. Life does not stop for the revolution to start. Life and the revolution fold together. The revolution keeps pace with the relentless flow of experience and, in doing so, loses some of its conspicuousness, gains pragmatic relevance, is made more manageable and doable, and, because of its close affinity with ongoing, everyday action, is eminently sensible. The form accommodates to the flow of experience and, in doing so, enables people to keep up with dynamic events.

6. *Plausibility*: The accounts of what is happening tell a coherent, meaningful story, a story of militant decency, a better today that replaces empty promises, and the creation of a new society. These are stories of possibilities being realized, and they provide reasonable explanations for what is happening and what can happen. The form gains its energy from stories of tangible accomplishments within an alternative social order.

7. *Enactment*: What is perhaps most characteristic of KOR is the dominance of action that creates a different order. People are counseled to "do what you think needs to be done." There is action at every turn – action such as lectures, publishing, providing medical or financial aid, performing small acts of decency, consumer protection, social work, concrete assistance in legal trials – action that even includes dissolving KOR itself. The form encourages action. Perhaps more accurately, the form is action.

Conclusion

The Mann Gulch firefighting crew and the KOR opposition group exemplify variations in organizational design that have an effect on the capability for sensemaking. Variations in sensemaking, in turn, affect enthusiasm, the willingness to sustain complex collaboration, and resourcefulness in the face of setbacks. Although Mann Gulch and KOR may seem far removed from organizing for global change, there is a sense in which they incorporate many of its conditions.

To see this parallel, consider the following more general and more stark rendering of the story of Mann Gulch.

Individuals who are strangers to one another
are spread out,
unable to communicate,
unfamiliar with the terrain,

in disagreement about who their leaders are, and
they're told to do something they've never done before,
or they will die.
They don't do it.
They die.

When people organize for global change, their organizational challenges look a lot like those in Mann Gulch. In organizing for global change, leaders also will face

1. Strangers with diverse experience
2. Face-to-face contact for intermittent, short periods
3. Unknown leaders
4. Temporary systems
5. Proposed solutions that make no sense
6. An inability to communicate and share experience
7. Terrain consisting of unfamiliar troubles (or opportunities)
8. Failures and possible fatalities

The context for efforts at global change may often bear an uncomfortable resemblance to the context at Mann Gulch. But if some of the organizational dysfunction at Mann Gulch can be understood as a failure to organize for sensemaking, then efforts at global change can be redesigned to strengthen this capability. That is what appears to have happened with the Worker's Defense Committee in Poland.

The promise of KOR is the suggestion that challenges such as those of Mann Gulch can be overcome. KOR is organized in such a way that

a community replaces strangers,
closeness replaces separation,
the familiar replaces the unfamiliar,
agreements replace disagreements,
acceptance replaces noncompliance, and
renewal replaces death.

References

Cooperrider, D. L. and Bilimoria, D. (1993). The challenge of global change for strategic management: Opportunities for charting a new course. In P. Shrivastava, A. Huff, and J. Dutton (Eds.), *Advances in Strategic Management*, Vol. 9 (pp. 99–142). Greenwich, CT: JAI.

Gilbert, D. T. (1991). How mental systems behave. *American Psychologist*, 46(2), 107–119.

Maclean, N. (1992). *Young Men and Fire*. Chicago, IL: University of Chicago Press.

Peters, T. J. and Waterman, R. H., Jr. (1982). *In Search of Excellence*. New York: Harper and Row.

Rothermel, R. C. (1993). *Mann Gulch Fire: A race that couldn't be run*. USDA, Forest Service, General Tech. Report INT-299.

Salancik, G. R. (1977). Commitment and the control of organizational behavior and belief. In B. M. Staw and G. R. Salancik (Eds.), *New Directions in Organizational Behavior* (pp. 1–54).

Chicago, IL: St. Clair.

Schell, J. (1987). Introduction. In A. Michnik, *Letters from Prison* (pp. xvii–xlii). Berkeley, CA: University of California Press.

Thoele, M. (1995). *Fire Line: The Summer Battles of the West*. Golden, CO: Fulcrum.

Weick, K. E. (1993). The collapse of sensemaking in organizations: The Mann Gulch disaster. *Administrative Science Quarterly*, 38, 628–652.

Weick, K. E. (1995). *Sensemaking in Organizations*. Thousand Oaks, CA: Sage.

Index